D1927662

CAT

INTERACTIVE TEXT

ADVANCED PAPER 7

PLANNING, CONTROL AND PERFORMANCE MANAGEMENT

BPP is the **official publisher** of training materials for the ACCA's CAT qualification. This Interactive Text which forms part of a suite of learning tools, has been specifically written to the **current syllabus** and Teaching Guide.

- Clear language and presentation
- Plenty of questions, examples and quizzes to demonstrate and practise techniques
- A question and answer bank prepared by BPP Learning Media authors

FOR EXAMS IN DECEMBER 2009 AND JUNE 2010

BPP LEARNING MEDIA

First edition 2003
Seventh edition June 2009

ISBN 9780 7517 6328 7
(Previous ISBN 9780 7517 4826 0)

British Library Cataloguing-in-Publication Data
A catalogue record for this book
is available from the British Library

Published by

BPP Learning Media Ltd
BPP House, Aldine Place
London W12 8AA

www.bpp.com/learningmedia

Printed in the United Kingdom

Your learning materials, published by BPP Learning Media Ltd, are printed on paper sourced from sustainable, managed forests.

We are grateful to the Association of Chartered Certified Accountants for permission to reproduce past examination questions. The suggested solutions in the exam answer bank have been prepared by BPP Learning Media Ltd, except where otherwise stated.

A note about copyright

Dear Customer

What does the little © mean and why does it matter?

Your market-leading BPP books, course materials and e-learning materials do not write and update themselves. People write them: on their own behalf or as employees of an organisation that invests in this activity. Copyright law protects their livelihoods. It does so by creating rights over the use of the content.

Breach of copyright is a form of theft – as well as being a criminal offence in some jurisdictions, it is potentially a serious breach of professional ethics.

With current technology, things might seem a bit hazy but, basically, without the express permission of BPP Learning Media:

- Photocopying our materials is a breach of copyright
- Scanning, ripcasting or conversion of our digital materials into different file formats, uploading them to facebook or emailing them to your friends is a breach of copyright

You can, of course, sell your books, in the form in which you have bought them – once you have finished with them. (Is this fair to your fellow students? We update for a reason.) But the e-products are sold on a single user licence basis: we do not supply 'unlock' codes to people who have bought them second-hand.

And what about outside the UK? BPP Learning Media strives to make our materials available at prices students can afford by local printing arrangements, pricing policies and partnerships which are clearly listed on our website. A tiny minority ignore this and indulge in criminal activity by illegally photocopying our material or supporting organisations that do. If they act illegally and unethically in one area, can you really trust them?

Contents

How to Use this Interactive Text

Aim of this Interactive Text

To provide the knowledge and practice to help you succeed in the examination for Paper 7 *Planning, Control and Performance Management.*

To pass the examination you need a thorough understanding in all areas covered by the syllabus and teaching guide.

Recommended approach

(a) To pass you need to be able to answer questions on **everything** specified by the syllabus and teaching guide. Read the text very carefully and do not skip any of it.

(b) Learning is an **active** process. Do **all** the questions as you work through the text so you can be sure you really understand what you have read.

(c) After you have covered the material in the Interactive Text, work through the **Question Bank**, checking your answers carefully against the **Answer Bank**.

(d) Before you take the exam, check that you still remember the material using the following quick revision plan.

    (i) Read through the **chapter topic list** at the beginning of each chapter. Are there any gaps in your knowledge? If so, study the section again.

    (ii) Read and learn the **key terms**.

    (iii) Look at the **exam alerts**. These show the ways in which topics might be examined.

    (iv) Read the **chapter roundups**, which are a summary of the **fast forwards** in each chapter.

    (v) Do the **quick quizzes** again. If you know what you're doing, they shouldn't take long.

    This approach is only a suggestion. You or your college may well adapt it to suit your needs.

    Remember this is a **practical** course.

    (a) Try to relate the material to your experience in the workplace or any other work experience you may have had.

    (b) Try to make as many links as you can to other papers at the Introductory and Intermediate levels.

For practice and revision use BPP Learning Media's Practice and Revision Kit, i-Pass and passcards.

Approach to examining the syllabus

Paper 7 is a three-hour written paper.

The format of the paper is:

	Marks
Ten multiple choice questions of two marks each	20
Four compulsory written questions	80
	100

Exams before June 2009 consisted of one 40-mark question and three 20-mark questions.

Analysis of past papers

These are the topics examined in past papers in the compulsory written questions.

Topic	Dec 2008	June 2008	Dec 2007	June 2007	Dec 2006	June 2006	Dec 2005	Jun 2005
Budget statements	•			•	•	•	•	
ROI, RI				•				
Balanced scorecard			•	•			•	
Benchmarking				•				
ABC				•			•	
Budget and actual profit, changes for activity, sampling					•			
Relevant costing	•				•		•	
Flexed budgets	•		•	•	•		•	
Variance calculations + Standard costing	•	•	•	•	•	•	•	•
Performance ratios		•	•	•		•		•
Sales, production, labour, materials budgets		•				•		
Incremental costs and revenues						•		
Breakeven, margin of safety, CVP	•	•						•
Sales forecasts	•							•
Value for money						•		
Non-financial indicators	•	•						•
Control charts					•			
Lifecycle costing						•	•	
ZBB			•		•	•		•
Marginal, absorption costing							•	•
Indexing, high-low, linear regression		•	•	•				•
Target costing								•

Topic	Dec 2008	June 2008	Dec 2007	June 2007	Dec 2006	June 2006	Dec 2005	Jun 2005
TQM	•			•				
Responsibility centres	•			•				

Questions and answers for all of these sittings can be downloaded from the ACCA website, together with examiner's comments on the paper. The latest questions and answers are in the BPP Learning Media Practice and Revision Kit.

Note that certain topics examined in previous sittings will no longer be examined from June 2009. These topics include decision-making and CVP analysis which are now tested in CAT 10.

Tackling multiple choice questions

MCQs are now part of all CAT exams. Papers 1 and 2 are examined by CBE, Papers 3 and 4 can be taken by CBE or by a written paper which is 40% MCQs. Paper 5 is now 24% MCQs and Papers 6 to 10 are 20% MCQs. All MCQs carry two marks.

The MCQs in your exam contain four possible answers. You have to **choose the option that best answers the question**. The three incorrect options are called distracters. There is a skill in answering MCQs quickly and correctly. By practising MCQs you can develop this skill, giving you a better chance of passing the exam.

You may wish to follow the approach outlined below, or you may prefer to adapt it.

Step 1 Skim read all the MCQs and identify what appear to be the easier questions.

Step 2 Attempt each question – **starting with the easier questions** identified in Step 1. Read the question **thoroughly**. You may prefer to work out the answer before looking at the options, or you may prefer to look at the options at the beginning. Adopt the method that works best for you.

Step 3 Read the four options and see if one matches your own answer. Be careful with numerical questions as the distracters are designed to match answers that incorporate common errors. Check that your calculation is correct. Have you followed the requirement exactly? Have you included every stage of the calculation?

Step 4 You may find that none of the options matches your answer.

- Re-read the question to ensure that you understand it and are answering the requirement
- Eliminate any obviously wrong answers
- Consider which of the remaining answers is the most likely to be correct and select the option

Step 5 If you are still unsure make a note and continue to the next question

Step 6 Revisit unanswered questions. When you come back to a question after a break you often find you are able to answer it correctly straight away. If you are still unsure have a guess. You are not penalised for incorrect answers, so **never leave a question unanswered!**

After extensive practice and revision of MCQs, you may find that you recognise a question when you sit the exam. Be aware that the detail and/or requirement may be different. If the question seems familiar read the requirement and options carefully – do not assume that it is identical.

P A R T

A

Cost accounting

Accounting for management

1

Topic list
1 The management function
2 The management accountant
3 Management information
4 The decision-making process
5 Management accounting information and decision making
6 External information
7 The maintenance and improvement of accounting information systems
8 Cost behaviour

Study guide reference

		Syllabus reference
1(a)	Describe the management function within an organisation and how this may vary according to the nature of the business	1
(b)	Describe the objectives of management accounting information in relation to short-term and long-term planning, control and performance measurement	1
(c)	Describe the role of the management accountant in an organisation	1
(d)	Describe the features of useful management information	1
(e)	Explain the limitations of management accounting information in providing guidance for managerial decision making	1
(f)	Explain how cost accounting systems can be maintained and improved	1
3(c)	Explain cost behaviour	1

1 The management function

FAST FORWARD

Managers have to **plan, control**, **organise**, **motivate** and **make decisions**.

1.1 The role of management

What do managers do? If you are under their control you probably think managers take long lunches, spend long holidays in exotic places and do very little work! If you are a manager, you may believe managers work very hard to ensure the organisation they work for is successful.

We are all managers in one sense – managers of our lives. The same management principles apply whether managing your own life, or managing a department.

1.2 You as a manager

Imagine your normal working day. Do you wake up each weekday and just hope that you will find some washed and ironed clothes in your wardrobe, that some milk will have magically appeared in your fridge or that a bus might happen to pass that will get you to the office on time? No! **You have to plan** for these things. They don't just happen.

What would happen if you decided to be extremely extravagant and ate at expensive restaurants every night? This might mean that your dream holiday to the Caribbean was no longer affordable. As manager of your life **you have to control what you do** to ensure that you can stick to your plans.

Suppose that you share a house with three other friends. Unless all of you like living in chaos, some sort of organisation is necessary to ensure that household duties are shared out equally. If you want to live in ordered surroundings **you need to organise yourself and others**.

Imagine it is 5.00 pm on Friday afternoon and you really fancy a few drinks in the pub after work. Your work colleagues are not keen on the idea. They would rather go home and watch television. How do you get them to do what you want them to do? You try to make them see that it would be better for them if they went to the pub instead of watching television. **You need to motivate them.**

There is one common activity running through the various aspects of managing your life. **Making decisions. It is difficult to plan, control, organise or motivate without making decisions.**

What does managing your life involve?

(a) Planning
(b) Controlling

(c) Organising
(d) Motivating
(e) Decision making

This is exactly what managers have to do to manage **staff**, the organisation's **products**, the organisation's **financial position** and the organisation's **public image**.

1.3 Planning

Management have to **plan for both the short term and the long term**. A long-range plan is necessary in order to anticipate any future needs or opportunities that require action to be taken either now or in the future. For example, management may need to consider building a new factory to meet anticipated increased demand for a product. Management should constantly be **thinking ahead**. They should **never be surprised by any gradual developments**. Planning therefore involves **converting the organisation's long-term objectives into a succession of short-term plans**. One such short term plan is the annual budget.

1.4 Controlling

Control is exercised by **comparing actual performance with the short-term plans** so that deviations from these short-term plans can be identified and corrective action taken. If the control process indicates that the long-term objectives are not achievable, the objectives can be changed before any serious damage to the company's future occurs.

1.5 Organising

Organising is the establishment of a **framework within which necessary activities can be performed**. For example, the designation of a member of staff to be responsible for a particular activity and the **definition of managers' responsibilities and lines of authority**. It requires the breakdown of the organisation into **manageable sections** such as departments and the **co-ordination of activities** in these sections.

1.6 Motivating

Managers need to influence employees to act in such a manner that will help achieve the organisation's objectives.

1.7 Decision making

Management is decision taking. Managers of all levels within an organisation take decisions

Types of decision	Detail
Strategic level	These **set or change the objectives or strategic targets of an organisation**. They include decisions about the selection of products and markets, the required levels of company profitability and the purchase or disposal of subsidiary companies or major fixed assets.
Tactical level	These are concerned with the **efficient and effective use of an organisation's resources** (sometimes referred to as the '4Ms': men, materials, machines and money). Tactical-level decisions therefore include setting budgets for the next period for sales, production and inventory levels, and setting measures of performance by which departmental results can be gauged.
Operational level	These are concerned with **ensuring that specific tasks are carried out effectively and efficiently**. They might include decisions concerning the allocation of particular staff to particular tasks and jobs or the action to take over customer complaints.

Question — Decisions

What strategic-level, tactical-level and operational-level decisions might an organisation take in relation to sales?

Answer

Here is our suggestion. Your answer is likely to be somewhat different.

(a) At the strategic level, senior management may decide that the company should increase sales by 5% per annum for at least five years.

(b) At the tactical level, the sales director and senior sales managers may decide to increase sales by 5% in the next year, with some provisional planning for future years. This would involve making decisions about direct sales resources, advertising, sales promotion and so on. Sales quotas could be assigned to each sales territory.

(c) At the operational level, the manager of a sales territory may make a decision regarding the weekly sales targets for each sales representative.

Key terms

Planning means formulating ways of proceeding. **Decision making** means choosing between various alternatives. These two terms are linked: you decide to plan in the first place and the plan you make is a collection of decisions.

Control is used in the sense of monitoring something so as to keep it on course, like the 'controls' of a car, not (or not merely) in the sense of imposing restraints, or exercising power over something.

Question — Planning and control

Mr and Mrs Average need to go to Sainsbury's to buy food and other household items. They make a list beforehand which sets out all the things they need. As they go round the supermarket they tick off the items on the list. If any particular item is not available they choose an alternative from the range on the shelves. They also buy a bottle of wine and two bars of chocolate. These were not on their original list.

(a) What part or parts of this activity would you describe as planning?

(b) There are several examples of decision making in this story. Identify three of them.

(c) What part or parts of this activity would you describe as control?

Answer

We would describe making the list as planning, but making the list is also an example of decision making, since Mr and Mrs Average have to decide what items will go on the list. Ticking off the items is control and choosing alternatives is 'control action' involving further decision making.

You should be able to answer the various parts of this question without further help.

1.8 The effect of the nature of the business on the management function

FAST FORWARD

The nature of an organisation will affect what the managers do in that organisation.

Our description of what management do is very general. In reality, although managers in most organisations will have to plan, control, organise, motivate and make decisions, what they have to plan, control, organise, motivate and make decisions about will be affected by the **nature of the organisation** in question.

For example, how useful is inflexible long-term planning in an organisation producing a product such as computer software (which has a very short shelf life)? Long term plans can be more easily made in an organisation operating in an **older, established industry**, where **patterns of demand are well known** and **unexpected occurrences are unlikely**.

Motivation is more **important in a labour-intensive organisation** (such as a supermarket chain) than in a machine-intensive organisation (such as a plant in which cars are assembled by robots).

The degree of organisation required will depend on the structure and size of the business, and the number of products it produces/services it provides. **Organising a huge company** which manufactures hundreds of different products in twenty different countries around the world will be **far more difficult than organising a small family-run business** which produces one product in one factory.

Control is vital in all organisations but the way in which control is exercised and the degree of control will vary from organisation to organisation. The **control process of standard costing and variance analysis is more suited to certain organisations** than others, as we will see later in the text. **Most organisations operate a budgetary control system but the sophistication of that system will vary**. Larger organisations tend to have more sophisticated control systems but that is not always the case.

Managers in all organisations take decisions. **Some managers might make decisions which involve millions of pounds** (such as whether or not to acquire a subsidiary), **others may make decisions which involve only a few pounds** (such as whether or not coffee and tea should be free to staff). **The type of decision will be affected by what the organisation does:** the manager in a hospital may make a decision which fundamentally affects the health of many people; the decision taken by the manager of a company which produces harmful chemicals may take a decision which could affect the environment.

Although you can generalise about what managers do, you should now appreciate that **every manager's role is unique**.

Question — **Management**

Have a chat with some managers in your organisation. What do they do? Do they plan, control, organise, motivate and make decisions? How do they do this? Why do they do this? Are they successful in what they are doing and if not, why not?

2 The management accountant

The management accountant can assist the manager to manage.

Assistance in planning

The management accountant assists planning by providing information. This information may be about pricing, capital expenditure projects, product costs or competition. In the **short-term planning process of budgeting**, the management accountant provides information on past costs and revenues which may be used as guidance. The management accountant is also involved in the budgeting process itself.

Assistance in controlling

The management accountant **supplies performance reports which compare actual performance with planned performance** and which therefore highlight those activities which are not conforming to plan.

Assistance in organising

By **ensuring that the accounting system is tailored to the organisational structure**, the management accountant reinforces the objectives of the organisational framework.

Assistance in motivating

Budgets prepared by the management accountant serve to motivate managers and subordinates to attempt to achieve the organisation's objectives. Formalised targets are more likely to motivate than vague comments.

Performance reports produced by the management accountant for the control process also motivate by communicating performance information in relation to the targets which have been set.

The management accountant also assists the motivation process by **identifying potential managerial problem areas** and highlighting those items which require investigation. A poorly designed budgeting process can have the opposite effect and **demotivate**.

Assistance in decision making

The management accountant is a vital cog in the organisation's decision-making process. He or she collects and analyses data, and presents information to managers to help in the decision-making process.

For example, suppose a component that an organisation currently manufactures in-house can now be purchased from a supplier. The management accountant provides information about the various costs and benefits associated with each option so that management can choose whether to buy-in the component or manufacture it in-house.

2.1 Management accounting

Having looked at the role of management accounting in terms of how it can meet the needs of management, we will now look at the discipline in more general terms.

The CIMA *Official Terminology* defines management accounting.

Key term

> **Management accounting** is the process of identification, measurement, accumulation, analysis, preparation, interpretation and communication of information used by management to plan, evaluate and control within an entity and to assure appropriate use of and accountability for its resources. Management accounting also comprises the preparation of financial reports for non-management groups such as shareholders, creditors, regulatory agencies and tax authorities.

The *Official Terminology* also describes the **core activities of management accounting**.

(a) **Participation in the planning process** at both strategic and operational levels. This involves the establishment of policies and the formulation of plans and budgets which will subsequently be expressed in financial terms.

(b) The initiation of and the **provision of guidance for management decisions**. This involves the generation, analysis, presentation and interpretation of appropriate relevant information.

(c) Contributing to the **monitoring and control** performance through the provision of reports on organisational (and organisational segment) performance, including comparisons of actual with planned or budgeted performance, and their analysis and interpretation.

Along with planning, control and decision making, **analysis** can also be described as one of the key processes of management accounting.

> 'This involves gathering data about past, present and planned activities, from both inside and, where relevant, outside of the company. The management accountant's role is to design mechanisms to capture operational data in a cost-effective manner and then to produce information in an appropriate form for presentation to management, for example, by producing monthly management accounts, efficiency studies on production methods and processes, product costs, etc ...'
>
> ('Accounting information systems: roles and processes', *ACCA Technician Bulletin*, June 2000)

FAST FORWARD

> Management accounting is therefore concerned with the collection of data, its analysis and processing into information, and the interpretation and communication of that information so as to assist management with planning, control and decision making.

Exam focus point

> In an exam, you are unlikely to be asked simply to 'state the functions of management accounting' or to 'describe the managerial role'. It is more likely that a particular scenario will be provided and you will have to 'state the functions' or 'describe the role' with reference to the scenario. And make sure you do refer to the scenario. Apply the general information we have provided to the circumstances of the question.

2.2 Financial accounting

'Financial accounting, can be defined as the **periodic reporting of accounting information**, as **required by statute for shareholders, government agencies** (most notably HM Revenue and Customs) and other **parties external to the business**. As such, **various rules and conventions** are necessary to ensure **consistency** between sets of accounts. Financial accounting is predominantly **based upon past** transactions and events. There is a requirement for companies to prepare three financial statements each year, a **income statement**, a **balance sheet** and a **cash flow statement**. Between them, these statements reveal the **monetary performance and value** of the company.

Without accurate and **independently verified** accounting statements, it would be very **difficult to attract funds for investment** from either the inventory market or from financial institutions such as banks or venture capitalists.'

This useful summary (with BPP's emphasis) was produced in an article entitled 'Accounting information systems: roles and processes' (*ACCA Technician Bulletin,* June 2000).

2.3 Management accounting compared with financial accounting

You should by now have realised that there are huge differences between financial accounting and management accounting and hence between the information each provides and the value of that information for particular purposes.

The following table summarises the main differences between management accounting and financial accounting.

Management accounting	Financial accounting
A management accounting system produces information that **is used within an organisation**, by managers and employees.	A financial accounting system produces information that is **used by parties external to the organisation**, such as shareholders, banks and receivables.
Management accounting **helps management to record, plan and control activities and aids the decision-making process.**	Financial accounting provides a **record of the performance** of an organisation over a defined period and the **state of affairs** at the end of that period.
There is **no legal requirement** for an organisation to use management accounting.	Limited companies must, **by law**, prepare financial accounts.
Management accounting can **focus on specific areas of an organisation's activities**. Information may aid a decision rather than be an end product of a decision.	Financial accounting **concentrates on the organisation as a whole**, aggregating revenues and costs from different operations. Financial accounts are an end in themselves.
Management accounting information may be **monetary** or alternatively **non-monetary**.	Most financial accounting information is of a **monetary** nature.
Management accounting provides both an **historical record** of the immediate past and a **future planning tool**.	Financial accounting presents an essentially **historical picture** of past operations.

Management accounting	Financial accounting
No strict rules govern the way in which management accounting operates. The management accounts and information are prepared in a **format that is of use to managers**.	Financial accounting must operate within a **framework determined by law, by IASs, SSAPs and by FRSs**. In principle the financial accounts of different organisations can be easily compared.

Question

Differences

Fill in the spaces in the following table.

	Financial accounting	Management accounting
Time horizon		
Principal objectives		
Report recipients		
Outputs		
Regulatory framework		

Answer

This is adapted from 'Accounting information systems: roles and processes', an article in the June 2000 edition of *ACCA Technician Bulletin.*

	Financial accounting	Management accounting
Time horizon	Past	Past, present and future
Principal objectives	Stewardship of business for the benefit of shareholders	To improve the economy, efficiency and effectiveness of operations
Report recipients	External parties - shareholders - government	Internal parties - directors - company managers
Outputs	(Usually) annual summaries - Income statement - balance sheet - cash flow statement	Detailed monthly and annual management accounts, showing results by product and function

	Financial accounting	Management accounting
Regulatory framework	Accounting concepts (as laid down by the Accounting Standards Board) plus statutory requirements of the Companies Acts	None prescribed, although the guidance and formats of CIMA *Official Terminology* tend to be followed in many organisations

Question

Management accounts

Which of the following statements about management accounts is/are true?

(i) They must be stated in purely monetary terms
(ii) Limited companies must, by law, prepare management accounts
(iii) They serve as a future planning tool and are not used as an historical record

A (i), (ii), (iii)
B (i) and (ii)
C (ii) only
D None of the statements are correct

Answer

D Management accounts often incorporate non-monetary measures. Therefore **statement (i)** is incorrect.

There is no legal requirement to prepare management accounts. Therefore **statement (ii)** is incorrect.

Management accounts do serve as a future planning tool, but they are also useful as an historical record of performance. Therefore **statement (iii)** is incorrect.

3 Management information

FAST FORWARD

Management information should be relevant, complete, accurate, clear and timely. It should inspire confidence and be communicated to the right manager, manageable in terms of volume, communicated by an appropriate channel of communication and provided at a cost which is less than the benefits it provides.

We now know that management accounting involves the collection of **data** and its analysis and processing into **information.**

3.1 Data and information

We therefore need to make a **distinction between data and information**.

Key term

Data is the raw material for data processing. Data relates to facts, events and transactions.

Information is data that has been processed in such a way as to be meaningful to the person who receives it.

An example demonstrates the difference. Many companies providing a product or service need to find out about consumer opinion, and employ market research organisations to do so. A typical market research survey employs a number of researchers who request a sample of the public (or the target market) to answer a number of questions relating to the product. Several hundred questionnaires may be completed.

Individually, a completed questionnaire would not tell the company very much, only the views of one consumer. In this case, the **individual questionnaires are data. Once they have been processed, and analysed, the resulting report is information**: the company will use this information in decision making.

The quality of source data affects the value of information. **Information is worthless if the source data is flawed.** If the researchers filled in questionnaires themselves, inventing the answers, then the conclusions drawn from the processed data would be wrong, and poor decisions would be made.

3.2 Management information

Management information is information **used by managers to help control the business**. The information provided by the **management accountant** is therefore **management information**.

3.3 Useful management information

What factors are important for the successful **conversion** of data to good management information?

Features of useful management information

(a) It should be **relevant** for its purpose.
(b) It should be **complete** for its purpose.
(c) It should be sufficiently **accurate** for its purpose.
(d) It should be **clear** to the manager using it.
(e) The manager using it should have **confidence** in it.
(f) It should be **communicated** to the appropriate manager.
(g) Its **volume** should be **manageable**.
(h) It should be **timely** (in other words communicated at the most appropriate time).
(i) It should be communicated by an appropriate **channel of communication.**
(j) It should be provided at a **cost which is less than the value of the benefits** it provides.

Let us have a look at these qualities in a bit more detail.

(a) **Relevance**. Information must be relevant to the purpose for which a manager wants to use it. In practice, far too many reports fail to 'keep to the point' and contain purposeless, irritating paragraphs which only serve to vex the managers reading them.

(b) **Completeness**. An information user should have all the information he needs to do his job properly. If he does not have a complete picture of the situation, he might well make bad decisions.

(c) **Accuracy**. Information should obviously be accurate because using incorrect information could have serious and damaging consequences. However, information should only be accurate enough for its purpose and there is no need to go into unnecessary detail for pointless accuracy.

(d) **Clarity**. Information must be clear to the user. If the user does not understand it properly he cannot use it properly. Lack of clarity is one of the causes of a breakdown in communication. It is therefore important to choose the most appropriate presentation medium or channel of communication.

(e) **Confidence**. Information must be trusted by the managers who are expected to use it. However not all information is certain. Some information has to be certain, especially operating information, for example, related to a production process. Strategic information, especially relating to the environment, is uncertain. However, if the assumptions underlying it are clearly stated, this might enhance the confidence with which the information is perceived.

(f) **Communication**. Within any organisation, individuals are given the authority to do certain tasks, and they must be given the information they need to do them. An office manager might be made responsible for controlling expenditures in his office, and given a budget expenditure limit for the year. As the year progresses, he might try to keep expenditure in check but unless he is told throughout the year what is his current total expenditure to date, he will find it difficult to judge whether he is keeping within budget or not.

(g) **Volume**. There are physical and mental limitations to what a person can read, absorb and understand properly before taking action. An enormous mountain of information, even if it is all relevant, cannot be handled. Reports to management must therefore be **clear** and **concise** and in many systems, control action works basically on the 'exception' principle.

(h) **Timing**. Information which is not available until after a decision is made will be useful only for comparisons and longer-term control, and may serve no purpose even then. Information prepared too frequently can be a serious disadvantage. If, for example, a decision is taken at a monthly meeting about a certain aspect of a company's operations, information to make the decision is only required once a month, and weekly reports would be a time-consuming waste of effort.

(i) **Channel of communication**. There are occasions when using one particular method of communication will be better than others. For example, job vacancies should be announced in a medium where they will be brought to the attention of the people most likely to be interested. The channel of communication might be the company's in-house journal, a national or local newspaper, a professional magazine, a job centre or school careers office. Some internal memoranda may be better sent by 'electronic mail'. Some information is best communicated informally by telephone or word-of-mouth, whereas other information ought to be formally communicated in writing or figures.

(j) **Cost**. Information should have some value, otherwise it would not be worth the cost of collecting and filing it. The benefits obtainable from the information must also exceed the costs of acquiring it, and whenever management is trying to decide whether or not to produce information for a particular purpose (for example whether to computerise an operation or to build a financial planning model) a cost/benefit study ought to be made.

In some situations, one of the features of useful management information might be **traded off** in favour of another.

(a) If management information is produced to such a high degree of **accuracy**, then this may mean that it is delivered late and therefore not **timely**.

(b) If management information is '**too complete**', the **costs** to produce it might outweigh the **value of the benefits**.

(c) If management information is **'too complete'**, its volume may be **excessive** and **unmanageable** (and therefore **difficult to understand**).

Question

Value of information

The value of information lies in the action taken as a result of receiving it. What questions might you ask in order to make an assessment of the value of information provided in your organisation?

Answer

(a) What information is provided?
(b) What is it used for?
(c) Who uses it?
(d) How often is it used?
(e) Does the frequency with which it is used coincide with the frequency with which it is provided?
(f) What is achieved by using it?
(g) What other relevant information is available which could be used instead?

An assessment of the value of information can be derived in this way, and the cost of obtaining it should then be compared against this value. On the basis of this comparison, it can be decided whether certain items of information are worth having. It should be remembered that there may also be intangible benefits which may be harder to quantify.

4 The decision-making process

FAST FORWARD

The **decision-making process** has six steps.

- Identify objectives
- Search for alternative courses of action
- Collect data about the alternative courses of action
- Select the appropriate course of action
- Implement the decision
- Compare actual and planned outcomes and take corrective action as necessary

Although termed the decision-making process, the steps set out below actually **incorporate planning and control.**

Step 1 **Identify objectives**

The organisation's **goals or objectives must be defined** to ensure that managers are able to assess which of the courses of action available is the most appropriate for the organisation. The objectives of many profit-making organisations include the maximisation of profit. Non-profit-making organisations such as hospitals and charities are likely to have an objective based on providing the most effective services with the resources available.

Step 2 **Search for alternative courses of action**

The next step is to find a **number of possible courses** of action that enable the objectives to be achieved. A profit-making organisation might need to consider the following.

- Developing new products to sell in existing markets
- Developing new products to sell in new markets
- Developing new markets in which to sell existing products

Step 3 **Collect data about the alternative courses of action**

The type of data that needs collecting will depend on the type of decision. If the decision is concerned with the long-term future of the organisation, the management accountant will need to collect data about the environment in which the organisation operates and about the organisation's capabilities. If the decision is more concerned with the short-term future of the organisation (such as deciding on the selling price for a product), data on the selling price of competitors' products will have to be collected.

Step 4 **Select the appropriate course of action**

The course of action which **best satisfies the organisation's objectives** should be selected.

Step 5 **Implement the decision**

The decision chosen should be implemented. Suppose an organisation has decided that it should raise the price of product X by $4 from $45 per unit to $49 per unit. The price will be raised and the sales budget will then be prepared on the basis of a selling price of $49.

Step 6 **Compare actual and planned outcomes and take any necessary corrective action if the planned results have not been achieved**

The final stage in the process involves comparing actual results with planned and taking control action required.

Exam focus point

If you are required to describe the steps in the decision-making process for a particular organisation, make sure that you tailor your description to the specific circumstances described in the question.

Question — Decisions

Try to discover how decision making is carried out in your organisation? Is it similar to the process we have discussed above? If it is different, is it better? If it is better, why is it better?

5 Management accounting information and decision making

FAST FORWARD

Management accounting information is, in general, unsuitable for decision making.

The **information required for decision making is different from the information provided by conventional management accounts. Decision-making information should be relevant**. However, absorption costing (a widely-used method of costing products and services which we will be looking at later) provides information that in many situations is misleading and irrelevant.

All decision making is concerned with the future and so there will **always be some degree of uncertainty** surrounding the possible outcomes of a decision. **Information for decision making should therefore incorporate uncertainty** in some way. The methods of incorporating uncertainty are outside the scope of this syllabus, but you should realise that if management accounting information does not take account of uncertainty it is unsuitable for decision making. If an attempt to incorporate uncertainty is made the information should be more suitable for decision making but can **never be risk free**.

Question — Uncertainty

Can you think of any factors which contribute to the uncertainty an organisation might face?

Answer

Here are a few suggestions. You probably thought of others.

The actions of competitors
Inflation
Interest rate changes
New government legislation
Possible shortages of material or labour
Possible industrial disputes

6 External information

In order to fulfil their role, the management accountant requires information. Some of that information will come from **inside the organisation** (such as from its financial accounting records or the personnel department) but the management accountant may have to look **outside the organisation** for other information.

Exam focus point

Exam questions involving external information can be prepared for by considering now what types and sources of such information are important to **your** organisation.

6.1 Primary external sources of information

An organisation's files are full of invoices, letters, advertisements and so on received from customers and suppliers. These documents provide data from an **external primary source**. A primary source of data is, as the term implies, **as close as you can get to the origin of an item of data**: the eyewitness to an event, the place in question, the document under scrutiny.

The **advantage** of using a primary source of data is that the **user** of the information **knows where it came from, the circumstances under which it was collected, and any limitations or inadequacies in it.**

6.2 Secondary external sources of information

FAST FORWARD

The main **secondary external data sources** are Governments, banks, newspapers, trade journals, information bureaux, consultancies, libraries and information services.

Secondary external sources of data are stores of data collected by outside organisations. The data is collected for general rather than specific purposes and so there are a number of possible **limitations**.

(a) The user will be unaware of any limitations which might be present.
(b) The data may not be suitable for the purpose it is being used for.
(c) The data may be out of date.

Secondary data sources may be satisfactory in certain situations, or they may be the only convenient means of obtaining an item of data. It is essential that the secondary external source used is **accurate** and **reliable**.

Despite the limitations of secondary external data sources, they can be valuable in some situations. There are four main secondary external data **sources**.

(a) Governments
(b) Banks
(c) Newspapers
(d) Trade journals

6.3 Governments

Official statistics are supplied by many Governments. In Great Britain, official statistics are supplied by the Office for National Statistics (ONS), and include the following.

Title	Detail
The *Annual Abstract of Statistics*	This is a general reference book for the United Kingdom which includes data on climate, population, social services, justice and crime, education, defence, manufacturing and agricultural production.
The *Monthly Digest*	An abbreviated version of the *Annual Abstract of Statistics.*
Financial Statistics	A monthly compilation of financial data. It includes statistics on Government income, expenditure and borrowing, financial institutions, companies, the overseas sector, the money supply, exchange rates, interest rates and share prices.
Economic Trends and *Regional Trends*	The main purpose of these publications is to indicate trends using tables, maps and charts.
The United Kingdom National Accounts (The Blue Book)	A source of data on the gross national product, the gross national income and the gross national expenditure. It gives a clear indication of how the nation makes and spends its money.
The United Kingdom Balance of Payments (The Pink Book)	This annual publication gives data on the inflows and outflows of private capital in the United Kingdom.
Social trends	This annual publication provides data on the population, income, householders, families and many other aspects of British life and work.

Monthly statistics are also published by many Government departments. For example, the Department of Employment in Britain publishes *The Department of Employment Gazette* which gives details of retail prices, employment, unemployment, unfilled job vacancies and other statistics relating to employment.

The Department of Trade and Industry in Britain publishes *British Business* on a weekly basis. It includes data on production, prices and trade.

Population data is published by many Governments around the world, and includes population numbers, births, deaths, marriages and so on. In Britain the Government carries out a full census of the whole population every ten years.

6.4 Banks

The Bank of England issues a quarterly magazine which includes data on banks in the UK, the money supply and Government borrowing and financial transactions.

6.5 Financial newspapers

Financial newspapers contain detailed business data and information. Financial newspapers include the *Financial Times*, the *Wall Street Journal*, the *Singapore Business Times* and the *Nikkei Weekly*. Such newspapers provide data on foreign exchange rates, interest rates, gilts and other inventory prices.

6.6 Trade journals

Most industries are served by one or more trade journals. Journals contain data on new developments in the industry, articles about competitors' products, details of industry costs and prices and so on.

6.7 Other sources

(a) **Advice or information bureaux**. Provide information in the form of advice, information leaflets or fact sheets.

(b) **Consultancies**. These include general market research organisations such as MORI and Gallup. There are also specialist market research companies which provide data on specific industries.

(c) **Specific reference works**. Different businesses will have different reference works or so called 'bibles' which are always used as a point of reference.

(d) **Libraries and information services**. Most countries have free public library systems. Educational institutes and business organisations may also provide library services which are available to their members.

(e) **Electronic sources** such as local and national radio and TV, teletext and the **Internet**. The **Internet is becoming more important** as a data source. Many of the sources described in this section can be accessed through their **Website** on the Internet.

7 The maintenance and improvement of accounting information systems

FAST FORWARD

Accounting information systems must be flexible so they can adapt to changes.

The concepts introduced in this section are covered in greater detail later in the text. This section is included to relate these concepts specifically to the maintenance and improvement of accounting information systems.

Key term

An **Accounting Information System** is a computer system or a related group of systems which collect and present accounting information.

Before computers information systems grew **informally**, with each manager making sure that he or she received all the information required to do the job. Information was often obtained from frequent face-to-face contact and co-operation between staff. Such an informal system works best in **very small organisations**.

The introduction of computers forced management to consider its information needs in detail. This is especially the case in larger companies.

In the early days of computing, systems were developed in a haphazard fashion. Systems development usually involved simply automating existing manual procedures rather than forming part of a planned strategy.

Now it is recognised that systems give better information if they are **formally planned**.

In relation to this chapter it is important to realise that even well planned systems will require **on-going maintenance and improvement**. This is because **changes** will occur over time within three areas.

(a) The environment
(b) The organisation's structure
(c) Technology

As a result of these changes the **information requirements** of managers are likely to change too. The accounting information system must be **flexible** enough to **adapt** to provide the necessary information.

Maintenance of the accounting information system involves those activities designed to ensure the current level of service can be maintained.

An **improvement** involves providing an existing service more efficiently, or a new service. For example reduced processing time for account queries, or the ability to present figures in a previously unavailable format such as a chart.

The accounting system should therefore be subject to a culture of **continuous improvement** in the same way as other systems and processes.

The concepts of continuous improvement, quality and total quality management are covered in Chapter 20. **Be sure you can apply these concepts to accounting information systems.**

8 Cost behaviour

Key term

Cost behaviour is 'The variability of input costs with activity undertaken.'

CIMA *Official Terminology*

8.1 Basic principles of cost behaviour

We will be examining the techniques of cost accounting in the remaining chapters of Part A, so we conclude this introductory chapter with a revision of the nature and behaviour of costs generally.

The basic principle of cost behaviour is that as the level of activity rises, costs will usually rise. It will probably cost more to produce 2,000 units of output than it will cost to produce 1,000 units; it will usually cost more to make five telephone calls than to make one call and so on. The problem for the accountant is to determine, for each item of cost, the way in which costs rise and by how much as the level of activity increases.

8.2 Fixed costs

A **fixed cost** is a cost that tends to be unaffected by increases or decreases in the volume of output. Fixed costs are a **period charge**, in that they relate to a span of time; as the time span increases, so too will the fixed costs. A sketch graph of a fixed cost would look like this.

Graph of fixed cost

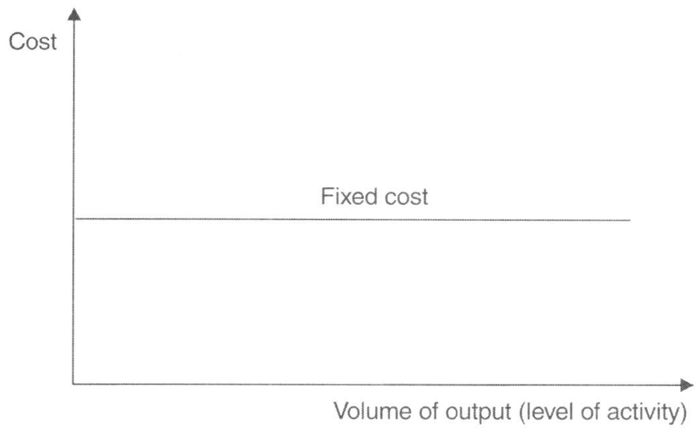

Examples of fixed costs

(a) The salary of the managing director (per month or per annum)
(b) The rent of a single factory building (per month or per annum)
(c) Straight line depreciation of a single machine (per month or per annum)

Key term

A **step cost** is a cost which is fixed in nature but only within certain levels of activity.

Consider the depreciation of a machine which may be fixed if production remains below 1,000 units per month. If production exceeds 1,000 units, a second machine may be required, and the cost of depreciation (on two machines) would go up a step. A sketch graph of a step cost could look like this.

Graph of step cost

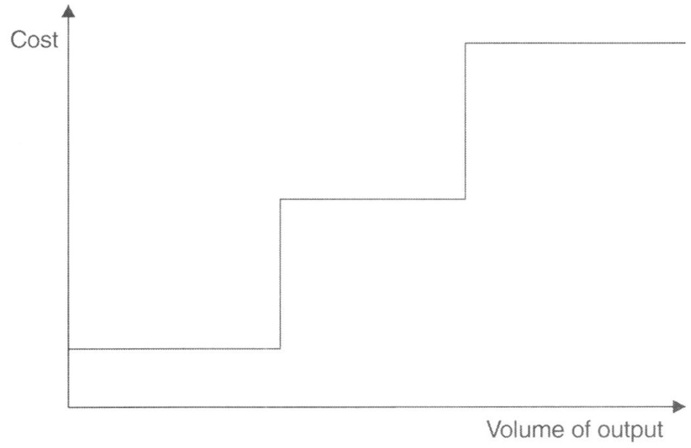

Other examples of step costs are as follows.

(a) Rent is a step cost in situations where accommodation requirements increase as output levels get higher.
(b) Basic pay of employees is nowadays usually fixed, but as output rises, more employees (direct workers, supervisors, managers and so on) are required.

8.3 Variable costs

A **variable cost** is a cost that tends to vary directly with the volume of output. The variable cost **per unit** is the same amount for each unit produced whereas **total** variable cost increases as volume of output increases. A sketch graph of a variable cost would look like this.

Graph of variable cost

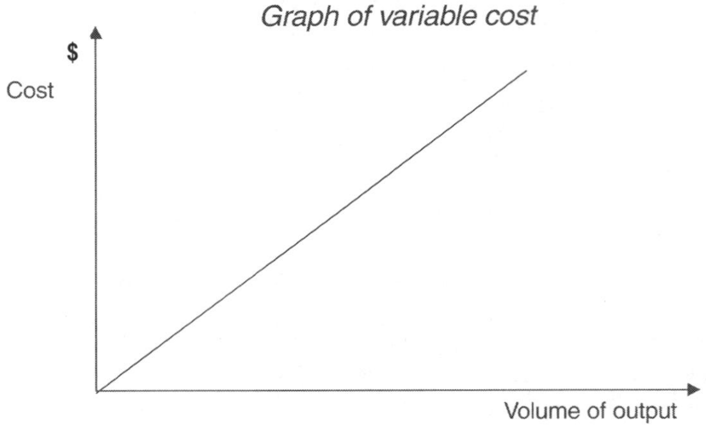

Examples of variable costs

(a) The cost of raw materials (where there is no discount for bulk purchasing since bulk purchase discounts reduce the unit cost of purchases).

(b) Direct labour costs are usually classed as a variable cost even though basic wages are often fixed.

(c) Sales commission is variable in relation to the volume or value of sales.

8.4 Non-linear variable costs

Although variable costs are usually assumed to be linear, there are situations where variable costs are **curvilinear**. Have a look at the following graphs.

Graph (a)

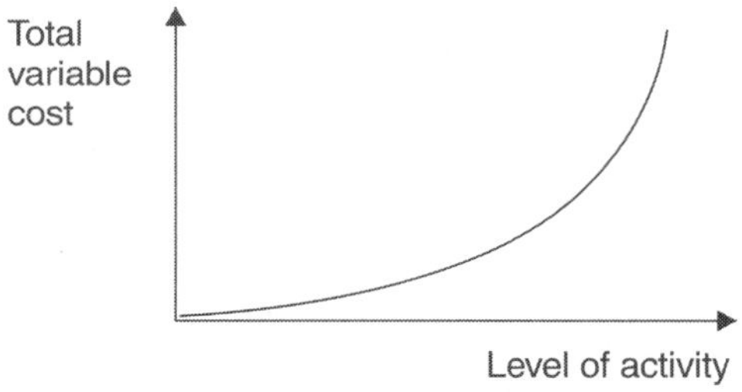

Graph (b)

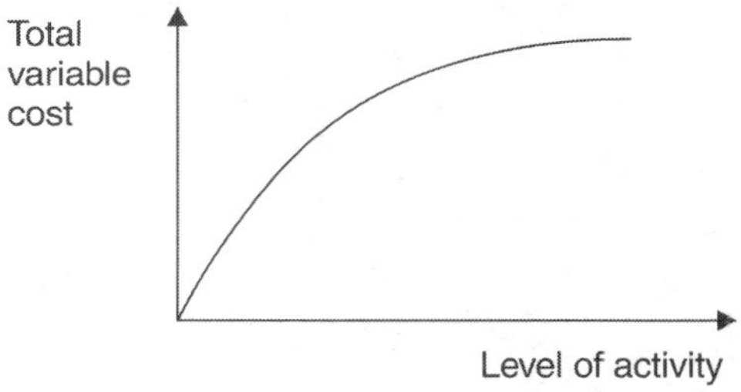

Graph (a) becomes steeper as levels of activity increase. Each additional unit of activity is adding more to total variable cost than the previous unit. Graph (b) becomes less steep as levels of activity increase. Each additional unit is adding less to total variable cost than the previous unit.

Semi-variable costs (or semi-fixed costs or mixed costs)

Key term

A **semi-variable/semi-fixed/mixed cost** is 'A cost containing both fixed and variable components and which is thus partly affected by a change in the level of activity'.

CIMA *Official Terminology*

Examples of semi-variable costs include the following.

(a) **Electricity and gas bills**. There is a basic charge plus a charge per unit of consumption.

(b) **Sales representative's salary**. The sales representative may earn a basic monthly amount of, say, $1,000 and then commission of 10% of the value of sales made.

The behaviour of a semi-variable cost can be presented graphically.

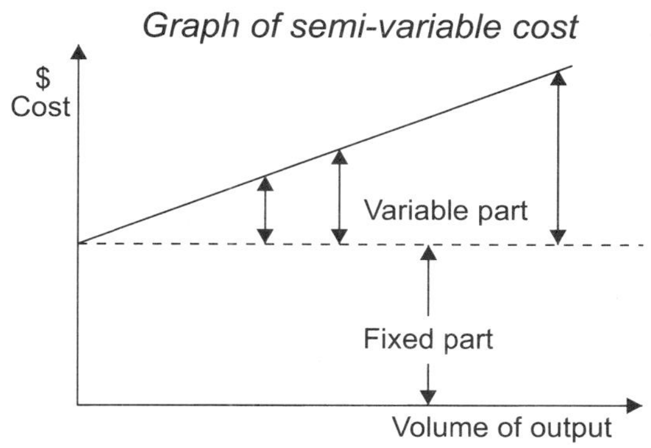

8.5 Cost behaviour and total and unit costs

If the variable cost of producing a unit is $5 per unit then it will remain at that cost per unit no matter how many units are produced. However if the business's fixed costs are $5,000 then the fixed cost *per unit* will decrease the more units are produced: one unit will have fixed costs of $5,000 per unit; if 2,500 are produced the fixed cost per unit will be $2; if 5,000 are produced the fixed cost per unit will be only $1. Thus as the level of activity increases the total costs *per unit* (fixed cost plus variable cost) will decrease.

In sketch graph form this may be illustrated as follows.

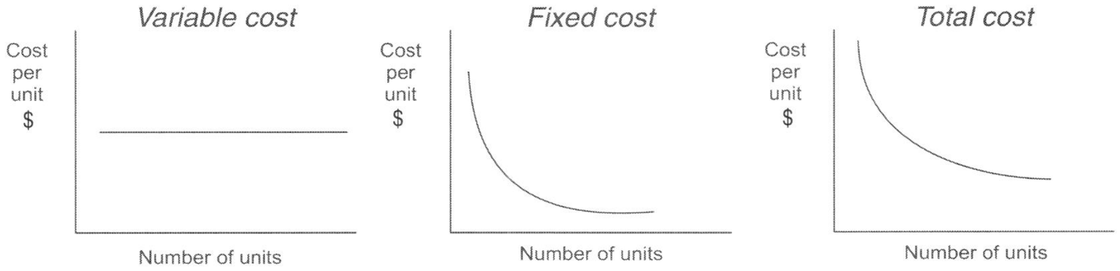

8.6 Assumptions about cost behaviour

It is often possible to assume that, within the normal or relevant range of output, costs are either fixed, variable or semi-variable.

Chapter Roundup

- Managers have to **plan, control, organise, motivate** and **make decisions**.
- The nature of an organisation will affect what the managers do in that organisation.
- Management accounting is therefore concerned with the collection of data, its analysis and processing into information, and the interpretation and communication of that information so as to assist management with planning, control and decision making.
- **Management information** should be relevant, complete, accurate, clear and timely. It should inspire confidence and be communicated to the right manager, manageable in terms of volume, communicated by an appropriate channel of communication and provided at a cost which is less than the benefits it provides.
- The **decision-making process** has six steps.
  - Identify objectives
  - Search for alternative courses of action
  - Collect data about the alternative courses of action
  - Select the appropriate course of action
  - Implement the decision
  - Compare actual and planned outcomes and take corrective action as necessary
- **Management accounting information** is, in general, unsuitable for decision making.
- The main **secondary external data sources** are Governments, banks, newspapers, trade journals, information bureaux, consultancies, libraries and information services.
- Accounting information systems must be flexible so they can adapt to changes.

Quick Quiz

1 Motivating involves comparing actual performance with planned performance, identifying deviations from plan and taking corrective action as necessary. True or false?

2 According to the definition of management accounting provided in the CIMA *Official Terminology*, management accounting involves the preparation of information for non-management groups such as creditors. True or false?

3 Good monetary information is always provided to the nearest cent. True or false?

4 The objective of *all* organisations is the maximisation of profit. True or false?

5 Information provided by conventional management accounts is ideal for decision making. True or false?

6 Which of the following is **not** an essential quality of good information?

A It should be relevant for its purposes
B It should be communicated to the right person
C It should be completely accurate
D It should be timely

7 Which of the following is/are primary sources of data?

(i) Historical records of transport costs to be used to prepare forecasts for budgetary planning

(ii) The *Annual Abstract of Statistics*, published by the Office for National Statistics in the United Kingdom

(iii) Data collected by a telephone survey to monitor the effectiveness of a bank's customer services

A (i) and (ii)
B (i) and (iii)
C (i) only
D (iii) only

Answers to Quick Quiz

1 False. What is described is control.

2 True.

3 False. Information should only be accurate enough for its purpose.

4 False. Profit maximisation is the objective of a lot of profit-making organisations but non-profit-making organisations in particular will have different objectives.

5 False.

6 Complete accuracy is not necessarily an **essential** quality of good information. It needs to be **sufficiently accurate** for its purpose, and often there is no need to go into unnecessary detail for pointless accuracy.

Relevance (**option A**) is an essential quality of good information. Busy managers should not be forced to waste their time reading pages of unnecessary information.

Communication of the information to the right person (**option B**) is essential. Individuals who are given the authority to do certain tasks must be given the information they need to do them.

The correct timing of information (**option D**) is essential. Information which is not available until after a decision is made will be useful only for comparisons and longer-term control, and may serve no purpose even then. Information prepared too frequently can also be a waste of time and resources.

7 D Data collected by survey for a particular project are a primary data source.

Historical records of transport costs were not collected specifically for the preparation of forecasts, therefore these are secondary data.

The *Annual Abstract of Statistics* is a source of secondary external data.

Now try the questions below from the Exam Question Bank

Number	Level	Marks	Time
Section A: Q1	MCQ	N/A	N/A
Section B: Q1	Preparation	10	18 mins

1.2 What do management accountants do with overheads?

There were two schools of thought as to the correct method of dealing with overheads.

(a) **Absorption costing**
(b) **Marginal costing**

A modern version of absorption costing called **activity based costing (ABC)** is gaining in popularity.

2 A reminder of absorption costing

FAST FORWARD

Absorption costing aims to include within the total cost of a product an appropriate share of the organisation's total overhead.

Key term

Absorption costing is a method of product costing which aims to include in the total cost of a product (unit, job, process and so on) an appropriate share of the organisation's total overhead. An appropriate share is generally taken to mean an amount which reflects the amount of time and effort that has gone into producing a unit or completing a job.

Knowledge brought forward from earlier studies

Absorption costing

- Product costs are built up using absorption costing by a process of **allocation**, **apportionment** and **overhead absorption**.
- **Allocation** is the process by which whole cost items are charged directly to a cost unit or cost centre. **Direct costs** are allocated directly to cost units. **Overheads** clearly identifiable with cost centres are allocated to those cost centres but costs which cannot be identified with one particular cost centre are allocated to general overhead cost centres. The cost of a warehouse security guard would therefore be charged to the warehouse cost centre but heating and lighting costs would be charged to a general overhead cost centre.
- The **first stage of overhead apportionment** involves sharing out (or apportioning) the overheads within **general overhead cost centres** between the other cost centres using a fair basis of apportionment (such as floor area occupied by each cost centre for heating and lighting costs).
- The **second stage of overhead apportionment** is to apportion the costs of **service cost centres** (both directly allocated and apportioned costs) to production cost centres.
- The final stage in absorption costing is the **absorption** into product costs (using overhead absorption rates) of the overheads which have been allocated and apportioned to the production cost centres.
- Costs allocated and apportioned to non-production cost centres are usually deducted from the full cost of production to arrive at the cost of sales.

The **theoretical justification** for using absorption costing is that all production overheads are incurred in the production of the organisation's output and so each unit of the product receives some benefit from these costs. Each unit of output should therefore be charged with some of the overhead costs.

Practical reasons for using absorption costing

(a) **Inventory valuations**

Inventory in hand must be valued for two reasons.

(i) For the closing inventory figure in the statement of financial position (balance sheet)
(ii) For the cost of sales figure in the income statement

The valuation of inventories will affect profitability during a period because of the way in which the cost of sales is calculated.

Calculation of cost of sales

	The cost of goods produced
+	the value of opening inventories
–	the value of closing inventories
=	the cost of goods sold.

In absorption costing closing inventories are valued at a fully absorbed factory cost rather than at prime cost (where fixed overheads have not been absorbed). They are not valued at the full cost of sales, because the only costs incurred in producing goods for finished inventory are factory costs.

(b) **Pricing decisions**

Many companies attempt to set selling prices **by calculating the full cost of production or sales** of each product, and then adding a margin for profit. In our example, the company might have fixed a gross profit margin at 25% on factory cost, or 20% of the sales price, in order to establish the unit sales price of $10. 'Full cost plus pricing' can be particularly useful for companies which do jobbing or contract work, where each job or contract is different, so that a standard unit sales price cannot be fixed. Without using absorption costing, a full cost is difficult to ascertain.

(c) **Establishing the profitability of different products**

This argument in favour of absorption costing states that if a company sells more than one product, it will be difficult to judge **how profitable each individual product is**, unless overhead costs are shared on a fair basis and charged to the cost of sales of each product.

2.1 Statement of Standard Accounting Practice 9 (SSAP 9)

Of these three arguments, the problem of valuing inventories is perhaps the most significant. **Absorption costing is recommended in financial accounting** by the *Statement of Standard Accounting Practice* on inventories and long-term contracts (SSAP 9). SSAP 9 deals with financial accounting systems and not with cost accounting systems. The cost accountant is (in theory) free to value inventories by whatever method seems best, but where companies integrate their financial accounting and cost accounting systems into a single system of accounting records, the valuation of closing inventories will be determined by SSAP 9.

SSAP 9 states that costs of all inventories should comprise those costs which have been incurred in the normal course of business in **bringing the product to its 'present location and condition'**. These costs incurred will include all related production overheads, even though these overheads may accrue on a time basis. In other words, in financial accounting, closing inventories should be valued at full factory cost, and it may therefore be convenient and appropriate to value inventories by the same method in the cost accounting system.

For many purposes absorption costing is, however, less useful as a costing method than marginal costing. In some situations, **absorption costing can be misleading** in the information it supplies.

Question — Absorption costing

In relation to calculating total absorption cost, label the following descriptions in the correct order as Steps 1 – 5.

Description		**Step**
A	Apportion fixed costs over departments	
B	Establish the overhead absorption rate	
C	Choose fair methods of apportionment	
D	Apply the overhead absorption rate to products	
E	Reapportion service departments costs	

Answer

A = 2
B = 4
C = 1
D = 5
E = 3

3 Overhead allocation, apportionment and absorption

FAST FORWARD

There are three stages in absorption costing: **allocation**, **apportionment** and **absorption**.

Work through the following example and activity in order to remind yourself of the basic principles of absorption costing. If you have trouble remembering how to perform absorption costing calculations, refer back to your Paper 4 Interactive Text and revise the basic principles.

FAST FORWARD

Apportionment has two stages: **general overhead apportionment** and **service department cost apportionment.**

3.1 Example: overhead apportionment

Millie has incurred the following overhead costs.

	$'000
Depreciation of factory	100
Factory repairs and maintenance	60
Factory office costs (treat as production overhead)	150
Depreciation of equipment	80
Insurance of equipment	20
Heating	39
Lighting	10
Canteen	90
	549

Information relating to the production and service departments in the factory is as follows.

	Department			
	Production 1	*Production* 2	*Service* 100	*Service* 101
Floor space (square metres)	1,200	1,600	800	400
Volume (cubic metres)	3,000	6,000	2,400	1,600
Number of employees	30	30	15	15
Book value of equipment	$30,000	$20,000	$10,000	$20,000

Required

Determine how the overhead costs should be apportioned between the four departments.

3.2 Solution

Costs are apportioned using the following general formula.

$$\frac{\text{Total overhead cost}}{\text{Total value of apportionment base}} \times \text{value of apportionment base of cost centre}$$

For example, heating for department 1 = $\frac{\$39,000}{13,000} \times 3,000 = \$9,000$

Item of cost	Basis of apportionment	Total cost	To Department 1	2	100	101
		$	$	$	$	$
Factory depreciation	(floor area)	100	30.0	40	20.0	10.0
Factory repairs	(floor area)	60	18.0	24	12.0	6.0
Factory office costs	(number of employees)	150	50.0	50	25.0	25.0
Equipment depreciation	(book value)	80	30.0	20	10.0	20.0
Equipment insurance	(book value)	20	7.5	5	2.5	5.0
Heating	(volume)	39	9.0	18	7.2	4.8
Lighting	(floor area)	10	3.0	4	2.0	1.0
Canteen	(number of employees)	90	30.0	30	15.0	15.0
Total		549	177.5	191	93.7	86.8

FAST FORWARD

Service department costs can be apportioned to production departments either directly, or using the **repeated distribution method**.

Question

Overhead apportionment

Pippin has three production departments (forming, machines and assembly) and two service departments (maintenance and general).

The following is an analysis of budgeted overhead costs for a twelve-month period.

	$	$
Rent and rates		8,000
Power		750
Light, heat		5,000
Repairs, maintenance:		
Forming	800	
Machines	1,800	
Assembly	300	
Maintenance	200	
General	100	
		3,200
Departmental expenses:		
Forming	1,500	
Machines	2,300	
Assembly	1,100	
Maintenance	900	
General	1,500	
Cfwd		7,300

	$	$
Bfwd		7,300
Depreciation:		
Plant		10,000
Fixtures and fittings		250
Insurance:		
Plant		2,000
Buildings		500
Indirect labour:		
Forming	3,000	
Machines	5,000	
Assembly	1,500	
Maintenance	4,000	
General	2,000	
		15,500
		52,500

Other available data are as follows

	Floor area sq.ft	Plant value $	Fixtures & fittings $	Effective horse - power	Direct cost for year $	Labour hours worked	Machine hours worked
Forming	2,000	25,000	1,000	40	20,500	14,400	12,000
Machines	4,000	60,000	500	90	30,300	20,500	21,600
Assembly	3,000	7,500	2,000	15	24,200	20,200	2,000
Maintenance	500	7,500	1,000	5	-	-	-
General	500	-	500	-	-	-	-
	10,000	100,000	5,000	150	75,000	55,100	35,600

Required

Using the data provided apportion overheads to the five departments.

Answer

	Basis	Forming $	Machines $	Assembly $	Maint'nce $	General $	Total $
Directly allocated overheads:							
Repairs, maintenance		800	1,800	300	200	100	3,200
Departmental expenses		1,500	2,300	1,100	900	1,500	7,300
Indirect labour		3,000	5,000	1,500	4,000	2,000	15,500
Apportionment of other overheads:							
Rent, rates	1	1,600	3,200	2,400	400	400	8,000
Power	2	200	450	75	25	0	750
Light, heat	1	1,000	2,000	1,500	250	250	5,000
Dep'n of plant	3	2,500	6,000	750	750	0	10,000
Dep'n of F & F	4	50	25	100	50	25	250
Insurance of plant	3	500	1,200	150	150	0	2,000
Insurance of buildings	1	100	200	150	25	25	500
		11,250	22,175	8,025	6,750	4,300	52,500

Basis of apportionment:

1 floor area
2 effective horsepower
3 plant value
4 fixtures and fittings value

Exam focus point

If an **examination question** calls for **the apportionment of overhead** items, you may encounter one or two items for which two (or more) bases of apportionment may appear to be equally acceptable. **Explain** why you chose one basis in preference to another.

Question

More overheads

Using your solution to the last question and the following information about the apportionment of service department costs, apportion the costs of the two service departments of Pippin to the three production departments and hence determine the total overhead for those departments.

	Maintenance %	General %
Forming	20	30
Machines	50	60
Assembly	30	10
	100	100

Answer

Service department	Basis of apportionment	Total cost	Forming	Machines	Assembly
		$	$	$	$
Maintenance	2:5:3	6,750	1,350	3,375	2,025
General	3:6:1	4,300	1,290	2,580	430
		11,050	2,640	5,955	2,455
Previously allocated and apportioned costs		41,450	11,250	22,175	8,025
Total overhead		52,500	13,890	28,130	10,480

FAST FORWARD

Overheads are absorbed into products using an appropriate **absorption rate** based on budgeted costs and budgeted activity levels.

Question

Overhead absorption

Using your solution to the preceding question and the following information, determine suitable overhead absorption rates for Pippin's three production departments.

	Forming	Machines	Assembly
Budgeted direct labour hours per annum	5,556	790	5,240
Budgeted machine hours per annum	1,350	5,626	147

Answer

Forming (labour intensive) $\frac{\$13,890}{5,556}$ = $2.50 per direct labour hour

Machines (machine intensive) $\frac{\$28,130}{5,626}$ = $5 per machine hour

Assembly (labour intensive) $\frac{\$10,480}{5,240}$ = $2 per direct labour hour

4 Blanket and departmental absorption rates

A **blanket overhead absorption rate** is an absorption rate **used throughout a factory** and for **all jobs** and units of output irrespective of the department in which they were produced. If, for example, total overheads were $500,000 and there were 250,000 direct machine hours during the period, the blanket overhead rate would be $2 per direct machine hour and all jobs passing through the factory would be charged at that rate.

Such a rate is not appropriate, however, if there are a number of departments and jobs do not spend an equal amount of time in each department.

It is argued that if a single factory overhead absorption rate is used, some products will receive a higher overhead charge than they ought 'fairly' to bear, whereas other products will be under-charged. By using a **separate absorption rate for each department**, charging of overheads will be equitable and the full cost of production of items will be more representative of the cost of the efforts and resources put into making them. (Remember, however, that by using **only one absorption base** for each department inconsistencies may still occur.) An example may help to illustrate this point.

4.1 Example: separate absorption rates

AB has two production departments, for which the following budgeted information is available.

	Department Aye	*Department Bee*	*Total*
Budgeted overheads	$180,000	$100,000	$280,000
Budgeted direct labour hours	100,000 hrs	20,000 hrs	120,000 hrs

If a single factory overhead absorption rate is applied, the rate of overhead recovery would be:

$$\frac{\$280{,}000}{120{,}000 \text{ hours}} = \$2.33 \text{ per direct labour hour}$$

If separate departmental rates are applied, these would be:

Department Aye	*Department Bee*
$\frac{\$180{,}000}{100{,}000 \text{ hours}}$	$\frac{\$100{,}000}{20{,}000 \text{ hours}}$
= $1.80 per direct labour hour	= $5 per direct labour hour

Department Bee has a higher overhead cost per hour worked than department Aye.

Now let us consider two separate jobs.

(a) Job A has a prime cost of $100, takes 30 hours in department Bee and does not involve any work in department Aye.

(b) Job B has a prime cost of $100, takes 28 hours in department Aye and 2 hours in department Bee.

What would be the factory cost of each job, using the following rates of overhead recovery.

(a) A single factory rate of overhead recovery
(b) Separate departmental rates of overhead recovery

4.2 Solution

(a)

	Job A	*Job B*
Single factory rate	$	$
Prime cost	100	100
Factory overhead (30 × $2.33)	70	70
Factory cost	170	170

(b)

		Job A		*Job B*
Separate departmental rates		$		$
Prime cost		100		100.00
Factory overhead: department Aye		0	(28 × $1.80)	50.40
department Bee	(30 × $5)	150	(2 × $5)	10.00
Factory cost		250		160.40

Using a single factory overhead absorption rate, both jobs would cost the same. However, since job A is done entirely within department Bee where overhead costs are relatively higher, whereas job B is done mostly within department Aye, where overhead costs are relatively lower, it is arguable that job A should cost more than job B. This will occur if separate departmental overhead recovery rates are used to reflect the work done on each job in each department separately.

If all **jobs do not spend approximately the same time in each department** then, to ensure that all jobs are charged with their fair share of overheads, it is necessary to **establish separate overhead rates for each department**.

5 Over and under absorption of overheads

FAST FORWARD

Under-/over-absorbed overhead occurs when overheads incurred do not equal overheads absorbed.

You should have encountered reasons for over and under absorption of overheads in *Intermediate Accounting for Costs.*

So treat this section as a refresher reading through the paragraphs and follow the example and solution in 5.2 to 5.3.

Suppose that Norman budgeted to make 100 units of product Z at a cost of $3 per unit in direct materials and $4 per unit in direct labour. The sales price would be $12 per unit, and production overheads were budgeted to amount to $200. A unit basis of overhead recovery is in operation. During the period 120 units were actually produced and sold (for $12 each) and the actual cost of direct materials was $380 and of direct labour, $450. Overheads incurred came to $210.

Ignoring administration, selling and distribution overheads, the cost of sales of product Z and the company's profit would be calculated as follows.

	$
Direct materials	380
Direct labour	450
Overheads absorbed (120 units × $2*)	240
Full cost of sales, product Z	1,070
Sales of product Z (120 units × $12)	1,440
Profit, product Z	370

* *Note* ($200 ÷ 100 units)

You may already have noticed that the **actual overhead cost incurred**, $210, is **not the same as the overhead absorbed** into the cost of production, $240; nevertheless, in absorption costing $240 is the 'correct' cost. This **discrepancy between actual overheads incurred and the overheads absorbed**, which is an inevitable feature of absorption costing, is only **reconciled at the end of an accounting period, as the 'under absorption' or 'over absorption' of overhead.**

The rate of overhead absorption is based on estimates (of both numerator and denominator) and it is quite likely that either one or both of the estimates will not agree with what *actually* occurs. Actual overheads incurred will probably be either greater than or less than overheads absorbed into the cost of production.

(a) **Over absorption** means that the **overheads charged to the cost of sales are greater then the overheads actually incurred.**

(b) **Under absorption** means that **insufficient overheads have been included in the cost of sales.**

Suppose that the budgeted overhead in a production department is $80,000 and the budgeted activity is 40,000 direct labour hours. The overhead recovery rate (using a direct labour hour basis) would be $2 per direct labour hour.
Actual overheads in the period are, say $84,000 and 45,000 direct labour hours are worked.

	$
Overhead incurred (actual)	84,000
Overhead absorbed (45,000 × $2)	90,000
Over-absorption of overhead	6,000

In this example, the cost of produced units or jobs has been charged with $6,000 more than was actually spent. An adjustment to reconcile the overheads charged to the actual overhead is necessary and the over-absorbed overhead will be written as an adjustment to the profit and loss account at the end of the accounting period.

5.1 The reasons for under-/over-absorbed overhead

The overhead absorption rate is predetermined from budget estimates of overhead cost and the expected volume of activity. Under or over recovery of overhead will occur in three circumstances.

(a) **Actual overhead costs are different from budgeted overheads.**
(b) **The actual activity level is different from the budgeted activity level.**
(c) **Both actual overhead costs and actual activity level are different from the budgeted costs and level.**

5.2 Example: reasons for under/over absorption

Trevor has a budgeted production overhead of $25,000 and a budgeted activity of 12,500 direct labour hours and therefore a recovery rate of $2 per direct labour hour.

Required

Calculate the under-/over-absorbed overhead, and the reasons for the under/over absorption, in the following circumstances.

(a) Actual overheads cost $22,000 and 12,500 direct labour hours are worked.
(b) Actual overheads cost $25,000 and 9,000 direct labour hours are worked.
(c) Actual overheads cost $22,000 and 9,000 direct labour hours are worked.

5.3 Solution

(a)

	$
Actual overhead	22,000
Absorbed overhead (12,500 × $2)	25,000
Over-absorbed overhead	3,000

The reason for the over absorption is that although the actual and budgeted direct labour hours are the same, actual overheads cost less than expected.

(b)

	$
Actual overhead	25,000
Absorbed overhead (9,000 × $2)	18,000
Under-absorbed overhead	7,000

The reason for the under absorption is that although budgeted and actual overhead costs were the same, fewer direct labour hours were worked than expected.

(c)

	$
Actual overhead	22,000
Absorbed overhead (9,000 × $2)	18,000
Under-absorbed overhead	4,000

The reason for the under absorption is a combination of the reasons in (a) and (b).

6 An evaluation of absorption costing

We have already seen that for the purposes of external reporting, absorption costing must be used to value inventories. In later chapters we will consider its usefulness for management reporting and decision making.

7 The reasons for the development of activity based costing

FAST FORWARD

An alternative to the traditional methods of absorption costing is **activity based costing (ABC).** ABC involves the identification of the factors (cost drivers) which cause the costs of an organisation's major activities. Support overheads are charged to products on the basis of their usage of an activity.

Exam focus point

> A question in the June 2007 exam tested knowledge of ABC by asking candidates to use ABC to allocate overheads and then calculate a sales price using this data. Candidates were also required to state three benefits of using ABC and discuss two circumstances where ABC is the most appropriate approach to product costing.
>
> A question in the December 2005 exam required the calculation of a selling price based on activity based costing.
>
> Candidates were also asked to explain why activity based costing would be more useful in costing products than absorption costing.

The **absorption costing approach** that we have learned about so far in this chapter was **developed in a time** when most organisations produced only a narrow range of products and **when overhead costs were only a very small fraction of total costs**, direct labour and direct material costs accounting for the largest proportion of the costs. The value of over- or under-absorbed overhead was therefore not too significant.

Nowadays, however, the situation is different. With the advent of advanced manufacturing technology (AMT), **overheads are likely to be far more important.**

(a) Direct labour may account for as little as 5% of a product's cost.

(b) The accessibility of information technology now allows for more sophisticated overhead allocation methods than in the past.

In today's business environment it is difficult to justify the use of direct labour or direct material as the basis for allocating overheads. It is against this background that **activity based costing (ABC) has emerged**.

The traditional methods accurately allocate to products the costs of those resources that are used in proportion to the number of units produced of a particular product. Such resources include machine-related costs such as power and lubricants. Many resources are used in non-volume related support activities (which have increased due to AMT), such as setting-up, production scheduling, first item inspection and data processing, however. These support activities assist the efficient manufacture of a wide range of products and are not, in general, affected by changes in production volume. They tend to vary in the long term according to the range and complexity of the products manufactured rather than the volume of output.

The wider the range and the more complex the products, the more support services will be required. Consider, for example, factory X which produces 10,000 units of one product, the Alpha, and factory Y which produces 1,000 units each of ten slightly different versions of the Alpha. Support activity costs in the factory Y are likely to be a lot higher than in factory X but the factories produce an identical number of units. Take setting-up. Factory X will only need to set-up once whereas Factory Y will have to set-up the production run at least ten times for the ten different products. Factory Y will therefore incur more set-up costs.

Traditional costing systems, which assume that all products consume all resources **in proportion to their production volumes**, tend to allocate too great a proportion of overheads to high volume products (which cause relatively little diversity and hence use fewer support services) and too small a proportion of overheads to low volume products (which cause greater diversity and therefore use more support services). ABC attempts to overcome this problem.

The **major ideas behind activity based costing** are as follows.

(a) **Activities cause costs**. Activities include ordering, materials handling, machining, assembly, production scheduling and despatching.

(b) **Producing products creates demand** for the activities.

(c) **Costs are assigned to a product on the basis of the product's consumption of the activities.**

Key term

> **Activity based costing (ABC)** involves the identification of the factors which cause the costs of an organisation's major activities. Support overheads are charged to products on the basis of their usage of the factor causing the overheads.

8 Calculating product costs using ABC

Exam focus point

This was examined in December 2004. The examiner has since noted that ABC is a commonly used technique in business and commerce, and that candidates should practise this area.

An ABC system operates as follows.

Step 1 **Identify** an organisation's **major activities**.

Step 2 **Identify** the factors which determine the size of the costs of an activity/cause the costs of an activity. These are known as **cost drivers**.

Key term

A **cost driver** is the factor which causes the costs of an activity.

Look at the following examples.

Activity	Cost driver
Ordering	Number of orders
Materials handling	Number of production runs
Production scheduling	Number of production runs
Despatching	Number of despatches

For those costs that vary with production levels in the short term, ABC uses volume-related cost drivers such as labour or machine hours. The cost of oil used as a lubricant on machines would therefore be added to products on the basis of the number of machine hours, since oil would have to be used for each hour the machine ran.

Step 3 **Collect the costs of each activity into** what are known as **cost pools** (equivalent to cost centres under more traditional costing methods).

Step 4 **Charge support overheads to products on the basis of their usage of the activity. A product's usage of an activity is measured by the number of the activity's cost driver it generates.**

Suppose, for example, that the cost pool for the ordering activity totalled $100,000 and that there were 10,000 orders (the cost driver). Each product would therefore be charged with $10 for each order it required. A batch requiring five orders would therefore be charged with $50.

Before we move on, try an example for yourself so that you are clear how cost drivers are used to charge overheads to activities. This example only shows activity based costing so you can see how cost drivers are used to allocate costs to products.

8.1 Example: Fred Co

Fred make and sell a number of products. Products A and B are products for which market prices are available at which S can obtain a share of the market as detailed below. Estimated data for the forthcoming period is as follows.

(a) Product data

	Product A	*Product B*	*Product C*
Production/sales (units)	5,000	10,000	40,000
	$'000	$'000	$'000
Total direct material cost	80	300	2,020
Total direct labour cost	40	100	660

(b) Variable overhead cost is $1,500,000 of which 40% is related to the acquisition, storage and use of direct materials and 60% is related to the control and use of direct labour.

(c) It is current practice in S plc to absorb variable overhead cost into product units using overall company wide percentages on direct material cost and direct labour cost as the absorption bases.

Required

Prepare estimated unit product costs for Product A and Product B where variable overhead is charged to product units using an activity based costing approach where **cost drivers** have been estimated for material and labour related overhead costs as follows.

	Product A	*Product B*	*Product C*
Direct material related overheads – **cost driver is material bulk**. The bulk proportions **per unit** are:	4	1	1.5
Direct labour related overheads – **cost driver is number of labour operations** (not directly time related).			
Labour operations per product **unit** are:	6	1	2.0

8.2 Solution

ABC approach

	A	*B*
	$	$
Direct material cost per unit ($80,000/5,000, $300,000/10,000)	16.00	30.00
Direct labour cost per unit ($40,000/5,000, $100,000/10,000)	8.00	10.00
Variable overhead cost per unit (see below)	71.68	14.17
	95.68	54.17

Workings

(1) **Material-related overheads**

Remember the cost drivers stated in the question. Multiply these by the production/sales for each product. This gives you total cost driver for each product.

		Bulk
Number of cost drivers		'000
Product A	4 × 5,000	20
Product B	1 × 10,000	10
Product C	1.5 × 40,000	60
		90

Then divide overhead by the cost driver

∴ **Overhead per cost driver** = ($1,500,000 × 40%)/90,000
= $600,000 ÷ 90,000
= $6.67

(2) **Labour-related overheads**

Remember the cost driver is number of labour operations per **unit** so you need to multiply this by production sales to give the total cost drivers for each product.

		Labour operations
Number of cost drivers		'000
Product A	6 × 5,000	30
Product B	1 × 10,000	10
Product C	2 × 40,000	80
		120

Then divide overhead by the cost driver

∴ **Overhead per cost driver** = ($1,500,000 × 60%)/120,000
= $900,000 ÷ 120,000
= $7.50

Variable overhead per unit

	A	B
	$	$
Material related		
$6.67 (per above W1) × 4 or 1	26.68	6.67
Labour related		
$7.50 (per above W2) × 6 or 1	45.00	7.50
	71.68	14.17

Now try another example which compares and contrasts absorption costing and ABC activity based costing

8.3 Example: ABC

Suppose that Cooplan manufactures four products, W, X, Y and Z. Output and cost data for the period just ended are as follows.

	Output Units	*Number of production runs in the period*	*Material cost per unit*	*Direct labour hours per unit*	*Machine hours per unit*
			$		
W	10	2	20	1	1
X	10	2	80	3	3
Y	100	5	20	1	1
Z	100	5	80	3	3
		14			

Direct labour cost per hour is $5. Overhead costs are as follows.

	$
Short-run variable costs	3,080
Set-up costs	10,920
Production and scheduling costs	9,100
Materials handling costs	7,700
	30,800

Required

Calculate product costs using the following approaches.

(a) Absorption costing
(b) ABC

8.4 Solution

Using a conventional absorption costing approach and an absorption rate for overheads based on either direct labour hours or machine hours, the product costs would be as follows.

	W	X	Y	Z	Total
	$	$	$	$	$
Direct material	200	800	2,000	8,000	11,000
Direct labour	50	150	500	1,500	2,200
Overheads *	700	2,100	7,000	21,000	30,800
	950	3,050	9,500	30,500	44,000
Units produced	10	10	100	100	
Cost per unit	$95	$305	$95	$305	

* $30,800 ÷ 440 hours = $70 per direct labour or machine hour

Using activity based costing and assuming that the number of production runs is the cost driver for set-up costs, production and scheduling costs and materials handling costs and that machine hours are the cost driver for short-run variable costs, unit costs would be as follows.

	W	*X*	*Y*	*Z*	*Total*
	$	$	$	$	$
Direct material	200	800	2,000	8,000	11,000
Direct labour	50	150	500	1,500	2,200
Short-run variable overheads (W1)	70	210	700	2,100	3,080
Set-up costs (W2)	1,560	1,560	3,900	3,900	10,920
Production and scheduling costs (W3)	1,300	1,300	3,250	3,250	9,100
Materials handling costs (W4)	1,100	1,100	2,750	2,750	7,700
	4,280	5,120	13,100	21,500	44,000
Units produced	10	10	100	100	
Cost per unit	$428	$512	$131	$215	

Workings

1	$3,080 ÷ 440 machine hours	=	$7 per machine hour
2	$10,920 ÷ 14 production runs	=	$780 per run
3	$9,100 ÷ 14 production runs	=	$650 per run
4	$7,700 ÷ 14 production runs	=	$550 per run

Summary

Product	*Conventional costing Unit cost*	*ABC Unit cost*	*Difference*
	$	$	$
W	95	428	+333
X	305	512	+207
Y	95	131	+36
Z	305	215	–90

The figures suggest that the traditional volume-based absorption costing system is flawed.

(a) It under allocates overhead costs to low-volume products (here, W and X with ten units of output) and over allocates overheads to higher-volume products (here Z in particular).

(b) It under allocates overhead costs to less complex products (here W and Y with just one hour of work needed per unit) and over allocates overheads to more complex products (here X and particularly Z).

9 ABC versus traditional absorption costing

9.1 Allocation of overheads

Traditional absorption costing allocates overheads to production departments (cost centres) whereas **ABC systems assign overheads to each major activity** (cost pools). With ABC systems, lots of activity-based cost pools are established whereas with traditional absorption costing, overheads tend to be pooled by departments. This can result in many reapportionments of service department costs to ensure that all overheads are allocated to production departments. **ABC** establishes separate cost pools for support activities such as despatching and materials handing. As the costs of these activities are assigned directly to products through cost driver rates, **reapportionment of service department costs is avoided.**

9.2 Absorption of overheads

The principal difference between the two systems is the way in which overheads are absorbed into products. Traditional absorption costing uses usually two absorption bases (labour hours and/or machine hours) to charge overheads to products whereas **ABC uses many cost drivers as absorption bases** (number of orders, number of dispatches and so on). **Absorption rates under ABC should therefore be more closely linked to the causes of overhead costs.**

9.3 Cost drivers and absorption rates

FAST FORWARD

When using ABC, for costs that vary with production levels in the short term, the cost driver will be volume related (labour or machine hours). Overheads that vary with some other activity (and not volume of production) should be traced to products using transaction-based cost drivers such as production runs or number of orders received.

The principal idea of ABC is to focus attention on what causes costs to increase, the cost drivers. Just as there are no rules for what to use as the basis for absorbing costs in traditional absorption costing, there are also difficulties in choosing cost drivers.

(a) Those **costs that do vary with production volume**, such as power costs, should be **traced to products using production volume-related cost drivers** as appropriate, such as direct labour hours or direct machine hours.

(b) **Overheads which do not vary with output** but with some other activity should be **traced to products using transaction-based cost drivers**, such as number of production runs and number of orders received.

Focusing attention on what actually causes overheads and tracing overheads to products on the basis of the usage of the cost drivers ensures that a greater proportion of overheads are product related, whereas traditional costing systems allow overheads to be related to products in rather more arbitrary ways. It is this feature of ABC which produces, it is claimed, greater accuracy.

9.4 Further merits of activity based costing

Once the necessary information regarding cost drivers has been obtained, ABC is relatively simple to implement. Here are some other **advantages of ABC.**

(a) Because of the financial reporting requirement to value inventories at full cost, management accounting has not given sufficient priority to the need to provide meaningful product costs and has simply used absorption costing to produce the full cost. **ABC**, on the other hand, focuses attention on the nature of cost behaviour and **attempts to provide meaningful product costs**.

(b) ABC uses multiple cost drivers to allocate overhead costs to activities and then to products, and does not simply use a meaningless direct labour hour recovery rate or machine hour recovery rate, that assumes that overhead costs are related to volume of activity only. Only **ABC recognises that many overhead costs arise out of the diversity and complexity of operations**.

(c) The **complexity of manufacturing has increased**, with wider product ranges, shorter product life cycles, a greater importance being attached to quality and more complex production processes. **ABC recognises this complexity with its multiple cost drivers.**

(d) In a more competitive environment, companies must be able to assess product profitability realistically. **ABC facilitates a good understanding of what drives overhead costs.**

(e) In modern manufacturing systems, overhead functions include a lot of non-factory-floor activities such as product design, quality control, production planning, sales order planning and customer service. **ABC is concerned with all overhead costs**, including the costs of these functions, and so it takes management accounting beyond its 'traditional' factory floor boundaries.

9.5 Criticisms of ABC

It has been suggested by critics that **activity based costing has some serious flaws.**

(a) Some measure of (arbitrary) cost apportionment may still be required at the cost pooling stage for items like rent, rates and building depreciation. If an ABC system has many cost pools the amount of apportionment needed may be greater than ever.

(b) The ability of a single cost driver to explain fully the cost behaviour of all items in its associated pool is questionable.

(c) To have a usable cost driver, a cost must be caused by an activity that is measurable in quantitative terms and which can be related to production output. But not all costs can be treated in this way. For example, what drives the cost of the annual external audit?

(d) ABC is sometimes introduced because it is fashionable, not because it will be used by management to provide meaningful product costs or extra information. If management is not going to use ABC information, a traditional absorption costing system may be simpler to operate.

Question — Using ABC

(a) List the features of organisations that would find ABC particularly useful for product costing.

(b) Briefly explain the reasons why ABC is particularly suitable in a modern business environment and describe any situations where it is not appropriate.

Answer

(a) Here are our suggestions.

- (i) Production overheads are a high proportion of total production costs.
- (ii) The product range is wide and diverse.
- (iii) The amounts of overhead resources used by products varies.
- (iv) Volume is not the primary driver of overhead resource consumption.

(b) **Reasons for suitability**

- (i) Most modern organisations tend to have a high level of overhead costs, especially relating to support services such as maintenance and data processing. ABC, by the use of carefully chosen cost drivers, traces these overheads to product lines in a more logical and less arbitrary manner than traditional absorption costing.
- (ii) The determination and use of cost drivers helps to measure and improve the efficiency and effectiveness of support departments.
- (iii) Many costs included in general overheads can actually be traced to specific product lines using ABC. This improves product costing and cost management because the costs are made the responsibility of the line manager.
- (iv) ABC forces the organisation to ask such searching questions as 'What causes the demand for the activity?', 'What does the department achieve?', 'Does it add value?' and so on.
- (v) ABC systems may encourage reductions in throughput time and inventory and improvements in quality.

Unsuitable situations

- (i) A number of businesses have recently been split into several small autonomous sections. In this situation there may be no need for a sophisticated costing system such as ABC because staff should be aware of cost behaviour.
- (ii) ABC can work against modern manufacturing methods such as just-in-time (JIT). JIT seeks to reduce set-up time so that very small batches can be made economically.
- (iii) The aim of set-up time reduction is to allow more set-ups, not just to reduce set-up costs. The use of a cost driver based on the number of set-ups will therefore work against JIT principles as it will tend to encourage larger batches.

Chapter Roundup

- Absorption costing aims to include within the total cost of a product an appropriate share of the organisation's total overhead.
- There are three stages in absorption costing: **allocation**, **apportionment** and **absorption**.
- Apportionment has two stages: **general overhead apportionment** and **service department cost apportionment**.
- Service department costs can be apportioned to production departments either directly, or using the **repeated distribution method**.
- Overheads are absorbed into products using an appropriate **absorption rate** based on budgeted costs and budgeted activity levels.
- **Under-/over-absorbed overhead** occurs when overheads incurred do not equal overheads absorbed.
- An alternative to the traditional methods of absorption costing is **activity based costing (ABC).** ABC involves the identification of the factors (cost drivers) which cause the costs of an organisation's major activities. Support overheads are charged to products on the basis of their usage of an activity.
- When using ABC, for costs that vary with production levels in the short term, the cost driver will be volume related (labour or machine hours). Overheads that vary with some other activity (and not volume of production) should be traced to products using transaction-based cost drivers such as production runs or number of orders received.

Quick Quiz

1 What is overhead allocation?

2 What basis might be applied to apportion heat and light?

3 What is service cost centre cost apportionment?

4 Absorption rates are calculated using actual figures. True or false?

5 When should blanket overhead absorption rates be used?

6 Why does under- or over-absorbed overhead occur?

7 What are the major ideas of activity based costing?

8 What is a cost pool?

9 Match the following overheads with the most appropriate basis of apportionment.

Overhead	**Basis of apportionment**
(a) Depreciation of equipment	(1) Direct machine hours
(b) Heat and light costs	(2) Number of employees
(c) Canteen	(3) Book value of equipment
(d) Insurance of equipment	(4) Floor area

10 A direct labour hour basis is most appropriate in which of the following environments?

A Machine-intensive
B Labour-intensive
C When all units produced are identical
D None of the above

Answers to Quick Quiz

1 Overhead allocation is the process by which whole cost items are charged direct to a cost unit (in the case of direct costs) or to a cost centre (in the case of overheads).

2 Heat and light might be apportioned on the basis of floor area occupied by each cost centre or volume of space occupied by each cost centre.

3 Service cost centre cost apportionment involves apportioning the costs of service cost centres to production cost centres.

4 False. Absorption rates are calculated using budgeted figures.

5 Blanket absorption rates should be used if there is only one department or if jobs spend an equal amount of time in each department.

6 Under or over recovery of overhead will occur in the following circumstances.

(a) Actual overhead costs are different to budgeted overheads.
(b) The actual activity level is different to the budgeted activity level.
(c) Both actual overhead costs and actual activity level are different to the budgeted costs and level.

7 The major ideas behind activity based costing are as follows.

(a) Activities cause costs. Activities include ordering, materials handling, machining, assembly, production scheduling and despatching.

(b) Producing products creates demand for the activities.

(c) Costs are assigned to a product on the basis of the product's consumption of the activities.

8 A cost pool is like a cost centre in traditional absorption costing. The costs of an activity are collected into cost pools.

9 (a) (3)
(b) (4)
(c) (2)
(d) (3)

10 B

Now try the questions below from the Exam Question Bank

Number	Level	Marks	Time
Section A: Q2-Q4	MCQ	N/A	N/A
Section B: Q2	Preparation	10	18 mins

Absorption costing and marginal costing compared

Topic list
1 Marginal cost and contribution
2 The principles of marginal costing
3 Marginal costing and absorption costing and the calculation of profit
4 Marginal costing versus absorption costing: reporting to management
5 Marginal costing versus absorption costing: external reporting
6 Marginal costing versus absorption costing: decision making
7 Marginal costing versus absorption costing: a summary

Study guide reference

		Syllabus reference
3(a)	Explain the use of marginal costing in an organisation	1
(d)	Prepare management accounts and cost estimates using marginal costing principles	1
(e)	Reconcile marginal costing and absorption costing profits	1
(f)	Evaluate the use of marginal costing in specific situations	1
(g)	Compare and contrast the use of absorption and marginal costing	1
4(f)	Compare and contrast the use of absorption, marginal and activity based costing	1

1 Marginal cost and contribution

FAST FORWARD

Marginal cost is the variable cost of one unit of product or service.

Key term

Marginal cost is the cost of a unit of a product or service which would be avoided if that unit were not produced or provided.

The **marginal production cost per unit** of an item therefore usually consists of the following.

(a) **Direct materials**
(b) **Direct labour**
(c) **Variable production overheads**

Direct labour costs might be excluded from marginal costs when the work force is a given number of employees on a fixed wage or salary. Even so, it is not uncommon for direct labour to be treated as a variable cost, even when employees are paid a basic wage for a fixed working week.

Exam focus point

If in doubt, you should treat direct labour as a variable cost unless given clear indications to the contrary.

The **marginal cost of sales** usually consists of the **marginal cost of production adjusted for inventory movements plus the variable selling costs**, which would include items such as sales commission, and possibly some variable distribution costs.

1.1 Contribution

FAST FORWARD

Contribution is the difference between sales value and marginal or variable cost.

Key term

Contribution is the difference between sales value and the marginal cost of sales.

Contribution is of fundamental importance in marginal costing, and the term 'contribution' is really short for **'contribution towards covering fixed overheads and making a profit'**.

Question — Contribution

Product Zen is sold for $1,009.99. The direct material cost per unit is $320, the direct labour cost per unit is $192 and the variable production overhead cost per unit is $132. Fixed overheads per annum are $100,000 and the budgeted production level is 1,000 units.

Calculate the contribution per unit of product Zen.

Answer

	$	$
Selling price per unit		1,009.99
Marginal cost per unit		
Direct material	320	
Direct labour	192	
Variable production overhead	132	
		644.00
Contribution per unit		365.99

We do *not* include absorbed fixed overheads in the calculation of marginal cost per unit and contribution per unit.

Now try the following question yourself. Make sure that you **fully understand** how to calculate contribution before you move onto the principles of marginal costing.

Question

More on contribution

Cost and selling price details for product Q are as follows.

	$ per unit
Direct material	4.20
Direct labour	3.00
Variable overhead	1.00
Fixed overhead	2.80
	11.00
Profit	4.00
Selling price	15.00

Budgeted production for month	10,000 units
Actual production for month	12,000 units
Actual sales for month	11,200 units
Actual fixed overhead cost incurred during month	$31,000

Calculate the marginal costing profit for the month based on the above data

A $44,800
B $45,160
C $50,600
D $76,160

Answer

B

Contribution per unit	=	$15 – $(4.20 + 3.00 + 1.00)
	=	$6.80
Contribution for month	=	$6.80 × 11,200 units
	=	$76,160
Less fixed costs incurred	=	$31,000
Marginal costing profit		$45,160

Option A bases the profit on the actual sales volume at $4 per unit profit. This utilises a unit rate for fixed overhead which is not valid under marginal costing.

If you selected option C you used the correct method but you based your calculations on the units produced rather than the units sold.

If you selected option D you calculated the correct contribution but you forgot to deduct the fixed overhead.

2 The principles of marginal costing

FAST FORWARD

In **marginal costing**, fixed production costs are treated as period costs and are written off as they are incurred. Inventories are therefore valued at variable production cost. In absorption costing, fixed production costs are absorbed into the cost of units and inventories are valued at their full production cost. Inventory values calculated using absorption costing are therefore greater than those calculated using marginal costing.

Key term

Marginal costing is an alternative method of costing to absorption costing. In marginal costing, **only variable costs are charged as a cost of sale**. Closing inventories of work in progress and finished goods are valued at marginal (variable) production cost. Fixed costs are treated as a period cost, and are charged in full to the income statement of the accounting period in which they are incurred.

Principles of marginal costing

(a) Period fixed costs are the same, for any volume of sales and production (provided that the level of activity is within the organisation's normal levels of activity). Therefore, **by selling an extra item of product** or service the following will occur.

  (i) **Revenue will increase by the sales value of the item sold.**
  (ii) **Costs will increase by the variable cost per unit.**
  (iii) **Profit will increase by the amount of contribution earned from the extra item.**

(b) Similarly, if the volume of sales falls by one item, the profit will fall by the amount of contribution earned from the item.

(c) Profit measurement should therefore be **based on an analysis of total contribution**. Since fixed costs relate to a period of time, and do not change with increases or decreases in sales volume, it is **misleading to charge units of sale with a share of fixed costs**. Absorption costing is therefore misleading, and it is more appropriate to deduct fixed costs from total contribution for the period to derive a profit figure.

(d) When a unit of product is made, the extra costs incurred in its manufacture are the variable production costs. Fixed costs are unaffected, and no extra fixed costs are incurred when output is increased. It is therefore argued that the **valuation of closing inventories should be at variable production cost** (direct materials, direct labour, direct expenses (if any) and variable production overhead) because these are the only costs properly attributable to the product.

2.1 Example: marginal costing principles

Gush makes a product, the Drip, which has a variable production cost of $6 per unit and a sales price of $10 per unit. At the beginning of April there were no opening inventories and production during the month was 20,000 units. Fixed costs for the month were $45,000 (production, administration, sales and distribution). There were no variable marketing costs.

Required

Calculate the contribution and profit for April using marginal costing principles, if sales were as follows.

(a) 10,000 Drips
(b) 15,000 Drips
(c) 20,000 Drips

2.2 Solution

The first stage in the profit calculation must be to identify the variable cost of sales, and then the contribution. Fixed costs are deducted from the total contribution to derive the profit. All closing inventories are valued at marginal production cost ($6 per unit).

	10,000 Drips		*15,000 Drips*		*20,000 Drips*	
	$	$	$	$	$	$
Sales (at $10 per unit)		100,000		150,000		200,000
Opening inventory	0		0		0	
Variable production cost	120,000		120,000		120,000	
	120,000		120,000		120,000	
Less value of closing inventory (at marginal cost)	60,000		30,000		–	
Variable cost of sales		60,000		90,000		120,000
Contribution		40,000		60,000		80,000
Less fixed costs		45,000		45,000		45,000
Profit/(loss)		(5,000)		15,000		35,000
Profit (loss) per unit		$(0.50)		$1		$1.75
Contribution per unit		$4		$4		$4

The conclusions which may be drawn from this example are as follows.

(a) The **profit per unit varies at differing levels of sales**, because the average fixed overhead cost per unit changes with the volume of output and sales.

(b) The **contribution per unit is constant at all levels of output and sales**. Total contribution, which is the contribution per unit multiplied by the number of units sold, increases in direct proportion to the volume of sales.

(c) Since the contribution per unit does not change, the **most effective way of calculating the expected profit at any level of output and sales** would be as follows.

   (i) **First calculate the total contribution.**
   (ii) **Then deduct fixed costs as a period charge in order to find the profit.**

(d) In our example the expected profit from the sale of 17,000 Drips would be as follows.

	$
Total contribution (17,000 × $4)	68,000
Less fixed costs	45,000
Profit	23,000

- **If total contribution exceeds fixed costs, a profit is made.**
- If **total contribution exactly equals fixed costs**, no profit and no loss is made, that is **breakeven point** is reached.
- If **total contribution is less than fixed costs**, there will be **a loss**.

Exam focus point

If asked to use a marginal costing format for a income statement, you need to highlight contribution and separate fixed and variable costs.

Question — Marginal cost

Plumber makes two products, the Loo and the Wash. Information relating to each of these products for April is as follows.

	Loo	*Wash*
Opening inventory	nil	nil
Production (units)	15,000	6,000
Sales (units)	10,000	5,000
Sales price per unit	$20	$30

Unit costs	$		$
Direct materials	8		14
Direct labour	4		2
Variable production overhead	2		1
Variable sales overhead	2		3

Fixed costs for the month	$
Production costs	40,000
Administration costs	15,000
Sales and distribution costs	25,000

Required

(a) Using marginal costing principles, calculate the profit in April. Use the approach set out above.
(b) Calculate the profit if sales had been 15,000 units of the Loo and 6,000 units of the Wash.

Answer

(a)

	$
Contribution from Loos (unit contribution = $20 – $16 = $4 × 10,000)	40,000
Contribution from Washes (unit contribution = $30 – $20 = $10 × 5,000)	50,000
Total contribution	90,000
Fixed costs for the period	80,000
Profit	10,000

(b) At a higher volume of sales, profit would be as follows.

	$
Contribution from sales of 15,000 Loos (× $4)	60,000
Contribution from sales of 6,000 Washes (× $10)	60,000
Total contribution	120,000
Less fixed costs	80,000
Profit	40,000

3 Marginal costing and absorption costing and the calculation of profit

FAST FORWARD

If the opening and closing inventory levels differ (assuming that the fixed overhead absorption rate remains constant), the profit reported for the accounting period under the two methods will be different. In the long run, however, total profit will be the same whatever method is used.

Absorption costing and marginal costing profits can be reconciled as follows:

	If inventory levels increase	*If inventory levels decrease*
	$	$
Marginal costing profit	X	X
Change in inventory level × fixed o/hd absorbed per unit	X	(X)
Absorption costing profit	X	X

Marginal costing as a cost accounting system is significantly different from absorption costing. It is an **alternative** method of accounting for costs and profit, which rejects the principles of absorbing fixed overheads into unit costs.

(a) **In marginal costing**

(i) **Closing inventories** are valued at marginal production cost.

(ii) **Fixed costs** are charged in full against the profit of the period in which they are incurred.

(b) **In absorption costing** (sometimes referred to as **full costing**)

(i) **Closing inventories** are valued at full production cost, and include a share of fixed production costs.

(ii) This means that the **cost of sales** in a period will include some fixed overhead incurred in a previous period (in opening inventory values) and will exclude some fixed overhead incurred in the current period but carried forward in closing inventory values as a charge to a subsequent accounting period.

Exam focus point

In the December 2005 exam, part of a question asked for an explanation of the differences between absorption and marginal costing including the effect on profit.

In the report on the June 2004 sitting (which included a question on comparisons between marginal costing and absorption costing), the examiner noted that 'only a minority of candidates managed to correctly adjust opening and closing **inventory** valuations from absorption to a marginal costing basis. Many ... seemed unaware of a suitable layout for a marginal costing statement' (as displayed in this chapter).

In **marginal costing**, it is necessary to **identify** the following.

- **Variable costs**
- **Contribution**
- **Fixed costs**

In **absorption costing** it is **not necessary to distinguish variable costs from fixed costs**.

3.1 Format for management accounts under absorption costing and marginal costing

In Chapter 1 we learnt that, unlike financial accounts, the **format of management accounts** is **not prescribed by law**. That **does not mean that there is no recommended format** to management accounts, however.

In an article in the *ACCA Technician Bulletin*, (May 2000) 'The format and meaning of management accounting information', the following structures were suggested.

Absorption costing

	$	$
Net turnover		X
Less:		
Direct materials	X	
Direct labour	X	
Total prime cost	X	
Total production overhead	X	
Production cost of sales		X
Gross (or factory) profit		X
Less:		
Selling overhead	X	
Distribution overhead	X	
Administrative expenses	X	
Research and development	X	
Total non-production overhead		X
Net profit before tax		X

Marginal costing

	$	$
Net turnover		X
Less:		
Direct materials	X	
Direct labour	X	
Total prime cost	X	
Variable production overhead	X	
Variable selling and distribution overhead	X	
Variable cost of sales		X
Contribution		X
Less **fixed costs**:		
Production overhead	X	
Selling overhead	X	
Distribution overhead	X	
Administrative expenses	X	
Research and development cost	X	
Total fixed cost		X
Net profit before tax		X

These structures **do not show under/over recovery of overheads using absorption costing or adjustments for opening and closing inventory** (these are both illustrated in examples to follow in this chapter).

As you will see as you work through the remainder of this chapter, you have to **take the information provided in the question into account** (a total figure you may be given for fixed costs, for example, or prime cost may be provided instead of direct materials and direct labour), but these structures do provide you with guidelines and a framework around which to construct your profit statements.

3.2 Example: marginal and absorption costing compared

Look back at the information contained in the last question. Suppose that the budgeted production for April was 15,000 units of the Loo and 6,000 units of the Wash, and production overhead is absorbed on the basis of budgeted direct labour costs.

Required

Calculate the profit if production was as budgeted, and sales were as follows.

(a) 10,000 units of the Loo and 5,000 units of the Wash
(b) 15,000 units of the Loo and 6,000 units of the Wash

Administration, sales and distribution costs should be charged as a period cost against profit.

3.3 Solution

Budgeted production overhead is calculated as follows.

	$
Fixed	40,000
Variable: Loos (15,000 × $2)	30,000
Washs (6,000 × $1)	6,000
Total	76,000

The production overhead absorption rate would be calculated as follows.

$$\frac{\text{Budgeted production overhead}}{\text{Budgeted direct labour cost}} = \frac{\$76{,}000}{(15{,}000 \times \$4) + (6{,}000 \times \$2)} \times 100\%$$

= 105.56% of direct labour cost

(a) If sales are 10,000 units of the Loo and 5,000 units of the Wash, profit would be as follows.

	Absorption costing		
	Loos	*Washes*	*Total*
	$	$	$
Costs of production			
Direct materials	120,000	84,000	204,000
Direct labour	60,000	12,000	72,000
Overhead (105.56% of labour)	63,333	12,667	76,000
	243,333	108,667	352,000
Less closing inventories	(1/3) 81,111	(1/6) 18,111	99,222
Production cost of sales	162,222	90,556	252,778
Administration costs			15,000
Sales and distribution costs			
Variable			35,000
Fixed			25,000
Total cost of sales			327,778
Sales	200,000	150,000	350,000
Profit			22,222

Note. There is no under-/over-absorption of overhead, since actual production is the same as budgeted production.

The profit derived using absorption costing techniques is different from the profit ($10,000) using marginal costing techniques at this volume of sales (see the earlier question).

(b) If production and sales are exactly the same, (15,000 units of the Loo and 6,000 units of the Wash) profit would be $40,000.

	$
Sales (300,000 + 180,000)	480,000
Cost of sales (352,000* + 15,000 + 48,000 + 25,000)	440,000
Profit	40,000

* No closing inventory if sales and production are equal.

This is the same as the profit calculated by marginal costing techniques in the earlier activity.

We can draw a number of conclusions from this example.

(a) Marginal costing and absorption costing are different techniques for assessing profit in a period.

(b) If there are **changes in inventories during a period**, so that opening inventory or closing inventory values are different, **marginal costing and absorption costing give different results for profit obtained**.

(c) If the **opening and closing inventory volumes and values are the same, marginal costing and absorption costing will give the same profit figure**. This is because the total cost of sales during the period would be the same, no matter how calculated.

Exam focus point

You must understand that in a period where production is greater than sales, absorption costing will show a higher profit than marginal costing (because closing inventory is valued at full production cost, and so some fixed overheads are carried forward to the next period). With marginal costing, by contrast, fixed production costs are written off against profit in the period they are incurred. As a result, the two costing methods will produce different profit figures. The examiner noted in his report on the June 2004 sitting that many candidates were unable to explain this.

3.4 The long-run effect on profit

In the long run, total profit for a company will be the same whether marginal costing or absorption costing is used. Different accounting conventions merely affect the profit of individual accounting periods.

3.5 Example: long-run effect on profit

Suppose that Hell makes and sells a single product, the Fire. At the beginning of 20X3, there are no opening inventories of the Fire, for which the variable production cost is $40 and the sales price $60 per unit. Fixed costs are $200,000 per year, of which $150,000 are fixed production costs.

	20X3	*20X4*
Sales	12,000 units	18,000 units
Production	15,000 units	15,000 units

Required

Determine the profit in each period using the following methods of costing.

(a) Absorption costing. Assume normal output is 15,000 units per period.
(b) Marginal costing.

3.6 Solution

It is important to notice that although production and sales volumes in each period are different (and therefore the profit for each period by absorption costing will be different from the profit by marginal costing), over the full period, total production equals sales volume, the total cost of sales is the same, and therefore the profit is the same by either method of accounting.

(a) **Absorption costing**: the absorption rate for fixed production overhead is:

$$\frac{\$150{,}000}{15{,}000 \text{ units}} = \$10 \text{ per unit}$$

	20X3		*20X4*		*Total*	
	$'000	$'000	$'000	$'000	$'000	$'000
Sales		720	1,080			1,800
Production costs						
Variable	600		600		1,200	
Fixed	150		150		300	
	750		750		1,500	
Add opening inventory b/f	–		150		–	
	750		900			
Less closing inventory c/f	150		–		–	
Production cost of sales	600		900		1,500	
Other costs	50		50		100	
Total cost of sales		650		950		1,600
Unadjusted profit		70		130		200
(Under-)/over-absorbed overhead		–		–		–
Profit		70		130		200

(b) **Marginal costing**

	20X3		20X4		Total	
	$'000	$'000	$'000	$'000	$'000	$'000
Sales		720		1,080		1,800
Variable production cost	600		600		1,200	
Add opening inventory b/f	–		120		–	
	600		720		1,200	
Less closing inventory c/f	120		–		–	
Variable production cost of sales		480		720		1,200
Contribution		240		360		1600
Fixed costs		200		200		400
Profit		40		160		200

Notes

(a) The total profit over the two periods is the same for each method of costing, but the profit in each period is different.

(b) In absorption costing, fixed production overhead of $30,000 is carried forward from 20X3 into 20X4 in inventory values, and becomes a charge to profit in 20X4. In marginal costing all fixed costs are charged in the year they are incurred, and so the profit in 20X3 is $30,000 lower and in 20X4 is $30,000 higher than the absorption costing profit.

3.7 Reconciling the profit figures given by the two methods

The difference in profits reported under the two costing systems is due to the different inventory valuation methods used.

If inventory levels increase between the beginning and end of a period, **absorption costing will report the higher profit**. This is because some of the fixed production overhead incurred during the period will be carried forward in closing **inventory** (which reduces cost of sales) to be set against sales revenue in the following period instead of being written off in full against profit in the period concerned.

If inventory levels decrease, absorption costing will report the lower profit because as well as the fixed overhead incurred, fixed production overhead which had been carried forward in opening **inventory** is released and is also included in cost of sales.

3.8 Example: reconciling profits

The profits reported under absorption costing and marginal costing for 20X3 in the example about Hell would be reconciled as follows.

	$'000
Marginal costing profit	40
Adjust for fixed overhead in inventory:	
Inventory increase of 3,000 units × $10 per unit	30
Absorption costing profit	70

Question — **Profit reconciliation**

Reconcile the profits reported under the two systems for 20X4 in the example about Hell.

Answer

	$'000
Marginal costing profit	160
Adjust for fixed overhead in inventory:	
Inventory decrease of 3,000 units × $10 per unit	(30)
Absorption costing profit	130

3.9 Reconciling ABC and marginal costing profits

ABC also involves absorption of fixed overheads. When this method is used closing inventories will include a share of fixed overheads. Where there is a movement in the level of inventories, ABC and marginal costing will yield different profits.

ABC and marginal costing profits can be reconciled as follows:

	If inventory levels increase	*If inventory levels decrease*
	$	$
Marginal costing profit	X	X
Change in inventory level × fixed o/hd absorbed per unit	X	(X)
ABC profit	X	X

You will notice that the method above is the same as that used when reconciling traditional absorption costing and marginal costing profits. This is because, although the approach to determining the absorption rate differs, with both ABC and traditional absorption costing closing inventory is valued at full production cost.

4 Marginal costing versus absorption costing: reporting to management

FAST FORWARD

When reporting to management, absorption costing can be used to manipulate profits by producing in excess of demand. On the other hand, marginal costing can give a misleading impression if demand is seasonal.

Because of differences in inventory valuations, the reported profit in any period is likely to differ according to the costing method used. Presumably, however, one method might be said to provide a more reliable guide to management about the organisation's profit position.

With marginal costing, contribution (sales minus variable costs) **varies in direct proportion to the volume of units sold**. Profits will increase as sales volume rises, by the amount of extra contribution earned. Since fixed cost expenditure does not alter, it can be argued that marginal costing gives an accurate picture of how a firm's cash flows and profits are affected by changes in sales volumes.

With absorption costing, in contrast, **there is no clear relationship between profit and sales volume**, and as sales volume rises the total profit will rise by the sum of the gross profit per unit plus the amount of overhead absorbed per unit. Arguably this is a confusing and unsatisfactory method of monitoring profitability.

If sales volumes are the same from period to period, marginal costing will report the same profit each period (given no change in selling prices or costs). In contrast, using absorption costing, profits can vary with the volume of production, even when the volume of sales is constant. **Absorption costing is therefore often criticised because of the possibility of manipulating profit, simply by changing output and inventory levels.**

4.1 Example: manipulating profits

Gloom budgeted to make and sell 10,000 units of its product in 20X1. The selling price is $10 per unit and the variable cost $4 per unit. Fixed production costs were budgeted at $50,000 for the year.

The company uses absorption costing and budgeted an absorption rate of $5 per unit.

During 20X1, it became apparent that sales demand would only be 8,000 units. The management, concerned about the apparent effect of the low volume of sales on profits, decided to increase production for the year to 15,000 units. Actual fixed costs were still expected to be $50,000 in spite of the significant increase in production volume.

Required

Calculate the profit at an actual sales volume of 8,000 units, using the following methods.

(a) Absorption costing (b) Marginal costing

4.2 Solution

(a) **Absorption costing**

	$	$
Sales (8,000 × $10)		80,000
Cost of production (15,000 × $9)	135,000	
Less: over-absorbed overhead	(25,000)	
		(110,000)
		(30,000)
Closing inventory (7,000 × $9)		63,000
Profit		33,000

(b) **Marginal costing**

	$	$
Sales		80,000
Cost of sales		
Cost of production (15,000 × $4)	60,000	
Closing inventory (7,000 × $4)	28,000	
		32,000
Contribution		48,000
Fixed costs		50,000
Loss		(2,000)

The difference in profits of $35,000 is explained by the difference in the increase in inventory values (7,000 units × $5 of fixed overhead per unit). With absorption costing, the expected profit will be higher than the original budget of (10,000 units × ($10 – 9)) $10,000 simply because $35,000 of fixed overheads will be carried forward in closing inventory values. By producing to absorb overhead rather than to satisfy customers, inventory levels will, of course, increase. Unless this inventory is sold, however, there may come a point when production has to stop and the inventory has to be sold off at lower prices.

Marginal costing would report a contribution of $6 per unit, or $48,000 in total for 8,000 units, which fails to cover the fixed costs of $50,000 by $2,000.

This argument is not conclusive, however, because **marginal costing is not so useful when sales fluctuate from month to month because of seasonal variations in sales demand**, but production per month is held constant in order to arrange for an even flow of output (and thereby prevent the cost of idle resources in periods of low demand and overtime in periods of high demand).

Consider the following example.

4.3 Example: seasonal variations in sales demand

High Scream budgets to make and sell 3,600 units of its product during 20X2 at a selling price of $5. Production variable costs are $3 per unit and fixed costs for the year are budgeted as $5,400 (divisible equally between the 12 months of the year). Sales demand in the first six months of the year will be only 200 units per month, but demand will double in the second six months to 400 per month. In order to save unnecessary production costs, the company has budgeted to spread production evenly over the year by producing 300 units per month.

Required

Calculate the profits each month using the following costing methods.

(a) Absorption costing
(b) Marginal costing

4.4 Solution

Absorption costing

(a) The fixed overhead absorption rate is $\frac{\$5,400}{3,600 \text{ units}} = \$1.50$ per unit

For each of the first six months of the year, profit per month would be as follows.

	$
Sales (200 units × $5)	1,000
Less full cost of sales (200 units × $4.50)	900
	100
Under-/over-absorbed overhead	0
Profit ($0.50 per unit)	100

For each of the second six months of the year, profit per month would be as follows.

	$
Sales (400 units × $5)	2,000
Less full cost of sales (400 units × $4.50)	1,800
	200
Under-/over-absorbed overhead	0
Profit ($0.50 per unit)	200

Total profit for the year would be 3,600 units × $0.50 = $1,800

(b) **Marginal costing**

For each of the first six months of the year, there would be a loss.

	$
Sales (200 units × $5)	1,000
Less variable cost of sales (200 units × $3)	600
Contribution ($2 per unit)	400
Less fixed costs	450
Loss	(50)

For each of the second six months of the year there would be a profit.

	$
Sales (400 units × $5)	2,000
Less variable cost of sales (400 units × $3)	1,200
Contribution ($2 per unit)	800
Less fixed costs	450
Profit	350

Total profit for the year would be $1,800

In this example it might be argued that in view of the deliberate policy of producing goods for inventory in the first half of the year, and selling out of inventory in the second half absorption costing would provide a better method of reporting profits month by month. At a profit of $0.50 per unit, total monthly profits double when sales double, which would conform to the expectations of the management of High Scream.

In contrast, marginal costing would report a loss in each of the first six months (which might cause unnecessary concern to management) and a misleadingly large jump into profitability in the second half of the year.

Other arguments in favour of absorption costing for internal profit reporting

(a) **Marginal costing fails to recognise the importance of working to full capacity**. With absorption costing, the effect of higher production volumes is to reduce unit costs (because the fixed cost per unit is lower) and if sales prices are based on the 'cost-plus' method, the relevance of output capacity to cost, price and sales demand should be apparent.

(b) **Selling prices based on marginal costing** might enable the firm to make a contribution on each unit of product it sells, but **the total contribution earned might be insufficient to cover all fixed costs.**

(c) **In the long run, all costs are variable**, and inventory values based on **absorption costing will give recognition to these long-run variable costs**.

There are also further **arguments in favour of marginal costing for internal profit reporting.**

(a) **Separating fixed and variable costs helps management to make short-run pricing decisions concerning incremental profits.**

(b) **Fixed costs (such as depreciation, rent or salaries) relate to a period of time and should be charged against the revenues of the period in which they are incurred.**

5 Marginal costing versus absorption costing: external reporting

FAST FORWARD

IAS 2 recommends the use of absorption costing for the valuation of inventories in financial accounts.

It **might be argued that absorption costing is preferable** to marginal costing in management accounting, **in order to be consistent with the requirement of IAS 2**. This argument might be especially relevant when a firm has an integrated or combined accounting system for its financial and management accounts.

However, with a flexible accounting information system, it should be relatively easy for a firm to maintain its accounts on a marginal costing basis, and when financial accounts are prepared, to convert its inventory values into fully absorbed costs.

Question — **Inventory valuation**

If your organisation holds inventory, find out how it is valued. Is it valued on a marginal costing basis or an absorption costing basis?

6 Marginal costing versus absorption costing: decision making

FAST FORWARD

Marginal costing is more useful for decision making, in short-run pricing decisions and situations where extra production will make a positive contribution.

Suppose that a sales manager has an item of product which he is having difficulty in selling. Its historical full cost is $80, made up of variable costs of $50 and fixed costs of $30. A customer offers $60 for it.

(a) If there is no other customer for the product, $60 would be better than nothing and the product should be sold to improve income and profit by this amount.

(b) If the company has spare production capacity which would otherwise not be used, it would be profitable to continue making more of the same product, if customers are willing to pay $60 for each extra unit made. This is because the additional costs are only $50 so that the profit would be increased marginally by $10 per unit produced.

(c) In absorption costing terms, the product makes a loss of $20, which would discourage the sales manager from accepting a price of $60 from the customer. His decision would be a bad one.

   (i) If the product is not sold for $60, it will presumably be scrapped eventually, so the choice is really between making a loss in absorption costing terms of $20, or a loss of $80 when the inventory is written off, whenever this happens.

   (ii) If there is demand for some extra units at $60 each, the absorption costing loss would be $20 per unit, but at the end of the year there would be an additional contribution to overheads and profit of $10 per unit. In terms of absorption costing the under-absorbed overhead would be reduced by $30 (the fixed cost part of the product's full cost) for each extra unit made and sold.

Absorption costing information about unit profits is therefore **irrelevant in short-run decisions in which fixed costs do not change** (such as short-run tactical decisions seeking to make the best use of existing facilities). In such circumstances the decision rule is to choose the alternative which maximises contribution.

We will be looking in more detail at decision making and the type of information required later in the text.

Question — **Marginal costing and decisions**

Comment briefly on the usefulness of marginal costing for decision making.

Answer

Marginal costing is useful in decision making because it separates variable and fixed costs and focuses on the costs which will change as the result of a decision, that is variable costs and stepped fixed costs. Attention is focused on activity-related variable costs, and hence management can easily see how costs and profit will be affected by changes in sales volume.

In particular, focusing on marginal costs may aid pricing, in that a mark-up on variable costs will often be a convenient price (for example in the retail industry).

Marginal costing information is also better in short-term decisions about whether to make a few extra units of a product. In these circumstances fixed costs will not change. With absorption costing extra fixed costs will be absorbed. Hence it may appear that the few extra units are making a negative contribution, when in fact sales value exceeds actual extra costs incurred.

7 Marginal costing versus absorption costing: a summary

No absolute recommendation of the costing method which should be used can be given. **Although any technique can be used for internal purposes, absorption costing must be used for external reporting**. An understanding of the behaviour of costs and the implications of contribution is vital for accountants and managers, and **the use of marginal costing for decision making is universal**.

Question

Which of the following are arguments in favour of marginal costing?

(a) Closing inventory is valued in accordance with IAS 2.
(b) It is simple to operate.
(c) There is no under or over absorption of overheads.
(d) Fixed costs are the same regardless of activity levels.
(e) The information from this costing method may be used for decision making.

Answer

(b), (c), (d), (e)

Chapter Roundup

- **Marginal cost** is the variable cost of one unit of product or service.
- **Contribution** is the difference between sales value and marginal or variable cost.
- In **marginal costing**, fixed production costs are treated as period costs and are written off as they are incurred. Inventories are therefore valued at variable production cost. In absorption costing, fixed production costs are absorbed into the cost of units and inventories are valued at their full production cost. Inventory values calculated using absorption costing are therefore greater than those calculated using marginal costing.
- If the opening and closing inventory levels differ (assuming that the fixed overhead absorption rate remains constant), the profit reported for the accounting period under the two methods will be different.
- In the long run, however, total profit will be the same whatever method is used.
- Absorption costing and marginal costing profits can be reconciled as follows:

	If inventory levels increase	*If inventory levels decrease*
	$	$
Marginal costing profit	X	X
Change in inventory level × fixed o/hd absorbed per unit	X	(X)
Absorption costing profit	X	X

- When reporting to management, absorption costing can be used to manipulate profits by producing in excess of demand. On the other hand, marginal costing can give a misleading impression if demand is seasonal.
- **IAS 2** recommends the use of absorption costing for the valuation of inventories in financial accounts.
- Marginal costing is more useful for decision making, in short-run pricing decisions and situations where extra production will make a positive contribution.

Quick Quiz

1 What does the marginal production cost per unit consist of?

2 How is contribution calculated?

3 How are inventories valued using marginal costing?

4 If the opening and closing inventory volumes and values are the same, marginal costing and absorption costing give the same profit figure. True or false?

5 If inventory levels increase between the beginning and end of a period, does absorption costing or marginal costing produce the higher inventory figure?

6 'Fixed costs (such as depreciation and rent) relate to a period of time and should be charged against the revenues of the period in which they are incurred' is an argument used in favour of absorption costing for internal profit reporting. True or false?

7 and 8 Cost and selling price details for product Q are as follows.

	$ per unit
Direct material	4.20
Direct labour	3.00
Variable overhead	1.00
Fixed overhead	2.80
	11.00
Profit	4.00
Selling price	15.00

Budgeted production for month	10,000 units
Actual production for month	12,000 units
Actual sales for month	11,200 units
Actual fixed overhead cost incurred during month	$31,000

(a) Based on the above data, the marginal costing profit for the month is

A $44,800
B $45,160
C $50,600
D $76,160

(b) Based on the above data, the absorption costing profit for the month is

A $42,200
B $44,800
C $45,160
D $47,400

Answers to Quick Quiz

1 The marginal production cost per unit usually consists of direct materials, direct labour and variable production overheads.

2 Contribution is calculated as the difference between sales value and the marginal cost of sales.

3 Inventories are valued at marginal (variable) production cost.

4 True

5 Absorption costing produces the higher figure.

6 False. This is an argument in favour of marginal costing.

7 and 8 (a) B

Contribution per unit	=	\$15 – \$(4.20 + 3.00 + 1.00)
	=	\$6.80
Contribution for month	=	\$6.80 × 11,200 units
	=	\$76,160
Less fixed costs incurred	=	\$31,000
Marginal costing profit		\$45,160

Option A bases the profit on the actual sales volume at \$4 per unit profit. This utilises a unit rate for fixed overhead which is not valid under marginal costing.

If you selected option C you used the correct method but you based your calculations on the units produced rather than the units sold.

If you selected option D you calculated the correct contribution but you forgot to deduct the fixed overhead.

(b) D

	\$
Sales 11,200 units × \$15	168,000
Absorption costs for 11,200 units (× \$11)	123,200
	44,800
Over absorbed fixed overhead for month (see working)	2,600
Absorption costing profit	47,400

Working	\$
Overhead absorbed into production (12,000 units × \$2.80)	33,600
Overhead incurred	31,000
Overhead over absorbed	2,600

If you selected **option A** you calculated all the figures correctly but you subtracted the over absorbed overhead instead of adding it to profit.

Option B makes no allowance for the over absorbed overhead, and **option C** is the marginal costing profit.

Now try the questions below from the Exam Question Bank

Number	Level	Marks	Time
Section A: Q5-Q6	MCQ	N/A	N/A
Section B: Q3	Examination	20	36 mins

4

Job, batch, contract, service and process costing

Topic list
1 Costing methods
2 Job costing
3 Batch costing
4 Contract costing
5 Service industry costing
6 Service department costing
7 Job costing and services
8 Framework for dealing with process costing

Study guide reference

		Syllabus reference
2(b)	Apply absorption costing principles in a job, contract, batch, service or process costing context	1
3(b)	Apply marginal costing principles in a job, contract, batch, service or process costing context	1
4(d)	Apply activity based costing principles in a job, contract, batch, service or process costing context	1

1 Costing methods

Exam focus point

The contents of this chapter are included in order to remind you about job, batch, contract, service and process costing methods. **For your examination, the main thing that you need to appreciate is how overhead will be charged under these costing methods.**

A costing method is designed to suit the way goods are processed or manufactured or the way services are provided. Each organisation's costing method will therefore have unique features but costing methods of firms in the same line of business will more than likely have common aspects. Organisations involved in completely different activities, such as hospitals and car part manufacturers, will use very different methods.

We will be considering five important costing methods. Job, batch, contract, service and process costing will be covered in this chapter.

Note that we describe the full absorption costing method in each case. This is because this is the more complex method. It may be adapted to the use of marginal costing principles simply by treating all overhead costs as period charges rather than by including them in calculations of product costs. A similar comment applies to the use of activity based costing. As you know, this simply amounts to a different approach to determining the absorption rate to apply for overheads.

2 Job costing

FAST FORWARD

Job costing is the costing method used where each cost unit is separately identifiable. The work is undertaken to customers' special requirements, is of comparatively short duration, is usually carried out within a factory or workshop and moves through processes and operations as a continuously identifiable unit.

Job costing is covered in your earlier studies and the examiner is looking at how overhead would be charged to jobs using marginal, absorption and activity based costing approaches. Therefore we will concentrate on overhead costs and how these are charged. We will also look at a full worked example so you can revise your knowledge.

Key terms

A **job** is a cost unit which consists of a single order or contract.

Job costing is a costing method applied where work is undertaken to customers' special requirements and each order is of comparatively short duration.

Knowledge brought forward from earlier studies

- The aim of **job costing** is simply to collect the cost information shown below.

	$
Direct materials	X
Direct labour	X
Direct expenses	X
Direct cost	X
Production overhead	X
Total production cost	X
Administration overhead	X
Selling overhead	X
Cost of sales	X

To the final figure is added a profit **'mark-up'** and the total is the selling price of the job.

- Job costs for each job are recorded in a job account which includes the cost information shown above.
- Direct costs are recorded as the job is performed.
- The job is debited with the appropriate job share of production overhead.
- Once the job is complete, the job account is charged with the appropriate administration and selling overhead.
- The difference between the agreed selling price and the total actual cost will be the supplier's profit or loss.
- Many organisations use cost plus pricing to price a job. Cost plus pricing is a method of determining the sales price by calculating the full cost of a product and adding a percentage mark-up for profit.

Exam focus point

An exam question including job costing may ask you to accumulate costs to arrive at a job cost, and then determine a job price by adding a certain amount of profit. To do this, you need to remember the following crucial formula.

	%
Cost of job	100
+ profit	25
	125

Profit may be expressed either as a percentage of job cost (such as 25% (25/100) mark up) or as a percentage of price (such as 20% (25/125) margin).

The June 2007 exam asked for a gross **margin** on sales so you needed to work backwards from sales.

2.1 Taking account of overheads

(a) **Production overheads charged to jobs**

(i) The **estimated production overheads** to be included in the job cost will be calculated from **overhead absorption rates** in operation and the estimate of the basis of the absorption rate (for example, direct labour hours). This assumes the job estimate is to include overheads (in a competitive environment management may feel that if overheads are to be incurred irrespective of whether or not the job is taken on, the minimum estimated quotation price should be based on variable costs only).

(ii) The actual production overhead to be included in the job cost will be calculated from the overhead absorption rate and the actual results (such as labour hours coded to the job in question). **Inaccurate overhead absorption rates can seriously harm an organisation**; if jobs are over priced, customers will go elsewhere and if jobs are under priced revenue will fail to cover costs.

(b) **Administration, selling and distribution overheads**

The organisation may absorb **non-production overheads** using any one of a variety of methods (percentage on full production cost, for example) and estimates of these costs and the actual costs should be included in the estimated and actual job cost.

If, for example, an outside haulage contractor will be required for delivery of the job to the customer, then an estimate of this cost should be obtained and the invoice value charged to the ledger once the cost has been incurred.

Question — **Activity based costing**

Can you think of a costing technique which might be particularly appropriate for attributing **non-production overheads** to jobs?

Answer

Activity based costing

2.2 Example: job costing

In order to identify the costs incurred in carrying out a range of work to customer specification in its factory, a company has a job costing system. This system identifies costs directly with a job where this is possible and reasonable. In addition, production overhead costs are absorbed into the cost of jobs at the end of each month, at an actual rate per direct labour hour for each of the two production departments and the company absorbs non-production overheads at a rate of 5% of production cost per job.

One of the jobs carried out in the factory during the month just ended was Job No 123. The following information has been collected relating specifically to this job.

(a) 400 kilos of Material Y were issued from stores to Department A.

(b) 76 direct labour hours were worked in Department A at a basic wage of $4.50 per hour. Six of these hours were classified as overtime at a premium of 50%.

(c) 300 kilos of Material Z were issued from stores to Department B.

(d) Department B returned 30 kilos of material Z to the storeroom, being excess to requirements for the job.

(e) 110 direct labour hours were worked in Department B at a basic wage of $4.00 per hour. 30 of these hours were classified as overtime at a premium of 50%. All overtime worked in Department B in the month is a result of the request of a customer for early completion of another job which had been originally scheduled for completion in the month following.

(f) Department B discovered defects in some of the work, which was returned to Department A for rectification. Three labour hours were worked in Department A on rectification (these are additional to the 76 direct labour hours in Department A noted above). Such rectification is regarded as a normal part of the work carried out generally in the department.

(g) Department B damaged five kilos of material Z which then had to be disposed of. Such losses of material are not expected to occur.

(h) Total costs incurred during the month on all jobs in the two production departments were as follows.

	Department A	Department B
	$	$
Direct materials issued from stores (note (i))	6,500	13,730
Direct materials returned to stores	135	275
Direct labour, at basic wage rate (note (ii))	9,090	11,200
Indirect labour, at basic wage rate	2,420	2,960
Overtime premium	450	120
Lubricants and cleaning compounds	520	680
Maintenance	720	510
Other	1,200	2,150

Notes

(i) This includes, in Department B, the scrapped Material Z. This was the only material scrapped in the month.

(ii) All direct labour in Department A is paid a basic wage of $4.50 per hour, and in Department B $4.00 per hour. Department A direct labour includes a total of 20 hours spent on rectification work.

(i) Materials are priced at the end of each month on a weighted average basis. Relevant information of material inventory movements during the month, for Material Y and Z, is as follows.

	Material Y	Material Z
Opening inventory	1,050 kilos (value $529.75)	6,970 kilos (value $9,946.50)
Purchases	600 kilos at $0.50 per kilo 500 kilos at $0.50 per kilo 400 kilos at $0.52 per kilo	16,000 kilos at $1.46 per kilo
Issues from stores	1,430 kilos	8,100 kilos
Returns to stores	–	30 kilos

Required

Prepare a list of the costs that should be assigned to Job No 123. Provide an explanation of your treatment of each item.

2.3 Solution

Job 123: Costs

Materials	$	**Explanation**
Material Y (W1)	202.00	The question states that this specifically relates to Job No 123.
Material Z (W2)	391.50	As above. The figure takes account of the fact that of the 300 kilos initially issued to the job, 30 kilos were returned and are therefore not included. The lost five kilos are discussed in W2.

Labour

Department A 76 hrs × \$4.50 per hr	342.00	As material Y
Department B 110 hrs × \$4 per hr	440.00	As material Y. (Overtime is not a consideration at this stage.) In neither the case of dept A or dept B was the overtime worked specifically at the request of the Job 123 customer and so the overtime premium should not be a direct cost of Job 123.

Overheads

Department A 76 hrs × \$2.70 per hour (W3)	205.20	The explanation of items included in overheads, and the calculation of absorption rates, are shown at W3.
Department B 110 hrs × \$2.25 per hour (W3)	247.50	
Non-production 5% × \$1,828.20	91.41	5% of the total of materials, labour and production overheads.

Workings

1 **Cost of material Y issued to Job 123**

This is priced at the month-end weighted average.

	kg	\$
Balance b/f	1,050	529.75
plus, at 50c per kg	600	300.00
plus, at 50c per kg	500	250.00
plus, at 52c per kg	400	208.00
	2,550	1,287.75

Hence weighted average is $\frac{\$1,287.75}{2,550\text{ kg}} = 50\frac{1}{2}$ c per kg

So cost of inventory issued to Job 123 is 400 kg × $50\frac{1}{2}$ c per kg = \$202

2 **Cost of material Z issued to Job 123**

Also priced at the month-end weighted average

	kg	\$
Balance b/f	6,970	9,946.50
plus, at \$1.46 per kg	16,000	23,360.00
	22,970	33,306.50

Hence weighted average is $\frac{\$33,306.50}{22,970} = \$1.45$ per kg

So cost of inventory issued to Job 123 is (300 – 30)kg × \$1.45 per kg = \$391.50

It is assumed that the five kilos damaged in Department B will be charged to Job 123, just as any adverse material usage would be charged to the job in hand. An alternative approach would be to regard the loss of the five kilos as an exceptional item and charge it as an overhead cost to an appropriate overhead cost centre (eg abnormal wastage in Department B).

3 **Rates of overhead absorption**

(a) **Departmental costs**

Department	*A*	*B*	*Explanation*
	$	$	
Rectification work 20 hrs × $4.50 per hr	90	-	Rectification is **normal** and part of work carried out **generally** in the dept.
Indirect labour	2,420	2,960	Their time is not allocated to any particular job, but all jobs benefit indirectly.
Overtime premium	450	-	The inclusion of over-time premium in over-heads ensures that all jobs bear the same direct wage rate, regardless of whether they were performed in what is classified as overtime, or not. All overtime in Dept B, however, is specifically attributable to another job because the over-time was incurred at the specific request of the customer for the job.
Lubricants	520	680	Each job benefits from these in a general way.
Maintenance	720	510	
Other	1,200	2,150	
	5,400	6,300	

(b)

Departmental direct labour hours		$\frac{11,200}{\$4/\text{hr}}$	
Hours worked	2,020 hrs	2,800 hrs	
Less			
Rectification work	(20) hrs	-	Included in overheads
Direct labour hrs	2,000 hrs	2,800 hrs	
Hence absorption rates			
=	$\frac{\$5,400}{2,000 \text{ hrs}}$	$\frac{\$6,300}{2,800 \text{ hrs}}$	
=	$2.70 per hr	$2.25 per hr	

Question

Job cost

The following information relates to job 56763/40, which is being carried out by Handley Ltd to meet a customer's order.

	Department V	Department Q
Direct materials used	$5,000	$3,000
Direct labour hours	400 hours	200 hours
Direct labour rate per hour	$4	$5
Production overhead per direct labour hour	$4	$4
Administration and other overhead	20% of full production cost	
Profit margin	25% of sales price	

Required

Calculate the selling price of job 56763/40.

Answer

	Department V	Department Q	Total
	$	$	$
Direct materials	5,000	3,000	8,000
Direct labour	1,600	1,000	2,600
Production overhead	1,600	800	2,400
Full production cost			13,000
Other overheads			2,600
Cost of the job			15,600
Profit (25% of sales=$33\frac{1}{3}$% of cost)			5,200
Sales price			20,800

2.4 Job costing for internal services

It is possible to use a job costing system **to control the costs of an internal service department**, such as the maintenance department or the printing department. If a job costing system is used it is possible to **charge the user departments for the cost of specific jobs carried out, rather than apportioning the total costs of these service departments** to the user departments using an arbitrarily determined apportionment basis.

An internal job costing system for service departments will have the following advantages.

Advantages	Comment
Realistic apportionment	The identification of expenses with jobs and the subsequent charging of these to the department(s) responsible means that costs are borne by those who incurred them.
Increased responsibility and awareness	User departments will be aware that they are charged for the specific services used and may be more careful to use the facility more efficiently. They will also appreciate the true cost of the facilities that they are using and can take decisions accordingly.
Control of service department costs	The service department may be restricted to charging a standard cost to user departments for specific jobs carried out or time spent. It will then be possible to measure the efficiency or inefficiency of the service department by recording the difference between the standard charges and the actual expenditure.
Planning information	This information will ease the planning process, as the purpose and cost of service department expenditure can be separately identified.

3 Batch costing

FAST FORWARD

Batch costing is similar to job costing in that each batch of similar articles is separately identifiable. The cost per unit manufactured in a batch is the total batch cost divided by the number of units in the batch.

Key term

A **batch** is a group of similar articles which maintains its identity during one or more stages of production and is treated as a cost unit.

In general, the **procedures for costing batches are very similar to those for costing jobs**.

(a) The **batch is treated as a job during production** and the costs are collected in the manner already described in this chapter.

(b) Once the batch has been completed, the **cost per unit can be calculated as the total batch cost divided into the number of units in the batch**.

3.1 Example: batch costing

Tuffin manufactures Wrens to order and has the following budgeted overheads for the year, based on normal activity levels.

Production departments	Budgeted Overheads	Budgeted activity
	$	
Bluffing	12,000	3,000 labour hours
Puffing	20,000	2,000 labour hours

Selling and administrative overheads are 25% of factory cost. An order for 500 Wrens, made as Batch 73N97, incurred the following costs.

Materials	$24,000
Labour	200 hours in the bluffing department at $5 per hour
	400 hours in the puffing department at $10 per hour

$1,000 was paid for the hire of special equipment for testing the accuracy of the puffing of the Wrens.

Required

Calculate the cost per unit for Batch 73N97.

3.2 Solution

The first step is to calculate the overhead absorption rate for the production departments.

Buffing = $\frac{\$12,000}{3,000}$ = $4 per labour hour

Puffing = $\frac{\$20,000}{2,000}$ = $10 per labour hour

Total cost – Batch 73N97

	$	$
Direct material		24,000
Direct expense		1,000
Direct labour 200 × $5 =	1,000	
400 × $10 =	4,000	
		5,000
Prime cost		30,000
Overheads 200 × $4 =	800	
400 × $10 =	4,000	
		4,800
Factory cost		34,800
Selling and administrative cost (25% of factory cost)		8,700
Total cost		43,500

Cost per unit = $\frac{\$43,500}{500}$ = $87

4 Contract costing

FAST FORWARD

Contract costing is a form of job costing which applies where the job is on a large scale and for a long duration. The majority of costs relating to a contract are direct costs.

Imagine trying to build up job costs on a job ticket in the way described in the previous chapter during the excavation of the tunnel under the English Channel or the construction of a skyscraper. It would be impossible. In industries such as building and construction work, civil engineering and shipbuilding, job costing is not usually appropriate. Contract costing is.

Key term

A **contract** is a cost unit or cost centre which is charged with the direct costs of production and an apportionment of head office overheads.

Contract costing is the name given to a method of job costing where the job to be carried out is of such magnitude that a formal contract is made between the customer and supplier. It applies where work is undertaken to customers' special requirements and each order is of long duration (compared with the time to which job costing applies). The work is usually constructional and *in general* the method is similar to job costing, although there are, of course, a few differences.

4.1 Features of contract costing

(a) A **formal contract** is made between customer and supplier.

(b) Work is undertaken to **customers' special requirements**.

(c) The work is for a **relatively long duration**. Large jobs may take a long time to complete, perhaps two or three years. Even when a contract is completed within less than twelve months, it is quite possible that the work may have begun during one financial year and ended during the supplier's next financial year; therefore the profit on the contract will relate to more than one accounting period.

(d) The work is frequently **constructional** in nature.

(e) The method of costing is **similar to job costing**.

(f) The work is frequently **based on site**.

(g) It is not unusual for a site to have its **own cashier and time-keeper**.

The problems which may arise in contract costing are as follows.

Problem	Comment
Identifying direct costs	Because of the large size of the job, many cost items which are usually thought of as production overhead are charged as direct costs of the contract (for example supervision, hire of plant, depreciation or loss in value of plant which is owned, sub-contractors' fees or charges and so on).
Low indirect costs	**Because many costs normally classed as overheads are charged as direct costs of a contract, the absorption rate for overheads should only apply a share of the cost of those cost items which are not already direct costs.** For most contracts the only item of indirect cost would be a charge for head office expenses.
Difficulties of cost control	Because of the size of some contracts and some sites, there are often cost control problems (material usage and losses, pilferage, labour supervision and utilisation, damage to and loss of plant and tools, vandalism and so on).
Dividing the profit between different accounting periods	When a contract covers two or more accounting periods, how should the profit (or loss) on the contract be divided between the periods? This problem is, fortunately, outside the scope of your syllabus.

4.2 Overhead costs

Overhead costs are added periodically (for example at the end of an accounting period) and are based on predetermined overhead absorption rates for the period. You may come across examples where a share of head office general costs is absorbed as an overhead cost to the contract, but this should not happen if the contract is unfinished at the end of the period, because only **production** overheads should be included in the value of any closing work in progress.

4.3 Contract accounts

The **account for a contract is a job account, or work in progress account**, and is a record of the direct materials, direct labour, direct expenses and overhead charges on the contract. A typical contract account might appear as shown below. Check the items in the account carefully, and notice how the cost (or value) of the work done emerges as work in progress.

On an unfinished contract, where no profits are taken mid-way through the contract, this cost of work in progress is carried forward as a closing inventory balance.

4.4 Example: a contract account

CONTRACT 794 – TEN-LANE MOTORWAY

	$'000		$'000
Book value of plant on site b/d	14,300	Materials returned to stores or transferred to other sites	2,100
Materials requisition from stores	15,247	Proceeds from sale of materials on site and jobbing work for other customers	600
Materials and equipment purchased	36,300	Book value of plant transferred	4,800
Maintenance and operating costs of plant and vehicles	14,444	Materials on site c/d	7,194
Hire charges for plant and vehicles not owned	6,500	Book value of plant on site c/d	6,640
Tools and consumables	8,570		21,334
Direct wages	23,890	Cost of work done c/d (balancing item)	139,917
Supervisors' and engineers' salaries (proportion relating to time spent on the contract)	13,000		
Other site expenses	12,000		
Overheads (apportioned perhaps on the basis of direct labour hours)	17,000		
	161,251		161,251
Materials on site b/d	7,194		
Book value of plant on site b/d	6,640		
Cost of work done b/d	139,917		

5 Service industry costing

FAST FORWARD

Service costing can be used by companies operating in a **service industry** or by companies wishing to establish the **cost of services carried out by some of their departments.**

Key term

Service costing is 'Cost accounting for services or functions, eg canteens, maintenance, personnel. These may be referred to as service centres, departments or functions'.

CIMA *Official Terminology*

5.1 What are service organisations?

Service organisations do not make or sell tangible goods. Profit-seeking service organisations include accountancy firms, law firms, management consultants, transport companies, banks, insurance companies and hotels. Almost all not-for-profit organisations – hospitals, schools, libraries and so on – are also service organisations.

Service costing differs from the other costing methods (product costing methods) for a number of reasons.

(a) With many services, the cost of direct materials consumed will be relatively small compared to the labour, direct expenses and overheads cost. In product costing the direct materials are often a greater proportion of the total cost.

(b) Because of the difficulty of identifying costs with specific cost units in service costing, the indirect costs tend to represent a higher proportion of total cost compared with product costing.

(c) The output of most service organisations is often **intangible** and hence difficult to define. A unit cost is therefore difficult to calculate.

(d) The service industry includes such a wide range of organisations which provide such different services and have such different cost structures that costing will vary considerably from one service to another.

5.2 Unit cost measures

FAST FORWARD

One main problem with service costing is being able to define a realistic cost unit that represents a suitable measure of the service provided. If the service is a function of two activity variables, a **composite cost unit** may be more appropriate.

A particular problem with service costing is the difficulty in defining a realistic cost unit that represents a suitable measure of the service provided. Frequently, a **composite cost unit** may be deemed more appropriate if the service is a function of two activity variables. Hotels, for example, may use the **'occupied bed-night'** as an appropriate unit for cost ascertainment and control.

A company operating a fleet of delivery vehicles may use the **'tonne/kilometre'** as a cost unit. This involves recording and monitoring the cost of carrying one tonne for one kilometre. The cost per tonne/kilometre is comparable regardless of the length of the journey and provides a valid cost unit for control purposes. The construction of this composite cost unit is demonstrated later in the chapter.

Typical cost units used by companies operating in a service industry are shown below.

Service	Cost unit
Road, rail and air transport services	Passenger/kilometre, tonne/kilometre
Hotels	Occupied bed-night
Education	Full-time student
Hospitals	Patient-day
Catering establishments	Meal served

Each organisation will need to ascertain the cost unit most appropriate to its activities. If a number of organisations within an industry use a common cost unit, valuable **comparisons** can be made between similar establishments. This is particularly applicable to hospitals, educational establishments and local authorities. Unit costs are also useful control measures as we shall see in the examples that follow.

Exam focus point

Make sure that you are familiar with suitable composite cost units for common forms of service operation eg transport.

FAST FORWARD

$$\textbf{Cost per service unit} = \frac{\text{Total costs for period}}{\text{Number of service units in the period}}$$

Whatever cost unit is decided upon, the calculation of a cost per unit is as follows.

Key term

$$\text{Cost per service unit} = \frac{\text{Total costs for period}}{\text{Number of service units in the period}}$$

The following examples will illustrate the principles involved in service industry costing and the further considerations to bear in mind when costing services.

5.2.1 Example: costing an educational establishment

A university offers a range of degree courses. The university organisation structure consists of three faculties each with a number of teaching departments. In addition, there is a university administrative/management function and a central services function.

(a) The following cost information is available for the year ended 30 June 20X3.

(i) **Occupancy costs**
Total $1,500,000

Such costs are apportioned on the basis of area used which is as follows.

	Square metres
Faculties	7,500
Teaching departments	20,000
Administration/management	7,000
Central services	3,000

(ii) **Administrative/management costs**

Direct costs: $1,775,000
Indirect costs: an apportionment of occupancy costs

Direct and indirect costs are charged to degree courses on a percentage basis.

(iii) **Faculty costs**

Direct costs: $700,000
Indirect costs: an apportionment of occupancy costs and central service costs

Direct and indirect costs are charged to teaching departments.

(iv) **Teaching departments**

Direct costs: $5,525,000
Indirect costs: an apportionment of occupancy costs and central service costs plus all faculty costs

Direct and indirect costs are charged to degree courses on a percentage basis.

(v) **Central services**

Direct costs: $1,000,000
Indirect costs: an apportionment of occupancy costs

(b) Direct and indirect costs of central services have, in previous years, been charged to users on a percentage basis. A study has now been completed which has estimated what user areas would have paid external suppliers for the same services on an individual basis. For the year ended 30 June 20X3, the apportionment of the central services cost is to be recalculated in a manner which recognises the cost savings achieved by using the central services facilities instead of using external service companies. This is to be done by apportioning the overall savings to user areas in proportion to their share of the estimated external costs.

The estimated external costs of service provision are as follows.

	$'000
Faculties	240
Teaching departments	800
Degree courses:	
Business studies	32
Mechanical engineering	48
Catering studies	32
All other degrees	448
	1,600

(c) Additional data relating to the degree courses is as follows.

		Degree course	
	Business studies	*Mechanical engineering*	*Catering studies*
Number of undergraduates	80	50	120
Apportioned costs (as % of totals)			
Teaching departments	3.0%	2.5%	7%
Administration/management	2.5%	5.0%	4%

Central services are to be apportioned as detailed in (b) above.

The total number of undergraduates from the university in the year to 30 June 20X3 was 2,500.

Required

(a) Calculate the average cost per undergraduate for the year ended 30 June 20X3.

(b) Calculate the average cost per undergraduate for each of the degrees in business studies, mechanical engineering and catering studies, showing all relevant cost analysis.

5.2.2 Solution

(a) The average cost per undergraduate is as follows.

	Total costs for university $'000
Occupancy	1,500
Admin/management	1,775
Faculty	700
Teaching departments	5,525
Central services	1,000
	10,500
Number of undergraduates	2,500
Average cost per undergraduate for year ended 30 June 20X3	$4,200

(b) Average cost per undergraduate for each course is as follows.

	Business studies $	*Mechanical engineering* $	*Catering studies* $
Teaching department costs (W1 and using % in question)	241,590	201,325	563,710
Admin/management costs (W1 and using % in question)	51,375	102,750	82,200
Central services (W2)	22,400	33,600	22,400
	315,365	337,675	668,310
Number of undergraduates	80	50	120
Average cost per undergraduate for year ended 30 June 20X3	$3,942	$6,754	$5,569

Workings

1 Cost allocation and apportionment

Cost item	*Basis of apportionment*	*Teaching departments*	*Admin/ management*	*Central services*	*Faculties*
		$'000	$'000	$'000	$'000
Direct costs	allocation	5,525	1,775	1,000	700
Occupancy costs	area used	800	280	120	300
Central services reapportioned	(W2)	560	-	(1,120)	168
Faculty costs reallocated	allocation	1,168	-	-	(1,168)
		8,053	2,055	-	-

2 Apportioning savings to user areas on the basis given in the question gives the same result as apportioning internal costs in proportion to the external costs.

	External costs	*Apportionment of internal central service costs*
	$'000	$'000
Faculties	240	168.0
Teaching	800	560.0
Degree courses:		
Business studies	32	22.4
Mechanical engineering	48	33.6
Catering studies	32	22.4
All other degrees	448	313.6
	1,600	1,120.0

Question

Service costs

Briefly describe cost units that are appropriate to a transport business.

Answer

The cost unit is the basic measure of control in an organisation, used to monitor cost and activity levels. The cost unit selected must be measurable and appropriate for the type of cost and activity. Possible cost units which could be suggested are as follows.

Cost per kilometre

- Variable cost per kilometre
- Fixed cost per kilometre

This is not particularly useful for control purposes because it will tend to vary with the kilometres run.

- Total cost of each vehicle per kilometre – this suffers from the same problem as above
- Maintenance cost of each vehicle per kilometre

Cost per tonne-kilometre

This can be more useful than a cost per kilometre for control purposes, because it combines the distance travelled and the load carried, both of which affect cost.

Cost per operating hour

Once again, many costs can be related to this cost unit, including the following.

- Total cost of each vehicle per operating hour
- Variable costs per operating hour
- Fixed costs per operating hour

Question

Carry operates a small fleet of delivery vehicles. Expected costs are as follows.

Loading	1 hour per tonne loaded
Loading costs:	
Labour (casual)	$2 per hour
Equipment depreciation	$80 per week
Supervision	$80 per week
Drivers' wages (fixed)	$100 per man per week
Petrol	10c per kilometre
Repairs	5c per kilometre
Depreciation	$80 per week per vehicle
Supervision	$120 per week
Other general expenses (fixed)	$200 per week

There are two drivers and two vehicles in the fleet.

During a slack week, only six journeys were made.

Journey	*Tonnes carried (one way)*	*One-way distance of journey Kilometres*
1	5	100
2	8	20
3	2	60
4	4	50
5	6	200
6	5	300

Required

Calculate the expected average full cost per tonne/kilometre for the week.

Answer

Variable costs

Journey	*1*	*2*	*3*	*4*	*5*	*6*
	$	$	$	$	$	$
Loading labour	10	16	4	8	12	10
Petrol (both ways)	20	4	12	10	40	60
Repairs (both ways)	10	2	6	5	20	30
	40	22	22	23	72	100

Total costs

	$
Variable costs (total for journeys 1 to 6)	279
Loading equipment depreciation	80
Loading supervision	80
Drivers' wages	200
Vehicles depreciation	160
Drivers' supervision	120
Other costs	200
	1,119

Journey	Tonnes	*One-way distance* Kilometres	Tonne/kilometres
1	5	100	500
2	8	20	160
3	2	60	120
4	4	50	200
5	6	200	1,200
6	5	300	1,500
			3,680

Cost per tonne/kilometre $\frac{\$1,119}{3,680} = \$0.304$

Note that the large element of fixed costs may distort this measure but that a variable cost per tonne/kilometre of $279/3,680 = $0.076 may be useful for budgetary control.

6 Service department costing

FAST FORWARD

Service department costing is also used to establish a specific cost for an **internal service** which is a service provided by one department for another, rather than sold externally to customers eg canteen, maintenance.

Service department costing is used to establish a specific cost for an **'internal service'** which is a service provided by one department for another, rather than sold externally to customers. Examples of some internal service departments include the following.

- Canteen
- Data processing
- Maintenance

The purposes of service department costing

The costing of internal services has two basic purposes.

(a) **To control the costs and efficiency in the service department.** If we establish a distribution cost per tonne/km, a canteen cost per employee, a maintenance cost per machine hour, job cost per repair, or a mainframe computer operating cost per hour, we can do the following in order to establish control measures.
   (i) Compare actual costs against a target or standard
   (ii) Compare actual costs in the current period against actual costs in previous periods

(b) **To control the costs of the user departments, and prevent the unnecessary use of services.** If the costs of services are charged to the user departments in such a way that the charges reflect the use actually made by each user department of the service department's services then the following will occur.
   (i) The overhead costs of user departments will be established more accurately. Some service department variable costs might be identified as costs which are directly attributable to the user department.
   (ii) If the service department's charges for a user department are high, the user department might be encouraged to consider whether it is making an excessively costly and wasteful use of the service department's service.
   (iii) The user department might decide that it can obtain a similar service at a lower cost from an external service company and so the service department will have priced itself out of the market. This is clearly not satisfactory from the point of view of the organisation as a whole.

Service costing also provides a **fairer basis** for charging service costs to user departments, instead of charging service costs as overheads on a broad direct labour hour basis, or similar arbitrary apportionment basis. This is because service costs are related more directly to **use**.

Some examples of situations where the costing of internal services would be useful are as follows.

(a) If repair costs in a factory are costed as jobs with each bit of repair work being given a job number and costed accordingly, repair costs can be charged to the departments on the basis of repair jobs actually undertaken, instead of on a more generalised basis, such as apportionment according to machine hour capacity in each department. Departments with high repair costs could then consider their high incidence of repairs, the age and reliability of their machines, or the skills of the machine operators.

(b) If mainframe computer costs are charged to a user department on the basis of a cost per hour, the user department would make the following assessment.

   (i) Whether it was getting good value from its use of the mainframe computer.

   (ii) Whether it might be better to hire the service of a computer bureau, or perhaps install a stand-alone microcomputer system in the department.

Question — Service costs

The maintenance department of FA charges user departments for its services as follows.

- A predetermined hourly rate for labour hours worked on maintenance jobs
- Specifically identifiable materials are charged at actual cost

The budgeted maintenance labour hours for the latest period were 800 hours, during which maintenance costs of $8,400 were budgeted to be incurred.

During the period, 22 maintenance hours were worked in production department 1, and materials costing $18 were used on these maintenance jobs.

The correct charge to production department 1 for its use of the maintenance service department during the period is

A $28.50 B $231.00 C $249.00 D $399.82

Answer

Predetermined labour hour rate for maintenance = $8,400/800
= $10.50 per hour

∴ Charge to production department 1:

	$
Maintenance labour (22 hours × $10.50)	231
Materials	18
	249

Therefore the correct answer is C.

7 Job costing and services

Service costing is one of the subdivisions of **continuous operation costing** and as such should theoretically be applied when the services result from a sequence of continuous or repetitive operations or processes. Service costing is therefore ideal for catering establishments, road, rail and air transport services and hotels. However, just because an organisation provides a service, it does not mean that service costing should automatically be applied.

Remember that job costing applies where work is undertaken to customers' special requirements. An organisation may therefore be working in the service sector but may supply one-off services which meet particular customers' special requirements; in such a situation job costing may be more appropriate than service costing. For example, a consultancy business, although part of the service sector, could use job costing.

(a) Each job could be given a separate number.
(b) Time sheets could be used to record and analyse consultants' time.
(c) The time spent against each job number would be shown as well as, for example, travelling time and mileage.
(d) Other costs such as stationery could be charged direct to each job as necessary.

8 Framework for dealing with process costing

FAST FORWARD

Process costing is used when there is a continuous flow of identical units.

Key term

Process costing is a costing method used where it is not possible to identify separate units of production, or jobs, usually because of the continuous nature of the production processes involved.

It is common to identify process costing with **continuous production** such as the following.

- Oil refining
- The manufacture of soap
- Paint
- Food and drink

The features of process costing which make it different from job or batch costing are as follows.

(a) In process costing it is not possible to build up cost records of the cost of each individual unit of output because production in progress is an **indistinguishable homogeneous mass**. Therefore process costing is an **averaging method** whereby costs are aggregated and divided by units produced.
(b) **Overheads** are often high in process industries such as oil refineries and they are usually absorbed through direct labour hours, process hours or material value.
(c) There is often a **loss in process** due to spoilage, wastage, evaporation and so on.
(d) The **output** of one process becomes the **input** to the next until the finished product is made in the final process.
(e) Output from production may be a single product, but there may also be a **by-product** (or by-products) and/or **joint products**.

As earlier in the Chapter, we based this section on the full absorption costing method. Don't forget that it is easy to adapt this to marginal costing by treating overheads as period charges, or to use activity based methods to establish the overhead absorption rate.

Exam focus point

Note that the contents of this section are mainly to remind you of the way in which process costing calculations are performed. It is highly unlikely that the examiner will set a detailed question on process costing. **You must, however, be able to apply absorption costing principles in a process costing context.**

Direct labour and production overhead may be treated together in an examination question as **conversion cost**.

8.1 Example: basics of process costing

Suppose that Fred and Ginger make top hats for Ascot. Production of the hats involves two processes, shaping and colouring. During the year to 31 March 20X3, 1,000,000 units of material worth $500,000 were input to the first process, shaping. Direct labour costs of $200,000 and production overhead costs of $200,000 were also incurred in connection with the shaping process. There were no opening or closing inventories in the shaping department. The process account for shaping for the year ended 31 March 20X3 is as follows.

PROCESS 1 (SHAPING) ACCOUNT

	Units	$		Units	$
Direct materials	1,000,000	500,000	Output to Process 2	1,000,000	900,000
Direct labour		200,000			
Production overheads		200,000			
	1,000,000	900,000		1,000,000	900,000

This is an averaging method whereby costs are pooled together for production. The cost per unit is therefore $900,000/1,000,000 = $0.90.

Chapter Roundup

- **Job costing** is the costing method used where each cost unit is separately identifiable. The work is undertaken to customers' special requirements, is of comparatively short duration, is usually carried out within a factory or workshop and moves through processes and operations as a continuously identifiable unit.
- **Batch costing** is similar to job costing in that each batch of similar articles is separately identifiable. The cost per unit manufactured in a batch is the total batch cost divided by the number of units in the batch.
- **Contract costing** is a form of job costing which applies where the job is on a large scale and for a long duration. The majority of costs relating to a contract are direct costs.
- **Service costing** can be used by companies operating in a **service industry** or by companies wishing to establish the **cost of services carried out by some of their departments**.
- One main problem with service costing is being able to define a realistic cost unit that represents a suitable measure of the service provided. If the service is a function of two activity variables, a **composite cost unit** may be more appropriate.
- **Cost per service unit** = $\frac{\text{Total costs for period}}{\text{Number of service units in the period}}$
- **Service department costing** is also used to establish a specific cost for an **internal service** which is a service provided by one department for another, rather than sold externally to customers eg canteen, maintenance.
- **Process costing** is used when there is a continuous flow of identical units.

Quick Quiz

1 Why might inaccurate absorption rates harm an organisation?
2 What is cost plus pricing?
3 What are the likely features of a computerised job costing system?
4 What are the advantages of an internal job costing system for some departments?
5 How is the cost per unit calculated in batch costing?
6 List the features of contract costing.

7 Cost per service unit = ______________________________

8 What are the distinguishing features of process costing?

9 Which of the following are not characteristics of job costing?

I Customer driven production
II Complete production possible within a single accounting period
III Homogeneous products

A I and II only
B I and III only
C II and III only
D III only

10 The following information is available for contract AF3.

Contract price	$15 million
Cost of work to date	$5,040,000
Estimated costs to completion	$3,960,000

The amount of profit to be recognised on the contract is

A $0 B $3,360,000 C $6,000,000 D $8,400,000

Answers to Quick Quiz

1 If jobs are overpriced, customer will go elsewhere. If jobs are underpriced, revenue will fail to cover costs.

2 Cost plus pricing involves adding a desired profit margin to the total costs to arrive at a selling price.

3 (a) Every job will be given a *job code number*, which will determine how the data relating to the job is stored.

(b) A separate set of codes will be given for the *type of costs* that any job is likely to incur. Thus 'direct wages', say, will have the same code whichever job they are allocated to.

(c) In a sophisticated system, costs can be analysed both by *job* (for example all costs related to Job 456), but also by *type* (for example direct wages incurred on all jobs). It is thus easy to perform control analysis and to make comparisons between jobs.

(d) A job costing system might have facilities built into it which incorporate other factors relating to the performance of the job. In complex jobs, sophisticated planning techniques might be employed to ensure that the job is performed in the minimum time possible: time management features may be incorporated into job costing software.

4 (a) Realistic apportionment
(b) Increased responsibility and awareness
(c) Control of service department costs
(d) Availability of planning information

5 Total costs ÷ number of units in batch = cost per unit

6 (a) A formal contract is made between customer and supplier.
(b) Work is undertaken to customers' special requirements.
(c) The work is for a relatively long duration.
(d) The work is frequently constructional in nature.
(e) The method of costing is similar to job costing.
(f) The work is frequently based on site.
(g) It is not unusual for a site to have its own cashier and time-keeper.

7 $\text{Cost per service unit} = \dfrac{\text{Total costs for period}}{\text{Number of service units in the period}}$

8 (a) The continuous nature of production in many processes means that there will usually be closing work in progress which must be valued

(b) There is often a loss in process due to spoilage, waste, evaporation and so on.

(c) Output from production may be a single product, by-product and/or joint products.

9 D

10 B Total cost to completion = \$5,040,000 + \$3,960,000 = \$9,000,000

Percentage of total cost incurred to date = \$5,040,000/\$9,000,000 = 56%

Therefore it is acceptable to recognise a profit. This eliminates option A.

$$\text{Profit to be recognised} = \frac{\text{Cost of work done}}{\text{Estimated total cost of contract}} \times \text{estimated total profit}$$

$$= \frac{£5,040,000}{£9,000,000} \times \$(15,000,000 - 9,000,000)$$

$$= \$3,360,000$$

Now try the questions below from the Exam Question Bank

Number	Level	Marks	Time
Section A: Q7	MCQ	N/A	N/A
Section B: Q4	Examination	20	36 mins

PART B

Planning and control

The collection of data

5

Topic list
1 Data and information
2 Types of data
3 Sources of data
4 Secondary data
5 Sampling
6 Sampling methods
7 Benchmarking

Study guide reference

		Syllabus reference
5(a)	Describe sources of information from within and outside the organisation	2
	(i) Describe sources of information from suppliers and customers	2
	(ii) Describe sources of information from suppliers and customers	2
	(iii) Discuss sampling techniques (random, systematic, stratified, multistage, cluster and quota)	2
	(iv) Choose an appropriate sampling method in a specific situation	2
	(v) Describe sources of information from government, trade associations and the financial press	2
	(vi) Describe benchmarking	2
	(vii) Discuss the advantages and disadvantages of benchmarking	2
	(viii) Select appropriate benchmarks at strategic, tactical and operational levels in a specific situation	2
	(Note: Derivation of random samples will not be examined.)	
25(g)	Discuss the role of benchmarking in performance measurement	2

1 Data and information

FAST FORWARD

Data are the raw materials for data processing. **Information** is data that has been processed.

Quantitative data are data that can be measured. A **'variable'** is something which can be measured.

Qualitative data cannot be measured but have **attributes** (an attribute is something an object either has or does not have).

1.1 What are data?

Key term

Data is a 'scientific' term for facts, figures, information and processing. Data are the raw materials for data processing.

Examples of data include the following.

(a) The number of tourists who visit Hong Kong each year
(b) The sales turnovers of all restaurants in Salisbury
(c) The number of people (with black hair) who pass their driving test each year

1.2 What is information?

Key term

Information is data that has been processed in such a way as to be meaningful to the person who receives it. Information is anything that is communicated.

The **quality of source data** affects the value of information. Information is worthless if the source data is flawed. If the researchers filled in questionnaires themselves, inventing the answers, then the conclusions drawn from the processed data would be wrong, and poor decisions would be made.

1.3 Quantitative and qualitative data

Quantitative data are data that can be measured (think of measuring quantities). Examples of quantitative data include the following.

(a) The temperature on each day of January in Singapore. This can be **measured** in degrees Fahrenheit or Celsius.

(b) The time it takes you to swim 50 lengths. This can be **measured** in hours and minutes.

Qualitative data are data that cannot be measured but which reflect some quality of what is being observed. The data are said to have **attributes**. An **attribute** is something an object has either got or not got. It cannot be measured. An example of **qualitative data** is whether someone is male or female. Whether you are male or female is an **attribute** because the sex of a person cannot be measured.

1.4 Quantitative and qualitative information

Just as data may be quantitative or qualitative, so too may information.

(a) **Quantitative information** is information which is capable of being expressed in numbers. It is usually financial in nature.

(b) **Qualitative information** is information which may not be expressed very easily in terms of numbers. Information of this nature is more likely to reflect the quality of something.

An example of **quantitative information** is 'The Chairman of the company has announced that the turnover for the year is **$4 million.**' You can see how this information is easily expressed in numerical terms.

An example of **qualitative information** is 'The standard of the books produced was **very high.**' This information cannot easily be expressed in terms of numbers, as the standard of something is usually described as being very high, quite low, or average and so on.

2 Types of data

Data may be **primary** (collected specifically for the purpose of a survey) or **secondary** (collected for some other purpose).

The main **characteristics of good information**

Relevance	Confidence-inspiring
Completeness	Properly communicated
Accuracy	Clarity

Discrete data/variables can only take on a countable number of values. **Continuous** data/ variables can take on any value.

We have already seen how data can be classified as being **quantitative** (can be measured (variables)) or qualitative (cannot be measured, has an **attribute**). We shall now consider the ways in which data may be further classified as follows.

(a) Primary and secondary data
(b) Discrete and continuous data
(c) Sample and population data

Primary and secondary data

(a) **Primary data** are data collected especially for a specific purpose. Raw data are primary data which have not been processed at all, and which are still just a list of numbers.

(b) **Secondary data** are data which have already been collected elsewhere, for some other purpose, but which can be used or adapted for the survey being conducted.

2.1 Discrete and continuous data

Quantitative data may be further classified as being **discrete** or **continuous.**

(a) **Discrete data** are data which can only taken on a finite or countable number of values within a given range.

(b) **Continuous data** are data which can take on any value. They are measured rather than counted.

An example of discrete data is the number of goals scored by Arsenal against Chelsea in the FA Cup Final: Arsenal could score 0, 1, 2, 3 or even 4 goals (**discrete variables** =0, 1, 2, 3, 4), but they cannot score 1½ or 2½ goals.

Continuous data include the heights of all the members of your family, as these can take on any value: 1.542m, 1.639m and 1.492m for example. **Continuous variables** = 1.542, 1.639, 1.492.

2.2 Sample and population data

(a) **Sample data** are data arising as a result of investigating a sample. A sample is a selection from the population.

(b) **Population data** are data arising as a result of investigating the population. A population is the group of people or objects of interest to the data collector.

The diagram below should help you to remember the ways in which data may be classified.

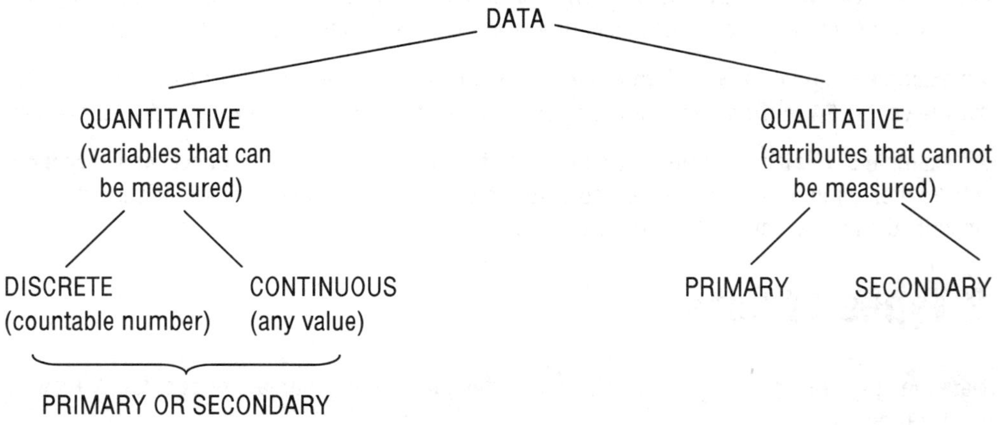

Question

Data

Look through the following list of surveys and decide whether each is collecting qualitative data or quantitative data. If you think the data is quantitative, indicate whether it is discrete or continuous.

(a) A survey of accountancy textbooks, to determine how many diagrams they contain.

(b) A survey of greetings cards on a newsagent's shelf, to determine whether or not each has a price sticker on it.

(c) A survey of the results in a cost accounting examination, to determine what percentage of marks the students obtained.

(d) A survey of heights of telegraph poles in Papua New Guinea, to find out if there is any variation across the country.

(e) A survey of swimmers to find out how long they take to swim a kilometre.

Answer

(a) The number of diagrams in an accountancy text book is an example of **quantitative** data, because it can be measured. Because the number of diagrams can only be counted in whole number steps, the resulting data is **discrete.** You cannot for example have 42½ diagrams, but you can have 42 or 43 diagrams.

(b) Whether or not a greetings card has a price sticker on it is not something that can be measured. This is therefore an example of **qualitative** data, as a greetings card either has a price sticker on it, or it does not have a price sticker on it.

(c) The results of a cost accounting examination can be measured, and are therefore an example of **quantitative** data. The examination results can only take on whole number values between 0% and

100%, and the data are therefore **discrete.** (It may be possible to score 62½%, or 64½%, but it is not possible to score 62.41%, so the variable is not continuous.)

(d) The heights of telegraph poles is an example of **quantitative** data as they can be measured. Since the telegraph poles may take on any height, the data is said to be **continuous.**

(e) The time taken to swim a kilometre may be measured and is therefore **quantitative** data. Because the time recorded can take on any value, in theory, the data is said to be **continuous**.

Now we know what sorts of data we may come across, and how it is classified, we can take a look at the different **sources of data.**

3 Sources of data

FAST FORWARD

Data may be obtained from an **internal** source or an **external** source.

3.1 Internal sources of data

3.1.1 The accounting records

There is no need for us to give a detailed description of the constituents of the accounting records. You are by now very familiar with the idea of a system of sales ledgers and purchase ledgers, general ledgers and cost ledgers. These records provide a history of an organisation's business. Some of this data is of great value outside the accounts department, for example sales data for the marketing function. Other data, like cheque numbers or employees' PAYE codes, is of purely administrative value within the accounts department.

You will also be aware that to maintain the **integrity of its accounting records**, an organisation of any size will have systems for and controls over transactions. These also give rise to valuable data. A inventory control system is the classic example. Besides actually recording the monetary value of purchases and inventory in hand for external financial reporting purposes, the system will include purchase orders, goods received notes, goods returned notes and so on, and these can be analysed to provide management information about speed of delivery, say, or the quality of supplies.

3.1.2 Other internal sources

Much of the data that are not strictly part of the financial accounting records are in fact closely tied in to the accounting system.

(a) **Data relating to personnel** will be linked to the payroll system. Additional data may be obtained from this source if, say, a project is being costed and it is necessary to ascertain the availability and rate of pay of different levels of staff, or the need for and cost of recruiting staff from outside the organisation.

(b) **Much data will be produced by a production department** about machine capacity, fuel consumption, movement of people, materials, and work in progress, set up times, maintenance requirements and so on. A large part of the traditional work of cost accounting involves ascribing costs to the physical information produced by this source.

(c) **Many service businesses** – notably accountants and solicitors – need to keep detailed records of the time spent on various activities, both to justify fees to clients and to assess the efficiency of operations.

3.2 External sources of data

We hardly need say that an organisation's files are also full of invoices, letters, advertisements and so on received from customers and suppliers. These documents provide data from an external source. There are many occasions when an active search outside the organisation is necessary.

(a) A **primary source** of data is, as the term implies, as close as you can get to the origin of an item of data: the eyewitness to an event, the place in question, the document under scrutiny.

(b) A **secondary source**, again logically enough, provides 'second-hand' data: books, articles, verbal or written reports by someone else.

You will remember that **primary data** are data collected especially for a specific purpose. The **advantage** of such data is that the investigator knows where the data came from and is aware of any inadequacies or limitations in the data. Its **disadvantage** is that it can be very expensive to collect primary data.

Management accountants often collect primary data when they carry out investigations. A good example would be the establishment of the direct cost of a product. This might be carried out by analysing materials invoices and wages costs over a representative period.

4 Secondary data

FAST FORWARD

The main sources of **secondary data** are: Governments; banks; newspapers; trade journals; information bureaux; consultancies; libraries and information services.

Secondary data are data which have already been collected elsewhere, for some other purpose, but which can be used or adapted for the survey being conducted.

Advantage of secondary data	Disadvantage of secondary data
They are cheaply available	Since the investigator did not collect the data, he is therefore unaware of any inadequacies or limitations of the data.

Secondary data sources may be satisfactory in certain situations, or they may be the only convenient means of obtaining an item of data. It is essential that there is good reason to believe that the secondary data used is **accurate** and **reliable**.

External sources of data may have been obtained for many different reasons, and care should be taken to ensure that it is used properly. This is because the data will have been collected for a specific purpose, and then used as secondary data.

Despite the limitations of secondary data, they can be very valuable in many situations. The main secondary data sources are as follows.

(a) Governments
(b) Banks
(c) Newspapers
(d) Trade journals

We considered these sources of secondary data in some detail in Chapter 1. Read that chapter to remind yourself of the sources and their characteristics.

4.1 The internet

The **Internet** is a global network connecting millions of computers. The Internet allows any computer with a telecommunications link to **send and receive information** to and from any other suitably equipped computer.

A **website** is a collection of images and text that **provide information** which may be viewed on the World Wide Web. Most organisations now have a website. Some sites are able to **process transactions** (known as electronic commerce or **e-commerce**).

Connection to the Internet is made via an **Internet Service Provider** (ISP). ISPs, such as AOL and Virgin provide their **own information services** in addition to Internet access and e-mail capability.

Users access the Internet through interface programs called **browsers.** The most popular and best known is **Microsoft Internet Explorer**.

Browser software packages provide a facility to **store Internet addresses** so that users can access frequently-visited sites without having to go through a long search process. So in business use, if you **regularly need up-to-date information**, say, on inventory market movements, new government legislation, or the activities of a competitor, you can simply click on the appropriate entry in a personal 'favourites' directory and be taken straight to the relevant site.

Searching the Net is done using a **search engine** such as Yahoo!, Google or AltaVista. These guide users to destinations throughout the web: the user simply types in a word or phrase to find related sites and documents.

All search engines work in a similar way. The illustrations that follow show the opening ('home') page of Google.co.uk. To perform a search, you simply click in an empty box (if the cursor isn't flashing there already), type in a word or words and click on Search or, for Google, on Google Search.

In the following example, the user is using the Google.co.uk search engine to find web pages from the UK containing information regarding share prices.

The results of the search are shown below

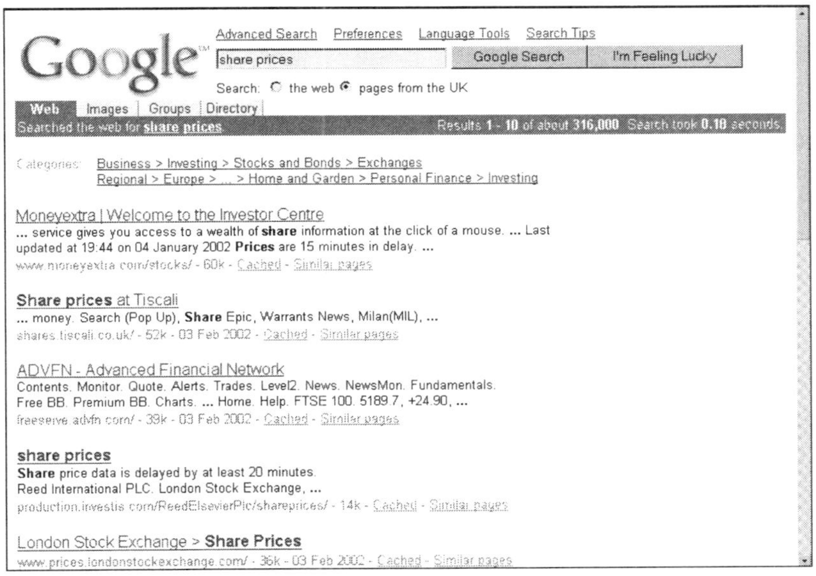

Google found hundreds of websites or documents relating to share information. To view a document, you simply click on the highlighted document title.

Remember, when you are looking at information on the Internet it is **not necessarily good information**, just because it is 'published'. **Anybody** can put information on the Internet. The **reliability** and **reputation** of the **provider is important**. For example, The Financial Times site, FT.com, is a respected source of financial information. On the other hand, a site such as 'Fred's Financial Advice' may contain unreliable information.

4.2 Information relating to customers and suppliers

Examples of the type of information a firm might wish to collect about customers and suppliers are as follows.

(a) Contact details
(b) Up-to-date price lists
(c) Share prices (historical and current)
(d) Key personnel in an organisation
(e) Copy of the latest set of published accounts
(f) Information relating to any recent press releases
(g) Information relating to any new projects that might currently be under consideration
(h) The organisation's mission statement

Question — **External data sources**

Which of the following are secondary external sources of data.

I *Economic Trends* (published by the Office for National Statistics in the United Kingdom).

II The *Singapore Business Times.*

III Data collected for a survey which was commissioned in order to determine whether Donald Ltd should launch a new product.

IV Historical records of expenditure on canteen costs in a hospital in order to prepare current forecasts.

A I and II only
B I, II and III only
C I, II and IV only
D I, II, III and IV

Answer

The correct answer is C.

Economic Trends and the *Singapore Business Times* are both sources of secondary external data. Historic expenditure data of canteen costs were not collected specifically for the preparation of forecasts, and are therefore also secondary data. Data collected through personal interview for a particular project are primary data.

5 Sampling

FAST FORWARD

Data are often collected from a **sample** rather than from a population. If the whole population is examined, the survey is called a **census**.

In many situations, it will not be practical to carry out a survey which considers every item of the **population**. For example, if a poll is taken to try to predict the results of an election, it would not be possible to ask all eligible voters how they are going to vote. To ask the whole population would take far too long and cost too much money.

In such situations where it is not possible to survey the whole population, a **sample** is selected. The results obtained from the sample are used to estimate the results of the whole population.

In situations where the whole population is examined, the survey is called a **census.** This situation is quite rare, which means that the investigator must choose a **sample.**

Disadvantages of a census

(a) The high cost of a census may exceed the value of the results obtained.
(b) It might be out of date by the time you complete it.

Advantages of a sample

(a) It can be shown mathematically that once a certain sample size has been reached, very little accuracy is gained by examining more items. The larger the size of the sample, however, the more accurate the results.
(b) It is possible to ask more questions with a sample.

5.1 The choice of a sample

One of the most important requirements of sample data is that they should be **complete.** That is, the data should **cover all areas** of the population to be examined. If this requirement is not met, then the sample will be **biased**.

6 Sampling methods

A **probability sampling method** is a sampling method in which there is a known chance of each member of the population appearing in the sample.

Probability sampling methods

- Random
- Stratified random
- Systematic
- Multistage
- Cluster

Random sampling requires the construction of a **sampling frame**. A sampling frame is a numbered list of all items in a population.

A **non-probability sampling method** is a sampling method in which the chance of each member of the population appearing in the sample is not known, for example, **quota sampling**.

You must be aware of the characteristics and advantages and disadvantages of the sampling methods covered in this chapter.

Once data have been collected they need to be **presented** and **analysed** It is important to remember that if data have not been collected properly, no amount of careful presentation or analysis can remedy this defect.

Exam focus point

In the December 2006 exam, candidates were tested on their knowledge of **stratified random sampling** and **cluster sampling**. Explanations and advantages of the two methods were needed for six marks.

6.1 Probability sampling methods

Key term

A **probability sampling method** is a sampling method in which there is a known chance of each member of the population appearing in the sample.

(a) Random sampling
(b) Stratified random sampling
(c) Systematic sampling
(d) Multistage sampling
(e) Cluster sampling

6.2 Random sampling

Key term

> A **simple random sample** is a sample selected in such a way that every item in the population has an equal chance of being included.

If a sample is selected using random sampling, it will be free from bias (since every item will have an equal chance of being selected). Once the sample has been selected, valid inferences about the population being sampled can be made.

For example, if you wanted to take a random sample of library books, it would not be good enough to pick them off the shelves, even if you picked them at random. This is because the books which were out on loan would stand no chance of being chosen. You would either have to make sure that all the books were on the shelves before taking your sample, or find some other way of sampling (for example, using the library index cards).

A random sample is not necessarily a perfect sample. For example, you might pick what you believe to be a completely random selection of library books, and find that every one of them is a detective thriller. It is a remote possibility, but it could happen. The only way to eliminate the possibility altogether is to take **100% survey (a census)** of the books, which, unless it is a tiny library, is impractical.

6.3 Sampling frames

If random sampling is used then it is necessary to construct a **sampling frame**

Key term

> A **sampling frame** is a numbered list of all items in a population.

Once a numbered list of all items in the population has been made, it is easy to select a random sample, simply by generating a list of random numbers.

For instance, if you wanted to select a random sample of children from a school, it would be useful to have a list of names:

0 J Absolam
1 R Brown
2 S Brown
...

Now the numbers 0, 1, 2 and so on can be used to select the random sample. It is normal to start the numbering at 0, so that when 0 appears in a list of random numbers it can be used.

Sometimes it is not possible to draw up a sampling frame. For example, if you wanted to take a random sample of Americans, it would take too long to list all Americans.

A sampling frame should have the following characteristics.

(a) **Completeness**. Are all members of the population included on the list?
(b) **Accuracy**. Is the information correct?
(c) **Adequacy**. Does it cover the entire population?
(d) **Up to dateness**. Is the list up to date?
(e) **Convenience**. Is the sampling frame readily accessible?
(f) **Non-duplication**. Does each member of the population appear on the list only once?

Two **readily available sampling frames** for the human population of Great Britain are the **council tax register** (list of dwellings) and the **electoral register** (list of individuals).

6.4 Drawbacks of random sampling

(a) Selected items are subject to the full range of variation inherent in the population.
(b) An unrepresentative sample may result.
(c) An adequate sampling frame might not exist.

(d) The numbering of the population might be laborious.
(e) It might be difficult to obtain the data if the selected items cover a wide area.
(f) It might be costly to obtain the data if the selected items cover a wide area.

6.5 Stratified random sampling

A variation on the random sampling method is **stratified random sampling**.

Key term

Stratified random sampling is a method of sampling which involves dividing the population into strata or categories. Random samples are then taken from each stratum or category.

In many situations, stratified sampling is the best method of choosing a sample. Stratified sampling is best demonstrated by means of an example.

6.6 Example: stratified sampling

The number of cost and management accountants in each type of work in a particular country are as follows.

Partnerships	500
Public companies	500
Private companies	700
Public practice	800
	2,500

If a sample of 20 was required the sample would be made up as follows.

		Sample
Partnerships	$\frac{500}{2,500} \times 20$	4
Public companies	$\frac{500}{2,500} \times 20$	4
Private companies	$\frac{700}{2,500} \times 20$	6
Public practice	$\frac{800}{2,500} \times 20$	6
		20

Advantages and disadvantages of stratification are as follows.

Advantages	Disadvantages
The sample selected will be representative since it guarantees that every important category will have elements in the final sample. **The structure of the sample will reflect that of the population** if the same proportion of individuals is chosen from each stratum. Each stratum is represented by a randomly chosen sample and therefore **inferences can be made about each stratum**. **Precision is increased**. Sampling takes place within strata and, because the range of variation is less in each stratum than in the population as a whole and variation between strata does not enter as a chance effect, higher precision is obtainable.	The main **disadvantage** of stratification is that it requires **prior knowledge of each item in the population**; sampling frames do not always contain such information.

6.7 Systematic sampling

Key term

Systematic sampling is a sampling method which works by selecting every nth item after a random start.

If it were decided to select a sample of 20 from a population of 800, then every 40th (800 ÷ 20) item after a random start in the first 40 should be selected. The starting point could be found using the lottery method or random number tables. If (say) 23 was chosen, then the sample would include the 23rd, 63rd, 103rd, 143rd ... 783rd items. The gap of 40 is known as the **sampling interval**.

Advantages and disadvantages of systematic sampling

Advantages	Disadvantages
It is easy to use	It is possible that a biased sample might be chosen if there is a regular pattern to the population which coincides with the sampling method.
It is cheap	It is not completely random since some items have a zero chance of being selected.

6.8 Multistage sampling

Key term

Multistage sampling is a probability sampling method which involves dividing the population into a number of sub-populations and then selecting a small sample of these sub-populations at random.

Each sub-population is then divided further, and then a small sample is again selected at random. This process is repeated as many times as is necessary.

Multistage sampling is best demonstrated by means of an example.

6.9 Example: multistage sampling

A survey of spending habits is being planned to cover the whole of Britain. It is obviously **impractical to draw up a sampling frame**, so **random sampling is not possible**. Multistage sampling is to be used instead.

The country is divided into a number of areas and a small sample of these is selected at random. Each of the areas selected is subdivided into smaller units and again, a smaller number of these is selected at random. This process is repeated as many times as necessary and finally, a random sample of the relevant people living in each of the smallest units is taken. A fair approximation to a random sample can be obtained.

Thus, we might choose a random sample of eight areas, and from each of these areas, select a random sample of five towns. From each town, a random sample of 200 people might be selected so that the total sample size is $8 \times 5 \times 200 = 8{,}000$ people.

Advantages and disadvantages of multistage sampling

Advantages	Disadvantages
Fewer investigators are needed	There is the **possibility of bias** if, for example, only a small number of regions are selected.
It is not so costly to obtain a sample	The method is **not truly random** as once the final sampling areas have been selected the rest of the population cannot be in the sample. If the population is heterogeneous, the areas chosen should reflect the **full range of the diversity**. Otherwise, choosing some areas and excluding others (even if it is done randomly) will result in a biased sample.

6.10 Cluster sampling

Key term

Cluster sampling is a non-random sampling method that involves selecting one definable subsection of the population as the sample, that subsection taken to be representative of the population in question.

For example, the pupils of one school might be taken as a cluster sample of all children at school in one county.

Advantages and disadvantages of cluster sampling

Advantages	Disadvantages
It is a good alternative to multistage sampling if a satisfactory sampling frame does not exist.	The potential for considerable bias.
It is inexpensive to operate.	

Question — Systematic sampling

Which of the following are disadvantages of systematic sampling? Tick as appropriate.

☐ The sample chosen might be biased
☐ Some samples have a zero chance of being selected so sampling method is not completely random
☐ Prior knowledge of each item in the population is required

Answer

✓ The sample chosen might be biased
✓ Some samples have a zero chance of being selected so sampling method is not completely random
☐ Prior knowledge of each item in the population is required

Non-probability sampling methods

Key term

A **non-probability sampling method** is a sampling method in which the chance of each member of the population appearing in the sample is not known.

The only non-probability sampling method that you need to know about is **quota sampling.**

6.11 Quota sampling

Key term

In **quota sampling**, randomness is forfeited in the interests of cheapness and administrative simplicity. Investigators are told to interview all the people they meet up to a certain quota.

6.12 Example: quota sampling

Consider the figures in Paragraph 6.6, but with the following additional information relating to the sex of the cost and management accountants.

	Male	*Female*
Partnerships	300	200
Public companies	400	100
Private companies	300	400
Public practice	300	500

An investigator's quotas might be as follows.

	Male	*Female*	*Total*
Partnerships	30	20	50
Public companies	40	10	50
Private companies	30	40	70
Public practice	30	50	80
			250

Using quota sampling, the investigator would interview the first 30 male cost and management accountants in partnerships that he met, the first 20 female cost and management accountants in partnerships that he met and so on.

Advantages and disadvantages of quota sampling

Advantages	Disadvantages
It is **cheap** and **administratively easy**.	The method can result in certain **biases**. For example, an interviewer in a shopping centre may fill his quota by only meeting people who can go shopping during the week.
A much larger sample can be studied, and hence more information can be gained at a faster speed for a given outlay than when compared with a fully randomised sampling method.	The non-random nature of the method rules out any valid estimate of the **sampling error** (a concept you will meet later in your studies) in estimates derived from the sample.
Although a fairly detailed knowledge of the characteristics of a population is required, **no sampling frame is necessary** because the interviewer questions every person he meets up to the quota.	
It may be the **only possible approach** in certain situations, such as television audience research.	
Given suitable, trained and properly briefed field workers, quota sampling **yields enough accurate information** for many forms of commercial market research.	

The diagram below summaries the various sampling methods.

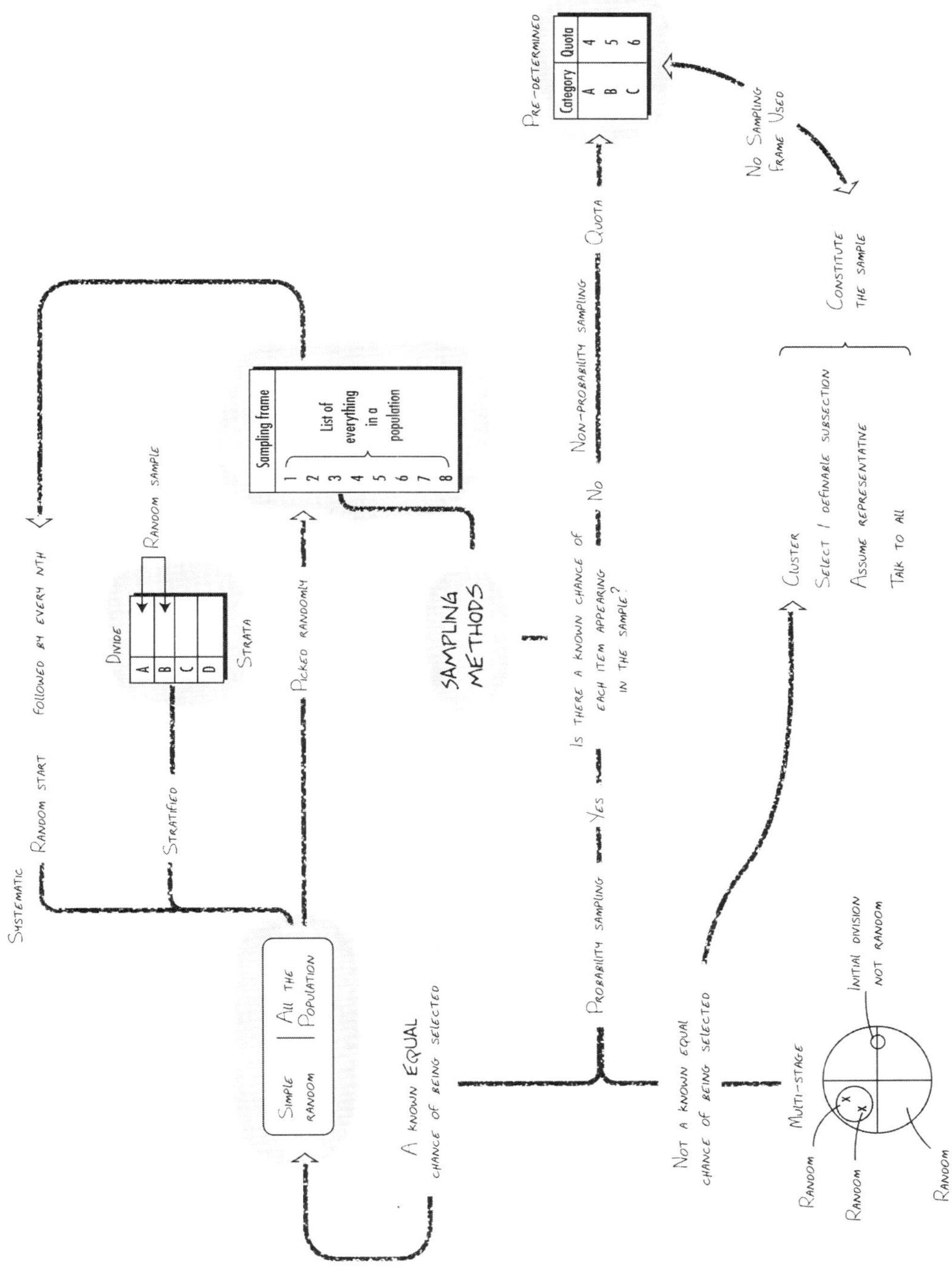

7 Benchmarking

Exam focus point

In the June 2007 exam, the examiner asked candidates to produce notes on two of three performance topics for ten marks each. One of these was benchmarking.

FAST FORWARD

Benchmarking is an attempt to identify best practices and by comparison of operations to achieve improved performance.

Benchmarking is another type of comparison exercise through which an organisation attempts to improve performance.

The idea is to seek the best available performance against which the organisation can monitor its own performance.

Key term

CIMA's *Official Terminology* defines **benchmarking** as 'The establishment, through data gathering, of targets and comparators, through whose use relative levels of performance (and particularly areas of underperformance) can be identified. By the adoption of identified best practices it is hoped that performance will improve.'

CIMA lists four types of benchmarking.

Type	Description
Internal benchmarking	A method of comparing one operating unit or function with another within the same industry
Functional benchmarking	Internal functions are compared with those of the best external practitioners of those functions, regardless of the industry they are in (also known as **operational** or **generic** benchmarking)
Competitive benchmarking	Information is gathered about direct competitors, through techniques such as reverse engineering*
Strategic benchmarking	A type of competitive benchmarking aimed at strategic action and organisational change

* **Reverse engineering**: buying a competitor's product and dismantling it, in order to understand its content and configuration

From this list you can see that a benchmarking exercise **does not necessarily have to involve the comparison of operations with those of a competitor**. Indeed, it might be difficult to persuade a direct competitor to part with any information which is useful for comparison purposes. Functional benchmarking, for example, does not always involve direct competitors. For instance a railway company may be identified as the 'best' in terms of on-board catering, and an airline company that operates on different routes could seek opportunities to improve by sharing information and comparing their own catering operations with those of the railway company.

A 1994 survey of the *The Times* Top 1,000 companies (half of which were in manufacturing) revealed that the business functions most subjected to benchmarking in the companies using the technique were **customer services, manufacturing, human resources and information services.**

7.1 Obtaining information

Financial information about competitors is **easier** to acquire than non-financial information. Information about **products** can be obtained from **reverse engineering**, **product literature**, **media comment** and **trade associations**. Information about **processes** (how an organisation deals with customers or suppliers) is more **difficult** to find.

Such information can be obtained from **group companies** or possibly **non-competing organisations in the same industry**.

7.2 Why use benchmarking?

7.2.1 For setting standards

Benchmarking allows **attainable standards** to be established following the examination of both **external and internal information**. If these standards are **regularly reviewed** in the light of information gained through benchmarking exercises, they can become part of a programme of **continuous improvement** by becoming increasingly demanding.

7.2.2 Other reasons

Anna Green, in her article *The Borrowers* in the October 1996 edition of Pass magazine, explains the **benefits** of benchmarking.

(a) Its flexibility means that it can be used in both the public and private sector and by people at different levels of responsibility.

(b) Cross comparisons (as opposed to comparisons with similar organisations) are more likely to expose radically different ways of doing things.

(c) It is an effective method of implementing change, people being involved in identifying and seeking out different ways of doing things in their own areas.

(d) It identifies the processes to improve.

(e) It helps with cost reduction.

(f) It improves the effectiveness of operations.

(g) It delivers services to a defined standard.

(h) It provides a focus on planning.

'Most importantly benchmarking establishes a desire to achieve continuous improvement and helps develop a culture in which it is easier to admit mistakes and make changes.'

Case Study

Two examples can be given of the successful application of benchmarking. One is *British Steel*, which started using benchmarking in 1988, comparing its overall performance against other major steel companies and obtaining detailed data from measurement against other steel plants. At present British Steel benchmarks costs, customer service, quality, reliability and responsiveness.

The second example is *British Airways* which has 'used benchmarking since 1987 to help transform itself from a stodgy, state-controlled enterprise to a leading world airline'. BA staff analyse their own business processes and identify the weakest elements, and then visit direct competitors with checklists and questions. Problems are often found to be shared and competitors are willing to pool information in pursuit of solutions.

Benchmarking works, it is claimed, for the following reasons.

(a) The comparisons are carried out by the managers who have to live with any changes implemented as a result of the exercise.

(b) Benchmarking focuses on improvement in key areas and sets targets which are challenging but 'achievable'. What is *really* achievable can be discovered by examining what others have achieved: managers are thus able to accept that they are not being asked to perform miracles.

Benchmarking has other advantages: it can provide **early warning of competitive disadvantage** and should lead to a greater incidence of **teamworking** and **cross-functional learning.**

Question

Benchmarking

We've looked at the advantages of benchmarking. Can you think of any disadvantages?

Answer

- Difficulties in deciding which activities to benchmark
- Identifying the 'best in class' for each activity
- Persuading other organisations to share information
- Successful practices in one organisation may not transfer successfully to another
- The danger of drawing incorrect conclusions from inappropriate comparisons

Chapter Roundup

- **Data** are the raw materials for data processing. **Information** is data that has been processed.
- **Quantitative data** are data that can be measured. A **'variable'** is something which can be measured.
- **Qualitative data** cannot be measured, but have **attributes** (an attribute is something an object either has or does not have).
- Data may be **primary** (collected specifically for the purpose of a survey) or **secondary** (collected for some other purpose).
- The main **characteristics of good information**

Relevance	Confidence-inspiring
Completeness	Properly communicated
Accuracy	Clarity

- **Discrete** data/variables can only take on a countable number of values. **Continuous** data/ variables can take on any value.
- Data may be obtained from an **internal** source or an **external** source.
- The main sources of **secondary data** are: Governments; banks; newspapers; trade journals; information bureaux; consultancies; libraries and information services.
- Data are often collected from a **sample** rather than from a population. If the whole population is examined, the survey is called a **census**.
- A **probability sampling method** is a sampling method in which there is a known chance of each member of the population appearing in the sample.

  Probability sampling methods

  - Random
  - Stratified random
  - Systematic
  - Multistage
  - Cluster

- Random sampling requires the construction of a **sampling frame**. A sampling frame is a numbered list of all items in a population.
- A **non-probability sampling method** is a sampling method in which the chance of each member of the population appearing in the sample is not known, for example, **quota sampling**.
- You must be aware of the characteristics and advantages and disadvantages of the sampling methods covered in this chapter.
- Once data have been collected they need to be **presented** and **analysed** It is important to remember that if data have not been collected properly, no amount of careful presentation or analysis can remedy this defect.
- Benchmarking is an attempt to identify best practices and by comparison of operations to achieve improved performance.

Quick Quiz

1 Fill in the blanks in the statements below using the words in the box.

Data can be either (1) .... (have variables) or (2) .... (have (3) ....). Variables can be either (4) .... (eg 0, 1, 2, 3) or (5) .... (eg 0.54, 0.612, 0.117). Data may also be classified as (6) .... (collected for a specific survey) or (7) .... (collected for some other purpose).

• Quantitative	• Continuous	• Attributes	• Primary
• Secondary	• Qualitative	• Discrete	

2 List four main secondary data sources.

3 What is the main advantage of using primary data over secondary data?

4 Identify the following as either primary or secondary data.

	Primary data	Secondary data
Annual Abstract of Statistics		
Wall Street Journal		
Investigator's survey		
Survey questionnaire		
Management Accounting		
BPP's website		

5 Fill in the blanks in the boxes below using the words in the box.

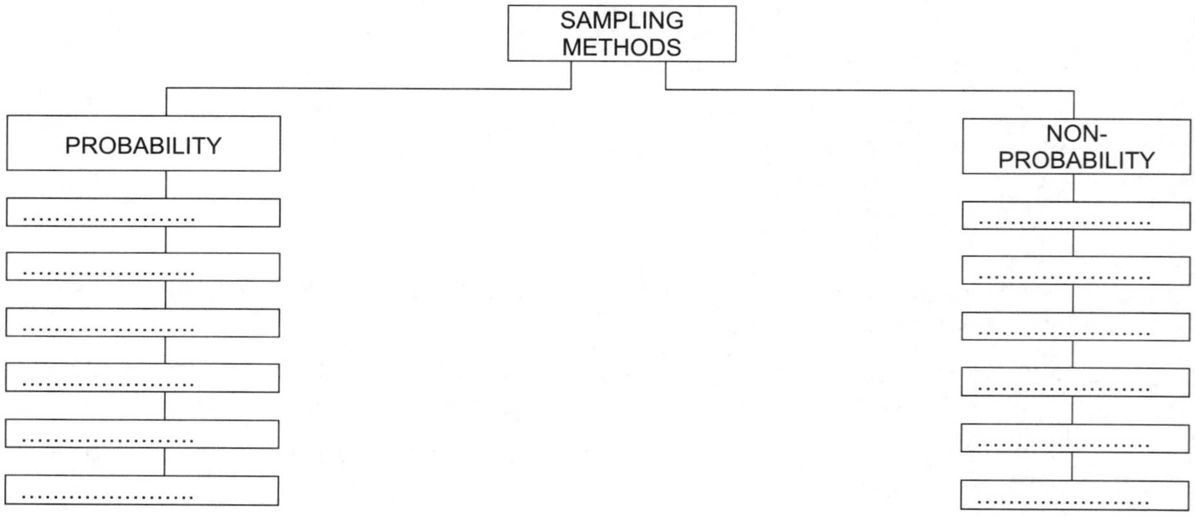

• Multistage	• Random	• Cluster
• Stratified	• Quota	• Systematic

6 A simple random sample is a sample selected in such a way that every item in the population has an equal chance of being included.

True ☐

False ☐

7 I If a sample is selected using random sampling, it will be free from bias
II A sampling frame is a numbered list of all items in a sample
III Cluster sampling is a non-probability sampling method
IV In quota sampling, investigators are told to interview all the people they meet up to a certain quota

Which of the above statements are true?

A I, II, III and IV
B I, II and IV only
C I and II only
D I and IV only

8 The essence of systematic sampling is that

A Each element of the population has an equal chance of being chosen
B Members of various strata are selected by the interviewers up to predetermined limits
C Every nth item of the population is selected
D Every element of one definable sub-section of the population is selected

9 *Match the type of benchmarking to the descriptions.*

Type of benchmarking

Internal; functional; competitive; strategic

Descriptions

(a) Information is gathered about direct competitors

(b) Internal functions are compared with those of the best external practitioners of those functions, regardless of the industry they are in

(c) One operating unit or function is compared with another within the same industry

(d) A type of competitive benchmarking aimed at strategic action and organisational change

Answers to Quick Quiz

1 (1) Quantitative (2) Qualitative (3) Attributes (4) Discrete
(5) Continuous (6) Primary (7) Secondary

2 (a) Governments (c) Newspapers
(b) Banks (d) Trade journals

3 The user of the information knows where it came from, the circumstances under which it was collected and any limitations or inadequacies in it.

4

Primary data	**Secondary data**
Investigator's survey	Wall Street Journal
Survey questionnaire	*Annual Abstract of Statistics*
	Management Accounting
	BPP's website

5

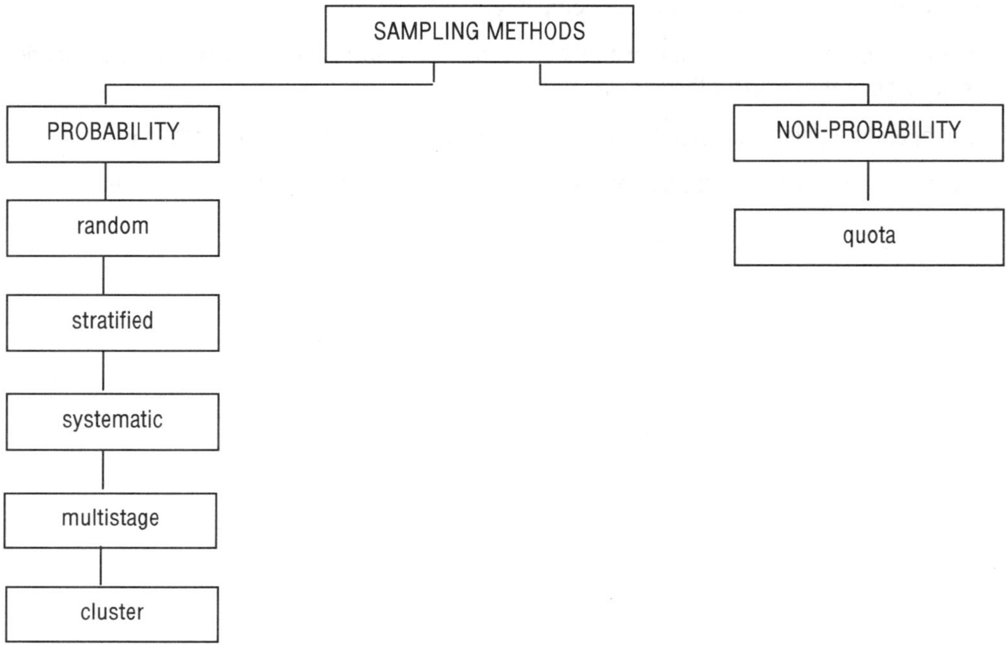

6 True

7 D

8 C

9 Internal benchmarking (c)
Functional benchmarking (b)
Competitive benchmarking (a)
Strategic benchmarking (d)

Now try the questions below from the Exam Question Bank

Number	Level	Marks	Time
Section A: Q8	MCQ	N/A	N/A
Section B: Q5	Preparation	10	18 mins

6

Presentation of information

Topic list
1 Presenting, disseminating and interpreting information
2 Written reports
3 Planning a report
4 General points on style
5 The format of reports
6 Presenting and interpreting information in tables
7 Presenting and interpreting information in charts
8 Presenting and interpreting information in frequency distributions and histograms
9 Using index numbers

Study guide reference

		Syllabus reference
6(a)	Presentation of information	3
	(i) Prepare written reports representing management information in suitable formats according to purpose	3
	(ii) Present information using tables, charts and graphs (bar charts, histograms, frequency polygons)	3
	(iii) Interpret information (including the above tables, charts and graphs) presented in management reports	3
6(b)	Indices	3
	(i) Calculate price and quantity indices on Laspeyres' and Paasche bases	3
	(ii) Discuss advantages and disadvantages of Laspeyres' and Paasche indices	3
	(iii) Adjust raw data using appropriate indices	3
25(h)	Produce reports highlighting key areas for management attention and recommendations for improvement	3

1 Presenting, disseminating and interpreting information

As we saw in Chapter 1, the management accountant is involved in the **presentation**, **dissemination** and **interpretation** of information. In this chapter we will be looking at the ways in which information can be presented, disseminated and interpreted.

Question — Information manager

Why might the management accountant be known as the information manager?

Answer

The management accountant is called the information manager because management accounting is concerned with the collection of data, its analysis and processing into information, and the interpretation and communication of that information so as to assist management with planning, control and decision making.

Exam focus point

In an article about presentation techniques for better examination performance, the examiner wrote, 'If the question specifically asks that you prepare a report, memorandum, letter, briefing notes etc, then that is exactly what you should do. There are often a couple of marks just for the application of the correct format.'

2 Written reports

FAST FORWARD

The purpose of a **report** must be clear, and certain general principles should be followed in planning and giving structure to a report.

Stylistic qualities of reports include objectivity and balance and ease of understanding.

To keep the main body of the report short enough to hold the reader's interest, detailed explanations, charts and tables of figures should be put into **appendices**. The main body of the report should make cross-reference to the appendices in appropriate places.

Exam focus point

The examiner has stressed that in the exam he expects around 40% of the answer to be narrative which may include reports. It is worth reading this chapter carefully and practising your report writing skills as well as general written responses to questions.

As an example, in the December 2005 exam, out of the 100 marks available, 51 were for explaining, suggesting, and giving (or stating) knowledge rather than calculating figures.

2.1 What is a report?

There are a variety of formats and styles of reports.

(a) You may think of reports as **extensive, complex documents**, but a **single page may be sufficient** in many contexts.

(b) **Routine reports are produced at regular intervals**. An example of a routine report is a budgetary control report, the preparation of which we will be looking at later in this text. **Special reports may be commissioned for 'one-off' planning and decision-making purposes** such as a report on a proposed project or particular issue.

(c) Reports may be **for professional purposes**, or they may be **for a wider audience** who will not all necessarily understand or require the same information.

Reports are meant to be **useful**. The information contained in a business report might be used in several ways.

(a) **To assist management**, as they rarely have time to carry out their own detailed investigations into the matters on which they make decisions; their time, moreover, is extremely expensive.

(b) **As a permanent record and source of reference**, should details need to be confirmed or recalled in the future.

(c) **To convey information** or suggestions/ideas to other interested parties (eg in a report for a committee).

2.2 Reports and their purpose

Reports are usually intended to **initiate a decision or action**. The decisions or actions might be the following types.

(a) **Control action**. If the report describes what has happened in the past, a control action may be taken in an attempt to prevent a repeat of this behaviour.

(b) **Planning decisions**. Reports that are commissioned to advise on a certain course of action will include a **recommendation** about what decision should be taken.

2.3 The report and the report users

(a) A special **'one-off' report** will be **commissioned by a manager**, who will then expect to **make a decision** on the basis of what the report tells him. For example, the board of directors of a company might call for a report on the financial viability of a new product or investment, and they will expect to decide whether or not to undertake the product development or the investment on the basis of the report's findings.

(b) **Routine reports,** such as performance reports, might be **required because they are a part of established procedures.** The managers receiving the reports will not have commissioned them specifically, but they will be expected to act on anything out-of-the-ordinary that the report tells them.

(c) **Some reports arise out of a particular event**, on which regulations prescribe the writing of a report. For example, a leaving report must be written following an employee's resignation.

(d) **Individual responsibilities** often include the requirement to write reports. The secretary at a meeting will have to report to members the procedures and decisions taken.

Whether the report is 'one-off' or routine, there is an **obligation on the part of the person requesting the report to state the use to which it will be put.** In other words, the purpose of the report must be clear to both its writers and its users.

The report writer should communicate information in an unbiased way. Information should be communicated impartially, so that the report user can make his own judgements. This has the following implications.

(a) Any assumptions, evaluations and recommendations by the report writer should be clearly 'signalled' as such.

(b) Points should not be over-weighted (or omitted as irrelevant) without honestly evaluating how **objective** the selection is.

(c) Facts and findings should be **balanced** against each other.

(d) A firm **conclusion** should, if possible, be reached. It should be clear how and why it was reached.

Question — **Report writing**

When writing a report, what can you do to ensure that the particular needs and abilities of the users of your report will be met?

Answer

(a) Avoid 'jargon', overly technical terms and specialist knowledge the user may not share.

(b) Keep vocabulary, sentence and paragraph structures as simple as possible, for clarity (without patronising an intelligent user).

(c) Bear in mind the type and level of detail that will interest the user and be relevant to his/her purpose.

(d) In a business context, the user may range from senior manager to junior supervisor, to non-managerial employee (such as in the case of minutes of a meeting) to complete layman (customer, press and so on). Vocabulary, syntax and presentation, the amount of detail gone into, the technical matter included and the formality of the report structure should all be influenced by such concerns.

2.4 Timeliness

As with all information a report may be of no use at all if it is not produced **on time**. There is no point in presenting a report to influence a decision if the decision has already been made. The timescales within which the report user is working must be known, and the time available to produce the report planned accordingly.

3 Planning a report

Question — Report planning

Which of the following questions should you ask yourself before writing a report?

(a) Who is the user?
(b) What type of report will be most useful to him/her?
(c) What exactly does he/she need to know, and for what purpose?
(d) How much information is required, how quickly and at what cost?
(e) Do you need to give judgements, recommendations etc (or just information)?

A a, b, c
B b, e
C c, d, e
D a, b, c, d, e

Answer

D All of these are important and you should know the answers before you embark on writing your report.

Questions when planning a report

(a) **Who am I writing to?** For example, directors need a different approach to fellow accountants.

(b) **What information do I need to provide?** What is relevant to the user's requirements?

(c) **Do I need to follow a line of reasoning?** If so, what is the most logical way in which data can be grouped, and sequenced, to make my reasoning clear?

(d) **Do I need to include my own personal views?** If so, at what point: final recommendation, throughout?

(e) **What can I do to make the report easier to read?**

- (i) Are there suitable sections or sub-headings I can use to indicate effectively each stage of the information/argument?
- (ii) Is the subject of the report too technical for the users? What vocabulary should I use to help them understand?
- (iii) Do I have a clear introduction to 'ease' the readers in to the subject, and a clear conclusion that will draw everything together for them?
- (iv) Are there any diagrams, graphs or tables that I can use to make my findings clearer?

Use the above questions as a checklist for planning a report. You can then jot down a 'skeleton' of the headings and sub-headings you have decided on. The formal headings of standard business reports may be useful to help you to organise your thoughts – but may not be necessary. What is important is that a **structure that helps readers understand** the report is adopted.

3.1 Example: report plan

A manager would like your views on the use of flexible working hours in your organisation. In due course, you are to write him a report considering the advantages and disadvantages to all concerned, and give your conclusions. Your task now is to prepare a plan for the report.

3.2 Solution

You should consider the following.

(a) A **brief** introduction to flexible working hours may not be amiss (as if the manager has not considered how flexi-time might work).

(b) The central section of the report might be structured: **Advantages –** Party 1, party 2, party 3. **Disadvantages –** Party 1, party 2, party 3.

(c) We have chosen to take the 'concerned' parties in turn, and consider the advantages and disadvantages for each. Don't just consider yourself and the staff, but '*all* concerned.'

The plan below is only a suggestion: the ideas for content should be your own.

REPORT PLAN

I INTRODUCTION

How flexible working hours operate (briefly), core period and flexible hours. Debit/credit of hours per week or month.

II EFFECTS

1 **Staff**

(a) **Advantages**

(i) Reduced stress: vagaries of traffic etc no longer a major worry
(ii) Flexibility: fitting in with family patterns, shop hours etc
(iii) Morale enhanced by discretion in own work patterns
(iv) Favourable results for morale, attendance etc in trial schemes

(b) **Disadvantages**

(i) Reduced discipline: some staff may take advantage
(ii) Fluctuating work patterns may be psychologically disruptive
(iii) Friction may result from scheduling to cover non-core periods

2 **Management**

(a) **Advantages**

(i) Morale and attendance advantages (for staff) may help management as well

(ii) Fewer idle staff (wastage) during quieter periods

(b) **Disadvantages**

(i) Planning, administering, controlling scheme
(ii) Cost of mechanical logging in/out devices

3 **Customers**

(a) **Advantages**

(i) High morale of staff hopefully leads to better service

(b) **Disadvantages**

(i) Possible bottlenecks of work during flexi-periods: delays
(ii) Possible discontinuity of service (personnel changing through day)

III CONCLUSIONS

1 Disadvantages: few and can be overcome with good management.
2 Advantages: fundamental, shown to be effective elsewhere.
3 Recommend trial scheme of flexi-time with a view to introducing it later in full.

4 General points on style

There are certain stylistic requirements in the writing of reports.

(a) **Objectivity and balance.** Even in a report designed to persuade as well as inform, avoid subjective value judgements and emotions: bias can undermine the credibility of the report and its recommendations.

(i) Emotional or otherwise loaded words should be avoided.

(ii) In more formal reports, first person subjects should be replaced with third person:

	It became clear that...
I/we found that...	(Your name) found that...
	Investigation revealed that...

(iii) Colloquialisms and abbreviated forms should be avoided in formal written English: colloquial (informal) 'I've', 'don't' etc should be replaced by 'I have' and 'do not'. You should not use expressions like 'blew his top': formal phrases should be used, such as 'showed considerable irritation'.

(b) **Ease of understanding**

(i) Avoid technical language and complex sentence structures.

(ii) The material will have to be logically organised.

(iii) Relevant themes should be signalled by appropriate headings or highlighted for easy scanning.

(iv) The layout of the report should display data clearly and attractively. Figures and diagrams should be used with discretion. Highlight key figures which appear within large tables of numbers.

Various display techniques may be used to make the content of a report easy to identify and digest. For example, **the relative importance of points should be signalled, each point may be referenced, and the body of text should be broken up to be easy on the eye.** These aims may be achieved as follows.

(a) **Headings**

Spaced out or enlarged CAPITALS may be used for the main title.

Important headings, such as sections of the report, may be in CAPITALS.

Underlining or *Italics* may be used for subheadings.

(b) **References**

Each section or point in a formal report should have a code for easy identification and reference.

Use different labelling for each type of heading	**Alternatively a 'decimal' system may be used:**
MAIN SECTION HEADINGS	
I,II,III,IV,V etc	1 Heading 1
A,B,C,D,E etc	1.1 Subheading 1
SUBSECTIONS	1.1.1 Subheading 1, Point 1
1,2,3,4,5 etc	1.1.2 Subheading 1, Point 2
	1.2 Subheading 2
POINTS AND SUBPOINTS	1.2.1 (a) Subheading 2, Point 1, Subpoint (a),
(a), (b), (c) etc	2 Heading 2
(i), (ii), (iii) etc	

(c) **Spacing**

Intelligent use of spacing separates headings from the body of the text for easy scanning, and also makes a large block more attractive and 'digestible'.

Question

Rewrite the following sentence so that it is more suitable for inclusion into a report.

'I've had a good hard look but try as I might I've not been able to find out who's been nicking money from the petty cash box. I'd prefer it if you'd take over now.'

Answer

This is one suggestion as to how the sentence could be rewritten.

'Despite thorough investigations it has been impossible to find an explanation for the differences that have been occurring between petty cash records and the petty cash float. It is clear the investigations should now be carried out at a higher level.'

5 The format of reports

5.1 General principles

When a **formal request is made by a superior for a report** to be prepared, such as in a formally-worded memorandum or letter, it is likely the **format and style of the report** expected is to be **formal as well**.

An **informal request** for a report – 'Can you jot down a few ideas for me about...' or 'Let me know what happens, will you?' – **will result in an informal report**, in which the structure will be less rigid, and the style slightly more personal (depending on the relationship perceived to exist between the writer and user).

If in doubt, it is better (more courteous and effective) to be too formal than informal.

The purpose of reports and their subject matter vary widely, but there are certain **generally accepted principles of report writing**.

Feature	Detail
Title	The title should be as short as possible whilst indicating clearly what the report is about.
Identification of report writer, report user and date	**If the report is extensive**, it should open with a list of contents.
Contents page	
Terms of reference	The introductory section of the report should include the terms of reference. The terms of reference will explain not only the **purpose** of the report but also any **restrictions** on its **scope**. When **timescale** is important, this too should be specified.
Sources of information	Sources of information should be acknowledged in the report. Alternatively, if the report is based on primary research, the nature of the fact-finding should be explained, perhaps in an appendix to the report.
Sections	The main body of the report should be divided into sections, each with a clear heading. These headings (or sub-headings) should if possible be standardised when reports are produced regularly (such as budgetary control reports). Paragraphs should be numbered, for ease of reference. Each paragraph should be concerned with just one basic idea.

Feature	Detail
Appendices	To keep the main body of the report short enough to hold the reader's interest, detailed explanations, charts and tables of figures should be put into appendices. The main body of the report should make cross-references to the appendices in appropriate places.
Summary of recommendations	A report will usually contain **conclusions or recommendations** about the **course of action** to be taken by the report user. These conclusions or recommendations should perhaps be stated at the beginning of the report (after the introduction and statement of terms of reference). The main body of the report can then follow and should lead the report user through the considerations that led the report writer to these conclusions. The conclusions or recommendations should then be re-stated at the end of the main body of the report.
Prominence of important items	The most significant items in a report should be given prominence.

Exam focus point

If you are asked to prepare a report in an exam, the best choice of headings in the main body of the report will be in line with the question requirement, eg (a) The basic idea of cost reduction; (b) Key factors to bear in mind; (c) Suggestions for cost reduction possibilities etc.

We are going to look at three main types of report.

(a) The short formal report
(b) The short informal report
(c) The memorandum report

You should not feel bound to use the following headings in a report in an exam, but the guidelines on report sections may be helpful, should you wish to follow them.

5.2 The short formal report

The short formal report is **used in formal contexts** such as where middle management is reporting to senior management. It should be laid out according to certain basic guidelines. It will be split into logical sections, each referenced and headed appropriately.

SHORT FORMAL REPORT

TITLE	At the top of every report (or on a title page, for lengthy ones) appears the title of the report (its subject) and, as appropriate, *who* has prepared it, *for whom* it is intended, the *date* of completion, and the *status* of the report ('Confidential' or 'Urgent').
I	TERMS OF REFERENCE or INTRODUCTION Here is laid out the scope and purpose of the report: what is to be investigated, what kind of information is required, whether recommendations are to be made etc.
II	PROCEDURE or METHOD This outlines the steps taken to make an investigation, collect data etc. Telephone calls or visits made, documents consulted, computations made etc should be briefly described, with the names of other people involved.
III	FINDINGS In this section the information itself is set out. The content should be clearly structured in chronological order, order of importance, or any other *logical* relationship.
IV	CONCLUSIONS This section allows for a summary of main findings.
V	RECOMMENDATIONS Here, if asked to do so in the terms of reference, the writer of the report may suggest the solution to the problem investigated so that the recipient will be able to make a decision if necessary.

5.3 The short informal report

The short informal report is used **for less complex and lower-level information.** You, as assistant management accountant (or similar), could be asked to prepare such a report for the Management Accounts Manager.

The structure of the informal report is less developed: it will be shorter and less complex in any case, so will not require elaborate referencing and layout. There will be three main sections, each of which may be headed in any way appropriate to the context in which the report is written.

SHORT INFORMAL REPORT

To: (the name and title of the person to whom the report is addressed)

From: (the name and title of the report writer)

Date:

Reference: (if necessary)

Subject: (brief description of the reason for or content of the report)

1 **Background or Situation or Introduction**

This sets the context of the report. Include anything that will help the reader to understand the rest of the report: the reason why it was requested, the current situation, and any other background information on people and things that will be mentioned in the following detailed section. This section may also contain the equivalent of 'terms of reference' and 'procedure' ('method').

2 **Findings or Analysis of the situation**

Here is set out the detailed information gathered, narrative of events or other substance of the report as required by the user. This section may or may not require subheadings: concise prose paragraphs may be sufficient.

3 **Action or Solution or Conclusion**

The main thrust of the findings may be summarised in this section and conclusions drawn, together with a note of the outcome of events, or action required, or recommendations as to how a problem might be solved.

5.4 The memorandum report

In informal reporting situations within an organisation, the 'short informal report' may well be presented in A4 memorandum format, which incorporates title headings and can thereafter be laid out at the writer's discretion. An ordinary memorandum **may be used for flexible, informal reports**: aside from the convenient title headings, there **are no particular requirements for structure, headings or layout**. The writer may consider whatever is logical, convenient and attractive for the reader.

Exam focus point

Where you are asked to produce a memorandum you should use the same title headings as for the short informal report (to, from, date, reference and subject). There may be presentation marks awarded for using these title headings.

6 Presenting and interpreting information in tables

FAST FORWARD

Tables are a simple way of presenting information about two variables.

Key term

A **table** is a matrix of information in rows and columns, with the rows and columns having titles.

Since a table is **two-dimensional**, it can only show two variables. For example, the resources required to produce items in a factory could be tabulated, with one dimension (rows or columns) representing the items produced and the other dimension representing the resources.

Resources for production: all figures in pounds

	Products				
	Athens	*Benidorm*	*Corfu*	*Dassia*	*Total*
Resources					
Direct material M_1	X	X	X	X	X
Direct material M_2	X	X	X	X	X
Direct labour grade S_1	X	X	X	X	X
Direct labour grade S_2	X	X	X	X	X
Direct expenses	X	X	X	X	X
Overheads	X	X	X	X	X
Total	X	X	X	X	X

6.1 Guidelines for tabulation

Once you have established what the table's two dimensions are, you should apply the following guidelines when presenting information in tabular form.

(a) The table should be given a clear **title**.
(b) All columns should be **clearly labelled**.
(c) Where appropriate, there should be clear **sub-totals**.
(d) A **total column** may be presented (usually the right-hand column.)
(e) A **total figure** is often advisable at the bottom of each column of figures.
(f) Information presented should be easy to read.

Exam focus point

Tabulation of data in reports is a common requirement in exams.

6.2 Example: tables

The total sales revenue of a certain trading company in year 8 was $10,000,000. Sales were made to three different regions, central, north and south. $6,000,000 of sales were to the central region and $3,000,000 were to the north region. The organisation makes four products, the L, the U, the C and the Y. Sales of the L totalled $1,100,000, sales of the U also totalled $1,100,000, while sales of the C totalled $2,900,000.

Sales to the central region were $3,500,000 of the Y, $1,500,000 of the C and $500,000 of the L, whilst in the north region, sales of the Y totalled $1,000,000, sales of the C totalled $1,100,000 and sales of the L $500,000.

Required

Draw up a table to show all the details of sales in the organisation and interpret the data by providing suitable secondary statistics to describe the distribution of sales across the three regions.

6.3 Solution

The basic table required has the following two dimensions.

(a) Regions
(b) Products

Secondary statistics are supporting figures that are **supplementary,** and which clarify or amplify the main pieces of information. A major example of secondary statistics is **percentages**. In this example, we could show one of the following.

(a) The percentage of the total sales in each region of each product
(b) The percentage of the total sales of each product made in each region

In this example, (a) has been selected but you might consider that (b) would be more suitable. Either could be suitable, depending of course on what purposes the information is being collected and presented for.

Analysis of sales

	Region							
Products	*Central*		*North*		*South*		*Total*	
	$m	%	$m	%	$m	%	$m	%
L	0.5	8.3	0.5	16.7	0.1**	10	1.1	11
U	0.5*	8.3	0.4*	13.3	0.2**	20	1.1	11
C	1.5	25.0	1.1	36.7	0.3**	30	2.9	29
Y	3.5	58.4	1.0	33.3	0.4**	40	4.9*	49
Total	6.0	100.0	3.0	100.0	1.0	100	10.0	100

* Balancing figure to make up the column total

** Balancing figure then needed to make up the row total

The percentages calculated allow us to **interpret** the information in the table. For example, we can see that nearly 50% of the organisation's sales are of product Y, and that 25% of the Central region's sales are of product C. The percentages highlight additional information which was not readily discernible from the absolute figures.

If we had selected approach (b) however, different features would have been highlighted. We would have known, for example, the percentage of sales of the L made to the Southern region.

Question

Table

Draw up a table using the information in the example but this time interpret the information by adopting approach (b).

Answer

Analysis of sales

	Products									
Regions	*L*		*U*		*C*		*Y*		*Total*	
	$m	%	$m	%	$m	%	$m	%	$m	%
Central	0.5	0.455	0.5	0.454	1.5	0.517	3.5	0.714	6.0	60
North	0.5	0.455	0.4	0.364	1.1	0.379	1.0	0.204	3.0	30
South	0.1	0.090	0.2	0.182	0.3	0.104	0.4	0.082	1.0	10
	1.1	1.000	1.1	1.000	2.9	1.000	4.9	1.000	10.0	100

7 Presenting and interpreting information in charts

FAST FORWARD

Bar charts often convey the meaning or significance of data more clearly than would a table. Make sure that you are able to construct **bar charts**.

There are three main types of bar chart: **simple**, **component** (including percentage component) and **multiple** (or compound).

Instead of presenting information in a table, it might be preferable to give a visual display in the form of a **chart**.

The purpose of a chart is to convey the information in a way that will demonstrate its meaning or significance more clearly than a table would. Charts are not always more appropriate than tables. The **most suitable way of presenting information** will depend on the following.

(a) **What the information is intended to show**. Visual displays usually make one or two points quite forcefully, whereas tables usually give more detailed information.

(b) **Who is going to use the information**. Some individuals might understand visual displays more readily than tables.

7.1 Bar charts

Key term

> A **bar chart** is a method of presenting information in which quantities are shown in the form of bars on a chart, the length of the bars being proportional to the quantities.

The bar chart is one of the most common methods of presenting information in a visual form. There are three main types of bar chart.

(a) **Simple** bar charts
(b) **Component** bar charts, including **percentage component** bar charts
(c) **Multiple** (or compound) bar charts

7.2 Simple bar charts

A **simple bar chart** is a chart consisting of one or more bars, in which the length of each bar indicates the magnitude of the corresponding information.

7.3 Example: a simple bar chart

Barker Ltd's total sales for the years from year 1 to year 6 are as follows.

Year	*Sales*
	Units
1	8,000
2	12,000
3	11,000
4	14,000
5	16,000
6	17,000

The information could be shown on a simple bar chart as follows.

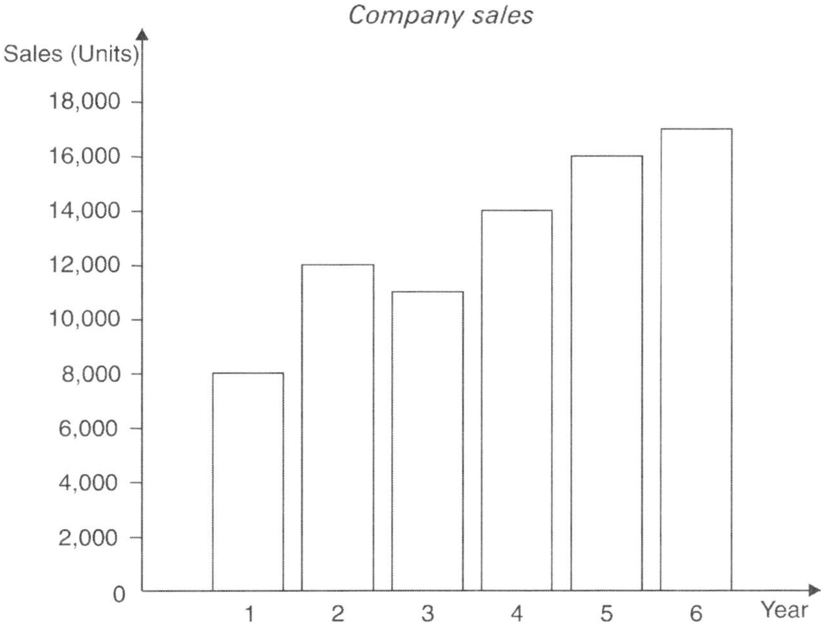

Each axis of the chart must be clearly **labelled**, and there must be a **scale**. This is vital when the reader comes to interpret the bar chart. Here, the y axis includes a scale for the level of sales, and so readers of the bar chart can see not only that sales levels have been **rising** year by year (with year 3 being an exception) but also **what** the actual sales levels have been each year.

Simple bar charts serve two interpretation purposes.

(a) They show the actual magnitude of each item.
(b) They enable one to compare magnitudes, by comparing the lengths of bars on the chart.

7.4 Component bar charts

A **component bar chart** is a bar chart that gives a breakdown of each total into its components.

7.5 Example: a component bar chart

Barker's sales for years 7 to 9 are as follows.

	Year 7	*Year 8*	*Year 9*
	Units	Units	Units
Region 1	10,000	12,000	17,000
Region 2	9,000	10,000	10,000
Region 3	5,000	6,000	7,000
Total	24,000	28,000	34,000

An interpretation of a component bar chart would show the following.

(a) How total sales have changed from year to year
(b) The components of each year's total

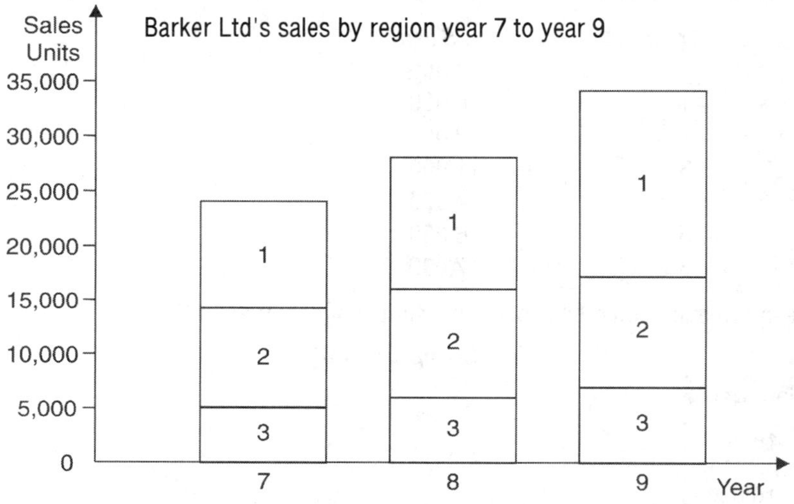

In this diagram the growth in sales is illustrated and the significance of growth in region 1 sales as the reason for the total sales growth is also fairly clear. The growth in region 1 sales would have been even clearer if region 1 had been drawn as the bottom element in each bar instead of the top one.

7.6 Percentage component bar charts

The **difference** between a **component bar chart** and a **percentage component bar chart** is that with a **component bar chart**, the total length of **each bar** (and the length of each component in it) **indicates magnitude**. A bigger amount is shown by a longer bar. With a **percentage component bar chart, total magnitudes are not shown**. If two or more bars are drawn on the chart, the total length of each bar is the same. The only varying lengths in a percentage component bar chart are the lengths of the sections of a bar, which vary according to the relative sizes of the components.

7.7 Example: a percentage component bar chart

The information in the previous example of sales of Barker could have been shown in a percentage component bar chart as follows.

Barker
Sales analysis by region year 7 to year 9

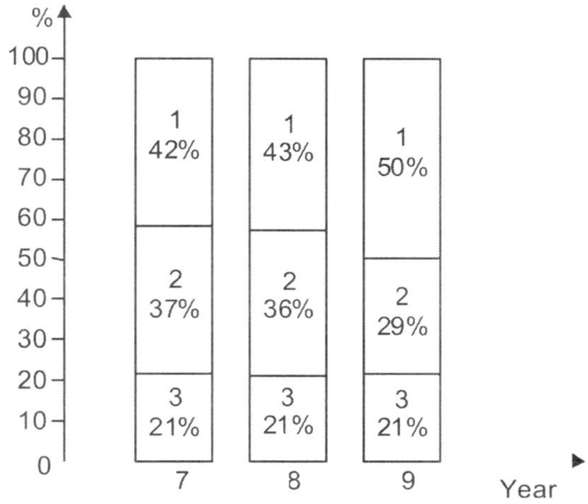

Working

	Year 7		*Year 8*		*Year 9*	
	$'000	%	$'000	%	$'000	%
Region 1	10,000	42	12,000	43	17,000	50
Region 2	9,000	37	10,000	36	10,000	29
Region 3	5,000	21	6,000	21	7,000	21
Total	24,000	100	28,000	100	34,000	100

This chart shows that sales in region 3 have remained a steady proportion of total sales, but the proportion of sales in region 1 in total sales has gone up quite considerably, while the proportion of sales in region 2 has fallen correspondingly.

7.8 Multiple bar charts (compound bar charts)

A **multiple bar chart** (or **compound bar chart**) is a bar chart in which two or more separate bars are used to present sub-divisions of information.

7.9 Example: a multiple bar chart

The information on Barker's sales could be shown in a multiple bar chart as follows.

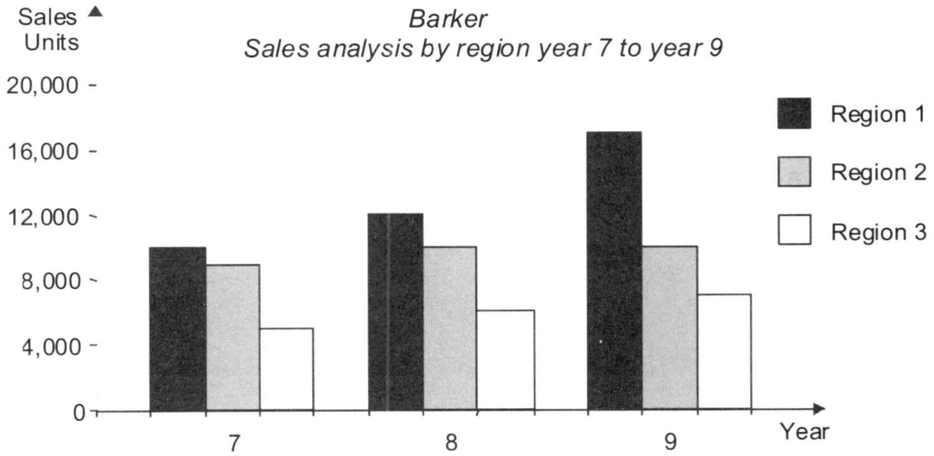

A multiple bar chart uses several bars for each total. In the above example, the sales in each year are shown as three separate bars, one for each region 1, 2 and 3.

Multiple bar charts are sometimes drawn with the bars horizontal instead of vertical.

Multiple bar charts present similar information to component bar charts, except for the following.

(a) Multiple bar charts do not show the grand total (in the above example, the total sales each year) whereas component bar charts do.

(b) Multiple bar charts illustrate the comparative magnitudes of the components more clearly than component bar charts.

8 Presenting and interpreting information in frequency distributions and histograms

FAST FORWARD

Frequency distributions are used if values of particular variables occur more than once. Make sure that you know the difference between grouped frequency and cumulative frequency distributions.

A frequency distribution can be represented pictorially by means of a histogram. The number of observations in a class is represented by the area covered by the bar, rather than by its height. **Frequency polygons** and **frequency curves** are perhaps more accurate methods of data presentation than the standard histogram.

8.1 Frequency distributions

Frequently the information collected by the management accountant is simply a mass of numbers.

0	4	5	6	5	3	4	2	5	3
7	6	4	9	5	8	6	2	4	5

The information could be arranged in order size (an array), however, and the lowest and highest items, as well as a typical items, could be identified.

Many sets of information contain a limited number of data values, even though there may be many occurrences of each value. It can therefore be useful to organise the information into what is known as a **frequency distribution (or frequency table).**

Key term

A **frequency distribution** is the distribution of the number of times the value of a particular variable occurs.

A frequency distribution for the information in Paragraph 8.1 (the number of days absence through sickness of 20 employees in the year) is as follows.

Days absence through sickness of employees in one year

Days	*Number of employees (frequency)*
0	1
1	0
2	2
3	2
4	4
5	5
6	3
7	1
8	1
9	1
	20

8.2 Interpretation of frequency distributions

When the numbers are arranged in this way it is immediately obvious that 4 and 5 days are the most common number of days absence per employee per year.

8.3 Grouped frequency distributions

Key term

A **grouped frequency distribution** is the distribution of the number of times a variable, the value of which falls within a particular range, occurs.

If there is a large set of data or if every (or nearly every) data item is different, it is often convenient to **group** frequencies together into **bands** or **classes**. For example, suppose that the monthly sales of product B over a period of 20 months was as follows, in units.

10,870	8,500	10,840	7,920
9,240	12,260	10,120	12,050
12,650	10,280	12,300	11,820
10,860	11,300	9,890	11,550
11,340	11,660	11,290	11,600

The range of sales from the lowest to the highest is 7,920 to 12,650, a range of 4,730 units. This range could be divided into classes of say, 1,000 units (the class width or class interval), and the number of months during which sales fell within each class could then be grouped into a single frequency, as follows.

Sales Units	*Number of months (frequency)*
7,000 – 7,999	1
8,000 – 8,999	1
9,000 – 9,999	2
10,000 – 10,999	5
11,000 – 11,999	7
12,000 – 12,999	4
	20

Note, however, that once items have been 'grouped' in this way their individual values are lost.

8.4 Grouped frequency distributions of continuous variables

As well as being used for discrete variables (as above), grouped frequency distributions (or grouped frequency tables) can be used to present data for **continuous variables** (ie variables which can **take on any value**, not just discrete values).

8.5 Example: a grouped frequency distribution for a continuous variable

Suppose we wish to record the weights of 50 different individuals. The information might be presented as a grouped frequency distribution, as follows.

Weight Kgs	*Number of individuals (frequency)*
Up to and including 45	1
Over 45, up to and including 50	3
Over 50, up to and including 55	8
Over 55, up to and including 60	16
Over 60, up to and including 65	18
Over 65	4
	50

Note the following points.

(a) It would be wrong to show the ranges as 0 – 45, 45 – 50, 50 – 55 and so on, because 45 kgs and 50 kg would then be values in two classes, which is not permissible. Although each value should only be in one class, we have to **make sure that each possible value can be included**. Classes such as 45-49, 50-54 would not be suitable since a weight of 49.5 kg would not belong in either class. Such classes could be used for discrete variables, however.

(b) There is an **open ended class** at each end of the range. This is because weights up to 45 kgs and over 65 kgs are thought to be uncommon in the group of individuals, so that a single 'open ended' class is used to group all the frequencies together.

8.6 Preparing grouped frequency distributions

To prepare a grouped frequency distribution, a decision must be made about **how wide each class should be**. In an examination, you might be told how many classes to use, or what the class interval should be. You should, however, generally observe the following guidelines.

(a) The size of each class should be **appropriate to the nature of the information being recorded**, and the most appropriate class interval varies according to circumstances.

(b) The **upper and lower limits of each class interval** should be suitable **'round' numbers** for class intervals which are in multiples of 5, 10, 100, 1,000 and so on. For example, if the class interval is 10, and items range in value from 23 to 62 (discrete values), the class intervals should be 20-29, 30-39, 40-49, 50-59 and 60-69, rather than 23-32, 33-42, 43-52 and 53-62.

(c) With **continuous variables**, either:

(i) the upper limit of a class should be 'up to and including ...' and the lower limit of the next class should be 'over ...'; or

(ii) the upper limit of a class should be 'less than...', and the lower limit of the next class should be 'at least ...'.

Question — Frequency distribution

The hours worked during the second week of May by the employees in a firm of accountants were as follows (in hours).

60	35	53	47	25	44	55	58	47	71
63	67	57	44	61	48	50	56	61	42
43	38	41	39	61	51	27	56	57	50
55	68	55	50	25	48	44	43	49	73
53	35	36	41	45	71	56	40	69	52
36	47	66	52	32	46	44	32	52	58
49	41	45	45	48	36	46	42	52	33
31	36	40	66	53	58	60	52	66	51
51	44	59	53	51	57	35	45	46	54
46	54	51	39	64	43	54	47	60	45

Required

Prepare a grouped frequency distribution classifying the hours into categories of five hours commencing with '25 hours and under 30 hours'.

Answer

We are told what classes to use, so the first step is to identify the lowest and highest values. The lowest value is 25 hours (in the first row) and the highest value is 73 hours (in the fourth row). This means that the class intervals must go up to '70 hours and under 75 hours'.

We can now set out the classes in a column, and then count the number of items in each class using tally marks.

Class interval	*Tally marks*	*Frequency*
Hours		
25 and less than 30	///	3
30 and less than 35	////	4
35 and less than 40	~~////~~ ~~////~~	10
40 and less than 45	~~////~~ ~~////~~ ~~////~~	15
45 and less than 50	~~////~~ ~~////~~ ~~////~~ ///	18
50 and less than 55	~~////~~ ~~////~~ ~~////~~ ~~////~~	20
55 and less than 60	~~////~~ ~~////~~ ///	13
60 and less than 65	~~////~~ ///	8
65 and less than 70	~~////~~ /	6
70 and less than 75	///	3
	Total	100

You should be able to interpret a grouped frequency distribution and express an interpretation in writing. In the example in Paragraph 8.5, an interpretation is fairly straightforward.

(a) Most weights fell between 45 kgs and 65 kgs.

(b) Most weights were in the middle of this range, with few people having weights in the lower and upper ends of the range.

8.7 Cumulative frequency distributions

Key term

A **cumulative frequency distribution** (or **cumulative frequency table**) shows the total number of times that a variable with a value above or below a certain amount occurs.

There are two possible cumulative frequency distributions for the grouped frequency distribution in Paragraph 8.3.

	Cumulative frequency		*Cumulative frequency*
≥ 7,000	20	< 8,000	1
≥ 8,000	19	< 9,000	2
≥ 9,000	18	<10,000	4
≥ 10,000	16	<11,000	9
≥ 11,000	11	<12,000	16
≥ 12,000	4	<13,000	20

8.8 Interpretation of cumulative frequency distributions

(a) The first cumulative frequency distribution shows that out of the total of 20 months, sales were 8,000 units or more in 19 months, 9,000 units or more in 18 months, 10,000 units or more in 16 months and so on.

(b) The second cumulative frequency distribution shows that, of the total of 20 months, sales were under 8,000 units in one month, under 9,000 units in two months, under 10,000 units in four months and so on.

It is often simpler to interpret information after it has been presented pictorially rather than as a table of figures. A frequency distribution can be represented pictorially by means of a histogram.

8.9 Histograms

Key term

A **histogram** is an information presentation method which is visually similar to a bar chart but frequencies are represented by **areas** covered by bars rather than by the **heights** of bars.

8.10 Histograms of frequency distributions with equal class intervals

Suppose that we want to draw a histogram of a frequency distribution with equal class intervals, as in the frequency distribution in Paragraph 8.3.

(a) The bars of the histogram will all have the same width.
(b) The heights will be proportional to the frequencies.

The histogram **looks almost identical to a bar chart except that the bars are joined together**. Because the bars are joined together, when presenting discrete data the data must be treated as continuous so that there are no gaps between class intervals. For example, for a cricketer's scores in various games the classes would have to be
≥ 0 but < 10, ≥ 10 but < 20 and so on, instead of 0-9, 10-19 and so on.

A histogram of the distribution in Paragraph 8.3 would be drawn as follows.

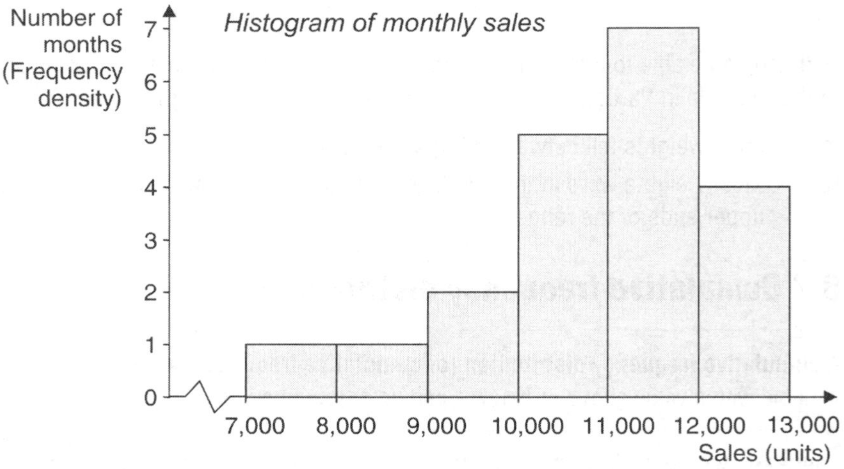

Note that the discrete data have been treated as continuous, the intervals being changed to >7,000 but ≤ 8,000, >8,000 but ≤ 9,000 and so on.

8.11 Histograms of frequency distributions with unequal class intervals

If a distribution has unequal class intervals, the **heights of the bars have to be adjusted** for the fact that the **bars do not have the same width**.

8.12 Example: a histogram with unequal class intervals

The direct costs of Compu's various products are as follows.

Unit direct costs	*Number of products*
Up to and including \$6	4
> \$6 ≤ \$8	6
> \$8 ≤ \$9	6
> \$9 ≤ \$12	6
More than \$12	3

The class intervals for unit direct costs are not all the same, and range from \$1 to \$3.

A histogram is **drawn as follows**.

(a) The **width of each bar on the chart must be proportionate to the corresponding class interval**. In other words, the bar representing costs of > \$6 ≤ \$8, a range of \$2, will be twice as wide as the bar representing costs of > \$8 ≤ \$9, a range of only \$1.

(b) A **standard width of bar must be selected**. This should be the size of class interval which occurs most frequently. In our example, class intervals \$1, \$2 and \$3 each occur once. An interval of \$2 will be selected as the standard width.

(c) **Open-ended classes must be closed off**. It is usual for the width of such classes to be the same as that of the adjoining class. In this example, the class 'up to and including $6' will become >$4 ≤ $6 and the class 'more than $12' will become >$12 ≤ $15.

(d) Each **frequency** is then **multiplied by (standard class width ÷ actual class width) to obtain the height of the bar** in the histogram.

(e) The **height of bars no longer corresponds to *frequency* but rather to frequency density** and hence the vertical axis should be labelled frequency density.

(f) Note that the **data is considered to be continuous** since the gap between, for example, $7.99 and $8 is very, very small.

Class interval	*Size of interval*	*Frequency*	*Adjustment*	*Height of bar*
> $4 ≤ $6	2	4	× 2/2	4
> $6 ≤ $8	2	6	× 2/2	6
> $8 ≤ $9	1	6	× 2/1	12
> $9 ≤ $12	3	6	× 2/3	4
> $12 ≤ $15	3	3	× 2/3	2

The first two bars will be of normal height.

The third bar will be twice as high as the class frequency (6) would suggest, to compensate for the fact that the class interval, $1, is only half the standard size.

The fourth and fifth bars will be two thirds as high as the class frequencies (6 and 3) would suggest, to compensate for the fact that the class interval, $3, is 150% of the standard size.

Histogram of direct costs: Compu

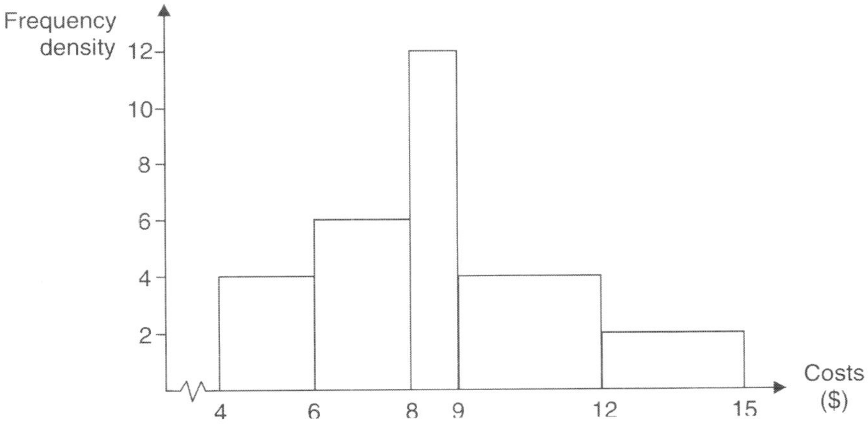

8.13 Interpretation of histograms

Bear in mind the following points when interpreting histograms.

(a) They indicate the range of the values, and whether it is narrow or wide.
(b) They indicate where the most frequently occurring value is.
(c) If class widths vary, they may be more difficult for the lay person to understand.
(d) They **assume frequencies occur evenly** throughout class intervals, and so are not 100% accurate.

Question — **Histogram**

The salary levels of Beswetherick's accounts department staff have been analysed as follows, into a grouped frequency distribution.

Salary	*Number of staff*
Up to $10,000	1
> $10,000 ≤ $12,000	10
> $12,000 ≤ $14,000	12
> $14,000 ≤ $18,000	8
> $18,000 ≤ $22,000	4
> $22,000	1

Required

Draw a histogram from this information.

Answer

Before drawing the histogram, we must decide on the following.

(a) A standard class width: $2,000 will be chosen.

(b) An open-ended class width. It is usual for the width to be the same as that of the adjoining class. In this example, the open-ended class width will therefore be $2,000 for class 'up to $10,000' and $4,000 for the class '> $22,000'.

Class interval	*Size of width* $	*Frequency*	*Adjustment*	*Height of block*
Up to $10,000	2,000	1	× 2/2	1
> $10,000 ≤ $12,000	2,000	10	× 2/2	10
> $12,000 ≤ $14,000	2,000	12	× 2/2	12
> $14,000 ≤ $18,000	4,000	8	× 2/4	4
> $18,000 ≤ $22,000	4,000	4	× 2/4	2
> $22,000	4,000	1	× 2/4	$^1/_2$

Histogram of accounts department staff's salary levels

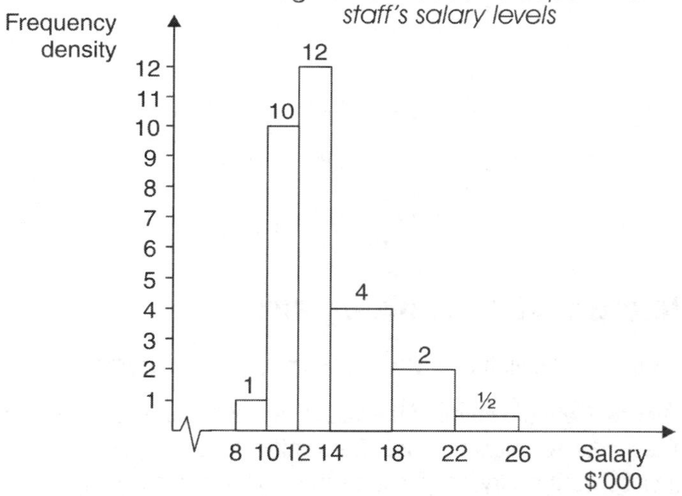

8.14 Frequency polygons

Key term

A **frequency polygon** is a chart derived from a histogram but, unlike the histogram, it makes the assumption that the frequency of occurrence of items is *not* evenly spread.

A **frequency polygon** is drawn from a histogram, in the following way.

(a) Mark the mid-point of the top of each bar in the histogram.

(b) Join up all these points with straight lines.

The ends of the diagram (the mid-points of the two end bars) should be joined to the base line at the mid-points of the next class intervals outside the range of observed data. These intervals should be taken to be of the same size as the last class intervals for observed data.

8.15 Example: a frequency polygon

The following grouped frequency distribution relates to the number of occasions during the past 40 weeks that a particular cost has been at a given level.

Cost $	*Number of occasions*
> 800 ≤ 1,000	4
> 1,000 ≤ 1,200	10
> 1,200 ≤ 1,400	12
> 1,400 ≤ 1,600	10
> 1,600 ≤ 1,800	4
	40

Required

Prepare a frequency polygon.

8.16 Solution

A histogram is first drawn, in the way described earlier. All classes are of the same width.

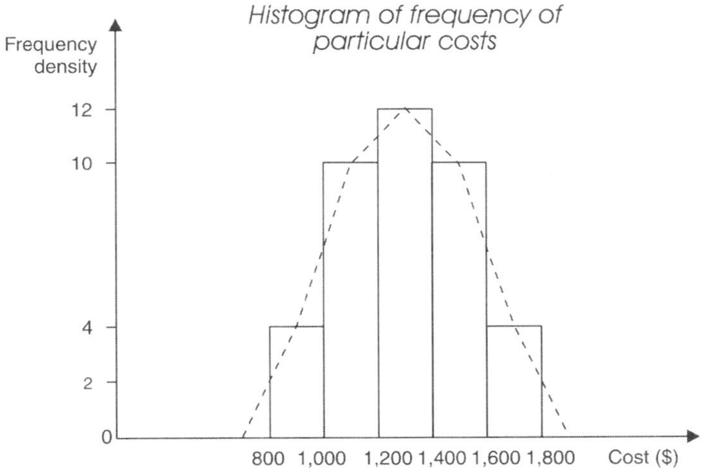

The mid-points of the class intervals outside the range of observed data are 700 and 1,900.

8.17 Frequency curves

Because a frequency polygon has straight lines between points, it too can be seen as an inaccurate way of presenting data. One method of obtaining greater accuracy would be to make the class intervals smaller. If the **class intervals of a distribution were made small enough** the frequency polygon would **become very smooth**. It would become a curve.

Exam focus point

There are always easy marks available for preparing tables and charts in an exam. Marks are awarded for neatness, using a ruler, labelling axes, providing a key where necessary, adding a clear heading and so on. **Don't** throw away these easy marks!

9 Using index numbers

FAST FORWARD

- An **index** is a measure, over time, of the average changes in the value (price or quantity) of a group of items relative to the situation at some period in the past.
- **Composite indices** cover more than one item.
- **Weighting** is used to reflect the importance of each item in the index.
- **Weighted aggregate indices** are found by applying weights and then calculating the index.
- There are two types of weighted aggregate index, the **Laspeyre** (which uses quantities/prices from the base period as the weights) and the **Paasche** (which uses quantities/prices from the current period as weights).
- **Fisher's ideal index** is the geometric mean of the Laspeyre and Paasche indices.
- Index numbers are a very useful way of summarising a large amount of data in a single series of numbers. You should remember, however, that any summary hides some detail and that index numbers should therefore be interpreted with caution.

Index numbers provide a standardised way of comparing the values, over time, of prices, wages, volume of output and so on. They are used extensively in business, government and commerce. No doubt you will be aware of some index numbers – for example, the RPI and the Financial Times All Share Index. This section will explain how to construct indices and will look at associated issues such as their limitations.

An index is a measure, over time, of the average changes in the values (prices or quantities) of a group of items. An index comprises a series of index numbers. Although it is possible to prepare an index for a single item, for example the price of an ounce of gold, such an index would probably be unnecessary. It is only when there is a group of items that a simple list of changes in their values over time becomes rather hard to interpret, and an index provides a useful single measure of comparison.

9.1 Price indices and quantity indices

An index may be a price index or a quantity index.

(a) **A price index measures the change in the money value of a group of items over time**. Perhaps the best known price index in the UK is the Retail Prices Index (RPI) which measures changes in the costs of items of expenditure of the average household.

(b) **A quantity index** (also called a volume index) **measures the change in the non-monetary values of a group of items over time**. An example is a productivity index, which measures changes in the productivity of various departments or groups of workers.

When **one commodity** only is under consideration, we have the following formulae.

(a) **Price index** = $\frac{P_n}{P_o} \times 100$

where P_n is the price for the period under consideration and P_0 is the price for the base period.

(b) **Quantity index** = $\frac{Q_n}{Q_o} \times 100$

where Q_n is the quantity for the period under consideration and Q_0 is the quantity for the base period.

9.2 Example: single-item indices

If the price of a cup of coffee was 40c in 20X0, 50c in 20X1 and 76c in 20X2, then using 20X0 as a base year the price index numbers for 20X1 and 20X2 would be as follows.

$$20X1 \text{ price index} = \frac{50}{40} \times 100 = 125$$

$$20X2 \text{ price index} = \frac{76}{40} \times 100 = 190$$

If the number of cups of coffee sold in 20X0 was 500,000, in 20X1 700,000 and in 20X2 600,000, then using 20X0 as a base year, the quantity index numbers for 20X1 and 20X2 would be as follows.

$$20X1 \text{ quantity index} = \frac{700,000}{500,000} \times 100 = 140$$

$$20X2 \text{ quantity index} = \frac{600,000}{500,000} \times 100 = 120$$

Given the values of some commodity over time (a time series), there are two ways in which index relatives can be calculated.

In the **fixed base method**, a base year is selected (index 100), and all subsequent changes are measured against this base. Such an approach should only be used if the basic nature of the commodity is unchanged over time.

In the **chain base method**, changes are calculated with respect to the value of the commodity in the period immediately before. This approach can be used for any set of commodity values but must be used if the basic nature of the commodity is changing over time.

9.3 Example: fixed base and chain base methods

The price of commodity was \$2.70 in 20X0, \$3.11 in 20X1, \$3.42 in 20X2 and \$3.83 in 20X3. Construct both a chain base index and a fixed base index for the years 20X0 to 20X3 using 20X0 as the base year.

9.4 Solution

Chain base index	20X0	100	
	20X1	115	(3.11/2.70 × 100)
	20X2	110	(3.42/3.11 × 100)
	20X3	112	(3.83/3.42 × 100)
Fixed base index	20X0	100	
	20X1	115	
	20X2	127	(3.42/2.70 × 100)
	20X3	142	(3.83/2.70 × 100)

The chain base relatives show the rate of change in prices from year to year, whereas the fixed base relatives show changes relative to prices in the base year.

9.5 Composite index numbers

Most practical indices cover more than one item and are hence termed **composite index numbers**. The RPI, for example, considers components such as food, alcoholic drink, tobacco and housing. An index of motor car costs might consider components such as finance payments, service costs, repairs, insurance and so on.

Suppose that the cost of living index is calculated from only three commodities: bread, tea and caviar, and that the prices for 20X1 and 20X2 were as follows.

	20X1	*20X2*
Bread	20c a loaf	40c a loaf
Tea	25c a packet	30c a packet
Caviar	450c a jar	405c a jar

A simple index could be calculated by adding the prices for single items in 20X2 and dividing by the corresponding sum relating to 20X1 (if 20X1 is the base year). In general, if the sum of the prices in the base year is ΣP_0 and the sum of the prices in the new year is ΣP_n, the index is $\frac{\Sigma P_n}{\Sigma P_0} \times 100$. The index, known as a **simple aggregate price index** would therefore be calculated as follows.

	P_0 20X1	P_n 20X2
	$	$
Bread	0.20	0.40
Tea	0.25	0.30
Caviar	4.50	4.05
	ΣP_0 = 4.95	ΣP_n = 4.75

Year	$\Sigma P_n / \Sigma P_0$	Simple aggregate price index
20X1	4.95/4.95 = 1.00	100
20X2	4.75/4.95 = 0.96	96

This type of index has a number of disadvantages. It ignores the amounts of bread, tea and caviar consumed (and hence the **importance** of each item), and the units to which the prices refer. If, for example, we had been given the price of a cup of tea rather than a packet of tea, the index would have been different.

To overcome these problems we can use **weighting**. A weighting factor can be thought of as an **indicator of the importance of the component** (such as alcohol in the RPI) with respect to the type of index being calculated.

9.6 Weighted aggregate indices

This method of weighting involves multiplying each component value by its corresponding weight and adding these products to form an aggregate. This is done for both the base period and the period in question. The aggregate for the period under consideration is then divided by the base period aggregate.

The general form of a **weighted aggregate index** is

$\frac{\Sigma wv_n}{\Sigma wv_o}$ where w is the weighting factor

v_o is the value of the commodity in the base period
v_n is the value of the commodity in the period in question

Price indices are usually weighted by quantities and quantity indices are usually weighted by prices.

Question

Weighted aggregate indexes

What are the formulae for calculating price and quantity weighted aggregate indices if base year weights are used?

Answer

Price index: $\frac{\Sigma Q_o P_n}{\Sigma Q_o P_o} \times 100$

where P_0 represents the prices of items in the base year
P_n represents the prices of items in the new year
Q_0 represents the quantities of the items consumed in the base year

Quantity index: $\frac{\Sigma P_o Q_n}{\Sigma P_o Q_o} \times 100$

where Q_0 represents the quantities consumed in the base year
Q_n represents the quantities consumed in the new year
P_0 represents the prices in the base year

9.7 Example: a price index

In the previous example of the cost of living index (Paragraph 9.5), the 20X2 index value could have been calculated as follows, assuming the quantities purchased by each household were as given below.

Item	*Quantity*	*Price in 20X1*		*Price in 20X2*	
	Q_0	P_0	P_0Q_0	P_n	P_nQ_0
Bread	6	20	120	40	240
Tea	2	25	50	30	60
Caviar	0.067	450	30	405	27
			200		327

$$\text{Index in 20X2} = \frac{327}{200} \times 100 = 163.5$$

We will now look at an example of a **quantity index**, which measures **changes in quantities** and uses **prices as weights**.

9.8 Example: a quantity index

The Falldown Construction Company uses four items of materials and components in a standard production job.

In 20X0 the quantities of each material or component used per job and their cost were as follows.

	Quantity	*Price per unit*
	Units	$
Material A	20	2
Material B	5	10
Component C	40	3
Component D	15	6

In 20X2 the quantities of materials and components used per job were as follows.

	Quantity
	Units
Material A	15
Material B	6
Component C	36
Component D	25

Using 20X0 as a base year, calculate the quantity index value in 20X2 for the amount of materials used in a standard job.

9.9 Solution

	Price P_o	*Quantity used* in 20X0 Q_o	P_oQ_o ($)	*Quantity used* in 20X2 Q_n	P_oQ_n ($)
Material A	$2	20	40	15	30
Material B	$10	5	50	6	60
Component C	$3	40	120	36	108
Component D	$6	15	90	25	150
			300		348

Quantity index = $\frac{348}{300} \times 100 = 116$

This would suggest that the company is using 16% more materials in 20X2 than in 20X0 on a standard job.

9.10 Laspeyre, Paasche and Fisher indices

Laspeyre and Paasche indices are special cases of weighed aggregate indices.

9.11 Laspeyre indices

Laspeyre indices use weights from the base period and are therefore sometimes called base weighted indices.

9.11.1 Laspeyre price index

A **Laspeyre price index** uses **quantities** consumed in the base period as weights. In the notation already used it can be expressed as follows.

Laspeyre price index = $\frac{\sum P_n Q_o}{\sum P_o Q_o} \times 100$

9.11.2 Laspeyre quantity index

A **Laspeyre quantity index** uses **prices** from the base period as weights and can be expressed as follows.

Laspeyre quantity index = $\frac{\sum P_o Q_n}{\sum P_o Q_o} \times 100$

9.12 Paasche indices

Paasche indices use **current time period weights**. In other words the weights are changed every time period.

9.12.1 Paasche price index

A **Paasche price index** uses **quantities** consumed in the current period as weights and can be expressed as follows.

Paasche price index = $\frac{\sum P_n Q_n}{\sum P_o Q_n} \times 100$

9.12.2 Paasche quantity index

A **Paasche quantity index** uses **prices** from the current period as weights and can be expressed as follows.

Paasche quantity index = $\frac{\sum P_n Q_n}{\sum P_n Q_o} \times 100$

9.13 Example: Laspeyre and Paasche price indices

The wholesale price index in Ruritania is made up from the prices of five items. The price of each item, and the average quantities purchased by manufacturing and other companies each week were as follows, in 20X0 and 20X2.

Item	*Quantity* 20X0 '000 units	*Price per unit* 20X0 Roubles	*Quantity* 20X2 '000 units	*Price per unit* 20X2 Roubles
P	60	3	80	4
Q	30	6	40	5
R	40	5	20	8
S	100	2	150	2
T	20	7	10	10

Required

Calculate the price index in 20X2, if 20X0 is taken as the base year, using the following.

(a) A Laspeyre index
(b) A Paasche index

9.14 Solution

Item					*Laspeyre*		*Paasche*	
	Q_o	P_o	Q_n	P_n	P_oQ_o	P_nQ_o	P_nQ_n	P_oQ_n
P	60	3	80	4	180	240	320	240
Q	30	6	40	5	180	150	200	240
R	40	5	20	8	200	320	160	100
S	100	2	150	2	200	200	300	300
T	20	7	10	10	140	200	100	70
					900	1,110	1,080	950

20X2 index numbers are as follows.

(a) Laspeyre index $= 100 \times \frac{1,110}{900} = 123.3$

(b) Paasche index $= 100 \times \frac{1,080}{950} = 113.7$

The Paasche index for 20X2 reflects the decline in consumption of the relatively expensive items R and T since 20X0. The Laspeyre index for 20X2 fails to reflect this change.

Question — Indexes

A baker has listed the ingredients he used and their prices, in 20X3 and 20X4, as follows.

	Kgs used *20X3* '000s	*Price per kg* *20X3* $	*Kgs used* *20X4* '000s	*Price per kg* *20X4* $
Milk	3	1.20	4	1.50
Eggs	6	0.95	5	0.98
Flour	1	1.40	2	1.30
Sugar	4	1.10	3	1.14

Required

Calculate the following quantity indices for 20X4 (with 20X3 as the base year).

(a) A Laspeyre index
(b) A Paasche index

Answer

Workings

	Q_o	P_o	Q_n	P_n	*Laspeyre* P_oQ_o	*Laspeyre* P_oQ_n	*Paasche* P_nQ_n	*Paasche* P_nQ_o
Milk	3	1.20	4	1.50	3.60	4.80	6.00	4.50
Eggs	6	0.95	5	0.98	5.70	4.75	4.90	5.88
Flour	1	1.40	2	1.30	1.40	2.80	2.60	1.30
Sugar	4	1.10	3	1.14	4.40	3.30	3.42	4.56
					15.10	15.65	16.92	16.24

Quantity index numbers for 20X4 are as follows.

(a) **Laspeyre method** = $100 \times \frac{15.65}{15.10} = 103.64$

(b) **Paasche method** = $100 \times \frac{16.92}{16.24} = 104.19$

9.15 Which to use – Paasche or Laspeyre ?

Both patterns of consumption and prices change and a decision therefore has to be made as to whether a Paasche or a Laspeyre index should be used.

The following points should be considered when deciding which type of index to use.

(a) A **Paasche index requires quantities to be ascertained each year**. A Laspeyre index only requires them for the base year. Constructing a Paasche index may therefore be costly.

(b) For the **Paasche index the denominator has to be recalculated each year** because the quantities/prices must be changed to current year consumption/price levels.

For the **Laspeyre index, the denominator is fixed**. The Laspeyre index can therefore be calculated as soon as current prices/quantities are known. The Paasche index, on the other hand, cannot be calculated until the end of a period, when information about current quantities/prices becomes available.

(c) The denominator of a Laspeyre index is fixed and therefore the Laspeyre index numbers for several different years can be **directly compared**. With the Paasche index, on the other hand, comparisons can only be drawn directly between the current year and the base year (although indirect comparisons can be made).

(d) The weights for a Laspeyre index become **out of date**, whereas those for the Paasche index are updated each year.

(e) A **Laspeyre price index** implicitly assumes that, whatever the price changes, the quantities purchased will remain the same. In terms of economic theory, no substitution of cheaper alternative goods and services is allowed to take place. Even if goods become relatively more expensive, it assumes that the same quantities are bought. As a result, the **index tends to overstate inflation**.

(f) The effect of current year weighting when using the Paasche price index means that greater importance is placed on goods that are relatively cheaper now than they were in the base year. As a consequence, the **Paasche price index** tends to **understate inflation**.

In practice, it is common to use a Laspeyre index and revise the weights every few years. (Where appropriate, a new base year may be created when the weights are changed.)

9.16 Fisher's ideal index

Because Laspeyre's index uses base period weights it tends to overstate any change in prices or quantities. When prices increase there is usually a reduction in the quantities consumed. The index numerator is therefore likely to be too large. Likewise, when prices decrease, quantities consumed increase, resulting in an under-weighting of those prices which have decreased and hence an overstatement of change. The Paasche index, on the other hand, tends to understate change.

To overcome these difficulties some statisticians prefer to use **Fisher's ideal index**. This index is found by taking the **geometric mean of the Laspeyre index and the Paasche index**.

Fisher's ideal index = $\sqrt{}$(Laspeyre × Paasche)

Question

Fisher's index

The Laspeyre index of retail prices for 20X7 (with a base year of 20X1) is 137.2. The corresponding Paasche index is 134.9.

Required

Calculate Fisher's ideal index.

Answer

$\sqrt{(137.2 \times 134.9)} = 136.0$

9.17 What items to include

The purpose to which the index is to be put must be carefully considered. Once this has been done, the items selected must be as **representative** as possible, taking into account this purpose. Care must be taken to ensure that the items are **unambiguously defined** and that their values are **readily ascertainable**.

For some indices, the choice of items might be relatively straightforward. For example, the **FT Actuaries All-Share Index**, compiled jointly by the Financial Times, the Institute of Actuaries and the Faculty of Actuaries, is made up of the share prices of approximately 800 companies quoted on The Inventory Exchange. The weights are based on the market capitalisations of the companies (the number of shares in issue multiplied by their market value).

For other indices, the choice of items will be more difficult. The Retail Prices Index is an excellent example of the problem. It would be impossible to include all items of domestic spending and a selective, **representative basket of goods** and services must be found, ranging from spending on mortgages and rents, to cars, public transport, food and drink, electricity, gas, telephone, clothing, leisure activities and so on.

9.18 Collecting the data

Data are required to determine the following.

(a) The values for each item
(b) The weight that will be attached to each item

Consider as an example a **cost of living index**. The prices of a particular commodity will vary from place to place, from shop to shop and from type to type. Also the price will vary during the period under consideration. The actual prices used must obviously be some sort of **average**. The way in which the average is to be obtained should be clearly defined at the outset.

When constructing a price index, it is common practice to use the **quantities consumed** as **weights**; similarly, when constructing a quantity index, the **prices** may be used as **weights**. Care must be taken in selecting the basis for the weighting. For example, in a cost of living index, it may be decided to use the consumption of a typical family as the weights, but some difficulty may be encountered in defining a typical family.

9.19 The choice of a base year

The **choice of a base date**, or base year is not significant, except that it should be **representative**. In the construction of a price index, the base year must not be one in which there were abnormally high or low prices for any items in the basket of goods making up the index. For example, a year in which there is a potato famine would be unsuitable as a base period for the Retail Prices Index.

9.20 The limitations and misinterpretation of index numbers

9.20.1 Limitations

Index numbers are usually only **approximations** of changes in price or quantity over time, and must be interpreted with care.

(a) As we have seen, weightings become **out of date over time**. Unless a Paasche index is used, the weightings will gradually cease to reflect current reality.

(b) **New products or items may appear, and old ones may cease to be significant**. For example, spending has changed in recent years, to include new items such as personal computers and video recorders, whereas the demand for twin tub washing machines has declined. These changes would make the weightings of a price index for such goods out of date.

(c) **The data used to calculate index numbers might be incomplete, out of date, or inaccurate**. For example, the quantity indices of imports and exports are based on records supplied by traders which may be prone to error or even deliberate falsification.

(d) **The base year of an index should be a normal year**, but there is probably no such thing as a perfectly normal year. Some error in the index will be caused by atypical values in the base period.

(e) The **'basket of items'** in an index is often **selective**. For example, the Retail Prices Index (RPI) is constructed from a sample of households and from a basket of less than 400 items.

(f) A **national index** may not be very relevant to an individual town or region. For example, if the national index of wages and salaries rises from 100 to 115, we cannot conclude that the wages and salaries of people in, say, Glasgow, have gone up by 15%.

(g) An index may **exclude important items**: for example, the RPI excludes payments of income tax out of gross wages.

9.20.2 Misinterpretation

You must be careful not to misinterpret index numbers. Several possible mistakes will be explained using the following example of a retail prices index.

	20X0		*20X1*		*20X2*
January	340.0	January	360.6	January	436.3
		February	362.5	February	437.1
		March	366.2	March	439.5
		April	370.0	April	442.1

(a) It would be wrong to say that prices rose by 2.6% between March and April 20X2. It is correct to say that prices rose 2.6 points, or

$$\frac{2.6}{439.5} = 0.6\%$$

(b) It would be correct to say that the annual rate of price increases (the rate of inflation) fell between March and April 20X2. It would be a mistake, however, to suppose that a fall in the rate of inflation means that prices are falling, therefore the price index is falling.

The rate of price increases has **slowed down**, but the trend of prices is still **upwards.**

(i) The annual rate of inflation from March 20X1 to March 20X2 is

$$\left(\frac{439.5 - 366.2}{366.2}\right) = 20\%$$

(ii) The annual rate of inflation from April 20X1 to April 20X2 is

$$\left(\frac{442.1-370.0}{370.0}\right) = 19.5\%$$

Thus the annual rate of inflation has dropped from 20% to 19.5% between March and April 20X2, even though prices went up in the month between March and April 20X2 by 0.6%. (The price increase between March and April 20X1 was over 1%. This is included in the calculation of the rate of inflation between March 20X1 and March 20X2, but is excluded in the comparison between April 20X1 and April 20X2 where it has been replaced by the lower price increase, 0.6%, between March and April 20X2.)

9.21 The Retail Prices Index (RPI) and Consumer Prices Index (CPI)

The Retail Prices Index measures the change in the cost of living. It is published monthly (on a Tuesday) near the middle of the month by the Office for National Statistics online. Since it measures the monthly change in the cost of living its principal use is as a **measure of inflation**.

The index measures the percentage changes, month by month, in the **average level of prices of 'a representative basket of goods'** purchased by the great majority of households in the United Kingdom. There are over 650 separate representative items that go to make up the RPI. It takes account of practically all wage earners and most small and medium salary earners.

In recent years, the Government has chosen to use the **Consumer Prices Index (CPI)** as the main measure of UK inflation for macroeconomic purposes. Thus the CPI is the basis for the government's inflation target: it is also used to make international comparisons.

The two main differences between the RPI and CPI are the exclusion of spending on many housing costs from the CPI and the inclusion of financial services in the CPI. Also, the CPI is calculated using a wider population and uses different mathematical formulae.

The **Family Expenditure Survey** is a continuing enquiry conducted by the Office for National Statistics into the general characteristics of households, their income and their expenditures. From this information the representative basket of goods is **divided into main groups**. Each group is divided into sections and these sections may be further split into separate items. Each group, section and specific item is weighted according to information from the Family Expenditure Survey to account for its relative importance in the basket.

Chapter Roundup

- The purpose of a **report** must be clear, and certain general principles should be followed in planning and giving structure to a report.
- Stylistic qualities of reports include objectivity and balance and ease of understanding.
- To keep the main body of the report short enough to hold the reader's interest, detailed explanations, charts and tables of figures should be put into **appendices**. The main body of the report should make cross-reference to the appendices in appropriate places.
- **Tables** are a simple way of presenting information about two variables.
- Bar charts often convey the meaning or significance of data more clearly than would a table. Make sure that you are able to construct **bar charts**.
- There are three main types of bar chart: **simple**, **component** (including percentage component) and **multiple** (or compound).
- **Frequency distributions** are used if values of particular variables occur more than once. Make sure that you know the difference between grouped frequency and cumulative frequency distributions.
- A frequency distribution can be represented pictorially by means of a histogram. The number of observations in a class is represented by the area covered by the bar, rather than by its height. **Frequency polygons** and **frequency curves** are perhaps more accurate methods of data presentation than the standard histogram.
- An **index** is a measure, over time, of the average changes in the value (price or quantity) of a group of items relative to the situation at some period in the past.
- **Composite indices** cover more than one item.
- **Weighting** is used to reflect the importance of each item in the index.
- **Weighted aggregate indices** are found by applying weights and then calculating the index.
- There are two types of weighted aggregate index, the **Laspeyre** (which uses quantities/prices from the base period as the weights) and the **Paasche** (which uses quantities/prices from the current period as weights).
- **Fisher's ideal index** is the geometric mean of the Laspeyre and Paasche indices.
- Index numbers are a very useful way of summarising a large amount of data in a single series of numbers. You should remember, however, that any summary hides some detail and that index numbers should therefore be interpreted with caution.

Quick Quiz

1. Why is it important to space out a report?
2. When should appendices be used in reports?
3. When would a memorandum report be used?
4. What are the main guidelines for tabulation?
5. Name the three main types of bar chart.
6. What is a cumulative frequency distribution?
7. When drawing a histogram what is the usual width of an open-ended class?
8. How would you draw a frequency polygon from a histogram?
9. What is the general form of a weighted aggregate index?
10. What type of weights do Laspeyre indices use?
11. Why might Fisher's ideal index be used?
12. In a histogram, one class is two thirds the width of the other classes.

    If the score in that class is 20, the correct height to plot on the histogram is

    A 13.33
    B 20.00
    C 30.00
    D 33.33

13. A histogram uses a set of bars to represent a grouped frequency table. To be correctly presented, the histogram must show the relationship of the rectangles to the frequencies by reference to the

    A Diagonal of each bar
    B Area of each bar
    C Width of each bar
    D Height of each bar

Answers to Quick Quiz

1 Intelligent use of spacing separates headings from the body of the text for easy scanning, and also makes a large block more attractive and 'digestible'.

2 Appendices should be used if the report will be too long and detailed to hold the reader's interest.

3 A memorandum would be used for flexible, informal reports.

4 (a) The table should be given a clear title.
(b) All columns should be clearly labelled.
(c) The information should be inserted into the appropriate places in the table.
(d) Where appropriate, there should be clear sub-totals.
(e) A total column may be presented; this would usually be the right-hand column.
(f) A total figure is often advisable at the bottom of each column of figures.
(g) Tables should not be packed with too much information so that reading the table is difficult.

5 (a) Simple bar charts
(b) Component bar charts, including percentage component bar charts
(c) Multiple (or compound) bar charts

6 A cumulative frequency distribution shows the total number of times that a value above or below a certain amount occurs.

7 It is usual for the width of an open-ended class to be the same as that of the adjoining class.

8 (a) Mark the mid-point of the top of each bar in the histogram.
(b) Join up all these points with straight lines.

9 $\frac{\sum wv_n}{\sum wv_o}$

10 Weights from the base period

11 The Laspeyre index tends to overstate change, while the Paasche index tends to understate it.

12 C Height of histogram = $\frac{20}{\frac{2}{3}}$ = 30

If you selected option A, you multiplied 20 by 2/3 instead of dividing it by 2/3.
Option B is incorrect because it represents the score in the class under consideration.
Option D represents the score in the class (20) plus 2/3 of 20 = 20 + 13.33 = 33.33.

13 B A histogram is a chart that looks like a bar chart except that the bars are joined together. On a histogram, frequencies are presented by the **area** covered by the bars.

Now try the questions below from the Exam Question Bank

Number	Level	Marks	Time
Section A: Q9-Q10	MCQ	N/A	N/A
Section B: Q6	Preparation	20	36 mins

7

Forecasting

Topic list
1 Forecasting and budgets
2 Cost forecasting: simple methods
3 The components of time series
4 Finding the trend
5 Finding the seasonal variations
6 Deseasonalisation
7 Sales forecasting: time series analysis
8 Forecasting problems
9 Forecasting and price movements
10 Linear regression analysis
11 Sales forecasting: the product life cycle

Study guide reference

		Syllabus reference
7(a)	Use the high-low method to estimate the fixed and variable elements of a cost	4
(b)	Explain the advantages and disadvantages of the high-low method	4
(c)	Construct scatter diagrams and lines of best fit	4
(d)	Describe the use of linear regression analysis in the analysis of cost data	4
(e)	Use linear regression coefficients to make forecasts of costs and revenues	4
(f)	Adjust historical and forecast data for price movements	4
(g)	Explain the advantages and disadvantages of linear regression analysis	4
(h)	Describe the product life cycle and explain its importance in forecasting	4
8(a)	Explain the principles of time series analysis (trend, seasonal variation and random elements)	4
(b)	Calculate moving averages	4
(c)	Determination of trend, including the use of regression analysis	4
(d)	Use trend and seasonal variation (additive and multiplicative) to make budget forecasts	4
(e)	Explain the advantages and disadvantages of time series analysis	4
(f)	Describe the concept of the product lifecycle and its implications for sales forecasting	4
	(Note: Derivation of regression coefficients will not be examined)	

Exam focus point

This is a key syllabus area. Key syllabus areas usually account for 80% or more of the marks available on the exam paper.

1 Forecasting and budgets

Exam focus point

The June 2005 exam included a 20 mark question covering a variety of forecasting techniques including price level index (Chapter 6), scattergraph (Section 2 of this chapter) and high-low technique (Section 2 of this chapter).

The production of a budget calls for the preparation of costs and sales forecasts. In fact, budgeting could be said to be as much a test of forecasting skills as anything else.

Key term

A **forecast** is an estimate of what might happen in the future.

A forecast is a **best estimate**, based on certain assumptions about the conditions that are expected to apply. A **budget**, in contrast, is a **plan** of what the organisation is aiming to achieve and what it has set as a target. A budget should be **realistic** and so it will be based to some extent on forecasts prepared. In preparing a budget, however, management will be trying to establish some control over the conditions that will apply in the future.

When a budget is set it will, for a short time, be the **same as the forecasts**. As actual **events progress** and the situation develops and changes, however, **new forecasts might be prepared** that differ from the budget targets. Management might be able to take **control action** to bring forecasts back into line with the budget; alternatively, management will have to accept that the budget will not be achieved, or it will be exceeded, depending on what the current forecasts indicate.

2 Cost forecasting: simple methods

FAST FORWARD

Simple methods of forecasting costs include the **scattergraph** and **high-low** techniques.

Cost forecasting involves the **measurement of historical costs to predict future costs**. The techniques used range from simple arithmetic and visual methods to advanced computer-based statistical systems. The sophisticated techniques are likely to be more reliable but, in practice, the simple techniques are more commonly used and should give estimates that are accurate enough for their purpose.

2.1 The scattergraph method

One cost forecasting technique is the **scattergraph** method.

Step 1 **Collect data of past volumes** of output and the **associated cost** of producing that output.

Step 2 **Plot this data on a graph** which has cost on the vertical axis and volume of output on the horizontal axis.

Step 3 **Draw a line of best fit** through the middle of the plotted points so that the distance of points above the line is the same as the distance of points below the line. This line represents the total cost at different volumes of output.

Scattergraph showing line of best fit

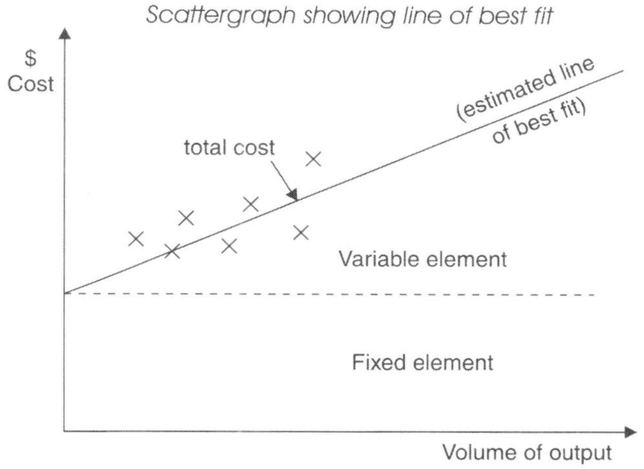

The **intersection of the line of best fit on the vertical axis is the fixed cost** (since the fixed cost is the cost of production when the volume of output is zero). Suppose the fixed cost is \$500 and that one of the plotted points (which is very close to the line or actually on it) represents output of 100 units and total cost of \$550. The variable cost of 100 units is therefore calculated as \$(550 – 500) = \$50 and so the variable cost per unit is \$0.50.

2.2 Preparing a forecast using the scattergraph method

Continuing with our example, if the expected volume of output is 200 units then the fixed cost is forecast to be \$500 and total variable costs are forecast to be 200 × \$0.50 = \$100, giving a total forecast cost of \$600.

Alternatively, the total forecast cost can be read directly from the total cost line, provided that the expected volume of output is contained within the range covered by the scattergraph.

The disadvantage of the scattergraph method for estimating costs is that the line of best fit is drawn by visual judgement and so is only a subjective approximation of total cost.

2.3 Example: forecasting using scattergraphs

Prepare a scattergraph of the following cost and volume data and forecast the total cost of production if the budgeted production volume in month 5 is 6,900 units.

Month	*Production cost*	*Production volume*
	$	Units
1	110,000	7,000
2	115,000	8,000
3	111,000	7,700
4	97,000	6,000

2.4 Solution

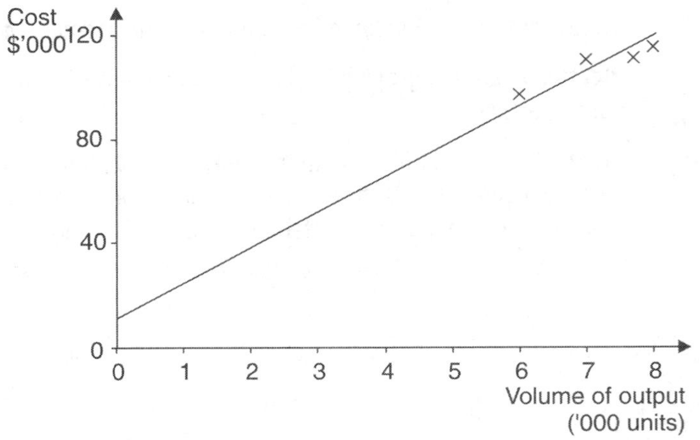

The point where the line cuts the vertical axis (approximately $12,000) is the fixed cost (the cost if there is no output). If we take the value of one of the plotted points which lies close to the line and deduct the fixed cost from the total cost, we can calculate the variable cost per unit.

Total cost for 8,000 units	= $115,000
Variable cost for 8,000 units	= $(115,000 – 12,000) = $103,000
Variable cost per unit	= $103,000/8,000 = $12.875
∴ Forecast production cost of 6,900 units	= $12,000 + ($12.875 × 6,900) = $100,837.50

Exam focus point

There were five marks available in the June 2005 exam for drawing a scattergraph of total industry sales. Yes, revenues as well as costs can be forecast using a scattergraph.

2.5 High-low method

(a) Records of costs in previous periods are reviewed and the costs of the following two periods are selected.

  (i) The period with the **highest** volume of activity

  (ii) The period with the **lowest** volume of activity

(b) The difference between the total cost of these two periods will be the **variable cost** of the difference in activity levels (since the same fixed cost is included in each total cost).

(c) The variable cost per unit may be calculated from this (difference in total costs ÷ difference in activity levels), and the **fixed cost** may then be determined by substitution.

(d) This method may be applied to annual sales figures or any other activity as well as costs. **So be prepared to use this outside the context of costs as candidates had to in the June 2005 exam.**

Exam focus point

Candidates could gain up to six marks in the June 2005 exam for using the high-low method to estimate a formula for industry sales. **Note this required the use of high-low to plot revenues rather than just costs.**

2.6 Example: the high-low method using revenues

The following information concerning sales revenues for a development, Cool Blue, for the last four months have been as follows.

Month	*Sales revenues*	*Website 'hits'*
	$	
1	110,000	70,000
2	115,000	80,000
3	111,000	77,000
4	97,000	60,000

Required

Calculate the revenues that should be expected in month five when hits is expected to be 75,000 units. Ignore inflation.

2.7 Solution

(a)

	Hits	*Revenue* $
High activity	80,000	115,000
Low activity	60,000	97,000
	20,000	18,000

Variable revenue per hit $18,000/20,000 = $0.90

(b) Substituting in either the high or low volume activity:

		High $		*Low* $
Total revenue		115,000		97,000
Variable revenue	(80,000 × $0.90)	72,000	(60,000 × $0.90)	54,000
Fixed revenue		43,000		43,000

(c) Estimated revenues when there are 75,000 hits:

	$
Fixed revenues	43,000
Variable revenues (75,000 × $0.90)	67,500
Total revenues	110,500

2.8 Example: the high-low method with stepped fixed costs

The following data relate to the overhead expenditure of contract cleaners (for industrial cleaning) at two activity levels.

Square metres cleaned	12,750	15,100
Overheads	$73,950	$83,585

When more than 20,000 square metres are industrially cleaned, it is necessary to have another supervisor and so the fixed costs rise to $43,350.

Required

Calculate the estimated overhead expenditure if 22,000 square metres are to be industrially cleaned.

2.9 Solution

	Units		$
High output	15,100	Total cost	83,585
Low output	12,750	Total cost	73,950
	2,350		9,635

$$\text{Variable cost} = \frac{\$9,635}{2,350}$$

= $4.10 per square metre

Estimated overhead expenditure if 22,000 square metres are to be industrially cleaned:

	$
Fixed costs	43,350
Variable costs (22,000 × $4.10)	90,200
	133,550

Question

Cost model

The Valuation Department of a large firm of surveyors wishes to develop a method of predicting its total costs in a period. The following past costs have been recorded at two activity levels.

	Number of valuations (V)	Total cost (TC)
Period 1	420	82,200
Period 2	515	90,275

The total cost model for a period could be represented as follows.

A TC = $46,500 + 85V
B TC = $42,000 + 95V
C TC = $46,500 – 85V
D TC = $51,500 – 95V

Answer

Although we only have two activity levels in this question we can still apply the high-low method.

	Valuations V	Total cost $
Period 2	515	90,275
Period 1	420	82,200
Change due to variable cost	95	8,075

∴ Variable cost per valuation = $8,075/95 = $85.

Period 2: fixed cost = $90,275 – (515 × $85)
= $46,500

Using good MCQ technique, you should have managed to eliminate C and D as incorrect options straightaway. The variable cost must be added to the fixed cost, rather than subtracted from it. Once you had calculated the variable cost as $85 per valuation (as shown above), you should have been able to select option A without going on to calculate the fixed cost (we have shown this calculation above for completeness).

3 The components of time series

- A **time series** is a series of figures or values recorded over time.
- There are four components of a time series: **trend**, **seasonal variations**, **cyclical variations** and **random variations**.

The **time series analysis** forecasting technique is usually used to forecast sales.

Exam focus point

This topic was examined in June 2004 as part of the 40-mark question.

Key term

A **time series** is a series of figures or values recorded over time.

The following are examples of time series.

(a) Output at a factory each day for the last month
(b) Monthly sales over the last two years
(c) Total annual costs for the last ten years
(d) Retail Prices Index each month for the last ten years
(e) The number of people employed by a company each year for the last 20 years

A graph of a time series is called a **historigram**. (Note the 'ri'; this is not the same as a histogram.) For example, consider the following time series.

Year	*Sales*
	$'000
1	20
2	21
3	24
4	23
5	27
6	30
7	28

The historigram is as follows.

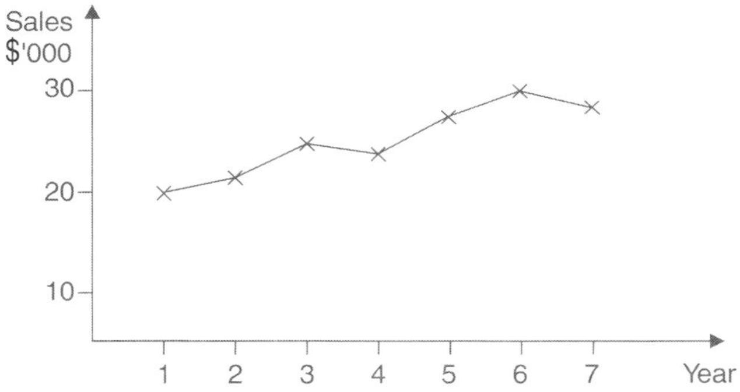

The horizontal axis is always chosen to represent time, and the vertical axis represents the values of the data recorded.

There are several features of a time series which it may be necessary to analyse in order to prepare forecasts.

(a) A **trend**
(b) **Seasonal variations** or fluctuations
(c) **Cycles**, or cyclical variations
(d) **Non-recurring, random variations**. These may be caused by unforeseen circumstances, such as a change in the government of the country, a war, the collapse of a company, technological change or a fire.

3.1 The trend

Key term

The **trend** is the underlying long-term movement over time in the values of the data recorded.

In the following examples of time series, there are three types of trend.

Year	Output per labour hour	Cost per unit	Number of employees
	Units	$	
4	30	1.00	100
5	24	1.08	103
6	26	1.20	96
7	22	1.15	102
8	21	1.18	103
9	17	1.25	98
	(A)	(B)	(C)

(a) In time series (A) there is a downward trend in the output per labour hour. Output per labour hour did not fall every year, because it went up between years 5 and 6, but the long-term movement is clearly a downward one.

(b) In time series (B) there is an upward trend in the cost per unit. Although unit costs went down in year 7 from a higher level in year 6, the basic movement over time is one of rising costs.

(c) In time series (C) there is no clear movement up or down, and the number of employees remained fairly constant around 100. The trend is therefore a static, or level one.

3.2 Seasonal variations

Key term

Seasonal variations are short-term fluctuations in recorded values, due to different circumstances which affect results at different times of the year, on different days of the week, at different times of day, or whatever.

Here are two examples of seasonal variations.

(a) Sales of ice cream will be higher in summer than winter.

(b) The telephone network may be heavily used at certain times of the day (such as mid-morning and mid-afternoon and much less used at other times (such as in the middle of the night).

Question — **Seasonal variations**

Can you think of some more examples of seasonal variations?

Answer

Here are some suggestions.

(a) Sales of overcoats will be higher in autumn than in spring.

(b) Shops might expect higher sales shortly before Christmas, or in their winter and summer sales.

(c) Sales might be higher on Friday and Saturday than on Monday.

'Seasonal' is a term which may appear to refer to the seasons of the year, but its meaning in time series analysis is somewhat broader, as the examples given above show.

Exam focus point

The terms 'trend' and 'seasonal variation' were examined in June 2004. The examiner noted that this was generally well done.

3.3 Example: a trend and seasonal variations

The number of customers served by a company of travel agents over the past four years is shown in the following historigram.

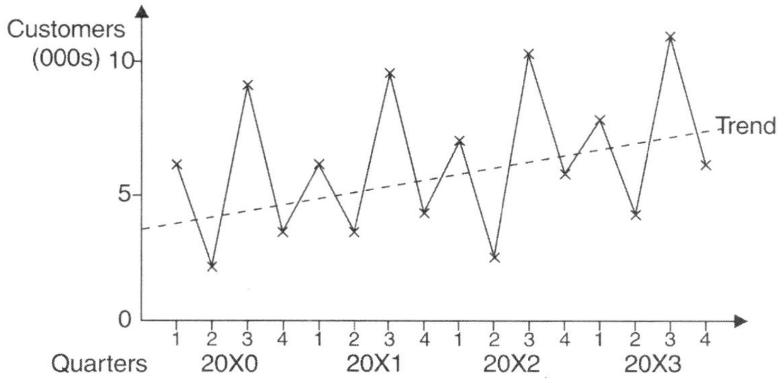

In this example, there would appear to be large seasonal fluctuations in demand, but there is also a basic upward trend.

3.4 Cyclical variations

Cyclical variations are **fluctuations which take place over a longer time period** than seasonal variations. It may take several years to complete the cycle. For example the sales of fashion items such as flared trousers could be said to be cyclical. The last cycle took approximately 30 years (mid 1960s to mid 1990s) to complete.

Question — Time series components

The following is an extract from a *Financial Times* article.

'It would be wrong to conclude too much from the encouraging 6 per cent growth in BT's inland call volumes in its final quarter. Even so, shareholders should be warmed by signs that its policy of boosting network usage is at long last bearing fruit.

The general economic recovery, of course, goes some way to explain the strong growth in calls. So do enforced price cuts. But the company's belated efforts to market its services also deserve some credit. Over the past year, charge card customers rose two-thirds, residential subscribers to extra services such as call diversion more than doubled, and freephone usage grew 30 per cent. Sunday calls have responded to lower week-end tariffs, though not enough to counterbalance the price cuts. Similarly, discounts targeted at business customers have slowed BT's loss of market share and helped it win back customers from Mercury.

BT realises it has so far exploited only a fraction of this growth opportunity. Britons use their phones much less intensively than their American counterparts. The company therefore plans to step up its marketing campaign in an attempt to create a 'high phone-usage culture'.

Investors, who have heard management promise similar things in the past, may be sceptical whether growth will materialise, given that BT's market share is bound to fall further.'

Required

Explain what the extract tells us about the following.

(a) The underlying *trend* in telephone usage in the UK and any factors influencing that trend
(b) *Short-term* (or 'seasonal') variations as they have affected BT's business
(c) *Cyclical variations* affecting BT's performance

Answer

(a) BT believes that it can accelerate the long-term trend towards higher phone usage in by increased effort in marketing its services. The long-term potential for growth can be seen from the fact that Britons use their phones much less than Americans. Only a fraction of this potential has been tapped so far. Although there is some evidence of this growth in the 6% increase in inland calls in

BT's final quarter, it is too early to be sure about whether this increase reflects the underlying trend.

(b) Types of 'seasonal' variation affecting BT are the fluctuations occurring over a weekly cycle and those occurring over the 24-hour period. The extract refers to changes over the weekly cycle. Calls made on Sundays have grown because of lower prices at the weekend, although this additional volume of business was not enough to outweigh the cut in price. (In other words, there was not a positive effect on revenue: there were more calls, but at lower prices).

(c) One of the main factors explaining the strong rise in calls in the final quarter is the cyclical variation arising from the general recovery in the economy. (Other factors are price cuts and improved marketing efforts.)

4 Finding the trend

FAST FORWARD

One method of finding the trend is by the use of **moving averages**. Remember that when finding the moving average of an even number of results, a second moving average has to be calculated so that trend values can relate to specific actual figures.

Look at these monthly sales figures.

	Sales
Year 6	$'000
August	0.02
September	0.04
October	0.04
November	3.20
December	14.60

It looks as though the business is expanding rapidly – and so it is, in a way. But when you know that the business is a Christmas card manufacturer, then you see immediately that the January sales will no doubt slump right back down again.

It is obvious that the business will do better in the Christmas season than at any other time – that is the seasonal variation with which the statistician has to contend. Using the monthly figures, how can he tell whether or not the business is doing well overall – whether there is a rising sales trend over time other than the short-term rise over Christmas?

One possibility is to compare figures with the equivalent figures of a year ago. However, many things can happen over a period of twelve months to make such a comparison misleading – for example, new products might now be manufactured and prices will probably have changed.

In fact, there are a number of ways of overcoming this problem of distinguishing trend from seasonal variations. One such method is called **moving averages**. This method attempts to **remove seasonal (or cyclical) variations from a time series by a process of averaging so as to leave a set of figures representing the trend.**

4.1 Finding the trend by moving averages

A **moving average** is an average of the results of a fixed number of periods. Since it is an average of several time periods, it is **related to the mid-point of the overall period**.

4.2 Example: moving averages

Year	*Sales*
	Units
20X0	390
20X1	380
20X2	460
20X3	450
20X4	470
20X5	440
20X6	500

Task

Take a moving average of the annual sales over a period of three years.

4.3 Solution

(a) Average sales in the three year period 20X0 – 20X2 were

$$\left(\frac{390+380+460}{3}\right) = \frac{1,230}{3} = 410$$

This average relates to the middle year of the period, 20X1.

(b) Similarly, average sales in the three year period 20X1 – 20X3 were

$$\left(\frac{380+460+450}{3}\right) = \frac{1,290}{3} = 430$$

This average relates to the middle year of the period, 20X2.

(c) The average sales can also be found for the periods 20X2 – 20X4, 20X3 – 20X5 and 20X4 – 20X6, to give the following.

Year	Sales	Moving total of 3 years' sales	Moving average of 3 year's sales (÷ 3)
20X0	390		
20X1	380	1,230	410
20X2	460	1,290	430
20X3	450	1,380	460
20X4	470	1,360	453
20X5	440	1,410	470
20X6	500		

Note the following points.

(i) The **moving average series has five figures** relating to the years from 20X1 to 20X5. The **original series had seven figures** for the years from 20X0 to 20X6.

(ii) There is an upward trend in sales, which is more noticeable from the series of moving averages than from the original series of actual sales each year.

Exam focus point

Do not rush headlong into averaging over a certain number of time periods in an exam, but over what period a moving average should be taken. The moving average which is most appropriate will depend on the circumstances and the nature of the time series.

- A moving average which takes an average of the results in many time periods will represent results over a longer term than a moving average of two or three periods.
- On the other hand, with a moving average of results in many time periods, the last figure in the series will be out of date by several periods. In the example above, the most recent average related to 20X5. With a moving average of five years' results, the final figure in the series would relate to 20X4.

- When there is a known cycle over which seasonal variations occur, such as all the days in the week or all the seasons in the year, the most suitable moving average would be one which covers one full cycle.

4.3.1 Moving averages of an even number of results

In the previous example, moving averages were taken of the results in an *odd* number of time periods, and the average then related to the mid-point of the overall period.

If a moving average were taken of results in an even number of time periods, the basic technique would be the same, but the mid-point of the overall period would not relate to a single period. For example, suppose an average were taken of the following four results.

Spring	120	
Summer	90	
Autumn	180	average 115
Winter	70	

The average would relate to the mid-point of the period, between summer and autumn.

The trend line average figures need to relate to a particular time period; otherwise, seasonal variations cannot be calculated. To overcome this difficulty, we **take a moving average of the moving average**. An example will illustrate this technique.

4.4 Example: moving averages over an even number of periods

Calculate a moving average trend line of the following results of Linden Ltd.

Year	*Quarter*	*Volume of sales '000 units*
20X5	1	600
	2	840
	3	420
	4	720
20X6	1	640
	2	860
	3	420
	4	740
20X7	1	670
	2	900
	3	430
	4	760

4.5 Solution

A moving average of four will be used, since the volume of sales would appear to depend on the season of the year, and each year has four quarterly results. The moving average of four does not relate to any specific period of time; therefore a second moving average of two will be calculated on the first moving average trend line.

Year	Quarter	*Actual volume of sales* '000 units (A)	*Moving total of 4 quarters' sales* '000 units (B)	*Moving average of 4 quarters' sales* '000 units (B ÷ 4)	*Mid-point of 2 moving averages Trend line* '000 units (C)
20X5	1	600			
	2	840			
	3	420	2,580	645.0	650.00
	4	720	2,620	655.0	657.50
20X6	1	640	2,640	660.0	660.00
	2	860	2,640	660.0	662.50
	3	420	2,660	665.0	668.75
	4	740	2,690	672.5	677.50
20X7	1	670	2,730	682.5	683.75
	2	900	2,740	685.0	687.50
	3	430	2,760	690.0	
	4	760			

By taking a mid point (a moving average of two) of the original moving averages, we can relate the results to specific quarters (from the third quarter of 20X5 to the second quarter of 20X7).

Question — **Trend in sales**

What can you say about the trend in sales of Linden Ltd in Paragraph 4.5 above?

Answer

The trend in sales is upward.

4.6 Moving averages on graphs

One way of displaying the trend clearly is to show it by plotting the moving average on a graph.

4.7 Example: moving averages on graphs

Actual sales of Slap-It-On suntan lotion for 20X5 and 20X6 were as follows.

	Sales $'000 *20X5*	$'000 *20X6*
January	100	110
February	120	130
March	200	220
April	200	210
May	240	230
June	250	240
July	210	250
August	210	300
September	200	150
October	110	110
November	90	80
December	50	40
	1,980	2,070

Task

Calculate the trend in the suntan lotion sales and display it on a graph. (*Hint.* Calculate an annual moving total.)

4.8 Solution

20X6	*Sales*	*Moving total*	*Moving average (trend)*
	$'000	$'000	$'000
January	110	1,990	165.83
February	130	2,000	166.67
March	220	2,020	168.33
April	210	2,030	169.17
May	230	2,020	168.33
June	240	2,010	167.50
July	250	2,050	170.83
August	300	2,140	178.33
September	150	2,090	174.17
October	110	2,090	174.17
November	80	2,080	173.33
December	40	2,070	172.50

There is one very important point not immediately obvious from the above table, and that is to do with the time periods covered by the moving total and moving average.

(a) The moving total, as we have seen, is the total for the previous twelve months. The figure of $1,990, for instance, represents total sales from February 20X5 to January 20X6.

(b) The moving average is the average monthly sales over the previous twelve months. The figure of $165.83, for instance, represents average monthly sales for each month during the period February 20X5 to January 20X6.

When **plotting a moving average on a graph**, it is therefore important to remember that the **points should be located at the mid-point of the period to which they apply**. For example, the figure of $165.83 (moving average at end of January 20X6) relates to the 12 months ending January 20X6 and so it must be plotted in the *middle* of that period (31 July 20X5).

The moving data on suntan lotion sales could be drawn on a graph as follows.

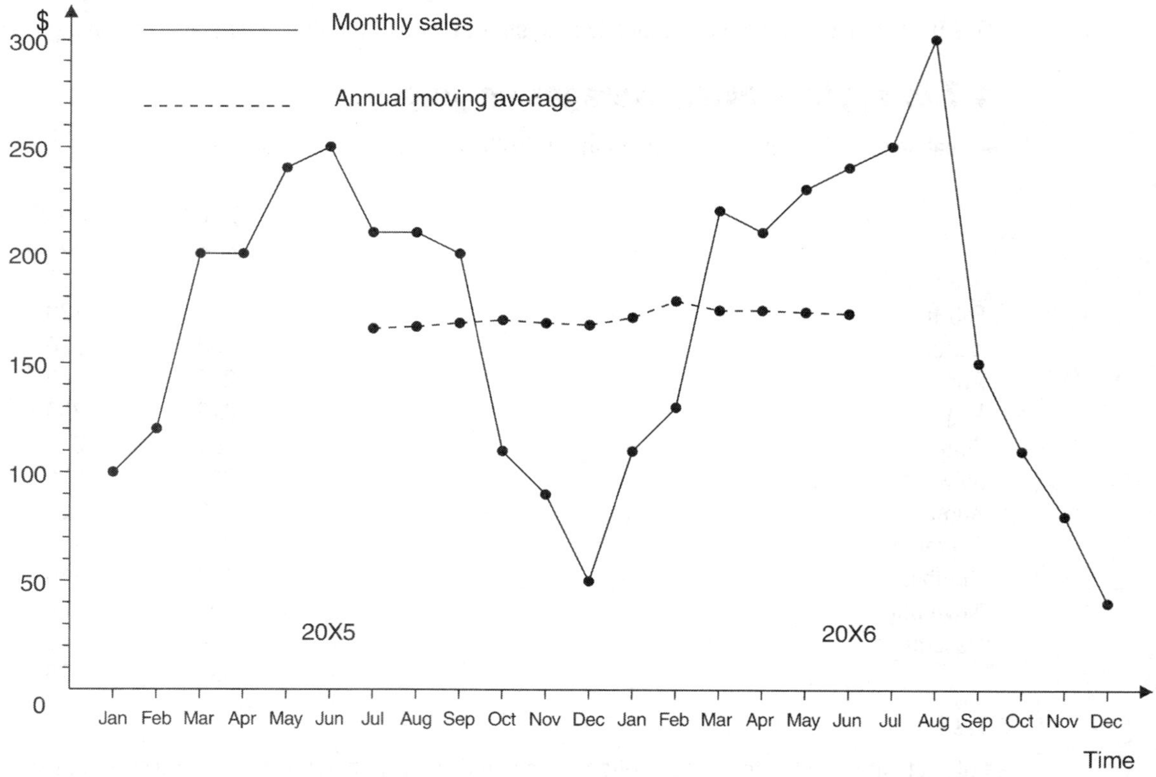

Points to note about this graph are as follows.

(a) The annual moving average can only be plotted from July 20X5 to May 20X6 as we have no data prior to January 20X5 or after December 20X6.

(b) The moving average has the effect of smoothing out the seasonal fluctuations in the ordinary sales graph (which is the reason why moving averages are used in the first place).

5 Finding the seasonal variations

FAST FORWARD

Seasonal variations are the difference between actual and trend figures **(additive model).** An average of the seasonal variations for each time period within the cycle must be determined and then adjusted so that the total of the seasonal variations sums to zero.

Once a trend has been established, we can find the **seasonal variations**.

The actual and trend sales for Linden Ltd (as calculated in Paragraph 4.5) are set out below. The **difference between the actual results for any one quarter and the trend figure for that quarter** will be the seasonal variation for that quarter.

5.1 Additive model

Year	*Quarter*	*Actual*	*Trend*	*Seasonal variation*
20X5	1	600		
	2	840		
	3	420	650.00	–230.00
	4	720	657.50	62.50
20X6	1	640	660.00	–20.00
	2	860	662.50	197.50
	3	420	668.75	–248.75
	4	740	677.50	62.50
20X7	1	670	683.75	–13.75
	2	900	687.50	212.50
	3	430		
	4	760		

The variation between the actual result for any one particular quarter and the trend line average is not the same from year to year, but an **average of these variations can be taken**.

	Q_1	Q_2	Q_3	Q_4
20X5			–230.00	62.50
20X6	–20.00	197.50	–248.75	62.50
20X7	–13.75	212.50		
Total	–33.75	410.00	–478.75	125.00
Average (÷ 2)	–16.875	205.00	–239.375	62.50

Our estimate of the 'seasonal' or quarterly variation is almost complete, but there is one more important step to take. Variations around the basic trend line should cancel each other out, and add up to zero. At the moment, they do not. We therefore **spread the total of the variations** (11.25) **across the four quarters** (11.25 ÷ 4) **so that the final total of the variations sum to zero.**

	Q_1	Q_2	Q_3	Q_4	Total
Estimated quarterly variations	– 16.8750	205.0000	–239.3750	62.5000	11.250
Adjustment to reduce variations to 0	–2.8125	–2.8125	–2.8125	–2.8125	–11.250
Final estimates of quarterly variations	–19.6875	202.1875	–242.1875	59.6875	0
These might be rounded as follows	QI: –20,	QI: 202,	QI:-242,	QI: 60,	Total: 0

Question

Additive model

The results of an additive time series model analysing production are shown below.

	Weekly production '000 units
Week 1	–4
Week 2	+5
Week 3	+9
Week 4	–6

Which of the following statements is/are true in relation to the data shown in the table above?

I Production is on average 9,000 units above the trend in week 3.
II Production is on average 4% below the trend in week 1.
III Production is on average 5% above the trend in week 2.
IV Production in week 4 is typically 6% below the trend.

A I only
B I and II only
C I and III only
D II and IV only

Answer

A I With an additive model, the weekly component represents the average value of actual production minus the trend for that week, so a component of +9 means production is 9,000 units above the trend.

This is the only correct statement.

If you selected option B, C or D, you have confused the additive variation of –4, +5 and –6 (actually –4,000 units, +5,000 units and –6,000 units respectively) with the multiplicative variation of –4%, +5% and –6% respectively. Multiplicative variations are covered later in this chapter.

Exam focus point

The examiner is unlikely to ask you to derive the seasonal variations in a time series, but it is important that you have a good understanding of how to do it.

5.2 A weakness in moving average analysis

The moving average calculations described so far in this chapter are based on an **additive model** which means that we add the values for a number of periods and take the average of those values.

An additive model has the important **drawback** that when there is a **steeply rising or a steeply declining trend, the moving average trend will either get ahead of or fall behind the real trend.**

5.3 Examples

Suppose that we were to take a three-period moving average of the following sales figures.

	Actual sales $'000	Three- year moving total $'000	Moving average $'000
20X1	1,000		
20X2	1,200	3,700	1,233
20X3	1,500	4,800	1,600
20X4	2,100	6,600	2,200
20X5	3,000	9,300	3,100
20X6	4,200	12,900	4,300
20X7	5,700	18,000	6,000
20X8	8,100		

In this example sales are on a steeply rising trend, which means that the moving average value for each year consistently overstates sales because it is partly influenced by the value of sales in the next year. The moving average value for 20X7, for example, is $6,000, which is $300 above actual sales for 20X7. This is because the moving average is partly based on the higher sales value in 20X8. The consequences are as follows.

(a) The trend sales is not a good representation of actual sales.
(b) The trend will probably be unsuitable for forecasting.

5.4 Seasonal variations using the multiplicative model

The method of estimating the seasonal variations in the above example was to use the differences between the trend and actual data. This model **assumes that the components of the series are independent** of each other, so that an increasing trend does not affect the seasonal variations and make them increase as well, for example.

The alternative is to use the **multiplicative model** whereby each actual figure is expressed as a proportion of the trend.

It may be easier to understand this model if we state this as an equation. The example below uses the equation to calculate the seasonal variation.

Key term

The **proportional (multiplicative) model** summarises a time series as $Y = T \times S \times R$ (or Y = T*S*R).

The **trend component** will be the **same whichever model is used** but the values of the **seasonal and random components** will **vary according to the model being applied**. In our examples, we assume that the random component is small and so can be ignored for our purposes. So the multiplicative model will be $Y = T \times S$.

Refer back to our example, Linden Ltd taking the first two years of data only. We can use the equation here to work out the seasonal variations. The trend is calculated in exactly the same way as before. So if $Y = T \times S$ then $S = Y/T$ and we can calculate **S = Y/T** for the multiplicative model.

Year	*Quarter*	*Actual (Y)*	*Trend (T)*	*Seasonal percentage (Y/T)*
20X5	1	600		
	2	840		
	3	420	650.00	0.646
	4	720	657.50	1.095
20X6	1	640	660.00	0.970
	2	860	662.50	1.298
	3	420		
	4	740		

Suppose that seasonal variations for the next four quarters are 0.628, 1.092, 0.980 and 1.309 respectively. The summary of the seasonal variations expressed in proportional terms is therefore as follows.

Year	Q_1	Q_2	Q_3	Q_4
	%	%	%	%
20X5			0.646	1.095
20X6	0.970	1.298	0.628	1.092
20X7	0.980	1.309		
Total	1.950	2.607	1.274	2.187
Average	0.975	1.3035	0.637	1.0935

Instead of summing to zero, as **with the additive approach**, the **averages should sum (in this case) to 4.0, 1.0 for each of the four quarters.** They actually sum to 4.009 so 0.00225 has to be deducted from each one.

	Q_1	Q_2	Q_3	Q_4
Average	0.97500	1.30350	0.63700	1.09350
Adjustment	–0.00225	–0.00225	–0.00225	–0.00225
Final estimate	0.97275	1.30125	0.63475	1.09125
Rounded	0.97	1.30	0.64	1.09

Note that the **proportional model is better than the additive model when the trend is increasing or decreasing over time**. In such circumstances, seasonal variations are likely to be increasing or decreasing too. The additive model simply adds absolute and unchanging seasonal variations to the trend figures whereas the proportional model, by multiplying increasing or decreasing trend values by a constant seasonal variation factor, takes account of changing seasonal variations.

6 Deseasonalisation

FAST FORWARD

Deseasonalised data are often used by economic commentators.

Economic statistics, such as unemployment figures, are often in 'seasonally adjusted' or 'deseasonalised' so as to ensure that the overall trend (rising, falling or stationary) is clear. All this means is that **seasonal variations (derived from previous data)** have been **taken out, to leave a figure which might be taken as indicating the trend.**

6.1 Example: deseasonalisation

Actual sales figures for four quarters, together with appropriate seasonal adjustment factors derived from previous data, are as follows.

Quarter	*Actual sales*	*Seasonal adjustments*
	$'000	$'000
1	150	+3
2	160	+4
3	164	–2
4	170	–5

Required

Deseasonalise these data.

6.2 Solution

We are reversing the normal process of applying seasonal variations to trend figures, so **we subtract positive seasonal variations (and add negative ones).**

Quarter	Actual sales $'000	Deseasonalised sales $'000
1	150	147
2	160	156
3	164	166
4	170	175

7 Sales forecasting: time series analysis

FAST FORWARD

Forecasting using time series analysis involves calculating a trend line, extrapolating the trend line and adjusting the forecasts by appropriate seasonal variations. The trend line can be extrapolated by eye or by using a common sense 'rule-of-thumb' approach.

The main idea behind time series analysis is the identification of the trend in the data and its separation from seasonal variations. Once that has been done forecasts of future values can be made as follows. Please note that you will not be asked to derive seasonal variations in a time series analysis. The information and inclusion in the following example are for completeness only

(a) **The trend line should be calculated.**

(b) **The trend line should be used to forecast future trend line values.**

(c) **These values should be adjusted by the average seasonal variation applicable to the future period, to determine the forecast for the period.**

Extending a trend line outside the range of known data, in this case forecasting the future from a trend line based on historical data, is known as **extrapolation**.

There are **two principal methods of calculating the forecast trend line**.

7.1 Inspection

The **trend line can be drawn by 'eye'** on a graph in such a way that it appears to lie evenly between the recorded points. **Forecasts can then be read off of an extrapolated trend line.**

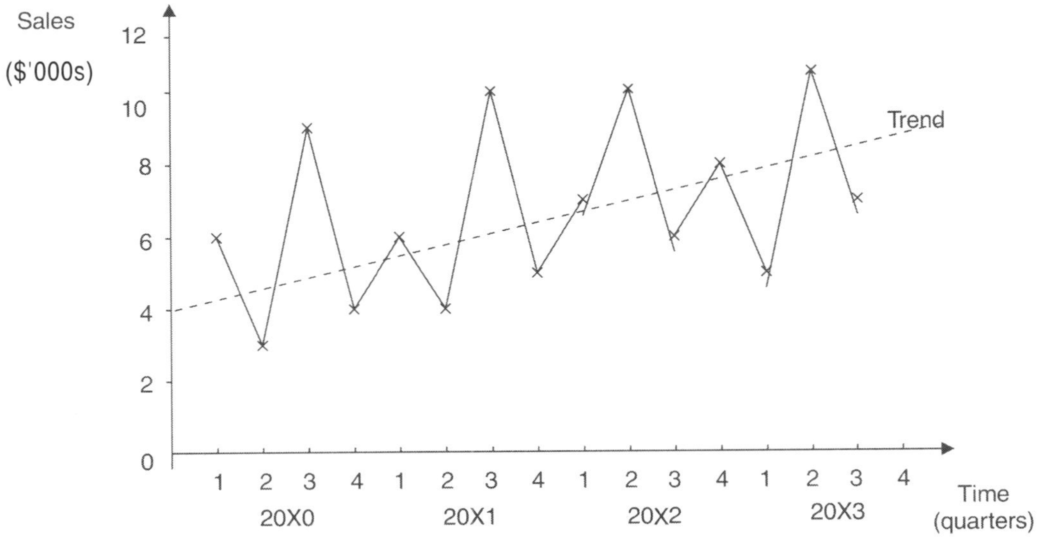

In the diagram above, for example, the trend for sales in 20X3 quarter 4 can be forecast as $9,000 by reading from the 'guessed' trend line. It could then be adjusted by the appropriate seasonal variation to determine the actual forecast.

7.2 Common sense 'rule-of-thumb' approach

This method is simply to **guess what future movements in the trend line might be, based on movements in the past**. It is not a mathematical technique, merely a common sense, rule-of-thumb approach. See if you can produce your own solution to the following problem.

7.3 Example: forecasting by rough approximation

The sales (in $'000) of swimwear by a large department store for each period of three months are as follows.

Quarter	*20X4*	*20X5*	*20X6*	*20X7*
	$'000	$'000	$'000	$'000
First		8	20	40
Second		30	50	62
Third		60	80	92
Fourth	24	20	40	

Task

(a) Using an additive model, find the centred moving average trend.

(b) Find the average seasonal variation for each quarter.

(c) Predict sales for the last quarter of 20X7 and the first quarter of 20X8, stating any assumptions.

7.4 Solution

	Quarter	*4 quarter moving total*	*Centred moving total*	*Moving average(÷4)*
20X4	4			
20X5	1			
		122		
	2		120	30
		118		
	3		124	31
		130		
	4		140	35
		150		
20X6	1		160	40
		170		
	2		180	45
		190		
	3		200	50
		210		
	4		216	54
		222		
20X7	1		228	57
		234		
	2			
	3			

(a) The centred moving average trend is shown in the right hand column of the table.

(b) *Seasonal variations*

	Quarter 1	2	3	4	Total
Year 20X5		0.00	+29.00	–15.00	
20X6	–20.00	+5.00	+30.00	–14.00	
20X7	–17.00				
Total	–37.00	+5.00	+59.00	–29.00	
Average	–18.50	+2.50	+29.50	–14.50	–1
Adjust total variation to nil	+0.25	+0.25	+0.25	+0.25	+1
Average seasonal variation	–18.25	+2.75	+29.75	–14.25	

(c) We might guess that the trend line is rising steadily, by (57 – 40)/4 = 4.25 per quarter in the period 1st quarter 20X6 to 1st quarter 20X7 (57 being the prediction in 1st quarter 20X7 and 40 the prediction in 1st quarter 20X6).

Since the trend may be levelling off a little, a quarterly increase of +4 in the trend will be assumed.

		Trend	Seasonal variation	Forecast
1st quarter	20X7	57		
4th quarter	20X7 (+ (3 × 4))	69	−14.25	54.75
1st quarter	20X8 (+ (4 × 4))	73	−18.25	54.75

Rounding to the nearest thousand dollars, the forecast sales are $55,000 for each of the two quarters.

Question

Forecast sales

Sales of product X each quarter for the last three years have been as follows (in thousands of units). Trend values, found by a moving averages method, are shown in brackets.

Year	*1st quarter*	*2nd quarter*	*3rd quarter*	*4th quarter*
1	18	30	20 (18.75)	6 (19.375)
2	20 (20)	33 (20.5)	22 (21)	8 (21.5)
3	22 (22.125)	35 (22.75)	25	10

Average seasonal variations for quarters 1 to 4 are −0.1, +12.4, +1.1 and −13.4 respectively.

Required

Use the trend line and estimates of seasonal variations to forecast sales in each quarter of year 4.

Answer

The trend line indicates an increase of about 0.6 per quarter. This can be confirmed by calculating the average quarterly increase in trend line values between the third quarter of year 1 (18.75) and the second quarter of year 3 (22.75). The average rise is

$$\frac{22.75-18.75}{7} = \frac{4}{7} = 0.57, \text{ say } 0.6$$

Taking 0.6 as the quarterly increase in the trend, the forecast of sales for year 4, before seasonal adjustments (the trend line forecast) would be as follows.

Year	*Quarter*			*Trend line*
3	*2nd	(actual trend)	22.75, say	22.8
	3rd			23.4
	4th			24.0
4	1st			24.6
	2nd			25.2
	3rd			25.8
	4th			26.4

* last known trend line value.

(Note that you could actually plot the trend line figures on a graph, extrapolate the trend line into the future and read off forecasts from the graph using the extrapolated trend line.)

Seasonal variations should now be incorporated to obtain the final forecast.

	Quarter	*Trend line forecast*	*Average seasonal variation*	*Forecast of actual sales*
		'000 units	'000 units	'000 units
Year 4	1st	24.6	−0.1	24.5
	2nd	25.2	+12.4	37.6
	3rd	25.8	+ 1.1	26.9
	4th	26.4	−13.4	13.0

8 Forecasting problems

All forecasts are subject to error, but the likely errors vary from case to case.

(a) The **further into the future** the forecast is for, the **more unreliable** it is likely to be.

(b) The **less data** available on which to base the forecast, the **less reliable** the forecast.

(c) The **pattern** of trend and seasonal variations **cannot be guaranteed to continue** in the future.

(d) There is always the danger of **random variations** upsetting the pattern of trend and seasonal variation.

In summary, time series can be rather simplistic as it assumes past trends will continue indefinitely.

There are a number of changes that also may make it **difficult to forecast** future events.

Type of change	Examples
Political and economic changes	Create uncertainty. For example changes in interest rates, exchange rates or inflation can mean that future sales and costs are difficult to forecast.
Environmental changes	For example the opening of the channel tunnel might have a considerable impact on some companies' markets.
Technological changes	May mean that the past is not a reliable indication of likely future events. For example the availability of faster machinery may make it difficult to use current output levels as the basis for forecasting future production output.
Technological advances	Can also change the nature of production. The advent of advanced manufacturing technology is changing the cost structure of many firms. Direct labour costs are reducing in significance and fixed manufacturing costs are increasing. This causes forecasting difficulties because of the resulting changes in cost behaviour patterns, breakeven points and so on.
Social changes	Alterations in taste and fashion and changes in the social acceptability of different products can cause difficulties in forecasting future sales levels. For example tobacco.

9 Forecasting and price movements

Exam focus point

In the June 2005 exam, five marks were available for using a price level index explained in this section to restate industry sales figures.

FAST FORWARD

Data used in forecasting may need to be **adjusted using index numbers to take account** of any movements in prices that may have occurred, usually as a result **of inflation**.

Suppose that cost and volume of output data have been collected for a five-year period during which time inflation has been running at eight percent per annum. Even if the volume of output in two of the years is the same, the costs will be different because of inflation. We therefore need to remove the effects of inflation from the costs so that they can be compared on a **like-for-like basis.**

We remove the effects of price movements **by adjusting figures to a common basis using index numbers**. Index numbers show how prices have changed compared with the price at a certain point in time, the **base period**. The base period will have an index number of 100. If the index number for a year is 128, prices have increased by 28% since the base period.

The basic approach is as follows.

Step 1 Remove the effects of price movements by adjusting the data to a common basis, usually to the price level of the base period.

$$\text{Actual cost} \times \frac{100}{\text{Index for year in question}}$$

Step 2 Apply the forecasting technique to the data produced in step 1

Step 3 Adjust the forecast produced in step 2 to take account of price movements.

$$\text{Unadjusted forecast} \times \frac{\text{Index for year}}{100}$$

9.1 Example: forecasting and price movements

Move Away has recorded the following total costs during the last three years.

Year	*Volume of output*	*Total cost*
	Units	$
20X0	26,000	401,600
20X1	32,000	565,440
20X2	36,000	647,000

An index of the movement in prices over the three-year period is as follows.

	Price level index
20X0	100
20X1	120
20X2	125

Prices therefore increased by 20% between 20X0 and 20X1 and by 25% between 20X0 and 20X2. They did *not* increase by 5% between 20X1 and 20X2 but by ((125 – 120)/120) × 100% = 4.17%.

Let's take account of inflation.

Step 1 Adjust the data to a common basis, index level 100.

Year	*Actual cost*		*Cost at price level index = 100*
	$		
20X0	401,600	$\times \frac{100}{100} =$	401,600
20X1	565,440	$\times \frac{100}{120} =$	471,200
20X2	647,000	$\times \frac{100}{125} =$	517,600

The figures in the right hand column represent the costs if there had been no inflation between 20X0 and 20X2.

Step 2 The scattergraph method can now be applied to the costs (at price level index = 100) and it would show that fixed costs are $100,000 and variable cost per unit is $11.60 (in terms of 20X0 prices). If output in 20X4 is forecast to be 38,500 units, total costs (unadjusted for price movements) are forecast as follows.

	$
Variable costs (20X0 prices) ($11.60 × 38,500)	446,600
Fixed costs (20X0 prices)	100,000
Total costs (20X0 prices)	546,600

Step 3 If the average price level index for 20X4 is estimated to be 137, at 20X4 prices we can calculate total costs as $\$546,600 \times \frac{137}{100} = \$748,842$

Data used in time series analysis can be adjusted for price movements in exactly the same way.

Question

Average price level index (1)

Using the average price level index, adjust the following costs so that they can be used for forecasting.

Year	*Cost* $	*Average price level index*
20X0	145,000	100
20X1	179,200	112
20X2	209,100	123
20X3	201,600	144
20X4	248,000	160

Answer

Year	*Cost* $		*Adjusted cost* $
20X0	145,000	$\times \frac{100}{100}$	145,000
20X1	179,200	$\times \frac{100}{112}$	160,000
20X2	209,100	$\times \frac{100}{123}$	170,000
20X3	201,600	$\times \frac{100}{144}$	140,000
20X4	248,000	$\times \frac{100}{160}$	155,000

Question

Average price level index (2)

The scattergraph method was applied to the data in the last question (once the data had been adjusted for price movements). Fixed costs were estimated to be $80,000 and variable cost per unit to be $1 per unit. Forecast the total cost that should be expected in 20X5 if output is 85,000 units and the average price level index is 180.

Answer

Forecast at 20X0 price levels

	$
Fixed cost	80,000
Variable cost (85,000 × $1)	85,000
	165,000

Forecast at 20X5 price levels = $165,000 × $\frac{180}{100}$ = $297,000

10 Linear regression analysis

FAST FORWARD

Linear regression determines a line of best fit by the method of least squares.

Exam focus point

The examiner tested linear regression in June 2004 in a question that asked candidates to define 'trend' and 'seasonal variation' and also forecast sales from the data provided.

10.1 Linear relationships

A **linear relationship** can be expressed in the form of an equation which has the general form
y = a + bx

where y is the **dependent** variable depending for its value on the value of x

x is the **independent** variable whose value helps to determine the corresponding value of y

a is a **constant**, a fixed amount

b is a constant, being the **coefficient of x** (that is, the number by which the value of x should be multiplied to derive the value of y)

If there is a linear relationship between total costs and level of activity, y = total costs, x = level of activity, a = fixed cost (the cost when there is no activity level) and b = variable cost per unit.

The graph below is taken from chapter 1 and shows the behaviour of a semi-variable cost. This demonstrates a **linear** relationship graphically.

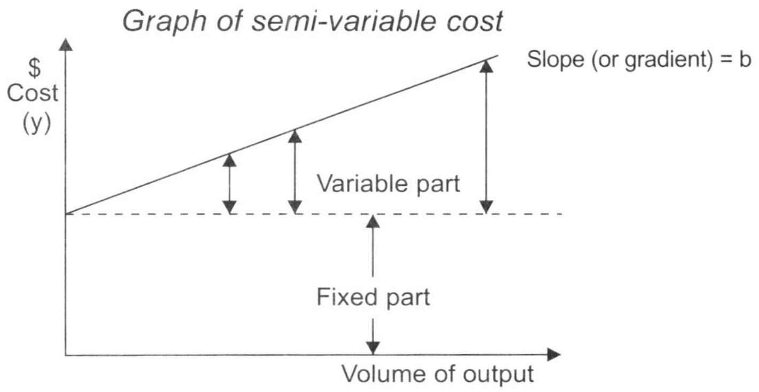

An example of a semi-variable is electricity cost, where there is a basic charge plus a charge per unit of consumption.

Using this example, the **independent variable** of output volume (x) helps us determine the **dependent variable** of electricity cost (y). The slope (b) reflects the variable cost of electricity per unit of output. The fixed cost element is the basic electricity charge (a).

The graph of a linear equation is a **straight line** and is determined by two things, the **gradient** (or slope) of the straight line and the point at which the straight line crosses the y axis (the **intercept**).

(a) Gradient = b in the equation y = a + bx = $(y_2 - y_1)/(x_2 - x_1)$ where (x_1, y_1), (x_2, y_2) are two points on the straight line

(b) Intercept = a in the equation y = a + bx

10.2 Linear regression analysis

Earlier in this chapter we looked at scattergraphs and the line of best fit.

You should recall that the scattergraph method is used to forecast costs or revenues by estimating a **line of best fit**.

Another method for estimating a line of best fit is using **linear regression analysis**.

Linear regression analysis, also known as the **'least squares technique'**, is a **statistical method** of estimating costs using historical data from a number of previous accounting periods.

The 'least squares technique' is a method for fitting a straight line through a set of points in such a way that the sum of the squared vertical distances (or deviations) from the observed points to the fitted line is minimised.

The relationships derived through use of linear regression are **likely to be more accurate** than plotting by eye or the 'high-low' method because:

(a) It provides a mathematical basis for the line of best fit rather than simply plotting by 'eye'.

(b) The 'least squares technique' uses many past observations to determine a line of best fit rather than just the two instances used in the 'high-low' method.

Linear regression analysis is used to derive a **line of best fit which has the general form**

y = a + bx where

y, the dependent variable = total cost
x, the independent variable = the level of activity
a, the intercept of the line on the y axis = the fixed cost
b, the gradient of the line = the variable cost per unit of activity.

Historical data is collected from previous periods and adjusted to a common price level to remove inflationary differences. This provides a number of readings for activity levels (x) and their associated costs (y). Then, by substituting these readings into the formulae below for a and b, estimates of the fixed cost and variable cost per unit are provided.

If $y = a + bx$, $b = \dfrac{n\Sigma xy - \Sigma x\Sigma y}{n\Sigma x^2 - (\Sigma x)^2}$ and $a = \dfrac{\Sigma y}{n} - \dfrac{b\Sigma x}{n}$

where n is the number of pair of data for x and y.

Attention!

Please note that the derivation of regression coefficients is not examinable so just use data provided.

10.3 The conditions suited to the use of linear regression analysis

The conditions which should apply if linear regression analysis is to be used to estimate costs are as follows.

(a) A **linear cost function should be assumed**. This assumption can be tested by measures of reliability, such as the correlation coefficient and the coefficient of determination (which ought to be reasonably close to 1). We will be looking at these concepts later in the chapter.

(b) When calculating a line of best fit, there will be a range of values for x. For example if the line y = 28 + 2.6x was predicted from data with output values ranging from x = 16 to x = 24, depending on the degree of correlation between x and y, we might safely use the estimated line of best fit to forecast values for y, provided that the value of x remains within the range 16 to 24. We would be on less safe ground if we used the equation to predict a value for y when x = 10, or 30, or any other value outside the range 16 to 24, because we would **have to assume that costs behave in the same way outside the range of x values used to establish the line in the first place.**

Key terms

Interpolation means using a line of best fit to predict a value within the two extreme points of the observed range.

Extrapolation means using a line of best fit to predict a value outside the two extreme points.

(c) The **historical data** for cost and output should be **adjusted to a common price level** (to overcome cost differences caused by inflation) and the historical data should also be **representative of current technology, current efficiency levels and current operations** (products made).

(d) As far as possible, **historical data should be accurately recorded** so that variable costs are properly matched against the items produced or sold, and fixed costs are properly matched against the time period to which they relate. For example, if a factory rental is $120,000 per annum, and if data is gathered monthly, these costs should be charged $10,000 to each month instead of $120,000 in full to a single month.

(e) Management should either be **confident that conditions** which have existed in the past **will continue into the future or amend the estimates** of cost produced by the linear regression analysis to **allow for expected changes** in the future.

(f) As with any forecasting process, the **amount of data available is very important**. Even if correlation is high, if we have fewer than about ten pairs of data, we must regard any forecast as being somewhat unreliable.

(g) It must be assumed that the **value of one variable, y, can be predicted or estimated from the value of one other variable, x.**

Question — Linear regression model

The relationship between total operating cost and quantity produced (in a manufacturing company) is given by the linear regression model TC = 5,000 + 500Q, where TC = total operating cost (in $) per annum and Q = quantity produced per annum (kg).

What reservations might you have about relying on the above model for decision-making purposes?

Answer

(a) The reliability of the model is unknown if we do **not know the correlation coefficient**. A low correlation would suggest that the model may be unreliable.

(b) The model is probably **valid only over a certain range** of quantity produced. Outside this range, the relationship between the two variables may be very different.

(c) The model is **based on past data**, and assumes that what has happened in the past will happen in the future.

(d) The model **assumes that a linear relationship exists** between the quantity produced per annum and the total operating costs per annum. It is possible that a non-linear relationship may exist.

(e) The **fixed costs** of $5,000 per annum may be **misleading** if they include an element of allocated costs.

10.4 Sales forecasting and linear regression

You could be asked to use data provided through linear regression analysis along with data from time series analysis to forecast sales.

10.4.1 Example: Linear regression analysis

Linear regression has been used to derive the quarterly trend in sales units of product S for Division P. The quarterly trend in sales units for Division P can be represented by the equation:

y = 2,000 + 30x

y is the forecast sales trend in units, x is the quarter number (where quarter 1 of 2008 = 1, quarter 2 of 2008 = 2, quarter 3 of 2008 = 3, etc.)

However product S is subject to seasonal variations which follow an additive model. The quarterly variations are set out below.

Quarter	*Seasonal variation in units*
1	+30
2	–50
3	–45
4	+35

Required

Using the information provided, forecast the sales (in units) for the final quarter of 2009.

10.4.2 Solution

The trend (y) is calculated using the equation given. The quarter is the eighth in the series (x = 8).

$y = 2,000 + 30x = 2,000 + (30 \times 8) = 2,240$.

However, you also need to adjust for seasonal variation. For the last quarter of a year this is +35.

Forecast sales units for quarter 4 in 2009 = 2,240 + 35 = 2,275 units.

10.4.3 Linear trend in sales

So far in the chapter we have looked at methods which assume a **linear** trend in sales. That is, sales follow a predictable pattern which can be plotted using methods including time series and linear regression analysis.

However, sales of products and services do not always follow a straight line.

Think about fashion products or fads for example. Sales often grow very fast and slump equally fast. In the next section we consider reasons why this might be the case when we look at the product life cycle.

11 Sales forecasting: the product life cycle

FAST FORWARD

The product life cycle model shows how sales of a product can be expected to vary with the passage of time.

A product will probably go through the stages of introduction, growth, maturity, decline and senility. Different levels of sales and profit can be expected at each stage. Note that the product life cycle is a **model** of what **might** happen, **not a law** prescribing what **will** happen. In other words, not all products go through these stages or even have a life cycle. However, the idea of a life cycle can be useful to experienced marketing staff when forecasting sales and profits.

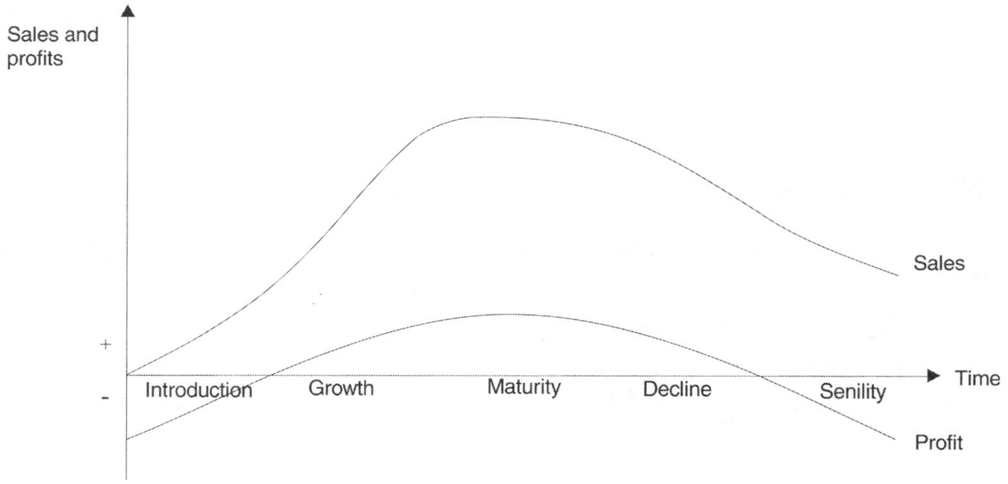

11.1 Introduction

(a) A new product takes time to find acceptance by would-be purchasers and there is a slow growth in sales. Unit costs are high because of low output and expensive sales promotion.

(b) The product for the time being is a loss-maker.

11.2 Growth

(a) If the new product gains market acceptance, sales will eventually rise more sharply and the product will start to make profits.

(b) As sales and production rise, unit costs fall.

11.3 Maturity

The rate of sales growth slows down and the product reaches a period of maturity which is probably the longest period of a successful product's life. Most products on the market will be at the mature stage of their life. Profits are good.

11.4 Decline

Eventually, sales will begin to decline so that there is over-capacity of production in the industry. Severe competition occurs, profits fall and some producers leave the market. The remaining producers seek means of prolonging the product life by modifying it and searching for new market segments. Many producers are reluctant to leave the market, although some inevitably do because of falling profits.

Chapter Roundup

- Simple methods of forecasting costs include the **scattergraph** and **high-low** techniques.
- A **time series** is a series of figures or values recorded over time.
- There are four components of a time series: **trend**, **seasonal variations**, **cyclical variations** and **random variations**.
- One method of finding the trend is by the use of **moving averages**. Remember that when finding the moving average of an even number of results, a second moving average has to be calculated so that trend values can relate to specific actual figures.
- Seasonal variations are the difference between actual and trend figures **(additive model).** An average of the seasonal variations for each time period within the cycle must be determined and then adjusted so that the total of the seasonal variations sums to zero.
- **Deseasonalised data** are often used by economic commentators.
- Forecasting using time series analysis involves calculating a trend line, extrapolating the trend line and adjusting the forecasts by appropriate seasonal variations. The trend line can be extrapolated by eye or by using a common sense 'rule-of-thumb' approach.
- **Data** used in forecasting may need to be adjusted using **index numbers** to take account of any movements in prices that have occurred, usually as a result of **inflation**.
- Linear regression determines a line of best fit by the method of least squares.
- The product life cycle model shows how sales of a product can be expected to vary with the passage of time.

Quick Quiz

1 What is the difference between a budget and a forecast?

2 What is the disadvantage of the scattergraph method?

3 When plotting moving averages on a graph, where should the plotted points be located?

4 Why are average seasonal variations adjusted to sum to zero?

5 What is the weakness of the additive model?

6 What is deseasonalised data?

7 What is extrapolation?

8 What factors affect the accuracy of forecasts?

9 What is the standard calculation for removing the effects of price movements from data?

10 If the relationship between production costs and output is connected by the linear relationship $y = 75x + 47{,}000$, what is 47,000?

A The number of units produced
B Total production costs
C The production cost if 75 units are produced
D The fixed production costs

11 Based on the last 7 periods, the underlying trend of sales is $y = 690.24 - 2.75x$. If the 8th period has a seasonal factor of –25.25, assuming an additive forecasting model, then the forecast for that period, in whole units is

A 643
B 646
C 668
D 671

12 Which of the following are necessary if forecasts obtained from a time series analysis are to be reliable?

I There must be no seasonal variation
II The trend must be increasing
III The model used must fit the past data
IV There must be no unforeseen events

A I and III only
B I and IV only
C II and III only
D III and IV only

Answers to Quick Quiz

1 A forecast is an estimate of what might happen in the future. It is a best estimate, based on certain assumptions about the conditions that are expected to apply. A budget, in contrast, is a plan of what the organisation is aiming to achieve and what it has set as a target. A budget should be realistic and so it will be based to some extent on forecasts prepared. In preparing a budget, however, management will be trying to establish some control over the conditions that will apply in the future.

2 The disadvantage of the scattergraph method for estimating costs is that the line of best fit is drawn by visual judgement and so is only a subjective approximation of total cost.

3 Points should be plotted at the midpoint of the period to which they apply.

4 Average seasonal variations are adjusted to sum to zero because variations around the basic trend line should cancel each other out and add up to zero.

5 An additive model has the important drawback that when there is a steeply rising or a steeply declining trend, the moving average trend will either get ahead of or fall behind the real trend.

6 Deseasonalised data is data from which the seasonal variations have been removed, leaving a figure which might be taken as indicating the trend.

7 Extrapolation is forecasting the future from a trend line based on historical data.

8 (a) The further into the future the forecast is for, the more unreliable it is likely to be.
(b) The less data available on which to base the forecast, the less reliable the forecast.
(c) The pattern of trend and seasonal variations cannot be guaranteed to continue in the future.
(d) There is always the danger of random variations upsetting the pattern of trend and seasonal variation.

9 $\text{Actual data} \times \dfrac{100}{\text{Index for time period in question}}$

10 D

11 A If $x = 8$, $y = 690.24 - (2.75 \times 8) = 668.24$

Forecast = trend + seasonal component = 668.24 – 25.25 = 642.99 = 643 (to the nearest unit)

If you selected option B, you calculated the forecast for the seventh period and deducted the seasonal component of the eighth period.

If you selected option C, you correctly forecast the trend for the eighth period but forgot to deduct the seasonal component.

If you selected option D, you simply calculated the trend for the seventh period instead of the eighth period.

12 D
I Provided the seasonal variation remains the same in the future as in the past, it will not make forecasts unreliable.
II Provided a multiplicative model is used, the fact that the trend is increasing need not have any adverse effect on the reliability of forecasts.
III If the model being used is inappropriate, for example, if an additive model is used when the trend is changing sharply, forecasts will not be very reliable.
IV Forecasts are made on the assumption that everything continues as in the past.

III and IV are therefore necessary and hence the correct answer is D.

Now try the questions below from the Exam Question Bank

Number	Level	Marks	Time
Section A: Q11	MCQ	N/A	N/A
Section B: Q7	Examination	20	36 mins

8

Planning and control systems

Topic list
1 The planning and control cycle
2 Factors affecting the design of planning and control systems
3 Responsibility centres
4 Controllable costs
5 Planning

Study guide reference

		Syllabus reference
9(a)	Link between planning cycles, budgets and forecasts	6
	(i) Describe the planning and control cycle in an organisation	6
	(ii) Explain how the design of the planning and control system will be affected by organisational structure, business objectives, the organisation's administrative procedures and the nature of the product/service market	6
	(iii) Compare short-term and long-term business plans and explain how they are related	6
16(a)	Responsibility accounting	6
	(i) Define the concept of responsibility accounting	6
	(ii) Explain its significance in control	6
	(iii) Evaluate the responsibility of managers in a given situation	6
	(iv) Explain the problem of joint responsibility	6
	(v) Design reports appropriate to a given responsibility structure	6
	(vi) Identify costs to be collected for a given responsibility structure	6
16(b)	Controllable and uncontrollable costs	6
	(i) Explain the concepts of controllable and uncontrollable costs	6
	(ii) Distinguish between controllable and uncontrollable costs in a given situation	6
17(a)	Define cost centres, revenue centres, profit centres and investment centres.	6

Exam focus point

This chapter covers a key syllabus area. Key syllabus areas usually account for 80% or more of the marks available on the exam paper.

1 The planning and control cycle

FAST FORWARD

There are seven steps in the planning and control cycle.

Step 1 Identify objectives

Step 2 Identity potential strategies

Step 3 Evaluate strategies

Step 4 Choose alternative courses of action

Step 5 Implement the long-term plan

Step 6 Measure actual results and compare with plan

Step 7 Respond to divergences from plan

The diagram below represents the planning and control cycle. **Planning** involves making choices between alternatives and is primarily a decision-making activity. The **control** process involves measuring and correcting actual performance to ensure that the strategies that are chosen and the plans for implementing them are carried out.

The planning and control cycle

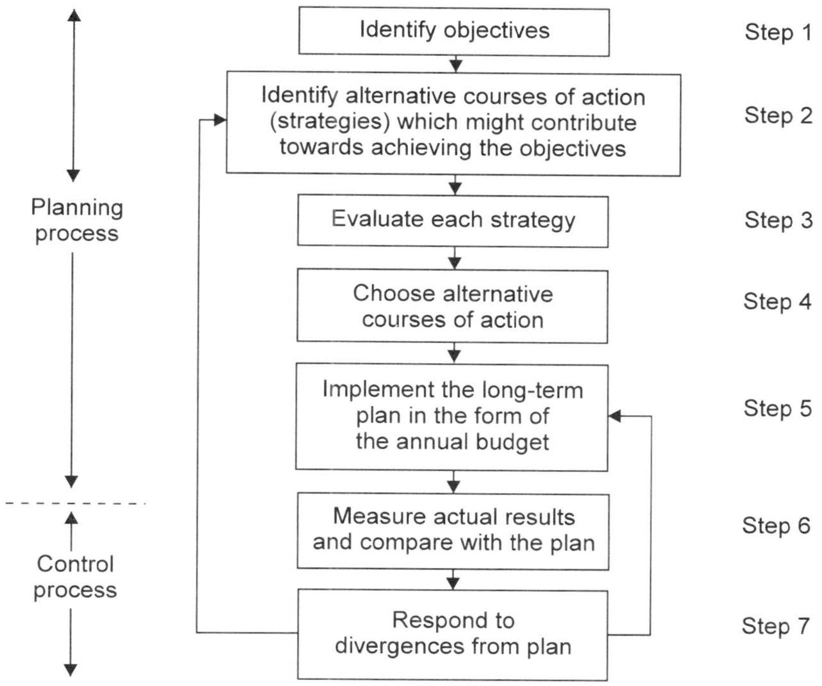

Step 1 **Identify objectives**

Objectives establish the direction in which the management of the organisation wish it to be heading. Typical objectives include the following.

(a) To maximise profits
(b) To increase market share
(c) To produce a better quality product than anyone else

Objectives answer the question: '**where do we want to be**?'.

Step 2 **Identify potential strategies**

Once an organisation has decided 'where it wants to be', the next step is to identify a range of possible courses of action or **strategies that might enable the organisation to get there.**

The organisation must therefore carry out an **information-gathering exercise** to ensure that it has a full **understanding of where it is now.** This is known as a '**position audit**' or '**strategic analysis**' and involves **looking** both **inwards** and **outwards**.

(a) The organisation must **gather information from all of its internal parts** to find out what resources it possesses: what its manufacturing capacity and capability is, what is the state of its technical know-how, how well it is able to market itself, how much cash it has in the bank, how much it could borrow and so on.
(b) It must also **gather information externally** so that it can assess its position in the environment. Just as it has assessed its **own strengths and weaknesses**, it must do likewise for its competitors (**threats**). Its market must be analysed (and any other markets that it is intending to enter) to identify possible new **opportunities**. The 'state of the world' must be considered. Is it in recession or is it booming? What is likely to happen in the future? This process is known as SWOT analysis.

Having carried out a strategic analysis, alternative strategies can be identified.

Step 3 **Evaluate strategies**

The strategies must then be evaluated **in terms of suitability, feasibility and acceptability in the context of the strategic analysis**. Management should select those strategies that have the greatest potential for achieving the organisation's objectives. One strategy may be chosen or several.

Step 4 **Choose alternative courses of action**

The next step in the process is to collect the **chosen strategies** together and **co-ordinate them into a long-term plan**, commonly expressed in financial terms.

Typically a long-term financial plan would show the following.

(a) Projected cash flows
(b) Projected long-term profits
(c) Capital expenditure plans
(d) Balance sheet forecasts
(e) A description of the long-term objectives and strategies in words

Step 5 **Implement the long-term plan**

The **long-term plan** should then be **broken down into smaller parts**. It is unlikely that the different parts will fall conveniently into successive time periods. Strategy A may take two and a half years, while Strategy B may take five months, but not start until year three of the plan. It is usual, however, to break down the plan as a whole into equal time periods (usually one year). The resulting **short-term plan** is called a **budget**.

Steps 6 and 7 **Measure actual results and compare with plan. Respond to divergences from plan**

At the end of the year actual results should be compared with those expected under the long-term plan. The **long-term plan should be reviewed** in the light of this comparison and the progress that has been made towards achieving the organisation's objectives should be assessed. Management can also **consider the feasibility of achieving the objectives** in the light of unforeseen circumstances which have arisen during the year. If the plans are now **no longer attainable then alternative strategies must be considered** for achieving the organisation's objectives, as indicated by the feedback loop (the arrowed line) linking step 7 to step 2. This aspect of control is carried out by senior management, normally on an annual basis.

The control of **day-to-day operations** is exercised by lower-level managers. At frequent intervals they must be provided with **performance reports** which consist of **detailed comparisons of actual results and budgeted results**. Performance reports provide **feedback information** by comparing planned and actual outcomes. Such reports should highlight those activities that do not conform to plan, so that managers can devote their scarce time to focusing on these items. Effective control requires that **corrective action** is taken so that **actual outcomes conform to planned outcomes**, as indicated by the feedback loop linking steps 5 and 7. Isolating past inefficiencies and the reasons for them will enable managers to take action that will avoid the same inefficiencies being repeated in the future. The system that provides reports that compare actual performance with budget figures is known as **responsibility accounting.**

Remember to apply this section (and the following section) to Chapter 1, Section 7, 'The maintenance and improvement of accounting information systems'.

Question — Planning cycle

Is your organisation's planning and control cycle similar to the one described here? If it differs, how does it differ? Why does it differ? Try to find out your organisation's objectives and the strategies it is adopting to attain those objectives.

2 Factors affecting the design of planning and control systems

We can divide the factors that affect the design of planning and control systems into three groups.

Factors	Examples
The environment	Its degree of predictability The degree of competition faced The number of different product markets faced The degree of hostility exhibited by competing organisations
Organisational structure	Size Interdependence of parts Degree of decentralisation Availability of resources
Technology	The nature of the production process The routineness/complexity of the production process The amount of variety in each task that has to be performed

2.1 Example: designing a planning and control system

The following example is very simplified but illustrates how the design of a planning and control system is affected by a number of factors.

Stable makes three different products, X, Y and Z. Until recently it had never had any competitors. Every month the managing director received a report from the management accountant in the following form (the numbers are for illustration only).

	$
Sales	10,000
Production costs	5,000
Gross profit	5,000
Administrative costs	1,000
Net profit	4,000

A few months ago another company, Turbulence & Co, entered the market for products X and Y, undercutting the prices charged by Stable. Turbulence started to win some of Stable's customers.

The managing director asked the management accountant for **information** about the **profitability** of its own versions of products X and Y. Sales information was easy to reanalyse, but to analyse production information in this way required a new system of coding to be introduced. Eventually the management accountant came up with the following report.

	X	*Y*	*Z*	*Total*
	$	$	$	$
Sales	3,000	3,000	4,000	10,000
Production costs	500	500	4,000	5,000
Gross profit	2,500	2,500	-	5,000
Administrative costs				1,000
Net profit				4,000

As a result of receiving this information the MD dropped the price of Stable's products X and Y. He divided the production function into two divisions, one to concentrate exclusively upon reducing the costs of product Z while maintaining quality.

The management accountant was asked to work closely with the division Z production manager in **designing a system to monitor and control costs**. He was also to work closely with the marketing managers of products X and Y so that the organisation **could respond rapidly to any further competitive**

pressures. Reports were to be made weekly and were to include as much information as could be determined about Turbulence's financial performance, pricing, marketing penetration and so on.

(a) The design of the system was originally determined by the facts that Stable faced a highly predictable environment, and that it was a highly centralised organisation.

(b) **The design of the new system is the result of a new set of circumstances**. The entry of Turbulence into two of Stable's markets required the system to adopt a product-based reporting structure with more externally-derived information in the case of products X and Y and more detailed analysis of internal information in the case of product Z. This is matched by a change in the structure of the organisation as a whole.

Let's now take a look at some of the specific ways in which the environment, organisational structure and technology impact on planning and control system design.

(a) **Environment**

 (i) The **more competition** an organisation faces, the **more sophisticated the planning and control system** needs to be.

 (ii) The type of competition faced (for example, competition on price as opposed to product rivalry) will influence the way in which planning and control information is used.

 (iii) The **more dynamic the environment** (that is, the more rapidly it changes), the **more frequently planning and control reports** will be required.

 (iv) The larger the number of product markets an organisation is in, the more decentralised its planning and control system will be.

(b) **Technology**

 (i) The nature of the production process (for example, jobbing on the one hand or mass production on the other) determines the amount of cost allocation rather than cost apportionment that can be done.

 (ii) The complexity of the 'task' that an organisation performs affects the planning and control system. (For example, a railway operator's 'task' of getting people from A to B involves keeping them fed via a catering division, which will need a different type of planning and control system to the transport division.)

(c) **Organisational structure**

The **more complex the structure** of an organisation, **the more planning and control that will be required** and hence the more complex the system.

Question **Organisation**

In what ways has the design of your organisation's planning and control system been affected by factors such as organisational structure?

Exam focus point

In an exam you may be asked to describe how various factors provided in a scenario will affect an organisation's planning and control system. Use your imagination (and your common sense)!

3 Responsibility centres

Exam focus point

The examiner asked candidates to define cost centres, profit centres and investment centres in the June 2007 exam. The part-question, for nine marks, also asked for an appropriate performance measure for each and a difficulty of each measure.

FAST FORWARD

Responsibility centres can be divided into three types.

- Cost centres
- Profit centres
- Investment centres

Key term

Responsibility accounting is a system of accounting that segregates revenue and costs into areas of personal responsibility in order to monitor and assess the performance of each part of an organisation.

A **responsibility centre** is a function or department of an organisation that is headed by a manager who has direct responsibility for its performance.

If a manager is to bear responsibility for the performance of his area of the business he will need information about its performance. In essence, a manager needs to know three things.

Requirements	Examples of information
What are his resources?	Finance, inventories of raw materials, spare machine capacity, labour availability, the balance of expenditure remaining for a certain budget, target date for completion of a job.
At what rate are his resources being consumed?	How fast is his labour force working, how quickly are his raw materials being used up, how quickly are other expenses being incurred, how quickly is available finance being consumed?
How well are the resources being used?	How well are his objectives being met?

Decisions must also be made as to the level of detail that is provided and the frequency with which information is provided. Moreover the cost of providing information must be weighed against the benefit derived from it.

In a traditional system managers are given monthly reports, but there is no logical reason for this except that it ties in with financial reporting cycles and may be administratively convenient. With modern systems, however, there is a danger of **information overload**, since information technology allows the information required to be made available much more frequently.

The task of the management accountant, therefore, is to learn from the managers of responsibility centres what information they need, in what form and at what intervals, and then to design a planning and control system that enables this to be provided.

It is to this end that responsibility centres are usually divided into different categories. Here we shall describe cost centres, profit centres and investment centres.

3.1 Cost centres

Key term

A **cost centre** acts as a collecting place for certain costs before they are analysed further.

Cost centres may include the following.

(a) A **department**
(b) A **machine** or group of machines
(c) A **project** (eg the installation of a new computer system)
(d) A **new product** (allowing development costs to be identified)

To charge actual costs to a cost centre, each cost centre will have a **cost code**. Items of expenditure will be recorded with the appropriate cost code. When costs are eventually analysed, there may well be some apportionment of the costs of one cost centre to other cost centres.

(a) The costs of those cost centres which receive an apportionment of shared costs should be divided into directly attributable costs (for which the cost centre manager is responsible) and shared costs (for which another cost centre is directly accountable).

(b) The **control system** should **trace shared costs back to the cost centres from which the costs have been apportioned**, so that their **managers can be made accountable** for the costs incurred.

Information about cost centres might be collected in terms of **total actual costs, total budgeted costs** and **total cost variances** (the differences between actual and budged costs) sub-analysed perhaps into efficiency, usage and expenditure variances. In addition, the information might be analysed in terms of **ratios**, such as the following.

(a) Cost per unit produced (budget and actual)
(b) Hours per unit produced (budget and actual)
(c) Efficiency ratio
(d) Selling costs per $ of sales (budget and actual)
(e) Transport costs per tonne/kilometre (budget and actual)

3.2 Profit centres

Key term

A **profit centre** is any unit of an organisation (for example, division of a company) to which both revenues and costs are assigned, so that the profitability of the unit may be measured.

Profit centres differ from cost centres in that they **account for both costs and revenues** and the **key performance measure** of a profit centre is therefore **profit**.

For profit centres to have any validity in a planning and control system based on responsibility accounting, **the manager of the profit centre must have some influence over both revenues and costs**, that is, a say in both sales and production policies.

A profit centre manager is likely to be a fairly senior person within an organisation, and a profit centre is likely to cover quite a large area of operations. A profit centre might be an entire division within the organisation, or there might be a separate profit centre for each product, product range, brand or service that the organisation sells. Information requirements will be similarly focused, as appropriate.

In the hierarchy of responsibility centres within an organisation, there are likely to be several cost centres within a profit centre.

3.3 Revenue centres

A **revenue centre** is similar to a cost centre and a profit centre but is accountable for **revenues** only.

For revenue centres to have any validity in a planning and control system based on responsibility accounting, revenue centre managers should normally have control over how revenues are raised.

3.4 Investment centres

Key term

An **investment centre** is a profit centre whose performance is measured by its return on capital employed.

This implies that the **investment centre manager has some say in investment policy** in his area of operations as well as being responsible for costs and revenues.

Several profit centres might share the same capital items, for example the same buildings, stores or transport fleet, and so investment centres are likely to include several profit centres, and provide a basis for control at a very senior management level, like that of a subsidiary company within a group.

Control can be exercised by reporting information such as **profit/sales ratios, asset turnover ratios, cost/sales ratios**, and **cost variances**. In addition, the performance of investment centres can be measured by divisional comparisons.

3.5 Traceable and controllable costs

The main problem with measuring controllable performance is in deciding which costs are **controllable** and which costs are **traceable**. The performance of the manager of the division is indicated by the **controllable profit** (and it is on this that he is judged) and the success of the division as a whole is judged on the **traceable profit**.

Consider, for example, depreciation on divisional machinery. Would this be included as a controllable fixed cost or a traceable fixed cost? Because profit centre managers are only responsible for the **costs and revenues** under their control, this means that they do not have control over the investment in fixed assets. The depreciation on divisional machinery would therefore be a **traceable fixed cost** judging the performance of the division, and not of the individual manager.

Question — Cost, profit and investment centres

Find out if your organisation has a system of cost, profit and investment centres. What is the scope of planning and control within each centre?

4 Controllable costs

4.1 Controllable costs and uncontrollable costs

Managers of responsibility centres should only be held accountable for costs over which they have some influence. From a motivation point of view this is important because it can be very demoralising for managers who feel that their performance is being judged on the basis of something over which they have no influence. It is also important from a control point of view in that control reports should ensure that information on costs is reported to the manager who is able to take action to control them.

Key term

A **controllable cost** is 'A cost that can be controlled, typically by a cost, profit or investment centre manager'. (CIMA *Official Terminology*)

Responsibility accounting attempts to associate costs, revenues, assets and liabilities with the managers most capable of controlling them. As a system of accounting, it therefore distinguishes between controllable and uncontrollable costs. Most **variable costs** within a department are thought to be **controllable in the short term** because managers can influence the efficiency with which resources are used, even if they cannot do anything to raise or lower price levels.

A cost which is not controllable by a junior manager or supervisor might be controllable by a senior manager. For example, there may be high direct labour costs in a department caused by excessive overtime working. The supervisor may feel obliged to continue with the overtime in order to meet production schedules, but his senior may be able to reduce costs by deciding to hire extra full-time staff, thereby reducing the requirements for overtime.

A cost which is not controllable by a manager in one department may be controllable by a manager in another department. For example, an increase in material costs may be caused by buying at higher prices than expected (controllable by the purchasing department) or by excessive wastage and spoilage (controllable by the production department) or by a faulty machine producing a high number of rejects (controllable by the maintenance department).

Some costs are **non-controllable**, such as increases in expenditure items due to inflation. Other costs are **controllable, but in the long term rather than the short term**. For example, production costs might be reduced by the introduction of new machinery and technology, but in the short term, management must attempt to do the best they can with the resources and machinery at their disposal.

4.2 The controllability of fixed costs

It is often assumed that all fixed costs are non-controllable in the short run. This is not so.

(a) **Committed fixed costs** are those costs arising from the possession of plant, equipment, buildings and an administration department to **support the long-term needs of the business**. These costs (depreciation, rent, administration salaries) are largely **non-controllable in the short term** because they have been committed by longer-term decisions affecting longer-term needs. When a company decides to cut production drastically, the long-term committed fixed costs will be reduced, but arrangements for settling redundancy terms and the sale of assets cannot be made quickly and in the short term.

(b) **Discretionary fixed costs**, such as advertising, sales promotion, research and development, training costs and consultancy fees are costs which are incurred as a result of a top management decision, but which could be **raised or lowered at fairly short notice** (irrespective of the actual volume of production and sales).

4.3 Controllability and apportioned costs

Managers should only be held accountable for costs over which they have some influence. This may seem quite straightforward in theory, but it is not always so easy in practice to distinguish controllable from uncontrollable costs. **Apportioned overhead costs provide a good example**.

Suppose that a manager of a production department in a manufacturing company is made responsible for the costs of his department. These costs include **directly attributable overhead items** such as the costs of indirect labour employed in the department, the cost of metered power units consumed and indirect materials consumed in the department. However, the department's overhead costs also include an apportionment of costs from other costs centres, such as the following.

(a) Rent and rates for the building which the department shares with other departments.
(b) Share of the costs of the maintenance department
(c) A share of the costs of the central data processing department

Should the production manager be held accountable for any of these apportioned costs?

(a) Managers should not be held accountable for costs over which they have no control. In this example, apportioned rent and rates costs would not be controllable by the production department manager.

(b) Managers should be held accountable for costs over which they have some influence. In this example, it is the responsibility of the maintenance department manager to keep maintenance costs within budget and of the DP manager to keep central DP costs within budget. But their costs will be partly variable and partly fixed, and the variable cost element will depend on the volume of demand for their services (the rate of usage of the service). If the production department's staff treat their equipment badly we might expect higher repair costs, and the production department manager should therefore be made accountable for the repair costs that his department makes the maintenance department incur on its behalf.

Question — **Committed and discretionary costs**

Try to discover some of your organisation's committed fixed costs and discretionary fixed costs.

5 Planning

FAST FORWARD

Planning must cover both the long term and the short term.

An organisation should never be surprised by developments which occur gradually over an extended period of time because the organisation should have implemented a planning process. **Planning involves establishing objectives and selecting appropriate strategies to achieve those objectives**. It therefore forces management to think ahead systematically in both the short term and the long term.

The planning process

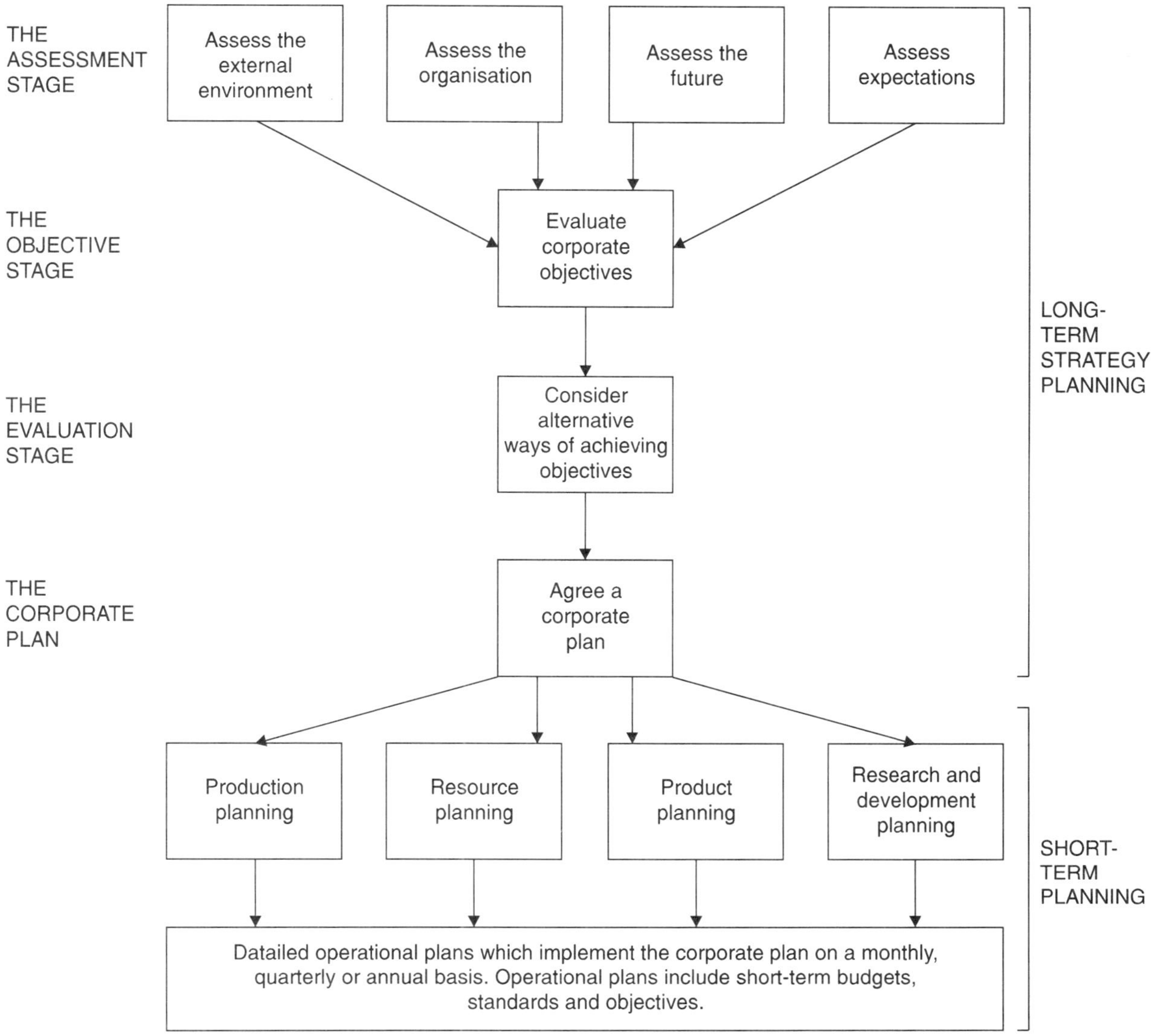

5.1 Long-term planning

Long-term planning, also known as **corporate planning**, involves selecting appropriate strategies so as to prepare a long-term plan to attain the objectives. The time span covered by a long-term plan depends on the organisation, the industry in which it operates and the particular environment involved. Typical periods are 2, 5, 7 or 10 years although longer periods are frequently encountered.

Long-term planning is a detailed, lengthy process, essentially incorporating three stages and ending with a corporate plan.

5.2 Short-term planning

The long-term corporate plan serves as the long-term framework for the organisation as a whole but for operational purposes it is necessary to **convert the corporate plan into a series of short-term plans**, usually covering one year, which relate to sections, functions or departments. The annual process of short-term planning should be seen as stages in the progressive fulfilment of the corporate plan as each short-term plan steers the organisation towards its long-term objectives. It is therefore vital that, to obtain the maximum advantage from short-term planning, some sort of long-term plan exists.

Question

Planning

More investigative work is needed from you here!

How is planning carried out in your organisation? Is there both long-term and short-term planning? What does each type of planning entail?

Answer

The activities in this chapter have required you to do some investigate work and to find out how planning and control is carried out in your organisation. Don't ignore these activities; the results of your investigations could well provide you with information that you can use in an exam.

Remember that this is a practical course and you need to relate the material covered to your work experience.

Chapter Roundup

- There are seven steps in the planning and control cycle.

  Step 1 Identify objectives

  Step 2 Identity potential strategies

  Step 3 Evaluate strategies

  Step 4 Choose alternative courses of action

  Step 5 Implement the long-term plan

  Step 6 Measure actual results and compare with plan

  Step 7 Respond to divergences from plan

- Responsibility centres can be divided into three types.
  – Cost centres
  – Profit centres
  – Investment centres
- Planning must cover both the long term and the short term.

Quick Quiz

1 What is the usual name for a short-term plan?

2 What is another name for strategic analysis?

3 What is responsibility accounting?

4 What is a profit centre?

5 Which of the following is an example of a discretionary cost?

A Material costs
B Advertising expenditure
C Cost of heating and lighting
D Salaries

6 Over which of the following can an investment centre manager exercise control?

I Controllable costs in the division
II Selling prices of the division's output
III The division's output volumes
IV Investment in the division's non-current assets and working capital

A All of them
B II and III
C I only
D IV only

Answers to Quick Quiz

1 A budget

2 Position audit

3 Responsibility accounting is a system of accounting that segregates revenue and costs into areas of personal responsibility in order to monitor and assess the performance of each part of an organisation.

4 A profit centre is any unit of an organisation (for example, division of a company) to which both revenues and costs are assigned, so that the profitability of the unit may be measured.

5 B A discretionary cost is a cost whose amount, within a particular time period, is determined by, and can be altered by, the budget holder.

6 A

Now try the questions below from the Exam Question Bank

Number	Level	Marks	Time
Section A: Q12	MCQ	N/A	N/A
Section B: Q8	Examination	20	36 mins

The budgetary process

9

Topic list
1 The functions of a budget
2 Administration of the budget
3 The budget preparation timetable
4 Functional budgets
5 Cash budgets
6 Budgeted income statement and statement of financial position (balance sheet)
7 The master budget
8 Computers and budgeting
9 Limiting factors

Study guide reference

		Syllabus reference
9(b)	Principal budget factors (demand, capacity and resource)	
	(i) Explain the importance of the principal budget factor in constructing a budget	6
	(ii) Describe principal budget factors (demand, capacity and resource)	6
	(iii) Identify the principal budget factor in a specific situation	
10(a)	Order of budget preparation	
	(i) Describe the order of budget construction relating to a specific limiting factor	6
	(ii) Prepare functional and departmental and master budgets in an appropriate order in a given situation	6
10(b)	Coordination of sub-budgets	
	(i) Explain the budget preparation timetable	6
	(ii) Describe relevant documentation produced and the management accountant's role in its production	6
	(iii) Describe the involvement of staff at all levels in the organisation in the budget preparation process and the effect on employee motivation of the approach adopted	6
	(iv) Describe the sources of information required for budget preparation and their likely limitations	6
10(c)	Revisions for limiting factors	
	(i) Explain how management might plan for variations in capacity levels	6
	(ii) Prepare budgets under varying capacity levels	6
11(a)	Prepare sales budgets	6
11(b)	Prepare functional budgets (production, raw materials usage and purchases, labour, fixed overheads)	6
11(c)	Discuss the preparation of discretionary expense budgets	6
11(d)	Prepare capital budgets	6
11(e)	Prepare cash budgets	6
11(f)	Prepare master budgets (profit and loss account and balance sheet)	6
12(b)	Use of computer based models	
	(i) Outline the role of spreadsheet models in budget construction	6
	(ii) Prepare simple spreadsheet formulae for budget construction	6
	(iii) Describe financial modelling software	6
	(iv) Describe 'what if' analysis and scenario planning	6
15(c)	Use of relevant computer packages	
	(i) Discuss the use of spreadsheets in flexing budgets	
	(ii) Prepare spreadsheet formulae for budget flexing	6

BPP LEARNING MEDIA

Exam focus point

This chapter covers a key syllabus area. Key syllabus areas usually account for 80% or more of the marks available on the exam paper.

1 The functions of a budget

FAST FORWARD

The functions of a **system of budgeting** are as follows.

- To ensure the achievement of the organisation's objectives
- To compel planning
- To communicate ideas and plans
- To co-ordinate activities
- To provide a framework for responsibility accounting
- To establish a system of control
- To motivate employees to improve their performance

A budget is a **quantified plan of action** for a forthcoming accounting period.

Key term

A **budget** is an organisation's plan for a forthcoming period, expressed in money terms.

A budget has two main purposes.

(a) To **compel planning**
(b) To **establish a system of control** by comparing budgeted and actual results

We shall be looking at these, and others, in more detail later on in this section of the chapter.

(a) **To compel planning**

Planning involves looking ahead into the future and setting out detailed plans. Plans are generally known as **budgets** and we shall be looking at the **budgetary process** in detail in this chapter and the next.

(b) **To establish a system of control**

Control over actual performance is provided by the comparisons of actual results against the budget plan. In the next section of this Interactive Text we will be looking at what happens when actual figures differ from expected **standards** and calculating **variances** to provide a basis for **control reporting**.

Exam focus point

Budget preparation is a key syllabus area.

There is no point in an organisation preparing a budget and not using it as a **control tool**. A beautifully laid out budgeted profit and loss account filed in the management accountant's file and never looked at again is worthless. The organisation should gain from both the actual preparation process and from the budget once it has been prepared.

Budgets are not prepared in isolation and then filed away; they have a number of important functions in an organisation.

Function	Detail
Ensure the achievement of the organisation's objectives	**Quantified expressions** of objectives are drawn up as targets to be achieved within the timescale of the budget plan.
Compel planning	Planning **forces management to look ahead**, to set out detailed plans for achieving the targets for each department, operation and (ideally) each manager and to anticipate problems.

Function	Detail
Communicate ideas and plans	A **formal system** is necessary to ensure that each person affected by the plans is aware of what he or she is supposed to be doing. Communication might be one-way, with managers giving orders to subordinates, or there might be a two-way dialogue.
Co-ordinate activities	The activities of different departments need to be **co-ordinated** to ensure maximum integration of effort towards **common goals**. This implies, for example, that the purchasing department should base its budget on production requirements and that the production budget should in turn be based on sales expectations.
Provide a framework for responsibility accounting	Budgets require that managers of budget centres are made **responsible** for the achievement of budget targets for the operations under their personal control.
Establish a system of control	Control over actual performance is provided by the comparisons of **actual results against the budget** plan. Departures from budget can then be **investigated** and the reasons for the departures can be divided into **controllable** and **uncontrollable** factors.
Motivate employees to improve their performance	The interest and commitment of employees can be retained if there is a system which lets them know how well or badly they are performing. The identification of controllable reasons for departures from budget with managers responsible provides an **incentive for improving future performance**.

2 Administration of the budget

FAST FORWARD

The **budget manual** is a collection of instructions governing the responsibilities of persons and the procedures, forms and records relating to the preparation and use of budgetary data.

Managers responsible for preparing budgets should ideally be the managers responsible for carrying out the budget.

The **budget committee** is the co-ordinating body in the preparation and administration of budgets.

Having seen why organisations prepare budgets, we will now turn our attention to the administrative procedures that ensure that the budget process works effectively.

2.1 The budget period

Key term

The **budget period** is the time period to which the budget relates.

Except for capital expenditure budgets, the budget period is commonly the accounting year (sub-divided into 12 or 13 control periods).

2.2 Budget documentation: the budget manual

Key term

The **budget manual** is a collection of instructions governing the responsibilities of persons and the procedures, forms and records relating to the preparation and use of budgetary data.

One of the functions of the budget is to improve communication. A budget manual should be produced so that everyone can refer to it for information and guidance about the budgeting process. The budget manual does *not* contain the actual budgets for the forthcoming period; it is more of an **instruction/information manual about the way budgeting operates** in a particular organisation.

A budget manual will usually be prepared by the management accountant.

Content	Detail
Explanation of the objectives of the budgeting process	• The purpose of budgetary planning and control • The objectives of the various stages of the budgeting process • The importance of budgets in the long-term planning and administration of the enterprise
Organisational structures	• An organisation chart • A list of individuals holding budget responsibilities
Outline of the principal budgets	• Relationship between them
Administrative details	• Membership, and terms of reference, of the budget committee • The sequence in which budgets are to be prepared • A timetable
Procedural matters	• Specimen forms and instructions for completing them • Specimen reports • Account codes (or a chart of accounts) • The name of the budget officer to whom enquiries must be sent

2.3 Responsibility for the preparation of budgets

Managers responsible for preparing budgets should ideally be the managers who are responsible for carrying out the budget. For example, the sales manager should draft the sales budget and selling overhead cost centre budget and the purchasing manager should draft the material purchases budget.

2.4 Budget committee

The **co-ordination** and **administration of budgets** is usually the **responsibility of a budget committee** (with the managing director as chairman). The budget committee is **assisted by a budget officer** who is usually an accountant. Every part of the organisation should be represented on the committee, so there should be a **representative from sales**, **production**, **marketing** and so on. Functions of the budget committee include the following.

(a) Co-ordination of the preparation of budgets, which includes the issue of the budget manual
(b) Issuing of timetables for the preparation of functional budgets
(c) Allocation of responsibilities for the preparation of functional budgets
(d) Provision of information to assist in the preparation of budgets
(e) Communication of final budgets to the appropriate managers
(f) Comparison of actual results with budget and the investigation of variances
(g) Continuous assessment of the budgeting and planning process, in order to improve the planning and control function

Question — Budgets

(a) Try to obtain a copy of your organisation's budget manual. Is it user friendly? Could it provide more useful information?

(b) Attempt to determine who is on your organisation's budget committee. What role do they play?

3 The budget preparation timetable

The **budget preparation process** is as follows.

- Communicating details of the budget policy and budget guidelines.
- Determining the factor that restricts output
- Preparation of the sales budget
- Initial preparation of budgets
- Negotiation of budgets with superiors
- Co-ordination and review of budgets
- Final acceptance of the budgets
- Budget review

The **principal budget factor** should be identified at the beginning of the budgetary process, and the budget for this is prepared before all the others.

The procedures involved in preparing a budget will differ from organisation to organisation, but the step-by-step approach described here is indicative of the steps followed by many organisations. The preparation of a budget may take weeks or months and the budget committee may meet several times before an organisation's budget is finally agreed.

Step 1 **Communicating details of the budget policy and budget guidelines**

The long-term plan is the starting point for the preparation of the annual budget. Managers responsible for preparing the budget must be aware of the way it is affected by the long-term plan so that it becomes part of the process of meeting the organisation's objectives. For example, if the long-term plan calls for a more aggressive pricing policy, the budget must take this into account. Managers should also be provided with important guidelines for wage rate increases, changes in productivity and so on, as well as information about industry demand and output.

Step 2 **Determining the factor that restricts output**

Key term

The **principal budget factor** (or **key budget factor** or **limiting budget factor)** is the factor that limits an organisation's performance for a given period and is often the starting point in budget preparation.

For example, a company's sales department might estimate that it could sell 1,000 units of product X, which would require 5,000 hours of grade A labour to produce. If there are no units of product X already in inventory, and only 4,000 hours of grade A labour available in the budget period, then the company would be unable to sell 1,000 units of X because of the shortage of labour hours. Grade A labour would be a limiting budget factor, and the company's management must choose one of the following options.

(a) Reduce budgeted sales by 20%.

(b) Try to increase the availability of grade A labour by 1,000 hours (25%) by recruitment or overtime working.

(c) Try to sub-contract the production of 1,000 units to another manufacturer, but still profit on the transaction.

In most organisations the principal budget factor is sales demand: a company is usually restricted from making and selling more of its products because there would be no sales demand for the increased output at a price which would be acceptable/profitable to the company. The principal budget factor may also be machine capacity, distribution and selling resources, the availability of key raw materials or the availability of cash. Once this factor is defined then the rest of the budget can be prepared. For example, if sales are the principal budget factor then the production manager can only prepare his budget after the sales budget is complete.

However in the public sector, the principal budget factor will not be profit related. You need to think about the limiting factor for these organisations in terms of activity, for insurance consultant availability, cash budget or accommodation.

Exam focus point

> In the December 2005 exam candidates were asked to explain what a principal budget factor is and suggest what this could be for a hospital. Three marks were available for this activity.

Question

Principal budget factor

In the NHS and other public sector organisations, the principal budget factor may not be the same as that faced by private sector organisations.

Required

List three or four limiting factors that would apply to public sector organisations.

Answer

Remember that state-run organisations providing services free at the point of consumption often face almost unlimited demand for their services. Therefore resources available usually comprise the limiting factor:

(a) Cash from government grants and ministries
(b) Trained staff such as nurses and doctors
(c) Equipment such as MRI scanners and hospital beds

Step 3 **Preparation of the sales budget**

For many organisations, the principal budget factor is sales volume. The sales budget is therefore often the primary budget from which the majority of the other budgets are derived.

Before the sales budget can be prepared a **sales forecast** has to be made. Chapter 7 highlighted the link between forecasts and budgets and outlined some sales forecasting methods (such as time series analysis).

Sales forecasting is complex and involves the consideration of a number of factors.

(a) Past sales patterns
(b) The economic environment
(c) Results of market research
(d) Anticipated advertising
(e) Competition
(f) Changing consumer taste
(g) New legislation
(h) Distribution
(i) Pricing policies and discounts offered
(j) Legislation
(k) Environmental factors

Management can use a number of forecasting methods.

(a) Sales personnel can be asked to provide estimates.
(b) Market research can be used (especially if an organisation is considering introducing a new product or service).
(c) Various mathematical techniques can be used to estimate sales levels.
(d) Annual contracts, under which major customers set out in advance monthly ranges of possible sales, can be reviewed.

On the basis of the sales forecast and the production capacity of the organisation, a sales budget will be prepared. This may be subdivided, possible subdivisions being by product, by sales area or by management responsibility.

Step 4 **Initial preparation of budgets**

Budget	Detail
Finished goods inventory budget	Decides the planned increase or decrease in finished inventory levels.

Budget	Detail
Production budget	Stated in units of each product and is calculated as the sales budget in units plus the budgeted increase in finished goods inventories or minus the budgeted decrease in finished goods inventories.
Budgets of resources for production	**Materials usage budget** is stated in quantities and perhaps cost for each type of material used. It should take into account budgeted losses in production. **Machine utilisation budget** shows the operating hours required on each machine or group of machines. **Labour budget or wages budget** will be expressed in hours for each grade of labour and in terms of cost. It should take into account budgeted idle time.
Overhead cost budgets	**Production overheads** **Administration overheads** **Selling and distribution overheads** **Research and development department overheads**
Raw materials inventory budget	Decides the planned increase or decrease of the level of inventories.
Raw materials purchase budget	Can be prepared in quantities and value for each type of material purchased once the raw material usage requirements and the raw materials inventory budget are known.
Overhead absorption rate	Can be calculated once the production volumes are planned, and the overhead cost centre budgets prepared.

Step 5 **Negotiation of budgets with superiors**

Once a manager has prepared his draft budget he should submit it to his superior for approval. The superior should then incorporate this budget with the others for which he or she is responsible and then submit this budget for approval to his or her superior. This process continues until the final budget is presented to the budget committee for approval.

At each stage of the process, the **budget** would be **negotiated between the manager who had prepared the budget and his/her superior** until agreed by both parties.

Step 6 **Co-ordination of budgets**

It is unlikely that the above steps will be problem-free. The budgets must be reviewed in relation to one another. Such a **review may indicate that some budgets are out of balance with others and need modifying**. The budget officer must identify such inconsistencies and bring them to the attention of the manager concerned. The **revision of one budget may lead to the revision of all budgets**. During this process the budgeted income statement and budgeted balance sheet and cash budget should be prepared to ensure that all of the individual parts of the budget combine into an acceptable master budget.

Step 7 **Final acceptance of the budget**

When all the budgets are in harmony with one another they are summarised into a **master budget** consisting of a budgeted income statement, budgeted balance sheet and cash budget.

Step 8 **Budget review**

The budgeting process does not stop once the budgets have been agreed. Actual results should be compared on a regular basis with the budgeted results. The frequency with which such comparisons are made depends very much on the organisation's circumstances and the sophistication of its control systems but it should occur at least monthly. Management should receive a report detailing the differences and should investigate the reasons for the differences. **If the differences are within the control of management, corrective action should be taken** to bring the reasons for the difference under control and to ensure that such inefficiencies do not occur in the future.

The **differences may have occurred, however, because the budget was unrealistic to begin with or because the actual conditions did not reflect those anticipated (or could have possibly been anticipated)**. This would therefore invalidate the remainder of the budget.

The **budget committee**, who should meet periodically to evaluate the organisation's actual performance, **may need to reappraise the organisation's future plans in the light of changes to anticipated conditions and to adjust the budget to take account of such changes**.

The important point to note is that the budgeting process does not end for the current year once the budget period has begun: budgeting should be seen as a continuous and dynamic process.

Question

Budget preparation

A company that manufactures and sells a range of products, with sales potential limited by market share, is considering introducing a system of budgeting.

Required

(a) List (in order of preparation) the budgets that need to be prepared.

(b) State which budgets the master budget will comprise.

(c) Consider how the work outlined in (a) and (b) can be co-ordinated in order for the budgeting process to be successful.

Answer

(a) The sequence of budget preparation will be roughly as follows.

  (i) Sales budget
  (The market share limits demand and so sales is the principal budget factor. All other activities will depend upon this forecast.)

  (ii) Finished goods inventory budget (in units)

  (iii) Production budget (in units)

  (iv) Production resources budgets (materials, machine hours, labour)

  (v) Overhead budgets for production, administration, selling and distribution, research and development and so on

  (vi) Cash budget

(b) The master budget is the summary of all the budgets. It often includes a summary income statement, statement of financial position (balance sheet) and cash budget.

(c) Procedures for preparing budgets can be contained in a budget manual which shows which budgets must be prepared when and by whom, what each functional budget should contain and detailed directions on how to prepare budgets including, for example, expected price increases, rates of interest, rates of depreciation and so on.

The formulation of budgets can be co-ordinated by a budget committee comprising the senior executives of the departments responsible for carrying out the budgets: sales, production, purchasing, personnel and so on.

The budgeting process may also be assisted by the use of a spreadsheet/computer budgeting package.

4 Functional budgets

Exam focus point

A full twenty-mark question in the June 2006 exam covered production and labour budgets. The budgets had to be prepared and then adjusted for changes in inventory and labour hours.

Key term

Functional (or **departmental) budgets** are the budgets for the various functions and departments of an organisation. They therefore include production budgets, marketing budgets, sales budgets, personnel budgets, purchasing budgets and research and development budgets.

We will look at the preparation of a number of types of functional budget in this chapter but the general principles covered can be applied in most situations.

You must work through the examples here and make sure that you understand the principles well as this area is regularly examined.

4.1 Production cost budget

If the principal budget factor was production capacity then the production cost budget would be the first to be prepared.
To assess whether production is the principal budget factor, the **production capacity available** must be determined. This should take into account the following factors.

(a) **Available labour**, including idle time, overtime and standard output rates per hour

(b) **Availability of raw materials** including allowances for losses during production

(d) **Maximum machine hours available**, including expected idle time and expected output rates per machine hour

It is, however, normally sales volume that is the constraint and therefore the production budget is prepared after the sales budget and the finished goods inventory budget.

The **production cost budget** will show the **quantities** and **costs** for **each product** and product group and will tie in with the sales and inventory budgets. This co-ordinating process is likely to show any shortfalls or excesses in capacity at various times over the budget period. If there is likely to be a shortfall then consideration should be given to overtime, subcontracting, machine hire, new sources of raw materials or some other way of increasing output. A significant shortfall means that production capacity is, in fact, the limiting factor.

If capacity exceeds sales volume for a length of time then consideration should be given to product diversification, a reduction in selling price (if demand is price elastic) and so on.

Once the production budget has been finalised, the labour, materials and machine budgets can be drawn up. These budgets will be based on budgeted activity levels, existing inventory positions and projected labour and material costs.

4.2 Example: the preparation of the production budget and direct labour budget

Pearson manufactures two products, P and L, and is preparing its budget for 20X3. Both products are made by the same grade of labour, grade G. The company currently holds 800 units of P and 1,200 units of L in inventory, but 250 of these units of L have just been discovered to have deteriorated in quality, and must therefore be scrapped. Budgeted sales of P are 3,000 units and of L 4,000 units, provided that the company maintains finished goods inventories at a level equal to three months' sales.

Grade G labour was originally expected to produce one unit of P in two hours and one unit of L in three hours, at an hourly rate of $2.50 per hour. In discussions with trade union negotiators, however, it has been agreed that the hourly wage rate should be raised by 50c per hour, provided that the times to produce P and L are reduced by 20%.

Required

Prepare the production budget and direct labour budget for 20X3.

4.3 Solution

The expected time to produce a unit of P will now be 80% of 2 hours = 1.6 hours, and the time for a unit of L will be 2.4 hours. The hourly wage rate will be $3, so that the direct labour cost will be $4.80 for P and $7.20 for L (thus achieving a saving for the company of 20c per unit of P produced and 30c per unit of L).

(a) *Production budget*

		Product P			*Product L*	
		Units	Units		Units	Units
Budgeted sales			3,000			4,000
Closing inventories	(3/12 × 3,000)	750		(3/12 × 4,000)	1,000	
Opening inventories (minus inventories scrapped)		800			950	
(Decrease)/increase in inventories			(50)			50
Production			2,950			4,050

(b) *Direct labour budget*

	Grade G	*Cost*
	Hours	$
2,950 units of product P	4,720	14,160
4,050 units of product L	9,720	29,160
Total	14,440	43,320

It is assumed that there will be no idle time among grade G labour which, if it existed, would have to be paid for at the rate of $3 per hour.

4.4 Labour budget

A useful concept in budgeting for labour requirements is the standard hour.

Key term

A **standard hour** is the quantity of work achievable at standard performance, expressed in terms of a standard unit of work done in a standard period of time.

Budgeted output of different products or jobs in a period can be converted into standard hours of production, and a labour budget constructed accordingly.

Standard hours are particularly useful when management wants to monitor the production levels of a variety of dissimilar units. For example product A may take five hours to produce and product B, seven hours. If four units of each product are produced, instead of saying that total output is eight units, we could state the production level as
(4 × 5) + (4 × 7) standard hours = 48 standard hours.

4.5 Example: direct labour budget based on standard hours

Canaervon manufactures a single product, the close, with a single grade of labour. Its sales budget and finished goods inventory budget for period 3 are as follows.

Sales	700 units
Opening inventories, finished goods	50 units
Closing inventories, finished goods	70 units

The goods are inspected only when production work is completed, and it is budgeted that 10% of finished work will be scrapped.

The standard direct labour hour content of the close is three hours. The budgeted productivity ratio for direct labour is only 80% (which means that labour is only working at 80% efficiency).

The company employs 18 direct operatives, who are expected to average 144 working hours each in period 3.

Required

(a) Prepare a production budget.

(b) Prepare a direct labour budget.

(c) Comment on the problem that your direct labour budget reveals, and suggest how this problem might be overcome.

4.6 Solution

(a) *Production budget*

	Units
Sales	700
Add closing inventory	70
	770
Less opening inventory	50
Production required of 'good' output	720
Wastage rate	10%

Total production required $720 \times \frac{100^*}{90} = 800\,\text{units}$

(* Note that the required adjustment is 100/90, not 110/100, since the waste is assumed to be 10% of total production, not 10% of good production.)

(b) Now we can prepare the direct labour budget.

Standard hours per unit	3
Total standard hours required = 800 units × 3 hours	2,400 hours
Productivity ratio	80%

Actual hours required $2{,}400 \times \frac{100}{80} = 3{,}000\,\text{hours}$

(c) If we look at the direct labour budget against the information provided, we can identify the problem.

	Hours
Budgeted hours available (18 operatives × 144 hours)	2,592
Actual hours required	3,000
Shortfall in labour hours	408

The (draft) budget indicates that there will not be enough direct labour hours to meet the production requirements. This problem might be overcome in one, or a combination, of the following ways.

(a) Reduce the closing inventory requirement below 70 units. This would reduce the number of production units required.

(b) Persuade the workforce to do some overtime working.

(c) Perhaps recruit more direct labour if long-term prospects are for higher production volumes.

(d) Discuss with the workforce (or their union representatives) the following possibilities.

(i) Improve the productivity ratio, and so reduce the number of hours required to produce the output.

(ii) If possible, reduce the wastage rate below 10%.

4.7 Material purchases budget

Question — Material budget

Taylors manufactures two products, W and S, which use the same raw materials, R and T. One unit of W uses 3 litres of R and 4 kilograms of T. One unit of S uses 5 litres of R and 2 kilograms of T. A litre of R is expected to cost $3 and a kilogram of T $7.

Budgeted sales for 20X2 are 8,000 units of W and 6,000 units of S; finished goods in inventory at 1 January 20X2 are 1,500 units of W and 300 units of S, and the company plans to hold inventories of 600 units of each product at 31 December 20X2.

Inventories of raw material are 6,000 litres of R and 2,800 kilograms of T at 1 January, and the company plans to hold 5,000 litres and 3,500 kilograms respectively at 31 December 20X2.

The warehouse and stores managers have suggested that a provision should be made for damages and deterioration of items held in store, as follows.

Product W :	loss of 50 units
Product S :	loss of 100 units
Material R :	loss of 500 litres
Material T :	loss of 200 kilograms

Required

Prepare a material purchases budget for the year 20X2.

Answer

To calculate material purchase requirements, it is first of all necessary to calculate the budgeted production volumes and material usage requirements.

	Product W		*Product S*	
	Units	Units	Units	Units
Sales		8,000		6,000
Provision for losses		50		100
Closing inventory	600		600	
Opening inventory	1,500		300	
(Decrease)/increase in inventory		(900)		300
Production budget		7,150		6,400

	Material R		*Material T*	
	Litres	Litres	Kg	Kg
Usage requirements				
To produce 7,150 units of W		21,450		28,600
To produce 6,400 units of S		32,000		12,800
Usage budget		53,450		41,400
Provision for losses		500		200
		53,950		41,600
Closing inventory	5,000		3,500	
Opening inventory	6,000		2,800	
(Decrease)/increase in inventory		(1,000)		700
Material purchases budget		52,950		42,300
Cost per unit		$3 per litre		$7 per kg
Cost of material purchases		$158,850		$296,100
Total purchases cost		$454,950		

Exam focus point

> The preparation of a material purchases budget will often require you to manipulate the expression:
>
> opening inventory + purchases – closing inventory = material used in production
>
> A material purchases figure is therefore given by:
>
> closing inventory + material used in production – opening inventory
>
> Likewise a production budget may require manipulation of the expression:
>
> opening inventory + units produced – closing inventory = sales

Now try the following question which draws together budget preparation for functional budgets. Remember the order in which budgets must be prepared using the steps in Section 3.

Question — Functional budget

XYZ company produces three products X, Y and Z. For the coming accounting period budgets are to be prepared based on the following information.

Budgeted sales

Product X	2,000 at $100 each
Product Y	4,000 at $130 each
Product Z	3,000 at $150 each

Budgeted usage of raw material

	RM11	*RM22*	*RM33*
Product X	5	2	-
Product Y	3	2	2
Product Z	2	1	3
Cost per unit of material	$5	$3	$4

Finished inventories budget

	Product X	*Product Y*	*Product Z*
Opening	500	800	700
Closing	600	1,000	800

Raw materials inventory budget

	RM11	*RM22*	*RM33*
Opening	21,000	10,000	16,000
Closing	18,000	9,000	12,000

	Product X	*Product Y*	*Product Z*
Expected hours per unit	4	6	8
Expected hourly rate (labour)	$9	$9	$9

Fill in the blanks.

(a) **Sales budget**

	Product X	*Product Y*	*Product Z*	*Total*
Sales quantity	☐	☐	☐	
Sales value	$ ☐	$ ☐	$ ☐	$ ☐

(b) **Production budget**

	Product X Units	*Product Y* Units	*Product Z* Units
Budgeted production	☐	☐	☐

(c) **Material usage budget**

	RM11 Units	RM22 Units	RM33 Units
Budgeted material usage			

(d) **Material purchases budget**

	RM11	RM22	RM33
Budgeted material purchases	$	$	$

(e) **Labour budget**

Budgeted total wages	$

Answer

(a)

	Product X	*Sales budget* *Product Y*	*Product Z*	*Total*
Sales quantity	2,000	4,000	3,000	
Sales price	$100	$130	$150	
Sales value	$ 200,000	$ 520,000	$ 450,000	$ 1,170,000

(b)

	Production budget		
	Product X	*Product Y*	*Product Z*
	Units	Units	Units
Sales quantity	2,000	4,000	3,000
Closing inventories	600	1,000	800
	2,600	5,000	3,800
Less opening inventories	500	800	700
Budgeted production	2,100	4,200	3,100

(c)

		Material usage budget		
	Production	*RM11*	*RM22*	*RM33*
	Units	Units	Units	Units
Product X	2,100	10,500	4,200	-
Product Y	4,200	12,600	8,400	8,400
Product Z	3,100	6,200	3,100	9,300
Budgeted material usage		29,300	15,700	17,700

(d)

	Material purchases budget		
	RM11	*RM22*	*RM33*
	Units	Units	Units
Budgeted material usage	29,300	15,700	17,700
Closing inventories	18,000	9,000	12,000
	47,300	24,700	29,700
Less opening inventories	21,000	10,000	16,000
Budgeted material purchases	26,300	14,700	13,700

Standard cost per unit	$5	$3	$4
Budgeted material purchases	$131,500	$44,100	$54,800

(e)

Product	Production	Hours required per unit	Labour budget Total hours	Rate per hour	Cost
	Units			$	$
X	2,100	4	8,400	9	75,600
Y	4,200	6	25,200	9	226,800
Z	3,100	8	24,800	9	223,200
Budgeted total wages					525,600

4.8 Budgets for departments not involved in manufacturing

Budgets are also prepared for those departments and functions not involved in manufacturing. An organisation may therefore also prepare an administration budget, a marketing budget, a research and development budget and so on. Such budgets do *not* take as their starting point the sales budget (if sales are the principal budget factor) because the level of administration costs, say, is unlikely to vary in proportion to the level of sales. Instead the administration cost budget will be drawn up following meetings between the management accountant and various members of staff ranging from the managing director down to office managers and supervisors. In Chapter 11, we will be examining a method of budgeting called zero based budgeting, which is ideal for budgeting in such cases.

The example below shows a typical marketing cost budget. Notice that only the selling and agency commission varies directly with the level of sales.

ABC: MARKETING COST BUDGET

Description/detail of cost items	$'000
Salaries and wages of marketing staff	X
Advertising expenses	X
Travelling and distribution costs	X
Market research activities	X
Promotional activities and marketing relations	X
Selling and agency commission ($2^1/_2$% of sales)	X
	X

4.9 Co-ordination of functional budgets

It is vital that the functional budgets are prepared in the correct order (for example, the material usage budget should be prepared after the production budget) and that the **overall process is co-ordinated** to ensure that the budgets are all in balance with each other. There is little point in the material usage budget being based on a budgeted production level of 10,000 units if the budgeted production level specified in the production budget is 15,000 units.

FAST FORWARD

Once prepared, the **functional budgets** must be reviewed to ensure they are consistent with one another.

5 Cash budgets

Key term

A **cash budget** is a detailed budget of cash inflows and outflows incorporating both revenue and capital items.

A cash budget is thus a statement in which estimated future cash receipts and payments are tabulated in such a way as to show the forecast cash balance of a business at defined intervals. Cash budgets are examined in paper 10 so we will not dwell on them here. You only need to understand how they fit into the budgetary process for your Paper 7 exam.

6 Budgeted income statement and statement of financial position (balance sheet)

Exam focus point

In the December 2005 exam, up to twelve marks could be earned for preparing an income and expenditure budget for a hospital department. A question in the June 2006 exam asked for a **budgeted profit statement** under two circumstances. Those were where a product is discontinued and where it is retained. There were fourteen marks available in total for the two calculations.

As well as wishing to forecast its cash position, a business might want to estimate its profitability and its financial position for a coming period. This would involve the preparation of a budgeted income statement and balance sheet, along with the cash budget which form the master budget.

Just like historical financial statements, **budgeted accounts are based on the accruals concept**. If you keep this point in mind you will often be able to cut through the deliberately confusing detail of examination questions to prepare an answer very quickly.

6.1 Example: preparing a budgeted income statement and statement of financial position (balance sheet)

Using the information below, you are required to prepare Peter Blair's budgeted income statement for the six months ending on 31 March 20X4 and a budgeted balance sheet as at that date.

6.1.1 Example

Peter Blair has worked for some years as a sales representative, but has recently been made redundant. He intends to start up in business on his own account, using $15,000 which he currently has invested with a building society. Peter maintains a bank account showing a small credit balance, and he plans to approach his bank for the necessary additional finance. Peter asks you for advice and provides the following additional information.

(a) Arrangements have been made to purchase fixed assets costing $8,000. These will be paid for at the end of September 20X3 and are expected to have a five-year life, at the end of which they will possess a nil residual value.

(b) Inventories costing $5,000 will be acquired on 28 September 20X3 and subsequent monthly purchases will be at a level sufficient to replace forecast sales for the month.

(c) Forecast monthly sales are $3,000 for October, $6,000 for November and December, and $10,500 from January 20X4 onwards.

(d) Selling price is fixed at the cost of stock plus 50%.

(e) Two months' credit will be allowed to customers but only one month's credit will be received from suppliers of inventory.

(f) Running expenses, including rent but excluding depreciation of fixed assets, are estimated at $1,600 per month.

(g) Blair intends to make monthly cash drawings of $1,000.

(h) Peter has prepared a cash budget for his bank manager. This shows a closing bank balance of $12,100 outdrawn at 31 March 20X4.

Required

Prepare a budgeted income statement and statement of financial position (balance sheet) for the six months to 31 March 20X4.

6.2 Solution

6.2.1 Notes to help you

Payments to suppliers could be a little tricky. We are told that selling price = cost of sales × 150% = cost of sales × 150/100, and so cost of sales is 100/150 × sales. Thus for March cost of sales is 100/150 × $10,500 = $7,000. These goods will be purchased in March but not paid for until April.

The income statement

The income statement is straightforward. The first figure is sales, which can be computed very easily from the information in the question. It is sufficient to add up the monthly sales figures given there; for the income statement there is no need to worry about any closing receivables. Similarly, cost of sales is calculated directly from the information on gross margin contained in the question.

Depreciation is over five years so the depreciation rate is 20%.

FORECAST TRADING AND INCOME STATEMENT
FOR THE SIX MONTHS ENDING 31 MARCH 20X4

	$	$
Sales (3,000 + (2 × 6,000) + (3 × 10,500))		46,500
Cost of sales (2/3 × $46,500)		31,000
Gross profit		15,500
Expenses		
Running expenses (6 × $1,600)	9,600	
Depreciation ($8,000 × 20% × 6/12)	800	
		10,400
Net profit		5,100

Items will be shown in the balance sheet as follows.

(a) Inventory will comprise the initial purchases of $5,000 (as month-end inventory levels are constant).

(b) Receivables will comprise sales made in February and March (not paid until April and May respectively).

(c) Payables will comprise purchases made in March (not paid for until April).

(d) The bank overdraft is the closing cash figure computed in the cash budget.

FORECAST STATEMENT OF FINANCIAL POSITION (BALANCE SHEET) AT 31 MARCH 20X4

ASSETS	$	$
Non-current assets $(8,000 – 800 depreciation)		7,200
Current assets		
Inventories	5,000	
Receivables (2 × $10,500)	21,000	
		26,000
		33,200
EQUITY AND LIABILITIES		
Proprietor's interest		
Capital introduced		15,000
Profit for the period	5,100	
Less drawings	6,000	
Deficit retained		(900)
		14,100
Current liabilities		
Bank overdraft	12,100	
Trade payables (March purchases)	7,000	
		19,100
		33,200

Budget questions are often accompanied by a large amount of sometimes confusing detail. This should not blind you to the fact that many figures can be entered very simply from the logic of the trading situation described. For example in the case of Blair you might feel tempted to begin a T-account to compute the closing receivables figure. This kind of working is rarely necessary, since you are told that receivables take two months to pay. Closing receivables will equal total credit sales in the last two months of the period.

Similarly, you may be given a simple statement that a business pays rates at $1,500 a year, followed by a lot of detail to enable you to calculate a prepayment at the beginning and end of the year. If you are preparing a budgeted income statement for the year do not lose sight of the fact that the rates expense can be entered as $1,500 without any calculation at all.

7 The master budget

Key term

When all the functional budgets have been prepared, they are summarised and consolidated into a **master budget** which consists of the budgeted income statement, budgeted balance sheet and cash budget and which provides the overall picture of the planned performance for the budget period

FAST FORWARD

The **master budget** consists of a budgeted income statement, a budgeted statement of financial position (balance sheet) and a cash budget.

7.1 Example: a master budget

Plagued Engineering produces two products, Niks and Args. The budget for the forthcoming year to 31 March 20X8 is to be prepared. Expectations for the forthcoming year include the following.

(a) PLAGUED ENGINEERING
STATEMENT OF FINANCIAL POSITION (BALANCE SHEET) AS AT 1 APRIL 20X7

ASSETS	$	$
Non-current assets		
Land and buildings		45,000
Plant and equipment at cost	187,000	
Less accumulated depreciation	75,000	
		112,000
Current assets		
Raw materials	7,650	
Finished goods	23,600	
Debtors	19,500	
Cash	4,300	
		55,050
		212,050
EQUITY AND LIABILITIES		
Capital and assets		
Share capital		150,000
Accumulated profits		55,250
		205,250
Current liabilities		
Payables		6,800
		212,050

(b) *Finished products*

The sales director has estimated the following.

		Niks	*Args*
(i)	Demand for the company's products	4,500 units	4,000 units
(ii)	Selling price per unit	$32	$44
(iii)	Closing inventory of finished products at 31 March 20X8	400 units	1,200 units
(iv)	Opening inventory of finished products at 1 April 20X7	900 units	200 units
(v)	Unit cost of this opening inventory	$20	$28
(vi)	Amount of plant capacity required for each unit of product		
	Machining	15 min	24 min
	Assembling	12 min	18 min
(vii)	Raw material content per unit of each product		
	Material A	1.5 kilos	0.5 kilos
	Material B	2.0 kilos	4.0 kilos
(viii)	Direct labour hours required per unit of each product	6 hours	9 hours

Finished goods are valued on a FIFO basis at full production cost.

(c) *Raw materials*

		Material A	*Material B*
(i)	Closing inventory requirement in kilos at 31 March 20X8	600	1,000
(ii)	Opening inventory at 1 April 20X7 in kilos	1,100	6,000
(iii)	Budgeted cost of raw materials per kilo	$1.50	$1.00

Actual costs per kilo of opening inventories are as budgeted cost for the coming year.

(d) *Direct labour*

The standard wage rate of direct labour is $1.60 per hour.

(e) *Production overhead*

Production overhead is absorbed on the basis of machining hours, with separate absorption rates for each department. The following overheads are anticipated in the production cost centre budgets.

	Machining department	*Assembling department*
	$	$
Supervisors' salaries	10,000	9,150
Power	4,400	2,000
Maintenance and running costs	2,100	2,000
Consumables	3,400	500
General expenses	19,600	5,000
	39,500	18,650

Depreciation is taken at 5% straight line on plant and equipment. A machine costing the company $20,000 is due to be installed on 1 October 20X7 in the machining department, which already has machinery installed to the value of $100,000 (at cost). Land worth $180,000 is to be acquired in December 20X7.

(f) *Selling and administration expenses*

	$
Sales commissions and salaries	14,300
Travelling and distribution	3,500
Office salaries	10,100
General administration expenses	2,500
	30,400

(g) There is no opening or closing work in progress and inflation should be ignored.

(h) Budgeted cash flows are as follows.

	Quarter 1	*Quarter 2*	*Quarter 3*	*Quarter 4*
Receipts from customers	70,000	100,000	100,000	40,000
Payments:				
Materials	7,000	9,000	10,000	5,000
Wages	33,000	20,000	11,000	15,000
Other costs and expenses	10,000	100,000	205,000	5,000

Required

Prepare the following for the year ended 31 March 20X8 for Plagued Engineering Ltd.

(a) Sales budget
(b) Production budget (in quantities)
(c) Plant utilisation budget
(d) Direct materials usage budget
(e) Direct labour budget
(f) Factory overhead budget
(g) Computation of the factory cost per unit for each product
(h) Direct materials purchases budget
(i) Cost of goods sold budget
(j) Cash budget
(k) A budgeted income statement account and balance sheet

7.2 Solution

(a) *Sales budget*

	Market demand	*Selling price*	*Sales value*
	Units	$	$
Niks	4,500	32.00	144,000
Args	4,000	44.00	176,000
			320,000

(b) *Production budget*

	Niks	*Args*
	Units	Units
Sales requirement	4,500	4,000
(Decrease)/increase in finished goods inventory	(500)	1,000
Production requirement	4,000	5,000

(c) *Plant utilisation budget*

Product		*Machining*		*Assembling*	
	Units	Hours per unit	Total hours	Hours per unit	Total hours
Niks	4,000	0.25	1,000	0.20	800
Args	5,000	0.40	2,000	0.30	1,500
			3,000		2,300

(d) *Direct materials usage budget*

		Material A	*Material B*
		kg	kg
Required for production:			
Niks:	4,000 × 1.5 kilos	6,000	–
	4,000 × 2.0 kilos	–	8,000
Args:	5,000 × 0.5 kilos	2,500	–
	5,000 × 4.0 kilos	–	20,000
Material usage		8,500	28,000
Unit cost		$1.50 per kilo	$1.00 per kilo
Cost of materials used		$12,750	$28,000

(e) *Direct labour budget*

Product	Production Units	Hours required per unit	Total hours	Rate per hour $	Cost $
Niks	4,000	6	24,000	1.60	38,400
Args	5,000	9	45,000	1.60	72,000
			Total direct wages		110,400

(f) *Production overhead budget*

	Machining dept $	*Assembling dept* $
Production overhead allocated and apportioned (excluding depreciation)	39,500	18,650
Depreciation costs		
(i) Existing plant		
(5% of $100,000 in machining)	5,000	
(5% of $87,000 in assembly)		4,350
(ii) Proposed plant		
(5% of $^6/_{12}$ × $20,000)	500	
Total production overhead	45,000	23,000
Total machine hours (see (c))	3,000 hrs	2,300 hrs
Absorption rate per machine hour	$15	$10

(g) *Cost of finished goods*

		Niks $		*Args* $
Direct material A	1.5 kg × $1.50	2.25	0.5 kg × $1.50	0.75
B	2.0 kg × $1.00	2.00	4.0 kg × $1.00	4.00
Direct labour	6 hrs × $1.60	9.60	9 hrs × $1.60	14.40
Production overhead				
Machining department	15 mins at $15 per hr	3.75	24 min at $15 per hr	6.00
Assembling department	12 mins at $10 per hr	2.00	18 mins at $10 per hr	3.00
Production cost per unit		19.60		28.15

(h) *Direct material purchases budget*

	A kg	*B* kg
Closing inventory required	600	1,000
Production requirements	8,500	28,000
	9,100	29,000
Less opening inventory	1,100	6,000
Purchase requirements	8,000	23,000
Cost per unit	$1.50	$1.00
Purchase costs	$12,000	$23,000

(i) *Cost of goods sold budget* (Using FIFO)

	Niks Units		$	*Args* Units		$
Opening inventories	900	(× 20.00)	18,000	200	(× 28.00)	5,600
Cost of production	4,000	(× 19.60)	78,400	5,000	(× 28.15)	140,750
	4,900		96,400	5,200		146,350
Less closing inventories	400	(× 19.60)	7,840	1,200	(× 28.15)	33,780
Cost of sales	4,500		88,560	4,000		112,570

Notes

(i) The cost of sales of Niks = 900 units at $20 each plus 3,600 units at $19.60 each.
(ii) The cost of sales of Args = 200 units at $28 each plus 3,800 units at $28.15 each.

(j) MASTER BUDGET

Cash budget for year to 31.3.X8

	Quarter 1	*Quarter 2*	*Quarter 3*	*Quarter 4*	*Total*
	$	$	$	$	$
Receipts	70,000	100,000	100,000	40,000	310,000
Payments					
Materials	7,000	9,000	10,000	5,000	31,000
Labour	33,000	20,000	11,000	15,000	79,000
Other costs and expenses	10,000	100,000	205,000	5,000	320,000
	50,000	129,000	226,000	25,000	430,000
Receipts less payments	20,000	(29,000)	(126,000)	15,000	(120,000)
Opening cash balance b/f	4,300	24,300	(4,700)	(130,700)	4,300
Closing cash balance c/f	24,300	(4,700)	(130,700)	(115,700)	(115,700)

Budgeted income statement for year to 31.3.X8

	Niks	*Args*	*Total*
	$	$	$
Sales	144,000	176,000	320,000
Less cost of sales	88,560	112,570	201,130
Gross profit	55,440	63,430	118,870
Less selling and administration			30,400
Net profit			88,470

Note. There will be no under-/over-absorbed production overhead in the budgeted income statement.

Budgeted statement of financial position (balance sheet) at 31.3.X8

	$	$	$
ASSETS			
Fixed assets			
Land and buildings (W1)			225,000
Plant and equipment at cost (W2)		207,000	
Less accumulated depreciation (W3)		84,850	
			122,150
			347,150
Current assets			
Raw materials (W4)		1,900	
Finished goods (W5)		41,620	
Receivables (W6)		29,500	
			73,020
			420,170
EQUITY AND LIABILITIES			
Capital and reserves			
Share capital		150,000	
Retained profit (W9)		143,720	
			293,720
Current liabilities			
Payables (W7)		10,750	
Bank overdraft (W8)		115,700	
			126,450
			420,170

Workings

1

	$
Opening balance at 1.4.X7	45,000
Addition	180,000
Cost at 31.3.X8	225,000

2

	$
Opening balance at 1.4.X7	187,000
Addition	20,000
Cost at 31.3.X8	207,000

3

	$
Opening balance at 1.4.X7	75,000
Addition in period	5,000
((f)(i) and (ii) of solution)	4,350
Accumulated depreciation at 31.3.X8	500
	84,850

4

	A	*B*	*Total*
Closing inventory (kgs)	600	1,000	
Cost per kg	× $1.50	× $1.00	
Value of closing inventory	$900	$1,000	
			$1,900

5

	Niks	*Args*	*Total*
Closing inventory (units)	400	1,200	
Cost per unit ((g) of solution)	× $19.60	× $28.15	
	$7,840	$33,780	
			$41,620

6

	$
Opening balance	19,500
Sales ((a) of solution)	320,000
Receipts (from cash budget)	(310,000)
Closing balance	29,500

7

		$	$
Opening balance at 1.4.X7			6,800
Land		180,000	
Machine		20,000	
Labour		110,400	
Production overhead	39,500		
	18,650		
		58,150	
Materials	12,000		
	23,000		
		35,000	
Expenses		30,400	
			433,950
			440,750
Cash payments (from cash budget)			(430,000)
Closing balance at 31.3.X8			10,750

8 From cash budget $115,750 overdrawn

9

	$
Retained profit b/f	55,250
Profit for year	88,470
Retained profit c/f	143,720

Exam focus point

Part of the 40 mark question on the December 2004 paper involved the preparation of sales, production and purchases budgets. In his report on the sitting, the examiner noted that 'this is very much a standard requirement in budgeting questions'. Given that budgeting is a key syllabus area, you must make sure that you can comfortably prepare each of the components of a master budget with the exception of a cash budget as this is examined in Paper 10.

Question — **Master budget**

Of what does the master budget comprise?

A The budgeted income statement

B The budgeted cash flow, budgeted income statement and budgeted statement of financial position (balance sheet)

C The entire set of budgets prepared

D The budgeted cash flow

Answer

B This is basic knowledge.

8 Computers and budgeting

Exam focus point

Candidates were asked to explain three advantages of using computer spreadsheet packages in a question in the December 2005 exam.

Budgeting used to be a very **time consuming** task. The examples we have looked at have demonstrated the need for a great number of numerical manipulations to produce a budget. These examples are far more simple than situations in the real world, so you can imagine the complexity of the budgetary process which even small organisations have to undergo. It is likely that the process will encounter problems. Functional budgets will be out of balance with each other and require modification. The revision of one budget may well lead to the revision of all of the budgets. The manual preparation of a master budget and a cash budget in the real world would therefore be daunting.

Computers can recalculate these inter-related budgets in an instant. A computerised system has a number of advantages.

(a) A computer has the ability to **process a larger volume of data**.
(b) A computerised system can process data **more rapidly** than a manual system.
(c) Computerised systems tend to be more **accurate** than manual systems.
(d) Computers have the ability to **store large volumes** of data in a readily accessible form.
(e) **Numerous scenarios** can be evaluated quickly.

A computerised budget model is ideal for taking over the manipulation of numbers, leaving staff to get involved in the real planning process.

Budgeting is usually computerised using either a computer **program written specifically** for the organisation or by a **commercial spreadsheet package**. Both methods of computerisation of the budgeting process will involve a **mathematical model** which represents the real world in terms of financial values. The model will consist of several, or many, interrelated variables, a variable being an item in the model which has a value.

A cash budgeting model, for example, should include all the factors (variables) which have a significant influence on cash flow. Variables would include time taken by debtors to pay what they owe, cash sales and credit sales, other cash expenses, and capital expenditure.

Once the **planning model** has been constructed, the same model can be used week by week, month after month, or year after year, simply by changing the values of the variables to produce new results for cash inflows, cash outflows, net cash flows and cash/bank balance.

A major advantage of budget models is the ability to **evaluate different options** and carry out **'what if' analysis**. By changing the value of certain variables (for example altering the ratio of cash sales to credit sales, increasing the amount of bad debts or capital expenditure, increasing the annual pay award to the workforce and so on) management are able to assess the effect of potential changes in their environment.

Spreadsheets can be used to **flex** budgets to reflect changes in activity – especially useful for variance analysis.

Computerised models can incorporate actual results, period by period, and carry out the necessary calculations to produce budgetary control reports.

The use of a model allows the budget for the remainder of the year to be adjusted once it is clear that the circumstances on which the budget was originally based have changed.

Key term

A **spreadsheet** is 'The term commonly used to describe many of the modelling packages available for microcomputers, being loosely derived from the likeness to a "spreadsheet of paper" divided into rows and columns'. (CIMA *Computing Terminology)*

A spreadsheet is a type of general purpose software package with **many business applications**, not just accounting ones. It **can be used to build a model**, in which data is presented in **cells** at the intersection of these **rows and columns**. It is up to the model builder to determine what data or information should be presented in the spreadsheet, how it should be presented and how the data should be manipulated by the spreadsheet program. The most widely used spreadsheet packages are Lotus 1-2-3 and Excel.

The idea behind a spreadsheet to **construct a model**.

(a) Identify what data goes into each row and column by **inserting text** (for example, column headings and row identifications).

(b) **Specify how the numerical data in the model should be derived**.

  (i) **Insertion into the model via keyboard input**.

  (ii) **Calculation from other data in the model** by means of a formula specified within the model itself. The model builder must insert these formulae into the spreadsheet model when it is first constructed.

  (iii) **Retrieval from data on a disk file** from another computer application program or module.

8.1 The advantages of spreadsheets

The uses of spreadsheets are really only limited by your imagination, and by the number of rows and columns in the spreadsheet, but some of the more **common accounting applications** are listed below.

(a) Balance sheets
(b) Cash flow analysis/forecasting
(c) General ledger
(d) Inventory records
(e) Job cost estimates
(f) Market share analysis and planning
(g) Profit projections
(h) Profit statements
(i) Project budgeting and control
(j) Sales projections and records
(k) Tax estimation

The great value of spreadsheets derives from their **simple format** of rows, columns and cells of data, and the ability of the data **users to have direct access themselves** to their spreadsheet models via their own PCs. Spreadsheets bring computer modelling within the everyday reach of data users.

8.2 The disadvantages of spreadsheets

Spreadsheets have disadvantages if they are not properly used.

(a) A **minor error in the design** of a model can **affect the validity of data** throughout the spreadsheet. Such errors can be very difficult to trace.

(b) Even if it is properly designed in the first place, it is very **easy to corrupt** a model by accidentally changing a cell or inputting data in the wrong place.

(c) It is possible to **become over-dependent on them**, so that simple one-off tasks that can be done in seconds with a pen and paper are done on a spreadsheet instead.

(d) The possibility for experimentation with data is so great that it is possible to **lose sight of the original intention** of the spreadsheet.

(e) Spreadsheets **cannot take account of qualitative factors** since they are invariably difficult to quantify. Decisions should not be made on the basis of quantitative information alone.

In summary, spreadsheets should be seen as a **tool in planning and decision making**. The user must make the decision.

8.3 'What if?' analysis

Once a model has been constructed the consequences of changes in any of the variables may be tested by asking **'what if?' questions, a form of sensitivity analysis**. For example, a spreadsheet may be used to develop a cash budget, such as that shown below.

	A	B	C	D
1		Month 1	Month 2	Month 3
2	Sales	1,000	1,200	1,440
3	Cost of sales	(650)	(780)	(936)
4	Gross profit	350	420	504
5				
6	Receipts:			
7	Current month	600	720	864
8	Previous month	-	400	480
9		-	-	-
10		600	1,120	1,344
11	Payments	(650)	(780)	(936)
12		(50)	340	408
13	Balance b/f	-	(50)	290
14	Balance c/f	(50)	290	698

Typical 'what if?' questions for sensitivity analysis

(a) What if the cost of sales is 68% of sales revenue, not 65%?

(b) What if payment from debtors is received 40% in the month of sale, 50% one month in arrears and 10% two months in arrears, instead of 60% in the month of sale and 40% one month in arrears?

(c) What if sales growth is only 15% per month, instead of 20% per month?

Using the spreadsheet model, the answers to such questions can be obtained simply and quickly, using the editing facility in the program. The information obtained should **provide management with a better understanding of what the cash flow position in the future might be**, and **what factors are critical to ensuring that the cash position remains reasonable**. For example, it might be found that the cost of sales must remain less than 67% of sales value to achieve a satisfactory cash position.

You have covered spreadsheet formulae in CAT 2. So have a go at the example below. If you struggle go back to your CAT 2 text or passcards.

Question

(a) Write out the formulae that would appear in column C of the spreadsheet shown above.

(b) Comment on the effect on the cash balances if *all* of the 'what if?' conditions listed in Section 8.3 applied. Perform the calculations manually, then if you have access to a spreadsheet package, you could use it to check your answer.

(c) Which cells in column C would have to be changed, and how, if the 'what if?' conditions applied?

(d) How could the design of the spreadsheet model be improved to facilitate sensitivity analysis?

Answer

(a)

C2:	B2*1.2	C10:	@ SUM(C7..C9) or = SUM (C7...C9)
C3:	C2*0.65	C11:	C3
C4:	C2 + C3	C12:	C10 + C11
C7:	C2*0.6	C13:	B14
C8:	B2*0.4	C14:	C12 + C13

Note that the figures are entered into each cell as either positive or negative and so C4, for example, is calculated by *adding* 1,200 and –780.

(b)

A	*B*		*C*		*D*
	Month 1		*Month 2*		*Month 3*
Sales	1,000	(+15%)	1,150	(+15%)	1,323
Cost of sales (68%)	680		782		900
Gross profit	320		368		423
Receipts					
Current month (40%)	400		460		529
Previous month (50%)	–		500		575
Two months in arrears (10%)	–		–		100
	400		960		1,204
Payments	(680)		(782)		(900)
	(280)		178		304
Balance b/f	–		(280)		(102)
Balance c/f	(280)		(102)		202

The cash position would be substantially worse if all of the 'what if?' conditions occurred simultaneously. Although the cash balance would become positive during month 3, the closing balance would be much lower. If these conditions were to apply then management would need to make arrangements to finance a large short-term deficit during months 1 and 2.

(c)

C2:	B2*1.15
C3:	C2*0.68
C7:	C2*0.4
C8:	B2*0.5
C9:	Blank (but D9 would have B2*0.1)

(d) It would be much easier to conduct sensitivity analysis if the items that are variable were allocated specific cells outside the body of the cash flow table. For example rows 15–19 could contain the following.

	A		B
15	Cost of sales/Sales		0.68
16	Receipts	- current month	0.40
17		- 1 month in arrears	0.50
18		- 2 months in arrears	0.10
19	Sales growth		1.15

The formulae in row C would then read as follows.

C2	B2*B19
C3	C2*B15
C7	C2*B16
C8	B2*B17
C9	A2*B18

(Note that B17, for example, is an absolute cell address whereas C2 is a relative cell address.)

Further sensitivity analysis could be conducted simply by changing the values in cells B15–B19, rather than having to rewrite each column each time a variable is changed.

9 Limiting factors

Key term

A **limiting factor** or **key factor** is 'Anything which limits the activity of an entity. An entity seeks to optimise the benefit it obtains from the limiting factor'.

(CIMA *Official Terminology)*

FAST FORWARD

If **resources are limiting factors, contribution will be maximised** by **earning** the biggest possible contribution per unit of limiting factor.

Where there is just one limiting factor, the technique for establishing the contribution-maximising product or service mix is to rank the products or services in order of contribution-earning ability per unit of limiting factor.

Where there is a maximum potential sales demand for an organisation's products or services, they should still be ranked in order of contribution-earning ability per unit of the limiting factor. The contribution-maximising decision, however, will be to produce the top-ranked products (or to provide the top-ranked services) up to the sales demand limit.

If an organisation has to produce more of a particular product or products than the level established by ranking according to contribution per unit of limiting factor, the products should be ranked in the normal way but the optimum production plan must first take into account the minimum production requirements. The remaining resource must then be allocated according to the ranking.

An organisation might be faced with just one limiting factor (other than maximum sales demand) but there might also be several scarce resources, with two or more of them putting an effective limit on the level of activity that can be achieved.

9.1 Examples of limiting factors

(a) **Sales**. There may be a limit to sales demand.

(b) **Labour**. The limit may be either in terms of total quantity or of particular skills.

(c) **Materials**. There may be insufficient available materials to produce enough units to satisfy sales demand.

(d) **Manufacturing capacity**. There may not be sufficient machine capacity for the production required to meet sales demand.

It is assumed in limiting factor analysis that management would select a product mix or service mix that would maximise profit and that profit is maximised when contribution is maximised (given no change in fixed cost expenditure incurred). In other words, marginal costing ideas are applied.

(a) Contribution will be maximised by earning the biggest possible **contribution per unit of limiting factor**. For example if grade A labour is the limiting factor, contribution will be maximised by earning the biggest contribution per hour of grade A labour worked.

(b) The limiting factor decision therefore involves the determination of the contribution earned per unit of limiting factor by each different product.

(c) If the sales demand is limited, the profit-maximising decision will be to produce the top-ranked product(s) up to the sales demand limit.

In limiting factor decisions, we generally assume that fixed costs are the same whatever product or service mix is selected, so that the only relevant costs are variable costs.

When there is just one limiting factor, the technique for establishing the contribution-maximising product mix or service mix is to rank the products or services in order of contribution-earning ability per unit of limiting factor.

9.2 Example: limiting factor decision

Sausage makes two products, the Mash and the Sauce. Unit variable costs are as follows.

	Mash	*Sauce*
	$	$
Direct materials	1	3
Direct labour ($3 per hour)	6	3
Variable overhead	1	1
	8	7

The sales price per unit is $14 per Mash and $11 per Sauce. During July the available direct labour is limited to 8,000 hours. Sales demand in July is expected to be as follows.

Mash	3,000 units
Sauce	5,000 units

Required

Determine the production budget that will maximise profit, assuming that fixed costs per month are $20,000 and that there are no opening inventory of finished goods or work in progress.

9.3 Solution

Step 1 Confirm that the limiting factor is something other than sales demand.

	Mash	*Sauces*	*Total*
Labour hours per unit	2 hrs	1 hr	
Sales demand	3,000 units	5,000 units	
Labour hours needed	6,000 hrs	5,000 hrs	11,000 hrs
Labour hours available			8,000 hrs
Shortfall			3,000 hrs

Labour is the limiting factor on production.

Step 2 Identify the contribution earned by each product per unit of scarce resource, that is, per labour hour worked.

	Mash	*Sauce*
	$	$
Sales price	14	11
Variable cost	8	7
Unit contribution	6	4
Labour hours per unit	2 hrs	1 hr
Contribution per labour hour (= per unit of limiting factor)	$3	$4

Although Mashes have a higher unit contribution than Sauces, two Sauces can be made in the time it takes to make one Mash. Because labour is in short supply it is more profitable to make Sauces than Mashes.

Step 3 Determine the budgeted production and sales. Sufficient Sauces will be made to meet the full sales demand, and the remaining labour hours available will then be used to make Mashes.

(a)

Product	*Demand*	*Hours required*	*Hours available*	*Priority for manufacture*
Sauces	5,000	5,000	5,000	1st
Mashes	3,000	6,000	3,000 (bal)	2nd
		11,000	8,000	

(b)

Product	*Units*	*Hours needed*	*Contribution per unit*	*Total*
			$	
Sauces	5,000	5,000	4	20,000
Mashes (balance)	1,500	3,000	6	9,000
		8,000		29,000
Less fixed costs				20,000
Profit				9,000

9.4 Conclusion

(a) Unit contribution is *not* the correct way to decide priorities.

(b) Labour hours are the scarce resource, therefore **contribution per labour hour** is the correct way to decide priorities.

(c) The Sauce earns $4 contribution per labour hour, and the Mash earns $3 contribution per labour hour. Sauces therefore make more profitable use of the scarce resource, and should be manufactured first.

Question — Limiting factor

The following details relate to three products made by DSF.

	V	A	L
	$ per unit	$ per unit	$ per unit
Selling price	120	170	176
Direct materials	30	40	60
Direct labour	20	30	20
Variable overhead	10	16	20
Fixed overhead	20	32	40
	80	118	140
Profit	40	52	36

All three products use the same direct labour and direct materials, but in different quantities.

In a period when the labour used on these products is in short supply, the most and least profitable use of the labour is

	Most profitable	Least profitable
A	L	V
B	L	A
C	V	A
D	A	L

Answer

The correct answer is B.

	V	A	L
	$	$	$
Selling price per unit	120	170	176
Variable cost per unit	60	86	100
Contribution per unit	60	84	76
Labour cost per unit	$20	$30	$20
Contribution per $ of labour	$3	$2.80	$3.80
Ranking	2	3	1

9.5 Two potentially limiting factors

You may be asked to deal with situations where two limiting factors (and also demand) are **potentially** limiting. The approach in these situations is to find out which factor (if any) prevents the business from fulfilling maximum demand.

9.6 Example: Two potentially limiting factors

Lucky manufactures and sells three products, X, Y and Z, for which budgeted sales demand, unit selling prices and unit variable costs are as follows.

	X		*Y*		*Z*	
Budgeted sales demand	550 units		500 units		400 units	
	$	$	$	$	$	$
Unit sales price		16		18		14
Variable costs: materials	8		6		2	
labour	4		6		9	
		12		12		11
Unit contribution		4		6		3

The company has existing inventories of 250 units of X and 200 units of Z, which it is quite willing to use up to meet sales demand.

All three products use the same direct materials and the same type of direct labour. In the next year, the available supply of materials will be restricted to $4,800 (at cost) and the available supply of labour to $6,600 (at cost).

Required

Determine what product mix and sales mix would maximise the company's profits in the next year.

9.7 Solution

There **appear to be two scarce resources**, direct materials and direct labour. This is not certain, however, and because there is a limited sales demand as well, either of the following might apply.

- There is **no limiting factor at all**, except sales demand.
- There is **only one scarce resource** that prevents the full potential sales demand being achieved.

Step 1 Establish which of the resources, if any, is scarce.

	X	*Y*	*Z*
	Units	Units	Units
Budgeted sales	550	500	400
Inventories in hand	250	0	200
Minimum production to meet demand	300	500	200

	Minimum production to meet sales demand	*Required materials at cost*	*Required labour at cost*
	Units	$	$
X	300	2,400	1,200
Y	500	3,000	3,000
Z	200	400	1,800
Total required		5,800	6,000
Total available		4,800	6,600
(Shortfall)/Surplus		(1,000)	600

Materials are a limiting factor, but labour is not.

Step 2 **Rank** X, Y and Z in order of contribution earned per $1 of direct materials consumed.

	X	*Y*	*Z*
	$	$	$
Unit contribution	4	6	3
Cost of materials	8	6	2
Contribution per $1 materials	$0.50	$1.00	$1.50
Ranking	3rd	2nd	1st

Step 3 **Determine a production plan.** Z should be manufactured up to the limit where units produced plus units in inventory will meet sales demand, then Y second and X third, until all the available materials are used up.

Ranking	*Product*	*Sales demand less units in inventories*	*Production quantity*		*Materials cost*
		Units	Units		$
1st	Z	200	200	(× $2)	400
2nd	Y	500	500	(× $6)	3,000
3rd	X	300	175	(× $8)	* 1,400
		Total available			4,800

* Balancing amount using up total available.

Step 4 **Draw up a budget.** The profit-maximising budget is as follows.

	X	*Y*	*Z*
	Units	Units	Units
Opening inventory	250	0	200
Add production	175	500	200
Sales	425	500	400

	X	*Y*	*Z*	*Total*
	$	$	$	$
Revenue	6,800	9,000	5,600	21,400
Variable costs	5,100	6,000	4,400	15,500
Contribution	1,700	3,000	1,200	5,900

9.8 Restricted freedom of action

In certain circumstances an organisation faced with a limiting factor on production and sales **might not be able to produce the profit-maximising product mix** because the mix and/or volume of products that can be produced and sold is also restricted by a factor other than a scarce resource.

(a) The organisation might have **contracted to supply a certain number of products** to a customer.

(b) The organisation might have to produce and sell a minimum quantity of one or more of its products to **provide a complete product range and/or to maintain customer goodwill.**

(c) The organisation might need to **maintain a certain market share** of one or more of its products.

In each of these cases, the organisation might have to **produce more of a particular product or products than the level established by ranking** according to contribution per unit of limiting factor.

The basic approach to dealing with such situations is to **rank the products in the normal way** but the **optimum production plan must take into account the minimum production requirements. The remaining resource must then be allocated according to the ranking.**

Work carefully through the following example which illustrates this approach.

9.9 Example: restricted freedom of action

Harvey is currently preparing its budget for the year ending 30 September 20X2. The company manufactures and sells three products, Beta, Delta and Gamma.

The unit selling price and cost structure of each product is budgeted as follows.

	Beta	*Delta*	*Gamma*
	$	$	$
Selling price	100	124	32
Variable costs:			
Labour	24	48	6
Materials	26	7	8
Overhead	10	5	6
	60	60	20
Contribution per unit	40	64	12

Direct labour rate is budgeted at $6 per hour, and fixed costs at $1,300,000 per annum. The company has a maximum production capacity of 228,000 direct labour hours.

A meeting of the board of directors has been convened to discuss the budget and to resolve the problem as to the quantity of each product which should be made and sold. The sales director presented the results of a recent market survey which reveals that market demand for the company's products will be as follows.

Product	*Units*
Beta	24,000
Delta	12,000
Gamma	60,000

The production director proposes that since Gamma only contributes $12 per unit, the product should no longer be produced, and the surplus capacity transferred to produce additional quantities of Beta and Delta. The sales director does not agree with the proposal. Gamma is considered necessary to complement the product range and to maintain customer goodwill. If Gamma is not offered, the sales director believes that sales of Beta and Delta will be seriously affected. After further discussion the board decided that a minimum of 10,000 units of each product should be produced. The remaining production capacity would then be allocated so as to achieve the maximum profit possible.

Required

Prepare a budget statement which clearly shows the maximum profit which could be achieved in the year ending 30 September 20X2.

9.10 Solution

Step 1 **Ascertain whether labour hours are a scarce resource.**

	Units demanded	*Labour hours per unit*	*Total labour hours*
Beta	24,000	4 ($24/$6)	96,000
Delta	12,000	8 ($48/$6)	96,000
Gamma	60,000	1 ($6/$6)	60,000
			252,000

Step 2 **Rank the products**

Since only 228,000 hours are available we need to establish which product earns the greatest contribution per labour hour.

	Beta	*Delta*	*Gamma*
Contribution	40	64	12
Labour hours	4	8	1
Contribution per labour hour	$10	$8	$12
Ranking	2nd	3rd	1st

Step 3 Determine a production plan.

The optimum production plan must take into account the requirement that 10,000 units of each product are produced, and then allocate the remaining hours according to the above ranking.

		Hours
Beta	10,000 units × 4 hours	40,000
Delta	10,000 units × 8 hours	80,000
Gamma	10,000 units × 1 hour	10,000
		130,000
Gamma	50,000 units × 1 hour (full demand)	50,000
Beta	12,000 units × 4 hours (balance)	48,000
		228,000

Step 4 Draw up a budget.

BUDGET STATEMENT

	$
Contribution	
Beta (22,000 units × $40)	880,000
Delta (10,000 units × $64)	640,000
Gamma (60,000 units × $12)	720,000
	2,240,000
Fixed costs	1,300,000
Profit	940,000

Question — Profit-maximising mix

Jam Ltd makes two products, the K and the L. The K sells for $50 per unit, the L for $70 per unit. The variable cost per unit of the K is $35, that of the L $40. Each unit of K uses 2 kgs of raw material. Each unit of L uses 3 kgs of material.

In the forthcoming period the availability of raw material is limited to 2,000 kgs. Jam is contracted to supply 500 units of K. Maximum demand for the L is 250 units. Demand for the K is unlimited.

What is the profit-maximising product mix?

	K	L
A	250 units	625 units
B	1,250 units	750 units
C	625 units	250 units
D	750 units	1,250 units

Answer

The correct answer is C.

	K	*L*
Contribution per unit	\$15	\$30
Contribution per unit of limiting factor	\$15/2 = \$7.50	\$30/3 = \$10
Ranking	2	1

Production plan	*Raw material used*
	kg
Contracted supply of K (500 × 2 kg)	1,000
Meet demand for L (250 × 3 kg)	750
Remainder of resource for K (125 × 2 kg)	250
	2,000

Chapter Roundup

- The functions of a **system of budgeting** are as follows.
  - To ensure the achievement of the organisation's objectives
  - To compel planning
  - To communicate ideas and plans
  - To co-ordinate activities
  - To provide a framework for responsibility accounting
  - To establish a system of control
  - To motivate employees to improve their performance
- A budget is a **quantified plan of action** for a forthcoming accounting period.
- The **budget manual** is a collection of instructions governing the responsibilities of persons and the procedures, forms and records relating to the preparation and use of budgetary data.
- Managers responsible for preparing budgets should ideally be the managers responsible for carrying out the budget.
- The **budget committee** is the co-ordinating body in the preparation and administration of budgets.
- The **budget preparation process** is as follows.
  - Communicating details of the budget policy and budget guidelines.
  - Determining the factor that restricts output
  - Preparation of the sales budget
  - Initial preparation of budgets
  - Negotiation of budgets with superiors
  - Co-ordination and review of budgets
  - Final acceptance of the budgets
  - Budget review
- The **principal budget factor** should be identified at the beginning of the budgetary process, and the budget for this is prepared before all the others.
- Once prepared, the **functional budgets** must be reviewed to ensure they are consistent with one another.
- The **master budget** consists of a budgeted income statement, a budgeted statement of financial position (balance sheet) and a cash budget.
- **If resources are limiting factors**, contribution will be maximised by earning the biggest possible contribution per unit of limiting factor.

- **Where there is just one limiting factor**, the technique for establishing the contribution-maximising product or service mix is to rank the products or services in order of contribution-earning ability per unit of limiting factor.
- **Where there is a maximum potential sales demand for an organisation's products or services**, they should still be ranked in order of contribution-earning ability per unit of the limiting factor. The contribution-maximising decision, however, will be to produce the top-ranked products (or to provide the top-ranked services) up to the sales demand limit.
- If an organisation has to produce more of a particular product or products than the level established by ranking according to contribution per unit of limiting factor, the products should be ranked in the normal way but the optimum production plan must first take into account the minimum production requirements. The remaining resource must then be allocated according to the ranking.

Quick Quiz

1 What are the functions of a system of budgeting?

2 What are the functions of a budget committee?

3 What is meant by the term principal budget factor?

4 What are the eight steps in the preparation of a budget?

5 How can a shortfall in capacity be overcome?

6 Explain the concept of the standard hour.

7 The master budget consists of the sales budget and the cash budget. True or false?

8 Marginal costing ideas are applied in limiting factor analysis. True or false?

9 Which of the following are functional budgets?

I Purchasing budget
II Cash budget
III Sales budget
IV Marketing cost budget

A I and II
B None of the above
C All of the above
D I, III and IV

10 When preparing a material purchases budget, what is the quantity to be purchased?

A Materials required for production – opening inventory of materials – closing inventory of materials
B Materials required for production – opening inventory of materials + closing inventory of materials
C Opening inventory of materials – materials required for production – closing inventory of materials
D Opening inventory of materials + closing inventory of materials – materials required for production

Answers to Quick Quiz

1 To ensure the achievement of the organisation's objectives
To compel planning
To communicate ideas and plans
To co-ordinate activities
To provide a framework for responsibility accounting
To establish a system of control
To motivate employees to improve their performance

2 (a) Co-ordination of the preparation of budgets, which includes the issue of the budget manual
(b) Issuing of timetables for the preparation of functional budgets
(c) Allocation of responsibilities for the preparation of functional budgets
(d) Provision of information to assist in the preparation of budgets
(e) Communication of final budgets to the appropriate managers
(f) Comparison of actual results with budget and the investigation of variances
(g) Continuous assessment of the budgeting and planning process, in order to improve the planning and control function

3 A principal budget factor is the factor that limits an organisation's performance for a given period.

4 (a) Communicating details of the budget policy and budget guidelines
(b) Determining the factor that restricts output
(c) Preparation of the sales budget
(d) Initial preparation of budgets
(e) Negotiation of budgets with superiors
(f) Co-ordination of budgets
(g) Final acceptance of the budgets
(h) Budget review

5 Consideration should be given to overtime, subcontracting, machine hire and/or new sources of materials.

6 A standard hour is the quantity of work achievable at standard performance, expressed in terms of a standard unit of work done in a standard period of time.

7 False. The master budget consists of the budgeted income statement, the budgeted balance sheet and the cash budget.

8 True

9 D A functional budget is a budget of income and/or expenditure for a particular department or process. A cash budget does not relate to a function.

10 B It may help you to think in terms of the inputs to a material purchases budget (opening inventory and purchases) and the outputs (closing inventory and the quantity used in production). The inputs should equal the outputs. Any one of the inputs or outputs can then be determined by manipulating opening inventory + purchases = closing inventory + used in production.

Now try the questions below from the Exam Question Bank

Number	Level	Marks	Time
Section A: Q13	MCQ	N/A	N/A
Section B: Q9	Examination	20	36 mins

10

Making budgets work

Topic list
1 Fixed and flexible budgets
2 Preparing flexible budgets
3 Flexible budgets and budgetary control
4 Incremental and zero based budgeting systems
5 The main features of zero based budgeting systems
6 The advantages and limitations of zero based budgets
7 Using zero based budgeting
8 Rolling budgets
9 Behavioural implications of budgeting
10 Participation and performance evaluation
11 The use of budgets as targets
12 The management accountant and motivation

Study guide reference

		Syllabus reference
12(a)	Alternative approaches to budgeting	6
	(i) Describe the main features of zero-based budgeting	
	(ii) Explain the advantages and limitations of zero-based budgets	
	(iii) Compare the use of incremental and zero-based budgeting systems	
	(iv) Describe when zero-based budgets are commonly used	
	(v) Describe the main features of a rolling budget	
13(a)	Fixed versus flexible budgets	7
	(i) Explain the importance of flexible budgets in control	
	(ii) Explain the disadvantages of fixed budgets in control	
	(iii) Identify situations where fixed or flexible budgetary control would be appropriate	
13(b)	Preparation	7
	(i) Flex a budget to a given level of volume	
	(ii) Prepare formulae appropriate for flexing a budget	
13(c)	Impact of capacity variations	7
	(i) Prepare flexed budgets at various output levels	
	(ii) Estimate profit at various output levels	
18	Budgetary control – budgets and the behaviour of managers and other employees	7
18(a)	Motivation	
	(i) Define motivation	
	(ii) Explain the importance of motivation in performance management	
	(iii) Identify factors in a budgetary planning and control system that influence motivation	
	(iv) Explain the impact of targets upon motivation	
	(v) Evaluate managerial incentive schemes	
18(b)	Participation	
	(i) Discuss the advantages and disadvantages of a participative approach to budgeting	
	(ii) Explain top down, bottom up, and budget challenging approaches to budgeting	
18(c)	Goal congruence and dysfunctional decision-making	
	(i) Define goal congruence and dysfunctional decision-making	
	(ii) Explain the importance of goal congruent behaviour	
	(iii) Discuss causes of dysfunctional behaviour in a specific situation	
	(iv) Identify dysfunctional behavior in a specific situation	
	(v) Amend budgeting procedures to encourage goal congruent behaviour	
	(vi) Describe ideal attainable, current and basic standards	

BPP LEARNING MEDIA

Exam focus point

This chapter covers a key syllabus area. Key syllabus areas usually account for 80% or more of the marks available in the exam paper.

In the June 2007 exam, there were eleven marks available for preparing a flexed budget statement and using this to calculate variances. In the December 2007 exam, knowledge of flexible budgets was tested a written question.

1 Fixed and flexible budgets

1.1 Fixed budgets

FAST FORWARD

Fixed budgets remain unchanged regardless of the level of activity; **flexible budgets** are designed to flex with the level of activity.

Comparison of a fixed budget with the actual results for a different level of activity is of little use for control purposes. Flexible budgets should be used to show what cost and revenues should have been for the actual level of activity.

Key term

A **fixed budget** is a budget which is designed to remain unchanged regardless of the volume of output or sales achieved.

The master budget prepared before the beginning of the budget period is known as the **fixed budget**. The term 'fixed' has the following meaning.

(a) The budget is **prepared on the basis of an estimated volume of production** and an **estimated volume of sales**, but no plans are made for the event that actual volumes of production and sales may differ from budgeted volumes.

(b) When actual volumes of production and sales during a control period (month or four weeks or quarter) are achieved, a fixed budget is **not adjusted (in retrospect) to the new levels of activity**.

The major purpose of a fixed budget is at the planning stage, when it seeks to define the broad objectives of the organisation.

1.2 Flexible budgets

Exam focus point

Flexible budgets made an appearance in the December 2005 exam when candidates were asked to flex a previously prepared income and expenditure budget.

Flexible budgeting was tested thoroughly in the December 2006 exam in the longer forty mark question. Candidates had to prepare a flexed budget profit statement for sixteen marks.

Key term

A **flexible budget** is a budget which, by recognising different cost behaviour patterns, is designed to change as volumes of output change.

Flexible budgets may be used in one of two ways.

(a) **At the planning stage**. For example, suppose that a company expects to sell 10,000 units of output during the next year. A master budget (the fixed budget) would be prepared on the basis of these expected volumes. However, if the company thinks that output and sales might be as low as 8,000 units or as high as 12,000 units, it may prepare **contingency flexible budgets**, at volumes of, say 8,000, 9,000, 11,000 and 12,000 units. There are a number of advantages of planning with flexible budgets.

    (i) It is possible to find out well in advance the costs of lay-off pay, idle time and so on if output falls short of budget.

(ii) Management can decide whether it would be possible to find alternative uses for spare capacity if output falls short of budget (could employees be asked to overhaul their own machines for example, instead of paying for an outside contractor?).

(iii) An estimate of the costs of overtime, subcontracting work or extra machine hire if sales volume exceeds the fixed budget estimate can be made. From this, it can be established whether there is a limiting factor which would prevent high volumes of output and sales being achieved.

(b) **Retrospectively**. At the end of each month (control period) or year, flexible budgets can be used to compare actual results achieved with what results should have been under the circumstances. Flexible budgets are an essential factor in **budgetary control** and overcome the practical problems involved in monitoring the budgetary control system.

(i) Management needs to be informed about how good or bad actual performance has been. To provide a **measure of performance**, there must be a **yardstick** (budget or standard) against which actual performance can be measured.

(ii) Every business is **dynamic**, and actual volumes of output cannot be expected to conform exactly to the fixed budget. Comparing actual costs directly with the fixed budget costs is meaningless (unless the actual level of activity turns out to be exactly as planned).

(iii) For **useful control information**, it is necessary to compare **actual results at the actual level of activity achieved against the results that should have been expected at this level of activity**, which are shown by the flexible budget.

Question — **Flexible budgets**

Why might flexible budgets be particularly useful to the car industry during a recession?

Answer

During a recession the car industry often has to put workers on a three- or four-day week due to lack of demand for its products. Budgets therefore have to be reassessed to match the reduced production time available.

2 Preparing flexible budgets

Flexible budgeting uses the principles of marginal costing. In estimating future costs it is often necessary to begin by looking at cost behaviour in the past. For costs which are wholly fixed or wholly variable no problem arises. But you may be presented with a cost which appears to have behaved in the past as a mixed cost (partly fixed and partly variable). The **high-low method** may be used for estimating the level of such a cost in a future period.

2.1 High-low method

(a) To estimate the fixed and variable elements of semi-variable costs, records of costs in previous periods are reviewed and the **costs of the following two periods** are selected.

(i) **The period with the highest volume of output**

(ii) **The period with the lowest volume of output**

(*Note*. The periods with the highest/lowest output may not be the periods with the highest/lowest cost.)

(b) The **difference** between the total cost of the high output and the total cost of the low output will be the **variable cost of the difference in output levels** (since the same fixed cost is included in each total cost).

(c) The **variable cost per unit** may be calculated from this (**difference in total costs ÷ difference in output levels**), and the **fixed cost** may then also be determined (**total cost at either output level – variable cost for output level chosen**).

Exam focus point

The high-low technique was a useful technique for answering a question on flexible budgets on the December 2004 paper. Students also needed to use the technique to calculate variable and fixed overhead costs in the June 2008 paper.

2.2 Example: the high-low method

The costs of operating the maintenance department of a television manufacturer for the last four months have been as follows.

Month	*Cost*	*Production volume*
	$	Units
1	110,000	7,000
2	115,000	8,000
3	111,000	7,700
4	97,000	6,000

Required

Calculate the costs that should be expected in month five when output is expected to be 7,500 units. Ignore inflation.

2.3 Solution

(a)

	Units		$
High output	8,000	total cost	115,000
Low output	6,000	total cost	97,000
Variable cost of	2,000		18,000
Variable cost per unit	$18,000/2,000 =		$9

(b) Substituting in either the high or low volume cost:

		High		*Low*
		$		$
Total cost		115,000		97,000
Variable costs	(8,000 × $9)	72,000	(6,000 × $9)	54,000
Fixed costs		43,000		43,000

(c) Estimated costs of 7,500 units of output:

	$
Fixed costs	43,000
Variable costs (7,500 × $9)	67,500
Total costs	110,500

Question — **High-low**

Using the high-low method and the following information, determine the cost of electricity in July if 2,750 units of electricity are consumed.

Month	*Cost*	*Electricity consumed*
	$	Units
January	204	2,600
February	212	2,800
March	200	2,500
April	220	3,000
May	184	2,100
June	188	2,200

Answer

	Units		$
High units	3,000	total cost =	220
Low units	2,100	total cost =	184
	900		36

Variable cost per unit = $\frac{\$36}{900}$ = \$0.04

Substituting:

	$
Total cost of 3,000 units	220
Variable costs (3,000 × \$0.04)	120
Fixed cost	100

Total cost in July = \$(100 + (2,750 × 0.04)) = \$210

We can now look at a full example of preparing a flexible budget.

2.4 Example: preparing a flexible budget

(a) Prepare a budget for 20X6 for the direct labour costs and overhead expenses of a production department at the activity levels of 80%, 90% and 100%, using the information listed below.

(i) The direct labour hourly rate is expected to be \$3.75.
(ii) 100% activity represents 60,000 direct labour hours.
(iii) Variable costs

Indirect labour	\$0.75 per direct labour hour
Consumable supplies	\$0.375 per direct labour hour
Canteen and other welfare services	6% of direct and indirect labour costs

(iv) Semi-variable costs are expected to relate to the direct labour hours in the same manner as for the last five years.

Year	*Direct labour hours*	*Semi-Variable Costs* $
20X1	64,000	20,800
20X2	59,000	19,800
20X3	53,000	18,600
20X4	49,000	17,800
20X5 (estimate)	40,000	16,000

(v) *Fixed overhead per labour hour at 100% activity*

	$
Depreciation	0.30
Maintenance	0.20
Insurance	0.10
Rates	0.25
Management salaries	0.40

(vi) Inflation is to be ignored.

(b) Calculate the **budget cost allowance (ie expected expenditure)** for 20X6 assuming that 57,000 direct labour hours are worked.

2.5 Solution

(a)

	80% level 48,000 hrs	90% level 54,000 hrs	100% level 60,000 hrs
	$'000	$'000	$'000
Direct labour	180.00	202.50	225.0
Other variable costs			
Indirect labour	36.00	40.50	45.0
Consumable supplies	18.00	20.25	22.5
Canteen etc	12.96	14.58	16.2
Total variable costs ($5.145 per hour)	246.96	277.83	308.7
Semi-variable costs (W)	17.60	18.80	20.0
Fixed costs			
Depreciation (60 × $0.3)	18.00	18.00	18.0
Maintenance (60 × $0.2)	12.00	12.00	12.0
Insurance (60 × $0.1)	6.00	6.00	6.0
Rates (60 × $0.25)	15.00	15.00	15.0
Management salaries (60 × $0.4)	24.00	24.00	24.0
Budgeted costs	339.56	371.63	403.7

Working

Using the high/low method:

	$
Total cost of 64,000 hours	20,800
Total cost of 40,000 hours	16,000
Variable cost of 24,000 hours	4,800
Variable cost per hour ($4,800/24,000)	$0.20

	$
Total cost of 64,000 hours	20,800
Variable cost of 64,000 hours (× $0.20)	12,800
Fixed costs	8,000

Semi-variable costs are calculated as follows.

			$
60,000 hours	(60,000 × $0.20) + $8,000	=	20,000
54,000 hours	(54,000 × $0.20) + $8,000	=	18,800
48,000 hours	(48,000 × $0.20) + $8,000	=	17,600

(b) The budget cost allowance for 57,000 direct labour hours of work would be as follows.

		$
Variable costs	(57,000 × $5.145)	293,265
Semi-variable costs	($8,000 + (57,000 × $0.20))	19,400
Fixed costs		75,000
		384,665

Note that in each case the fixed costs remain the same when the level of activity changes and **are not flexed**.

2.6 The measure of activity in flexible budgets

The preparation of a flexible budget requires an estimate of the way in which costs (and revenues) vary with the level of activity.

Sales revenue will clearly vary with sales volume, and direct material costs (and often direct labour costs) will vary with production volume. In some instances, however, it may be appropriate to budget for overhead costs as mixed costs (part-fixed, part-variable) which vary with an 'activity' which is neither production nor sales volume. Taking production overheads in a processing department as an illustration, the total overhead costs will be partly fixed and partly variable. The variable portion may vary with the direct labour hours worked in the department, or with the number of machine hours of operation. The better measure of activity, labour hours or machine hours, may only be decided after a close analysis of historical results.

Exam focus point

In an exam **do not fall into the trap of flexing fixed costs**. Do not forget that they remain unchanged regardless of the level of activity. In the December 2008 exam there was a question on flexing a budget. Many candidates incorrectly flexed the fixed costs. Even if fixed overheads are initially expressed on a 'per unit' basis in the question, remember that once you have calculated the total fixed cost for a given activity level, it will remain unchanged when activity levels alter.

The **measure of activity used to estimate variable costs should satisfy certain criteria**.

Criteria	Detail
Derived from the activity that causes particular costs to vary	
Independent of variable factors other than its own volume	For example, if labour hours are the measure of activity, the level of activity should be measured in labour hours, and not the labour cost of those hours (the latter being prone to the effect of a price change).
Stable	In this respect, a standard unit of output provides a better measure than actual units. For example, if total costs are assumed to vary with direct labour hours, it would be more appropriate to choose 'standard hours produced' as a measure of activity than 'actual hours worked' because the actual hours may have been worked efficiently or inefficiently, and the variations in performance would probably affect the actual costs incurred.

3 Flexible budgets and budgetary control

FAST FORWARD

A prerequisite of flexible budgeting is a knowledge of cost behaviour.

The differences between the components of the fixed budget and the actual results are known as **budget variances.**

Key term

Budgetary control is the practice of establishing budgets which identify areas of responsibility for individual managers (for example production managers, purchasing managers and so on) and of regularly comparing actual results against expected results. The differences between actual results and expected results are called **variances** and these are used to provide a guideline for control action by individual managers.

We will be looking at variances in some detail later in the text.

Individual managers are held responsible for **investigating differences** between budgeted and actual results, and are then expected to **take corrective action** or amend the plan in the light of actual events.

The wrong approach to budgetary control is to compare actual results against a fixed budget. Consider the following example.

Tree manufactures a single product, the bough. Budgeted results and actual results for June are shown below.

	Budget	*Actual results*	*Variance*
Production and sales of the bough (units)	2,000	3,000	
	$	$	$
Sales revenue (a)	20,000	30,000	10,000 (F)
Direct materials	6,000	8,500	2,500 (A)
Direct labour	4,000	4,500	500 (A)
Maintenance	1,000	1,400	400 (A)
Depreciation	2,000	2,200	200 (A)
Rent and rates	1,500	1,600	100 (A)
Other costs	3,600	5,000	1,400 (A)
Total costs (b)	18,100	23,200	5,100
Profit (a)–(b)	1,900	6,800	4,900 (F)

(a) In this example, the variances are meaningless for purposes of control. **Costs were higher than budget because the volume of output was also higher**; variable costs would be expected to increase above the budgeted costs. There is no information to show whether control action is needed for any aspect of costs or revenue.

(b) For control purposes, it is necessary to know the following.

- (i) Were actual costs higher than they should have been to produce and sell 3,000 boughs?
- (ii) Was actual revenue satisfactory from the sale of 3,000 boughs?
- (iii) Has the volume of units made and sold varied from the budget favourably or adversely?

Correct approach to budgetary control

(a) **Identify fixed and variable costs.**

(b) **Produce a flexible budget using marginal costing techniques.**

In the previous example of Tree, let us suppose that we have the following information regarding cost behaviour.

(a) Direct materials and maintenance costs are variable.

(b) Although basic wages are a fixed cost, direct labour is regarded as variable in order to measure efficiency/productivity.

(c) Rent and rates and depreciation are fixed costs.

(d) Other costs consist of fixed costs of $1,600 plus a variable cost of $1 per unit made and sold.

Now that the cost behaviour patterns are known, a budget cost allowance can be calculated for each item of expenditure. This allowance is shown in **a flexible budget** as the **expected expenditure on each item for the relevant level of activity**. The budget cost allowances are calculated as follows.

(a)	Variable cost allowances	= original budgets × (3,000 units/2,000 units)
	eg material cost allowance	= $6,000 × $^3/_2$ = $9,000
(b)	Fixed cost allowances	= as original budget
(c)	Semi-fixed cost allowances	= original budgeted fixed costs + (3,000 units × variable cost per unit)
	eg other cost allowances	= $1,600 + (3,000 × $1) = $4,600

The budgetary control analysis should be as follows.

	Fixed budget (a)	Flexible budget (b)	Actual results (c)	Budget variance (b)–(c)
Production & sales (units)	2,000	3,000	3,000	
	$	$	$	$
Sales revenue	20,000	30,000	30,000	0
Variable costs				
Direct materials	6,000	9,000	8,500	500 (F)
Direct labour	4,000	6,000	4,500	1,500 (F)
Maintenance	1,000	1,500	1,400	100 (F)
Semi-variable costs				
Other costs	3,600	4,600	5,000	400 (A)
Fixed costs				
Depreciation	2,000	2,000	2,200	200 (A)
Rent and rates	1,500	1,500	1,600	100 (A)
Total costs	18,100	24,600	23,200	1,400 (F)
Profit	1,900	5,400	6,800	1,400 (F)

Note. (F) **denotes a favourable variance and (A) an adverse or unfavourable variance**. Adverse variances are sometimes denoted as (U) for 'unfavourable'.

We can **analyse** the above as follows.

(a) In selling 3,000 units the expected profit should have been, not the fixed budget profit of $1,900, but the flexible budget profit of $5,400. Instead, actual profit was $6,800 ie $1,400 more than we should have expected. One of the reasons for the improvement is that, **given actual output and sales** of 3,000 units, **costs were lower than expected** (and sales revenue exactly as expected).

	$
Direct materials cost variance	500 (F)
Direct labour cost variance	1,500 (F)
Maintenance cost variance	100 (F)
Other costs variance	400 (A)
Fixed cost variances	
Depreciation	200 (A)
Rent and rates	100 (A)
	1,400 (F)

Profit was therefore increased by $1,400 because costs were lower than anticipated.

(b) Another reason for the improvement in profit above the fixed budget profit is the **sales volume**. Tree sold 3,000 boughs instead of 2,000 boughs, with the following result.

	$	$
Sales revenue increased by		10,000
Variable costs increased by:		
direct materials	3,000	
direct labour	2,000	
maintenance	500	
variable element of other costs	1,000	
Fixed costs are unchanged		6,500
Profit increased by		3,500

Profit was therefore increased by $3,500 because sales volumes increased.

(c) A full variance analysis statement would be as follows.

	$	$
Fixed budget profit		1,900
Variances		
Sales volume	3,500 (F)	
Direct materials cost	500 (F)	
Direct labour cost	1,500 (F)	
Maintenance cost	100 (F)	
Other costs	400 (A)	
Depreciation	200 (A)	
Rent and rates	100 (A)	
		4,900 (F)
Actual profit		6,800

If management believes any variance is significant enough to warrant investigation, they will investigate to see whether any corrective action is necessary or whether the plan needs amending in the light of actual events.

Question

Budgetary control

The budgeted and actual results of Crunch for September were as follows. The company uses a marginal costing system. There were no opening or closing inventories.

Sales and production	*Fixed budget* 1,000 units		*Actual* 700 units	
	$	$	$	$
Sales		20,000		14,200
Variable cost of sales				
Direct materials	8,000		5,200	
Direct labour	4,000		3,100	
Variable overhead	2,000		1,500	
		14,000		9,800
Contribution		6,000		4,400
Fixed costs		5,000		5,400
Profit/(loss)		1,000		(1,000)

Required

Prepare a budget that will be useful for management control purposes.

Answer

We need to prepare a flexible budget for 700 units.

	Budget 1,000 units	Per unit	*Flexed budget* 700 units	*Actual* 700 units	*Variances*
	$	$	$	$	$
Sales	20,000	(20)	14,000	14,200	200 (F)
Variable costs					
Direct material	8,000	(8)	5,600	5,200	400 (F)
Direct labour	4,000	(4)	2,800	3,100	300 (A)
Variable production overhead	2,000	(2)	1,400	1,500	100 (A)
	14,000	(14)	9,800	9,800	
Contribution	6,000		4,200	4,400	
Fixed costs	5,000	(N/A)	5,000	5,400	400 (A)
Profit/(loss)	1,000		(800)	(1,000)	200 (A)

Note that the differences between actual results (what revenues and costs *were* for 700 units) and the flexed budget (what revenues and costs *should* be for 700 units) have been noted in the right hand column as *variances.* (F) denotes a situation where actual results were better than the flexible budget results whereas (A) denotes a situation where actual results were worse than flexible budget results.

By flexing the budget in the exercise above we removed the effect on sales revenue of the difference between budgeted *sales volume* and actual *sales volume.* But there is still a variance of $200 (F). This means that the actual *selling price* must have been different to the budgeted selling price, resulting in a $200 (F) selling price variance.

3.1 Factors to consider when preparing flexible budgets

The mechanics of flexible budgeting are, in theory, fairly straightforward. In practice, however, there are a number of **points that must be considered before figures are flexed**.

(a) The **separation of costs into their fixed and variable elements** is not always straightforward.

(b) Fixed costs may behave in a **step-line** fashion as activity levels increase/decrease.

(c) Account must be taken of the **assumptions** upon which the original fixed budget was based. Such assumptions might include the constraint posed by limiting factors, the rate of inflation, judgements about future uncertainty, the demand for the organisation's products and so on.

3.2 Fixed and flexible budgets: a summary

Attempt the following activity to ensure that you understand the difference between fixed and flexible budgets and that you are aware of their advantages, disadvantages and uses.

Question — Fixed and flexible budgets

Explain the differences between a fixed budget and a flexible budget. Describe the way in which fixed budgets and flexible budgets are useful for planning and control.

Answer

Fixed and flexible budgets: the differences

A fixed budget will not change to take into account variations in production, sales or expenses actually experienced. A flexible budget can do this by adjusting expected total costs for the level of production achieved. The original budget based on a given volume is 'flexed' to the actual volume by analysing budgeted costs over budgeted volume and multiplying by actual units produced.

Fixed and flexible budgets: their uses

Both sorts of budget are used essentially for cost control, although they also provide management with a yardstick to measure achievement and may thus encourage the attainment of objectives.

Fixed budgets are useful at the planning stage as they provide a common ground for the preparation of all the many types of budget. At the end of the period, actual results may be compared with the fixed budget and analysed for control. However, this analysis may be distorted by uncorrected errors underlying the estimates on which the fixed budget was constructed.

A flexible budget may be needed at the planning stage to complement the master budget; output may be budgeted at a number of different possible levels for instance. During the period the flexible budget may then be updated to the actual level of activity and the results compared.

As a result flexible budgets assist management control by providing more dynamic and comparable information. Relying only on a fixed budget would give rise to massive variances; since forecast volume is very unlikely to be matched, the variances will contain large volume differences. Flexible budgets are more likely to pinpoint actual problem areas on which control may be exercised.

Exam focus point

> Flexible budgets are a key syllabus area. You should be able to explain why budget variances should be based upon flexed budget figures.

4 Incremental and zero based budgeting systems

FAST FORWARD

> The traditional approach to budgeting, known as **incremental budgeting**, bases the budget on the current year's results plus an extra amount for estimated growth or inflation. It encourages **slack** and wasteful spending to creep into budgets.

The **traditional approach** to budgeting is to **base next year's budget on the current year's results plus an extra amount for estimated growth or inflation next year.** This approach is known as **incremental budgeting** since it is concerned mainly with the increments in costs and revenues which will occur in the coming period.

Incremental budgeting is a reasonable procedure if current operations are as effective, efficient and economical as they can be, and the organisation and the environment are largely unchanged.

Question — Incremental budgeting

Can incremental budgeting be used to budget for rent? What about for advertising expenditure?

Answer

Incremental budgeting is appropriate for budgeting for rent, which may be estimated on the basis of current rent plus an increment for the annual rent increase. Advertising expenditure, on the other hand, is not so easily quantifiable and is more discretionary in nature. Using incremental budgeting for advertising expenditure could allow slack and wasteful spending to creep into the budget.

In general, however, it is an **inefficient form of budgeting** as it **encourages slack** and **wasteful spending** to creep into budgets. Past inefficiencies are perpetuated because cost levels are rarely subjected to close scrutiny.

To ensure that inefficiencies are not concealed, alternative approaches to budgeting have been developed. One such approach is **zero based budgeting (ZBB)**, the use of which was pioneered by *P Pyhrr* in the United States in the early 1970s.

5 The main features of zero based budgeting systems

FAST FORWARD

> The principle behind **zero based budgeting (ZBB)** is that the budget for each cost centre should be made from 'scratch' or zero. Every item of expenditure must be justified in its entirety in order to be included in the next year's budget.
>
> There is a three-step approach to ZBB.
>
> – Define **decision packages**
> – Evaluate and rank packages
> – Allocate resources
>
> ZBB is particularly useful for the following.
>
> – Budgeting for discretionary costs
> – Rationalisation measures

5.1 The principles of zero based budgeting

ZBB rejects the assumption inherent in incremental budgeting that next year's budget can be based on this year's costs. Every aspect of the budget is examined in terms of its cost and the benefits it provides and the selection of better alternatives is encouraged.

Exam focus point

Candidates were asked to explain zero-based budgeting and give two advantages of using it in the December 2006 exam. There were eight marks available for this task.

Key term

Zero based budgeting involves preparing a budget for each cost centre from a zero base. Every item of expenditure has then to be justified in its entirety in order to be included in the next year's budget.

5.2 Implementing zero base budgeting

The implementation of ZBB involves a number of steps but of greater importance is the **development of a questioning attitude** by all those involved in the budgetary process. Existing practices and expenditures must be challenged and searching questions, such as the following must be asked.

(a) Does the activity need to be carried out?
(b) What would be the consequences if the activity was not carried out?
(c) Does the activity benefit the organisation?
(d) Is the current level of provision current?
(e) Are there alternative ways of providing the function?
(f) How much should the activity cost?
(g) Is the expenditure worth the benefits achieved?

The basic approach of ZBB has three steps.

Step 1 Define decision packages

A **decision package** is a comprehensive **description of a specific organisational activity which management can use to evaluate the activity and rank it in order of priority against other activities.** Managers prepare decision packages for the activities within the budget centre for which they have responsibility

There are two types of decision package.

(a) **Mutually exclusive packages** contain **alternative methods of getting the same job done**. The best option among the packages must be selected by comparing costs and benefits and the other packages are then discarded. For example, an organisation might consider two alternative decision packages for the preparation of the payroll: Package 1 might be in-house preparation of the payroll whereas Package 2 could involve the use of an outside agency.

(b) **Incremental packages divide one aspect of an activity into different levels of effort**. The 'base' package will describe the minimum amount of work that must be done to carry out the activity and the other packages describe what additional work could be done, at what cost and for what benefits.

Suppose that a cost centre manager is preparing a budget for maintenance costs. He might first consider two mutually exclusive packages. Package A might be to keep a maintenance team of two men per shift for two shifts each day at a cost of $60,000 per annum, whereas package B might be to obtain a maintenance service from an outside contractor at a cost of $50,000. A cost-benefit analysis will be conducted because the quicker repairs obtainable from an in-house maintenance service might justify its extra cost.

If we now suppose that package A is preferred, the budget analysis must be completed by describing the incremental variations in this chosen alternative.

(a) The 'base' package would describe the minimum requirement for the maintenance work. This might be to pay for one man per shift for two shifts each day at a cost of $30,000.

(b) Incremental package 1 might be to pay for two men on the early shift and one man on the late shift, at a cost of $45,000. The extra cost of $15,000 would need to be justified, for example by savings in lost production time, or by more efficient machinery.

(c) Incremental package 2 might be the original preference, for two men on each shift at a cost of $60,000. The cost-benefit analysis would compare its advantages, if any, over incremental package 1.

(d) Incremental package 3 might be for three men on the early shift and two on the late shift, at a cost of $75,000; and so on.

Question

ZBB

What might the base package for a personnel department cover? What might incremental packages cover?

Answer

The base package might cover the recruitment and dismissal of staff. Incremental packages might cover training, pension administration, trade union liaison, staff welfare and so on.

Step 2 **Evaluate and rank packages**

Each activity (decision package) is evaluated and ranked on the basis of its benefit to the organisation.

The ranking process provides managers with a technique to **allocate scarce resources** between different activities. Minimum work requirements (those that are essential to get a job done) will be given high priority and so too will work which meets legal obligations. In the accounting department these would be minimum requirements to operate the payroll, purchase ledger and sales ledger systems, and to maintain and publish a set of accounts which satisfies the external auditors.

The **ranking process can be lengthy** because large numbers of different packages will have been prepared by managers throughout the organisation. In large organisations the number of packages might be so huge that senior management cannot do the ranking unaided. In such circumstances, the following occurs.

(a) Cost centre managers will be asked to rank the packages for their own cost centre.

(b) The manager at the next level up the hierarchy of seniority will consolidate the rankings of his or her subordinates into a single ranking list for the group of cost centres, using the rankings of each cost centre as a guide.

(c) These consolidated rankings will be passed in turn one stage further up the management hierarchy for further consolidation. At higher levels of consolidation, the ranking process might be done by a committee of managers rather than by an individual.

Once a consolidated ranking of packages has been prepared, it should be reviewed to make sure that there is a general agreement that the rankings are reasonable and there are no anomalies in them.

Step 3 Allocate resources

Resources in the budget are then **allocated** according to the funds available and the evaluation and ranking of the competing packages. Packages involving small expenditures can be dealt with by junior managers but senior managers must make decisions involving larger amounts of expenditure. The ZBB process must, however, run through the entire management structure.

6 The advantages and limitations of zero based budgets

6.1 The advantages of implementing ZBB

(a) It is possible to identify and **remove inefficient or obsolete operations.**

(b) It forces employees to **avoid wasteful expenditure**.

(c) It can **increase motivation**.

(d) It provides a **budgeting and planning tool** for management which responds to changes in the business environment; 'obsolescent' items of expenditure are identified and dropped.

(e) The **documentation** required **provides** all management with a co-ordinated, in-depth **appraisal of an organisation's operations.**

(f) It **challenges the status quo** and forces an organisation to examine alternative activities and existing expenditure levels.

(g) In summary, ZBB should result in a **more efficient allocation of resources** to an organisation's activities and departments.

6.2 The disadvantages of ZBB

The major disadvantage of zero based budgeting is the **time and energy required**. The assumptions about costs and benefits in each package must be continually updated and new packages developed as soon as new activities emerge. The following problems might also occur.

(a) **Short-term benefits** might be **emphasised** to the detriment of long-term benefits.

(b) The **false idea that all decisions have to be made in the budget might be encouraged**. Management must be able to meet unforeseen opportunities and threats at all times, and must not feel restricted from carrying out new ideas simply because they were not approved by a decision package, cost benefit analysis and the ranking process.

(c) It may be a **call for management skills** both in constructing decision packages and in the ranking process **which the organisation does not possess**. Managers may therefore have to be trained in ZBB techniques so that they can apply them sensibly and properly.

(d) It may be **difficult to 'sell' ZBB to managers as a useful technique** for the following reasons.

    (i) Incremental costs and benefits of alternative courses of action are hard to quantify accurately.

    (ii) Employees or trade union representatives may resist management ideas for changing the ways in which work is done.

(e) The organisation's **information systems may not be capable of providing suitable** incremental cost and incremental benefit **analysis**.

(f) **The ranking process can be difficult**. Managers face three common problems.

    (i) A large number of packages may have to be ranked.

    (ii) There is often a conceptual difficulty in having to rank packages which managers regard as being equally vital, for legal or operational reasons.

    (iii) It is difficult to rank completely different types of activity, especially where activities have qualitative rather than quantitative benefits – such as spending on staff welfare and working conditions – where ranking must usually be entirely subjective.

In summary, perhaps the **most serious drawback to ZBB is that it requires a lot of management time and paperwork**. One way of obtaining the benefits of ZBB but of overcoming the drawbacks is to apply it selectively on a rolling basis throughout the organisation. This year finance, next year marketing, the year after personnel and so on. In this way all activities will be thoroughly scrutinised over a period of time.

7 Using zero based budgeting

ZBB can be used by both **profit-making** and **non-profit-making** organisations. It is popular in the US and Canada but its adoption has been slow in the UK.

The procedures of zero base budgeting do not lend themselves easily to direct manufacturing costs where standard costing, work study and the techniques of management planning and control have long been established as a means of budgeting expenditure.

ZBB is best applied to expenditure incurred in **departments that support** the essential production function. These include marketing, finance, quality control, repairs and maintenance, production planning, research and development, engineering design, personnel, data processing, sales and distribution. In many organisations, these expenses make up a large proportion of the total expenditure. These activities are less easily quantifiable by conventional methods and are **more discretionary** in nature.

ZBB can also be successfully applied to **service industries** and **non-profit-making organisations** such as local and central government departments, educational establishments, hospitals and so on.

ZBB can be applied in any organisation where alternative levels of provision for each activity are possible and where the costs and benefits are separately identifiable.

7.1 Particular uses of ZBB

(a) **Budgeting for discretionary cost items** such as advertising, R & D and training costs. The priorities for spending money could be established by ranking activities and alternative levels of spending or service can be evaluated on an incremental basis. For example, is it worth spending $2,000 more to increase the numbers trained on one type of training course by 10%? If so, what priority should this incremental spending on training be given, when compared with other potential training activities?

(b) **Rationalisation measures.** 'Rationalisation' means cutting back on production and activity levels, and cutting costs. ZBB can be used to make rationalisation decisions when an organisation is forced to make spending cuts. (This use of ZBB might explain any unpopularity it might have among managers.)

Question — ZBB again

Think about what the base package and incremental packages might cover in your department if your organisation used ZBB.

8 Rolling budgets

FAST FORWARD

Rolling budgets (continuous budgets) are budgets which are continuously updated by adding a further period (say a month or a quarter) and deducting the earliest period.

As an organisation and the environment it operates in are dynamic (always changing) management may decide to introduce a system of **rolling budgets** (also called **continuous budgets**).

Key term

A **rolling budget** is a budget which is continuously updated by adding a further accounting period (a month or quarter) when the earlier accounting period has expired.

Rolling budgets are an attempt to prepare targets and plans which are **more realistic and certain**, particularly with a regard to price levels, by **shortening the period between preparing budgets.**

Instead of preparing a period budget annually for the full budget period, there would be **budgets every one, two, three or four months** (three to six, or even twelve budgets each year). **Each of these budgets**

would plan for the next twelve months so that the current budget is extended by an extra period as the current period ends: hence the name rolling budgets.

Computerised budget models enable rolling budgets to be maintained relatively easily.

8.1 Advantages and disadvantages of rolling budgets

(a) They **reduce the element of uncertainty** in budgeting. Rolling budgets concentrate detailed planning and control on short-term prospects where the degree of **uncertainty is smaller**.

(b) They force managers to reassess the budget regularly, and to **produce budgets** which are **up to date in the light of current events and expectations**. For example, if annual budgets are formulated by adding an allowance for inflation to last year's figures, there is a danger that the annual rate of inflation will be over-estimated so that the budgets will be too high and thus encourage overspending by departments. In contrast, quarterly **budgets prepared on a rolling basis are likely to predict inflation rates more accurately** because shorter-term forecasts are used.

(c) **Planning and control will be based on a recent plan** instead of a fixed annual budget that might have been made many months ago and which is no longer realistic.

(d) Realistic budgets are likely to have a **better motivational influence** on managers.

(e) There is **always a budget which extends for several months ahead**. For example, if rolling budgets are prepared quarterly there will always be a budget extending for the next 9 to 12 months. If rolling budgets are prepared monthly there will always be a budget for the next 11 to 12 months. This is not the case when fixed annual budgets are used.

Question

Disadvantages

What do you see as the disadvantages of rolling budgets?

Answer

(a) A system of rolling budgets calls for the routine preparation of a new budget at regular intervals during the course of the one financial year. This involves more time, effort and money in budget preparation.

(b) Frequent budgeting might have an off-putting effect on managers who doubt the value of preparing one budget after another at regular intervals, even when there are major differences between the figures in one budget and the next.

(c) Revisions to the budget might involve revisions to standard costs too, which in turn would involve revisions to inventory valuations. This could mean that a large administrative effort is required in the accounts department every time a rolling budget is prepared to bring the accounting records up to date.

8.1.1 Rolling budgets or updated annual budgets

If the expected changes are not likely to be continuous there is a strong argument that routine updating of the budget is unnecessary. **Instead the annual budget could be updated whenever changes become foreseeable**, so that a budget might be updated once or twice, and perhaps more often, during the course of the year.

When a fixed budget is updated, a 'rolling' budget would probably not be prepared. For example, if a budget is updated in month 8 of the year, the updated budget would relate to months 8–12 at the end of the financial year. It would not be extended to month 7 of the following year.

9 Behavioural implications of budgeting

FAST FORWARD

Used correctly a budgetary control system can **motivate** but it can also produce undesirable **negative reactions**.

The purpose of a budgetary control system is to assist management in planning and controlling the resources of their organisation by providing appropriate control information. The information will only be valuable, however, if it is interpreted correctly and used purposefully by managers *and* employees.

The correct use of control information therefore depends not only on the content of the information itself, but also on the behaviour of its recipients. This is because control in business is exercised by people. Their attitude to control information will colour their views on what they should do with it and a number of behavioural problems can arise.

(a) The **managers who set the budget** or standards are **often not the managers** who are then made **responsible for achieving budget targets.**

(b) The **goals of the organisation as a whole**, as expressed in a budget, **may not coincide with the personal aspirations of individual managers**.

(c) **Control is applied at different stages by different people**. A supervisor might get weekly control reports, and act on them; his superior might get monthly control reports, and decide to take different control action. Different managers can get in each others' way, and resent the interference from others.

9.1 Motivation

Motivation is what makes people behave in the way that they do. It comes from individual attitudes, or group attitudes. Individuals will be motivated by personal desires and interests. These may be in line with the objectives of the organisation, and some people 'live for their jobs'. Other individuals see their job as a chore, and their motivations will be unrelated to the objectives of the organisation they work for.

It is therefore vital that the goals of management and the employees harmonise with the goals of the organisation as a whole. This is known as **goal congruence**. Although obtaining goal congruence is essentially a behavioural problem, **it is possible to design and run a budgetary control system which will go some way towards ensuring that goal congruence is achieved**. Managers and employees must therefore be favourably disposed towards the budgetary control system so that it can operate efficiently.

The management accountant should therefore try to ensure that employees have positive attitudes towards **setting budgets, implementing budgets** (that is, putting the organisation's plans into practice) and feedback of results (**control information**). If this desirable state of affairs does not exist the organisation is at risk of under-performing as a result of dysfunctional decision-making.

Key term

Goal congruence is the state which leads individuals or groups to take actions that are in their self-interest and also in the best interest of the organisation.

CIMA Official Terminology

Dysfunctional decision making occurs when goal congruence does not exist or is impaired. Managers and others take decisions that promote their self-interest at the expense of the interest of the organisation.

9.1.1 Poor attitudes when setting budgets

If managers are involved in preparing a budget, poor attitudes or hostile behaviour towards the budgetary control system can begin at the **planning stage.**

(a) Managers may **complain that they are too busy** to spend much time on budgeting.

(b) They may **build 'slack' into their expenditure estimates**.

(c) They may argue that **formalising a budget plan on paper is too restricting** and that managers should be allowed flexibility in the decisions they take.

(d) They may set budgets for their budget centre and **not coordinate** their own plans with those of other budget centres.

(e) They may **base future plans on past results**, instead of using the opportunity for formalised planning to look at alternative options and new ideas.

On the other hand, **managers may not be involved in the budgeting process**. Organisational goals may not be communicated to them and they might have their budget decided for them by senior management or administrative decision. It is **hard for people to be motivated to achieve targets set by someone else.**

9.1.2 Poor attitudes when putting plans into action

Poor attitudes also arise **when a budget is implemented**.

(a) Managers might **put in only just enough effort** to achieve budget targets, without trying to beat targets.

(b) A formal budget might **encourage rigidity and discourage flexibility**.

(c) **Short-term planning** in a budget **can draw attention away from the longer-term consequences** of decisions.

(d) There might be **minimal cooperation and communication** between managers.

(e) Managers will often try to make sure that they **spend up to their full budget allowance, and do not overspend**, so that they will not be accused of having asked for too much spending allowance in the first place.

9.1.3 Poor attitudes and the use of control information

The **attitude of managers towards the accounting control information** they receive **might reduce the information's effectiveness**.

(a) Management accounting control reports could well be seen as having a relatively **low priority** in the list of management tasks. Managers might take the view that they have more pressing jobs on hand than looking at routine control reports.

(b) Managers might **resent control information**; they may see it as **part of a system of trying to find fault with their work**. This resentment is likely to be particularly strong when budgets or standards are imposed on managers without allowing them to participate in the budget-setting process.

(c) If budgets are seen as **pressure devices** to push managers into doing better, control reports will be resented.

(d) Managers **may not understand the information** in the control reports, because they are unfamiliar with accounting terminology or principles.

(e) Managers might have a **false sense of what their objectives should be**. A production manager might consider it more important to maintain quality standards regardless of cost. He would then dismiss adverse expenditure variances as inevitable and unavoidable.

(f) **If there are flaws in the system of recording actual costs**, managers will dismiss control information as unreliable.

(g) **Control information** might be **received weeks after the end of the** period to which it relates, in which case managers might regard it as out-of-date and no longer useful.

(h) Managers might be **held responsible for variances outside their control**.

It is therefore obvious that accountants and senior management should try to implement systems that are acceptable to budget holders and which produce positive effects.

9.1.4 Pay as a motivator

Many researchers agree that **pay can be an important motivator**, when there is a formal link between higher pay (or other rewards, such as promotion) and achieving budget targets. Individuals are likely to work harder to achieve budget if they know that they will be rewarded for their successful efforts. There are, however, problems with using pay as an incentive.

(a) A serious problem that can arise is that **formal reward and performance evaluation systems can encourage dysfunctional behaviour**. Many investigations have noted the tendency of managers to pad their budgets either in anticipation of cuts by superiors or to make the subsequent variances more favourable. And there are numerous examples of managers making decisions in response to performance indices, even though the decisions are contrary to the wider purposes of the organisation.

(b) The targets must be challenging, but fair, otherwise individuals will become dissatisfied. **Pay can be a demotivator as well as a motivator**!

10 Participation and performance evaluation

FAST FORWARD

There are basically two ways in which a budget can be set: from the **top down (imposed** budget) or from the **bottom up (participatory** budget). Many writers refer to a third style (negotiated). There are three ways of using budgetary information to evaluate managerial performance (**budget constrained style, profit conscious style, non-accounting style**).

10.1 Participation

It has been argued that **participation** in the budgeting process **will improve motivation** and so will improve the quality of budget decisions and the efforts of individuals to achieve their budget targets (although obviously this will depend on the personality of the individual, the nature of the task (narrowly defined or flexible) and the organisational culture).

There are basically two ways in which a budget can be set: from the **top down** (imposed budget) or from the **bottom up** (participatory budget).

10.2 Imposed style of budgeting

Key term

An **imposed/top-down budget** is 'A budget allowance which is set without permitting the ultimate budget holder to have the opportunity to participate in the budgeting process'. (CIMA *Official Terminology*)

In this approach to budgeting, **top management prepare a budget with little or no input from operating personnel** which is then imposed upon the employees who have to work to the budgeted figures.

The times when imposed budgets are effective

(a) In newly-formed organisations
(b) In very small businesses
(c) During periods of economic hardship
(d) When operational managers lack budgeting skills
(e) When the organisation's different units require precise coordination

There are, of course, advantages and disadvantages to this style of setting budgets.

(a) **Advantages**

 (i) Strategic plans are likely to be incorporated into planned activities.
 (ii) They enhance the coordination between the plans and objectives of divisions.
 (iii) They use senior management's awareness of total resource availability.
 (iv) They decrease the input from inexperienced or uninformed lower-level employees.
 (v) They decrease the period of time taken to draw up the budgets.

(b) **Disadvantages**

 (i) Dissatisfaction, defensiveness and low morale amongst employees. It is hard for people to be motivated to achieve targets set by somebody else.
 (ii) The feeling of team spirit may disappear.
 (iii) The acceptance of organisational goals and objectives could be limited.

(iv) The feeling of the budget as a punitive device could arise.

(v) Managers who are performing operations on a day to day basis are likely to have a better understanding of what is achievable.

(vi) Unachievable budgets could result if consideration is not given to local operating and political environments. This applies particularly to overseas divisions.

(vii) Lower-level management initiative may be stifled.

10.3 Participative style of budgeting

Key term

Participative/bottom-up budgeting is 'A budgeting system in which all budget holders are given the opportunity to participate in setting their own budgets'.

(CIMA *Official Terminology*)

In this approach to budgeting, **budgets are developed by lower-level managers who then submit the budgets to their superiors**. The budgets are based on the lower-level managers' perceptions of what is achievable and the associated necessary resources.

Question

Participative budgets

In what circumstances might participative budgets *not* be effective?

A In centralised organisations
B In well-established organisations
C In very large businesses
D During periods of economic affluence

Answer

The correct answer is A.

An imposed budget is likely to be most effective in a centralised organisation.

As well as in the circumstances in B, C and D, participative budgets are also effective when operational management have strong budgeting skills and when the organisation's different units act autonomously.

Advantages of participative budgets

(a) They are based on information from employees most familiar with the department.
(b) Knowledge spread among several levels of management is pulled together.
(c) Morale and motivation is improved.
(d) They increase operational managers' commitment to organisational objectives.
(e) In general they are more realistic.
(f) Co-ordination between units is improved.
(g) Specific resource requirements are included.
(h) Senior managers' overview is mixed with operational level details.
(i) Individual managers' aspiration levels are more likely to be taken into account.

Disadvantages of participative budgets

(a) They consume more time.
(b) Changes implemented by senior management may cause dissatisfaction.
(c) Budgets may be unachievable if managers are not qualified to participate.
(d) They may cause managers to introduce budgetary slack and budget bias.
(e) They can support 'empire-building' by subordinates.
(f) An earlier start to the budgeting process could be required.
(g) Managers may set 'easy' budgets to ensure that they are achievable.

10.4 Negotiated style of budgeting

Key term

A **negotiated budget** is 'A budget in which budget allowances are set largely on the basis of negotiations between budget holders and those to whom they report'.

(CIMA *Official Terminology*)

At the two extremes, budgets can be dictated from above or simply emerge from below but, in practice, different levels of management often agree budgets by a process of negotiation. In the imposed budget approach, operational managers will try to negotiate with senior managers the budget targets which they consider to be unreasonable or unrealistic. Likewise senior management usually review and revise budgets presented to them under a participative approach through a process of negotiation with lower level managers. **Final budgets are therefore most likely to lie between what top management would really like and what junior managers believe is feasible.** The budgeting process is hence a **bargaining process** and it is this bargaining which is of vital importance, **determining whether the budget is an effective management tool or simply a clerical device**.

10.5 Performance evaluation

A very important **source of motivation to perform well** (to achieve budget targets, perhaps, or to eliminate variances) is, not surprisingly, being **kept informed about how actual results are progressing, and how actual results compare with target**. Individuals should not be kept in the dark about their performance.

The information fed back about actual results should have the qualities of good information.

Question — Good information

Cast your mind back to your earlier studies. Which of the following is not a quality of good information?

A Relevant
B Complete
C Timely
D Cheap

Answer

The correct answer is D.

Good information is not necessarily cheap. The cost of providing it should be less than the value of the benefits it provides, however.

Here are the qualities of good information.

(a) Relevance
(b) Accuracy
(c) Inspires confidence
(d) Timely
(e) Cost of provision less than the value of benefits provided
(f) Completeness
(g) Clarity
(h) Appropriately communicated (channel and recipient)
(i) Manageable volume

10.6 Features of feedback

(a) Reports should be **clear** and **comprehensive**.

(b) The '**exception principle**' should be applied so that **significant variances** are highlighted for investigation.

(c) Reports should identify the **controllable** costs and revenues, which are the items that can be directly influenced by the manager who receives the report. It can be demotivating if managers feel that they are being held responsible for items which are outside their control and which they are unable to influence.

(d) Reports should be **timely**, which means they must be produced in good time to allow the individual to take control action before any adverse results get much worse.

(e) Information should be **accurate** (although only accurate enough for its purpose as there is no need to go into unnecessary detail for pointless accuracy).

(f) Reports should be communicated to the manager who has **responsibility** and **authority** to act on the matter.

Surprisingly research evidence suggests that **all too often accounting performance measures lead to a lack of goal congruence**. Managers seek to improve their performance on the basis of the indicator used, even if this is not in the best interests of the organisation as a whole. For example, a production manager may be encouraged to achieve and maintain high production levels and to reduce costs, particularly if his or her bonus is linked to these factors. Such a manager is likely to be highly motivated. But the need to maintain high production levels could lead to high levels of slow-moving inventory, resulting in an adverse effect on the company's cash flow.

The **impact of an accounting system on managerial performance** depends ultimately on how the information is used. Research by Hopwood has shown that there are three distinct ways of using budgetary information to evaluate managerial performance.

Style of evaluation	Comment
Budget constrained	'The manager's performance is primarily evaluated upon the basis of his ability to continually meet the budget on a short-term basis. This criterion of performance is stressed at the expense of other valued and important criteria and the manager will receive unfavourable feedback from his superior if, for instance, his actual costs exceed the budgeted costs, regardless of other considerations.'
Profit conscious	'The manager's performance is evaluated on the basis of his ability to increase the general effectiveness of his unit's operations in relation to the long-term purposes of the organisation. For instance, at the cost centre level one important aspect of this ability concerns the attention which he devotes to reducing long-run costs. For this purpose, however, the budgetary information has to be used with great care in a rather flexible manner.'
Non-accounting	'The budgetary information plays a relatively unimportant part in the superior's evaluation of the manager's performance.'

A summary of the effects of the three styles of evaluation is as follows.

		Style of evaluation	
	Budget constrained	*Profit conscious*	*Non-accounting*
Involvement with costs	HIGH	HIGH	LOW
Job-related tension	HIGH	MEDIUM	MEDIUM
Manipulation of the accounting reports (**bias**)	EXTENSIVE	LITTLE	LITTLE
Relations with the supervisor	POOR	GOOD	GOOD
Relations with colleagues	POOR	GOOD	GOOD

Research has shown no clear preference for one style over another.

10.7 Budgetary slack

Key term

> **Budgetary slack** is the difference between the minimum necessary costs and the costs built into the budget or actually incurred.

In the process of preparing budgets, managers might **deliberately overestimate costs and underestimate sales**, so that they will not be blamed in the future for overspending and poor results.

In controlling actual operations, managers must then **ensure that their spending rises to meet their budget**, otherwise they will be 'blamed' for careless budgeting.

A typical situation is for a manager to **pad the budget** and waste money on non-essential expenses so that he uses all his budget allowances. The reason behind his action is the fear that unless the allowance is fully spent it will be reduced in future periods thus making his job more difficult as the future reduced budgets will not be so easy to attain. Because inefficiency and slack are allowed for in budgets, achieving a budget target means only that costs have remained within the accepted levels of inefficient spending.

Conversely, it has been noted that, after a run of mediocre results, some managers **deliberately overstate revenues and understate cost estimates**, no doubt feeling the need to make an immediate favourable impact by promising better performance in the future. They may merely delay problems, however, as the managers may well be censured when they fail to hit these optimistic targets.

11 The use of budgets as targets

FAST FORWARD

> In certain situations it is useful to prepare an **expectations budget** and an **aspirations budget**.
>
> Management and the management accountant require strategies and methods for dealing with the **tensions** and **conflict** resulting from the **conflicting purposes** of a budget.

Once decided, budgets become targets. As targets, they can motivate managers to achieve a high level of performance. But **how difficult should targets be**? And how might people react to targets of differing degrees of difficulty in achievement?

(a) There is likely to be a **demotivating** effect where an **ideal standard** of performance is set, because adverse efficiency variances will always be reported. We consider performance standards in more detail in Chapter 11.

(b) A **low standard of efficiency** is also **demotivating**, because there is no sense of achievement in attaining the required standards, and there will be no impetus for employees to try harder to do better than this.

(c) A **budgeted level of attainment** could be 'normal': that is, the **same as the level that has been achieved in the past**. Arguably, this level will be **too low**. It might **encourage budgetary slack**.

It has been argued that **each individual has a personal 'aspiration level'**. This is a level of performance in a task with which the individual is familiar, which the individual undertakes for himself to reach. This aspiration level might be quite challenging and if individuals in a work group all have similar aspiration levels it should be possible to incorporate these levels within the official operating standards.

Some care should be taken, however, in applying this.

(a) If a manager's **tendency to achieve success is stronger than the tendency to avoid failure**, budgets with **targets of intermediate levels of difficulty** are the most **motivating**, and stimulate a manager to better performance levels. Budgets which are either too easy to achieve or too difficult are de-motivating, and managers given such targets achieve relatively low levels of performance.

(b) A manager's **tendency to avoid failure might be stronger than the tendency to achieve success**. (This is likely in an organisation in which the budget is used as a pressure device on subordinates by senior managers). Managers might then be discouraged from trying to achieve budgets of intermediate difficulty and tend to avoid taking on such tasks, resulting in poor levels of performance, worse than if budget targets were either easy or very difficult to achieve.

It has therefore been suggested that in a situation where budget targets of an intermediate difficulty *are* motivating, such targets ought to be set if the purpose of budgets is to motivate; however, although budgets which are set for **motivational purposes** need to be stated in terms of **aspirations rather than expectations**, budgets for planning and decision purposes need to be stated in terms of the best available estimate of expected actual performance. The **solution** might therefore be to have **two budgets**.

(a) A **budget for planning and decision making based on reasonable expectations**.

(b) A second **budget for motivational purposes**, with **more difficult targets of performance** (that is, targets of an intermediate level of difficulty).

These two budgets might be called an **'expectations budget'** and an **'aspirations budget'** respectively.

12 The management accountant and motivation

We have seen that budgets serve many purposes, but in some instances their purposes can conflict and have an effect on management behaviour. Management and the management accountant therefore require strategies and methods for dealing with the resulting tensions and conflict. For example, should targets be adjusted for uncontrollable and unforeseeable environmental influence? But what is then the effect on motivation if employees view performance standards as changeable?

Can performance measures and the related budgetary control system ever **motivate managers** towards achieving the organisation's goals?

(a) Accounting measures of performance **can't provide a comprehensive assessment** of what a person has achieved for the organisation.

(b) It is unfair as it is usually **impossible to segregate controllable and uncontrollable components of performance**.

(c) Accounting **reports tend to concentrate on short-term achievements**, to the exclusion of the long-term effects.

(d) Many accounting **reports try to serve several different purposes**, and in trying to satisfy several needs actually satisfy none properly.

The management accountant does not have the authority to do much on his or her own to improve hostile or apathetic attitudes to control information. There has to be support, either from senior management or from budget centre managers. However, the management accountant can do quite a lot to improve and then maintain the standard of a budgetary control reporting system.

(a) **How senior management can offer support**

    (i) Making sure that a **system of responsibility accounting is adopted**. We will discuss this in the next chapter.

    (ii) Allowing **managers to have a say in formulating their budgets**.

    (iii) Offering **incentives** to managers who meet budget targets.

    (iv) **Not regarding budgetary control information as a way of apportioning blame.**

(b) **Budget centre managers should accept their responsibilities**. In-house training courses could be held to encourage a collective, cooperative and positive attitude amongst managers.

(c) **How the management accountant can improve** (or maintain) the **quality of the budgetary control system**

    (i) **Develop a working relationship with operational managers**, going out to meet them and discussing the control reports.

    (ii) **Explain the meaning of budgets and control reports**.

    (iii) **Keep accounting jargon in these reports to a minimum.**

    (iv) Make **reports clear and to the point**, for example using the principle of reporting by exception.

    (v) Provide control information with a **minimum of delay.**

(vi) **Make control information as useful as possible**, by distinguishing between directly attributable and controllable costs over which a manager should have influence and apportioned or fixed costs which are unavoidable or uncontrollable.

(vii) Make sure that **actual costs are recorded accurately**.

(viii) Ensure that **budgets are up-to-date**, either by having a system of rolling budgets, or else by updating budgets or standards as necessary, and ensuring that standards are 'fair' so that control information is realistic.

Attention!

There are no ideal solutions to the conflicts caused by the operation of a budgetary control system. Management and the management accountant have to develop their own ways of dealing with them, taking into account their organisation, their business and the personalities involved.

Question

Participation in budgets

Discuss the behavioural aspects of participation in the budgeting process and any difficulties you might envisage.

Answer

The level of participation in the budgeting process can vary from zero participation to a process of group decision making. There are a number of behavioural aspects of participation to consider.

(a) **Communication**. Managers cannot be expected to achieve targets if they do not know what those targets are. Communication of targets is made easier if managers have participated in the budgetary process from the beginning.

(b) **Motivation**. Managers are likely to be better motivated to achieve a budget if they have been involved in compiling it, rather than having a dictatorial budget imposed on them.

(c) **Realistic targets**. A target must be achievable and accepted as realistic if it is to be a motivating factor. A manager who has been involved in setting targets is more likely to accept them as realistic. In addition, managers who are close to the operation of their departments may be more aware of the costs and potential savings in running it.

(d) **Goal congruence**. One of the best ways of achieving goal congruence is to involve managers in the preparation of their own budgets, so that their personal goals can be taken into account in setting targets.

Although participative budgeting has many advantages, difficulties might also arise.

(a) **Pseudo-participation**. Participation may not be genuine, but merely a pretence at involving managers in the preparation of their budgets. Managers may feel that their contribution is being ignored, or that the participation consists of merely obtaining their agreement to a budget which has already been decided. If this is the case then managers are likely to be more demotivated than if there is no participation at all.

(b) **Coordination**. If participative budgeting is well managed it can improve the coordination of the preparation of the various budgets. There is, however, a danger that too many managers will become involved so that communication becomes difficult and the process become complex.

(c) **Training**. Some managers may not possess the necessary skill to make an effective contribution to the preparation of their budgets. Additional training may be necessary, with the consequent investment of money and time. It may also be necessary to train managers to understand the purposes and advantages of participation.

(d) **Slack**. If budgets are used in a punitive fashion for control purposes then managers will be tempted to build in extra expenditure to provide a 'cushion' against overspending. It is easier for them to build in slack in a participative system.

Chapter Roundup

- **Fixed budgets** remain unchanged regardless of the level of activity; **flexible budgets** are designed to flex with the level of activity.
- Comparison of a fixed budget with the actual results for a different level of activity is of little use for control purposes. Flexible budgets should be used to show what cost and revenues should have been for the actual level of activity.
- A prerequisite of flexible budgeting is a knowledge of cost behaviour.
- The differences between the components of the fixed budget and the actual results are known as **budget variances**.
- The traditional approach to budgeting, known as **incremental budgeting**, bases the budget on the current year's results plus an extra amount for estimated growth or inflation. It encourages **slack** and wasteful spending to creep into budgets.
- The principle behind **zero based budgeting (ZBB)** is that the budget for each cost centre should be made from 'scratch' or zero. Every item of expenditure must be justified in its entirety in order to be included in the next year's budget.
- There is a three-step approach to ZBB.
  - Define **decision packages**
  - Evaluate and rank packages
  - Allocate resources
- ZBB is particularly useful for the following.
  - Budgeting for discretionary costs
  - Rationalisation measures
- **Rolling budgets** (**continuous budgets**) are budgets which are continuously updated by adding a further period (say a month or a quarter) and deducting the earliest period.
- Used correctly a budgetary control system can **motivate** but it can also produce undesirable **negative reactions**.
- There are basically two ways in which a budget can be set: from the **top down (imposed** budget) or from the **bottom up** (**participatory** budget). Many writers refer to a third style (negotiated).
- There are three ways of using budgetary information to evaluate managerial performance (**budget constrained style**, **profit conscious style**, **non-accounting style**).
- In certain situations it is useful to prepare an **expectations budget** and an **aspirations budget**.
- Management and the management accountant require strategies and methods for dealing with the **tensions** and **conflict** resulting from the **conflicting purposes** of a budget.

Quick Quiz

1 Distinguish between a fixed budget and a flexible budget.

2 Flexible budgets are normally prepared on a marginal cost basis. True or false?

3 What is the correct approach to budgetary control?

4 What are the two main reasons for differences between a fixed budget profit and actual profit?

5 What is incremental budgeting?

6 Name two types of decision package.

7 Describe two particular uses of ZBB.

8 What are continuous budgets?

9 In what circumstances are imposed budgets effective?

10 *Match the descriptions to the budgeting style.*

Description

(a) Budget allowances are set without the involvement of the budget holder

(b) All budget holders are involved in setting their own budgets

(c) Budget allowances are set on the basis of discussions between budget holders and those to whom they report

Budgeting style

Negotiated budgeting
Participative budgeting
Imposed budgeting

11 *Choose the appropriate words from those highlighted.*

An **expectations/aspirations** budget would be most useful for the purposes of planning and decision making based on reasonable expectations, whereas an **aspirations/expectations** budget is more appropriate for improving motivation by setting targets of an intermediate level of difficulty.

12 Which of the following definitions best describes zero based budgeting?

A A method of budgeting where an attempt is made to make the expenditure under each cost heading as close to zero as possible.

B A method of budgeting whereby all activities are re-evaluated each time a budget is formulated.

C A method of budgeting that recognises the difference between the behaviour of fixed and variable costs with respect to changes in output and the budget is designed to change appropriately with such fluctuations.

D A method of budgeting where the sum of revenues and expenditures in each budget centre must equal zero.

13 Which of the following statements are true?

I A flexible budget can be used to control operational efficiency.

II Incremental budgeting can be defined as a system of budgetary planning and control that measures the additional costs that are incurred when there are unplanned extra units of activity.

III Rolling budgets review and, if necessary, revise the budget for the next quarter to ensure that budgets remain relevant for the remainder of the accounting period.

A I and II only
B II and III only
C III only
D I only

Answers to Quick Quiz

1 A **fixed budget** is a budget which is designed to remain unchanged regardless of the volume of output or sales achieved.

A **flexible budget** is a budget which, by recognising different cost behaviour patterns, is designed to change if volumes of output change.

2 True.

3 The correct approach to budgetary control is as follows.

(a) Identify fixed and variable costs
(b) Produce a flexible budget using marginal costing techniques

4 A fixed budget profit might differ from an actual profit because costs were higher or lower than expected given the actual output and/or sales volumes were different to the level expected.

5 Incremental budgeting involves basing the budget on the current year's results plus an extra amount for estimated growth or inflation.

6 Mutually exclusive packages
Incremental packages

7 ZBB can be applied to support expenses, discretionary cost items and rationalisation measures.

8 Continuous budgets are rolling budgets.

9 (a) In newly-formed organisations
(b) In very small businesses
(c) During periods of economic hardship
(d) When operational managers lack budgeting skills
(e) When the organisation's different units require precise co-ordination

10 (a) Imposed budgeting
(b) Participative budgeting
(c) Negotiated budgeting

11 expectations
aspirations

12 B Zero based budgeting is a method of budgeting whereby all activities are re-evaluated each time a budget is formatted.

13 D A flexible budget can be used to control operational efficiency.

Now try the questions below from the Exam Question Bank

Number	Level	Marks	Time
Section A: Q14	MCQ	N/A	N/A
Section B: Q10	Examination	20	36 mins
Section B: Q11	Examination	20	36 mins

PART C

Standard costing

11

Standard costing

Topic list
1 The uses of standard costing
2 Setting standards
3 The behavioural implications of standard costing
4 Updating standards
5 Criticisms of standard costing
6 Budgets and standards compared

Study guide reference

		Syllabus reference
19(a)	Explain the operation of a standard costing system	5
(b)	Discuss the advantages of standard costing and variance analysis	5
(c)	Evaluate the appropriateness of standard costing in a specific situation	5
(d)	Discuss the value of standard costing in a modern manufacturing and service environment	5
(e)	Define standard absorption and standard marginal costing	5
(f)	Discuss the advantages and limitations of standard marginal and standard absorption costing	5
(g)	Prepare standard cost cards (product specification) for standard marginal and standard absorption costing	5

Exam focus point

This chapter covers a key syllabus area. Key syllabus areas usually account for 80% or more of the marks available on the exam paper.

1 The uses of standard costing

FAST FORWARD

A **standard** is a **predetermined unit of cost** for inventory valuation, budgeting and control.

1.1 What is a standard cost?

Key term

A **standard cost** is a carefully predetermined estimated unit cost.

Standard costs are usually drawn up for a unit of production or a unit of service rendered but it is also possible to have a standard cost per routine task completed, or a standard cost per $1 of sale. A standard cost per unit of production may include administration, selling and distribution costs, but in many organisations, the assessment of standards is confined to production costs only.

1.2 What is standard costing?

Key term

The CIMA *Official Terminology* definition of **standard costing** is 'A control technique that reports variances by comparing actual loss to pre-set standards so facilitating **management by exception**.'

Standard costing is the **preparation of standard costs** to be used in the following circumstances.

(a) To assist in **setting budgets** and **evaluating managerial performance.**

(b) To act as a **control device** by establishing standards, highlighting (via **variance analysis**) activities that do not conform to plan and thus alerting management to those areas that may be out of control and in need of corrective action.

(c) To enable the principle of **'management by exception'** to be practised. A standard cost, when established, is an average expected unit cost. Because it is only an average, actual results will vary to some extent above and below the average. Variances should only be reported where the difference between actual and standard is significant.

(d) To **provide a prediction of future costs** to be used in decision-making situations.

(e) To **value inventories and cost production** for cost accounting purposes. It is an alternative method of valuation to methods like FIFO, LIFO or replacement costing.

(f) To **motivate staff and management** by the provision of challenging targets.

(g) To **provide guidance on improvement of efficiency**.

Although the use of standard costs to simplify the keeping of cost accounting records should not be overlooked, we will be **concentrating** on the **control and variance analysis** aspect of standard costing.

1.3 When standard costing is used

Standard costing can be used in a variety of costing situations.

(a) Batch and mass production
(b) Process manufacture
(c) Jobbing manufacture (where there is standardisation of parts)
(d) Service industries (if a realistic cost unit can be established)

However, the **greatest benefit** from its use can be gained if there is a **degree of repetition** in the production process. It is therefore most suited to **mass production** and **repetitive assembly** work. However, a standard cost can be calculated **per task if there is a similarity of tasks**. In this way standard costing can be used by some **service organisations**.

2 Setting standards

FAST FORWARD

A **standard cost card** shows full details of the standard cost of each product.

A standard cost implies that a standard or target exists for every single element that contributes to the product: the types, usage and prices of materials and parts, the grades, rates of pay and times for the labour involved, the production methods, tools and so on. The standard cost for each part of the product is recorded on a **standard cost card**, an example of which is given below.

STANDARD COST CARD
Product: the Splodget, No 12345

	Cost	*Requirement*		
Direct materials			$	$
A	$2.00 per kg	6 kgs	12.00	
B	$3.00 per kg	2 kgs	6.00	
C	$4.00 per litre	1 litre	4.00	
Others			2.00	
				24.00
Direct labour				
Grade I	$4.00 per hour	3 hrs	12.00	
Grade II	$5.40 per hour	5 hrs	27.00	
				39.00
Variable production overheads	$1.00 per hour	8 hrs	8.00	
Fixed production overheads	$3.00 per hour	8 hrs	24.00	
Standard full cost of production			95.00	

Standard costs may be used in **both marginal and absorption costing systems**. The card illustrated has been prepared under an absorption costing system, with selling and administration costs excluded from the standard.

The **responsibility for setting** standard costs should be shared between **managers able to provide the necessary information** about levels of expected efficiency, prices and overhead costs. Standard costs are **usually revised once a year** (to allow for the new overheads budget, inflation in prices, and any changes in expected efficiency of materials usage or of labour). However they may be **revised more frequently if conditions are changing rapidly**.

2.1 Setting standards for materials costs

Direct material prices will be estimated by the purchasing department from their existing knowledge.

(a) Purchase contracts already agreed
(b) Pricing discussions with regular suppliers
(c) Quotations and estimates from potential suppliers
(d) The forecast movement of prices in the market
(e) The availability of bulk purchase discounts
(f) Material quality required

Price inflation can cause difficulties in setting realistic standard prices. Suppose that a material costs $10 per kilogram at the moment, and during the course of the next 12 months, it is expected to go up in price by 20% to $12 per kilogram. **What standard price should be selected?**

- The **current price** of $10 per kilogram
- The **expected price** for the year, say, $11 per kilogram

Either price would be possible, but neither would be entirely satisfactory.

(a) If the **current price** were used in the standard, the reported price variance would become adverse as soon as prices go up, which might be very early in the year. If prices go up gradually rather than in one big jump, it would be difficult to select an appropriate time for revising the standard.
(b) If an **estimated mid-year price** were used, price variances should be favourable in the first half of the year and adverse in the second half, again assuming that prices go up gradually. Management could only really check that in any month, the price variance did not become excessively adverse (or favourable) and that the price variance switched from being favourable to adverse around month six or seven and not sooner.

Standard costing for materials is therefore more **difficult in times of inflation but it is still worthwhile**.

(a) Usage and efficiency variances will still be meaningful.
(b) Inflation is measurable: there is no reason why its effects cannot be removed from the variances reported.
(c) Standard costs can be revised, so long as this is not done too frequently.

2.2 Setting standards for labour rates

Direct labour rates per hour will be set by discussion with the personnel department and by reference to the payroll and to any agreements on pay rises and/or bonuses with trade union representatives of the employees. A separate average hourly rate or weekly wage will be set for each different labour grade/type of employee (even though individual rates of pay may vary according to age and experience).

2.3 Setting standards for material usage and labour efficiency

To estimate the materials required to make each product (material usage) and also the labour hours required (labour efficiency), **technical specifications** must be prepared for each product by production experts (either in the production department or the work study department).

Material usage and labour efficiency standards are known as **performance standards**.

2.4 Types of performance standard

FAST FORWARD

Performance standards are used to set efficiency targets. There are four types: ideal, attainable, current and basic.

The setting of standards raises the problem of how demanding the standard should be. Should the standard represent a perfect performance or an easily attainable performance? The type of performance standard used can have behavioural implications. There are four types of standard.

Type of standard	Description
Ideal	These are based on **perfect operating conditions**: no wastage, no spoilage, no inefficiencies, no idle time, no breakdowns. Variances from ideal standards are useful for pinpointing areas where a close examination may result in large savings, but they are likely to have an unfavourable motivational impact because reported variances will always be adverse. Employees will often feel that the goals are unattainable and not work so hard.
Attainable	These are based on the hope that a standard amount of work will be carried out efficiently, machines properly operated or materials properly used. **Some allowance is made for wastage and inefficiencies.** If well-set they provide a useful psychological incentive by giving employees a realistic, but challenging target of efficiency. The consent and co-operation of employees involved in improving the standard are required.
Current	These are based on **current working conditions** (current wastage, current inefficiencies). The disadvantage of current standards is that they do not attempt to improve on current levels of efficiency.
Basic	These are **kept unaltered over a long period of time**, and may be out of date. They are used to show changes in efficiency or performance over a long period of time. Basic standards are perhaps the least useful and least common type of standard in use.

Exam focus point

Six marks were on offer in the December 2007 exam for an explanation of 'ideal' and 'attainable' standards and the merits of each.

Ideal standards, attainable standards and current standards each have their supporters and it is by **no means clear which of them is preferable**.

Question

Standards

Which of the following statements is not true?

A Variances from ideal standards are useful for pinpointing areas where a close examination might result in large cost savings.

B Basic standards may provide an incentive to greater efficiency even though the standard cannot be achieved.

C Ideal standards cannot be achieved and so there will always be adverse variances. If the standards are used for budgeting, an allowance will have to be included for these 'inefficiencies'.

D Current standards or attainable standards are a better basis for budgeting, because they represent the level of productivity which management will wish to plan for.

Answer

The correct answer is B.

Statement B is describing ideal standards, not basic standards.

2.5 Setting standards for overheads

The **standard overhead absorption rate** is the same as the **predetermined overhead absorption rate** as calculated for an absorption costing system.

The **standard absorption rate** will **depend** on the **planned production volume** for a period. Production volume will **depend on two factors**.

(a) **Production capacity** (or **'volume capacity'**) measured perhaps in standard hours of output.

(b) **Efficiency of working**, by labour or machines, allowing for rest time and contingency allowances. This will depend on the type of performance standard to be used (ideal, current, attainable and so on).

Suppose that a department has a workforce of ten employees, each of whom works a 36 hour week to make standard units, and each unit has a standard production time of two hours. The expected efficiency of the workforce is 125%.

(a) **Budgeted capacity**, in direct labour hours, would be 10 × 36 = 360 production hours per week.

(b) **Budgeted efficiency** is 125% so that the workforce should take only 1 hour of actual production time to produce 1.25 standard hours of output.

(c) This means in our example that **budgeted output** is 360 production hours × 125% = 450 standard hours of output per week. At two standard hours per unit, this represents production activity or volume of 225 units of output per week.

Output, capacity and efficiency are interrelated items, and you should check your understanding of them by attempting the following problem.

Question — Budgeted output

ABC Ltd carries out routine office work in a sales order processing department, and all tasks in the department have been given standard times. There are 40 clerks in the department who work on average 140 hours per month each. The efficiency ratio of the department is 110%.

Required

Calculate the budgeted output in the department.

Answer

Capacity	=	40 × 140 = 5,600 hours per month
Efficiency	=	110%
Budgeted output	=	5,600 × 110% = 6,160 standard hours of work per month

2.5.1 Capacity levels

Capacity levels are needed to establish a standard absorption rate for production overhead, when standard absorption costing is used. Any one of three capacity levels might be used for budgeting.

Key terms

Full capacity is 'output achievable if sales orders, supplies and workforce were all available '.

Practical capacity is 'full capacity less an allowance for known unavoidable volume losses'.

Budgeted capacity is 'standard hours planned for the budget period, taking account of, for example, budgeted sales, workforce availability and expected efficiency '.

(CIMA *Official Terminology)*

(a) **Full capacity** is the **theoretical** capacity, assuming continuous production without any stoppages due to factors such as machine downtime, supply shortages or labour shortages. Full capacity would be associated with **ideal standards**.

(b) **Practical capacity** acknowledges that **some stoppages are unavoidable**, such as maintenance time for machines, and resetting time between jobs, some machine breakdowns and so on. Practical capacity is below full capacity, and would be associated with **attainable standards**.

(c) **Budgeted capacity** is the capacity (labour hours, machine hours) **needed to produce the budgeted output**, and would be associated with **current standards**, which relate to current conditions but may not be representative of normal practical capacity over a longer period of time.

Idle capacity would be defined as the **practical capacity** in a period **less the budgeted capacity** measured in standard hours of output. It represents unused capacity that ought to be available, but which is not needed because the budgeted volume is lower than the practicable volume that could be achieved.

2.5.2 Capacity ratios

Capacity ratios can be calculated. They provide similar information to fixed overhead variances (which we cover in the next chapter).

Question — Ratios

Given the following information, calculate an idle capacity ratio, a production volume ratio and an efficiency ratio and explain their meanings.

Full capacity	10,000 standard hours	Standard hours produced	6,500
Practical capacity	8,000 standard hours	Actual hours worked	7,000
Budgeted capacity	7,500 standard hours		

Answer

Idle capacity ratio $= \dfrac{\text{Practical capacity - budgeted capacity}}{\text{Practical capacity}} \times 100\%$

$= \dfrac{8{,}000 - 7{,}500}{8{,}000} \times 100\% = 6.25\%.$

This means that 6.25% of practical capacity will be unused because budgeted volume is lower than the volume that could be achieved.

Production volume ratio $= \dfrac{\text{Standard hours produced}}{\text{Budgeted capacity}} \times 100\%$

$= \dfrac{6{,}500}{7{,}500} \times 100\% = 86^2/_3\%$

This means actual output was only $86^2/_3\%$ of budgeted output.

Efficiency ratio $= \dfrac{\text{Standard hours produced}}{\text{Actual hours worked}} \times 100\% = \dfrac{6{,}500}{7{,}000} \times 100\% = 92.86\%$

This means that the labour force were working at 92.86% efficiency.

2.6 Setting standards for selling price and margin

As well as standard costs, standard selling prices and standard margins can be set. The standard selling price will depend on a number of factors including the following.

(a) Anticipated market demand
(b) Competing products and competitors' actions
(c) Manufacturing costs
(d) Inflation estimates

The standard sales margin is the difference between the standard cost and the standard selling price.

3 The behavioural implications of standard costing

FAST FORWARD

An effective standard costing system should take account of **behavioural implications** in its design.

Setting standards and using them as a yardstick for cost control is not simply an exercise in dealing with numbers. It also involves dealing with people, and a standard costing system will only be **effective if it is designed with full understanding of its potential behavioural effects**. We have already seen how the type of performance standard used can have behavioural implications. For example the adverse variances which tend to be reported when ideal standards are used can be demotivating for the individuals who are working to achieve the standard.

Other behavioural implications to be considered in the design and operation of a standard costing system

(a) **Communication is of the utmost importance**. Because of the technical nature of much of the standard setting process, production employees and their supervisors may need to be involved. This will help to win their support for the resulting standards and they are more likely to be willing to work to achieve them. Moreover, the employees' practical knowledge will contribute towards a more accurate and useful standard for cost planning and control.

(b) **The variance reporting system should not be used punitively**. There must be no undue pressure or excessive blame attached to the non-achievement of standards. Managers who are treated in this way may resent the use of the standard costing system and thus reduce its effectiveness.

(c) **Care must be taken to distinguish between controllable and non-controllable costs in variance reporting.** It can be demotivating for managers who feel that they are being held responsible for costs and variances over which they cannot exercise control.

(d) **Variance control reports must be produced promptly and accurately**. Inaccuracy will lead to managers losing faith in the value of the information and they may not bother to act upon it. Late information may cause frustration if managers feel that they could have acted earlier if they had known that problems existed.

4 Updating standards

When an organisation introduces a system of standard costing, it is quite possible that the standards initially set will not be the most accurate reflection of what occurs 'on average'. **Initial standards** may need **substantial revision** in the early period of a standard costing system's life before they are really useful measures for control purposes.

The evolution of standards does not stop after a couple of accounting periods, however. Standards must be **continuously reviewed** to ensure that they do **mirror** what is **currently happening** and that they are the **most accurate 'average'**.

Out-of-date standards will produce **variances** that are **illogical bases** for planning, control, decision making or performance evaluation. Current operational performance cannot be compared to out-of-date standards.

'Labour and material usage standards normally are set by the industrial engineering department. Material price normally is considered the responsibility of purchasing. Similarly, the labour rates are set by the personnel department. As the production processes change (improve), past standards become less than realistic, and should be revised. It is the responsibility of departments that originally created the standard to inform the accounting department about the need for revising the standards.

But, unfortunately, some managers prefer to keep the old standards because the new improved production process makes their performance look better with old standards.'

(LU Tatikonda, 'Production Managers Need a Course in Cost Accounting', *Management Accounting* (*June 1987*), published by Institute of Management Accountants, Montvale, N J)

4.1 Improvement of the standard setting process

Standard setting procedures may be refined and extended to enable more accurate standards to be set.

(a) **Work study** methods may be established within the organisation. These enable accurate estimates of labour time to be made.

(b) The introduction of **computerised information systems** provides more reliable standards.

With CADCAM (computer-aided design/computer aided manufacture) systems the planning of manufacturing requirements can be **computerised**, with the useful spin-off that standard costs can also be constructed by computer, thus saving administrative time and expense while providing far more accurate standards.

4.2 Revision of standards

In practice standard costs are usually revised **once a year** to allow for the new overheads budget, inflation in prices and wage rates, and any changes in expected efficiency of material usage, labour or machinery.

Some argue that standards should be revised **as soon as there is any change in the basis upon which they were set.** Clearly, for example, if a standard is based on the cost of a material that is no longer available or the use of equipment which has been replaced, it is meaningless to compare actual performance using the new material and equipment with the old standard.

Coates, Rickwood and Stacey in their book *Management Accounting in Practice* put forward the following reasons for revising standards.

'(a) Manufacturing methods are **significantly** changed due to plant layout, machinery alterations, change in product design, use of different materials, etc.

(b) The relationship of normal capacity and actual activity is **significantly** out of balance.

(c) The disparity between the standard and expected performance is **so significant** that the standard as a measurement loses its value.

(d) An existing standard is discovered to be incorrectly set and a **significant** difference exists.'

(JB Coates, CP Rickwood, RJ Stacey, *Management Accounting in Practice,* CIMA)

Frequent changes in standards can cause **problems**.

(a) They may become **ineffective as motivators and measures of performance,** since it may be perceived that target setters are constantly 'moving the goal posts'.

(b) The **administrative effort** may be too time consuming (although the introduction of computer systems renders this objection less forceful).

Coates *et al* concede the following point.

'Revisions should be **held to a minimum**, despite the fact that standards may not be precise, in order to provide for relative comparisons between operating periods and/or versus budget.'

The most **suitable approach** would therefore appear to be a policy of revising the standards **whenever changes of a permanent and reasonably long-term nature occur**, but not in response to temporary 'blips' in price or efficiency.

5 Criticisms of standard costing

FAST FORWARD

There are a number of **criticisms** of the use of standard costing, particularly in the modern manufacturing environment.

Some commentators have argued that **traditional variance analysis is unhelpful and potentially misleading** in the modern organisation, and can make managers focus their attention on the wrong issues. Here are just two examples.

(a) **Efficiency variance**. Traditional variance analysis emphasises adverse efficiency variances should be avoided, which means that managers should try to prevent idle time and to keep up production. In a total quality management environment, just in time may be used (JIT being defined in CIMA *Official Terminology* as 'A system whose objective is to produce or procure products or components as they are required by a customer or for use, rather than for inventory.') In these circumstances, manufacturing to eliminate idle time could result in the manufacture of unwanted products that must be held in store and might eventually be scrapped. Efficiency variances could focus management attention on the wrong problems.

(b) **Materials price variance**. In a JIT environment the key issues in materials purchasing are supplier reliability, materials quality, and delivery in small order quantities. Purchasing managers should not be shopping around every month looking for the cheapest price. Many JIT systems depend on long-term contractual links with suppliers, which means that material price variances are not relevant for management control purposes.

Other criticisms of using standard costing in today's environment

(a) Variance analysis concentrates on only a **narrow range of costs**, and does not give sufficient attention to issues such as quality and customer satisfaction.

(b) Standard costing places **too much emphasis on direct labour costs**. Direct labour is only a small proportion of costs in the modern manufacturing environment and so this emphasis is not appropriate.

(c) Many of the variances in a standard costing system focus on the control of **short-term variable costs**. In most modern manufacturing environments, the majority of costs, including direct labour costs, tend to be fixed in the short run.

(d) The use of standard costing relies on the existence of **repetitive operations** and relatively **homogeneous** output. Nowadays many organisations are forced continually to respond to customers' changing requirements, with the result that output and operations are not so repetitive.

(e) Standard costing systems were **developed** when the **business environment** was more **stable** and **less prone to change**. The current business environment is more dynamic and it is not possible to assume stable conditions.

(f) Standard costing systems **assume** that **performance to standard is acceptable**. Today's business environment is more focused on continuous improvement.

(g) Most standard costing systems produce **control statements weekly or monthly**. The modern manager needs much more prompt control information in order to function efficiently in the dynamic business environment.

This long list of criticisms of standard costing may lead you to believe that such systems have little use in today's business environment. Standard costing systems can be **adapted to remain useful**, however.

Question — Standard costing

Can you think of some ways in which a standard costing system could be adapted so that it is useful in the modern business environment?

Answer

Here are some ideas.

(a) **Non-financial measures** can be included within management control reports. Examples include number of defects, percentage of on-time deliveries, and so on.

(b) Even when output is not standardised, it may be possible to identify a number of **standard components and activities** whose costs may be controlled effectively by the setting of standard costs and identification of variances.

(c) The use of computer power enables standards to be **updated rapidly** and more frequently, so that they remain useful for the purposes of control by comparison.

(d) The use of **ideal standards** and **more demanding performance levels** can combine the benefits of **continuous improvement** and standard costing control.

(e) **Information**, particularly of a non-financial nature, can be **produced more rapidly** with the assistance of **computers**. For example the use of on-line data capture can enable the continuous display of real time information on factors such as hours worked, number of components used and number of defects.

6 Budgets and standards compared

You will recall from your earlier studies that a **budget** is a **quantified monetary plan** for a **future period**, which **managers will try to achieve**. Its major function lies in **communicating plans** and **coordinating activities** within an organisation.

On the other hand, a **standard** is a **carefully predetermined quantity target** which can be **achieved in certain conditions**.

Budgets and standards are **similar** in the following ways.

(a) They both involve looking to the future and **forecasting** what is likely to happen given a certain set of circumstances.

(b) They are both **used for control purposes**. A budget aids control by setting financial targets or limits for a forthcoming period. Actual achievements or expenditures are then compared with the budgets and action is taken to correct any variances where necessary. A standard also achieves control by comparison of actual results against a predetermined target.

As well as being similar, **budgets and standards are interrelated**. For example, a standard unit production cost can act as the basis for a production cost budget. The unit cost is multiplied by the budgeted activity level to arrive at the budgeted expenditure on production costs.

There are, however, important differences between budgets and standards.

Budgets	Standards
Gives planned **total aggregate costs** for a function or cost centre	Shows the unit resource usage for a **single task**, for example the standard labour hours for a single unit of production
Can be prepared for **all functions**, even where output cannot be measured	Limited to situations where **repetitive actions** are performed and output can be measured
Expressed in **money terms**	**Need not be expressed in money terms**. For example a standard rate of output does not need a financial value put on it

In summary, budgets and standards are very similar and interrelated, but there are important differences between them.

Chapter Roundup

- A **standard** is a **predetermined unit of cost** for inventory valuation, budgeting and control.
- A **standard cost card** shows full details of the standard cost of each product.
- **Performance standards** are used to set efficiency targets. There are four types: ideal, attainable, current and basic.
- An effective standard costing system should take account of **behavioural implications** in its design.
- There are a number of **criticisms** of the use of standard costing, particularly in the modern manufacturing environment.

Quick Quiz

1 Match the types of performance standard to the correct descriptions.

Performance standards		*Descriptions*	
(a)	Ideal	(1)	If well set, can provide a useful psychological incentive
(b)	Attainable	(2)	Do not attempt to improve on current levels of efficiency
(c)	Current	(3)	Least common type of standard in use
(d)	Basic	(4)	Likely to have an unfavourable motivational effect

2 An attainable standard is based on perfect operating conditions. True or false?

3 Fill in the gaps.

(i) Budgets are prepared for .... costs; standards are for a ....

(ii) .... can be prepared for all functions; .... are only suitable for repetitive actions where output can be measured.

(iii) .... are expressed in money terms; .... need not be expressed in money terms.

4 Choose the appropriate words from those highlighted.

Standard costing places too much emphasis on **direct material costs/direct labour costs/ overheads**. **Direct material/direct labour/overheads is/are** a **small/large** proportion of costs in the modern manufacturing environment and so this emphasis is **appropriate/inappropriate**.

5 Four types of performance standard are

(a) ....

(b) ....

(c) ....

(d) ....

6 *Choose the correct words from those highlighted.*

A standard cost is a **planned/historical unit/total** cost.

Answers to Quick Quiz

1 (a) 4
(b) 1
(c) 2
(d) 3

2 False. An ideal standard is based on perfect operating conditions.

3 (i) aggregate total
single task

(ii) budgets
standards

(iii) budgets
standards

4 Standard costing places too much emphasis on direct labour costs. Direct labour is only a small proportion of costs in the modern manufacturing environment and so this emphasis is inappropriate.

5 (a) Ideal
(b) Attainable
(c) Current
(d) Basis

6 A standard cost is a **planned unit** cost.

Now try the questions below from the Exam Question Bank

Number	Level	Marks	Time
Section A: Q15	MCQ	N/A	N/A
Section B: Q12	Preparation	20	36 mins

Variance analysis

12

Topic list
1 Variances
2 Direct material cost variances
3 Direct labour cost variances
4 Variable production overhead variances
5 Fixed production overhead variances
6 Sales variances
7 Variances – controllable and non-controllable elements
8 Operating statements
9 Variances in a standard marginal costing system
10 Cost bookkeeping
11 Standard cost bookkeeping

Study guide reference

		Syllabus reference
14(a)	Calculate simple variances between flexed budget, fixed budgets and actual results for sales, costs and profits (i) Calculate sales price and sales margin volume variances (ii) Explain the meaning of budget variances (iii) Analyse the potential causes of budget variances	7
20(a)	Calculate material price and usage variances (price variances to be based upon usage or purchases)	5
(b)	Calculate labour rate and efficiency variances	5
(c)	Calculate fixed overhead expenditure, volume, capacity and efficiency variances	5
(d)	Calculate variable overhead expenditure and efficiency variances	5
(e)	Calculate sales margin volume and sales price variances	5
(f)	Undertake entries in a standard cost bookkeeping situation	5
21(a)	Prepare a reconciliation of standard to actual cost for an absorption costing system	5
(b)	Prepare a reconciliation of standard to actual cost for a marginal costing system	5
(c)	Prepare a reconciliation of budgeted to actual profit for an absorption costing system	5
(d)	Prepare a reconciliation of budgeted to actual profit for a marginal costing system	5
(e)	Prepare control reports suitable for presentation to management	5
22(a)	Subdivide variances to reflect responsibility structures	5
(b)	Calculate idle time variances	5
(c)	Analyse variances into controllable and non-controllable elements	5

Exam focus point

This chapter covers a key syllabus area. Key syllabus areas usually account for 80% or more of the marks available on the exam paper.

1 Variances

Exam focus point

In the June 2008 exam candidates were asked to calculate nine different variances for a total of eighteen marks.

Both the December and June 2007 exams tested variances. In the June exam this was for six marks as part of a flexible budget question. In December, this was for ten marks and asked for possible causes as well as calculations.

There were nine marks on offer in the December 2006 exam for the calculation of variances based on a flexed budget and actual outcome.

Candidates at the June 2006 sitting were asked to calculate a range of material, labour and overhead variances. They also needed to prepare a statement reconciling actual and standard cost. A total of thirteen marks were available for these requirements.

FAST FORWARD

- **Price, rate and expenditure variances** measure the difference between the actual amount of money paid and the amount of money that should have been paid for the actual quantity of materials or the actual number of hours of labour or variable overheads.
- **Usage and efficiency variances** are quantity variances. They measure the difference between the actual physical quantity of materials used or hours taken and the quantities that should have been used or taken for the actual volume of production. These physical differences are then converted into money values by applying the appropriate standard price or rate.
- The **idle time variance** is the number of hours of idle time valued at the standard rate per hour

Key term

A **variance** is the 'Difference between planned, budgeted, or standard cost and the actual cost incurred. The same comparisons may be made for revenues'.
(CIMA *Official Terminology*)

The process by which the **total difference between standard and actual** results is **analysed** is known as **variance analysis**.

Key term

Variance analysis is defined in CIMA *Official Terminology* as 'The evaluation of performance by means of variances, whose timely reporting should maximise the opportunity for managerial action'.

When **actual results are better than expected results**, we have a **favourable** variance (F). If, on the other hand, **actual results are worse than expected results**, we have an **adverse** variance (A).

Variances can be divided into three main groups.

(a) Variable cost variances
   (i) Direct material
   (ii) Direct labour
   (iii) Variable production overhead
(b) Fixed production overhead variances
(c) Sales variances

2 Direct material cost variances

Exam focus point

Three marks could be earned for suggesting the potential causes of direct material usage variances in the December 2006 exam.

The **direct material total variance** (the difference between what the output actually cost and what it should have cost, in terms of material) can be **divided into two sub-variances**.

(a) **The direct material price variance**

This is the **difference between the standard cost and the actual cost for the actual quantity of material used or purchased.** In other words, it is the difference between what the material did cost and what it should have cost.

(b) **The direct material usage variance**

This is the **difference between the standard quantity of materials that should have been used for the number of units actually produced, and the actual quantity of materials used, valued at the standard cost per unit of material.** In other words, it is the difference between how much material should have been used and how much material was used, valued at standard cost.

2.1 Example: direct material variances

Product X has a standard direct material cost as follows.

10 kilograms of material Y at $10 per kilogram = $100 per unit of X.

During period 4, 1,000 units of X were manufactured, using 11,700 kilograms of material Y which cost $98,600.

Required

Calculate the following variances.

(a) The direct material total variance
(b) The direct material price variance
(c) The direct material usage variance

2.2 Solution

(a) **The direct material total variance**

This is the difference between what 1,000 units should have cost and what they did cost.

	$
1,000 units should have cost (× $100)	100,000
but did cost	98,600
Direct material total variance	1,400 (F)

The variance is favourable because the units cost less than they should have cost.

Now we can break down the direct material total variance into its two constituent parts: the direct material price variance and the direct material usage variance.

(b) **The direct material price variance**

This is the difference between what 11,700 kgs should have cost and what 11,700 kgs did cost.

	$
11,700 kgs of Y should have cost (× $10)	117,000
but did cost	98,600
Material Y price variance	18,400 (F)

The variance is favourable because the material cost less than it should have.

(c) **The direct material usage variance**

This is the difference between how many kilograms of Y should have been used to produce 1,000 units of X and how many kilograms were used, valued at the standard cost per kilogram.

1,000 units should have used (× 10 kgs)	10,000 kgs
but did use	11,700 kgs
Usage variance in kgs	1,700 kgs (A)
× standard cost per kilogram	× $10
Usage variance in $	$17,000 (A)

The variance is adverse because more material than should have been used was used.

(d) **Summary**

	$
Price variance	18,400 (F)
Usage variance	17,000 (A)
Total variance	1,400 (F)

2.3 Materials variances and opening and closing inventory

Suppose that a company uses raw material P in production, and that this raw material has a standard price of $3 per metre. During one month 6,000 metres are bought for $18,600, and 5,000 metres are used in production. At the end of the month, inventory will have been increased by 1,000 metres. In variance analysis, the problem is to decide the **material price variance**. Should it be calculated on the basis of **materials purchased** (6,000 metres) or on the basis of **materials used** (5,000 metres)?

The answer to this problem depends on **how closing inventories** of the raw materials will be **valued**.

(a) If they are valued at **standard cost**, (1,000 units at $3 per unit) the price variance is calculated on material **purchases** in the period.

(b) If they are valued at **actual cost** (FIFO) (1,000 units at $3.10 per unit) the price variance is calculated on materials **used in production** in the period.

A **full standard costing system** is usually in operation and therefore the price variance is usually calculated on **purchases** in the period. The variance on the full 6,000 metres will be written off to the costing income statement even though only 5,000 metres are included in the cost of production.

There are two main **advantages** in extracting the material price variance at the time of **receipt**.

(a) If variances are extracted at the time of receipt they will be **brought to the attention of managers earlier** than if they are extracted as the material is used. If it is necessary to correct any variances then management action can be more timely.

(b) Since variances are extracted at the time of receipt, **all inventories will be valued at standard price**. This is administratively easier and it means that all issues from inventories can be made at standard price. If inventories are held at actual cost it is necessary to calculate a separate price variance on each batch as it is issued. Since issues are usually made in a number of small batches this can be a time-consuming task, especially with a manual system.

Question — Price variance

What is the price variance based on the information in Section 2.3 above?

A $3,100 (A)
B $600 (A)
C $3,100 (F)
D $600 (F)

Answer

The correct answer is B.

The price variance would be calculated as follows.

	$	
6,000 metres of material P purchased should cost (× $3)	18,000	
but did cost	18,600	
Price variance	600	(A)

3 Direct labour cost variances

The calculation of direct labour variances is very similar to the calculation of direct material variances.

The **direct labour total variance** (the difference between what the output should have cost and what it did cost, in terms of labour) can be **divided into two sub-variances**.

(a) **The direct labour rate variance**

This is similar to the direct material price variance. If is the **difference between the standard cost and the actual cost for the actual number of hours paid for**.

In other words, it is the difference between what the labour did cost and what it should have cost.

(b) **The direct labour efficiency variance**

This is similar to the direct material usage variance. It is the **difference between the hours that should have been worked for the number of units actually produced, and the actual number of hours worked, valued at the standard rate per hour.**

In other words, it is the difference between how many hours should have been worked and how many hours were worked, valued at the standard rate per hour.

3.1 Example: direct labour variances

The standard direct labour cost of product X is as follows.

2 hours of grade Z labour at $5 per hour = $10 per unit of product X.

During period 4, 1,000 units of product X were made, and the direct labour cost of grade Z labour was $8,900 for 2,300 hours of work.

Required

Calculate the following variances.

(a) The direct labour total variance
(b) The direct labour rate variance
(c) The direct labour efficiency (productivity) variance

3.2 Solution

(a) **The direct labour total variance**

This is the difference between what 1,000 units should have cost and what they did cost.

	$
1,000 units should have cost (× $10)	10,000
but did cost	8,900
Direct labour total variance	1,100 (F)

The variance is favourable because the units cost less than they should have done.

Again we can analyse this total variance into its two constituent parts.

(b) **The direct labour rate variance**

This is the difference between what 2,300 hours should have cost and what 2,300 hours did cost.

	$
2,300 hours of work should have cost (× $5 per hr)	11,500
but did cost	8,900
Direct labour rate variance	2,600 (F)

The variance is favourable because the labour cost less than it should have cost.

(c) **The direct labour efficiency variance**

1,000 units of X should have taken (× 2 hrs)	2,000 hrs
but did take	2,300 hrs
Efficiency variance in hours	300 hrs (A)
× standard rate per hour	× $5
Efficiency variance in $	$1,500 (A)

The variance is adverse because more hours were worked than should have been worked.

(d) **Summary**

	$
Rate variance	2,600 (F)
Efficiency variance	1,500 (A)
Total variance	1,100 (F)

3.3 Idle time variance

A company may operate a costing system in which any idle time is recorded. Idle time may be caused by machine breakdowns or not having work to give to employees, perhaps because of bottlenecks in production or a shortage of orders from customers. When idle time occurs, the labour force is still paid wages for time at work, but no actual work is done. Time paid for without any work being done is unproductive and therefore inefficient. In variance analysis, **idle time is an adverse efficiency variance**.

When idle time is recorded separately, it is helpful to provide control information which identifies the cost of idle time separately, and in variance analysis, there will be an idle time variance **as a separate part of the total labour efficiency variance**. The remaining **efficiency variance** will then relate only to the productivity of the labour force during the **hours spent actively working**.

Question — Idle time variances

Idle time variances are always adverse.

True ☐

False ☐

Answer

True

3.4 Example: labour variances with idle time

Refer to the standard cost data in Paragraph 3.1. During period 5, 1,500 units of product X were made and the cost of grade Z labour was $17,500 for 3,080 hours. During the period, however, there as a shortage of customer orders and 100 hours were recorded as idle time.

Required

Calculate the following variances.

(a) The direct labour total variance
(b) The direct labour rate variance
(c) The idle time variance
(d) The direct labour efficiency variance

3.5 Solution

(a) **The direct labour total variance**

	$
1,500 units of product X should have cost (× $10)	15,000
but did cost	17,500
Direct labour total variance	2,500 (A)

Actual cost is greater than standard cost. The variance is therefore adverse.

(b) **The direct labour rate variance**

The rate variance is a comparison of what the hours paid should have cost and what they did cost.

	$
3,080 hours of grade Z labour should have cost (× $5)	15,400
but did cost	17,500
Direct labour rate variance	2,100 (A)

Actual cost is greater than standard cost. The variance is therefore adverse.

(c) **The idle time variance**

The idle time variance is the hours of idle time, valued at the standard rate per hour.

Idle time variance = 100 hours (A) × \$5 = \$500 (A)

Idle time is **always** an **adverse** variance.

(d) **The direct labour efficiency variance**

The efficiency variance considers the hours actively worked (the difference between hours paid for and idle time hours). In our example, there were (3,080 – 100) = 2,980 hours when the labour force was not idle. The variance is calculated by taking the amount of output produced (1,500 units of product X) and comparing the time it should have taken to make them, with the actual time spent **actively** making them (2,980 hours). Once again, the variance in hours is valued at the standard rate per labour hour.

1,500 units of product X should take (× 2 hrs)	3,000 hrs
but did take (3,080 – 100)	2,980 hrs
Direct labour efficiency variance in hours	20 hrs (F)
× standard rate per hour	× \$5
Direct labour efficiency variance in \$	\$100 (F)

(e) **Summary**

	\$
Direct labour rate variance	2,100 (A)
Idle time variance	500 (A)
Direct labour efficiency variance	100 (F)
Direct labour total variance	2,500 (A)

Attention!

Remember that, if idle time is recorded, the actual hours used in the **efficiency variance** calculation are the **hours worked and not the hours paid for**.

This also applies to idle time where this occurs when calculating **variable** and **fixed overhead efficiency variances**.

Question

Labour variances

Growler is planning to make 100,000 units per period of product AA. Each unit of AA should require 2 hours to produce, with labour being paid \$11 per hour. Attainable work hours are less than clock hours, so 250,000 hours have been budgeted in the period.

Actual data for the period was:

Units produced	120,000
Direct labour cost	\$3,200,000
Clock hours	280,000

Required

Calculate the following variances.

(a) Labour rate variance
(b) Labour efficiency variance
(c) Idle time variance

Answer

The information means that clock hours have to be multiplied by 200,000/250,000 (80%) in order to arrive at a realistic efficiency variance.

(a) **Labour rate variance**

	$'000	
280,000 hours should have cost (× $11)	3,080	
but did cost	3,200	
Labour rate variance	120	(A)

(b) **Labour efficiency variance**

120,000 units should have taken (× 2 hours)	240,000	hrs
but did take (280,000 × 80%)	224,000	hrs
Variance in hours	16,000	hrs (F)
× standard rate per hour	× $11	
Labour efficiency variance	$176,000	(F)

(c) **Idle time variance**

280,000 × 20%	56,000	hrs
	× $11	
	$616,000	(A)

4 Variable production overhead variances

Suppose that the variable production overhead cost of product X is as follows.

2 hours at $1.50 = $3 per unit

During period 6, 400 units of product X were made. The labour force worked 820 hours, of which 60 hours were recorded as idle time. The variable overhead cost was $1,230.

Calculate the following variances.

(a) The variable overhead total variance
(b) The variable production overhead expenditure variance
(c) The variable production overhead efficiency variance

Since this example **relates to variable production costs**, the total variance is **based on actual units of production**. (If the overhead had been a **variable selling cost**, the variance would be **based on sales volumes**.)

	$	
400 units of product X should cost (× $3)	1,200	
but did cost	1,230	
Variable production overhead total variance	30	(A)

In many variance reporting systems, the variance analysis goes no further, and expenditure and efficiency variances are not calculated. However, the adverse variance of $30 may be explained as the **sum of two factors**.

(a) The hourly rate of spending on variable production overheads was higher than it should have been, that is there is an **expenditure variance**.

(b) The labour force worked inefficiently, and took longer to make the output than it should have done. This means that spending on variable production overhead was higher than it should have been, in other words there is an **efficiency (productivity) variance**. The variable production overhead efficiency variance is exactly the same, in hours, as the direct labour efficiency variance, and occurs for the same reasons.

It is usually assumed that **variable overheads are incurred during active working hours**, but are not incurred during idle time (for example the machines are not running, therefore power is not being consumed, and no indirect materials are being used). This means in our example that although the labour force was paid for 820 hours, they were actively working for only 760 of those hours and so variable production overhead spending occurred during 760 hours.

(a) **The variable production overhead expenditure variance**

This is the difference between the amount of variable production overhead that should have been incurred in the actual hours actively worked, and the actual amount of variable production overhead incurred.

	$	
760 hours of variable production overhead should cost (× $1.50)	1,140	
but did cost	1,230	
Variable production overhead expenditure variance	90	(A)

(b) **The variable production overhead efficiency variance**

If you already know the direct **labour efficiency variance**, the variable production overhead efficiency variance is **exactly the same in hours**, but **priced at the variable production overhead rate per hour**. In our example, the efficiency variance would be as follows.

400 units of product X should take (× 2 hrs)	800 hrs	
but did take (active hours)	760 hrs	
Variable production overhead efficiency variance in hours	40 hrs	(F)
× standard rate per hour	× $1.50	
Variable production overhead efficiency variance in $	$60	(F)

(c) **Summary**

	$	
Variable production overhead expenditure variance	90	(A)
Variable production overhead efficiency variance	60	(F)
Variable production overhead total variance	30	(A)

5 Fixed production overhead variances

FAST FORWARD

The **total fixed production overhead variance** may be broken down into two parts as usual: an **expenditure variance** and a **volume variance**. The volume variance may in turn be split into an **efficiency variance** and a **capacity variance**.

The method of calculating variances is essentially the same for labour, materials and variable overheads. As we will see, fixed production overhead variances are very different. In an absorption costing system, they are simply **an attempt to explain the under or over absorption of fixed overheads**.

The **fixed production overhead total variance** may be broken down into **two parts** as usual.

(a) **An expenditure variance**

(b) **A volume variance. This in turn may be split into two parts.**

   (i) An efficiency variance

   (ii) A capacity variance

The fixed production overhead volume variance sometimes causes confusion and may need more explanation. The most important point is that the **volume variance applies to fixed production overhead costs only** and not to variable production overheads.

(a) Variable production overheads incurred change with the volume of activity. If the master budget is to work for 300 hours and variable overheads are incurred and absorbed at a rate of $6 per hour, the variable overhead budget will be $1,800. If only 200 hours are actually worked, the variable overhead absorbed will be $1,200 and the expected expenditure will also be $1,200, so that there will be no under or over absorption of overhead because of volume changes.

(b) Fixed production overheads are different because the level of expenditure does not change as the number of hours worked varies. If the master budget is to work for 300 hours and fixed overheads are budgeted to be $2,400, the fixed overhead absorption rate will be $8 per hour. If actual hours worked are only 200 hours, the fixed overhead absorbed will be $1,600, but expected expenditure will be unchanged at $2,400. There is an under absorption of $800 because of the volume variance of 100 hours shortfall multiplied by the absorption rate of $8 per hour.

Attention!

> You will find it easier to calculate and understand fixed production overhead variances if you keep in mind the whole time the fact that you are trying to explain the reasons for any under- or over-absorbed production overhead. Remember that the absorption rate is calculated as budgeted fixed production overhead ÷ budgeted level of activity.

Generally the level of activity used in the overhead absorption rate will be units of production or hours of activity. More often than not, if just one product is being produced, the level of activity is in terms of units produced. If, however, more than one product is produced, units of output are converted to standard hours.

You will remember from your earlier studies that if either the budgeted overhead expenditure or the budgeted activity level or both are incorrect then we will have under- or over-absorbed overhead.

(a) The fixed overhead **expenditure variance** measures the under or over absorption caused by the **actual overhead expenditure being different from budget**.

(b) There are two reasons why the **actual production or hours of activity may be different from the budgeted production or budgeted number of hours** used in calculating the absorption rate.

  (i) The **work force may have been working at a more or less efficient rate than standard** to produce a given output. This is measured by the fixed overhead **efficiency variance**.

  (ii) Regardless of the level of efficiency, the **total number of hours worked could have been less or more than was originally budgeted** (employees may have worked a lot of overtime or there may have been a strike). Other things being equal, this could lead to under- or over-absorbed fixed overhead and the effect is measured by the fixed overhead **capacity variance**.

5.1 How to calculate the variances

Key terms

> **Fixed overhead total variance** is the difference between fixed overhead incurred and fixed overhead absorbed (the under - or over-absorbed fixed overhead).
>
> **Fixed overhead expenditure variance** is the difference between the budgeted fixed overhead expenditure and actual fixed overhead expenditure.
>
> **Fixed overhead volume variance** is the difference between actual and budgeted production volume multiplied by the standard absorption rate per *unit*.
>
> **Fixed overhead efficiency variance** is the difference between the number of hours that actual production should have taken, and the number of hours actually taken (that is, worked) multiplied by the standard absorption rate per *hour*.
>
> **Fixed overhead capacity variance** is the difference between budgeted hours of work and the actual hours worked, multiplied by the standard absorption rate per *hour*.

You should now be ready to work through an example to demonstrate all of the fixed overhead variances.

5.2 Example: fixed overhead variances

Suppose that a company budgets to produce 1,000 units of product E during August. The expected time to produce a unit of E is five hours, and the budgeted fixed production overhead is $20,000. The standard fixed production overhead cost per unit of product E will therefore be 5 hours at $4 per hour (= $20 per unit). Actual fixed production overhead expenditure in August turns out to be $20,450. The labour force manages to produce 1,100 units of product E in 5,400 hours of work.

Required

Calculate the fixed production overhead total variance and its sub-variances.

5.3 Solution

(a) **Fixed production overhead total variance**

	$
Fixed overhead incurred	20,450
Fixed overhead absorbed (1,100 units × $20 per unit)	22,000
Fixed production overhead total variance (= under-/over-absorbed overhead)	1,550 (F)

The variance is favourable because more overheads were absorbed than budgeted.

(b) **Fixed production overhead expenditure variance**

	$
Budgeted fixed overhead expenditure	20,000
Actual fixed overhead expenditure	20,450
Fixed production overhead expenditure variance	450 (A)

The variance is adverse because expenditure was greater than budgeted.

(c) **Fixed production overhead volume variance**

The production volume achieved was greater than expected. The fixed production overhead volume variance measures the difference at the standard rate.

	$
Actual production at standard rate (1,100 × $20 per unit)	22,000
Budgeted production at standard rate (1,000 × $20 per unit)	20,000
Fixed production overhead volume variance	2,000 (F)

The variance is favourable because output was greater than expected.

This **volume variance arises for two reasons**.

(i) The labour force may have worked efficiently, and produced output at a faster rate than expected. More overhead will be absorbed if units are produced more quickly. This efficiency variance is exactly the same in hours as the direct labour efficiency variance (and variable overhead efficiency variance), but is valued in $ at the standard absorption rate for fixed overhead.

(ii) The labour force may have worked longer hours than budgeted, and therefore potentially produced more output, so there may be a capacity variance.

(d) **Fixed production overhead efficiency variance**

The efficiency variance is calculated in the same way as the labour efficiency variance.

1,100 units of product E should take (× 5 hrs)	5,500 hrs
but did take	5,400 hrs
Efficiency variance in hours	100 hrs (F)
× standard fixed overhead absorption rate per hour	× $4
Fixed production overhead efficiency variance in $	$400 (F)

The labour force has produced 5,500 standard hours of work in 5,400 actual hours and so output is 100 standard hours (or 20 units of product E) higher than budgeted for this reason and the variance is favourable.

(e) **Fixed production overhead capacity variance**

The capacity variance is the difference between the budgeted and actual hours of work.

Budgeted hours of work	5,000 hrs
Actual hours of work	5,400 hrs
Capacity variance in hours	400 hrs (F)
× standard fixed overhead absorption rate per hour	× $4
Fixed production overhead capacity variance in $	$1,600 (F)

Since the labour force worked 400 hours longer than budgeted, we should expect output to be 400 standard hours (or 80 units of product E) higher than budgeted and hence the variance is favourable.

Question

Lots of variances

Brain produces and sells one product only, the Blob, the standard cost for one unit being as follows.

	$
Direct material A – 10 kilograms at $20 per kg	200
Direct wages – 5 hours at $6 per hour	30
Fixed production overhead	50
Total standard cost	280

The fixed overhead included in the standard cost is based on an expected monthly output of 900 units.

During April the actual results were as follows.

Production	800 units
Material A	7,800 kg used, costing $159,900
Direct wages	4,200 hours worked for $24,150
Fixed production overhead	$47,000

Required

(a) Calculate material price and usage variances.
(b) Calculate labour rate and efficiency variances.
(c) Calculate fixed production overhead expenditure and volume variances.
(d) Calculate fixed production overhead efficiency and capacity variances.

Answer

(a) **Material price variance**

	$
7,800 kgs should have cost (× $20)	156,000
but did cost	159,900
Price variance	3,900 (A)

Material usage variance

800 units should have used (× 10 kgs)	8,000 kgs
but did use	7,800 kgs
Usage variance in kgs	200 kgs (F)
× standard cost per kilogram	× $20
Usage variance in $	$4,000 (F)

(b) **Labour rate variance**

	$
4,200 hours should have cost (× $6)	25,200
but did cost	24,150
Rate variance	1,050 (F)

Labour efficiency variance

800 units should have taken (× 5 hrs)	4,000 hrs
but did take	4,200 hrs
Efficiency variance in hours	200 hrs (A)
× standard rate per hour	× $6
Labour efficiency variance in $	$1,200 (A)

(c) **Fixed production overhead expenditure variance**

	$	
Budgeted expenditure ($50 × 900)	45,000	
Actual expenditure	47,000	
Expenditure variance	2,000	(A)

Fixed production overhead volume variance

	$	
Budgeted production at standard rate (900 × $50)	45,000	
Actual production at standard rate (800 × $50)	40,000	
Volume variance	5,000	(A)

(d) **Fixed production overhead efficiency variance**

Fixed production overhead standard rate per hour = $50/5 = $10 per hour

From the labour efficiency variance,		
Efficiency variance in hours	200 hrs	(A)
x standard fixed production overhead absorption rate per hour	× $10	
Fixed production overhead efficiency variance in $	$2,000	(A)

Fixed production overhead capacity variance

Budgeted hours of work (900 units × 5 hours)	4,500 hrs	
Actual hours of work	4,200 hrs	
Capacity variance in hours	300 hrs	(A)
x standard fixed production overhead absorption rate per hour	× $10	
Fixed production overhead capacity variance in $	$3,000	(A)

Check:	efficiency variance	+	capacity variance	=	volume variance
	$2,000 (A)	+	$3,000 (A)	=	$5,000 (A)

6 Sales variances

FAST FORWARD

The **selling price variance** is the difference between what revenue should have been for the quantity sold and the actual revenue.

The **sales volume variance** is the difference between the actual and budgeted sales volumes, valued at the standard profit or contribution margin per unit.

Exam focus point

Sales variances were examined in December 2008. Candidates were asked to calculate sales price and sales volume contribution variances. Candidates were also asked to explain the meaning of each variance.

6.1 Selling price variance

The **selling price variance** is a measure of the effect on expected profit of a different selling price to budgeted selling price. It is calculated as the **difference between what the sales revenue should have been for the actual quantity sold, and what it was.**

Suppose that the budgeted selling price of product X is $15. Actual sales in year 3 were 2,000 units at $15.30 per unit. The selling price variance is calculated as follows.

	$	
Sales revenue from 2,000 units should have been (× $15)	30,000	
but was (× $15.30)	30,600	
Selling price variance	600	(F)

The variance is favourable because the price was higher than expected.

BPP LEARNING MEDIA

6.2 Sales volume profit variance

The **sales volume profit variance** is the difference between the actual units sold and the budgeted quantity, valued at the standard profit per unit. In other words, it measures **the increase or decrease in standard profit as a result of the sales volume being higher or lower than budgeted.**

Suppose that a company budgets to sell 8,000 units of product J for $12 per unit. The standard full cost per unit is $7. Actual sales were 7,700 units, at $12.50 per unit.

The sales volume profit variance is calculated as follows.

Budgeted sales volume	8,000 units
Actual sales volume	7,700 units
Sales volume variance in units	300 units (A)
× standard profit per unit ($(12–7))	× $5
Sales volume variance	$1,500 (A)

The variance is adverse because actual sales were less than budgeted.

Question

Sales variances

Jasper has the following budget and actual figures for year 4.

	Budget	*Actual*
Sales units	600	620
Selling price per unit	$30	$29

Standard full cost of production = $28 per unit.

The selling price variance and the sales volume profit variances are

	Selling price variance	*Sales volume profit variance*
A	$620 (F)	$40 (A)
B	$600 (A)	$40 (F)
C	$620 (A)	$40 (F)
D	$620 (A)	$600 (F)

Answer

The correct answer is C.

	$
Sales revenue for 620 units should have been (× $30)	18,600
but was (× $29)	17,980
Selling price variance	620 (A)
Budgeted sales volume	600 units
Actual sales volume	620 units
Sales volume variance in units	20 units (F)
× standard profit per unit ($(30 – 28))	× $2
Sales volume profit variance	$40 (F)

6.3 The significance of sales variances

The possible **interdependence** between sales price and sales volume variances should be obvious to you. A reduction in the sales price might stimulate bigger sales demand, so that an adverse sales price variance might be counterbalanced by a favourable sales volume variance. Similarly, a price rise would give a favourable price variance, but possibly at the cost of a fall in demand and an adverse sales volume variance.

It is therefore important in analysing an unfavourable sales variance that the overall consequence should be considered, that is, has there been a counterbalancing favourable variance as a direct result of the unfavourable one?

7 Variances – controllable and non-controllable elements

Variances can be split into two parts as follows.

(a) Controllable variances
(b) Non-controllable variances

Controllable variances are those variances which can be controlled by management. **Non-controllable variances**, on the other hand, are those variances which are caused by unknown unpredictable factors, such as the following.

(a) Inflation
(b) Currency fluctuations
(c) National wage rate agreements
(d) Theft

Controllable and non-controllable elements of variances are best explained by means of an example.

7.1 Example: controllable and non-controllable elements of variances

Lansdale produced 1,100 units of Product P5 in May 20X2. These units should have used 6,600 litres of Liquid L1 which should have cost $237,600. Instead, 9,350 litres were purchased and used at a cost of $359,975.

During May 20X2, 1,500 litres of the liquid L1 purchased were stolen.

Required

Calculate the material usage variance, separating it into its controllable and non-controllable elements.

7.2 Solution

1,100 units should have used (litres)	6,600	
but did use (litres)	9,350	
Usage variance in litres	2,750	(A)
× standard cost per litre	$36	
Material usage variance	$99,000	(A)

Of the excess 2,750 litres used, 1,500 litres were because of theft. Therefore $54,000 (1,500 litres × $36) of the total materials usage variance were due to theft and therefore not controllable by management. This variance can be analysed as follows.

	$
Total variance	99,000
Variance due to theft (non-controllable)	54,000
Variance controllable by management	45,000

Let's have a look at another example.

7.3 Example: controllable and non-controllable elements of variances again

Ray uses a particular metal in its factory to produce one of its products. The standard cost per kg of the metal is $10. During year 7, 2,000 kgs were purchased at a cost of $16,000. The index of material prices stood at 350.9 when the standard was set but at 315.81 when the material was purchased.

Required

Subdivide the material price variance into its controllable and non-controllable elements.

7.4 Solution

Revised standard cost per kg = $\$10 \times \dfrac{315.81}{350.9} = \$9$

Actual cost per kg = $\dfrac{\$16,000}{2,000\,\text{kg}} = \$8$

Material price variance

	$	
2,000 kg did cost	16,000	
but should have cost (2,000 kg × $10)	20,000	
Material price variance	4,000	(F)

The material price variance can be subdivided into its controllable and non-controllable elements as follows.

	$	
Total variance	4,000	(F)
Variance due to inflation (see working)	(2,000)	(F)
Variance controllable by management	2,000	(F)

Working

	$	
2,000 kg should have cost (× $9*)	18,000	
but did cost	16,000	
	2,000	(F)

* Revised standard cost per kg

Question — Controllable variances

Martin contracted to buy a quantity of material for $10 per metre when the rate of exchange between the UK pound and the US dollar was $1.60. In April 20X1, when the exchange rate was $1.68, the company paid for 1,600 metres.

Required

Subdivide the material price variance into its controllable and non-controllable elements.

Answer

Material price variance

	£	
1,600 metres should have cost (× $10/1.60)	10,000	
but did cost (× $10/1.68)	9,524	
Material price variance	476	(F)

Analysis

	£	
Total variance	476	(F)
Variance due to currency fluctuations	(476)	(F)
Variance controllable by management	–	

Note that in this activity, the material price variance is entirely due to the non-controllable element (currency fluctuations) and that none of the variance is controllable by management.

8 Operating statements

FAST FORWARD

An **operating statement/statement of variances** is a report, usually to senior management, at the end of a control period, reconciling budgeted profit for the period to actual profit.

So far, we have considered how variances are calculated without considering how they combine to **reconcile the difference between budgeted profit and actual profit** during a period. This reconciliation is usually presented as a report to senior management at the end of each control period. The report is called an operating statement or statement of variances.

Key term

The CIMA *Official Terminology* definition of an **operating statement** is 'A regular report for management of actual costs and revenues, as appropriate. Usually compares actual with budget and shows variances'.

An extensive example will now be introduced, both to revise the variance calculations already described, and also to show how to combine them into an operating statement.

8.1 Example: variances and operating statements

Sydney manufactures one product, and the entire product is sold as soon as it is produced. There are no opening or closing inventories and work in progress is negligible. The company operates a standard costing system and analysis of variances is made every month. The standard cost card for the product, a boomerang, is as follows.

STANDARD COST CARD – BOOMERANG		$
Direct materials	0.5 kilos at $4 per kilo	2.00
Direct wages	2 hours at $2.00 per hour	4.00
Variable overheads	2 hours at $0.30 per hour	0.60
Fixed overhead	2 hours at $3.70 per hour	7.40
Standard cost		14.00
Standard profit		6.00
Standing selling price		20.00

Selling and administration expenses are not included in the standard cost, and are deducted from profit as a period charge.

Budgeted output for the month of June 20X7 was 5,100 units. Actual results for June year 7 were as follows.

Production of 4,850 units was sold for $95,600.
Materials consumed in production amounted to 2,300 kgs at a total cost of $9,800.
Labour hours paid for amounted to 8,500 hours at a cost of $16,800.
Actual operating hours amounted to 8,000 hours.
Variable overheads amounted to $2,600.
Fixed overheads amounted to $42,300.
Selling and administration expenses amounted to $18,000.

Required

Calculate all variances and prepare an operating statement for the month ended 30 June 20X7.

8.2 Solution

		$
(a)	2,300 kg of material should cost (× $4)	9,200
	but did cost	9,800
	Material price variance	600 (A)

(b)	4,850 boomerangs should use (× 0.5 kgs)	2,425 kg
	but did use	2,300 kg
	Material usage variance in kgs	125 kg (F)
	× standard cost per kg	× $4
	Material usage variance in $	$ 500 (F)

		$
(c)	8,500 hours of labour should cost (× $2)	17,000
	but did cost	16,800
	Labour rate variance	200 (F)
(d)	4,850 boomerangs should take (× 2 hrs)	9,700 hrs
	but did take (active hours)	8,000 hrs
	Labour efficiency variance in hours	1,700 hrs (F)
	× standard cost per hour	× $2
	Labour efficiency variance in $	$3,400 (F)
(e)	Idle time variance 500 hours (A) × $2	$1,000 (A)

		$
(f)	8,000 hours incurring variable o/hd expenditure should cost (× $0.30)	2,400
	but did cost	2,600
	Variable overhead expenditure variance	200 (A)
(g)	Variable overhead efficiency variance in hours is the same as the labour efficiency variance:	
	1,700 hours (F) × $0.30 per hour	$ 510 (F)

		$
(h)	Budgeted fixed overhead (5,100 units × 2 hrs × $3.70)	37,740
	Actual fixed overhead	42,300
	Fixed overhead expenditure variance	4,560 (A)

		$
(i)	Actual production at standard rate (4,850 units × $7.40)	35,890
	Budgeted production at standard rate (5,100 units × $7.40)	37,740
	Fixed overhead volume variance	1,850 (A)
(j)	Fixed overhead efficiency variance in hours is the same as the labour efficiency variance:	
	1,700 hrs (F) × $3.70 per hour	$6,290 (F)
(k)	Budgeted hours of work (5,100 units × 2 hours)	10,200 hrs
	Actual hours of work	8,000 hrs
	Capacity variance in hours	2,200 hrs (A)
	× standard fixed overhead absorption rate per hour	× $3.70
	Fixed overhead capacity variance in $	$8,140 (A)
(l)	Revenue from 4,850 boomerangs should be (× $20)	97,000
	but was	95,600
	Selling price variance	1,400 (A)
(m)	Budgeted sales volume	5,100 units
	Actual sales volume	4,850 units
	Sales volume profit variance in units	250 units
	× standard profit per unit	× $6 (A)
	Sales volume profit variance in $	$1,500 (A)

There are several ways in which an operating statement may be presented. Perhaps the most common format is one which reconciles budgeted profit to actual profit. In this example, **sales and administration costs will be introduced at the end of the statement**, so that we shall **begin with 'budgeted profit before sales and administration costs'**.

Sales variances are reported first, and the **total of the budgeted profit and the two sales variances** results in a figure for **'actual sales minus the standard cost of sales'**. The **cost variances** are then reported, and an **actual profit** (before sales and administration costs) calculated. **Sales and administration costs** are then **deducted** to reach the **actual profit**.

SYDNEY – OPERATING STATEMENT JUNE YEAR 7

		$	$
Budgeted profit before sales and administration costs			30,600
Sales variances: price		1,400 (A)	
volume		1,500 (A)	
			2,900 (A)
Actual sales minus the standard cost of sales			27,700
Cost variances	(F)	(A)	
	$	$	
Material price		600	
Material usage	500		
Labour rate	200		
Labour efficiency	3,400		
Labour idle time		1,000	
Variable overhead expenditure		200	
Variable overhead efficiency	510		
Fixed overhead expenditure		4,560	
Fixed overhead efficiency	6,290		
Fixed overhead capacity		8,140	
	10,900	14,500	3,600 (A)
Actual profit before sales and admin costs c/f			24,100
Sales and administration costs			18,000
Actual profit, June 20X7			6,100
Check		$	$
Sales			95,600
Materials		9,800	
Labour		16,800	
Variable overhead		2,600	
Fixed overhead		42,300	
Sales and administration		18,000	
			89,500
Actual profit			6,100

9 Variances in a standard marginal costing system

FAST FORWARD

In a **standard marginal costing system**, there will be no fixed production overhead volume variance and the sales volume variance will be valued at standard contribution margin not standard profit margin.

In all of the examples we have worked through so far, a system of standard absorption costing has been in operation. If an organisation uses **standard marginal costing** instead of standard absorption costing, there will be two differences in the way the variances are calculated.

(a) In marginal costing, fixed costs are not absorbed into product costs and so there are no fixed cost variances to explain any under or over absorption of overheads. There will, therefore, be **no fixed overhead volume variance**. There will be a fixed overhead expenditure variance which is calculated in exactly the same way as for absorption costing systems.

(b) The **sales volume variance** will be valued at **standard contribution margin** (sales price per unit minus variable costs of sale per unit), **not** standard **profit** margin. It will be called the **sales volume contribution variance.**

9.1 Preparing a marginal costing operating statement

Returning once again to the example of Sydney, the variances in a system of standard marginal costing would be as follows.

(a) There is **no fixed overhead volume variance**, and therefore no variances for fixed overhead efficiency and capacity.

(b) The standard contribution per unit of boomerang is $(20 – 6.60) = $13.40 and so the **sales volume contribution variance** of 250 units (A) is valued at (× $13.40) = $3,350 (A).

The other variances are unchanged. However, this operating statement differs from an absorption costing operating statement in the following ways.

(a) It **begins with the budgeted contribution** ($30,600 + budgeted fixed production costs $37,740 = $68,340).

(b) The subtotal before the analysis of cost variances is **actual sales** ($95,600) **less the standard variable cost of sales** (4,850 × $6.60) = $63,590.

(c) **Actual contribution** is highlighted in the statement.

(d) Budgeted fixed production overhead is adjusted by the fixed overhead expenditure variance to show the **actual fixed production overhead expenditure**.

Therefore a **marginal costing** operating statement might look like this.

SYDNEY – OPERATING STATEMENT JUNE 20X7

	$	$	$
Budgeted contribution		68,340	
Sales variances: volume	3,350 (A)		
price	1,400 (A)		
			4,750 (A)
Actual sales minus the standard variable cost of sales			63,590
	(F)	(A)	
	$	$	
Variable cost variances			
Material price		600	
Material usage	500		
Labour rate	200		
Labour efficiency	3,400		
Labour idle time		1,000	
Variable overhead expenditure		200	
Variable overhead efficiency	510		
	4,610	1,800	
			2,810 (F)
Actual contribution			66,400
Budgeted fixed production overhead		37,740	
Expenditure variance		4,560 (A)	
Actual fixed production overhead			42,300
Actual profit before sales and administration costs			24,100
Sales and administration costs			18,000
Actual profit			6,100

Notice that the actual profit is the same as the profit calculated by standard absorption costing because there were no changes in inventory levels. Absorption costing and marginal costing do not always produce an identical profit figure.

Exam focus point

In June 2005, the examiner asked candidates to explain differences between standard absorption costing and standard marginal costing for sales volume variances, fixed overhead variances and inventory valuation and therefore profit.

10 Cost bookkeeping

FAST FORWARD

There are two types of cost accounting system – **interlocking** and **integrated**.

Key term

Integrated accounts. 'A set of accounting records that integrates both financial and cost accounts using a common input of data for all accounting purposes'.

CIMA *Official Terminology*

Exam focus point

You studied cost bookkeeping in your earlier studies (Paper 4) so look through the following example for revision purposes. You are highly unlikely to encounter a detailed cost bookkeeping question in your examination – but make sure that you can remember the basic principles (you will need to apply these when we go on to the next section of this chapter: standard cost bookkeeping).

Knowledge brought forward from earlier studies

In Intermediate Paper 4 *Accounting for costs,* cost bookkeeping is covered in some depth.

The two types of cost bookkeeping systems, **interlocking** and **integrated** are explained and examples of both are given.

At this level, the examiner will not examine detailed cost bookkeeping. However, he expects you to have the knowledge from your previous studies.

We have included an example of integrated accounts in Section 10.1 for you to work through. Make sure you are confident with this before you move on to Section 11.

10.1 Example: integrated accounts

Using the information given below for October, you are required to prepare the following accounts.

(a) Raw materials control
(b) Work in progress control
(c) Finished goods control
(d) Production overhead control
(e) Wages and salaries control
(f) Selling and administration overhead control
(g) Cost of sales
(h) Trading and profit and loss

Balances as at 1 October

	$'000
Raw materials control	10
Work in progress control	15
Finished goods control	18

Transactions for October

		$'000
Materials received from suppliers on credit		50
Materials issued to production		42
Materials issued to production service departments		5
Direct wages incurred		30
Production indirect wages incurred		13
Selling and administration salaries incurred		12
Production expenses paid as incurred		8
Selling and administration expenses paid as incurred		9
Provision for depreciation:	production equipment	3
	selling and administration equipment	2
Wages and salaries paid:	direct wages	28
	production indirect wages	13
	selling and administration salaries	12
Production completed and transferred to finished goods store		90
Production cost of goods sold		97
Sales on credit		145

Production overhead is absorbed at the rate of 80 per cent of direct wages incurred.

10.2 Solution

The figures in brackets refer to the explanations which follow after the ledger accounts.

RAW MATERIALS CONTROL

	$'000		$'000
Balance b/d	10	Work in progress (1)	42
Payables	50	Production overhead control (1)	5
		Balance c/d	13
	60		60
Balance b/d	13		

WORK IN PROGRESS CONTROL

	$'000		$'000
Balance b/d	15	Finished goods control (4)	90
Raw materials control (1)	42	Balance c/d (4)	21
Wages and salaries control (2)	30		
Production overhead control (3)	24		
	111		111
Balance b/d	21		

FINISHED GOODS CONTROL

	$'000		$'000
Balance b/d	18	Cost of sales (5)	97
Work in progress control (4)	90	Balance c/d (5)	11
	108		108
Balance b/d	11		

PRODUCTION OVERHEAD CONTROL

	$'000		$'000
Raw materials control (1)	5	Work in progress control (3)	24
Wages and salaries control (2)	13	Under absorption to income statement (8)	
Bank (6)	8		5
Provision for depreciation (6)	3		
	29		29

WAGES AND SALARIES CONTROL

	$'000		$'000
Bank (7)	53	Work in progress control (2)	30
Balance c/d (7)	2	Production overhead control (2)	13
		Selling and admin o/h control (2)	12
	55		55
		Balance b/d	2

SELLING AND ADMINISTRATION OVERHEAD CONTROL

	$'000		$'000
Bank (6)	9	Income statement	23
Wages and salaries control (2)	12		
Provision for depreciation (6)	2		
	23		23

COST OF SALES

	$'000		$'000
Finished goods control (5)	97	Income statement	97

TRADING AND INCOME STATEMENT CONTROL

	$'000		$'000
Cost of sales (5)	97	Sales – receivables	145
Gross profit c/d	48		
	145		145
Under-absorbed overhead (8)	5	Gross profit b/d	48
Selling and admin o/h	23		
Net profit for October	20		
	48		48

Notes

(1) The materials issued to production are charged as **direct materials** to work in progress. The materials issued to production service departments are **indirect materials**. The cost of indirect materials is 'collected' in the production overhead control account, pending its later absorption, along with all the other production overheads, into the value of work in progress.

(2) The wages and salaries **incurred** are debited to the relevant control accounts:

(a) Direct wages to work in progress

(b) Indirect wages to production overhead control

(c) Selling and administration salaries to selling and administration overhead control

The credit entry for wages **incurred** is made in the wages and salaries control account.

(3) Once the direct material and direct wages have been debited to work in progress, the next step is to **absorb production overheads**, using the predetermined overhead absorption rate. The work in progress account is charged with 80 per cent of wages incurred: $30,000 × 80% = $24,000.

(4) Now that all of the elements of production cost have been charged to work in progress, the **production cost of goods completed** can be transferred to the finished goods control account. The balance on the work in progress account represents the inventory at the end of October.

(5) The **production cost of goods sold** is transferred from the finished goods account to the cost of sales account. The balance on the finished goods account represents the inventory at the end of October.

(6) The production expenses incurred and the depreciation on production machinery are debited in the production overhead control account. Thus they are 'collected' with the other production overheads, for later **absorption into work in progress**.

(7) The total amount of wages **paid** ($28,000 + $13,000 + $12,000) is debited to the wages and salaries control account. The balance remaining on the account is the difference between the wages paid and the wages incurred. This represents a $2,000 accrual for wages, which is carried down into next month's accounts.

(8) The balance remaining on the production overhead control account is the difference between the production overhead incurred, and the amount absorbed into work in progress. On this occasion the overhead is **underabsorbed** and is transferred as a debit in the income statement.

Question

Raw material control

The following information relates to E for March.

Opening balance of raw materials	$12,000
Raw materials purchased on credit	$80,000
Raw materials issued: to production	$73,000
to production maintenance	$8,000
Raw materials returned to supplier	$2,000

Required

Complete the raw materials inventory control account for March.

Answer

RAW MATERIALS INVENTORY CONTROL

	$		$
Balance b/d	12,000	Work in progress	73,000
Payables	80,000	Production overhead control	8,000
		Creditors	2,000
		Balance c/d	9,000
	92,000		92,000
Balance b/d	9,000		

11 Standard cost bookkeeping

FAST FORWARD

The general principle in standard cost bookkeeping is that **cost variances should be recorded as early as possible.** They are recorded in the relevant account in which they **arise** and the appropriate double entry is taken to a variance account.

Adverse variances are **debited** in the relevant variance account; **favourable** variances are **credited** in the relevant variance account.

Now that you know how to calculate variances you need to be able to incorporate them into a standard cost bookkeeping system.

Don't be put off by the sound of standard cost bookkeeping. It is no more complicated than the bookkeeping you have looked at so far. It is simply an extension of the basic system and is used when an organisation runs a standard costing system.

The general principle in standard cost bookkeeping is that cost variances should be recorded as **early as possible**. They are recorded in the relevant account **where they arise** and the appropriate double entry is taken to a variance account. Examples are as follows.

(a) **Material price variances** are apparent when materials are purchased, and they are therefore recorded in the **stores account**. If a price variance is adverse, we should credit the stores account and debit a variance account with the amount of the variance.

(b) **Material usage variances** do not occur until output is actually produced in the factory, and they are therefore recorded in the **work in progress account**. If a usage variance is favourable, we should debit the work in progress account and credit a variance account with the value of the variance.

There are some possible variations in accounting method between one organisation's system and others, especially in the method of recording overhead variances, but the following are the basic principles.

(a) The **material price variance** is recorded in the **stores control account**.

(b) The **labour rate variance** is recorded in the **wages control account**.

(c) The following variances are recorded in the **work in progress account**.
   (i) Material usage variance
   (ii) Idle time variance
   (iii) Labour efficiency variance
   (iv) Variable overhead efficiency variance

(d) The **production overhead expenditure variance** will be recorded in the **production overhead control account.**

(e) The **production overhead volume variance** may be recorded in the **fixed production overhead account**. (*Note.* Alternatively, you may find the volume variance recorded in the **work in progress account**.)

(f) **Sales variances do not appear in the books of account.** Sales are recorded in the sales account at actual invoiced value.

(g) The balance of variances in the variance accounts at the end of a period may be **written off to the income statement.**

The actual process is best demonstrated with an example. Work carefully through the one which follows, ensuring that you know how the various variances are recorded. This example assumes the use of an **integrated system**.

11.1 Example: cost bookkeeping and variances

Zed operates an integrated accounting system and prepares its final accounts monthly. You are provided with the following information.

Balances as at 1 October	$'000
Plant and machinery, at cost	600
Inventory – raw materials	520
Wages payable	40
Inventory – finished goods	132

Data for the month of October	
Materials purchased on credit	400,000 kgs at $4.90 per kg
Issued to production	328,000 kgs
Direct wages incurred	225,000 hours at $4.20 per hour
Direct wages paid	$920,000
Production overhead incurred on credit	$1,490,000
Sales	$4,875,000
Production and sales	39,000 units

Additional data	
Depreciation allowance	plant and machinery, 20% pa on cost
Inventories of raw materials and finished goods	maintained at standard

Standard data	
Direct material price	$5.00 per kg
Direct material usage	8 kgs per unit
Direct wages	$4.00 per hour
Direct labour	6 hours per unit
Production overhead	absorbed at 150% of standard direct wages
Budgeted output	10,000 units per week

Required

(a) Calculate the appropriate cost variances for October.

(b) Show the following ledger accounts for October.

  (i) Stores ledger control account
  (ii) Direct wages control account
  (iii) Production overhead control account
  (iv) Work in progress control account
  (v) Finished goods control account
  (vi) Cost of sales control account
  (vii) Sales account
  (viii) Variances account
  (ix) Income statement

11.2 Solution

(a) We will begin by determining the standard unit cost and calculating the variances.

Standard cost per unit	$
Direct materials (8 kgs × $5)	40
Direct labour (6 hrs × $4)	24
Production overhead (150% × $24)	36
	100

Direct material price variance	$'000
400,000 kgs should cost (× $5)	2,000
but did cost (400,000 × $4.90)	1,960
	40 (F)

Direct material usage variance	
39,000 units should use (× 8)	312,000 kgs
but did use	328,000 kgs
Variance in kg	16,000 kgs (A)
× standard price per kg	× $5
	$80,000 (A)

Direct labour rate variance	$'000
225,000 hours should cost (× $4)	900
but did cost (225,000 × $4.20)	945
	45 (A)

Direct labour efficiency variance	
39,000 units should take (× 6 hrs)	234,000 hrs
but did take	225,000 hrs
Variance in hours	9,000 hrs (F)
× standard rate per hour	× $4
	$36,000 (F)

Production overhead expenditure variance	$'000	$'000
Budgeted expenditure (10,000 units × 4 wks × $36)		1,440
Actual expenditure		
Incurred on credit	1,490	
Depreciation (20% × 1/12 × $600)	10	
		1,500
		60 (A)

Production overhead volume variance	$'000
Actual production at standard rate (39,000 × $36)	1,404
Budgeted production at standard rate (10,000 × 4 wks × $36)	1,440
	36 (A)

(b) (i) STORES LEDGER CONTROL ACCOUNT

	$'000		$'000
Balance b/f	520	Work in progress	
Payables		(328,000 × $5)	1,640
(400,000 × $4.90)	1,960	Balance c/d	880
Material price variance	40		
	2,520		2,520
Balance b/d	880		

Notes

(1) Materials are issued from store at standard price.

(2) The material price variance is recorded in this account. It is a favourable variance, therefore it is recorded as a credit in the variance account.

(ii) DIRECT WAGES CONTROL ACCOUNT

	$'000		$'000
Bank	920	Balance b/f	40
Balance c/d	65	Work in progress	
		(225,000 hrs × $4)	900
		Labour rate variance	45
	985		985
		Balance b/d	65

Notes

(1) Labour hours are charged to work in progress at the standard rate per hour.

(2) The labour rate variance is recorded in this account. It is an adverse variance, therefore it is recorded as a debit in the variance account.

(iii) PRODUCTION OVERHEAD CONTROL ACCOUNT

	$'000		$'000
Payables	1,490	Work in progress	
Depreciation on plant		(39,000 × $36)	1,404
and machinery	10	Production overhead expenditure variance	60
		Production overhead volume variance	36
	1,500		1,500

Notes

(1) Production is charged with the standard rate for the units produced.

(2) The production overhead expenditure variance is shown in this account

(3) In this example, the volume variance is shown in the overhead account.

(4) Both are adverse variances, therefore they are both recorded as debits in the variance account.

(iv) WORK IN PROGRESS CONTROL ACCOUNT

	$'000		$'000
Stores ledger control	1,640	Finished goods	
Direct wages control	900	(39,000 × $100)	3,900
Production overhead control	1,404	Direct material usage	
Direct labour		variance	80
efficiency variance	36		
	3,980		3,980

Notes

(1) Output is transferred to the finished goods account at standard production cost.
(2) The efficiency variances appear in this account.

(v) FINISHED GOODS CONTROL ACCOUNT

	$'000		$'000
Balance b/f	132	Cost of sales (39,000 × $100)	3,900
Work in progress	3,900	Balance c/d	132
	4,032		4,032
Balance b/d	132		

(vi) COST OF SALES CONTROL ACCOUNT

	$'000		$'000
Finished goods	3,900	Income statement	3,900

(vii) SALES ACCOUNT

	$'000		$'000
Income statement	4,875	Bank/receivables	4,875

(viii) VARIANCES ACCOUNT

	$'000		$'000
Wages (labour rate)	45	Stores (material price)	40
WIP (prodn o/h expenditure)	60	WIP (labour efficiency)	36
WIP (prodn o/h volume)	36	Income statement	145
WIP (material usage)	80		
	221		221

Exam focus point

The variances are recorded in a variances account as part of the double entry system. The balance on the account at the end of the period is written off to the income statement. Sometimes a separate account is used for each variance, but the double entry principles would be the same. An adverse variance is debited in the relevant variance account; a favourable variance is credited in the variance account.

(ix) INCOME STATEMENT

	$'000		$'000
Cost of sales	3,900	Sales	4,875
Variances	145		
Gross profit for month	830		
	4,875		4,875

11.3 Example: journal entries

Suppose that 4 kgs of material A are required to make one unit of product TS, each kilogram costing $10. It takes direct labour 5 hours to make one unit of product TS. The labour force is paid $4.50 per hour.

During the period the following results were recorded.

Material A: 8,200 kgs purchased on credit *	$95,000
Material A: kgs issued to production*	8,200 kgs
Units of product TS produced*	1,600
Direct labour hours worked*	10,000
Cost of direct labour*	$32,000

Required

(a) Calculate the following variances for the period.

(i) Material price variance
(ii) Material usage variance
(iii) Labour rate variance
(iv) Labour efficiency variance

(b) Prepare journal entries for the transactions marked * above, together with the variances calculated in (a).

Note

You should make the following assumptions.

(i) An integrated accounting system is maintained.
(ii) There are no opening or closing inventories of work in progress.

11.4 Solution

(a)

		$
(i)	8,200 kgs should cost (× $10)	82,000
	but did cost	95,000
	Material price variance	13,000 (A)
(ii)	1,600 units of TS should use (× 4 kgs)	6,400 kgs
	but did use	8,200 kgs
	Usage variance in kgs	1,800 kgs (A)
	× standard price per kg	× $10
	Material usage variance	$18,000 (A)
(iii)		$
	10,000 hours should cost (× $4.50)	45,000
	but did cost	32,000
	Labour rate variance	13,000 (F)
(iv)	1,600 units of TS should take (× 5 hrs)	8,000 hrs
	but did take	10,000 hrs
	Efficiency variance in hrs	2,000 hrs (A)
	× standard rate per hour	× $4.50
	Labour efficiency variance	$9,000 (A)

(b)

(i)		$	$
	Stores ledger control account (8,200 kgs × $10)	82,000	
	Material price variance	13,000	
	Payables		95,000
	The purchase of materials on credit		
(ii)	Work in progress control account	82,000	
	Stores ledger control account		82,000
	The issue of material A to production		

		$	$
(iii)	Material usage variance	18,000	
	Work in progress control account		18,000
	The recording of the material A usage variance		
(iv)	Work in progress control account (10,000 hrs × $4.50)	45,000	
	Direct labour control account		32,000
	Direct labour rate variance		13,000
	The charging of labour to work in progress		
(v)	Direct labour efficiency variance	9,000	
	Work in progress control account		9,000
	The recording of the labour efficiency variance		
(vi)	Finished goods control account (1,600 × $62.50 (W))	100,000	
	Work in progress control account		100,000
	The transfer of finished goods from work in progress		

Working

Standard cost of product TS

	$
Material A (4 kgs × $10)	40.00
Direct labour (5 hrs × $4.50)	22.50
	62.50

Question — Integrated accounts

A company uses raw material J in production. The standard price for material J is $3 per metre. During the month 6,000 metres were purchased for $18,600, of which 5,000 metres were issued to production.

Required

Show the journal entries to record the above transactions in integrated accounts in the following separate circumstances.

(a) When raw material inventory is valued at standard cost, that is the direct materials price variance is extracted on receipt.

(b) When raw materials inventory is valued at actual cost, that is the direct materials price variance is extracted as the materials are used.

Answer

(a)

	$	$
Raw material inventory (6,000 × $3)	18,000	
Direct material price variance	600	
Payables		18,600
Purchase on credit of 6,000 metres of material J		
Work in progress (5,000 × $3)	15,000	
Raw material inventory		15,000
Issue to production of 5,000 metres of J		

(b)	Raw material inventory	18,600	
	Payables		18,600
	Purchase on credit of 6,000 metres of material J		
	Work in progress	15,000	
	Direct material price variance (5,000 × \$(3.10 – 3.00))	500	
	Raw material inventory		15,500
	Issue to production of 5,000 metres of material J		

Note that in both cases the material is charged to work in progress at standard price. In (b) the price variance is extracted only on the material which has been used up, the inventory being valued at actual cost.

Chapter Roundup

- **Price, rate and expenditure variances** measure the difference between the actual amount of money paid and the amount of money that should have been paid for the actual quantity of materials or the actual number of hours of labour or variable overheads.
- **Usage and efficiency variances** are quantity variances. They measure the difference between the actual physical quantity of materials used or hours taken and the quantities that should have been used or taken for the actual volume of production. These physical differences are then converted into money values by applying the appropriate standard price or rate.
- The **idle time variance** is the number of hours of idle time valued at the standard rate per hour.
- The **total fixed production overhead variance** may be broken down into two parts as usual: an **expenditure variance** and a **volume variance**. The volume variance may in turn be split into an **efficiency variance** and a **capacity variance.**
- The **selling price variance** is the difference between what revenue should have been for the quantity sold and the actual revenue.
- The **sales volume variance** is the difference between the actual and budgeted sales volumes, valued at the standard profit or contribution margin per unit.
- An **operating statement/statement of variances** is a report, usually to senior management, at the end of a control period, reconciling budgeted profit for the period to actual profit.
- In a **standard marginal costing system**, there will be no fixed production overhead volume variance and the sales volume variance will be valued at standard contribution margin not standard profit margin.
- There are two types of cost accounting system – **interlocking** and **integrated.**
- The general principle in standard cost bookkeeping is that **cost variances should be recorded as early as possible**. They are recorded in the relevant account in which they **arise** and the appropriate double entry is taken to a variance account.
- **Adverse** variances are **debited** in the relevant variance account; **favourable** variances are **credited** in the relevant variance account.

Quick Quiz

1 Choose the appropriate words from those highlighted.

If material price variances are extracted **at the time of receipt/as the material is used**, they will be brought to the attention of managers earlier than if they are extracted **at the time of receipt/as the material is used**.

And if variances are extracted **at the time of receipt/as material is used**, all inventories will be valued at **standard price/actual price**, which is administratively easier.

2 Idle time is a favourable efficiency variance. True or false?

3 Fill in the blanks.

Fixed production overhead volume variance = ... variance + ... variance

4 Choose the appropriate word from those highlighted.

Actual labour hours worked were higher than the budgeted labour hours for the period. The fixed overhead capacity variance will therefore be **adverse/ favourable**.

5 Fill in the blank.

Sales volume variance = (actual sales volume – budgeted sales volume) × ....

6 Which of the following statements about the fixed production overhead volume variance is true?

A It is the same in a standard marginal costing system as in a standard absorption costing system.
B It does not exist in a standard absorption costing system.
C It does not exist in a standard marginal costing system.
D It is made up of an expenditure variance and an efficiency variance.

7 Subdivide the following variances.

(a) Direct materials cost variance

(b) Direct labour cost variance

(c) Variable production overhead variance

8 Adverse material usage variances might occur for the following reasons.

I Defective material
II Excessive waste
III Theft
IV Unforeseen discounts received

A I
B I and II
C I, II and III
D I, II, III and IV

Answers to Quick Quiz

1 at the time of receipt
as the material is used
at the time of receipt
standard price

2 False. It is an adverse efficiency variance.

3 fixed production overhead capacity variance + fixed production overhead efficiency variance

4 favourable

5 Absorption costing system: standard profit per unit

Marginal costing system: standard contribution per unit

6 C. This variance does not exist in a standard marginal costing system.

7 (a) → Price
→ Usage

(b) → Rate
→ Efficiency

(c) → Expenditure
→ Efficiency

8 C

Now try the questions below from the Exam Question Bank

Number	Level	Marks	Time
Section A: Q16-Q17	MCQ	N/A	N/A
Section B: Q13	Preparation	10	18 mins

13

What variances mean

Topic list
1 Variances and variance analysis
2 Potential causes of variances
3 Interrelationships between variances
4 Variance analysis reports
5 To investigate or not to investigate?
6 Control limits and control charts
7 Control action

Study guide reference

		Syllabus reference
15(a)	Presentation of budgetary control reports for management	5
	(i) Prepare control accounts suitable for presentation to management	
	(ii) Discuss the relative significance of variances	
(b)	Recommendation of appropriate control action	
	(i) Explain potential actions to eliminate variances	
	(ii) Discuss the advantages and disadvantages of particular actions	
23(a)	Significance and identification of possible reasons for variances	5
	(i) Discuss the causes of variances in general	
	(ii) Identify potential causes of variances in a specific situation	
	(iii) Explain the potential interrelationships between variances	
	(iv) Discuss the meaning and significance of variances	
(b)	Factors to consider before investigation	
	(i) Explain the significance of cost of investigation, cost of correction, benefit of correction, and probability of successful correction in variance investigation	
	(ii) Calculate the expected benefit of variance investigation	
	(iii) Discuss the role of control charts in variance investigation	
(c)	Recommend control action	
	(i) Explain potential courses of action to correct a variance	
	(ii) Evaluate courses of action to correct a variance in specific circumstances	

Exam focus point

This chapter covers a key syllabus area. Key syllabus areas usually account for 80% or more of the marks available on the exam paper.

1 Variances and variance analysis

This chapter builds on your earlier studies of variances. We shall start by revising the different types of sales and cost variances.

The revision of these variances is most usefully carried out by working through an extensive example which covers the different types of variance that you need to be able to calculate.

FAST FORWARD

- **Variances** measure the difference between actual results and expected results.
- An **expense variance** is the difference between standard expense cost and actual expense cost.

1.1 Example: variance calculation

Pink Perpetuity manufactures wooden toys. One of their products, a set of wooden building blocks (code WBB01), has the following standard unit cost and selling price.

		$	$
Direct materials			
Wood	2 units at $7.50 per unit	15	
Other materials		15	
			30
Direct labour	2 hours at $6 per hour		12
Variable production overheads	2 hours at $4 per hour		8
Fixed production overheads	2 hours at $8 per hour		16
Standard cost			66
Selling price			80
Standard profit, before marketing and administrative expenses			14

Budgeted production and sales for period 9 of 20X9 were 500 units of WBB01.

During period 9 of 20X9, actual results were as follows.

Production of building blocks (WBB01)		570 units
Sales of building blocks (WBB01)		475 units
Sales revenue		$42,000
Costs		
Wood purchased:	quantity	1,200 units
	cost	$9,400
Wood used		1,450 units
Other materials purchased and used		$8,200
Direct labour:	hours worked and paid for	1,300 hours
	labour cost	$7,400
Variable production overheads		$4,700
Fixed production overheads		$8,500

Inventories of wood are valued at standard cost, and inventories of finished goods are valued at standard full production cost.

Required

Calculate the following variances

(a) Material price variance for wood
(b) Material usage variance for wood
(c) Total material cost variance for other materials
(d) Labour rate variance
(e) Labour efficiency variance
(f) Total variable overhead variance
(g) Variable overhead expenditure variance
(h) Variable overhead efficiency variance
(i) Fixed overhead expenditure variance
(j) Fixed overhead volume variance
(k) Fixed overhead volume efficiency variance
(l) Fixed overhead volume capacity variance
(m) Selling price variance
(n) Sales volume variance

1.2 Solution

(a) **Material price variance for wood**

Inventories are valued at standard costs, and so price variances must be calculated on quantities purchased, rather than quantities used.

Key term

> The **material price variance** is the difference between the standard cost and the actual cost of the *actual* quantity of material used or purchased. In other words, it is the difference between what the material did cost and what it should have cost.

FAST FORWARD

Material price variances are extracted at the time of receipt of the materials, not the time of usage.

	$	
1,200 units of wood were purchased and cost	9,400	
but should cost (× $7.50)	9,000	
Material price variance for wood	400	(A)

(b) **Material usage variance for wood**

Key term

> The **material usage variance** is the difference between the standard quantity of materials that *should* have been used for the number of units *actually* produced, and the actual quantity of materials used, valued at the standard cost per unit of material. In other words, it is the difference between how much material should have been used and how much material was used, valued at standard cost.

570 units of WBB01 were made and used	1,450	units of materials
but 570 units should use (× 2)	1,140	units of materials
Usage variance in units	310	units (A)
× standard cost per unit of wood	× $7.50	
Usage variance in $	$2,325	(A)

(c) **Material cost variance for other materials**

We are not given a breakdown into units of material and price per unit of material, and so the only materials variance we can calculate is the **total cost variance**.

Key term

> The **material total variance** is the difference between what the output actually cost and what it should have cost, in terms of material. It can be divided into the material price variance and the material usage variance.

	$	
570 units of WBB01 did cost	8,200	in other materials
but should cost (× $15)	8,550	
Other materials cost variance	350	(F)

(d) **Labour rate variance**

Key term

> The **labour rate variance** is the difference between the standard cost and the actual cost for the actual number of hours paid for. In other words, it is the difference between what the labour did cost and what it should have cost.

	$	
1,300 hours were paid for and cost	7,400	
but should cost (× $6)	7,800	
Labour rate variance	400	(F)

(e) **Labour efficiency variance**

Key term

> The **labour efficiency variance** is the difference between the hours that *should* have been worked for the number of units *actually* produced, and the actual number of hours worked, valued at the standard rate per hour. In other words, it is the difference between how many hours should have been worked and how many hours were worked, valued at the standard rate per hour.

570 units of WBB01 took	1,300	hours
but should take (× 2 hrs)	1,140	hours
Efficiency variance, in hours	160	hours (A)
× standard cost per labour hour	× $6	
Efficiency variance in $	$960	(A)

(f) **Total variable overhead variance**

Key term

> The **variable overhead total variance** is the difference between what the output should have cost and what it did cost, in terms of variable production overhead.

FAST FORWARD

> The **variable production overhead total variance** can be subdivided into the variable production overhead **expenditure** variance and the variable production overhead **efficiency** variance.

	$	
570 units of WBB01 did cost	4,700	
but should cost (× $8)	4,560	
Variable overhead total variance	140	(A)

(g) **Variable overhead expenditure variance**

Key term

> The **variable overhead expenditure variance** is the difference between the amount of variable production overhead that should have been incurred in the actual hours actively worked, and the actual amount of variable production overhead incurred.

	$	
1,300 hours of working did cost	4,700	
but should cost (× $4)	5,200	
Variable overhead expenditure variance	500	(F)

(h) **Variable overhead efficiency variance**

This is exactly the same in hours as the direct labour efficiency variance and is valued at the standard cost per hour for variable overhead.

Key term

> The **variable overhead efficiency variance** is the difference between the standard number of hours that should have been worked for the number of units actually produced, and the actual number of hours worked, valued at the variable production overhead rate per hour.

160 hours (A) × $4 per hour $640 (A)

		$	
Check	Expenditure variance	500	(F)
	Efficiency variance	640	(A)
	Total variance	140	(A)

(i) **Fixed overhead expenditure variance**

This is under- or over-absorption of overhead because actual fixed overhead expenditure differed from budgeted expenditure.

Key term

> **Fixed overhead expenditure variance** is the difference between the budgeted fixed production overhead expenditure and actual fixed production overhead expenditure.

	$	
Budgeted fixed overhead	8,000	
Actual fixed overhead	8,500	
Expenditure variance	500	(A)

(j) **Fixed overhead volume variance**

Key term

> **Fixed overhead volume variance** is the difference between actual and budgeted production/volume multiplied by the standard absorption rate per **unit**.

Budgeted production volume of WBB01	500 units
Actual production volume	570 units
Total volume variance, in units or std hours	70 units (F)
× standard fixed overhead cost per unit	× $16
Total volume variance in $	$1,120 (F)

Like efficiency and usage variances, a volume variance is a quantity variance, measured in units, and converted into money values at standard cost. Producing a bigger quantity than budgeted will create over-absorption of fixed overhead, and so is a favourable variance.

(k) **Fixed overhead volume efficiency variance**

Key term

> **Fixed overhead volume efficiency variance** is the difference between the number of hours that actual production should have taken, and the number of hours actually taken (that is, worked) multiplied by the standard absorption rate per **hour**.

160 hrs (A) × $8 per hour $1,280 (A)

(l) **Fixed overhead volume capacity variance**

Key term

> **Fixed overhead volume capacity variance** is the difference between budgeted hours of work and the actual hours worked, multiplied by the standard absorption rate per **hour**.

Budgeted production hours (500 units × 2 hrs)	1,000 hours
Actual production hours	1,300 hours
Volume capacity variance in hours	300 hours (F)
× standard fixed overhead rate per hour	× $8
Volume capacity variance in $	$2,400 (F)

The capacity and efficiency variances add up to the total volume variance of $1,120 (F).

(m) **Selling price variance**

Key term

> The **selling price variance** is a measure of the effect on expected profit of a different selling price to standard selling price. It is calculated as the difference between what the sales revenue should have been for the actual quantity sold, and what it was.

	$
475 units of WBB01 should have sold for (× $80)	38,000
but did sell for	42,000
Selling price variance	4,000 (F)

(n) **Sales volume variance**

In a standard full costing system, the sales volume variance is valued in terms of standard profit margin.

Key term

> The **sales volume variance** is the difference between actual units sold and the budgeted quantity, valued at the standard profit per unit. In other words, it measures the effect on expected profit of the sales volume being higher or lower than budgeted.

Budgeted sales volume of WBB01	500 units
Actual sales volume	475 units
Sales volume variance	25 units (A)
× standard profit margin per unit	× $14
Sales volume variance	$350 (A)

Once variances have been calculated, they are analysed using a technique known as **variance analysis.**

The examiner wrote an article in May 2006 *Student Accountant* on the subject of understanding the causes of variances. You may want to read this as useful information when answering questions.

Key term

Variance analysis is the process by which the total difference between standard and actual results is analysed.

2 Potential causes of variances

Exam focus point

In the December 2005 exam, six marks were available for an explanation and cause of labour rate, idle time and labour efficiency variances.

There were up to seven marks available for drafting a memorandum explaining the meaning of controllable and non-controllable price variances. This was part of a longer question testing variance analysis.

2.1 General causes of variances

Managers need to understand the causes of variances so that the correct action can be taken in the future. There are four general causes of variances.

(a) **Unrealistic standards.** The budget may be overly optimistic and unachievable as a result.

(b) **Incorrectly recorded actual costs.** A variance from budgeted costs may arise if actual costs are incorrectly recorded or allocated.

(c) **Random events.** Occasionally events occur which are virtually impossible to predict and are not expected to re-occur. If this is the case no action is needed. The event will have been out of management's control.

(d) **Operating inefficiency.** If this is the cause of a variance then it could be within management's control and appropriate action may be needed. Variances arising from operating inefficiency are covered in more detail in the rest of this section.

2.2 Material price variances

An **adverse** price variance would suggest that the **managers responsible for buying decisions have paid too much for the materials**, and should be more careful in future. There are **reasons** why a large adverse or favourable price variance might occur, however, which are **outside the buying management's control**.

Reason	Comment
Inflation	A general increase in the price of materials.
Seasonal variations in prices	If material prices fluctuate seasonally, the standard price might be an average price for the year as a whole, on the assumption that it is impractical to buy a whole year's supply in the cheap season and store it until needed. In such a situation, price variances should be favourable for purchases in the cheap season and adverse for purchases in the more expensive season.
Rush orders	If buying managers are asked to make an order for immediate delivery, they might have to forgo a bulk purchase discount, or pay more for the quick supply lead time. The responsibility for the resulting adverse price variance should therefore belong to whoever made the rush order necessary in the first place.

Price variances should be **reported in the period when the purchases are made**, not when the materials are issued from stores and used. This is mainly because control information about price variances ought to be made available as soon as possible after the buying decision which gave rise to the variance, that is when the materials are bought.

2.3 Materials usage variances

A materials usage variance indicates that the quantity of materials consumed was larger or smaller than standard. It could indicate that materials **wastage** was higher or lower than it should have been or that the quantity of **rejects** was above or below standard. Wastage costs money, and should be kept to a minimum. The size of a materials usage variance, however, just like the size of a labour efficiency variance, **depends on the standard rate of usage** (or efficiency) and **whether the standard was attainable or ideal.**

In certain circumstances it could be worthwhile calculating mix and yield variances in order to carry out further analysis.

2.4 Labour rate variances

It might be tempting to think that the rate variance is something that operational managers can do little about, since rates of pay will be agreed at a senior level. A rate variance might, however, be due to **unexpected overtime working** (with overtime paid at a premium rate) or **productivity bonuses** added on to basic rates. To some extent, these should be **controllable by operational managers.**

2.5 Labour efficiency variances

The labour efficiency variance indicates that the actual production time needed to do the work was longer or less than expected. Inefficiency costs money: after all, if it takes three hours to make a unit of product instead of two hours, the unit cost of production will be higher and the profit from selling the unit will be less.

A standard time for labour to produce an item of work will normally take into account contingency allowances for down time and rest periods. Whether or not there is an allowance for these factors will depend on the type of performance standard used (ideal, attainable and so on). In a production industry based on batch production or jobbing work, the standard time will include an allowance for setting up times and clearing up times for each batch or job finished.

An **adverse** labour efficiency variance might indicate **poor labour productivity** in a period, for which a badly-motivated workforce or weak supervision might be to blame, but other causes of a variance might be as follows.

(a) Excessively **high down times**, due to a serious machine break down, or a bottleneck in production which left many of the workforce idle and waiting for work

(b) **Shorter batch runs** than expected, which increase the amount of setting up time and cleaning up time between batches, when no physical output is being produced

2.6 Overhead variances

Variances are supposed to provide management with control information. For example, an adverse material price variance of $100 tells management that the material used cost $100 more than it should have cost. But what about information provided by overhead variances? What control information can mangers get from the fact that there is an adverse fixed overhead capacity variance of $450 or that there is a favourable fixed overhead efficiency variance of $690? The information is not nearly so clear or understandable as that provided by labour and material variances, is it? But why is this?

2.6.1 Fixed overhead volume variance

Unlike expenditure variances or variable cost efficiency variances, the fixed overhead volume variance and its sub-divisions are **not a true reflection of the extra or lower cash spending** by an organisation as a result of the variance occurring. This is because the variances are valued in terms of overhead absorption rates; the estimates used in the calculation of these rates are often quite arbitrary but it is these absorption rates which determine the values assigned to the overhead variances.

Together with the expenditure variance, the fixed overhead volume variance shows the under- or over-absorbed fixed overhead. Under/over absorption is simply a book balancing exercise, however, which occurs as a result of the cost ascertainment process of absorption costing, and the level of under-/over-absorbed overhead depends on the accuracy of the original estimates used in calculating the absorption rates. The level of under/over absorption is not control information, it is simply a figure used to balance the books.

The fixed overhead efficiency and capacity variances are of **some relevance for control, however**. They **provide a measure of the difference between budgeted production volume and actual production volume,** and management should obviously be interested in whether budgeted output was achieved, and if not, why not.

Perhaps it would be more useful, however, if the losses or gains in output were valued in terms of contribution rather than in terms of absorption rates (which have arbitrary elements and were designed for quite a different purpose). The existence of a fixed overhead volume variance can therefore be important; it is only the monetary value given to the variance that can be misleading to managers.

2.6.2 Variable overhead efficiency variance

This arises because labour is either more or less efficient than standard. Variable production overheads tend to be incurred in direct proportion to production hours worked, and so if the workforce spends too much time on a job, it will incur not only more labour cost than it should, but also more variable overhead cost too.

2.6.3 Expenditure variances

The **fixed overhead expenditure variance** probably provides the **most useful** management information as the size of the variance can be said to be controllable.

(a) It does have its limitations, however. It is made up of a price component and a usage component. It can therefore vary if there are changes in charges (for example salary increases) or if quantities change (for example if more staff are taken on).

(b) For such variances to have any practical value as a control measure, the variances for each cost centre need to be calculated, and reported to the managers responsible. Within each overhead cost centre, the manager should be able to analyse the total variance into indirect materials cost variances, indirect labour cost variances and excess or favourable spending on other items, such as depreciation, postage and so on.

2.7 Selling price variance

FAST FORWARD

The **selling price variance** measures the effect on profit of a different selling price to standard selling price.

This is perhaps the variance with the **most obvious meaning**. A selling price variance indicates by how much actual selling prices of products or services have exceeded or been less than standard.

Selling price variances will be **common**. Many companies sell their products to customers at a discount, with the size of the discount depending on the size of the order or who the customer is. (For example, regular customers might be given a minimum discount on their purchases, regardless of order quantity). The standard selling price might ignore discounts altogether, or it might have an allowance for the average expected discount. In either event, the actual sales prices and standard sales prices will usually differ.

2.8 Sales volume variance

A sales volume variance will result in **higher-than-expected sales revenue if it is favourable, but there will be an off-setting increase in the cost of sales**. Similarly, an adverse sales volume variance will result in lower-than-expected sales revenue, but there will be an offsetting reduction in the cost of sales.

The **net effect** of a sales volume variance is an **increase or reduction in profitability**, which is valued in terms of profit margin when a standard absorption costing system is in use and in terms of contribution margin, when a standard marginal costing system is in use.

2.9 Summary

Variance	Favourable	Adverse
Material price	Unforeseen discounts received Greater care in purchasing Change in material standard	Price increase Careless purchasing Change in material standard
Material usage	Material used of higher quality than standard More efficient use of material Errors in allocating material to jobs	Defective material Excessive waste or theft Stricter quality control Errors in allocating material to jobs
Labour rate	Use of workers at a rate of pay lower than standard	Wage rate increase
Idle time	**The idle time variance is always adverse**	Machine breakdown Illness or injury to worker
Labour efficiency	Output produced more quickly than expected because of worker motivation, better quality materials etc Errors in allocating time to jobs	Lost time in excess of standard Output lower than standard set because of lack of training, sub-standard materials etc Errors in allocating time to jobs
Fixed overhead expenditure	Savings in costs incurred More economical use of services	Increase in cost of services used Excessive use of services Change in type of service used
Overhead expenditure variances ought to be traced to the individual cost centres where the variances occurred.		
Fixed overhead efficiency	See labour efficiency	See labour efficiency
Fixed overhead capacity	Actual time worked greater than budget (eg overtime working)	Excessive idle time Shortage of plant capacity

Question

Reported variance

M absorbs fixed production overhead at a predetermined rate based on budgeted output. Extracts from the variance analysis for April are as follows.

Fixed production overhead expenditure variance	\$6,000 (F)
Fixed production overhead efficiency variance	\$8,000 (A)
Fixed production overhead capacity variance	\$7,000 (F)

Consider the following statements concerning production in April.

Statement

1 The fixed production overhead was over-absorbed by \$5,000
2 Production output was higher than budget
3 Labour hours worked were higher than budget
4 Labour hours worked were more than the standard allowance for the actual output

Which of these statements are consistent with the reported variances?

A Statements 1 and 4 only
B Statements 2 and 3 only
C Statements 1, 2 and 3 only
D Statements 1, 3 and 4 only

Answer

The correct answer is D.

Statement 1 is correct because over-absorbed fixed overhead is represented by a favourable total overhead variance.

If the production output was higher than budget, the volume variance, ie the sum of the efficiency and capacity variances would be favourable. Statement 2 is incorrect.

If labour hours were higher than budget then the capacity variance would be favourable. Statement 3 is correct.

If labour takes longer than the standard time allowance then the efficiency variance is adverse. Statement 4 is correct.

Question

Standard costing and inflation

Jot down ideas for answering the following questions.

(a) Explain the problems concerning control of operations that a manufacturing company can be expected to experience in using a standard costing system during periods of rapid inflation.

(b) Suggest three methods by which the company could try to overcome the problems to which you have referred in answer to (a) above, indicating the shortcomings of each method.

Answer

(a)

(i) Inflation should be budgeted for in standard prices. But **how** can the rate of inflation and the timing of inflationary increases be accurately **estimated**? Who decides **how much inflationary 'allowance'** should be added to each manager's expenditure budget?

(ii) How can actual expenditure be judged against a **realistic 'standard' price level**. Ideally, there would be an external price index (for example, one published by the government's Office for National Statistics) but even external price indices are not reliable guides to the prices an organisation ought to be paying.

(iii) The existence of inflation tends to **eliminate the practical value of price variances** as a pointer to controlling spending.

(iv) Inflation affects operations more directly. Usually costs go up before an organisation can put up the prices of its own products to customers. Inflation therefore tends to **put pressure on a company's cash flows**.

(v) To provide useful and accurately-valued variances (accurate efficiency variances as well as reliable price variances) the **standard costs ought to be revised frequently**. This would be an administrative burden on the organisation.

(vi) If the organisation uses standard costs for pricing or inventory valuation, frequent revisions of the standard would be necessary to keep prices ahead of costs or inventories sensibly valued.

(b) To overcome the problems, we could suggest the following.

(i) **Frequent revision** of the standard costs. **Problem** – the administrative burden.

(ii) **Incorporating estimates** of the rate of inflation and the timing of inflation into budget expenditure allowances and standard costs. **Problem** – accurate forecasting.

(iii) Constructing **internal indices** of material prices to measure what actual price levels should have been. **Problem** – the administrative burden of constructing and maintaining the index.

(iv) A **determined effort** by management to **keep costs down**, and resist unnecessary spending. Cost control can minimise the damaging effects of price inflation. **Problem** – obtaining the cooperation of all management and employees in cost control efforts.

3 Interrelationships between variances

Individual variances should not be looked at in isolation. One variance might be interrelated with another, and much of it might have occurred only because the other, interrelated, variance occurred too. This needs to be taken into account when deciding whether or not to investigate a variance (see also section 5 of this chapter). **When two variances are interdependent (interrelated) one will usually be adverse and the other one favourable**. Here are some examples.

Interrelated variances	Explanation
Materials price and material usage	If cheaper materials are purchased in order to obtain a favourable price variance, materials wastage might be higher and an adverse usage variance may occur. If the cheaper material is more difficult to handle, there might be an adverse labour efficiency variance too. If a decision is made to purchase more expensive material, the price variance will be adverse but the usage variance might be favourable if the material is easier to use or of a higher quality.
Labour rate and labour efficiency/material usage	If employees are paid higher rates for experience and skill, using a highly skilled team to do some work might lead to an adverse rate variance and a favourable efficiency variance and possibly a favourable material usage variance (experienced staff are less likely to waste material, for example). In contrast, a favourable rate variance might indicate a larger-than-expected proportion of inexperienced workers in the workforce, which could result in an adverse labour efficiency variance, and perhaps poor materials handling and high rates of rejects and hence an adverse materials usage variance.
Selling price and sales volume	The connection between selling price and sales volume is perhaps an obvious one. A reduction in the selling price might stimulate bigger sales demand, so that an adverse selling price variance might be counterbalanced by a favourable sales volume variance. Similarly, a price rise would give a favourable price variance, but possibly at the cost of a fall in demand and an adverse sales volume variance.
Variable and fixed production overhead efficiency variances and other variances	Because the variable and fixed production overhead efficiency variances are the same, in hours, as the labour efficiency variance, any interrelationships between other variances and the labour efficiency variance apply equally to the variable and fixed production overhead efficiency variances. So if there is an interrelationship between a favourable labour rate variance and an adverse labour efficiency variance, there will also be interrelationships between the favourable labour rate variance and adverse variable and fixed production overhead efficiency variances.

Because cost accountants analyse total variances into component elements (materials price and usage, labour rate and efficiency, and so on) they should not lose sight of the overall 'integrated' picture of events, and any interdependence between variances should be reported whenever it is suspected to have occurred.

Question — Interdependent variances

If two variances are **interdependent**, both must be either favourable or adverse.

True ☐

False ☐

Answer

False. Favourable material price and adverse material usage variances might be interdependent, for example.

Exam focus point

Ensure that you can provide possible reasons for various variances occurring and that you are aware of the interdependence between variances.

4 Variance analysis reports

Once the operating statement has been prepared it is usually included in a report presented to management at the end of each control period. The operating statement may be included within the body of the report or may form an appendix.

An operating statement provides an overview of the differences between planned costs and actual costs. Total cost variances may be reported in some organisations whereas, in others, each total variance may be broken down into the constituent components. Whatever the degree of detail, it is likely that **most recipients of the report will require some explanation. Many of the managers receiving the report will be functional managers** (production managers, sales managers and so on) rather than accounting or finance managers. **They may find it difficult to interpret an operating statement.**

The report should therefore highlight significant variances and make recommendations for possible management action.

4.1 Example: variance reports

Searcher, a manufacturing firm, operates a standard marginal costing system. It makes a single product, the SE, using a single raw material, EKS.

Standard costs relating to the SE have been calculated as follows.

Standard cost schedule – SE

	$ per unit
Direct material EKS, 10 kg at $15 per kg	150
Direct labour, 5 hours at $9 per hour	45
	195
Variable production overheads, 5 hours at $3 per hour	15
	210
Standard selling price	250
Standard contribution	40

Budgeted fixed production overheads per control period are $25,000.

During control period 13, although budgeted production and sales were 950 units, 1,000 units were produced and then sold for $275,000.

Other information regarding actual performance during control period 13 is as follows.

Direct material EKS

11,000 kg were purchased during the period, actual cost being $144,000.

There were no opening or closing inventories of raw material EKS.

Direct labour

5,200 hours were worked during the period, total wages being $48,360.

Variable production overhead

The actual cost for the period was $16,800.

Fixed production overheads

The actual cost for the period was $30,000.

Required

Produce a report for management which includes a statement reconciling budgeted and actual profit and which explains the key features of the variances and makes recommendations for management action.

4.2 Solution

REPORT

To: Managers of Searcher
From: A Student
Date: 13 November 20X7
Subject: Variance Report – control period 13

This report contains an operating statement showing a reconciliation of budgeted and actual profit for control period 13. Key features of the statement are explained and recommendations for management action are provided.

The calculation of budgeted profit and the operating statement variances are contained in the appendix to this report.

OPERATING STATEMENT FOR CONTROL PERIOD 13

		$	$
Budgeted profit			13,000
Sales variances: price		25,000 (F)	
volume		2,000 (F)	
			27,000 (F)
Actual sales minus standard cost of sales			40,000 (F)
	$ (F)	$ (A)	
Cost variances			
Direct labour rate		1,560	
Direct labour efficiency		1,800	
Direct material price	21,000		
Direct material usage		15,000	
Variable production overhead rate		1,200	
Variable production overhead efficiency		600	
Fixed production overhead		5,000	
	21,000	25,160	4,160 (A)
Actual profit			35,840

Explanation of variances and recommendations for management action

Direct labour rate variance

An adverse variance arises because the labour force were paid an average of ($48,360/5,200) = $9.30 per hour instead of the standard cost of $9 per hour. If this is a new agreed rate the standard should be revised. It may, however, be due to a short-term need to recruit temporary labour at rates more expensive than standard or to overtime working or bonus payments. The production manager and/or the personnel department should be contacted for further information.

Direct labour efficiency variance

An adverse variance of $1,800 has arisen because the labour force took 200 hours more to produce 1,000 units than the standard allowance. The production manager should be asked to explain the variance. Possible causes are lack of training or machine breakdown, but the material variances may also offer a clue as to the explanation.

Material price variance

Materials were purchased for $13.09 per kg in the period (a price $1.91 less than standard) giving rise to a favourable price variance of $21,000. However this appears to have been at the expense of quality, to judge from the usage variance. The purchasing manager should be asked to explain why the cheaper materials were purchased.

Material usage variance

1,000 kg more than standard were used to make 1,000 units. This seems most likely to be because cheaper, poor quality materials were purchased, probably resulting in excessive waste. It is possible that the need for rectification work due to poor materials also explains why the labour force was less efficient than standard.

Total variable production overhead variance

An adverse variance of $1,800 has arisen. Variable overhead varies in line with labour costs and thus $600 of the variance is explicable by reference to the extra labour hours worked. The remainder is due to an increase in variable overhead costs: the actual rate per hour was $16,800/5,200 hours = $3.23, as opposed to the standard rate of $3. For further explanation we need to know what the overhead comprises and who is responsible for the expenditure.

Fixed production overhead variance

Fixed production overheads in the period were $30,000, representing an increase of 20% over the budgeted figures of $25,000. A breakdown of the total figure is needed before control action can be recommended.

Selling price variance

The favourable selling price variance of $25,000 indicates that each unit of SE was sold for $275 instead of the standard price of $250. The reason for this significant price increase should be investigated; the sales manager will no doubt be able to provide information. We may have increased our prices following price rises by our competitors. Alternatively, there may have been an increase in demand for the SE, leading to a shortage of the product, with the result that we were able to increase our prices.

Sales volume variance

Sales volumes were 50 greater than budgeted, resulting in a favourable sales volume variance of $2,000. Despite the fact that we increased the selling price of the SE we were able to increase volumes, possibly because there is a shortage of the product following increased demand. Again, the sales manager will have the appropriate information.

Appendix

	$
Calculation of budgeted profit	
Budgeted contribution ($40 × 950)	38,000
Budgeted fixed overheads	25,000
	13,000

Calculation of variances

	$
5,200 hours should cost (× $9)	46,800
but did cost	48,360
Direct labour rate variance	1,560 (A)

1,000 units should take (× 5 hours)	5,000 hrs
but did take	5,200 hrs
Direct labour efficiency variance in hrs	200 hrs (A)
× standard rate per hour	× $9
Direct labour efficiency variance in $	1,800 (A)

	$
11,000 kg should cost (× $15)	165,000
but did cost	144,000
Direct materials price variance	21,000 (F)
1,000 units should use (× 10kg)	10,000 kgs
but did use	11,000 kgs
Direct materials usage variance in kgs	1,000 kgs (A)
× standard cost per kg	× $15
Direct materials usage variance in $	$15,000 (A)

	$
5,200 hrs of variable production overhead should cost (× $3)	15,600
but did cost	16,800
Variable production overhead rate variance	1,200 (A)
Variable production overhead efficiency variance in hrs (same as labour efficiency variance)	200 hrs (A)
× standard cost per hr	× $3
Variable production overhead efficiency variance	$600 (A)

	$
Budgeted fixed production overhead expenditure	25,000
Actual fixed production overhead expenditure	30,000
Fixed production overhead variance	5,000 (A)

	$
1,000 units should have sold for (× $250)	250,000
but did sell for	275,000
Selling price variance	25,000 (F)
Budgeted sales volume	950 units
Actual sales volume	1,000 units
Sales volume variance in units	50 units (F)
× standard contribution per unit	× $40
Sales volume variance	$2,000 (F)

Exam focus point

In the exam you may well be required to produce a report explaining the key features of variances and making recommendations for management action. Don't forget the information about effective report writing included earlier.

5 To investigate or not to investigate?

FAST FORWARD

Materiality, **controllability** and **variance trend** should be considered before a decision about whether or not to investigate a variance is taken.

One way of deciding whether or not to investigate a variance is to only investigate those variances which exceed pre-set tolerance limits.

Before management decide whether or not to investigate the reasons for the occurrence of a particular variance, there are a **number of factors which should be considered.**

Exam focus point

These factors were examined in December 2004.

5.1 Materiality

Small variations in a single period between actual and standard are bound to occur and are unlikely to be significant. Obtaining an 'explanation' of the reasons why they occurred is likely to be time-consuming and irritating for the manager concerned. For such variations **further investigation is not worthwhile**.

5.2 Controllability

If there is a general worldwide price increase in the price of an important raw material there is nothing that can be done internally to control the effect of this. If a central decision is made to award all employees a 10% increase in salary, staff costs in division A will increase by this amount and the variance is not controllable by division A's manager. **Uncontrollable variances call for a change in the standard, not an investigation into the past.**

5.3 Variance trend

Although small variations in a single period are unlikely to be significant, small variations that occur consistently may need more attention. Variance trend is more important that a single set of variances for one accounting period. The trend **provides an indication of whether the variance is fluctuating within acceptable control limits or becoming out of control.**

(a) If, say, an efficiency variance is $1,000 adverse in month 1, the obvious conclusion is that the process is out of control and that corrective action must be taken. This may be correct, but what if the same variance is $1,000 adverse every month? The *trend* indicates that the process is in control and the standard has been wrongly set.

(b) Suppose, though, that the same variance is consistently $1,000 adverse for each of the first six months of the year but that production has steadily fallen from 100 units in month 1 to 65 units by month 6. The variance trend in absolute terms is constant, but relative to the number of units produced, efficiency has got steadily worse.

5.4 Reliability/variability

Are the figures accurate? If mistakes were made in recording the numbers, it may be that no problem exists. On the other hand, some costs can be very volatile (such as certain raw materials) so a variance would not be surprising.

5.5 Cost v benefit

If a variance would cost more to investigate than could be gained by that investigation, there is no justification for it.

Individual variances should therefore not be looked at in isolation; variances should be scrutinised for a number of successive periods if their full significance is to be appreciated.

Question — Variance trends

What might the following variance trend information indicate?

(a) Regular, perhaps fairly slight, increases in adverse price variances
(b) A rapid, large increase in adverse price variances
(c) Gradually improving labour efficiency variances
(d) Worsening trends in machine running expense variances

Answer

(a) Such variances usually indicate the workings of general inflation.

(b) These variances may indicate a sudden scarcity of a resource. It may soon be necessary to seek out cheaper substitutes.

(c) These may signal the existence of a learning curve, or the success of a productivity bonus scheme.

(d) These may indicate that equipment is deteriorating and will soon need repair or even replacement.

5.6 The significance of variances

A variance can be considered significant if it will influence management's actions and decisions. Significant variances usually need investigating.

Variances which are **simply random** deviations, in other words fluctuations which have arisen by chance, are **uncontrollable**. This is because a standard cost is really only an **average** expected cost and is not a rigid specification. Some variances either side of this average must be expected to occur and are hence outside management's control.

The problem for both management and the accountant is therefore to decide whether a variation from standard is attributable to chance and hence *not* significant or whether it is due to a controllable cause and therefore significant.

6 Control limits and control charts

FAST FORWARD

Control limits may be illustrated on a **control chart**.

Exam focus point

Control charts were examined in the December 2006 exam. Candidates were asked to explain how they would be used in deciding to investigate variances, and a diagram of a control chart was required.

Because standard costs are only estimates of average costs, it would be incorrect to treat them as being rigid. **Tolerance limits should be set, and only variances which exceed these limits should be reported as being significant and investigated. The following variances would lie within the tolerance limits.**

(a) **Normal variations around average performance**, with variations above and below the average (adverse and favourable variances) cancelling each other out in the course of time.

(b) **Minor operational variances** which are too small to justify the cost of investigation and control action by management. Small variances might 'sort themselves out' in time, and only if they persist and grow larger should investigative action be worthwhile.

(c) A **minor planning error** in the standard cost for the year.

The control limits may be illustrated on a **variance control chart** as follows.

Variance control chart

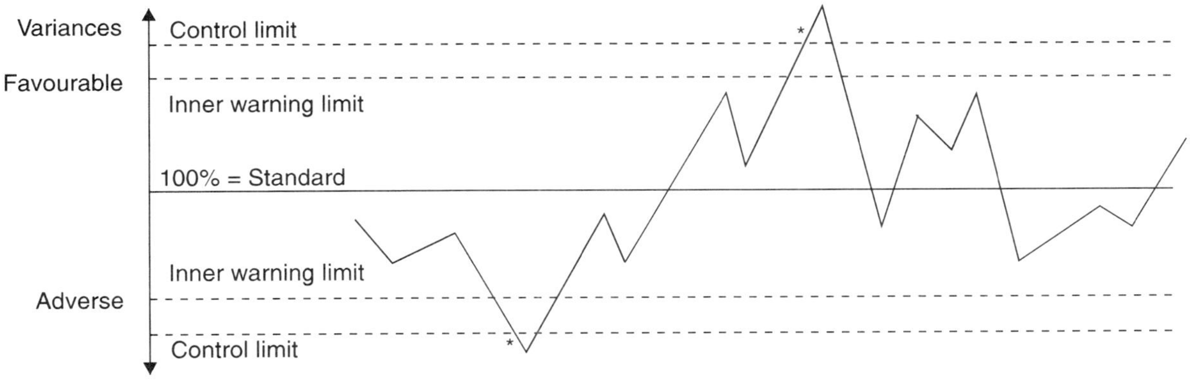

*Notify as an exception

There are several **ways of establishing control** limits.

(a) Management might establish a rule that any **variance should be deemed significant if it exceeds a certain percentage of standard**, for example if it exceeds 10% of standard in any one period based on judgement or experience.

(b) Management can use **statistics, and estimate** not only the standard cost, but the **expected standard deviation** (a measure of the spread or dispersion) of actual costs around the standard. Variances would then be deemed significant if actual costs were significantly different from standard.

Not all variances which are outside the control limits require detailed investigation. Often the cause is already known. **A variance will only be investigated if the expected value of benefits from investigation and any control action exceed the costs of investigation.**

For example it may be known from past experience that the cost of investigating a particular variance is \$150 and that cost savings amounting to \$1,200 can be made if the variance is corrected successfully. However it is also known that there is only a 30% possibility of the variance being corrected once the cause is found.

Expected value of an investigation = (\$1,200 × 0.3) – \$150 = \$210

In this particular case it is worth investigating the variance.

Question

Variance investigation

Every month the operating statement of Jefferson shows a direct material efficiency variance of between \$1,500 and \$2,500 relating to a product that is only to be produced for a further six months. The company management accountant believes that if the variance is investigated, there is a 70% chance that its cause can eliminated. The cost of the investigation, however, is \$5,000.

Should the investigation take place?

Answer

Minimum possible cost saving = 6 × \$1,500 = \$9,000

Expected value of the benefit of investigating the variance	= 70% × \$9,000
	= \$6,300
Cost of investigation	= \$5,000

∴ Expected benefits exceed the costs

∴ The investigation is worthwhile.

Another approach is to **look at the variances over a number of accounting periods**, instead of just looking at variances in a single period.

The variance in each period is added to the total of the variances that have occurred over a longer period of time. If the variances are not significant, the total will simply fluctuate in a random way above and below the average (favourable and unfavourable variances), to give an insignificant total or cumulative sum. If the cumulative sum develops a positive or negative drift, it may exceed a set tolerance limit. Then the situation must be investigated, and control action will probably be required. The cumulative sum of variances over a period of time can be shown on a **cusum chart**.

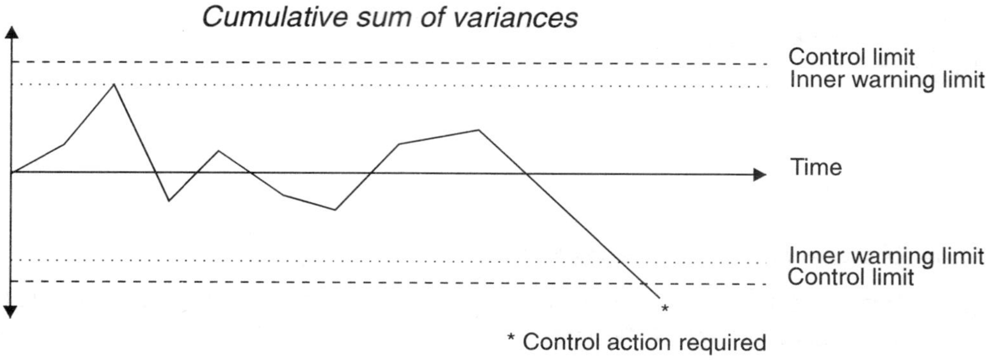

The advantage of the multiple period approach is that **trends are detectable earlier**, and control action can be introduced sooner than might have been the case if only current-period variances were investigated.

7 Control action

FAST FORWARD

A variance should only be investigated if the expected value of benefits from investigation and any control action exceed the costs of investigation.

If the cause of a variance is controllable, action can be taken to bring the system back under control in future. If the variance is uncontrollable, but not simply due to chance, it will be necessary to review forecasts of expected results, and perhaps to revise the budget.

If a variance is assessed as significant then control action may be necessary.

Since a variance compares historical actual costs with standard costs, it is a statement of what has gone wrong (or right) in the past. By taking control action, managers can do nothing about the past, but they can use their analysis of past results to identify where the 'system' is out of control. If the **cause of the variance is controllable, action can be taken to bring the system back under control in future. If the variance is uncontrollable, on the other hand, but *not* simply due to chance, it will be necessary to revise forecasts of expected results, and perhaps to revise the budget.**

It may be possible for control action to restore actual results back on course to achieve the original budget. For example, if there is an adverse labour efficiency variance in month 1 of 1,100 hours, control action by the production department might succeed in increasing efficiency above standard by 100 hours per month for the next 11 months.

It is also possible that control action might succeed in restoring better order to a situation, but the improvements might not be sufficient to enable the company to achieve its original budget. For example if for three months there has been an adverse labour efficiency in a production department, so that the cost per unit of output was $8 instead of a standard cost of $5. Control action might succeed in improving efficiency, so that unit costs are reduced to $7, $6 or even $5, but the earlier excess spending means that the profit in the master budget will not be achieved.

Depending on the situation and the control action taken, the action may take immediate effect, or it may take several weeks or months to implement. The effect of control action might be short-lived, lasting for only one control period; but it is more likely to be implemented with the aim of long-term improvement.

7.1 Possible control action

The **control action which may be taken will depend on the reason why the variance occurred**. Some reasons for variances are outlined in the paragraphs below.

7.2 Measurement errors

In practice it may be extremely difficult to establish that 1,000 units of product A used 32,000 kg of raw material X. Scales may be misread, the pilfering or wastage of materials may go unrecorded, items may be wrongly classified (as material X3, say, when material X8 was used in reality), or employees may make adjustments to records to make their own performance look better.

An investigation may show that **control action is required to improve the accuracy of the recording system** so that measurement errors do not occur.

7.3 Out of date standards

Price standards are likely to become out of date when changes to the costs of material, power, labour and so on occur, or in **periods of high inflation**. In such circumstances an **investigation of variances is likely to highlight a general change in market prices** rather than efficiencies or inefficiencies in acquiring resources.

Standards may also be out of date where operations are subject to **technological development** or if **learning curve effects** have not been taken into account. Investigation of this type of variance will provide information about the inaccuracy of the standard and **highlight the need to frequently review and update standards.**

7.4 Efficient or inefficient operations

Spoilage and better quality material/more highly skilled labour than standard are all likely to affect the efficiency of operations and hence cause variances. **Investigation** of variances in this category should **highlight the cause of the inefficiency or efficiency and will lead to control action to eliminate the inefficiency being repeated** or action to **compound the benefits of the efficiency**. For example, stricter supervision may be required to reduce wastage levels.

7.5 Random or chance fluctuations

A standard is an **average** figure. It represents the midpoint of a range of possible values and therefore actual results are likely to deviate unpredictably within the predictable range.

As long as the variance falls within this range, it will be classified as a random or chance fluctuation and **control action will not be necessary**.

Question — Report on variances

As the management accountant of the ABC Production Co you have prepared the following variance report for the general manager.

VARIANCE REPORT: SEPTEMBER 20X5

	Variance (Adverse) $	*Variance (Favourable)* $	*Total variance* $
Material			(2,000)
Usage	5,500		
Price		3,500	
Labour			(1,500)
Utilisation	3,000		
Rate		1,500	
Overhead			(500)
Price		4,500	
Efficiency	2,000		
Capacity	3,000		

Actual costs for September 20X5 were as follows.

	$
Materials	$100,000
Labour	$80,000
Overheads	$75,000
Total	$255,000

The general manager tells you that he is quite satisfied with this result because the total adverse variance of $4,000 is only 1.57% of total costs.

Required

Write a brief report to the General Manager giving *your own* interpretation of the month's results.

Answer

REPORT ON RESULTS FOR SEPTEMBER 20X5

1 TERMS OF REFERENCE

This report provides a management accounting interpretation of the company's results for September 20X5. The report was prepared by A N Employee, Management Accountant and submitted to A Boss, General Manager, on XX October 20X5.

2 METHOD

Using the management accounting department's variance report for September 20X5 and actual cost data for the month, the company's results were analysed.

3 FINDINGS

Total variance

The total variance may only be 1.57% of total costs but this total disguises a number of significant adverse and favourable variances which need investigating.

Materials variances

The fact that there is a favourable price variance and an adverse usage variance could indicate interdependence. The purchasing department may have bought cheap materials but these cheaper materials may have been more difficult to work with so that more material was required per unit produced. The possibility of such an interdependence should be investigated. Whether or not there is an interdependence, both variances do require investigation since they represent 5.5% (usage) and 3.5% (price) of the actual material cost for the month.

Labour variances

Again there could be an interdependence between the adverse utilisation variance and the favourable rate variance, less skilled (and lower paid) employees perhaps having worked less efficiently than standard. Discussions with factory management should reveal whether this is so. Both variances do need investigation since they again represent a high percentage (compared with 1.57%) of the actual labour cost for the month (3.75% for the utilisation variance and 1.875% for the rate variance).

Overhead variances

An investigation into the fixed and variable components of the overhead would facilitate control information. The cause of the favourable price variance, which represents 6% of the total overhead costs for the month, should be encouraged.

The adverse overhead variances in total represent 6.67% of actual overhead cost during the month and must therefore be investigated. The capacity variance signifies that actual hours of work were less than budgeted hours of work. The company is obviously working below its planned capacity level. Efforts should therefore be made to increase production so as to eradicate this variance.

4 CONCLUSION

It is not the total of the monthly variances which should be considered but the individual variances, as a number of them represent significant deviations from planned results. Investigations into their causes should be performed and control action taken to ensure that either performance is back under control in future if the cause of the variance can be controlled, or the forecasts of expected results are revised if the variance is uncontrollable.

Question — Control problems

Jot down ideas for answering the following questions.

(a) Explain the problems concerning control of operations that a manufacturing company can be expected to experience in using a standard costing system during periods of rapid inflation.

(b) Suggest a method by which the company could try to overcome the problems to which you have referred in answer to (a) above, indicating the shortcoming of the method.

Answer

(a) (i) Inflation should be budgeted for in standard prices. But how can the rate of inflation and the timing of inflationary increases be accurately estimated? Who decides how much inflationary 'allowance' should be added to the standards?

(ii) How can actual expenditure be judged against a realistic 'standard' price level. Ideally, there would be an external price index (for example, one published by the government's Office for National Statistics) but even external price indices are not reliable guides to the prices an organisation ought to be paying.

(iii) The existence of inflation tends to eliminate the practical value of price variances as a pointer to controlling spending.

(iv) Inflation affects operations more directly. Usually costs go up before an organisation can put up the prices of its own products to customers. Inflation therefore tends to put pressure on a company's cash flows.

(v) To provide useful and accurately-valued variances the standard costs ought to be revised frequently. This would be an administrative burden on the organisation.

(vi) If the organisation uses standard costs for pricing or inventory valuation, frequent revisions of the standard would be necessary to keep prices ahead of costs or inventories sensibly valued.

(b) To overcome the problems, we could suggest the following.

 (i) Frequent revision of the standard costs. *Problem* – the administrative burden.

 (ii) Incorporating estimates of the rate of inflation and the timing of inflation into standard costs. *Problem* – accurate forecasting.

Chapter Roundup

- **Variances** measure the difference between actual results and expected results.
- An **expense variance** is the difference between standard expense cost and actual expense cost.
- Material price variances are extracted at the time of receipt of the materials, not the time of usage.
- The **variable production overhead total variance** can be subdivided into the variable production overhead **expenditure** variance and the variable production overhead **efficiency** variance.
- The **selling price variance** measures the effect on profit of a different selling price to standard selling price.
- **Materiality**, **controllability** and **variance trend** should be considered before a decision about whether or not to investigate a variance is taken.
- One way of deciding whether or not to investigate a variance is to only investigate those variances which exceed pre-set tolerance limits.
- **Control limits** may be illustrated on a **control chart**.
- A variance should only be investigated if the expected value of benefits from investigation and any control action exceed the costs of investigation.
- If the cause of a variance is controllable, action can be taken to bring the system back under control in future. If the variance is uncontrollable, but not simply due to chance, it will be necessary to review forecasts of expected results, and perhaps to revise the budget.

Quick Quiz

1 If an organisation uses standard marginal costing instead of absorption costing:

(a) Which variance would no longer be calculated?
(b) Which variance would be different and why?

2 Fixed production overhead volume variances do not occur in a standard absorption costing system. True or false?

3 What does variance trend show?

4 What three types of variance would lie within tolerance limits?

5 Describe the two ways of establishing control limits.

6 What are the four basic reasons why variances occur?

7 A regular report for management of actual cost and revenue, and usually comparing actual with budget (and showing variances) is known as

A Bank statement
B Variance statement
C Budget statement
D Operating statement

8 A favourable sales price variance can result from a combination of a lower than budgeted sales volume and a higher than standard selling price.

True ☐

False ☐

Answers to Quick Quiz

1 (a) There would be no fixed overhead volume variance

(b) The sales volume variance would be different because it would be calculated using the standard contribution per unit rather than the standard profit per unit.

2 False. They do not occur in standard marginal costing systems.

3 Variance trend provides an indication of whether a variance is fluctuating within acceptable limits or becoming out of control.

4 Normal variations around average performance, minor operational variances and variances due to minor planning errors in the standard cost will lie within tolerance limits.

5 (a) Management might establish a rule that any variance should be deemed significant if it exceeds a certain percentage of standard, for example if it exceeds 10% of standard in any one period based on judgement or experience.

(b) Management can use statistics, and estimate not only the standard cost, but the expected standard deviation (a measure of the spread or dispersion) of actual costs around the standard. Variances would then be deemed significant if actual costs were significantly different from standard.

6 Variances occur because of measurement errors, out of date standards, efficient or inefficient operations and random/chance fluctuations.

7 D

8 **False**. The variance is **favourable** if the actual price is higher than standard.

Now try the questions below from the Exam Question Bank

Number	Level	Marks	Time
Section A: Q18	MCQ	N/A	N/A
Section B: Q14	Examination	20	36 mins

PART D

Management accounting applications

14

Performance measurement

Topic list
1 Performance measurement and the planning and control system
2 Goals and objectives
3 Commercial goals and objectives
4 Performance measures
5 Measuring profitability and productivity
6 Performance measures based on the statement of financial position (balance sheet)
7 External considerations

Study guide reference

		Syllabus reference
24(a)	Performance hierarchy	8
	(i) Discuss the purpose of mission statements and their role in performance measurement	8
	(ii) Discuss the purpose of strategic and operational and tactical objectives and their role in performance measurement	
(b)	External considerations	8
	(i) Discuss the impact of economic and market conditions on performance measurement	
(c)	Discuss the impact of government regulation on performance measurement	8
25(a)	Discuss and calculate measures of financial performance – profitability, liquidity, activity and gearing	8
(b)	Discuss the importance of non-financial performance measures	8
(c)	Discuss the relationship between short-term and long-term performance	8
26(a)	Perspectives of the balanced scorecard	8
	(iii) Discuss critical success factors and key performance indicators and their link to objectives and mission statements	
	(iv) Establish critical success factors and key performance indicators in a specific situation	
(b)	Economy, efficiency and effectiveness	8
	(i) Explain the concepts of economy, efficiency and effectiveness	
	(ii) Describe performance indicators for economy, efficiency and effectiveness	
	(iii) Establish performance indicators for economy, efficiency and effectiveness in a specific situation	

Exam focus point

This chapter covers a key syllabus area. Key syllabus areas usually account for 80% or more of the marks available on the exam paper.

1 Performance measurement and the planning and control system

FAST FORWARD

The higher direction of an organisation requires a clear vision, in general terms, of what the organisation should be doing in the longer term and how it should go about doing it. This may be encapsulated in a **mission statement**.

Performance measurement aims to establish how well something or somebody is doing in relation to a planned activity. The 'thing' may be one of the following.

(a) A machine
(b) A factory
(c) An organisation as a whole

The 'body' may be one of the following

(a) An individual employee
(b) A manager
(c) A group of people

Performance measurement is a **vital part** of the **control process.** The essence of control is that **actual performance is compared with a standard or target that was established earlier. For machines, processes**, departments and individuals such targets are laid down by the budgetary process and published in the budget itself. At a higher level, when we are trying to control the whole organisation, a slightly more complex process is required.

To begin with, the normal budgetary control process has benefit at this level. The forecast income statement and statement of financial position, which are the final product of the budget process, obviously represent overall targets for the organisation. However, these targets are not sufficient for the proper control of a large organisation: they only provide guidance for a very short period and only in terms of decisions that have already been taken. Even if a new process is scheduled to come into operation during the next year, that is the result of decisions long past. The budgetary process offers little guidance for the longer-term progress of the organisation.

We must now take a brief look at the world of strategic management. It is in this arena that the wider direction of the organisation is determined. Strategic managers must look several years into the future and decide what they want the organisation to do and where they want it to go. An important part of this process is the design and refinement of the organisational **mission statement**. This should encapsulate the **vision** of top management: what it is they are trying to achieve and, in general terms, how they wish to achieve it.

1.1 Elements of mission

Purpose. Why does the company exist?

(a) To create wealth for shareholders?
(b) To satisfy the needs of **all stakeholders** (including employees, society at large, for example)?

Strategy. Mission provides the commercial logic for the organisation, and so defines two things

(a) The **products or services** it offers and therefore its competitive position.
(b) The **competences** by which it hopes to prosper, and its way of competing.

Strategic scope. An organisation's strategic scope is defined by the **boundaries** its managers set for it. These boundaries may be set in terms of geography, market, business method, product or any other parameter that **defines the nature of the organisation**.

Policies and standards of behaviour. The mission needs to be converted into everyday performance. For example, a firm whose mission covers excellent customer service must deal with simple matters such as politeness to customers, speed at which phone calls are answered and so forth.

Values and culture. Values are the basic, perhaps unstated, beliefs of the people who work in the organisation.

The values of the business as a **collective entity** are in tune with the **personal values** of the individuals working for it. In conflicts of ethics, clashes between organisational and personal values are hard to resolve if someone's principles disagree with what the organisation wants.

For there to be a strong, motivating sense of mission, the four elements above must be mutually reinforcing.

1.2 The importance of mission

Although hard to quantify (and hence, from an accounting viewpoint, of dubious value) mission is taken seriously by many firms.

(a) Values and feelings are integral elements of **consumers' buying decisions**, as evidenced by advertising, branding and market research. Customers not only ask 'What do you sell?' but 'What do you stand for?'
(b) A respect for quantifiable information is part of the professional culture and training of the accountant; other people have different values and priorities.

(c) Studies into organisational behaviour suggest that employees are **motivated** by more than money. A sense of mission and values can help to motivate employees.

(d) Many firms take mission seriously in strategic management.

1.3 Mission statements

Mission statements are formal statements of an organisation's mission. They might be reproduced in a number of places (eg at the front of an organisation's annual report, on publicity material, in the chairman's office, in communal work areas and so on). There is no standard format, but they should possess certain characteristics.

(a) **Brevity** – easy to understand and remember
(b) **Flexibility** – to accommodate change
(c) **Distinctiveness –** to make the firm stand out

1.4 Mission and planning

Although the mission statement might be seen as a set of abstract principles, it can play an important **role in the planning process**.

(a) **Plans should outline the fulfilment of the organisation's mission**. To take the example of a religious organisation (the best example of a 'missionary organisation'), the mission of spreading the gospel might be embodied in plans to send individuals as missionaries to various parts of the world, plans for fund-raising activities, or even targets for the numbers of new converts.

(b) **Evaluation and screening**. Mission also acts as a yardstick by which plans are judged.

 (i) The mission of an ethical investment trust would preclude investing in tobacco firms.
 (ii) Mission helps to ensure consistency in decisions.

(c) **Implementation**. Mission also affects the implementation of a planned strategy, in the culture and business practices of the firm.

2 Goals and objectives

FAST FORWARD

A hierarchy of SMART goals and objectives cascades downwards from the mission statement, eventually providing the targets for the periodic budget process.

From the vision and mission, **goals** are derived.

(a) **Operational goals** can be expressed as objectives. Here is an example.
 Operational goal: 'Cut costs'. The objective: 'Reduce budget by 5%'

(b) **Non-operational goals** A university's goal might be to 'seek truth'.
 Not all goals can be measured.

In practice most organisations set themselves **quantified objectives** in order to enact the corporate mission. Many objectives are:

(a) **S**pecific
(b) **M**easurable
(c) **A**ttainable
(d) **R**esults-orientated
(e) **T**ime-bounded

There should be **goal congruence**. The goals set for different parts of the organisation should be consistent with each other.

2.1 Primary and secondary objectives

Some objectives are more important than others. In the hierarchy of objectives, there is a **primary corporate objective** and other **secondary objectives** which should combine to ensure the achievement of the overall corporate objective.

For example, if a company sets itself an objective of growth in profits, as its primary aim, it will then have to develop strategies by which this primary objective can be achieved. An objective must then be set for each individual strategy. Secondary objectives might then be concerned with sales growth, continual technological innovation, customer service, product quality, efficient resource management or reducing the company's reliance on debt capital.

2.2 Long-term objectives and short-term objectives

Objectives may be long-term and short-term. A company that is suffering from a recession in its core industries and making losses in the short term might continue to have a long term primary objective of achieving a growth in profits, but in the short term its primary objective might be survival.

3 Commercial goals and objectives

Objectives are normally **quantified** statements of what the organisation actually intends to achieve over a period of time.

Uses of objectives

(a) Objectives **orientate the activities** of the organisation towards the fulfilment of the organisation's mission, in theory if not always in practice.

(b) The mission of a **business**, whether stated or not, must include **profitability**.

(c) Objectives can also be used as standards **for measuring the performance** of the organisation and departments in it.

3.1 Corporate and unit objectives

Corporate objectives concern the firm as **a whole**, for example:

(a) Profitability
(b) Market share
(c) Growth
(d) Cash flow
(e) Return on capital employed
(f) Risk
(g) Customer satisfaction
(h) Quality
(i) Industrial relations
(j) Added value
(k) Earnings per share

Similar objectives can be developed for each **strategic business unit (SBU).** (An SBU is a part of the company that for all intents and purposes has its own distinct products, markets and assets.)

Unit objectives are specific to individual units of an organisation.

(a) **Commercial**

(i) Increase the number of customers by x% (an objective of a sales department)

(ii) Reduce the number of rejects by 50% (an objective of a production department)

(iii) Produce monthly reports more quickly, within 5 working days of the end of each month (an objective of the management accounting department)

(b) **Public sector**

(i) Introduce x% more places at nursery schools (an objective of a borough education department)

(ii) Respond more quickly to calls (an objective of a local police station, fire department or hospital ambulance service)

(c) **General**

   (i) Resources (eg cheaper raw materials, lower borrowing costs, 'top-quality college graduates')
   (ii) Market (eg market share, market standing)
   (iii) Employee development (eg training, promotion, safety)
   (iv) Innovation in products or processes
   (v) Productivity (the amount of output from resource inputs)
   (vi) Technology

3.2 Primary and secondary objectives

Some objectives are more important than others. There is a **primary corporate objective** (restricted by certain constraints on corporate activity) and other **secondary objectives** which are strategic objectives which should combine to ensure the achievement of the primary corporate objective.

(a) For example, if a company sets itself an objective of growth in profits, as its primary objective, it will then have to develop strategies by which this primary objective can be achieved.

(b) Secondary objectives might then be concerned with sales growth, continual technological innovation, customer service, product quality, efficient resource management (eg labour productivity) or reducing the company's reliance on debt capital.

3.3 Trade-off between objectives

When there are several key objectives, some might be achieved only **at the expense of others**. For example, a company's objective of achieving good profits and profit growth might have adverse consequences for the cash flow of the business, or the quality of the firm's products.

There will be a **trade-off** between objectives when strategies are formulated, and a choice will have to be made. For example, there might be a choice between the following two options.

Option A 15% sales growth, 10% profit growth, a $2 million negative cash flow and reduced product quality and customer satisfaction.

Option B 8% sales growth, 5% profit growth, a $500,000 surplus cash flow, and maintenance of high product quality/customer satisfaction.

If the firm chose option B in preference to option A, it would be trading off sales growth and profit growth for better cash flow, product quality and customer satisfaction. The long-term effect of reduced quality has not been considered.

3.4 Critical success factors

As long ago as 1955 *Lewis* made a study of *GEC's* management reporting system and found that it produced reports on the following factors.

(a)	Profitability	(e)	Personnel development
(b)	Market share	(f)	Employee attitudes
(c)	Productivity	(g)	Public responsibility
(d)	Product leadership	(h)	Balance between short-range and long-range goals

These are examples of 'critical success factors'.

Key term

> **A critical success factor** is a performance requirement that is fundamental to competitive success.

There are usually **fewer than ten** of these factors that any one executive should monitor. Furthermore, they are very time dependent so they should be **re-examined** as often as necessary to keep abreast of the current business climate.

Critical success factors can be set and used by **identifying objectives and goals, determining which factors are critical for accomplishing each objective** and then determining a small number of performance measures for each factor. For example, if next day delivery were an objective, an employee attitude survey that revealed indifference (or over-defensiveness) towards customer complaints about late deliveries would be an indication of failure.

Exam focus point

A question in the June 2004 examination linked critical success factors with the elements of the balanced score card (see Chapter 15).

4 Performance measures

FAST FORWARD

Performance measure can be divided into two groups.

- **Financial performance** measures
- **Non-financial performance measures**

Financial performance measures include **profit, revenue, costs, share price** and **cash flow.**

Non-financial performance measures include **product quality, reliability** and **customer satisfaction**.

Performance measures can be **quantitative** or **qualitative.**

Non-financial indicators (NFIs) are useful in a modern business environment.

Exam focus point

In the December 2007 exam, up to twelve marks were available for calculating ratios and statistics for a mobile phone company.

In the June 2008 exam, up to sixteen marks were available when students were expected to calculate five measures and make comments on their findings.

In June 2006, there were fourteen marks available for calculating four financial ratios and explaining the meaning of each ratio.

Performance measures were examined in the December 2006 exam when candidates were asked to calculate various measures of occupancy and fixed and variable unit costs.

4.1 Deciding what measures to use

When an organisation is content that it has set appropriate objectives it then becomes possible to consider how progress towards the achievement of these objectives is to be measured. This is what is meant by performance measurement. Just as different objectives are appropriate to each business, so different performance measures may be appropriate for any given objective. The choice of performance measures will vary from organisation to organisation.

Factors to consider	Detail
Measurement needs resources	This means people, equipment and time to collect and analyse information. The **costs and benefits** of providing resources to produce a performance indicator must be carefully weighed up.
Performance must be measured in relation to something	If not, measurement is meaningless. Overall performance should be measured against the **objectives** of the organisation. If the organisation has no clear objectives, the first step in performance measurement is to set them. The second is to identify the factors that are critical to the success of those objectives. These are the **critical success factors** discussed earlier.
Measures must be relevant	This means finding out what the organisation does and how it does it so that measures reflect what actually occurs.

Factors to consider	Detail
Measurement needs responses	Managers will only respond to measures that they find **useful**. The management accountant therefore needs to adopt a modern marketing philosophy to the provision of performance measures: satisfy customer wants, not pile 'em high and sell 'em cheap.

4.2 Monitoring performance measures

Once suitable performance measures have been selected they must be **monitored on a regular basis** to ensure that they are providing useful information. There is little point in an organisation devoting considerable resources to measuring market share if an increase in market share is not one of the organisation's objectives.

4.3 A range of performance measures

Performance measures may be divided into two groups.

(a) Financial performance measures
(b) Non-financial performance measures.

4.4 Financial performance measures

Financial performance is fundamental to businesses.

Measure	Example
Profit	**Profit** is the most common measure of all. Return on investment is also frequently used. 'ICI increased pre-tax profits to $233m'.
Revenue	'the US businesses contributed $113.9m of total group turnover of $409m'.
Costs	'The US dollar's fall benefited pre-tax profits by about $50m while savings from the cost-cutting programme instituted in 1991 were running at around $100m a quarter'.
Share price	'The group's shares rose 31c to 1,278c despite the market's fall'.
Cash flow	'Cash flow was also continuing to improve, with cash and marketable securities totalling $8.4bn on March 31, up from $8bn at December 31'.

Note that the monetary amounts stated are **only given meaning in relation to something else**. Financial results should be compared against a **yard-stick** such as the following.

(a) Budgeted **sales**, **costs** and **profits**
(b) **Standards** in a standard costing system
(c) The **trend** over time (last year/this year, say)
(d) The results of **other parts of the business**
(e) The results of **other businesses**
(f) The **economy** in general
(g) **Future potential** (for example the performance of a new business may be judged in terms of nearness to breaking even).

4.5 Non-financial performance measures

Exam focus point

In the December 2008 exam, students could earn up to eight marks where they were asked to suggest four non-financial measures that could be used to assess performance for a college or university.

The use of non-financial performance measures has increased in recent years.

A key reason why non-financial performance measures are used is that they are considered to be **leading indicators** of financial performance. For example if customer satisfaction is low this could imply a future fall in profits due to decreased sales demand. The non-financial measure of poor customer satisfaction has given an indication that the financial measure of future sales may change.

You can appreciate the benefits of non-financial performance indicators when you contrast them with financial performance measures and the effect both might have on management.

(a) **Non-financial performance measures** can provide managers with incentives to improve long-term financial performance. Focusing on customer satisfaction encourages repeat business which is good for long term profitability.

(b) **Financial performance measures** used alone may provide managers with shorter term incentives which could be detrimental to the business in the long term. For example price increases applied in the short term to meet financial targets could damage customer relations in the long term if quality has not improved.

4.6 Quantitative and qualitative performance measures

Quantitative information is capable of being expressed in numbers. Qualitative information is not numeric. Qualitative information can sometimes be converted into numeric through tools such as ranking scales. For example 1 = Good, 2 = Average, 3 = Poor.

(a) An example of a **quantitative** performance measure is 'You have been late for work **twice** this week and it's only Tuesday!'.

(b) An example of a **qualitative** performance measure is 'My bed is **very** comfortable'.

The first measure is likely to find its way into a **staff appraisal report**. The second would feature in a bed manufacturer's **customer satisfaction survey**. Both are indicators of whether their subjects are doing as good a job as they are required to do.

Qualitative measures are by nature **subjective** and **judgmental** but they can still be useful. They are especially valuable when they are derived from several **different sources**, as the likelihood of an unreliable judgement is reduced.

Consider the statement.

> 'Seven out of ten customers think our beds are very comfortable.'

This is a **quantitative measure** of customer satisfaction (7 out of 10), as well as a **qualitative measure** of the perceived performance of the beds (very comfortable).

4.6.1 Non-financial indicators

FAST FORWARD

Changes in cost structures, the competitive environment and the manufacturing environment have lead to an **increased use of NFIs.**

In recent years there have been significant changes in organisations. Changes in the cost structures, manufacturing and increased competition have meant that organisations need to look at new measures of performance.

These changes have led to a shift from treating financial figures as the foundation of performance measurement to treating them as one of a range of measures.

Changes in cost structures

Modern technology requires massive investment and product life cycles have got shorter. A greater proportion of costs are sunk and a large proportion of costs are planned, engineered or designed into a product/service before production/delivery. **At the time the product/service is produced/delivered, it is therefore too late to control costs.**

Changes in competitive environment

Financial measures do not convey the full picture of a company's performance, especially in a **modern business environment**.

> 'In today's worldwide competitive environment companies are competing in terms of product quality, delivery, reliability, after-sales service and customer satisfaction. None of these variables is directly measured by the traditional responsibility accounting system, despite the fact that they represent the major goals of world-class manufacturing companies.'

Changes in manufacturing environment

New manufacturing techniques and technologies focus on minimising throughput times, inventory levels and set-up times. But managers can reduce the costs for which they are responsible by increasing inventory levels through maximising output. If a performance measurement system **focuses principally on costs**, managers may **concentrate on cost reduction and ignore other important strategic manufacturing goals**.

Organisations are increasingly using quantitative and qualitative **non-financial indicators (NFIs)**. Here are some examples.

(a) Quality rating
(b) Number of customer complaints
(c) Number of warranty claims
(d) Lead times
(e) Rework
(f) Delivery to time
(g) Non-productive hours
(h) System (machine) down time

Unlike traditional variance reports, measures such as these can be **provided quickly** for managers, per shift or on a daily or even hourly basis as required. They are likely to be **easy to calculate**, and **easier** for non-financial managers **to understand** and therefore to use effectively.

Anything can be compared if it is meaningful to do so. The measures should be **tailored to the** circumstances. For example, the number of coffee breaks per 20 pages of text might indicate to you how hard you are studying!

Non-financial indicators typically combine elements from the table below.

Errors/failure	Time	Quantity	People
Defects	Second	Range of products	Employees
Equipment failures	Minute	Parts/components	Employee skills
Warranty claims	Hour	Units produced	Customers
Complaints	Shift	Units sold	Competitors
Returns	Cycle	Services performed	Suppliers
Stockouts	Day	kg/litres/metres	
Lateness/waiting	Month	m^2/m^3	
Misinformation	Year	Documents	
Miscalculation		Deliveries	
Absenteeism		Enquiries	

Traditional measures derived from these lists like 'kg (of material) per unit produced' or 'units produced per hour' are very common. What may at first seem a fairly **unlikely combination** may also be very revealing. For example, 'miscalculations per 1,000 invoices' would show how accurately the invoicing clerk was working.

Question — **Non-financial indicators**

Using the above chart make up five non-financial indicators and explain how each might be useful.

Answer

Here are five suggested indicators, showing you how to use the chart.

(a) Services performed late v total services performed
(b) Total units sold v total units sold by competitors (indicating market share)
(c) Warranty claims per month
(d) Documents processed per employee
(e) Equipment failures per 1,000 units produced

There are, of course, many other possibilities. Don't forget to explain how the ones that you chose might be useful.

Exam focus point

> If you are asked to suggest suitable performance measures in an exam, think about NFIs. Remember that anything can be compared if it is meaningful to do so.

4.6.2 Ratios

Ratios are a useful performance measurement technique.

(a) It is **easier to look at changes over time** by comparing ratios in one time period with the corresponding ratios for periods in the past.
(b) Ratios are often **easier to understand than absolute measures** of physical quantities or money values. For example, it is easier to understand that 'productivity in March was 94%' than 'there was an adverse labour efficiency variance in March of $3,600'.
(c) Ratios **relate one item to another, and so help to put performance into context**. For example the profit/sales ratio sets profit in the context of how much has been earned per $1 of sales, and so shows how wide or narrow profit margins are.
(d) Ratios can be used as **targets,** for example for productivity. Managers will then take decisions which will enable them to achieve their targets.
(e) Ratios provide a way of **summarising** an organisation's results, and **comparing** them with similar organisations.

4.6.3 Percentages

A percentage expresses one number as a proportion of another and **gives meaning to absolute numbers**. Market share, capacity levels, wastage and staff turnover are often expressed using percentages.

4.7 Economy, efficiency and effectiveness

Economy, efficiency and effectiveness are all generally desirable features of organisational performance.

(a) **Economy** lies in operating at minimum cost. However, an over-parsimonious approach will reduce **effectiveness.**
(b) **Effectiveness** is achieving established objectives. There are usually several ways to achieve objectives, some more costly than others.
(c) **Efficiency** consists of attaining desired results at minimum cost. It therefore combines **effectiveness** with **economy**.

You should be aware that some people use the word *efficiency* in a more restricted sense than that explained above, to mean the same thing as **productivity**; that is, the ratio of output to input. This is actually a specifically engineering use, as in *the efficiency of a motor*. The point of using the word in this way is to emphasise that it is possible to be very productive in doing the wrong thing: no amount of *efficiency* (in this sense) will make a company profitable if it brings the wrong products to market. You can recognise this use of *efficiency* because it becomes necessary to combine it with *effectiveness* in order to discuss good practice. Thus, if you come across an exam question that asks you how a company can improve its 'efficiency and effectiveness', *efficiency* is being used in the more restricted way. This usage is very common in the public sector, where people are frequently unsure of what their organisation's purpose is and precisely what it is supposed to be doing.

Exam focus point

In an article on performance measurement, the examiner stated that a good performance measure should:

- provide incentive to make decision which are in the best interest of the overall company (goal congruence)
- only include factors for which the manager/division can be held accountable
- recognise both the long-term and short-term objectives of the organisation

Attention!

When you use the ratios in this section in many cases you will use a profit figure and/or a capital employed figure. Unless you are told otherwise, use earning before interest and tax (EBIT) as profit, and shareholder funds plus long-term liabilities for capital employed. Please note that EBIT is the same as PBIT or profit before interest and tax.

5 Measuring profitability and productivity

FAST FORWARD

Profitability can be measured by **return on investment (ROI)/return on capital employee (ROCE), profit margin, gross profit margin** or **cost/sales ratios.**

5.1 Profitability

Exam focus point

Return on investment and residual income were the subject of a twenty mark question in the December 2006 exam. Candidates were asked to do calculations, explain what residual income is and state two advantages of residual income as a divisional performance measure.

5.1.1 Return on investment (ROI)

Key term

Return on investment (ROI) (also called **return on capital employed (ROCE)**) is calculated as (profit/capital employed) × 100% and shows how much profit has been made in relation to the amount of resources invested.

Profits alone do not show whether the return is sufficient, in view of the value of assets committed. Thus if company A and company B have the following results, company B would have the better performance.

	A	B
	$	$
Profit	5,000	5,000
Sales	100,000	100,000
Capital employed	50,000	25,000
ROI	10%	20%

The profit of each company is the same but company B only invested $25,000 to achieve that profit whereas company A invested $50,000.

ROI may be calculated in a number of ways, but management accountants prefer to exclude from profits all revenues and expenditures not related to the core operation of the business (such as interest payable and income from trade investments). **Profit before interest and tax** is therefore often used.

Similarly **all assets of a non-operational nature** (for example trade investments and intangible assets such as goodwill) **should be excluded** from capital employed.

Profits should be related to average capital employed. In practice many companies calculate the ratio **using year-end assets.** This can be misleading. If a new investment is undertaken near to year end and financed, for example, by an issue of shares, the capital employed will rise by the finance raised but profits will only have a month or two of the new investment's contribution.

What does the ROI tell us? What should we be looking for? There are **two principal comparisons** that can be made.

(a) The change in ROI from one year to the next
(b) The ROI being earned by other entities

5.1.2 Profit margin

Key term

The **profit margin (profit to sales ratio)** is calculated as (profit ÷ revenue) × 100%.

The profit margin provides a simple measure of performance for management. Investigation of unsatisfactory profit margins enables control action to be taken, either by reducing excessive costs or by raising selling prices.

5.2 Example: the profit to sales ratio

A company compares its year 2 results with year 1 results as follows.

	Year 2	Year 1
	$	$
Sales	160,000	120,000
Cost of sales		
Direct materials	40,000	20,000
Direct labour	40,000	30,000
Production overhead	22,000	20,000
Marketing overhead	42,000	35,000
	144,000	105,000
Profit	16,000	15,000
Profit to sales ratio	10%	12½%

Ratio analysis on the above information shows that there is a decline in profitability in spite of the $1,000 increase in profit, because the profit margin is less in year 2 than year 1.

5.2.1 Gross profit margin

The profit to sales ratio above was based on a profit figure which included non-production overheads. The **pure trading activities of a business can be analysed** using the gross profit margin, which is calculated as (gross profit ÷ turnover) × 100%.

For the company in Paragraph 5.2 the gross profit margin would be

((16,000 + 42,000)/160,000) × 100% = 36.25% in year 2 and ((15,000 + 35,000)/120,000) × 100% = 41.67% in year 1.

5.2.2 Cost/sales ratios

There are three principal ratios for analysing income statement information.

(a) Production cost of sales ÷ sales
(b) Distribution and marketing costs ÷ sales
(c) Administrative costs ÷ sales

When particular areas of weakness are found subsidiary ratios are used to examine them in greater depth. For example, for production costs the following ratios might be used.

(a) Material costs ÷ sales value of production
(b) Works labour costs ÷ sales value of production
(c) Production overheads ÷ sales value of production

5.3 Example: cost/sales ratios

Look back to the example above. A more detailed analysis would show that higher direct materials are the probable cause of the decline in profitability.

	Year 2	*Year 1*
Material costs/sales	25%	16.7%

Other cost/sales ratios have remained the same or improved.

5.4 Productivity

This is the quantity of the product or service produced **(output) in relation to** the resources put in (**input**). For example so many units produced per hour, or per employee, or per tonne of material. It measures **how efficiently resources are being used**.

Question — Performance measures

An invoicing assistant works in a department with three colleagues. She is paid $8,000 per annum. The department typically handles 10,000 invoices per week.

One morning she spends half an hour on the phone to her grandfather, who lives in Australia, at the company's expense. The cost of the call proves to be $32.

Required

From this scenario identify as many different performance measures as possible, explaining what each is intended to measure. Make any further assumptions you wish.

Answer

Invoices per employee per week: 2,500 (activity)

Staff cost per invoice: $0.06 (cost/profitability)

Invoices per hour: 2,500/(7 × 5) = 71.4 (productivity)

Cost of idle time: $32 + $2.20 (half-hourly rate) = $34.20 (cost/profitability)

You may have thought of other measures and probably have slight rounding differences.

Attention!

Where a ratio includes capital employed, you should use shareholders funds plus long-term liabilities unless you are told otherwise.

6 Performance measures based on the statement of financial position (balance sheet)

FAST FORWARD

Asset turnover is a measure of how well the assets of a business are being used to generate sales. It is calculated as (sales ÷ capital employed).

The **current ratio** is the 'standard' test of liquidity and is the ratio of current assets to current liabilities. The **quick ratio**, or **acid test ratio**, is the ratio of current assets less inventories to current liabilities.

6.1 Asset turnover

Key term

> **Asset turnover** is a measure of how well the assets of a business are being used to generate sales. It is calculated as (sales ÷ capital employed).

For example, suppose two companies each have capital employed of $100,000 and Company A makes sales of $400,000 per annum whereas Company B makes sales of only $200,000 per annum. Company A is making a higher turnover from the same amount of assets, in other words twice as much asset turnover as Company B, and this will help A to make a higher return on capital employed than B. Asset turnover is **expressed as 'x times' so that assets generate x times their value in annual turnover**. Here, Company A's asset turnover is 4 times and B's is 2 times.

6.1.1 Interrelationship between profit margin, asset turnover and ROI

Profit margin and asset turnover together explain the ROI. The relationship between the three ratios is as follows.

Profit margin × asset turnover = ROI

$$\frac{\text{Profit}}{\text{Sales}} \times \frac{\text{Sales}}{\text{Capital employed}} = \frac{\text{Profit}}{\text{Capital employed}}$$

6.2 Liquidity ratios: current ratio and quick ratio

Key term

> The **current ratio** is the 'standard' test of liquidity and is the ratio of current assets to current liabilities.

The idea behind the current ratio is that a company should have enough current assets that give a promise of 'cash to come' to meet its future commitments to pay off its current liabilities. Obviously, a ratio in excess of 1 should be expected. Otherwise, there would be the prospect that the company might be unable to pay its debts on time. In practice, a ratio comfortably in excess of 1 should be expected, but what is 'comfortable' varies between different types of businesses.

Companies are not able to convert all their current assets into cash very quickly. In particular, some manufacturing companies might hold large quantities of raw material inventories, which must be used in production to create finished goods inventories. Finished goods inventories might be warehoused for a long time, or sold on lengthy credit. In such businesses, **where inventory turnover is slow, most inventories are not very 'liquid' assets**, because the cash cycle is so long. For these reasons, we **calculate an additional liquidity ratio**, known as the quick ratio or acid test ratio.

Key term

> The **quick ratio**, or **acid test ratio**, is the ratio of current assets less inventories to current liabilities.

This ratio should ideally be at least 1 for companies with a slow inventory turnover. For companies with a fast inventory turnover, a quick ratio can be comfortably less than 1 without suggesting that the company is in cash flow trouble.

Both the current ratio and the quick ratio offer an indication of the company's liquidity position, but the absolute figures should not be interpreted too literally. It is often said that an acceptable current ratio is 1.5 and an acceptable quick ratio is 0.8, but these should only be used as a guide. Different businesses operate in very different ways. A supermarket, for example, might have a current ratio of 0.40 and a quick ratio of 0.16. due to low receivables (people do not buy groceries on credit), low cash (good cash management), medium inventories (high inventories but quick turnover, particularly in view of perishability) and very high payables (many supermarkets buy their supplies of groceries on credit).

What is important is the trend of these ratios, which will show whether liquidity is improving or deteriorating. If a supermarket has traded for the last 10 years (very successfully) with current ratios of 0.40 and quick ratios of 0.16 then it ought to be able to continue in business with those levels of liquidity. If in the following year the current ratio were to fall to 0.38 and the quick ratio to 0.09, further investigation would be needed. It is the relative position that is far more important than the absolute figures.

A current ratio and a quick ratio can get bigger than they need to be however. A company that has large volumes of inventories and receivables might be over-investing in working capital, and so tying up more funds in the business than it needs to. This would suggest poor management of (receivables) or inventories by the company.

Question

Liquidity ratio

The following details have been extracted from the accounts of PQR plc. The company's year ends on 31 March.

	Year 2	*Year 3*	*Year 4*
	$m	$m	$m
Revenue	100	103	108
Gross profit	33.0	34.0	35.6
Net profit	15	15	15
Non-current assets	64	72	68
Inventory	4	4	4
Receivables	8	11	15
Payables	5	6	6
Cash at bank	5	-	-
Bank overdraft	-	6	5

Required

(a) Calculate the following for each of the three years.

(i) Gross profit percentage
(ii) Net profit percentage
(iii) Quick ratio (acid test)

(b) Comment briefly on the ratios you have calculated

Answer

(a)

	Year 2	*Year 3*	*Year 4*
(i) Gross profit %	(33/100) × 100% = 33%	(34/103) × 100% = 33%	(35.6/108) × 100% = 33%
(ii) Net profit %	(15/100) × 100% = 15%	(15/103) × 100% = 14.56%	(15/108) × 100% = 13.9%
(iii) Quick ratio	(8 + 5)/5 = 2.6	11/(6 + 6) = 0.9	15/(6 + 5) = 1.4

(b) Revenue has risen only slightly over the three years with the gross profit margin remaining high at 33%. This suggests that selling prices and costs have been increased only in line with inflation.

Net profit margin has fallen. While the fall is not great it indicates that expenditure on overheads has increased. The fall should be investigated and an attempt made to ensure that the trend does not continue.

The quick ratio fell sharply in Year 3, although it has since recovered. The more worrying aspect of the changes to working capital is that there is less cash (a bank overdraft) and more receivables. It is worth enquiring whether this is due to poor credit control or extending credit in an effort to boost or maintain sales.

It appears from the above that the company is showing a healthy profit, but needs to pay attention to working capital. It should be emphasised, however, that it is difficult to draw conclusions without knowing the sector in which PQR operates or any details about the performance of its competitors.

6.3 Efficiency ratios: control of receivables, payables and inventory

FAST FORWARD

A rough measure of the average length of time it takes for a company's receivables to pay what they owe is the **accounts receivable collection period**. The **accounts payable payment period** is a rough measure of the average length of time it takes a company to pay what it owes.

The **inventory turnover period** indicates the average number of days that items of **inventory** are held for.

Inventory turnover is a measure of how vigorously a business is trading.

The **working capital period** (or **average age of working capital**) identifies how long it takes to convert the purchase of inventories into cash from sales.

6.3.1 Accounts receivable collection period

Key term

The estimated average **accounts receivable collection period** is a rough measure of the average length of time it takes for a company's receivables to pay what they owe and is calculated as (trade receivables/sales) × 365 days or (trade receivables/ sales) × 12 months.

The **estimate of receivables days is only approximate** because the balance sheet value of receivables might be abnormally high or low compared with the organisation's 'normal' level.

A supermarket should have a very low accounts receivable collection period since sales should not be on credit. Sales of most organisations, however, are usually made on 'normal credit terms' of payment within 30 days. A period significantly in excess of this might be representative of poor management of funds of a business. However, some companies must allow generous credit terms to win customers. Exporting companies in particular may have to carry large amounts of receivables, and so their average collection period might be well in excess of 30 days.

The **trend of the collection period over time is probably the best guide**. If the period is increasing year on year, this is indicative of a poorly managed credit control function (and potentially therefore a poorly managed company).

6.3.2 Inventory turnover period

Key term

Inventory turnover period is a calculation of the number of days inventory is held for and is calculated as (inventory ÷ cost of sales) × 365 days or (inventory ÷ cost of sales) × 12 months.

As with the average debt collection period, this is only an approximate estimated figure, but one which should be reliable enough for comparing changes year on year.

Presumably if we add together the inventory days and the receivable days, this should give us an indication of how soon inventory is convertible into cash. Both ratios therefore give us a further indication of the company's liquidity.

6.3.3 Inventory turnover

Key term

'Cost of sales ÷ inventory' is termed **inventory turnover**, and is a measure of how vigorously a business is trading.

A **lengthening inventory turnover period** from one year to the next indicates either a **slowdown in trading** or **a build-up in inventory levels**, perhaps suggesting that the investment in inventories is becoming excessive.

When you are interpreting inventory turnover data you should consider the type of organisation and the systems it operates.

(a) Obviously there should be a marked difference between the inventory turnover of a retail organisation such as a supermarket, and a manufacturing group.

(b) In an organisation which operates a just in time system you would expect to see very high inventory turnover, but you may also notice other effects such as low storage costs and higher prices paid for supplies.

6.3.4 Accounts payable payment period

Key term

Accounts payable payment period or **days** provides a rough measure of the average length of time it takes a company to pay what it owes. It is ideally calculated by the formula (payables/purchases) × 365 days or (payables/purchases) × 12 months. Cost of sales can be used as an approximation for purchases.

This ratio **often helps to assess a company's liquidity**. An increase is often a sign of lack of long-term finance or poor management of current assets, resulting in the use of extended credit from suppliers, increased bank overdraft and so on.

6.3.5 Working capital period

Working capital control is concerned with minimising funds tied up in net current assets while ensuring that sufficient inventory, cash and credit facilities are in place to enable trading to take place. Calculation of the ratio provides some insight into working capital control.

Key term

The **working capital period** (or **average age of working capital**) identifies how long it takes to convert the purchase of inventories into cash from sales and is calculated as (working capital/cost of sales) × 365 days. The ratio can also be calculated as (working capital/ operating costs) × 365 days.

Care needs to be taken when determining the ideal ratio. Reduce it too low and there may be insufficient inventory and other current assets to sustain the volume of trade, but taking too much credit from suppliers may jeopardise relationships and/or cause suppliers to increase prices.

A ratio in excess of a target indicates that working capital levels are probably too high and that management action is needed to reduce them. This may involve stringent control of debtors, a reduction in inventory levels and/or a more efficient use of available credit facilities. A debtors days ratio, inventory turnover period and creditors turnover period can be calculated to determine where the problem lies. The ratio has two principal limitations.

(a) It is based on the working capital level on one particular day, which may not be representative of working capital levels throughout the entire period.

(b) Working capital includes a figure for inventory which may be a very subjective valuation.

Question — Liquidity and working capital

Calculate liquidity and working capital ratios from the accounts of the DOG Group, a manufacturer of products for the construction industry. Discuss your results.

	Year 8	*Year 7*
	$m	$m
Revenue	2,065.0	1,788.7
Cost of sales	1,478.6	1,304.0
Gross profit	586.4	484.7
EXTRACT FROM THE STATEMENT OF FINANCIAL POSITION (BALANCE SHEET)		
Current assets		
Inventories	119.0	109.0
Receivables (note 1)	400.9	347.4
Short-term investments	4.2	18.8
Cash at bank and in hand	48.2	48.0
	572.3	523.2

Creditors: amounts falling due within one year		
Loans and overdrafts	49.1	35.3
Corporation taxes	62.0	46.7
Dividend	19.2	14.3
Payables (note 2)	370.7	324.0
	501.0	420.3

Notes	$m	$m
1 Trade receivables	329.8	285.4
2 Trade payables	236.2	210.8

Answer

	Year 8	*Year 7*
Current ratio	(572.3/501.0) = 1.14	(523.2/420.3) = 1.24
Quick ratio	(453.3/501.0) = 0.90	(414.2/420.3) = 0.99
Accounts receivable payment period	(329.8/2,065.0) × 365 = 58 days	(285.4/1,788.7) × 365 = 58 days
Inventory turnover period	(119.0/1,478.6) × 365 = 29 days	(109.0/1,304.0) × 365 = 31 days
Accounts payable payment period	(236.2/1,478.6) × 365 = 58 days	(210.8/1,304.0) × 365 = 59 days

DOG is a manufacturing group serving the construction industry, and so would be expected to have a comparatively lengthy accounts receivables' turnover period, because of the relatively poor cash flow in the construction industry. It is clear that management compensates for this by ensuring that they do not pay for raw materials and so on before they have sold their inventories of finished goods (hence the similarity of receivables and payables turnover periods).

DOG's current ratio is a little lower than average but its quick ratio is better than average and very little less than the current ratio. This suggests that inventory levels are strictly controlled, which is reinforced by the low inventory turnover period. It would seem that working capital is tightly managed, to avoid the poor liquidity which could be caused by a high accounts receivables payment period and comparatively high payables period.

6.4 Debt and gearing/leverage ratios

Debt ratios are concerned with how much the company **owes in relation to its size** and whether it is getting into heavier debt or improving its situation.

(a) When a company is heavily in debt, and seems to be getting even more heavily into debt, banks and other would-be lenders are very soon likely to refuse further borrowing and the company might well find itself in trouble.

(b) When a company is earning only a **modest profit** before interest and tax, and has a **heavy debt burden**, there will be very little profit left over for shareholders after the interest charges have been paid.

Leverage is an alternative term for gearing and the words have the same meaning.

6.4.1 Capital gearing or leverage

Capital gearing is concerned with the amount of debt in a company's **long-term** capital structure. **Gearing ratios** provide a long-term measure of liquidity.

Key term

$$\text{Gearing ratio} = \frac{\text{Prior charge capital (long-term debt)}}{\text{Prior charge capital + shareholders equity}}$$

Prior charge capital is long-term loans and preference shares (if any). It does not include loans repayable within one year and bank overdraft, unless overdraft finance is a permanent part of the business's capital.

6.4.2 Interest cover

The **interest cover** ratio shows whether a company is earning enough profits before interest and tax to pay its interest costs comfortably, or whether its interest costs are high in relation to the size of its profits, so that a fall in profit before interest and tax (PBIT) would then have a significant effect on profits available for ordinary shareholders.

Key term

$$\text{Interest cover} = \frac{\text{PBIT}}{\text{Interest charges}}$$

An interest cover of 2 times or less would be low, and it should really exceed 3 times before the company's interest costs can be considered to be within acceptable limits. Note it is usual to exclude preference dividends from 'interest' charges.

6.5 Limitations of income statement and statement of financial position (balance sheet) measures

(a) **On their own, they do not provide information to enable managers to gauge performance or make control decisions.** Yardsticks are needed for comparison purposes.

(b) The measures used **must be carefully defined**. For example, should 'return' equal profit before interest and taxation, profit after taxation, or profit before interest, taxation and investment income?

(c) Measures compared over a period of time at historical cost will not be properly comparable where **inflation** in prices has occurred during the period, unless an adjustment is made to the measures to make allowance for price level differences.

(d) The measures of **different companies** cannot be properly compared where each company uses a **different method to do the following**.
   (i) Value closing inventories (for example FIFO, LIFO, or marginal/absorbed cost)
   (ii) Apportion overheads in absorption costing
   (iii) Value non-current assets (for example at net book value, replacement cost and so on)
   (iv) Estimate the life of assets in order to calculate depreciation
   (v) Account for research and development costs
   (vi) Account for goodwill

(e) Remember that measures calculated using **historical costs** may not be a guide to the future.

Question — **Ratio calculations**

You are given summarised results of an electrical engineering business as follows.

INCOME STATEMENT FOR YEAR ENDED 31 DECEMBER YEAR 1

	$'000
Revenue	60,000
Cost of sales	42,000
Gross profit	18,000
Operating expenses	15,500
Profit	2,500

STATEMENT OF FINANCIAL POSITION (BALANCE SHEET) AT 31 DECEMBER YEAR 1

	$'000	$'000
Non-current assets		12,500
Current assets		
Inventory	14,000	
Receivables	16,000	
Cash	500	
		43,000

EQUITY AND LIABILITIES	
Capital and reserves	19,000
Current liabilities (payables only)	24,000
	43,000

Required

Calculate the following ratios, clearly showing the figures used in the calculations.

(a) Current ratio
(b) Quick/acid test ratio
(c) Inventory turnover in days
(d) Accounts receivable collection period in days
(e) Accounts payable payment period in days
(f) Gross profit percentage
(g) Net profit percentage
(h) ROCE
(i) Asset turnover

Answer

(a) Current ratio = (Current assets/current liabilities) = (30,500/24,000) = 1.27

(b) Acid test ratio = (Current assets – inventory/current liabilities) = (16,500/24,000) = 0.6875

(c) Inventory turnover = (Inventory/cost of sales) × 365 days = (14,000/42,000) × 365 = 122 days

(d) Accounts receivable collection period = (Receivables/sales) × 365 days = (16,000/60,000) × 365 = 97 days

(e) Accounts payable = (Payables/cost of sales) × 365 days = (24,000/42,000) × 365 = 209 days

(f) Gross profit % = (Gross profit/sales) × 100% = (18,000/60,000) × 100% = 30%

(g) Net profit % = (Net profit/sales) × 100% = (2,500/60,000)× 100% = 4.2%

(h) ROCE = (Profit/capital employed) × 100% = (2,500/19,000) × 100% = 13.16%

(i) Asset turnover = (Sales/capital employed) = (60,000/19,000) = 3.2 times

Question — Limitations of ratios

Comment on any limitations of the ratios used in the last question and of comparisons made using such ratios.

Answer

Limitations of the ratios and inter-company comparisons

There are a number of limitations of which management should be aware before drawing any firm conclusions from a comparison of these ratios.

(a) The ratios are merely averages, based on year-end balance sheet data, which may not be representative.

(b) These ratios could be affected by any new investment towards the end of the financial year. Such investment would increase the value of the assets or capital employed, but the profits from the investment would not yet have accumulated in the income statement. Generally, newer assets tend to depress the asset turnover and hence the ROCE in the short term. It is possible that this is the cause of our company's lower asset turnover and ROCE.

(c) Although the trade association probably makes some attempt to standardise the data, different member companies may be using different accounting policies, for example in calculating depreciation and valuing inventory.

(d) Our company's analyst may have used a different formula for calculating one or more of the ratios. For example, as noted above, there are a variety of ways of calculating capital employed. It is likely, however, that the trade association would provide information on the basis of calculation of the ratios.

(e) The member companies will have some activities in common, hence their membership of the trade association. Some may, however, have a diversified range of activities, which will distort the ratios and make direct comparison difficult.

6.6 Internal and external analysis

External analysis of companies' performance using **financial accounts** is relatively straightforward since the **range of possible measures** tends to be **limited** by the scarcity of the information available. We have covered most of these measures in this section and the previous one.

The **analysis of a company's internal management accounts** uses more or less the same measures as a starting point. The level of analysis and detail found in internal accounts tends to be much greater than in published financial accounts, however, and so more extensive analysis is possible.

In the October 2000 edition of the *ACCA Technician Bulletin,* the author of the article 'Internal Financial Analysis' illustrated how the performance of two sales regions could be analysed using **conventional ratios** and other **performance measures specific to the situation**.

(a) Initially, using observations based upon absolute figures (sales, level of debtors, bad debts written off)

(b) Then using the conventional debtor days ratio

(c) Finally, using other relationships that might give further insights (bad debts per $1,000 of sales, cost per employee, debts collected per employee)

In the exam, if you are required to carry out internal analysis, you will therefore need to suggest measures that are **appropriate** to the **specific scenario**. We look at such measures in the next chapter.

7 External considerations

FAST FORWARD

External conditions can affect performance.

So far we have looked in detail at some important aspects of performance measurement, but they have all been concerned with information pertaining to the internal processes of the organisation. This approach is necessary, but the analysis is not complete. The organisation is not sealed off from its environment: it is subject to the conditions present in that environment and its performance is influenced by them. We must always be aware when measuring performance of the influence of external conditions and changes in them.

For a commercial business, success is subject to general economic and market conditions.

(a) **Market conditions**. A business operates in a competitive environment and suppliers, customers and competitors all influence one another's operations. The entry of a new and dynamic competitor, for example is certain to have an effect on budgeted sales.

(b) **General economic conditions** influence businesses most obviously by raising or lowering overall demand and supply. The role of government is very important here since government economic policy affects demand in particular quite rapidly. Changes in interest rates are determined largely by government policy and have a direct effect on credit sales.

For non-profit organisations that do not trade, economic conditions and government policy are still important. Charities depending on donations will be subject to general feelings of prosperity or otherwise, while public bodies may have their available funds controlled directly or indirectly by government.

The general conclusion from these and similar considerations is that appropriate attention should be paid to general and specific external conditions when measuring performance. We have already seen some aspects of this when we considered the proper use of variances. Sales variances in particular are often traceable to external conditions. However, it is important that external conditions are not over-emphasised and used as an excuse. Judgement is needed here, both on the part of those responsible for interpreting the bald facts of numerical analysis, and on that of those to whom reports are submitted.

Finally, note that the effect of external conditions is not always adverse! Managers may be as quick to claim the credit for high performance caused by good conditions as they are to blame poor conditions for their own failings.

Chapter Roundup

- The higher direction of an organisation requires a clear vision, in general terms, of what the organisation should be doing in the longer term and how it should go about doing it. This may be encapsulated in a **mission statement**.
- A hierarchy of SMART goals and objectives cascades downwards from the mission statement, eventually providing the targets for the periodic budget process.
- Performance measure can be divided into two groups.
  - **Financial performance measures**
  - **Non-financial performance measures**
- Financial performance measures include **profit**, **revenue**, **costs**, **share price** and **cash flow**.
- Non-financial performance measures include **product quality**, **reliability** and **customer satisfaction**.
- Performance measures can be **quantitative** or **qualitative.**
- **Non-financial indicators (NFIs)** are useful in a modern business environment.
- Changes in cost structures, the competitive environment and the manufacturing environment have led to an **increased use of NFIs**.
- **Profitability** can be measured by **return on investment (ROI)/return on capital employed (ROCE), profit margin, gross profit margin** or **cost/sales ratios.**
- **Asset turnover** is a measure of how well the assets of a business are being used to generate sales. It is calculated as (sales ÷ capital employed).
- The **current ratio** is the 'standard' test of liquidity and is the ratio of current assets to current liabilities. The **quick ratio**, or **acid test ratio**, is the ratio of current assets less inventories to current liabilities.
- A rough measure of the average length of time it takes for a company's receivables to pay what they owe is the **accounts receivables collection period**. The **accounts payable payment period** is a rough measure of the average length of time it takes a company to pay what it owes.
- The **inventory turnover period** indicates the average number of days that items of **inventory** are held for.
- **Inventory turnover** is a measure of how vigorously a business is trading.
- The **working capital period** (or **average age of working capital**) identifies how long it takes to convert the purchase of inventories into cash from sales.
- **External conditions** can affect performance.

Quick Quiz

1 List five possible financial performance measures.

2 Costs are down by 15% is an example of a qualitative performance measure. True or false?

3 How is ROI calculated?

4 When should a current ratio in excess of 1 be expected?

5 Should the quick ratio for a company with fast inventory turnover be greater than 1?

6 ROCE is $\frac{\text{Profit before interest and tax}}{\text{Capital employed}} \times 100\%$

True ☐

False ☐

7 The debt ratio is a company's long-term debt divided by its net assets.

True ☐

False ☐

Answers to Quick Quiz

1 Profit, revenue, costs, share price and cash flow. Of course there are others.

2 False. It is quantitative.

3 (Profit ÷ capital employed) × 100%

4 A current ratio in excess of 1 should always be expected.

5 No, it may be less than 1.

6 **True**. Profit before interest and tax or PBIT is the figure used in the Question *Ratio calculations* in the chapter.

7 **False**. Refer to Section 6 if you are unclear what the ratio is made up of.

Now try the questions below from the Exam Question Bank

Number	Level	Marks	Time
Section A: Q19-Q21	MCQ	N/A	N/A
Section B: Q15	Examination	20	36 mins
Section B: Q16	Examination	40	72 mins

15

Applications of performance measures

Topic list
1 Performance measures for manufacturing businesses
2 Performance measures for manufacturing environments
3 Performance measures for services
4 Performance measures for non-profit-making organisations
5 Management performance measures
6 Responsibility centre performance measures
7 Non-financial objectives
8 The balanced scorecard

Study guide reference

		Syllabus reference
17(b)	Discuss performance measures appropriate to each type of responsibility centre (budget variances, contribution measures, controllable profit, traceable profit, return on investment and residual income)	8
(c)	Calculate controllable profit, traceable profit, return on investment and residual income in a specific situation	8
(d)	Distinguish between managerial performance and business unit performance	8
25(d)	Discuss the measurement of performance in service industry situations	8
(e)	Discuss the measurement of performance in non-profit seeking and public sector organisations	8
(f)	Discuss measures that may be used to assess managerial performance and the practical problems involved	8
26(a)	Perspectives of the balanced scorecard	8
	(i) Discuss the advantages and limitations of the balanced scorecard	
	(ii) Describe performance indicators for financial success, customer satisfaction, process efficiency and growth	
(b)	Economy, efficiency and effectiveness	8
	(iv) Discuss the meaning of each of the efficiency, capacity and activity ratios	
	(v) Calculate the efficiency, capacity and activity ratios in a specific situation	
(c)	Unit costs	8
	(i) Describe performance measures which would be suitable in job, batch, contract and process costing environments	
(d)	Resource utilisation	8
	(i) Describe measures of performance utilisation in service and manufacturing environments	
	(ii) Establish measures of resource utilisation in a specific situation	
(e)	Profitability	8
	(i) Calculate return on investment and residual income	
	(ii) Explain the advantages and limitations of return on investment and residual income	
(f)	Quality of service	8
	(i) Distinguish performance measurement issues in service and manufacturing industries	
	(ii) Describe performance measures appropriate for service industries	
(g)	(i) Establish performance measures for a service business in a specific situation	8

Exam focus point

This chapter covers a key syllabus area. Key syllabus areas usually account for 80% or more of the marks available on the exam paper.

1 Performance measures for manufacturing businesses

FAST FORWARD

In a customer-focused organisation, basic **measures for sales** can be supplemented by a host of others including customer rejects/returns: total sales.

Performance measures for **materials** and **labour** include **variances.**

Performance can be measured using the **standard hour.**

Efficiency, **activity** and **capacity ratios** provide useful information.

1.1 Performance measures for sales

Traditionally sales performance is measured in terms of price and volume variances, and a sales mix variance. Other possible measures include revenue targets and target market share. They may be analysed in detail: by country, by region, by individual products, by salesperson and so on.

In a customer-focused organisation the basic information 'Turnover is up by 14%' can be supplemented by a host of other indicators.

(a) **Customer rejects/returns: total sales**. This ratio helps to monitor customer satisfaction, providing a check on the efficiency of quality control procedures.

(b) **Deliveries late: deliveries on schedule**. This ratio can be applied both to sales made to customers and to receipts from suppliers. When applied to customers it provides an indication of the efficiency of production and production scheduling.

(c) **Flexibility measures** indicate how well able a company is to respond to customers' requirements. Measures could be devised to measure how quickly and efficiently **new products** are launched, and how well procedures meet **customer needs**.

(d) **Number of people served and speed of service**, in a shop or a bank for example. If it takes too long to reach the point of sale, future sales are liable to be lost.

(e) **Customer satisfaction questionnaires,** for input to the organisation's management information system.

1.2 Performance measures for materials

Traditional measures are **standard costs,** and price and usage **variances**. Many traditional systems also analyse **wastage**.

Measures used in **modern manufacturing environments** include the number of **rejects** in materials supplied, and the **timing and reliability of deliveries** of materials.

1.3 Performance measures for labour

Labour costs are traditionally measured in terms of **standard performance** (ideal, attainable and so on) and rate and efficiency **variances**.

Qualitative measures of labour performance concentrate on matters such as **ability to communicate, interpersonal relationships** with colleagues, **customers' impressions** and **levels of skills** attained.

Managers can expect to be judged to some extent by the performance of their staff. High profitability or tight cost control are not the only indicators of managerial performance!

1.4 Performance measures for overheads

Standards for variable overheads and efficiency variances are traditional measures. Various time based measure are also available.

(a) **Machine down time: total machine hours**. This ratio provides a measure of machine usage and efficiency.

(b) **Value added time: production cycle time**. Value added time is the direct production time during which the product is being made. The production cycle time includes non-value-added times such as set-up time, downtime, idle time and so on. The 'perfect' ratio is 100%, but in practice this optimum will not be achieved. A high ratio means non-value-added activities are being kept to a minimum.

1.5 Measures of performance using the standard hour

Sam manufactures plates, mugs and eggcups. Production during the first two quarters of 20X5 was as follows.

	Quarter 1	*Quarter 2*
Plates	1,000	800
Mugs	1,200	1,500
Eggcups	800	900

The fact that 3,000 products were produced in quarter 1 and 3,200 in quarter 2 does not tell us anything about Sam's performance over the two periods because plates, mugs and eggcups are so different. The fact that the production mix has changed is not revealed by considering the total number of units produced. The problem of how to **measure output when a number of dissimilar products are manufactured** can be overcome, however, by the **use of the standard hour**.

The standard hour (or standard minute) is the **quantity of work achievable at standard performance, expressed in terms of a standard unit of work done in a standard period of time.**

The standard time allowed to produce one unit of each of Sam's products is as follows.

	Standard time
Plate	$\frac{1}{2}$ hour
Mug	$\frac{1}{3}$ hour
Eggcup	$\frac{1}{4}$ hour

By measuring the standard hours of output in each quarter, a more useful output measure is obtained.

		Quarter 1		*Quarter 2*	
Product	*Standard hours per unit*	*Production*	*Standard hours*	*Production*	*Standard hours*
Plate	$\frac{1}{2}$	1,000	500	800	400
Mug	$\frac{1}{3}$	1,200	400	1,500	500
Eggcup	$\frac{1}{4}$	800	200	900	225
			1,100		1,125

The output level in the two quarters was therefore very similar.

1.6 Efficiency, activity and capacity ratios

Standard hours are useful in computing levels of **efficiency, activity and capacity**. Any management accounting reports involving budgets and variance analysis should incorporate control ratios. The three main control ratios are the efficiency, capacity and activity ratios.

(a) The **capacity ratio compares actual hours worked and budgeted hours**, and measures the **extent to which planned utilisation has been achieved.**

(b) The **activity** or **production volume ratio compares the number of standard hours equivalent to the actual work produced and budgeted hours.**

(c) **The efficiency ratio** measures the **efficiency of the labour force** by **comparing equivalent standard hours for work produced and actual hours worked.**

1.7 Example: ratios and standard hours

Given the following information about Sam for quarter 1 of 20X5, calculate a capacity ratio, an activity ratio and an efficiency ratio and explain their meaning.

Budgeted hours	1,100 standard hours
Standard hours produced	1,125 standard hours
Actual hours worked	1,200

1.8 Solution

$$\text{Capacity ratio} = \frac{\text{Actual hours worked}}{\text{Budgeted hours}} \times 100\% = \frac{1,200}{1,100} \times 100\% = 109\%$$

$$\text{Activity ratio} = \frac{\text{Standard hours produced}}{\text{Budgeted hours}} \times 100\% = \frac{1,125}{1,100} \times 100\% = 102\%$$

The overall activity or production volume for the quarter was 2% greater than forecast. This was achieved by a 9% increase in capacity.

$$\text{Efficiency ratio} = \frac{\text{Standard hours produced}}{\text{Actual hours worked}} \times 100\% = \frac{1,125}{1,200} \times 100\% = 94\%$$

The labour force worked 6% below standard levels of efficiency.

2 Performance measures for manufacturing environments

In a **jobbing** environment each job undertaken is unique. Products are made to the specific requirements of individual customers. This has a number of implications for performance measurement.

(a) Detailed planning should be undertaken and performance targets set. As so many variables are involved this is a complicated process, and the likelihood of targets not being achieved is significant.

(b) **Suppliers may be different for each job**, making it **harder to set standards** for quality, speed of delivery and so on.

(c) **Customer satisfaction** measures are particularly **important** in this environment (payment might depend contractually upon customer satisfaction). Feedback on performance should be obtained from the customer during the job.

(d) Because each job will be different the organisation will have to be extremely **flexible**. Measures of success in adapting to new requirements will provide a key indicator. Measures of **employee skills** will be equally important.

(e) It is likely that the job will need to be completed within a certain **time** and therefore an ongoing check must be kept of performance in relation to the **deadline**.

A **contract** or **project** is simply a large job that takes a considerable length of time. The same considerations apply regarding performance measurement as in a jobbing environment. The following are also relevant.

(a) The size and consequences of **overspending** may be huge.

(b) The longer timescale means that progress must be measured even more carefully, since there is more likelihood of slippage if **deadlines** seem a long way off.

In a **batch** production environment, products are more **standardised**, although some costs and activities may be unique to a specific batch. Standardisation of products means that materials requirements and labour and machinery capabilities are also more standardised. **Performance standards** can be set for materials quality and usage, labour efficiency, suppliers and so on.

The high degree of standardisation in a **process costing** environment means that it is **ideal for setting performance standards**. However, costs, materials usage/wastage, labour inefficiencies, machine breakdowns and so on cannot be traced to a specific item. These features can only be measured on an average per unit basis. A measure like 'cost per unit' in a processing environment reflects **average**

performance over a period of time. It may therefore be more difficult to improve upon existing performance standards as **inefficiencies may not be easily identifiable.**

3 Performance measures for services

FAST FORWARD

Performance measures covering the following **six 'dimensions'** have been suggested for service organisations.

- Competitive performance
- Financial performance
- Quality of service
- Flexibility
- Resource utilisation
- Innovation

3.1 Service businesses

A service business does not produce a physical product. Instead it provides a service, for example a haircut, or insurance.

(a) A service is **intangible**. The actual benefit being bought can not be touched.

(b) The production and consumption of a service are **simultaneous**, and therefore it cannot be inspected for quality in advance.

(c) Services are **perishable**, that is, they cannot be stored. For example a hairdresser cannot do haircuts in advance and keep them stocked away in case of heavy demand.

(d) A service is **heterogeneous**. The service received will vary each time. Services are more reliant on people. People are not robots, so how the service is delivered will not be identical each time.

Question — Service measures

Consider how the factors intangibility, simultaneity, perishability and heterogeneity apply to the various services that you use: public transport, your bank account, meals in restaurants, the postal service, your annual holiday and so on.

3.2 'Dimensions' of performance measurement

Performance measurement in service businesses is made more difficult because of the four factors listed above. However, performance measurement is possible, the key being to ensure what you are measuring has been clearly enough defined. A range of performance measures covering **six 'dimensions'** are used.

3.2.1 Competitive performance

Competitive performance focuses on factors such as sales growth, market share and ability to obtain new business.

3.2.2 Financial performance

Like any other business, a service business needs to plan, and its short-term plans can be drawn up in the form of a **budget**.

(a) There might be a **budgeted expenditure limit** for individual activities within the business.

(b) **Standard performance measures** (such as standard cost per unit of activity or standard quantity of 'output' per unit of resource used up (ie productivity)) can be established as targets.

Question — Productivity measure

A secretary working in a bank is paid $12,000 per annum and produces 4,500 letters a year. Devise a cost per unit of activity and a standard measure of productivity.

Answer

$\frac{\$12,000}{4,500}$ = $2.66 per letter

$\frac{4,500}{(365-52-52)}$ = 17.24 letters per working day, ignoring holidays.

Other answers are possible.

3.2.3 Quality of service

Service quality is measured principally by **qualitative measures**, although some quantitative measures are used by some businesses. An equipment hire company used a 'successful hire indicator'. This was expressed as a percentage. All hires has to be classified as successful or unsuccessful (based on equipment performance) when equipment was returned.

The following table shows the measures used to assess 4 quality factors and the means of obtaining the information by British Airports Authority (BAA), a transport facility service provider.

Service quality factors	Measures	Mechanisms
Access	Walking distances Ease of finding way around	Customer survey and internal operational data
Cleanliness/tidiness	Cleanliness of environment and equipment	Customer survey and management inspection
Comfort	Crowdedness of airport	Customer survey and management inspection
Friendliness	Staff attitude and helpfulness	Customer survey and management inspection

Question — Measuring service quality

What do you conclude are the two main means of measuring service quality at BAA?

Answer

Customer surveys and management inspection

3.2.4 Flexibility

Flexibility has three aspects.

Aspect	Detail
Speed of delivery	This is vital in some service industries. Measures include factors such as waiting time in queues. In other types of service it may be more a question of timeliness. Does the auditor turn up to do the annual audit during the appointed week? Is the audit done within the time anticipated by the partner or does it drag on for weeks? These aspects are all easily measurable in terms of 'days late'. Depending upon the circumstances 'days late' may also reflect on inability to cope with fluctuations in demand.
Ability to respond to customers' specifications	This will depend on the type of service. A professional service such as legal advice must be tailored exactly to the customer's needs. Performance is partly a matter of customer perception. Customer attitude surveys may be appropriate. Performance also depends on the diversity of skills possessed by the service organisation. This can be measured in terms of the mix of staff skills and the amount of time spent on training.
Coping with demand	This is measurable in quantitative terms. For example train companies can measure the extent of overcrowding. Customer queuing time can be measured for banks and retailers. Professional services can measure levels of overtime worked.

3.2.5 Resource utilisation measures

Resource utilisation is usually measured in terms of **productivity**. The ease with which this may be measured varies according to the service being delivered. The main input resource of a firm of accountants, for example, is the **time** of staff. The main output of an accountancy firm is **chargeable hours**. Productivity will therefore be measured as the ratio of chargeable hours to total hours.

Here are some resource utilisation ratios.

Business	Input	Output
Accountancy firms	Man hours available	Chargeable hours
Commonwealth Hotels	Rooms available	Rooms occupied
Railway companies	Train miles available	Passenger miles
Barclays Bank	Number of staff	Number of accounts

3.2.6 Innovation

Companies do not have to innovate to be successful, but it helps! Others will try to steal their market, and so others' innovations must at least be matched. In a modern environment in which product quality, product differentiation and continuous improvement are the order of the day, a company that can find innovative ways of satisfying customers' needs has an important **competitive advantage**

The **innovating process can be measured** in terms of **how much it costs to develop a new service, how effective the process is** (that is, how innovative is the organisation, if at all?), and **how quickly it can develop new services**. In more concrete terms this might translate into the following.

(a) The **amount of spending on research and development**, and whether these costs are recovered from new service sales (and how quickly).

(b) The **proportion of new services to total services** provided.

(c) The **time between identification of the customer need for a new service and making it available**.

Question

A service business has collected some figures relating to its year just ended.

	Budget	*Actual*
Customer enquiries		
New customers	6,000	9,000
Existing customers	4,000	3,000
Business won		
New customers	2,000	4,000
Existing customers	1,500	1,500
Types of services performed		
Service A	875	780
Service B	1,575	1,850
Service C	1,050	2,870
Employees		
Service A	5	4
Service B	10	10
Service C	5	8

Required

Calculate figures that illustrate competitiveness and resource utilisation.

Answer

Competitiveness can only be measured from these figures by looking at how successful the organisation is at converting enquiries into firm orders.

Percentage of enquiries converted into firm orders

	Budget	*Actual*
New customers (W1)	33%	44%
Existing customers (W1)	37.5%	50%

Resource utilisation can be measured by looking at average services performed per employee.

	Budget	*Actual*	*Rise*
Service A (W2)	175	195	+11.4%
Service B (W2)	157.5	185	+17.5%
Service C (W2)	175	358.75	+105.0%

Workings

1 For example 2,000/6,000 = 33%
2 For example 875/5 = 175

What comments would you make about the results of these calculations? How well is the business doing?

4 Performance measures for non-profit-making organisations

FAST FORWARD

Performance of **NPMOs** can be measured as follows.
- In terms of inputs and outputs
- By judgement
- By comparison

BPP LEARNING MEDIA

4.1 Non-profit-making organisations (NPMOs)

NPMOs include private sector organisations such as charities and churches and much of the public sector. Commercial organisations generally have market competition and the profit motive to guide the process of managing resources economically, efficiently and effectively. However, NPMOs **cannot** by definition **be judged by profitability** nor do they generally have to be successful against competition, so other methods of assessing performance have to be used.

A major problem with many NPMOs, particularly government bodies, is that it is **difficult to define their objectives**.

Question

Objectives

One of the objectives of a local government body could be 'to provide adequate street lighting throughout the area'.

(a) How could the 'adequacy' of street lighting be measured?

(b) Assume that other objectives are:

  (i) to improve road safety in the area; and
  (ii) to reduce crime.

  How much does 'adequate' street lighting contribute to each of these aims?

(c) What is an excessive amount of money to pay for adequately lit streets, improved road safety and reduced crime? How much is too little?

Answer

Mull over these questions and discuss them in class or with colleagues if possible. It is possible to suggest answers, perhaps even in quantitative terms, but the point is that there are no *easy* answers, and no right or wrong answers.

4.2 How can performance be measured?

Exam focus point

Economy, efficiency and effectiveness were all examined in the June 2006 exam. The meaning of and application of each to a scenario were required

Performance is often judged in terms of inputs and outputs. This ties in with the **'value for money'** criteria often used to assess NPMOs.

(a) **Economy** (spending money frugally)

(b) **Efficiency** (getting out as much as possible for what goes in)

(c) **Effectiveness** (getting done, by means of (a) and (b), what was supposed to be done)

Effectiveness is the relationship between an organisation's outputs and its objectives, **efficiency** is the relationship between inputs and outputs, and **economy** means controlling expenditure.

Problems with an NPMO

(a) NPMOs tend to have **multiple objectives**, so that even if they can all be clearly identified it is impossible to say which is the overriding objective.

(b) **Outputs can seldom be measured** in a way that is generally agreed to be meaningful. (For example, are good exam results alone an adequate measure of the quality of teaching?)

Here are four possible solutions.

Solutions	Detail
Inputs	Judging performance in this way is very common in everyday life. If somebody tells you that their suit cost $750, you would generally conclude that it was a good quality suit. The **drawback** is that you might also conclude that the person wearing the suit had been cheated. So it is with the inputs and outputs of a NPMO. Does the output justify the input?
Judgements	Accept that performance measurement must to some extent be subjective. **Judgements** can be made **by experts** in that particular non-profit-making activity **or by the persons who fund the activity**.
Comparisons	NPMOs can **compare** their performance **against each other** and **against the historical results** of their predecessors.
Unit cost measurements	Measures like 'cost per patient day' or 'cost of borrowing one library book' can be established to allow organisations to assess whether they are doing better or worse than their counterparts.

4.3 Example: Inputs and outputs

Suppose that at a cost of $40,000 and 4,000 hours (**inputs**) in an average year, two policemen travel 8,000 miles and are instrumental in 200 arrests (**outputs**). A large number of **possibly meaningful measures** can be derived from these few figures, as the table below shows.

		$40,000	*4,000 hours*	*8,000 miles*	*200 arrests*
Cost ($)	*$40,000*		$40,000/4,000 = $10 per hour	$40,000/8,000 = $5 per mile	$40,000/200 = $200 per arrest
Time (hours)	*4,000*	4,000/$40,000 = 6 minutes patrolling per $1 spent		4,000/8,000 = ½ hour to patrol 1 mile	4,000/200 = 20 hours per arrest
Miles	*8,000*	8,000/$40,000 = 0.2 of a mile per $1	8,000/4,000 = 2 miles patrolled per hour		8,000/200 = 40 miles per arrest
Arrests	*200*	200/$40,000 = 1 arrest per $200	200/4,000 = 1 arrest every 20 hours	200/8,000 = 1 arrest every 40 miles	

4.4 Performance measurement in the public sector

In public sector organisations, an increasing volume of information on performance and 'value for money' is produced for internal and external use. The ways in which performance can be measured depends very much upon which organisation is involved.

(a) The first question which would need to be asked is 'what are the **aims** and **objectives** of the organisation?' For example, the objective of Companies House is to maintain and make available records of company reports.

(b) The next question to ask is 'How can we tell if the organisation is **meeting** the objectives?' Quantified information - ie information in the form of numbers - will be useful, and this will consist mainly of output and performance measures and indicators. For these, targets can be set. Any individual organisational unit should have no more than a handful of key targets.

Individual targets are likely to fall under the headings:

(a) **Financial performance targets**
(b) **Volume of output targets**
(c) **Quality of service targets**
(d) **Efficiency targets**

4.5 Performance measurement in central government

Over recent years, much of the work of central government has been reorganised into semi-autonomous **executive agencies**, which we mentioned earlier in the chapter.

The following are examples of targets related to **financial performance** in executive agencies.

(a) **Full cost recovery** (National School of Government, Central Office of Information and others), plus unit cost targets
(b) **Commercial revenue** to offset costs (Met Office)
(c) **Non-Exchequer income** as a **percentage** of **total income** (National Engineering Laboratory)

Targets related to **output** can be difficult to set. In many cases the output of executive agencies is not tangible. For example, Historic Royal Palaces not only deals with visitors, whose numbers can be counted, but is also responsible for maintaining the fabric of royal palaces - an output which is more difficult to measure. In such cases, performance will be best measured by appraising the **progress** of the **project** as a whole.

Example of **quality** targets set for executive agencies include the following.

(a) **Timeliness**
    (i) Time to handle applications
    (ii) Car driving tests to be reduced to 6 weeks nationally (Driving Standards Agency)
(b) **Quality of product**
    (i) Number of print orders delivered without fault (HMSO)
    (ii) 95% business complaints handled within 5 days
    (iii) 85% overall customer satisfaction rating

Efficiency improvements may come through reducing the cost of inputs without reducing the quality of outputs. Alternatively, areas of activity affecting total costs may be reduced. Targets related to **efficiency** include the following.

(a) **Percentage reduction** in **price paid** for purchases of stationery and paper
(b) Reduction in the ratio of **cost of support services** to **total cost**
(c) 8.7% **efficiency increase** in the use of **accommodation**

4.6 Performance measurement in local government

The performance measures chosen by local authorities usually consist of **comparative statistics** and **unit costs**. Reporting on comparative statistics was recommended by the Department of the Environment in its code of practice *Local authority Annual Reports* (1982).

The following list illustrates the types of comparative statistics suggested in the code of practice.

PERFORMANCE MEASURES IN LOCAL GOVERNMENT	
For the authority's total expenditure and for each function	Net cost per 1,000 population Manpower per 1,000 population
Primary education, secondary education	Pupil/teacher ratio Cost per pupil
School meals	Revenue/cost ratio Pupils receiving free meals as a proportion of school roll
Home helps	Contract hours per 1,000 population over 65
Police	Population per police officer Serious offences per 1,000 population
Fire	Proportion of area at high risk
Public transport	Passenger journeys per week per 1,000 population
Highways	Maintenance cost per kilometre

5 Management performance measures

FAST FORWARD

Possible **management performance measures** include the following.

- Subjective measures
- Judgement of outsiders
- Upward appraisal
- Accounting measures

We have not so far **distinguished between measures of performance of individual managers** and **measures of performance of what it is they manage**

The distinction is very important. A manager may improve performance of a poorly performing division, but the division could still rank as one of the poorest performing divisions within the organisation. If the manager is assessed purely on the division's results then he will not appear to be a good performer.

The problem is deciding which performance measures should be used to measure management performance and which should be used to measure the performance of the business.

It is difficult to devise performance measures that relate specifically to a manager to judge his or her performance **as a manager**. It is possible to calculate statistics to assess the manager as an **employee** (days absent, professional qualifications obtained, personality and so on), but this does not measure managerial performance.

It is necessary to consider a manager in relation to his or her **area of responsibility**. If we want to know how good a manager is at marketing, the marketing performance of his or her division is the **starting point**. Then we must consider to what extent the manager is able to **influence** the performance, and the performance **trend.**

It is unreasonable to assess managers' performance in relation to matters that are beyond their control. Management performance measures should therefore **only include those items that are directly controllable by the manager in question.**

5.1 Possible management performance measures

Measures	Detail
Subjective measures	An example is ranking performance on a scale of 1 to 5. This approach is imprecise but does measure managerial performance rather than divisional performance. The process must be perceived by managers to be fair. The judgement should be made by somebody impartial, but close enough to the work of each manager to appreciate the efforts he has made and the difficulties he faces.
Judgement of outsiders	An organisation might, for example, set up a bonus scheme for directors under which they would receive a bonus if the share price outperforms the FT-SE 100 index for more than three years. This is fair in that the share price reflects many aspects of performance, but it is questionable whether they can all be influenced by the directors concerned.
Upward appraisal	This involves staff giving their opinions on the performance of their managers. To be effective this requires healthy working relationships.
Accounting measures	These can be used, but must be tailored according to what or whom is being judged.

6 Responsibility centre performance measures

Exam focus point

In the December 2006 exam candidates were asked to prepare a flexed budgeted profit statement showing budgeted contribution and traceable profit for **profit centres**.

The examiner considers this to be an important area so make sure that you read this section carefully. Study the example in this section and ensure you understand how a multi-divisional income statement is drawn up.

6.1 Typical performance measures

In order to ensure that junior managers in an organisation make decisions that are in the best interests of the organisation as a whole, senior managers generally introduce the following systems of performance measures.

Responsibility centre	Manager responsible for?	Financial performance measures
Cost centre	Costs	Variances
Revenue centre	Revenues only	Revenues
Profit centre	Costs and revenues	Controllable profit
Investment centre	Costs, revenues and assets	Return on Investment and Residual Income

We looked at variances in Part C of this Interactive Text, and we are now going to turn our attention to the following performance measures.

(a) Controllable profit
(b) Return on Investment (ROI)
(c) Residual Income (RI)

6.2 Traditional performance measures – cost centres

As we have already seen, variance analysis is often used as a way of measuring the performance of cost centres. Despite giving detailed explanations of why the variances have occurred, variance analysis as a performance indicator does have a number of disadvantages.

(a) It is concerned with controlling costs and inefficiencies in the short term only and may lead to conflict with an organisation's longer-term objectives.

(b) The variances are only as good as the standards on which they are based.

(c) It is not always obvious which managers are responsible for which variances. For example, are direct materials price variances the responsibility of the production manager or the purchasing manager, or both?

6.3 Traditional performance measures – profit centres

Profit centres often use controllable profit statements as a way of measuring the performance of both individual managers and their divisions. A proforma controllable profit statement is shown below.

6.4 Example: controllable profit statement

	Car sales	*Petrol*	*Total*
	$	$	$
Sales	315,000	25,000	340,000
Variable costs			
Plates, tax, MOT	(105,000)		(105,000)
Car valeting cost	(50,000)		(50,000)
Fuel	–	(15,000)	(15,000)
Contribution	160,000	10,000	170,000
Traceable fixed costs			
Fixed cleaning costs for showroom	(6,000)		(6,000)
Wages	(40,000)	(5,000)	(45,000)
Traceable profit	114,000	5,000	119,000
Common costs			
Building maintenance			(12,000)
Management salaries			(35,000)
Budgeted profit			72,000

The main problem with controllable profit statements is in deciding which costs are **controllable** and which costs are **traceable**. The performance of the manager of the division is indicated by the **controllable profit** (and it is on this that he is judged) and the success of the division as a whole is judged on the **traceable profit**.

Consider, for example, depreciation on divisional machinery. Would this be included as a controllable fixed cost or a traceable fixed cost? Because profit centre managers are only responsible for the **costs and revenues** under their control, this means that they do not have control over the investment in fixed assets. The depreciation on divisional machinery would therefore be a **traceable fixed cost** judging the performance of the division, and not of the individual manager.

6.5 Traditional performance measures – investment centres

Managers of investment centres have responsibility for costs, revenues and capital investment. Divisional performance is commonly measured using the following.

(a) **Return on Investment** (ROI)

(b) **Residual Income** (RI)

Return on Investment (ROI) is calculated as follows.

$$ROI = \frac{\text{Controllable (traceable) profit}}{\text{Controllable (traceable) investment}} \times 100\%$$

Residual Income (RI) is calculated as follows.

RI = Controllable (traceable) profit – imputed interest charge on controllable (traceable) investment

6.6 Example: calculation of ROI and RI

Division M is a division of MR plc. The following data relate to Division M.

Net assets	\$20m
Annual profit	\$5m
Cost of capital	15% per annum

MR plc is considering two proposals.

Proposal 1

Invest a further \$2m in fixed assets to earn an annual profit of \$0.40m.

Proposal 2

Dispose of fixed assets at their net book value of \$5.5m. This would lead to profits falling by \$1m per annum. Proceeds from the disposal of these fixed assets would not be credited to Division M (but to the Holding Company of MR plc instead).

Required

(a) Calculate the current Return on Investment and Residual Income for Division M.

(b) Consider each of the two proposals and show how the Return on Investment and Residual Income would change if these proposals were adopted.

6.7 Solution

(a) **Current Return on Investment**

Return on Investment $= \frac{\text{Traceable profit}}{\text{Traceable investment}} \times 100\%$

$= \frac{\$5m}{\$20m} \times 100\%$

$= 25\%$

Residual Income = Traceable profit – imputed interest charge on traceable investment

= \$5m – (15% × \$20m)

= \$5m – \$3m

= \$2m

The Return on Investment (25%) exceeds the cost of capital (15%) and the residual income is positive (+\$2m) and therefore Division M is performing well.

(b) Let us now look at the situations that would arise if proposals 1 and 2 were to be adopted.

Proposal 1

New traceable profit = \$5m + \$0.4m
= \$5.4m

∴ New traceable investment = \$20m + \$2m
= \$22m

∴ **New Return on Investment** $= \frac{£5.4m}{£22m} \times 100\%$
= 24.5%

∴ **New Residual Income** = \$5.4m – (15% × \$22m)
= \$5.4m – \$3.3m
= \$2.1m

Proposal 2

New traceable profit = \$5m – \$1m
= \$4m

New traceable investment = \$20m – \$5.5m
= \$14.5m

∴ **New Return on Investment** $= \frac{\$4m}{\$14.5m} \times 100\%$
= 27.6%

∴ **New Residual Income** = \$4m – (15% × \$14.5m)
= \$4m – \$2.18m
= \$1.82m

Summary

	Current	*Proposal 1*	*Proposal 2*
Return on Investment (%)	25	24.5	27.6
Residual Income (\$m)	2	2.1	1.82

Based on ROI alone, proposal 2 would appear the best showing a **relative** increase in return when proposal 1 shows a decrease.

However the RI suggests the opposite is true and proposal 1 is best. This is because RI focuses purely on the **absolute** result.

When considering proposal 2, divisional managers should also consider the asset rate of return.

$$\text{Asset rate of return} = \frac{\text{Change in profit}}{\text{Change in investment}}$$

$$= \frac{\$1m}{\$5.5m} \times 100\%$$

= 18.2%

Since MR plc's current rate of return is 25%, any asset which has a rate of return less than this should be disposed of. It is important to remember, therefore, that whichever proposal is accepted, it should lead to goal congruence.

6.8 Advantages of Return on Investment and Residual Income

Return on Investment is a relative measure, whereas **Residual Income** is an absolute measure. Consequently, Residual Income, as an absolute measure of performance is used to select proposals based on the absolute increase in profits, rather than the relative increases.

This can be demonstrated in the example above where the ROI increases to 29% with proposal 2, but the reality is that Residual Income only increases by an absolute value of \$0.2m. Residual Income therefore allows you to select a proposal that will maximise your wealth (in absolute terms).

Residual Income can also be related to the net present value (NPV) of a project, and supports the NPV approach. Therefore, organisations that maximise Residual Income will not necessarily, but are likely to maximise NPV in the long run (and hence shareholder wealth).

6.9 Disadvantages of Return on Investment and Residual Income

These performance measures have a number of common disadvantages.

(a) It can be difficult to identify controllable (traceable) profits.

(b) When organisations value assets at net book value, ROI and RI generally **increase** as assets get older. Consequently, management may hold on to out-of-date plant and machinery.

(c) Both ROI and RI involve a cost of capital figure which must be estimated. The cost of capital is difficult to calculate and is not known with certainty.

(d) Both ROI and RI measure divisional performance based on a single value. Most organisations these days are of such a complex nature that a single figure is unlikely to be adequate for an investment decision.

(e) As a general rule, most investment projects with positive NPVs have correspondingly low ROI and RI figures in early years. This can lead to the project being rejected in the first few years of a new investment, because the payoffs are long term.

Exam focus point

The advantages and disadvantages of RI were examined in June 2004.

7 Non-financial objectives

FAST FORWARD

Non-financial objectives include the welfare of employees and society in general and the fulfilment of responsibilities towards customers and suppliers.

A company may have important **non-financial objectives**, which will limit the achievement of financial objectives. Examples of non-financial objectives are as follows.

(a) **The welfare of employees**

A company might try to provide **good wages and salaries**, comfortable and safe working conditions, good training and career development, and good pensions. If redundancies are necessary, many companies will provide generous redundancy payments, or spend money trying to find alternative employment for redundant staff.

(b) **The welfare of management**

Managers will often take decisions to improve their **own circumstances**, even though their decisions will incur expenditure and so reduce profits. High salaries, company cars and other perks are all examples of managers promoting their own interests.

(c) **The provision of a service**

The major objectives of some companies will include fulfilment of a responsibility to **provide a service** to the public. Examples are the privatised British Telecom and British Gas. Providing a service is of course a key responsibility of government departments and local authorities.

(d) **The fulfilment of responsibilities towards customers**

Responsibilities towards **customers** include providing in good time a product or service of a **quality** that customers expect, and dealing **honestly and fairly** with customers. **Reliable supply arrangements**, also **after-sales service arrangements**, are important.

(e) **The fulfilment of responsibilities towards suppliers**

Responsibilities towards **suppliers** are expressed mainly in terms of **trading relationships**. A company's size could give it considerable power as a buyer. The company should not use its power unscrupulously. Suppliers might rely on getting prompt payment, in accordance with the agreed terms of trade.

(f) **The welfare of society as a whole**

The management of some companies is aware of the role that their company has to play in exercising **corporate social responsibility**. This includes **compliance with applicable laws and regulations** but is wider than that. Companies may be aware of their responsibility to minimise pollution and other harmful 'externalities' (such as excessive traffic) which their activities generate. In delivering 'green' environmental policies, a company may improve its corporate image as well as reducing harmful externality effects. Companies also may consider their **'positive' responsibilities**, for example to make a contribution to the community by local sponsorship.

Other non-financial objectives are growth, diversification and leadership in research and development.

7.1 Financial and non-financial objectives

Non-financial objectives do not negate financial objectives, but they do suggest that the simple theory of company finance, that the objective of a firm is to maximise the wealth of ordinary shareholders, is too simplistic. Financial objectives may have to be compromised in order to satisfy non-financial objectives.

8 The balanced scorecard

FAST FORWARD

The **balanced scorecard** measures performance in four different perspectives: customer satisfaction, financial success, process efficiency and growth.

So far in our discussion we have focussed on performance measurement and control from a financial point of view. Another approach, originally developed by Kaplan and Norton, is the use of what is called a 'balanced scorecard' consisting of a **variety of indicators both financial and non-financial.** This approach has developed over the years and is used by a wide range of companies. Consequently, different terminology may be used by different companies.

Exam focus point

The examiner has stated that he would use the term 'growth' rather than 'innovation and learning'. The terms he favours are shown in the tables in this section. The balanced scorecard was examined in June 2004.

Key term

The **balanced scorecard approach** is 'An approach to the provision of information to management to assist strategic policy formulation and achievement. It emphasises the need to provide the user with a set of information which addresses all relevant areas of performance in an objective and unbiased fashion. The information provided may include both financial and non-financial elements, and cover areas such as profitability, customer satisfaction, internal efficiency and innovation.' (CIMA *Official Terminology*)

The balanced scorecard focuses on **four different perspectives**, as follows.

Perspective	Question	Explanation
Customer satisfaction	What do existing and new customers value from us?	Gives rise to targets that matter to customers: cost, quality, delivery, inspection, handling and so on.
Process efficiency	What processes must we excel at to achieve our financial and customer objectives?	Aims to improve internal processes, decision making and resource utilisation.
Growth	Can we continue to improve and create future value?	Considers the business's capacity to maintain its competitive position through the acquisition of new skills and the development of new products.
Financial success	How do we create value for our shareholders?	Covers traditional measures such as growth, profitability and shareholder value but set through talking to the shareholder or shareholders direct.

The scorecard is 'balanced' in the sense that managers are required to think in terms of all four perspectives, to prevent improvements being made in one area at the expense of another.

The types of measure (**key performance indicators**) which may be monitored under each of the four perspectives include the following in the example on the next page. The list is not exhaustive but it will give you an idea of the possible scope of a balanced scorecard approach. The measures selected, particularly within the process efficiency perspective, will vary considerably with the type of organisation and its objectives.

Two examples of how a balanced scorecard might appear are given below. One refers to a restaurant which is a profit-making business. The other refers to a charity. Use these examples to think about how a balanced scorecard may appear in your own workplace.

Balanced Scorecard for a restaurant

Financial Success

GOALS	MEASURES (KPI)
To grow and open new restaurants	New restaurants opened
Profitable	Net profit margins

Customer Satisfaction

GOALS	MEASURES (KPI)
Great service	Excellent results on customer survey
Repeat business	Customers booking to come again
Innovative food	New menus on a regular basis

Process Efficiency

GOALS	MEASURES (KPI)
Timely food delivery	Time from order to delivery
Efficient staff	Processing of food order, few mistakes
Low food wastage	Amount of food discarded

Growth

GOALS	MEASURES (KPI)
Trained staff	Employees with relevant training and qualifications
New menu choices	Number of new dishes introduced

Balanced Scorecard for a charity

Financial Success

GOALS	MEASURES (KPI)
Income from charitable donations	Donations received
Improved margins	Lower costs and/or increased income from all sources

Customer Satisfaction

GOALS	MEASURES (KPI)
Continued donor support	Pledges given and direct debits set up
Donor involvement in initiatives	Fundraising and charity dinners

Process Efficiency

GOALS	MEASURES (KPI)
Reduce overheads	Lower overheads measured by monitoring and accounts
Claim back tax on gift aid	Improved reclaim times for gift aided donation

Growth

GOALS	MEASURES (KPI)
More projects supported	Number of projects given support
More fundraisers	Number of fundraisers recruited
More money pledged	Amount of donations promised

Exam focus point

Key performance indicators should be:

- specific as to profitability
- measurable and distinct
- relevant measuring achievement of a **critical success factor** (see Chapter 14)

Each organisation has to decide which performance measure to use under each heading. This was applied to a hotel chain in the June 2004 examination.

The balanced scorecard was also examined in December 2005 and June 2007 where the examiner asked for notes to help a manager understand what the balanced scorecard is.

There were eight marks available in the December 2007 exam for an analysis of performance using the balanced scorecard approach.

The following **important features** of this approach have been identified.

(a) It looks at both **internal and external matters** concerning the organisation.
(b) It is **related to the key elements of a company's strategy**.
(c) **Financial and non-financial measures** are linked together.

The balanced scorecard approach may be particularly useful for performance measurement in organisations which are unable to use simple profit as a performance measure. For example the **public sector** has long been forced to use a **wide range of performance indicators**, which can be formalised with a balanced scorecard approach.

Question — Balanced scorecard

For each of the following performance indicators, identify one balanced scorecard perspective being measured.

(a) Labour cost per unit manufactured
(b) Asset turnover
(c) Training expenditure as a percentage of sales turnover
(d) Return on capital employed
(e) Percentage of on-time deliveries
(f) Percentage of turnover generated by new products
(g) Percentage of quality control rejects

Answer

(a) Process efficiency (the improvement of internal processes)
(b) Process efficiency (the intensity of asset usage)
(c) Growth or possibly process efficiency
(d) Financial success
(e) Customer satisfaction, or possibly process efficiency
(f) Growth
(g) Process efficiency, or possibly customer satisfaction

8.1 Advantages and disadvantages

As with all techniques, problems can arise when it is applied.

Advantages	Explanation
All four perspectives considered by managers	Managers need to look at both **internal** and **external** matters affecting the organisation. They also need to link together **financial** and **non-financial** measures. Therefore they can see how factors in one area affect all other areas.
Consistency between objectives, control systems and staff	It can be difficult to incorporate objectives into control systems such as budgets. So targets set by a budget, say, may conflict with objectives. Moreover, staff may put their own interpretation on objectives against the actual intention of the original objective. The balanced scorecard should improve communication between different levels of the organisation. The balanced scorecard strives to keep all of these factors in balance.

Disadvantages	Explanation
Conflicting measures	Some measures in the scorecard such as research funding and cost reduction may naturally conflict. It is often difficult to determine the balance which will achieve the best results.
Selecting measures	Not only do appropriate measures have to be devised but the number of measures used must be agreed. Care must be taken that the impact of the results is not lost in a sea of information.
Expertise	Measurement is only useful if it initiates appropriate action. Non-financial managers may have difficulty with the usual profit measures. With more measures to consider this problem will be compounded.
Interpretation	Even a financially-trained manager may have difficulty in putting the figures into an overall perspective.

Chapter Roundup

- In a customer-focused organisation, basic **measures for sales** can be supplemented by a host of others including customer rejects/returns: total sales.
- Performance measures for **materials** and **labour** include **variances.**
- Performance can be measured using the **standard hour.**
- **Efficiency**, **activity** and **capacity ratios** provide useful information.
- Performance measures covering the following **six 'dimensions'** have been suggested for service organisations.
  - Competitive performance
  - Financial performance
  - Quality of service
  - Flexibility
  - Resource utilisation
  - Innovation
- Performance of **NPMOs** can be measured as follows.
  - In terms of inputs and outputs
  - By judgement
  - By comparison
- Possible **management performance measures** include the following.
  - Subjective measures
  - Judgement of outsiders
  - Upward appraisal
  - Accounting measures
- **Non-financial objectives** include the welfare of employees and society in general and the fulfilment of responsibilities towards customers and suppliers.
- The **balanced scorecard** measures performance in four different perspectives: customer satisfaction, financial success, process efficiency and growth.

Quick Quiz

1 What does the performance measure 'deliveries late: deliveries on schedule' indicate?

2 Suggest a measure for assessing machine usage and efficiency.

3 How is the efficiency ratio calculated?

4 What are the three aspects of flexibility?

5 What does 'economy' mean in terms of measuring the performance of an NPMO?

6 In the context of a balanced scorecard approach to performance measurement, to which of the four perspectives does each measure relate?

	Performance measure	*Perspective*
(a)	Time taken to develop new products	....
(b)	Percentage of on-time deliveries	....
(c)	Average set-up time	....
(d)	Return on capital employed	....

7 To which perspective of the balanced scorecard could the measure 'training day per employee' be most appropriately applied?

A Customer
B Internal
C Growth
D Financial

Answers to Quick Quiz

1 The efficiency of production and production scheduling.

2 Machine down time: total machine hours

3 (Standard hours produced ÷ actual hours worked) × 100%

4 Speed of delivery, ability to respond to customers' specifications and coping with demand.

5 Spending money frugally

6 (a) Growth
(b) Customer
(c) Internal
(d) Financial

7 C

Now try the questions below from the Exam Question Bank

Number	Level	Marks	Time
Section A: Q22-Q24	MCQ	N/A	N/A
Section B: Q17	Examination	20	36 mins

16

Pricing

Topic list
1 The importance of pricing
2 Factors affecting pricing policy
3 Full cost plus pricing
4 Marginal cost plus pricing
5 ABC plus pricing
6 Opportunity cost approach to pricing
7 Fixed price tenders

Study guide reference

		Syllabus reference
27(a)	Describe the factors which may influence an organisation's pricing policy	1,9
(b)	Prepare and justify cost-based approaches to pricing using absorption costing, marginal costing and opportunity costing approaches	1,9
(c)	Discuss the merits and limitations of cost-based approaches to pricing	1,9
(d)	Describe the procedure for preparing cost estimates for fixed price quotations and tenders	1,9

Exam focus point

This chapter covers a key syllabus area. Key syllabus areas usually account for 80% or more of the marks available on the exam paper.

1 The importance of pricing

Exam focus point

In the December 2005 exam, candidates were asked to calculate selling price using three approaches including marginal cost

Price can go by many names. Fares, rent, assessments and fees for example. All profit organisations and many non-profit-making organisations face the task of setting a price for their products or services.

In the past, setting a price was the single most important decision made by the sales department. In modern marketing philosophy, price, whilst important, is not necessarily the predominant factor. **Modern businesses** seek to interpret and **satisfy customer wants and needs by modifying existing products or introducing new products** to the range. This contrasts with **earlier production-oriented times** when the typical reaction was to **cut prices in order to sell more of an organisation's product.**

Nevertheless, **the pricing** of an organisation's products or services is **key to its profitability**.

2 Factors affecting pricing policy

FAST FORWARD

In practice in the modern world there are many more influences on pricing policy than the cost of a product or service.

Influence on pricing policy	Comment
Demand	Demand is the most important factor influencing the price of a product. In general, demand increases as prices are lowered.
Price sensitivity	This describes how demand for a product reacts to price changes. Sensitivity to price levels will vary amongst purchasers. **Those that can pass on the cost of purchases will be the least sensitive** to price. For example, the business traveller will be more concerned about the level of service and quality of food in looking for an hotel than price, since his or her employer will be paying the bill. In contrast, the family on holiday are likely to be very price sensitive when choosing an overnight stay.
Price perception	Price perception is **the way customers react to prices.** For example, customers may react to a price increase by buying more. They believe further price increases will follow so they 'stock up'.

Influence on pricing policy	Comment
Quality	In the absence of other information, customers tend to **judge quality by price**. A price change may send signals to customers concerning the quality of the product. A price rise may indicate improvements in quality, a price reduction may signal reduced quality, for example through the use of inferior components.
Intermediaries	If an organisation distributes products or services to the market through independent intermediaries, the **objectives of these intermediaries complicate the pricing decision**. Such intermediaries are likely to deal with a range of suppliers and their aims concern their own profits rather than those of suppliers.
Competitors	In setting prices, an organisation sends out signals to rivals. **Competitors are likely to react to these signals in some way**. In some industries (such as petrol retailing) **pricing moves in unison**; in others, price changes by one supplier may initiate a **price war**, with each supplier undercutting the others. Competition is discussed in more detail below.
Suppliers	If an organisation's suppliers **notice a price rise** for the organisation's products, they **may seek a rise** in the price for their supplies to the organisation on the grounds that it is now able to pay a higher price.
Inflation	In periods of inflation the organisation may need to change prices to reflect increases in the prices of supplies, labour, rent and so on. Such changes may be needed to keep relative (real) prices unchanged.
Newness	When a **new product** is introduced there are no existing reference points such as customer or competitor behaviour. **Pricing decisions are difficult to make** in these circumstances. It may be possible to seek alternative reference points, such as the price in another market where the new product has already been launched.
Incomes	In times of **rising incomes**, **price** may become **less important than product quality** or convenience of access (distribution). When income levels are **falling** and/or unemployment levels rising, **price** will become **more important.**
Product range	Products are often interrelated, for example complements or substitutes. With complementary products **pricing** is likely **to focus** on the profit from the **whole range** rather than the profit on each single product. For example the use of **loss leaders**: a very low price for one product is intended to make consumers buy additional products in the range which carry higher profit margins. A good example is selling razors at a loss whilst selling the blades for them at a higher profit margin, or selling the Monday edition of The Times newspaper cheaply to encourage new readers.
Ethics	Ethical considerations may be a further factor, for example whether or not to **exploit** short-term shortages through higher prices.
Substitute products	These are **products which could be transformed for the same use**. For example if the price of train travel rises it comes under competition from cheaper coach travel and more expensive air travel.

2.1 Product life cycle

FAST FORWARD

A typical product has a **life cycle** of four stages.

Exam focus point

Candidates were asked to explain and describe the product life cycle in the June 2006 exam. They were also required to explain its importance in sales and forecasting. There were upto twelve marks that could be earned for completing these requirements.

The product life concept is relevant to pricing policy. As explained earlier, the concept states that a typical product moves through four stages.

Stage	Detail
Introduction	The product is introduced to the market. Heavy **capital expenditure** will be incurred on product development and perhaps also on the purchase of new fixed assets and building up inventories for sale. On its introduction to the market, the product will begin to earn some revenue, but initially demand is likely to be small. Potential customers will be unaware of the product or service, and the organisation may have to spend further on **advertising** to bring the product or service to the attention of the market.
Growth	The product gains a bigger market as demand builds up. Sales revenues increase and the product begins to make a profit. The initial costs of the **investment** in the new product are gradually **recovered**.
Maturity	Eventually, the growth in demand for the product will slow down and it will enter a period of relative maturity. It will continue to be profitable. The product may be **modified or improved**, **as a means of sustaining its demand**.
Saturation and decline	At some stage, the market may reach 'saturation point'. Demand will start to fall. For a while, the product will still be profitable in spite of declining sales, but eventually it will become a **loss-maker** and this is the time when the organisation should decide to stop selling the product or service, and so the product's life cycle should reach its end. Remember, however, that some mature products will **never decline**: staple food products such as milk or bread are the best example.

Not all products follow this cycle, but it remains a useful tool when considering decisions such as pricing. **The life cycle concept is relevant when considering what pricing policy will be adapted**.

2.2 Markets

FAST FORWARD

The price that an organisation can charge for its products will be determined to a certain extent by the market (perfect competition, monopoly, oligarchy)in which it operates.

Key terms

Perfect competition: many buyers and many sellers all dealing in an identical product. Neither producer nor user has any market power and both must accept the prevailing market price.

Monopoly: one seller who dominates many buyers. The monopolist can use his market power to set a profit-maximising price.

Oligopoly: relatively few competitive companies dominate the market. Whilst each large firm has the ability to influence market prices, the unpredictable reaction from the other giants makes the final industry price indeterminate.

2.3 Competition

FAST FORWARD

Competition affects pricing policy.

In **established industries** dominated by a few major firms, a price initiative by one firm will usually be countered by a price reaction by competitors. In these circumstances, **prices tend to be stable**.

If a **rival cuts its prices** in the expectation of increasing its market share, a **firm has several options**.

(a) It will **maintain its existing prices** if the expectation is that only a small market share would be lost, so that it is more profitable to keep prices at their existing level. Eventually, the rival firm may drop out of the market or be forced to raise its prices.

(b) It may maintain its prices but respond with a **non-price counter-attack**. This is a more positive response, because the firm will be securing or justifying its current prices with a product change, advertising, or better back-up services.

(c) It may **reduce its prices**. This should protect the firm's market share so that the main beneficiary from the price reduction will be the consumer.

(d) It may **raise its prices** *and respond with a* **non-price counter-attack**. The extra revenue from the higher prices might be used to finance an advertising campaign or product design changes. A price increase would be based on a campaign to emphasise the quality difference between the firm's own product and the rival's product.

2.4 Price leadership

FAST FORWARD

A **price leader** indicates to the other firms in the market what the price will be.

Given that price competition can have disastrous consequences in conditions of oligopoly, it is not unusual to find that large corporations emerge as price leaders. The price leader **indicates to the other firms in the market what the price will be**, and **competitors then set their prices with reference to the leader's price**.

2.5 Market penetration pricing

FAST FORWARD

Market penetration **pricing** and **market skimming pricing** are pricing policies for new products.

This is a policy of **low prices** when the product is **first launched** in order to obtain sufficient penetration into the market. A penetration policy may be appropriate in a number of circumstances.

(a) If the firm wishes to **discourage new entrants** into the market

(b) If the firm wishes to **shorten the initial period of the product's life cycle** in order to enter the growth and maturity stages as quickly as possible

(c) If there are significant **economies of scale** to be achieved from a high volume of output, so that quick penetration into the market is desirable in order to gain unit cost reductions

(d) If **demand is likely to increase as prices fall**

2.6 Market skimming pricing

In contrast, market skimming involves charging **high prices** when a product is **first launched** and **spending heavily on advertising** and sales promotion to obtain sales. As the product moves into the **later stages** of its life cycle (growth, maturity and decline) **progressively lower prices** will be charged. The profitable 'cream' is thus skimmed off in stages until sales can only be sustained at lower prices.

The aim of market skimming is to gain **high unit profits early** in the product's life. High unit prices make it more likely that **competitors** will enter the market than if lower prices were to be charged.

When such a policy is appropriate

(a) Where the **product is new and different**, so that customers are prepared to pay high prices so as to be one up on other people who do not own it. For example the i-Pod.

(b) Where the strength of **demand** and the sensitivity of demand to price are **unknown**. It is better from the point of view of marketing to start by charging high prices and then reduce them if the demand is insufficient.

(c) Where products may have a **short life cycle**, and so need to recover their development costs and make a profit quickly.

3 Full cost plus pricing

FAST FORWARD

Using **full cost plus pricing**, the sales price is determined by calculating the full cost of the product and adding a percentage mark-up for profit. The approach is unlikely to arrive at a profit-maximising price.

Exam focus point

Candidates could earn up to six marks in the December 2005 exam for explaining advantages and disadvantages of cost plus pricing.

A traditional approach to pricing products is full cost plus pricing, whereby the sales price is determined by **calculating the full cost of the product and adding a percentage mark-up for profit.**

An adoption of full cost plus pricing is **target pricing** which means setting a price so as to achieve a target profit or return on capital employed.

In full cost plus pricing, the full cost may be a fully absorbed *production* cost only, or it may include some absorbed administration, selling and distribution overhead. The full cost might also include some opportunity costs as well, such as the opportunity cost of a production resource that is in short supply, so that **'full cost' need not be the cost as it might be established in the accounts**.

A business might have an idea of the percentage profit margin it would like to earn and so might decide on an average profit mark-up as a general guideline for pricing decisions. This would be particularly **useful for** businesses that carry out a large amount of **contract work** or **jobbing work**, for which individual job or contract prices must be quoted regularly to prospective customers.

However, the **percentage profit mark-up** does not have to be fixed, but can be **varied to suit the circumstances**. In particular, the percentage mark-up can be varied to suit demand conditions in the market.

The full cost plus approach to pricing is commonly used. Varying the size of the profit mark-up gives the pricing decisions much-needed flexibility so as to adapt to demand conditions.

3.1 Problems with full cost plus pricing

(a) Cost plus pricing **fails to recognise** that since demand may be determined by price, **there will be a profit-maximising combination of price and demand.** A cost plus based approach to pricing will be **most unlikely to arrive at the profit-maximising price**.

(b) Prices must be adjusted to market and demand conditions, the decision cannot simply be made on a cost basis only.

(c) That output volume, which is a key factor in the fixed overhead absorption rate, must be budgeted. Output volume will depend on demand. An estimate of demand depends on price. The calculation of a full cost plus price requires an overhead absorption rate. So, a full cost plus pricing **decision cannot be made without a knowledge of demand and demand cannot be estimated without a knowledge of price. This is a never ending loop.**

   (i) One solution is to estimate likely demand (which should be known from past experience in the case of established products) and calculate an absorption rate on this assumed volume of output. Provided that actual volume equals or exceeds the estimated volume of sales, the company will achieve (or exceed) its target profit.

(ii) Another solution is to set a price on the basis of a budgeted production volume and allow inventories to build up for a time if demand is below production volume at this price. A price review can be made when demand conditions are known better, and either of the following decisions could be taken.

(1) A price reduction could be made to stimulate demand if this seems appropriate.

(2) Production volumes could be reduced and prices raised if necessary in recognition of the lack of demand for the product at the original budgeted volumes.

(d) **Further disadvantages of full cost plus pricing**

(i) It **fails to allow for competition**. A company may need to match the prices of rival firms when these take a price-cutting initiative.

(ii) A full cost plus basis for a pricing decision is a means of ensuring that, in the long run, a company succeeds in covering all its fixed costs and making a profit out of revenue earned. However, in the short term it is **inflexible**.

(1) A firm tendering for a contract may quote a cost plus price that results in the contract going elsewhere, although a lower price would have been sufficient to cover all incremental costs and opportunity costs.

(2) In the short term, rapidly-changing environmental factors might dictate the need for lower (or higher) prices than long-term considerations would indicate.

(iii) Full cost plus prices tend to ignore opportunity costs.

(iv) Where more than one product is sold by a company, the price decided by a cost plus formula depends on the method of apportioning fixed costs between the products.

3.2 Example: full cost plus pricing with more than one product

Giraffe is attempting to decide sales prices for two products, Lyons and Tygers. The products are both made by the same workforce and in the same department. 30,000 direct labour hours are budgeted for the year. The budgeted fixed costs are $30,000 and it is expected that the department will operate at full capacity. Variable costs per unit are as follows.

		Lyons		*Tygers*
		$		$
Materials		4		4
Labour	(2 hours)	6	(3 hours)	9
Expenses	(1 machine hour)	2	(1 machine hour)	2
		12		15

Expected demand is 7,500 Lyons and 5,000 Tygers.

Required

Calculate the unit prices which give a profit of 20% on full cost if overheads are absorbed on the following bases.

(a) On a direct labour hour basis

(b) On a machine hour basis

3.3 Solution

(a) A direct labour hour basis

$$\frac{\text{Budgeted fixed costs}}{\text{Budgeted labour costs}} = \frac{\$30,000}{(15,000+15,000)} = \$1$$

Absorption rate $1 per direct labour hour

	Lyons	Tygers
	$	$
Variable costs	12.00	15.00
Overhead absorbed	2.00	3.00
	14.00	18.00
Profit (20%)	2.80	3.60
Price	16.80	21.60

The total budgeted profit would be $(21,000 + 18,000) = $39,000.

(b) *A machine hour basis*

$$\frac{\text{Budgeted fixed costs}}{\text{Budgeted machine hours}} = \frac{\$30,000}{(7,500+5,000)} = \frac{\$30,000}{12,500} = \$2.40$$

Absorption rate $2.40 per machine hour

	Lyons	Tygers
	$	$
Variable costs	12.00	15.00
Overhead absorbed	2.40	2.40
Full cost	14.40	17.40
Profit (20%)	2.88	3.48
Price	17.28	20.88

The total budgeted profit would be $(21,600 + 17,400) = $39,000.

(c) The different bases for charging overheads result in different prices for both Lyons (difference of 48c per unit) and Tygers (difference of 72c per unit).

It is unlikely that the expected sales demand for the products would be the same at both sales prices. It is questionable whether one (or either) product might achieve expected sales demand at the higher price. In other words, although the budgeted profit is $39,000 whichever overhead absorption method is used, this assumes that budgeted sales would be achieved regardless of the unit price of each product. This is an unrealistic basis on which to make a decision.

3.4 Advantages of full cost plus pricing

(a) Since the size of the profit margin can be varied at management's discretion, a decision based on a price in excess of full cost should ensure that a company working at normal capacity will cover all its fixed costs and make a profit. Companies may benefit from cost plus pricing in the following circumstances.

  (i) When they carry out large contracts which must make a sufficient profit margin to cover a fair share of fixed costs

  (ii) If they must justify their prices to potential customers (for example for government contracts)

  (iii) If they find it difficult to estimate expected demand at different sales prices

(b) It is a **simple, quick and cheap** method of pricing which can be delegated to junior managers. This may be particularly important with jobbing work where many prices must be decided and quoted each day.

Question — Mark-up

A product's full cost is $4.75 and it is sold at full cost plus 70%. A competitor has just launched a similar product selling for $7.99. How will this affect the first product's mark up?

Answer

Price needs to be reduced to $7.99

Mark-up therefore needs to be $\left(\frac{7.99-4.75}{4.75}\right) \times 100\% = 68\%$

The mark-up therefore needs to be reduced by 2%.

4 Marginal cost plus pricing

FAST FORWARD

Marginal cost plus pricing (mark-up pricing) involves adding a profit margin to the marginal cost of production or the marginal cost of sales.

Instead of pricing products or services by adding a profit margin on to full cost, a business might **add a profit margin on to marginal cost** (**either the marginal cost of production or else the marginal cost of sales**).

For example, if a company budgets to make 10,000 units of a product for which the variable cost of production is $3 a unit and the fixed production cost $60,000 a year, it might decide to fix a price by adding, say, $33^1/_3$% to full production cost to give a price of $9 × $1^1/_3$ = $12 a unit. Alternatively, it might decide to add a profit margin of, say, 250% on to the variable production cost, to give a price of $3 × 350% = $10.50.

Advantages of a marginal cost plus approach

(a) It is a **simple and easy** method to use.

(b) The **mark-up can be varied**, and so provided that a rigid mark-up is not used, mark-up pricing can be adjusted to reflect demand conditions.

(c) It draws management attention to contribution and the effects of higher or lower sales volumes on profit. This helps to **create a better awareness of** the concepts and implications of **marginal costing and breakeven analysis**. For example, if a product costs $10 a unit and a mark-up of 150% is added to reach a price of $25 a unit, management should be clearly aware that every additional $1 of sales revenue would add 60c to contribution and profit.

(d) Mark-up pricing is **convenient where there is a readily identifiable basic variable cost. Retail industries** are the most obvious example, and it is quite common for the prices of goods in shops to be fixed by adding a mark-up (20% or $33^1/_3$%, say) to the purchase cost. For example, a department store might buy in items of pottery at $3 each, add a mark-up of one third and resell the items at $4.

Drawbacks to marginal cost plus pricing

(a) Although the size of the mark-up can be varied in accordance with demand conditions, it **does not ensure that sufficient attention is paid to demand conditions, competitors' prices and profit maximisation**.

(b) It ignores fixed overheads in the pricing decision, but the price must be high enough to ensure that a profit is made after covering fixed costs. Pricing decisions **cannot ignore fixed costs altogether.**

Question

Profit margin

A product has the following costs.

	$
Direct materials	5
Direct labour	3
Variable overhead	7

Fixed overheads are $10,000 per month. Budgeted sales for the month are 400 units.

What profit margin needs to be added to marginal cost to break even?

Answer

To breakeven, total contribution = fixed costs. Let selling price = p. Unit contribution = p – 15

Total monthly contribution	= 400 (p – 15)
At breakeven point, 400(p – 15)	= 10,000
p – 15	= 25
p	= 40

$$\text{Profit margin} = \frac{40-15}{15} \times 100\% = 166\tfrac{2}{3}\%$$

Consider the following **cost/profit/sales structure.**

	%
Cost	80
Profit	20
Sales	100

The **profit added** to the full cost or marginal cost of a product may be expressed in one of two ways.

(a) Percentage of **cost of sales**, such as **25%** ($^{20}/_{80}$) **mark-up**
(b) Percentage of **sales**, such as **20%** ($^{20}/_{100}$) **margin**

Alternatively, the **cost/profit/sales structure** could be:

	%
Cost	100
Profit	20
Sales	120

(a) Mark-up = $^{20}/_{100}$ = 20%
(b) Margin = $^{20}/_{120}$ = 16.7%

Question

Mark-ups

(a) Product B's unit cost is $50. A selling price is set based on a margin of 15%. What is the selling price?

(b) Product L sells for $750. The mark-up is 10%. What is the unit cost of product L?

Answer

(a)

	$	%
Cost	50	85
Profit	?	15
Selling price	?	100

Selling price = $50/0.85 = $58.82

(b)

	$	%
Cost	?	100
Profit	?	10
Selling price	750	110

Cost = $750/1.1 = $681.82

Question

MC pricing

Which of the following are advantages of marginal cost plus pricing?

I It is simple and easy to use.
II The mark-up can be varied.
III It pays attention to profit maximisation.
IV It ignores fixed overheads in the pricing decision.

A I only
B II and III
C II, III and IV
D I and II

Answer

D **I:** The same can be said of full cost plus pricing.

II: The mark-up can be adjusted to reflect demand conditions.

III: Although the size of the mark-up can be varied in accordance with demand conditions, it is not a method of pricing which ensures that sufficient attention is paid to demand conditions, competitors' prices and profit maximisation.

IV: The price must be high enough to ensure that a profit is made after covering fixed costs.

5 ABC plus pricing

FAST FORWARD

ABC plus pricing is a full cost plus pricing method in which the overheads included in the cost are derived using activity based costing instead of traditional absorption costing.

The implication for **pricing if ABC is used** is that the full cost on which prices are based may be radically different from a price based on full cost determined using traditional absorption costing.

5.1 Example: activity based costing and pricing

ABP makes two products, X and Y, with the following cost patterns.

	Product X	*Product Y*
	$	$
Direct materials	27	24
Direct labour at $5 per hour	20	25
Variable production overheads at $6 per hour	3	6
	50	55

Production fixed overheads total $300,000 per month and these are absorbed on the basis of direct labour hours. Budgeted direct labour hours are 25,000 per month. However, the company has carried out an analysis of its production support activities and found that its 'fixed costs' actually vary in accordance with non volume-related factors.

Activity	*Cost driver*	*Product X*	*Product Y*	*Total cost*
				$
Set-ups	Production runs	30	20	40,000
Materials handling	Production runs	30	20	150,000
Inspection	Inspections	880	3,520	110,000
				300,000

Budgeted production is 1,250 units of product X and 4,000 units of product Y.

Required

Given that the company wishes to make a profit of 20% on full production costs calculate the prices that should be charged for products X and Y using the following.

(a) Full cost pricing
(b) Activity based cost pricing

5.2 Solution

(a) The **full cost and mark-up** will be calculated as follows.

	Product X	*Product Y*
	$	$
Variable costs	50.00	55.00
Fixed prod o/hds ($300,000/25,000 = $12 per direct labour hr)	48.00	60.00
	98.00	115.00
Profit mark-up (20%)	19.60	23.00
Selling price	117.60	138.00

(b) Using **activity based costing**, overheads will be allocated on the basis of cost drivers.

	X	*Y*	*Total*
	$	$	$
Set ups (30:20)	24,000	16,000	40,000
Materials handling (30:20)	90,000	60,000	150,000
Inspections (880:3,520)	22,000	88,000	110,000
Selling profit	136,000	164,000	300,000
Budgeted units	1,250	4,000	
Overheads per unit	$108.80	$41.00	

The price is then calculated as before.

	Product X	*Product Y*
	$	$
Variable costs	50.00	55.00
Production overheads	108.80	41.00
	158.80	96.00
Profit mark-up (20%)	31.76	19.20
Selling price	190.56	115.20

(c) **Commentary**

The results in (b) are radically different from those in (a). On this basis it appears that the company has **previously been making a huge loss** on every unit of product X sold for $117.60. If the market will not accept a price increase, it may be worth considering ceasing production of product X entirely. It also appears that there is scope for a reduction in the price of product Y, and this would certainly be worthwhile if demand for the product is elastic.

The pricing implications of activity based costing

Consider a business that produces a **large volume** standard product and a number of **variants** which are more refined versions of the basic product and sell in low volumes at a higher price. Such companies are common in practice in the modern business environment. In practice, also, such companies absorb fixed overheads on a conventional basis such as direct labour hours, and price their products by adding a mark up to full cost.

In the situation described, the **majority of the overheads** would be allocated to the **standard** range, and only a small percentage to the up-market products. The result would be that the profit margin achieved on the standard range would be much lower than that on the up-market range.

Thus the traditional costing and pricing system indicates that the firm might be wise to concentrate on its high margin, up-market products and drop its standard range. This is **absurd**, however. Much of the overhead cost incurred in such an organisation is the cost of support activities like production scheduling: the more different **varieties** of product there are, the higher the level of such activities will become. The cost of marketing and distribution also increase disproportionately to the volume of products being made.

The bulk of the overheads in such an organisation are actually the '**costs of complexity**'. Their arbitrary allocation on the basis of labour hours gives an entirely **distorted** view of production line profitability; many products that appear to be highly profitable actually make a loss if costs are allocated on the basis of what activities cause them.

The problem arises with **marginal cost-plus** approaches as well as with absorption cost based approaches, particularly in a modern manufacturing environment, where a relatively small proportion of the total cost is variable. The implication in both cases is that conventional costing should be abandoned in favour of ABC.

6 Opportunity cost approach to pricing

FAST FORWARD

The **opportunity cost approach to pricing** involves including the opportunity costs of the resources consumed in making and selling the item in the cost of the product and then adding a profit margin.

The opportunity cost approach to pricing can be used to **set a full cost plus price or marginal cost plus price which includes the opportunity costs of the resources consumed in making and selling the item.**

6.1 Example: full cost-plus pricing and opportunity costs

Oppo Ltd has begun to produce a new product, Product Tunity, for which the following cost estimates have been made.

	$
Direct materials	27
Direct labour: 4 hrs at $5 per hour	20
Variable production overheads: machining, ½ hr at $6 per hour	3
	50

Production fixed overheads are budgeted at $300,000 per month and because of the shortage of available machining capacity, the company will be restricted to 10,000 hours of machine time per month. The absorption rate will be a direct labour rate, however, and budgeted direct labour hours are 25,000 per month. It is estimated that the company could obtain a minimum contribution of $10 per machine hour on producing items other than product Tunity.

Required

The company wishes to make a profit of 20% on full production cost from product Tunity. Calculate the full cost plus price.

6.2 Solution

Let us begin by calculating a price based on *not* including opportunity costs.

	$
Direct materials	27.00
Direct labour (4 hours)	20.00
Variable production overheads	3.00
Fixed production overheads	
(at $\frac{\$300,000}{25,000}$ = $12 per direct labour hour)	48.00
Full production cost	98.00
Profit mark-up (20%)	19.60
Selling price per unit of product Tunity	117.60

The price if we include machine time opportunity costs is as follows.

	$
Full production cost as above	98.00
Opportunity cost of machine time:	
contribution forgone (½ hr × $10)	5.00
Adjusted full cost	103.00
Profit mark-up (20%)	20.60
Selling price per unit of product Tunity	123.60

The inclusion of opportunity costs therefore raises the price by $6.

7 Fixed price tenders

FAST FORWARD

Fixed price tenders involve an analysis of relevant costs. A margin is often added to the **minimum price.**

7.1 Special orders

A special order is a **one-off revenue earning opportunity**. These may arise in the following situations.

(a) When a business has a regular source of income but also has some **spare capacity** allowing it to take on extra work if demanded. For example a brewery might have a capacity of 500,000 barrels per month but only be producing and selling 300,000 barrels per month. It could therefore consider special orders to use up some of its spare capacity.

(b) When a business has no regular source of income and **relies exclusively** on its **ability to respond to demand**. A building firm is a typical example as are many types of sub-contractors. In the service sector consultants often work on this basis.

The reason for making the distinction is that in the case of (a), a firm would normally attempt to cover its longer-term running costs in its prices for its regular product. Pricing for special orders need therefore take no account of unavoidable fixed costs. This is clearly not the case for a firm in (b)'s position, where special orders are the only source of income for the foreseeable future.

Questions featuring pricing for special orders typically present a scenario in which a firm has to decide whether to submit a fixed price tender for a contract.

The basic approach in both situations is to determine the price at which the firm would break even if it undertook the work, that is, the minimum price that it could afford to charge.

7.2 Minimum pricing

A minimum price is the price that would have to be charged to cover the following.

(a) The **incremental costs** of producing and selling the item
(b) The **opportunity costs** of the resources consumed in making and selling the item

A minimum price would leave the business no better or worse off in financial terms than if it did not sell the item.

Features of minimum price

(a) **Based on relevant costs**
(b) **Unlikely to be charged** because it would not provide the business with any incremental profit

Calculating the minimum price is useful as it shows two things

(a) An absolute minimum below which the price should not be set.

(b) The incremental profit that would be obtained from any price that is actually charged in excess of the minimum. For example, if the minimum price is $20,000 and the actual price charged is $24,000, the incremental profit on the sale would be $4,000.

If resources are scarce, minimum prices must include an allowance for the opportunity cost of using the resources on the job.

7.3 Example: opportunity costs and minimum price

Minimax has just completed production of an item of special equipment for a customer, only to be notified that this customer has now gone into liquidation.

After much effort, the sales manager has been able to interest a potential buyer who might buy the machine if certain conversion work could first be carried out.

(a) The sales price of the machine to the original buyer had been fixed at $138,600 and had included an estimated normal profit mark-up of 10% on total costs. The costs incurred in the manufacture of the machine were as follows.

	$
Direct materials	49,000
Direct labour	36,000
Variable overhead	9,000
Fixed production overhead	24,000
Fixed sales and distribution overhead	8,000
	126,000

(b) If the machine is converted, the production manager estimates that the cost of the extra work required would be as follows.

Direct materials (at cost) $9,600
Direct labour
Department X: 6 workers for 4 weeks at $210 per worker per week
Department Y: 2 workers for 4 weeks at $160 per worker per week

(c) Variable overhead would be 20% of direct labour cost, and fixed production overhead would be absorbed as follows.

Department X: 83.33% of direct labour cost
Department Y: 25% of direct labour cost

(d) Additional information is available as follows.

(i) In the original machine, there are three types of material.

(1) Type A could be sold for scrap for $8,000.

(2) Type B could be sold for scrap for $2,400 but it would take 120 hours of casual labour paid at $3.50 per hour to put it into a condition in which it would be suitable for sale.

(3) Type C would need to be scrapped, at a cost to Minimax of $1,100.

(ii) The direct materials required for the conversion are already in inventory. If not needed for the conversion they would be used in the production of another machine in place of materials that would otherwise need to be purchased, and that would currently cost $8,800.

(iii) The conversion work would be carried out in two departments, X and Y. Department X is currently extremely busy and working at full capacity; it is estimated that its contribution to fixed overhead and profits is $2.50 per $1 of labour.

Department Y, on the other hand, is short of work but for organisational reasons its labour force, which at the moment has a workload of only 40% of its standard capacity, cannot be reduced below its current level of eight employees, all of whom are paid a wage of $160 per week.

(iv) The designs and specifications of the original machine could be sold to an overseas customer for $4,500 if the machine is scrapped.

(v) If conversion work is undertaken, a temporary supervisor would need to be employed for four weeks at a total cost of $1,500. It is normal company practice to charge supervision costs to fixed overhead.

(vi) The original customer has already paid a non-returnable deposit to Minimax of 12.5% of the selling price.

Required

Calculate the minimum price that Minimax should quote for the converted machine. Explain clearly how you have reached this figure.

7.4 Solution

The minimum price is the price which reflects the **opportunity costs** of the work. These are established as follows.

(a) **Past costs are not relevant**, and the $126,000 of cost incurred should be excluded from the minimum price calculation. It is necessary, however, to consider the alternative use of the direct materials which would be forgone if the conversion work is carried out.

BPP LEARNING MEDIA

	$
Type A	
Revenue from sales as scrap (note (i))	8,000
Type B	
Revenue from sales as scrap, minus the additional cash costs necessary to prepare it for sale ($2,400 – (120 × $3.50)) (note (i))	1,980
Type C	
Cost of disposal if the machine is not converted (a negative opportunity cost) (note (ii))	(1,100)
Total opportunity cost of materials types A, B and C	8,880

By agreeing to the conversion of the machine, Minimax would therefore lose a net revenue of $8,880 from the alternative use of these materials.

Notes

(i) Scrap sales would be lost if the conversion work goes ahead.
(ii) These costs would be incurred unless the work goes ahead.

(b) The cost of additional direct materials for conversion is $9,600, but this is an historical cost. The relevant cost of these materials is the $8,800 which would be spent on new purchases if the conversion is carried out. If the conversion work goes ahead, the materials in inventory would be unavailable for production of the other machine mentioned in item (d)(ii) of the question and so the extra purchases of $8,800 would then be needed.

(c) Direct labour in departments X and Y is a fixed cost and the labour force will be paid regardless of the work they do or do not do. The cost of labour for conversion in department Y is not a relevant cost because the work could be done without any extra cost to the company.

In department X, however, acceptance of the conversion work would oblige the company to divert production from other profitable jobs. The minimum contribution required from using department X labour must be sufficient to cover the cost of the labour and variable overheads and then make an additional $2.50 in contribution per direct labour hour.

Department X: costs for direct labour hours spent on conversion

6 workers × 4 weeks × $210 =	$5,040
Variable overhead cost $5,040 × 20% =	$1,008
Contribution forgone by diverting labour from other work $2.50 per $1 of labour cost = $5,040 × 250% =	$12,600

(d) Variable overheads in department Y are relevant costs because they will only be incurred if production work is carried out. (It is assumed that if the workforce is idle, no variable overheads would be incurred.)

Department Y 20% of (2 workers × 4 weeks × $160) = $256

(e) If the machine is converted, the company cannot sell the designs and specifications to the overseas company. $4,500 is a relevant (opportunity) cost of accepting the conversion order.

(f) Fixed overheads, being mainly unchanged regardless of what the company decides to do, should be ignored because they are not relevant (incremental) costs. The additional cost of supervision should, however, be included as a relevant cost of the order because the $1,500 will not be spent unless the conversion work is done.

(g) The non-refundable deposit received should be ignored and should not be deducted in the calculation of the minimum price. Just as costs incurred in the past are not relevant to a current decision about what to do in the future, revenues collected in the past are also irrelevant.

Estimate of minimum price for the converted machine

	$	$
Opportunity cost of using the direct materials types A, B and C		8,880
Opportunity cost of additional materials for conversion		8,800
Opportunity cost of work in department X		
Labour	5,040	
Variable overhead	1,008	
Contribution forgone	12,600	
		18,648
Opportunity cost: sale of designs and specifications		4,500
Incremental costs:		
Variable production overheads in department Y		256
Fixed production overheads (additional supervision)		1,500
Minimum price		42,584

Question

Fixed price contract

DDD has decided to price its jobs as follows.

(a) It calculates the minimum price for the job using relevant costs.
(b) It adds $5,000 to cover fixed costs.
(c) It adds a 10% profit margin to the total cost.

A customer who has work to be performed in May says he will award the contract to DDD Ltd if its bid is reduced by $5,000.

Required

Assess whether the contract should be accepted.

Answer

Yes or no. Yes, if there is no other work available, because DDD will at least earn a contribution towards fixed costs of 10% of the minimum cost. But no, if by accepting this reduced price it would send a signal to other prospective customers that they too could negotiate such a large reduction.

In setting the price, management must decide **how much profit** it would consider reasonable on the job. A simple cost-plus approach can be used (for example, add 10% to the minimum price) but the company management should **consider the effect that the additional jobs will have** on the activities engaged in by the company and whether these activities will create additional unforeseen costs.

Sometimes an organisation may depart from its typical price-setting routine and 'low-ball' bid jobs. A **low-ball bid** may be a minimum price or it may even be below the minimum price. The rationale behind low-ball bids is to obtain the job so as to have the opportunity to introduce products or services to a particular market segment. This type of approach cannot be sustained in the long term.

7.5 Qualitative factors

When setting the price management must consider qualitative as well as quantitative issues.

(a) Will setting a low bid price cause the customer (or others) to feel that a **precedent** has been established for future prices?

(b) Will the contribution margin on a bid set low enough to acquire the job, **earn a sufficient amount to justify the additional burdens** placed on management or employees by the activity?

(c) How, if at all, will fixed price tenders **affect the organisation's normal sales**?

(d) If the job is taking place during a period of low business activity (off-season or during a recession), is management willing to take the business at a **lower contribution or profit margin simply to keep a valued workforce employed?**

7.6 Monitoring costs against fixed prices

Once the tender has been submitted and accepted, management must ensure that actual costs do not exceed the estimated costs, since for every cost overrun profit is eroded. **Actual costs must be monitored. Variances** between actual and estimated costs must be **highlighted and, if significant, investigated**. Control action may be required.

Exam focus point

In an exam you could be asked to prepare a report in which you have to calculate the lowest possible price that could be quoted, based upon costs analysis.

Chapter Roundup

- In practice in the modern world there are many more influences on pricing policy than the cost of a product or service.
- A typical product has a **life cycle** of four stages.
- The price that an organisation can charge for its products will be determined to a certain extent by the market (**perfect competition, monopoly, oligopoly**) in which it operates.
- **Competition** affects pricing policy.
- A **price leader** indicates to the other firms in the market what the price will be.
- **Market penetration pricing** and **market skimming pricing** are pricing policies for new products.
- Using **full cost plus pricing**, the sales price is determined by calculating the full cost of the product and adding a percentage mark-up for profit. The approach is unlikely to arrive at a profit-maximising price.
- **Marginal cost plus pricing (mark-up pricing)** involves adding a profit margin to the marginal cost of production or the marginal cost of sales.
- **ABC plus pricing** is a full cost plus pricing method in which the overheads included in the cost are derived using activity based costing instead of traditional absorption costing.
- The **opportunity cost approach to pricing** involves including the opportunity costs of the resources consumed in making and selling the item in the cost of the product and then adding a profit margin.
- **Fixed price tenders** involve an analysis of relevant costs. A margin is often added to the **minimum price.**

Quick Quiz

1. Name ten influences (apart from cost) on pricing policy.
2. What are the four stages of the product life cycle?
3. What is an oligopoly?
4. What price is first charged for a product under a policy of market penetration pricing?
5. What form of pricing is useful for businesses that carry out a large amount of jobbing or contract work?
6. Describe two drawbacks to marginal cost plus pricing?
7. What costs does a minimum price cover?
8. What qualitative issues should management consider when submitting a fixed price quotation.
9. Using activity based costing how are overheads allocated?
10. What type of market condition involves a large number of suppliers offering similar but not identical products?

    A Perfect competition
    B Monopoly
    C Monopolistic competition
    D Oligopoly

Answers to Quick Quiz

1 Price sensitivity, price perception, quality, intermediaries, competitors, suppliers, newness, incomes, product range, ethics, substitute products

2 Introduction, growth, maturity, decline

3 A market dominated by relatively few competitive companies.

4 Low prices

5 Full cost plus pricing

6 (a) Although the size of the mark-up can be varied in accordance with demand conditions, it does not ensure that sufficient attention is paid to demand conditions, competitors' prices and profit maximisation.

(b) It ignores fixed overheads in the pricing decision, but the price must be high enough to ensure that a profit is made after covering fixed costs. Pricing decisions cannot ignore fixed costs altogether.

7 (a) The incremental costs of producing and selling the item

(b) The opportunity costs of the resources consumed in making and selling the item

8 (a) Will setting a low bid price cause the customer (or others) to feel that a precedent has been established for future prices?

(b) Will the contribution margin on a bid set low enough to acquire the job, earn a sufficient amount to justify the additional burdens placed on management or employees by the activity?

(c) How, if at all, will fixed price tenders affect the organisation's normal sales?

(d) If the job is taking place during a period of low business activity (off-season or during a recession), is management willing to take the business at a lower contribution or profit margin simply to keep a valued workforce employed?

9 Using **activity based costing** overheads are allocated on the basis of cost drivers.

10 A

Now try the questions below from the Exam Question Bank

Number	Level	Marks	Time
Section A: Q25	MCQ	N/A	N/A
Section B: Q18	Examination	20	36 mins

17

Quality

Topic list
1 The importance of quality in a business environment
2 Total quality management
3 Quality assurance procedures
4 Costs of quality
5 The costs and benefits of quality processes

Study guide reference

		Syllabus reference
26 (h)	(i) Discuss the importance of quality in organisations	9
	(ii) Establish measures of quality in a specific situation	
28(a)	Total Quality Management	9
	(i) Explain in general terms the costs of quality (prevention, appraisal, internal failure and external failure)	
	(ii) Establish measures of the cost of quality in specific situations	
	(iii) Calculate the costs and benefits of quality initiatives	

1 The importance of quality in a business environment

The modern business environment is remarkably different from the business environment of a decade or so ago. One change has been the **switch in emphasis away from quantity towards quality**. Consumers and **customers** have become **more sophisticated and discerning** in their requirements. They are no longer satisfied with accepting the late delivery of the same old unreliable products from an organisation which does not appear to care for its customers. They want new products, superior on-time delivery performance and an immediate response to their requests. Many organisations are therefore turning to quality to help them to survive the competitive modern business environment. **By developing new products quickly and supplying them on time at a consistently high level of quality such organisations are likely to become the success stories of the new millennium.**

Question — Success stories

In your opinion, what organisations are likely to become the success stories of the new millennium? Why?

2 Total quality management

Exam focus point

In the June 2007 exam, candidates were asked to produce explanatory notes on two of three measures, for ten marks each. One of these was TQM.

FAST FORWARD

Total quality management (TQM) is the process of applying a zero defect philosophy to the management of all resources and relationships within an organisation as a means of developing and sustaining a culture of continuous improvement which focuses on meeting customer expectations.

Quality combines the following criteria.

(a) How well made a product is, or how well performed if it is a service.
(b) How well it serves its purpose.
(c) How it measures up against its rivals.

Implications of these criteria

(a) That quality is something that **requires care on the part of the provider**.
(b) That quality is largely **subjective** – it is in the eye of the beholder, the **customer**.

The process of the management of quality

(a) Establishing **standards of quality** for a product or service.

(b) Establishing **procedures or production methods** which ought to ensure that these required standards of quality are met in a suitably high proportion of cases.

(c) **Monitoring** actual quality.

(d) Taking **control action** when actual quality falls below standard.

Take the postal service as an example. The postal service might establish a standard that 90% of first class letters will be delivered on the day after they are posted, and 99% will be delivered within two days of posting.

(a) Procedures would have to be established for ensuring that these standards could be met (attending to such matters as frequency of collections, automated letter sorting, frequency of deliveries and number of staff employed).

(b) Actual performance could be monitored, perhaps by taking samples from time to time of letters that are posted and delivered.

(c) If the quality standard is not being achieved, the management of the postal service should take control action (employ more postmen or advertise the use of postcodes again).

Quality management becomes **total when it is applied to everything a business does**.

Key term

Total quality management (TQM) is the process of applying a zero defect philosophy to the management of all resources and relationships within the firm as a means of developing and sustaining a culture of continuous improvement which focuses on meeting customers' expectations.

2.1 Get it right, first time

One of the basic principles of TQM is that the **cost of preventing mistakes is less than the cost of correcting them** once they occur. The aim should therefore be **to get things right first time**.

Every mistake, delay and misunderstanding, directly costs an organisation money through **wasted time and effort**, including time taken in pacifying customers. The **lost potential for future sales because of poor customer service must also be taken into account.**

2.2 Continuous improvement

A second basic principle of TQM is dissatisfaction with the *status quo*: the belief that it is **always possible to improve** and so the aim should be to **'get it more right next time'**.

2.3 Total quality management (TQM) and performance measures

Performance measures for **TQM** must embrace every activity of the organisation.

Because TQM embraces every activity of a business, **performance measures should not be confined to the production process.** Measures should also cover the work of sales, distribution and administration departments, the efforts of external suppliers and the reaction of external customers.

In many cases the measure used will be non-financial ones. They may be divided into three types.

Type of measure	Example
Measuring incoming supplies	Percentage of defective items per delivery Number of returns per supplier
Monitoring work done as it proceeds	Number of rejects per production run Ratio of waste material to used material
Measuring customer satisfaction	Complaints per 10,000 units sold Number of claims under warranty

2.4 The requirements of quality

Mark Lee Inman listed 'eight requirements of quality' in his article in the May 1995 *ACCA Students' Newsletter.*

(a) Accept that the only thing that matters is the **customer**.

(b) Recognise the importance of the **customer-supplier relationship**, where customers include internal customers: passing sub-standard material down to another division is not satisfactory.

(c) Move away from relying on inspecting to a predetermined level of quality and move towards **preventing the cause of the defect in the first place**.

(d) Each employee or group of **employees must be personally responsible** for defect-free production or service in their domain.

(e) There must be a move away from 'acceptable' quality levels. **Any level of defects is unacceptable.**

(f) **All departments** should try obsessively to get things right first time: this applies to misdirected telephone calls and typing errors as much as to production.

(g) **Quality certification** programmes should be introduced.

(h) The **cost of poor quality** should be emphasised: good quality generates savings.

Question — **Quality**

Which of the above 'requirements' has your organisation met? Does your organisation offer a quality product or service? If not, why not?

3 Quality assurance procedures

FAST FORWARD

Quality assurance procedures should not be confined to the production process but must also cover the work of sales, distribution and administration departments, the efforts of external suppliers and the reaction of external customers.

Quality control happens at various stages in the process of designing a product or service.

– Product design stage
– Production engineering stage
– Administration

Quality control is aimed at preventing the manufacture of defective items or the provision of defective services. **Inspection** is a technique for identifying when defective items are being produced at an unacceptable level.

Because TQM embraces every activity of a business, quality assurance procedures **cannot be confined to the production process** but must also cover the work of sales, distribution and administration departments, the efforts of external suppliers, and the reaction of external customers.

3.1 Quality assurance of goods inwards

The quality of output depends on the quality of input materials, and so quality control should include **procedures for acceptance and inspection of goods inwards and measurement of rejects**. Each supplier can be given a 'rating' for the quality of the goods they tend to supply, and preference with purchase orders can be given to well-rated suppliers. This method is referred to as **'vendor rating'**.

Under a **quality assurance scheme** the supplier guarantees the quality of goods supplied. Usually agreed inspection procedures and quality control standards are worked out by customer and supplier, and checks are made to ensure that they are being adhered to. This places the **onus on the supplier to carry out the necessary quality checks**, or face cancellation of the contract.

Suppliers' quality assurance schemes are being used increasingly, particularly where extensive sub-contracting work is carried out, for example in the motor industries. One such scheme is **BS EN ISO 9000** certification. This is a nationally promoted standard, awarded after audit and inspection of a company's operations. It certifies that the company is operating to a structure of written policies and procedures which are designed to ensure that it can consistently deliver a product or service to meet customer requirements.

Question — Quality assurance

Does your organisation have BS EN ISO 9000 certification? Do its competitors? Would it be worthwhile for your organisation to gain certification? If not, why not?

3.2 Inspection of output

This will take place at key stages in the production process, and provides a continual check that the production process is under control. The aim of inspection is not to sort out the bad products from the good. The **aim is to satisfy management that the production process is meeting required quality standards.**

The **inspection of samples** rather than testing of all items will keep inspection costs down. The greater the confidence in the reliability of production methods and process control, the smaller the samples will be. The aim of TQM is for the process never to go out of control.

3.3 Monitoring customer reaction

If sub-standard items or services are supplied, customer **complaints ought to be encouraged and monitored**, with a view to identifying quality weaknesses in product design, production engineering, production standards or the quality of raw materials in use.

3.4 Employees and quality

When **new technology or new practices** are introduced, **training** in the new way of working is vital if quality is to be maintained or improved.

A **quality orientation** requires well trained **and motivated** staff.

(a) Workers can be **motivated** by a positive approach to quality: producing quality work is a tangible and worthwhile objective. Where responsibility for quality checking has been given to the worker, job satisfaction may be increased. This sign of trust may promote a more positive and responsible attitude.

(b) Competition to meet and beat quality standards should be encouraged and rewarded. Quality circles (see below) may be set up, perhaps with responsibility for implementing improvements which they identify.

3.4.1 Empowerment

Workers themselves are frequently the best source of information about how (or how not) to improve quality. Empowerment therefore has two key aspects.

(a) Allowing workers to have the **freedom to decide how to do** the necessary work, using the skills they possess and acquiring new skills as necessary to be an effective team member.

(b) Making those workers **personally responsible** for achieving production targets and for quality control.

3.4.2 Quality circles

A quality circle consists of a group of employees who meet regularly to discuss **problems of quality** and **quality control** in their area of work, and perhaps to suggest ways of improving quality.

3.5 Design for quality

A TQM environment aims to get it right first time, and this means that **quality, not faults, must be designed into the organisation's products and operations from the outset**.

Quality needs to be 'built in' at various stages in the process of designing a product or service.

(a) **Product design stage**

The product or service specifications should provide a balance between price and quality (of sales and delivery, as well as manufacture). Whether the product or service will be competitive is dependent on this balance.

Modern manufacturing businesses use Computer Aided Design (CAD) in product design. CAD helps identify the following.

(i) Opportunities to **reduce the number of parts** in a product overall. The fewer the number of parts, the less parts there are to go wrong.

(ii) Opportunities to **use parts or materials that are already used** by other products. The more common parts overall, the less chance there is of a product failing to meet quality standards due to a rogue supplier.

(iii) Opportunities to **improve physical characteristics** such as shape, size or weight or positioning of controls and so on to make the product more user-friendly.

(b) **Production engineering stage**

Production engineering is the **process of designing the methods for making a product** (or service) **to the design specification**. It sets out to make production methods as efficient as possible.

(c) **Administration**

Information systems should be designed to get the required information to the right person at the right time; **distribution systems** should be designed to get the right item to the right person at the right time; and so on.

3.6 Quality control and inspection

A distinction should be made between **quality control** and **inspection**.

(a) **Quality control** involves setting controls for the process of manufacture or service delivery. It is a aimed at **preventing the manufacture of defective items** or the provision of defective services.

(b) **Inspection** is concerned with looking at products made, supplies delivered and services provided, to establish whether they are up to specification. It is a technique of **identifying when defective items are being produced at an unacceptable level.** Inspection is usually carried out at three main points.

(i) Receiving inspection – for raw materials and purchased components;
(ii) Floor or process inspection for WIP; and
(iii) Final inspection or testing for finished goods.

4 Costs of quality

FAST FORWARD

The costs associated with a concern for quality are:

- **prevention costs**
- **appraisal costs**
- **internal failure costs**
- **external failure costs**

When we talk about quality-related costs you should remember that a concern for **good quality saves money** as the requirement for expensive reworkings, the time spent dealing with complaints and the time and money spent recruiting new customers should be reduced.

Key terms

Prevention costs represent the cost of any action taken to investigate, prevent or reduce defects and failures, such as trials and training programmes.

Appraisal costs are the costs of assessing quality achieved, such as testing equipment.

Internal failure costs are costs arising within the organisation of failure to achieve the quality specified. They are discovered before the product is delivered and include 'down time' and scrap costs.

External failure costs are costs arising outside the manufacturing organisation of failure to achieve specified quality (after transfer of ownership to the customer), such as warranty claims or complaint investigations.

Exam focus point

Quality-related costs in a particular environment is a very examinable topic. They were specifically examined in December 2008, but candidates were expected to be able to apply them to a manufacturing business.

Quality-related cost	Example
Prevention costs	Quality engineering Design/development of quality control equipment and inspection equipment Maintenance of quality control equipment and inspection equipment Administration of quality control Training in quality control
Appraisal costs	Acceptance testing Inspection of goods inwards Inspection costs of in-house processing Performance testing
Internal failure costs	Failure analysis Re-inspection costs Losses from failure of purchased items Losses due to lower selling prices for sub-quality goods Costs of reviewing product specifications after failures
External failure costs	Administration of customer complaints section Costs of customer service section Product liability costs Cost of repairing products returned from customers Cost of providing replacement items due to sub-standard products or marketing errors

4.1 Example: cost of poor quality

A manufacturer's inspection procedures indicate that one faulty item out of every 1,000 good items produced is sent to a customer. The management regards this as acceptable, as a replacement will be supplied free of charge. Unit sales are 10,000,000 per year, and each unit costs $20 to manufacture and makes a profit of $5. It is probable that every customer who buys a faulty product will return it, and will thenceforth buy a similar product from another company. The average customer buys two units a year. Marketing costs per new customer are $10 per year.

(a) What is your best estimate of the net cost of this policy for a year?
(b) What name(s) would you give to quality-related costs of this type?
(c) Could the situation be improved by incurring other types of quality-related cost?

4.2 Solution

(a) Presumed number of bad units delivered a year = $\frac{10,000,000}{1,000}$ = 10,000

	$
Cost of defects 10,000 × $20	200,000
Cost of free replacement 10,000 × $20	200,000
Manufacturing cost	400,000
Marketing costs for replacement customers $10 × 10,000	100,000
Gross cost of poor quality	500,000
Less income from original sale	250,000
Net cost of poor quality	250,000

Although the cost of the original defective item is recovered, this does not alter the fact that the company does not get it right first time. The company has still suffered the cost of the replacement and the cost of replacing the customer by marketing to new customers.

(b) The cost of replacements is an external failure cost; the cost of defects and the new marketing costs are internal failure costs.

(c) It appears that the manufacturer already incurs *appraisal* costs, since there are inspection procedures for goods about to be despatched. The reason(s) for the fault should be established (a further *internal failure* cost) and the extent of the problem should be more precisely ascertained (further *appraisal* costs), since it is not certain that all dissatisfied customers return their goods, though it is highly likely that their business is lost. Once this has been done it will be possible to decide whether, by spending more on *prevention,* the overall cost of poor quality can be reduced.

Question — **Cost of quality**

(a) What do you see as the costs of training for quality?
(b) What costs are associated with design for quality?

Answer

(a) The costs of training for quality include:

(i) the cost of the non-productive time taken to learn new attitudes and skills;
(ii) the cost of qualified instructors or training courses and materials, as necessary;
(iii) the cost of mistakes when learning on the job, including wasted materials and lost time.

(b) Design for quality incurs costs such as the cost of employing design staff and of obtaining and using monitoring equipment for process control, obtaining and using inspection equipment, and employing quality control staff.

5 The costs and benefits of quality processes

Glyn Thomas in *Accounting Technician* provides a useful summary of the benefits of TQM.

> 'It makes quality the central concern of the business. Too often, quality is either confused with addressing customer complaints with inevitably leads to it being viewed negatively, or is viewed as a direct measure of the product or service itself. Instead, all activities that are involved should be considered. Quality should be inherent in every facet of the business and not just a "bolt-on extra".
>
> A key factor of QA is that it can apply to all or parts of your business, so there may be scope for partially introducing it and then expanding at a later date. Applied to the whole business however, it will allow a holistic approach to quality throughout the whole company and have an effect from shop floor through to ordering, sales and management.
>
> It **reduces wastage and mistakes**, and therefore **leads to contracts being completed on time without unnecessary remedial work**. In addition, due to built-in fault-logging procedures, it is **unlikely that problems will be duplicated in the future**.'

The Royal Bank of Scotland (*Management Accounting*, September 1996) explained why they choose to gain BS EN ISO 9000 registration.

> 'The benefits are manifold and can be applied to all sectors of business. The primary benefits **enable the business to sustain a competitive** edge and include:
>
> (a) a quality-focused environment with the **customer at the centre** of all activities;
>
> (b) processes are defined and managed consistently. This in turn leads to a **more efficient and effective organisation through effective planning and control;**
>
> (c) our quality management system is designed for **continuous self- and team-based improvement.** This can be achieved with our corrective action system and the process of internal quality audits.'

Question

Quality processes

(a) What are the potential benefits of training for quality?
(b) What are the potential benefits of quality control?

Answer

(a) The potential benefits of training for quality include:

 (i) improved quality of output;
 (ii) improved productivity;
 (iii) greater jobs satisfaction and commitment on the part of employees.

(b) The benefits of quality control come from savings in quality-related costs, from improvements in customer relations and hopefully (because of the quality of the final product) increased sales revenue due to increased sales demand.

When changes are made to products and procedures in order to enhance quality, both **costs** and **benefits** are likely to arise. We have already discussed the classic 'costs of quality': prevention costs; appraisal costs; internal failure costs; and external failure costs. Each of these categories is likely to include, at least potentially, a wide range of individually identifiable costs. The great thing about these costs from the accounting point of view is that they are usually fairly easy to quantify.

The benefits of improvements to quality are often less easy to identify and quantify. Where costs of failure can be eliminated or reduced, the benefit is reasonably clear. Similarly, if new working patterns successfully eliminate checks and other quality control procedures, it should not be too difficult to calculate the savings achieved. However, it is likely that there will be many occasions where benefits are very hard to measure. For example, to quote the Royal Bank of Scotland report quoted above, just how would you go about quantifying the costs and benefits of 'a quality-focussed environment with the customer at the centre of all activities'?

Fortunately you are unlikely to be asked to solve such conundrums in your examination. You should, however, be aware of their existence and be prepared to mention them in any discussion of the costs and benefits of quality initiatives.

Chapter Roundup

- **Total quality management (TQM)** is the process of applying a zero defect philosophy to the management of all resources and relationships within an organisation as a means of developing and sustaining a culture of continuous improvement which focuses on meeting customer expectations.
- **Quality assurance procedures** should not be confined to the production process but must also cover the work of sales, distribution and administration departments, the efforts of external suppliers and the reaction of external customers.
- **Quality control** happens at various stages in the process of designing a product or service.
  - Product design stage
  - Production engineering stage
  - Administration
- **Quality control** is aimed at preventing the manufacture of defective items or the provision of defective services. **Inspection** is a technique for identifying when defective items are being produced at an unacceptable level.
- The costs associated with a concern for quality are:
  - **prevention costs**
  - **appraisal costs**
  - **internal failure costs**
  - **external failure costs**

Quick Quiz

1 What are the four aspects of the process of managing quality?

2 What are the two basic principles of TQM?

3 The aim of TQM is for a process to go out of control less than 10% of the time. True or false?

4 What are the three main points at which inspection is usually carried out?

5 What are internal failure costs?

6 In a TQM environment, which of the following would be classified as an external failure cost?

I Cost of repairing products returned from customer
II Cost of customer service section
III Product liability costs
IV Cost of providing replacement items due to marketing errors

A None of the above
B All of the above
C I only
D III only

Answers to Quick Quiz

1 (a) Establishing standards of quality for a product or service

(b) Establishing procedures or production methods which ought to ensure that these required standards of quality are met in a suitably high proportion of cases

(c) Monitoring actual quality

(d) Taking control action when actual quality falls below standard

2 (a) Get it right first time
(b) Get it more right next time

3 False. The aim of TQM is for a process never to go out of control.

4 (a) Receiving inspection for raw materials and purchased components
(b) Floor or process inspection for WIP
(c) Final inspection or testing for finished goods

5 The costs arising within the organisation of failure to achieve the quality specified

6 B

Now try the questions below from the Exam Question Bank

Number	Level	Marks	Time
Section A: Q26	MCQ	N/A	N/A
Section B: Q19	Examination	20	36 mins

18

Cost management

Topic list
1 Cost control and cost reduction
2 Planning for cost reduction
3 The scope of cost reduction campaigns
4 Methods of cost reduction: improving efficiency
5 Methods of cost reduction: material costs
6 Methods of cost reduction: labour costs
7 Other aspects of cost reduction
8 Value analysis
9 The scope of value analysis
10 Carrying out a value analysis
11 Life cycle costing
12 Target costing

Study guide reference

		Syllabus reference
28(b)	Cost reduction and value enhancement recommendations	8
	(i) Compare cost control and cost reduction	
	(ii) Describe and evaluate cost reduction methods	
	(iii) Describe and evaluate value analysis	
(c)	Life cycle costing	9
	(i) Describe life cycle costing	
	(ii) Discuss the benefits of life cycle costing in a specific situation	
(d)	Target costing	9
	(i) Describe target costing	
	(ii) Discuss the link between target costing and pricing	
	(iii) Discuss the role of value engineering in target costing	

Exam focus point

This chapter covers a key syllabus area. Key syllabus areas usually account for 80% or more of the marks available on the exam paper.

1 Cost control and cost reduction

FAST FORWARD

Cost reduction is a planned and positive approach to reducing expenditure.

Cost reduction should not be confused with cost control.

Key term

Cost control is concerned with regulating the costs of operating a business and keeping costs within acceptable limits.

The limits will usually be the standard cost or target cost limits set out in the formal operational plan or budget. If actual costs differ from planned costs by a significant amount, cost control action will be necessary.

You might like to think of cost control as an exercise in good housekeeping; the wasteful use of valuable resources is avoided and efficiency and cost consciousness are encouraged.

Cost reduction, in contrast, **starts with an assumption that current cost levels**, or planned cost levels, **are too high**, even though cost control might be good and efficiency levels high.

Key term

Cost reduction is a planned and positive approach to reducing expenditure.

Cost control action ought to lead to a reduction in excessive spending. A **cost reduction programme**, on the other hand, **aims to reduce expected cost levels** to below current budgeted or standard levels by changing methods of working.

Cost control aims to reduce costs to budget or standard level, cost reduction aims to reduce costs to below budget or standard level, as budgets and standards do not necessarily reflect the cost and conditions which minimise costs.

2 Planning for cost reduction

FAST FORWARD

Cost reduction measures ought to be planned programmes to reduce costs rather than crash programmes to cut spending levels.

Exam focus point

Eight marks could be earned in the December 2005 exam for suggesting four actions to reduce the cost of products made.

There are two basic **approaches to cost reduction**.

(a) **Crash programmes to cut spending levels**

If an organisation is having problems with its profitability or cash flow, the management might decide **on an immediate programme to reduce spending**. Some current projects might be abandoned, capital expenditures deferred, employees made redundant or new recruitment stopped. The absence of careful planning might make such crash programmes look like panic measures. Poorly-planned crash programmes to reduce costs could result in reductions in operational efficiency. For example, decisions by a company to reduce the size of its legal department or its internal audit section might cut staff costs in the short term but increase costs in the longer term.

(b) **Planned programmes to reduce costs**

Many companies tend to introduce crash programmes for cost reduction in times of crisis and ignore the problem completely in times of prosperity. A far better approach is to have **continual assessments** of the organisation's products, production methods, services, internal administration systems and so on.

Cost reduction exercises should therefore be **planned** campaigns to cut expenditure; they should **preferably be continuous** and long-term, so that short-term cost reductions are not soon reversed and 'forgotten'.

Difficulties introducing cost reduction programmes

(a) There may be **resistance from employees** to the pressure to reduce costs. They may feel threatened by the change. The purpose and scope of the campaign should be fully explained to employees to reduce uncertainty and (hopefully) resistance.

(b) The programme may be limited to a small area of the business with the result that **costs are reduced in one cost centre, only to reappear as an extra cost in another cost centre**.

(c) Cost reduction campaigns are **often introduced as a rushed, desperate measure** instead of a carefully organised, well thought-out exercise.

Cost reduction does not happen of its own accord. **Managers must make positive decisions to reduce costs.**

(a) A planned programme of cost reduction must begin with the assumption that some costs can be significantly reduced. The benefits of cost savings must be worthwhile, and should exceed the costs of achieving them.

(b) Areas for potential cost reduction should be investigated, and unnecessary costs identified.

(c) Cost reduction measures should be proposed, agreed, implemented and then monitored.

Question — Cost reduction

Before looking for ways in which costs can be reduced it is useful to consider the reasons why unnecessary costs occur. Can you think of any examples?

Answer

Here are some thoughts. You may well have come up with different ideas.

(a) Lack of information, for example about new materials, products or processes
(b) Lack of ideas
(c) Genuine but incorrect beliefs, for example the belief that quantities are too small to justify mass production techniques
(d) Changed circumstances, for example a failure to take advantage of better processes that are now available

3 The scope of cost reduction campaigns

The scope of a cost reduction **campaign should embrace the activities of the entire company.** In a manufacturing company this would span purchasing and distribution levels within the organisation from the shop floor upwards. Non-manufacturing industries and public sector organisations should equally look at **all areas** of their activities.

A cost reduction campaign should have a **long-term aim as well as short-term objectives.**

(a) In the short term only variable costs, for the most part, are susceptible to cost reduction efforts. Many fixed costs (for example rent) are not easily changed.
(b) Some fixed costs are avoidable in the short term (for example advertising or sales promotion expenditure). These are called *discretionary fixed costs.*
(c) In the long term most costs can be either reduced or avoided. This includes fixed cost as well as variable cost expenditure items.

4 Methods of cost reduction: improving efficiency

FAST FORWARD

One way of reducing costs is to improve the efficiency of materials usage, the productivity of labour or the efficiency of machinery or other equipment.

One way of reducing costs is to improve the efficiency of material usage, the productivity of labour, or the efficiency of machinery or other equipment. There are several ways in which this might be done.

Improved materials usage might be achieved by reducing levels of wastage, where wastage is currently high.

Question — Reducing wastage

How can wastage be reduced?

Answer

Here are some suggestions.

(a) Changing the specifications for cutting solid materials.
(b) Introducing new equipment that reduces wastage in processing or handling materials.
(c) Identifying poor quality output at an earlier stage in the operational processes.
(d) Using better quality materials. Even though more expensive, better quality materials might save costs because they are less likely to tear or might last longer.

Improving labour productivity

(a) Giving pay incentives for better productivity.
(b) Changing work methods to eliminate unnecessary procedures and make better use of labour time.

(c) Improving the methods for achieving co-operation between groups or departments.

(d) Setting more challenging standards of efficiency. Standards should be tight but achievable. If efficiency standards are too lax, it is likely that the work force will put in the minimum effort needed to achieve the required standard. Given the right motivation among the work force, more challenging standards will encourage greater effort.

(e) Introducing standards where they did not exist before.

Improving the efficiency of equipment usage

(a) Making better use of equipment resources. For example, if an office PC is only in use for 50% of its available time, it might be possible to put another application on to it, and so improve office productivity.

(b) Achieving a better balance between preventive maintenance and machine 'down-time' for repairs.

Question

Improving efficiency

A machine may be maintained at one of three levels, 1, 2 and 3. The monthly costs of the maintenance work, and the monthly hours of production lost, are as follows.

Level	*Maintenance cost*	*Hours lost (cost $350/hour)*
	$	
1	4,000	14
2	5,200	10
3	6,700	6

Required

Determine which level of maintenance should be chosen.

Answer

Level	*Maintenance cost*	*Cost of hours lost*	*Total cost*
	$	$	$
1	4,000	4,900	8,900
2	5,200	3,500	8,700
3	6,700	2,100	8,800

Level 2 should be chosen, to give the lowest total monthly cost.

Once improved standards of efficiency have been set, as a means of reducing costs, it is important that cost *control* should be applied by management.

5 Methods of cost reduction: material costs

Materials costs can be reduced by attacking the costs of wastage. Other ways of reducing materials costs are as follows.

(a) A company could **obtain lower prices for purchases** of materials and components. Bulk purchase discounts might be obtainable. Alternatively, a more cost-conscious approach to buying, with a system of putting all major purchase contracts out to tender, might help to reduce prices.

(b) A company could **improve stores control and cut stores costs**. You should be aware of the **concept of the economic ordering quantity**, which is the size of order that will minimise the combined costs of ordering items for inventory and stockholding costs. Stockholding costs might be reduced by dealing with problems of obsolescence, deterioration of items in store or theft.

(c) It might be possible to **use alternative materials**. Cheaper substitute materials might be available.

Standardisation of parts and components might offer enormous cost reduction potential for some manufacturing industries. Can you think why this might be the case?

Answer

(a) If a manufacturer has fewer types of components to manufacture, he will be able to increase the length of production runs, and so reduce production costs. Non-standard parts tend to be produced in small runs, and unit costs will be higher as a consequence.

(b) Standardisation helps to cut purchasing cost for the following reasons.

   (i) There are fewer items to buy and inventory. The company can purchase in bulk, and so perhaps obtain bulk purchase discounts.

   (ii) It may be possible to buy standard parts from more than one supplier, and so purchasing will be more competitive.

6 Methods of cost reduction: labour costs

FAST FORWARD

Work study is a means of raising the productivity of an operating unit by the reorganisation of work. There are two main parts to work study: **method study** and **work measurement**.

Organisation and methods (O & M) is a term for techniques, including method study and work measurement, that are used in examining clerical, administrative and management procedures in order to make improvements.

Methods of reducing labour costs	Detail
Improving efficiency or productivity	
Changing the methods of work	A work study or O & M programme (see below) might be set up to look for cost savings from improved work methods.
Replacing people with machinery	The substitution of labour by automatic equipment can reduce costs substantially.

6.1 Work study

Key terms

Work study is a means of raising the production efficiency (productivity) of an operating unit by the reorganisation of work. There are two main parts to work study: method study and work measurement.

Method study is the systematic recording and critical examination of existing and proposed ways of doing work in order to develop and apply easier and more effective methods, and reduce costs.

Work measurement involves establishing the time for a qualified worker to carry out a specified job at a specified level of performance

Main objectives of a work study

(a) The analysis, design and improvement of work systems, work places and work methods

(b) The establishment of **standards** enable an organisation to determine labour and equipment requirements, assess performance, plan operations, cost operations and products and calculate realistic wage levels.

(c) The development and application of job evaluation schemes based on job descriptions

(d) The specification of plant facilities, layout and space utilisation

(e) The assessment of the most profitable alternative combinations of personnel, materials and equipment
(f) The development of procedures for the planning and control of work and material usage
(g) The development of procedures for presenting information to management about work performance

The use of work study has grown rapidly over the past decade. Why?

(a) Tangible results are produced quickly
(b) No large capital outlay is required
(c) It is, in its basic form, simple and readily grasped in outline, by all
(d) The facts it produces can be used to increase efficiency throughout the organisation
(e) There is no work to which it cannot be applied

The obvious application of work study is in production where it was first developed, but the technique is now applied in such industries as building and construction, agriculture, transport, hospitals, national and local government and service industries.

Direct observation methods of work study involve observing jobs in practice, but **synthetic methods** are used to estimate the work of work study content of jobs without having to observe them. An example of a synthetic method is a 'tick sheet' that a customer service person ticks after each customer is served.

6.2 Organisation and methods (O & M)

Key term

> **Organisation and methods (O&M)** is a term for techniques, including method study and work measurement, that are used to examine clerical, administrative and management procedures in order to make improvements.

O & M is **primarily concerned with office work** and looks in particular at areas such as the following.

(a) Organisation
(b) Duties
(c) Staffing
(d) Office layout
(e) Methods of procedure and documentation and the design of forms
(f) Office mechanisation

Work study and O & M are perhaps associated in your mind with establishing standard times for work, but remember that the real aim is to decide the **most efficient methods** of getting work done, as well as establishing standard times for work done by this method. More efficient methods and tighter standards will improve efficiency and productivity, and so reduce costs.

Question — O&M

Do you think a work study or O&M programme would discover any ways in which the work methods you use could be improved so as to reduce costs?

7 Other aspects of cost reduction

7.1 Finance costs

Finance costs might offer some scope for savings.

(a) There might be a finance cost in taking credit from suppliers, in the form of an **opportunity cost of failing to take advantage of discounts for early payment** that suppliers might be offering.

(b) Similarly, a company should give some thought to the credit terms it offers to customers. Finance tied up in working capital involves a cost. (This might be the interest charges on a bank overdraft, the cost of borrowing long-term finance, or the opportunity cost of the capital tied up.) Costs might be reduced by **reassessing policies for offering early payment discounts** to credit customers.

(c) A company might wish to reassess its sources of finance. **Is it borrowing at the lowest obtainable rates**?

(d) Savings might be achievable from **improved foreign exchange dealings**, for companies involved in buying and selling abroad.

7.2 Rationalisation

Where organisations grow, especially by means of mergers and takeovers, there is a tendency for work to be duplicated in different parts of the organisation. Two or three factories, for example, might make the same product, when it would be more economical to concentrate all production in one factory. The **elimination of unnecessary duplication and the concentration of resources** is a form of rationalisation. The end result of such rationalisation is therefore to reduce costs through greater efficiency.

7.3 Expense items

Expense items, other than materials and labour, may be a significant part of total costs, and these too should be controlled. Examples are as follows.

(a) **Capital expenditure proposals should be carefully evaluated.**

(b) Management should **continually question** the need for any cost item.

(c) Consultancy organisations may be used to advise companies how to reduce specialised expense items such as information technology (IT).

7.4 Control over spending decisions

Cost reduction might be achieved if improved control over spending decisions is achieved. Often, costly spending decisions are taken by managers without proper consideration of the long-term cost.

Authority for different types of spending is usually given to management at various levels in the hierarchy, depending on the nature of the cost. Consider the following example.

Nature of cost	*Authorised by*	*Based on a cost of*	*Ten year cost*
Purchase of equipment for $200,000: ten year life	Board	$200,000	$200,000
Hire of office manager; salary $20,000	Director	$20,000	$200,000
Hire of two secretaries; wages $200 per week each	Office Manager	$200/week each	$200,000
Wage deal, 100 employees getting an extra $400 a year	?	$40,000	$400,000

In the example the hire of two secretaries is as costly as the purchase of the equipment, yet the level of control is lower. It would make more sense for the hire of the secretaries to require the higher level of authorisation. The hire of labour is in many ways a more permanent investment than buying equipment. Machinery can be sold, but it is much more difficult to reduce staffing levels.

Question — Spending decisions

Find out who takes the spending decisions in your organisation. Are office managers able to commit your organisation to potentially high levels over the long-term, as in the example above?

Exam focus point

In an exam you might be provided with a lot of information about an organisation and asked to suggest ways in which its costs could be reduced. Make sure that you consider all of the areas that we have covered in this chapter.

8 Value analysis

FAST FORWARD

Value analysis is a planned, scientific approach to cost reduction, which reviews the material composition of a product and the product's design so that modifications and improvements can be made which do not reduce the value of the product to the customer or user.

Value engineering is the application of similar techniques to new products.

Value analysis considers four aspects of value: **cost value, exchange value, use value** and **esteem value**.

An approach to cost reduction, which embraces many of the techniques already mentioned, is value analysis (VA) and value engineering.

Key term

Value analysis is a planned, scientific approach to cost reduction, which reviews the material composition of a product and the product's design so that modifications and improvements can be made which do not reduce the value of the product to the customer or the user.

The **value of the product must therefore be kept the same or else improved, at a reduced cost.** The administration of a value analysis exercise should perhaps be the responsibility of a cost reduction committee.

Key term

Value engineering is the application of value analysis techniques to new products, so that new products are designed and developed to a given value at minimum cost.

8.1 What is different about value analysis?

Two features of value analysis distinguish it from other approaches to cost reduction.

(a) It encourages innovation and a more radical outlook for ways of reducing costs.

(b) It recognises the various types of value which a product or service provides, analyses this value, and then seeks ways of improving or maintaining aspects of this value at a lower cost. Other techniques often ignores this value aspect.

Not every exercise in value analysis results in suggestions for radically different ways of making a product or service. But value analysis can result in radical ideas for change, because ideas for cost reduction are not constrained by the existing product design.

Conventional cost reduction techniques try to achieve the lowest production costs for a specific product design whereas value analysis recognises that the real goal should be the least-cost method of making a product that achieves its desired function, not the least-cost method of accomplishing a product design to a mandatory and detailed specification.

8.2 Value

Four aspects of 'value' should be considered.

Key terms

Cost value is the cost of producing and selling an item.
Exchange value is the market value of the product or service.
Use value is what the article does, the purposes it fulfils.
Esteem value is the prestige the customer attaches to the product.

(a) Value analysis seeks to reduce unit costs, and so cost value is the one aspect of value to be reduced.
(b) Value analysis attempts to provide the same (or a better) use value at the lowest cost. Use value therefore involves considerations of the performance and reliability of the product or service.
(c) Value analysis attempts to maintain or enhance the esteem value of a product at the lowest cost.

Question — Value analysis

Classify the following features of a product, using the types of value set out above.

(a) The product can be sold for $27.50.
(b) The product is available in six colours to suit customers' tastes.
(c) The product will last for at least ten years.

Answer

(a) Exchange value
(b) Esteem value
(c) Use value

Value analysis involves the **systematic investigation of every source of cost and technique** of production with the aim of cutting all unnecessary costs. An unnecessary cost is an additional cost incurred without adding use, exchange or esteem value to a product.

There might be a **conflict between reducing costs and maintaining the aesthetic value** (esteem value) of a product. Whereas a value analysis exercise should not result in a sacrifice of the product's function in order to cut costs, it might result in a product that is not as pleasing aesthetically. Where cost cutting and aesthetics are incompatible, there should **be a clear direction from senior management** about which is more important.

9 The scope of value analysis

FAST FORWARD

Value analysis concentrates on product design, components, material costs and production methods.

Any commercial organisation should be continually seeking lower costs, better products and higher profits. These can be achieved in any of the following ways.

(a) Cost elimination or cost prevention
(b) Cost reduction
(c) Improving product quality and so selling greater quantities at the same price as before
(d) Improving product quality and so being able to increase the sales price

Value analysis can achieve all four of these objectives.

Question

Benefits of VA

What are the other possible benefits of a VA programme?

Answer

(a) Improved product performance and product reliability
(b) Improved product quality
(c) An increased product life, in terms of both the marketable life of the product (for the company) and the usable life of each product unit (for the customer)
(d) Possibly, shorter delivery 'lead times' to customers because of a shorter production cycle
(e) The increased use of standardisation (standard parts and components) which contributes to lower costs for the customer
(f) A more economic use of scarce resources
(g) Encouraging employees to show innovation and creative ideas

Three areas of special importance are as follows.

Area	Method
Product design	At the **design stage** value analysis is called **value engineering**. The designer should be cost conscious and avoid unnecessary complications. **Simple product design** can avoid production and quality control problems, thereby resulting in lower costs.
Components and material costs	The purchasing department should beware of lapsing into habit with routine buying decisions. Buyers ought to be **fully aware** of technology changes, and significant changes in material prices that new technology creates. The purchasing department has a crucial role to play in reducing costs and improving value by obtaining the desired quality materials at the lowest possible price.
Production methods	These ought to be reviewed continually, on a product-by-product basis, especially with changing technology.

10 Carrying out a value analysis

FAST FORWARD

The steps in a value analysis study are as follows.

- Select a product or service for investigation.
- Obtain and record information about it.
- Evaluate the product.
- Consider alternatives.
- Select the least-cost alternative.
- Make a recommendation.
- If accepted, implement the recommendation.
- After a period, evaluate the outcome and measure the cost savings.

Typical considerations in value analysis

(a) **Can a cheaper substitute material be found** which is as good, if not better, than the material currently used?
(b) **Can unnecessary weight or embellishments be removed** without reducing the product's desirability?

(c) **Is it possible to use standardised components** thereby reducing the variety of units used and produced? Variety reduction through standardisation facilitates longer production runs at lower unit costs.

(d) **Is it possible to reduce the number of components,** for example could a product be assembled safely with a smaller number of screws?

The origins of value analysis were in the engineering industry, but its principles and applications spread much wider. **Value analysis can be applied to services, or aspects of office work, or to management information systems** (for example the value of information, reports and so on).

10.1 The steps in value analysis

A value analysis study should be carried out by a team of experts, preferably with **varying backgrounds**, which blends experience, skill and imagination. A team will typically consist of three to seven members who collectively possess the necessary skills to examine the product, service or operation.

Value analysis should be an **inter-disciplinary exercise**, and ought to involve a management accountant but also managers concerned with method study and work measurement, estimating, engineering, planning, production, purchasing and marketing. Other experts might be called on to contribute to the team's work.

Steps in value analysis

Step 1 **Selecting a product or service for study**. The product selected should be one which accounts for a high proportion of the organisation's costs, since the **greatest cost savings should be obtainable from high cost areas**. The choice should also take into account the expected future life of the product and the stage of its 'life cycle' that it has reached. A product reaching the end of its marketable life is unlikely to offer scope for substantial savings, unless cost reduction measures would also extend the product's life.

Step 2 **Obtaining and recording information**. The questions to be asked include: What is the product or service supposed to do? Does it succeed? What are the costs of the product or service? Are there alternative ways of making or providing it? What do these alternatives cost?

Step 3 **Analysing the information and evaluating the product**. Each aspect of the product or service. Any cost reductions should be achieved without the loss of use or esteem value. (Or at least, cost savings must exceed any loss in value suffered.) The type of questions to be asked and answered in the analysis stage are as follows.

(a) Are all the parts necessary?
(b) Can the parts be obtained or made at a lower cost?
(c) Can standardised parts be used?
(d) Are all the features of the product or service necessary?
(e) Can any of the features be incorporated at a lower cost?
(f) Does the value provided by each feature justify its cost?
(g) Can the product be made or the service performed at a lower cost?

Step 4 **Considering alternatives**. From the analysis, a variety of options can be devised. This is the **'new ideas' stage** of the study, and alternative options would mix ideas for eliminating unnecessary parts or features, combining several features into one, standardising certain components or features, or introducing new methods of operation or new sources of supply (for example external purchase of components instead of in-house manufacture). New advances in technology might be considered, and a creative approach should underlie this phase of the exercise.

Step 5 **Selection of the least cost alternative**. The evaluation of each alternative should be recorded, and costs (and other aspects of value) compared.

Step 6 **Recommendation**. The **preferred alternative** should then be recommended to the decision makers for approval. The VA team itself will not have the authority to decide whether or not a cost reduction proposal should be implemented.

Step 7 **Implementation and follow-up**. Once a value analysis proposal is approved and accepted, its **implementation must be properly planned and co-ordinated**. The VA team should review the implementation and, where appropriate, improve the new product or method in the light of practical experience.

To be successful, **value analysis programmes must have the full backing of senior management**. Management must therefore do the following.

(a) Give the VA programme their visible **support**, for example acting as a member of a VA steering group, attending VA training sessions and so on.
(b) **Establish goals** for the programme to achieve.
(c) **Select the personnel** for the value analysis team and establish a VA 'organisation' within the company.
(d) Give the VA programme a **sufficient budget** to carry out its work properly.
(e) Insist on a **continuing audit** of the achievements of the VA programme.
(f) Give **rewards** to individuals and groups for outstanding achievements.

11 Life cycle costing

FAST FORWARD

Life cycle costing tracks and accumulates costs and revenues attributable to each product over the entire product life cycle.

A **product life cycle** can be divided into four phases.

–	Introduction	–	Maturity
–	Growth	–	Decline

11.1 What are life cycle costs?

A product's life cycle costs are incurred **from its design stage through development to market launch, production and sales, and finally to its eventual withdrawal from the market**. The component elements of a product's cost over its life cycle could therefore include the following.

(a) **Research & development costs**
(b) The **cost of purchasing any technical data** required
(c) Retirement and disposal costs
(d) **Training costs** (including initial operator training and skills updating)
(e) **Production costs**
(f) **Distribution costs**
(g) **Marketing costs**
(h) **Inventory costs** (holding spare parts, warehousing and so on)
(i) **Costs**

Life cycle costs can apply to services, customers and projects as well as to physical products.

Traditional cost accumulation systems are based on the financial accounting year and tend to dissect a product's life cycle into a series of 12-month periods. This means that traditional management accounting systems **do not accumulate costs over a product's entire life cycle** and **do not** therefore **assess a product's profitability over its entire life.** Instead they do it on a periodic basis.

Life cycle costing, on the other hand, **tracks and accumulates actual costs and revenues** attributable to each product **over the entire product life cycle.** Hence the total profitability of any given product can be determined.

Exam focus point

Life cycle costing was examined in December 2004, in the light of its particular application to a company scenario. The examiner noted that only 'a minority recognised that in competitive markets with short product life-cycles managers need to know the full cost of products over their entire cycle'.

Key term

Life cycle costing is the accumulation of costs over a product's entire life.

11.2 The product life cycle

Every product goes through a life cycle as covered earlier in the text.

(a) **Introduction**. The product is introduced to the market. Potential customers will be unaware of the product or service, and the organisation may have to spend further on advertising to bring the product or service to the attention of the market.

(b) **Growth**. The product gains a bigger market as demand builds up. Sales revenues increase and the product begins to make a profit.

(c) **Maturity**. Eventually, the growth in demand for the product will slow down and it will enter a period of relative maturity. It will continue to be profitable. The product may be modified or improved, as a means of sustaining its demand.

(d) **Decline**. At some stage, the market will have bought enough of the product and it will therefore reach 'saturation point'. Demand will start to fall. Eventually it will become a loss-maker and this is the time when the organisation should decide to stop selling the product or service.

The level of sales and profits earned over a life cycle can be illustrated diagrammatically as follows.

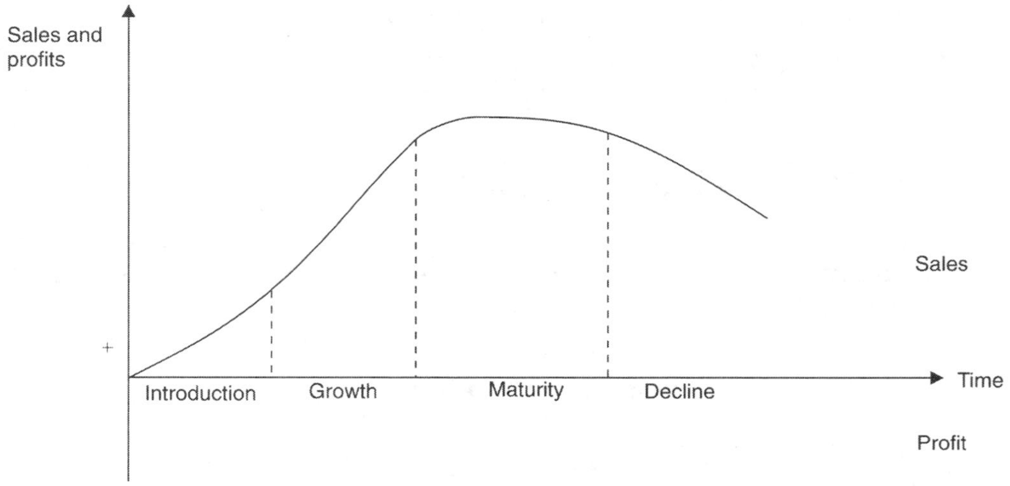

The horizontal axis measures the duration of **the life cycle**, which **can last** from, say, **18 months to several hundred years**. Children's crazes or fad products have very short lives while some products, such as binoculars (invented in the eighteenth century) can last a very long time.

11.3 Problems with traditional cost accumulation systems

Traditional cost accumulation systems do not tend to relate **research and development costs** to the products that caused them. Instead they **write off** these costs on an annual basis **against** the **revenue generated by existing products**. This makes the existing products seem **less profitable** than they really are. If research and development costs are not related to the causal product the true profitability of that product cannot be assessed.

Traditional cost accumulation systems usually **total all non-production costs** and record them as a **period expense**.

11.4 The value of life cycle costing

With life cycle costing, non-production costs are traced to individual products over complete life cycles.

(a) The total of these costs for each individual product can therefore be reported and compared with revenues generated in the future.

(b) The visibility of such costs is increased.

(c) **Individual product profitability can be more fully understood** by attributing *all* costs to products.

(d) As a consequence, **more accurate feedback information** is available on the organisation's success or failure in developing new products. In today's competitive environment, where the ability to produce new and updated versions of products is paramount to the survival of an organisation, this information is vital.

12 Target costing

FAST FORWARD

Target costing involves setting a target cost by subtracting a desired profit margin from a competitive market price.

Exam focus point

Three marks were available to candidates at the June 2005 sitting for defining target costing and explaining how it could be used in a particular scenario.

To compete effectively in today's competitive market, organisations must continually redesign their products with the result that **product life cycles** have become much **shorter.** The **planning, development and design stage** of a product is therefore **critical** to an organisation's cost management process. Considering possible **cost reductions at this stage** of a product's life cycle (rather than during the production process) is now one of the most **important** issues facing management accountants in industry.

Here are some examples of **decisions made at the design stage** which directly **impact on the cost of a product.**

(a) The number of different components
(b) Whether the components are standard or not
(c) The ease of changing over tools

Japanese companies have developed **target costing** as a **response to the problem of controlling and reducing costs over the product life cycle.**

Key terms

Target costing involves setting a target cost by subtracting a desired profit margin from a competitive market price.

Target cost is an estimate of a product cost which is determined by subtracting a desired profit margin from a competitive market price. This target cost may be less than the planned initial product cost but it is expected to be achieved by the time the product reaches the maturity stage of the product life cycle.

Target costing has its **greatest impact at the design stage** because a large percentage of a product's **life cycle costs are determined by decisions made early in its life cycle.**

The technique requires managers to **change** the way they think about the **relationship between cost, price and profit**.

(a) **Traditionally** the approach is to **develop a product**, **determine the production cost** of that product, **set a selling price**, with a **resulting profit** or loss.

(b) The **target costing approach** is to **develop a product**, **determine the market selling price and desired profit margin**, with a **resulting cost** which must be achieved.

Do you remember looking at cost plus pricing in Chapter 16? Cost plus pricing is a 'bottom up' approach where you start with full production costs and add a margin to arrive at a selling price. However it does not take account of market conditions.

In contrast, target costing is a 'top down' method and starts with a price that takes account of market conditions and deducts a desired margin to arrive at a target cost.

In 'Product costing/pricing strategy' (*ACCA Students Newsletter*, August 1999), a useful summary of the **steps in the implementation of the target costing process** was provided.

Step 1 Determine a product specification of which an adequate sales volume is estimated.

Step 2 Set a selling price at which the organisation will be able to achieve a desired market share.

Step 3 Estimate the required profit based on return on sales or return on investment.

Step 4 Calculate the target cost = target selling price – target profit.

Step 5 Compile an estimated cost for the product based on the anticipated design specification and current cost levels.

Step 6 Calculate cost gap = estimated cost – target cost.

Step 7 Make efforts to close the gap. This is more likely to be successful if efforts are made to 'design out' costs prior to production, rather than to 'control out' costs during the production phase.

Step 8 Negotiate with the customer before making the decision about whether to go ahead with the project.

When a product is first manufactured, its target cost may well be much lower than its currently-attainable cost, which is determined by current technology and processes. Management can then set **benchmarks for improvement** towards the target costs, by improving technologies and processes. Various techniques can be employed.

(a) Reducing the **number of components**
(b) Using **standard components** wherever possible
(c) **Training** staff in more efficient techniques
(d) Acquiring new, more efficient **technology**
(e) Cutting out **non-value-added activities** (identified using **activity analysis** etc)
(f) Using **different materials**
(g) Using **cheaper staff**

These techniques are known as **value-engineering**.

Even if the product can be produced within the target cost the story does not end there. Target costing can be applied throughout the entire life cycle. **Once the product goes into production target costs will therefore gradually be reduced**. These reductions will be **incorporated into the budgeting process**. This means that **cost savings** must be **actively sought** and made **continuously** over the life of the product.

Chapter Roundup

- **Cost reduction** is a planned and positive approach to reducing expenditure.
- Cost reduction measures ought to be planned programmes to reduce costs rather than crash programmes to cut spending levels.
- One way of reducing costs is to improve the efficiency of materials usage, the productivity of labour or the efficiency of machinery or other equipment.
- **Work study** is a means of raising the productivity of an operating unit by the reorganisation of work. There are two main parts to work study: **method study** and **work measurement**.
- **Organisation and methods (O & M)** is a term for techniques, including method study and work measurement, that are used in examining clerical, administrative and management procedures in order to make improvements.
- **Value analysis** is a planned, scientific approach to cost reduction, which reviews the material composition of a product and the product's design so that modifications and improvements can be made which do not reduce the value of the product to the customer or user.
- **Value engineering** is the application of similar techniques to new products.
- **Value analysis** considers four aspects of value: **cost value, exchange value, use value** and **esteem value**.
- Value analysis concentrates on product design, components, material costs and production methods.
- The steps in a value analysis study are as follows.
  - Select a product or service for investigation.
  - Obtain and record information about it.
  - Evaluate the product.
  - Consider alternatives.
  - Select the least-cost alternative.
  - Make a recommendation.
  - If accepted, implement the recommendation.
  - After a period, evaluate the outcome and measure the cost savings.
- **Life cycle costing** tracks and accumulates costs and revenues attributable to each product over the entire product life cycle.
- A **product life cycle** can be divided into four phases.
  - Introduction
  - Growth
  - Maturity
  - Decline
- **Target costing** involves setting a target cost by subtracting a desired profit margin from a competitive market price.

Quick Quiz

1 What are the main difficulties of introducing cost reduction programmes?

2 Suggest five ways in which labour productivity might be improved.

3 What is method study?

4 In which areas of office work might an O & M study be applied?

5 Define the four aspects of value to be considered in a value analysis exercise.

6 *Match the following costs to the appropriate life cycle cost classification.*

Costs	*Classifications*
Design	Inventory costs
Energy costs	Acquisition costs
Warehousing	Maintenance costs
Transportation	Operation costs
Customer service	Product distribution costs

7 Life cycle costing is the profiling of cost over a product's production life.

☐ True

☐ False

8 *Fill in the blanks using words from the list (a) to (h).*

Target cost = ... minus ....

Cost gap = ... minus ....

(a) target cost
(b) cost gap
(c) budgeted selling price
(d) production cost
(e) target selling price
(f) estimated cost
(g) estimated selling price
(h) target profit

9 *Choose the correct words from those highlighted*

Value **engineering/analysis** is cost avoidance or cost prevention before production whereas value **engineering/analysis** is cost reduction during production.

10 When are the bulk of a product's lifecycle costs normally determined?

A At the design/development stage
B When the product is introduced to the market
C When the product is in its growth stage
D On disposal

Answers to Quick Quiz

1 The major difficulties with introducing cost reduction programmes are as follows.

(a) There may be resistance from employees to the pressure to reduce costs, usually because the nature and purpose of the campaign has not been properly explained to them, and because they feel threatened by the change.

(b) The programme may be limited to a small area of the business with the result that costs are reduced in one cost centre, only to reappear as an extra cost in another cost centre.

(c) Cost reduction campaigns are often introduced as a rushed, desperate measure instead of a carefully organised, well thought-out exercise.

2 Labour productivity might be improved by the following methods.

(a) Giving pay incentives for better productivity.

(b) Changing work methods to eliminate unnecessary procedures and make better use of labour time.

(c) Improving the methods for achieving co-operation between groups or departments.

(d) Setting more challenging standards of efficiency to aim for. Given the right motivation among the work force, more challenging standards will encourage greater effort.

(e) Introducing standards where they did not exist before.

3 Method study is the systematic recording and critical examination of existing and proposed ways of doing work in order to develop and apply easier and more effective methods, and reduce costs.

4 (a) Organisation
(b) Duties
(c) Staffing
(d) Office layout
(e) Methods of procedure and documentation and the design of forms
(f) Office mechanisation

5 (a) *Cost value* is the cost of producing and selling an item.
(b) *Exchange value* is the market value of the product or service.
(c) *Use value* is what the article does, the purposes it fulfils.
(d) *Esteem value* is the prestige the customer attaches to the product.

6

Cost	*Classification*
Design	Acquisition costs
Energy costs	Operation costs
Warehousing	Inventory costs
Transportation	Product distribution costs
Customer service	Maintenance costs

7 False. It also looks at development costs and so on which are incurred prior to production, and any dismantling costs, which are incurred once production ceases.

8 Target cost = estimated selling price minus target profit
Cost gap = estimated cost – target cost

9 **Value engineering**, **value analysis**

10 A

Now try the questions below from the Exam Question Bank

Number	Level	Marks	Time
Section A: Q27	MCQ	N/A	N/A
Section B: Q20	Examination	20	36 mins

Exam question and answer bank

Examiner's Sample Multiple Choice Questions

1 Four years ago material X cost \$5 per kg and the price index most appropriate to the cost of material X stood at 150.

The same index now stands at 430.

What is the best estimate of the current cost of material X per kg?

A \$1.74 (\$5 × 150 ÷ 430)
B \$9.33 (\$5 × (430 – 150) ÷ 150
C \$14.33 (\$5 × 430 ÷ 150)
D \$21.50 (\$5 × 430 ÷ 100) **(2 marks)**

2 Which of the following is the best description of a rolling budget?

A A budget that is continuously updated by adding a further accounting period when the earliest accounting period has expired.

B A budget that is adjusted for known changes in volume during the accounting period.

C A budget that, by recognising cost behaviour patterns, is designed to change as volume of activity changes.

D A budget that is prepared by higher levels of management and then communicated to lower levels of management.

(2 marks)

3 In the last year a division's controllable return on investment was 25% and its controllable profit was \$80,000. The cost of finance appropriate to the division was 18% per annum.

What was the division's controllable residual income in the last year?

A \$5,600 \$80,000 × (0.25 – 0.18)
B \$22,400 \$80,000 – (\$80,000 ÷ 0.25 × 0.18)
C \$74,400 \$80,000 – (\$80,000 × (0.25 – 0.18)
D \$76,400 \$80,000 – (\$80,000 × 0.25 × 0.18) **(2 marks)**

4 The standard raw material cost for a unit of production is 2 kg at \$4.00 per kg. Purchases for a period were 13,000 kg at an actual cost of \$4.50 per kg. Raw material inventory, which are valued at standard cost, increased by \$8,000 in the period. Budgeted production for the period was 6,000 units but actual production was only 5,000 units.

What was the raw material usage variance for the period?

A \$20,000 Adverse (5,000 × 2kg – (13,000kg + \$8,000 ÷ \$4.00/kg) × \$4.00
B \$4,000 Adverse (5,000 × 2kg – (13,000kg – \$8,000 ÷ \$4.00/kg) × \$4.00
C \$4,000 Favourable (6,000 × 2kg – (13,000kg – \$8,000 ÷ \$4.00/kg) × \$4.00
D \$12,000 Favourable (13,000kg – 5,000 × 2kg) × \$4.00 **(2 marks)**

5 A government body uses measures based upon the 'three Es' to the measure value for money generated by a publicly funded hospital. It considers the most important performance measure to be 'cost per successfully treated patient'.

Which of the three E's best describes the above measure?

A Economy (A measure of cost related to input)
B Effectiveness (A measure of output related to objectives)
C Efficiency (A measure of output related to input)
D Externality (Not one of the three Es) **(2 marks)**

6 The following observations have been made of total overhead cost.

Output level (units)	5,000	10,000
Total overhead cost ($)	14,000	27,000

The variable element of total overhead cost is known to increase by $1 per unit at output levels above 7,000 units.

What is the variable element of total overhead cost at an output level of 5,000 units?

A $2.00 per unit ($27,000 – $14,000 – 3,000 units × $1) ÷ (10,000 units – 5,000 units)
B $2.60 per unit ($27,000 – $14,000) ÷ (10,000 units – 5,000 units)
C $3.20 per unit ($27,000 – $14,000 + 3,000 units × $1) ÷ (10,000 units – 5,000 units)
D $3.60 per unit ($27,000 – $14,000) ÷ (10,000 units – 5,000 units) + $1 **(2 marks)**

7 The following statements have been made about linear regression analysis:

(i) It provides more accurate estimates than the high low technique.
(ii) It can only be used to estimate variable cost.
(iii) It assumes that cost behaviour is linear.
(iv) It only takes into account two observations of cost and output.

Which of the following statements about the use of linear regression analysis in cost estimation are true?

A (i) and (ii)
B (i) and (iii)
C (ii) and (iii)
D (iii) and (iv) **(2 marks)**

8 A manufacturing company always carries finished goods inventory equal to 20% of the next month's budgeted sales.

Sales for the current month are 2,000 units and are budgeted to be 20% higher next month.

How many units will be produced in the current month?

A 2,080
B 1,920 (400 + 2000 – 480)
C 2,000 (no adjustment)
D 2400 (2000 + 400) **(2 marks)**

9 A company charges a price of $10 per unit in order to earn a 20% MARGIN on sales. It plans to change its price so as to earn a 30% MARK-UP on cost.

What will be the percentage change in price?

A 4.0 % increase ($10 × 80% × 130% – $10) ÷ $10 × 100%
B 10.0 % increase (30% – 20%)
C 50.0% increase (30 – 20) ÷ 20 × 100%
D 62.5 % increase ($10 ÷ 80% × 130% – $10) ÷ $10 × 100% **(2 marks)**

10 Which of the following are components of a time series analysis?

(i) Trend
(ii) Seasonal variation
(iii) Cyclical variation

A (i) and (ii) only
B (i) and (iii) only
C (ii) and (iii) only
D (i), (ii) and (iii) **(2 marks)**

Section A: Multiple Choice Questions

1 The sales manager has prepared a manpower plan to ensure that sales quotas for the forthcoming year are achieved. This is an example of:

A Strategic planning
B Tactical planning
C Operational planning
D Corporate planning

2 Having attended a course on activity based costing (ABC) you decide to experiment by applying the principles of ABC to the four products currently made and sold by your company. Details of the four products and relevant information are given below for one period.

Product	*P1*	*P2*	*P3*	*P4*
Output in units	120	100	80	120
Costs per unit:	$	$	$	$
Direct material	40	50	30	60
Direct labour	28	21	14	21

The four products are similar and are usually produced in production runs of 20 units.

The total of the production overhead for the period has been analysed as follows.

	$
Set up costs	5,250
Stores receiving	3,600
Inspection/quality control	2,100
Materials handling and despatch	4,620

You have ascertained that the following 'cost drivers' are to be used for the costs shown.

Cost	Cost driver
Set up costs	Number of production runs
Stores receiving	Requisitions raised
Inspection/quality control	Number of production runs
Materials handling and despatch	Orders executed

The number of requisitions raised on the stores was 20 for each product and the number of orders executed was 42, each order being for a batch of 10 of a product.

Required

(a) The total costs for each product using activity based costing are:

(i) $ ______ for P1

(ii) $ ______ for P2

(iii) $ ______ for P3

(iv) $ ______ for P4

(b) The unit costs are:

(i) $ ______ for P1

(ii) $ ______ for P2

(iii) $ ______ for P3

(iv) $ ______ for P4

3 Factory overheads can be absorbed by which of the following methods?

(i) Direct labour hours
(ii) Machine hours
(iii) As a % of prime cost
(iv) $x per unit

A (i), (ii), (iii) or (iv)
B (i) or (ii) only
C (i), (ii) or (iii) only
D (ii), (iii) or (iv) only

4 Which of the following would be the most appropriate basis for apportioning machinery insurance costs to cost centres within a factory?

A The number of machines in each cost centre
B The floor area occupied by the machinery in each cost centre
C The value of the machinery in each cost centre
D The operating hours of the machinery in each cost centre

5 Identify which of the following relate to either

A = Absorption costing
M = Marginal costing

		A or M
(a)	Closing inventories valued at marginal production cost	
(b)	Closing inventories valued at full production cost	
(c)	Cost of sales include some fixed overhead incurred in previous period in opening inventory values	
(d)	Fixed costs are charged in full against profit for the period	

6 A company producing a single product reported the following profits.

Basis	**Profit**
Marginal costing	$100,000
Absorption costing	$110,000

Fixed overheads per unit for the period were $5.

Which of the following statements are true?

(i) Closing inventory levels are 2,000 units higher than opening inventory
(ii) Opening inventory levels are 2,000 units higher than closing inventory
(iii) It is impossible to say whether inventory levels have changed
(iv) More units were produced than sold during the period

A (iv) only
B (ii) and (iv)
C (iii) only
D (i) and (iv)

7 Match up the following services with their typical cost units

Service		**Cost unit**
Hotels		Patient-day
Education	?	Meal served
Hospitals		Full-time student
Catering organisations		Occupied bed-night

8 A company which makes rechargeable batteries selects some of the batteries for examination. The procedure used chooses two random numbers, say n and m. Starting at the nth battery, every battery at an interval of m is then chosen for examination.

This type of sampling is known as:

A Stratified
B Systematic
C Random
D Multistage

The following data relates to question 9

The distribution of average weekly wages paid to direct labour employees at the factory of Parrots Co is as follows.

Weekly average wage $	*Number of employees*	*Frequency density*	*Cumulative frequency*
51 and < 61	13	A	
61 and < 66	12	B	
66 and < 71	16	C	
71 and < 76	21		E
76 and < 81	25		F
81 and < 86	20		
86 and < 91	14		
91 and < 101	9	D	G

9 Using a standard interval size of $5, calculate the frequency densities corresponding to the letters A, B, C and D.

A = [ ]

B = [ ]

C = [ ]

D = [ ]

10 Which of the following statements about a Paasche **price** index are true?

(i) It is a type of weighted aggregate index
(ii) It uses quantities consumed in the current period as weights
(iii) It uses prices from the current period as weights
(iv) It becomes out of date more quickly than the Laspeyre index

A (i) and (ii)
B (i) and (iii)
C (ii) and (iv)
D (iii) and (iv)

11 In a time series analysis, the multiplicative model is used to forecast sales and the following seasonal variations apply.

Quarter	*1*	*2*	*3*	*4*
Seasonal variation	0.45	1.22	1.31	?

The seasonal variation for quarter 4 is

A 0.02
B 1.02
C 1.98
D 2.98

12 What is another name for corporate planning?

A Strategic planning
B Organisational planning
C Cost centre planning
D Long-term planning

13 Which of the following is unlikely to be contained with a budget manual?

A Organisational structures
B Objectives of the budgetary process
C Selling overhead budget
D Administrative details of budget preparation

14 Fill in the blanks with the word 'fixed' or the word 'flexible'.

(a) At the planning stage, a .... budget can show what the effects would be if the actual outcome differs from the prediction.

(b) At the end of each period, actual results may be compared with the relevant activity level in the .... budget as a control procedure.

(c) Master budgets are .... budgets.

15 Standard costing provides which of the following? Tick all that apply.

(a)	Targets and measures of performance	☐
(b)	Information for budgeting	☐
(c)	Simplification of inventory control systems	☐
(d)	Actual future costs	☐

16 SG Co has extracted the following details from the standard cost card of one of its products.

Direct labour 3.5 hours @ $9.20 per hour

During period 4, SG Co produced 1,600 units of product and incurred direct labour cost of $55,100 for 5,800 hours.

The direct labour rate and efficiency variances for period 4 were

	Rate	*Efficiency*
	$	$
A	1,740 adverse	1,840 adverse
B	1,740 adverse	1,900 adverse
C	1,740 adverse	1,840 favourable
D	1,740 favourable	1,840 favourable

17 BA Co has budgeted to make and sell 4,200 units of product X during the period.

The standard variable overhead cost per unit is $4.

During the period covered by the budget, the actual results were:

Production and sales of X	5,000 units
Variable overhead incurred	$17,500

The variable overhead total variance for the period was

A $2,500 favourable
B $700 favourable
C $2,500 adverse
D $700 adverse

18 Which of the following would help to explain a favourable sales volume variance?

(i) Increased competitor activity led to a reduction in the number of units sold.

(ii) Customers were given discounts at a higher level than standard in order to encourage increased sales.

(iii) The unit cost of production was lower than standard and selling prices were maintained at the standard level, so that a higher contribution was achieved per unit sold.

(iv) Higher quality material supplies led to improvements in the quality of the final output, which customers found attractive.

A (i), (ii) and (iv) only
B (ii), (iii) and (iv) only
C (ii) and (iv) only
D (ii) only

19 *Choose the correct terms from those highlighted.*

ROCE = **profit margin/EBITDA/EPS ×/÷ ROI/RI/asset turnover**

20 The following information relates to P Limited at 31 December 20X0.

	$
Inventories	1,550
Short term payables	2,100
Receivables	1,300
Cash at bank	1,250

Which of the following is the quick ratio for P Limited to two decimal places?

A 1.95
B 1.21
C 0.62
D 0.74

21 Which of the following is a non-financial performance measure?

A Share price
B Delivery time
C Cash flow
D Revenue

22 *Match the definition to the term.*

Terms	*Definition*
(a) Economy	(1) Ensuring outputs succeed in achieving objectives
(b) Efficiency	(2) Getting out as much as possible for what goes in
(c) Effectiveness	(3) Spending money frugally

23 Which of the following is a feature of the Residual Income performance measure?

A It is a relative measure
B It measures divisional performance based on multiple values
C It generally decreases as assets get older
D It helps you to select a proposal that will maximise wealth in absolute terms

24 Which of the following is **not** a perspective associated with the balanced scorecard?

A Customer satisfaction
B Financial success
C Reliability
D Growth

25 The cost of a job is $100,000

(a) If profit is 25% of the job cost, the price of the job = $ [ ]

(b) If there is a 25% margin, the price of the job = $ [ ]

26 Match the cost to the correct cost category

Costs

(a) Administration of quality control
(b) Product liability costs
(c) Acceptance testing
(d) Losses due to lower selling prices for sub-quality goods

Cost categories

(i) Prevention costs
(ii) Appraisal costs
(iii) Internal failure costs
(iv) External failure costs

27 *Match the terms to the correct definitions*

Terms

Cost value
Exchange value
Use value
Esteem value

Definitions

(a) The prestige the customer attaches to the product
(b) The market value of the product
(c) What the product does
(d) The cost of producing and selling the product

Section B: Questions

1 Wilton, MacDonald, Pearce & Co — 18 mins

Wilton, MacDonald, Pearce & Co, a medium-sized firm of architects, are about to absorb Butcher, Fowler & Partners, a similar sized firm. They have engaged you as management accountant. Part of your duties will be to review the management accounting function of the combined practice and to recruit an assistant. You have an appointment tomorrow morning with the senior partner to discuss these issues.

Required

Jot down notes to use in tomorrow's meeting which cover the following points.

(a) The functions of management accounting, with particular reference to Wilton, MacDonald, Pearce & Co

(b) The personal attributes you would expect the assistant management accountant to possess

(10 marks)

2 Products L and M — 18 mins

A company manufactures two products, L and M, using the same equipment and similar processes. An extract of the production data for these products in one period is shown below.

	L	*M*
Quantity produced (units)	5,000	7,000
Direct labour hours per unit	1	2
Machine hours per unit	3	1
Set-ups in the period	10	40
Orders handled in the period	15	60

Overhead costs	$
Relating to machine activity	220,000
Relating to production run set-ups	20,000
Relating to handling of orders	45,000
	285,000

Required

Calculate the production overheads to be absorbed by one unit of each of the products using the following costing methods.

(a) A traditional costing approach using a direct labour hour rate to absorb overheads

(b) An activity based costing approach, using suitable cost drivers to trace overheads to products

Comment on your results.

(10 marks)

3 ABC — 36 mins

The following data have been extracted from the budgets and standard costs of ABC Limited, a company which manufactures and sells a single product.

	$ per unit
Selling price	45.00
Direct materials cost	10.00
Direct wages cost	4.00
Variable overhead cost	2.50

Fixed production overhead costs are budgeted at $400,000 per annum. Normal production levels are thought to be 320,000 units per annum.

Budgeted selling and distribution costs are as follows.

Variable	$1.50 per unit sold
Fixed	$80,000 per annum

Budgeted administration costs are $120,000 per annum.

The following patterns of sales and production are expected during the first six months of 20X3.

	January – March	*April – June*
Sales (units)	60,000	90,000
Production (units)	70,000	100,000

There is no inventory on 1 January 20X3.

Required

Prepare profit statements for each of the two quarters, in a columnar format, using:

(a) marginal costing; and
(b) absorption costing.

(20 marks)

4 Twist and Tern Co **36 mins**

(a) Twist and Tern Co is a company that carries out jobbing work. One of the jobs carried out in February was job 1357, to which the following information relates.

Direct material Y:	400 kilos were issued from stores at a cost of $5 per kilo.
Direct material Z:	800 kilos were issued from stores at a cost of $6 per kilo.
	60 kilos were returned.
Department P:	320 labour hours were worked, of which 100 hours were done in overtime.
Department Q:	200 labour hours were worked, of which 100 hours were done in overtime.

Overtime work is not normal in Department P, where basic pay is $8 per hour plus an overtime premium of $2 per hour. Overtime work was done in Department Q in February because of a request by the customer of another job to complete his job quickly. Basic pay in Department Q is $10 per hour and overtime premium is $3 per hour.

Overhead is absorbed at the rate of $3 per direct labour hour in both departments.

(i) The direct materials cost of job 1357 is $ ☐.

(ii) The direct labour cost of job 1357 is $ ☐.

(iii) The full production cost of job 1357 is $ ☐.

(10 marks)

(b) A printing firm is proposing offering a leaflet advertising service to local traders.

The following costs have been estimated for a batch of 10,000 leaflets.

Setting up machine	6 hours at $10 per hour
Artwork	$20 per batch
Paper	$1.80 per 100 sheets
Other printing materials	$15
Direct labour cost	4 hours at $6 per hour

Fixed overheads allocated to this side of the business are $1,000 per annum incurred at an even rate throughout the year. Overheads are recovered on the basis of orders received, which are expected to be two per week for 50 weeks in the year.

The management requires 25% profit on selling price.

(i) The selling price, to the nearest cent, per thousand leaflets, for quantities of:

(1) 5,000 leaflets is $ [ ]

(2) 10,000 leaflets is $ [ ]

(ii) During the latest week, the firm sold two batches of 10,000 leaflets and one batch of 5,000 leaflets. All costs and selling prices were as estimated.

The profit for the week was $ [ ]

(10 marks)

(Total = 20 marks)

5 Test the market — 18 mins

Describe four methods a brewery could employ to test the market for a new canned beer. Discuss the relative advantages and disadvantages of each method chosen.

(10 marks)

6 Lemmi Bank — 36 mins

Income for Lemmi Bank in 20X0, 20X1 and 20X2 is made up as follows.

	20X0	*20X1*	*20X2*
	$'000	$'000	$'000
Interest income	3,579	2,961	2,192
Commission income	857	893	917
Other income	62	59	70

Required

Using the above data, draw the following.

(a) A simple bar chart
(b) A component bar chart
(c) A percentage component bar chart
(d) A compound bar chart

(20 marks)

7 Product costing system — 36 mins

A company, which manufactures a range of products, has decided to introduce a product costing system. As a first step it wishes to analyse the behaviour of its costs.

The following data is available for the previous four periods.

	Period 1	*Period 2*	*Period 3*	*Period 4*
Total costs ($)	190,760	224,020	236,100	255,600
Total output (units)	64,200	79,350	80,170	85,620
Period inflation (note 1)		5%	4%	3%

Note 1. Average prices in period 2 were 5% higher than period 1 etc.

Required

(a) Adjust the total costs in each period to Period 4 price levels.

(b) Using the high-low method, applied to the adjusted costs in answer to part (a), establish a linear function of the form:

$y = a + bx$

to represent total costs.

(c) Plot the adjusted costs for the four periods (ie at Period 4 prices) on a scattergraph and draw the linear cost function, established in part (b), on the graph.

(d) Using the linear function established in (b) above, estimate costs in the following period (Period 5) when output is expected to be 87,500 units and period inflation is forecast at 2%.

(e) Outline limitations of the analysis carried out in answer to parts (a) to (d).

(20 marks)

8 Planning and control systems — 36 mins

A significant proportion of the management accounting activity within most organisations is concerned with the production and reporting of information for control purposes.

Some commentators have asserted that the control aspect of management accounting is over emphasised. This over emphasis is, they believe, to the detriment of the prime functions of management accounting which are to produce information to assist planning and decision making.

Required

Discuss the above assertion and give your view of its validity. You may draw upon your own experience where relevant.

(20 marks)

9 Zap plc — 36 mins

(a) Sales are often considered to be the principal budget factor of an organisation.

Explain the meaning of the 'principal budget factor' and, assuming that it is sales, explain how sales may be forecast, making appropriate reference to the use of statistical techniques and the use of microcomputers. **(10 marks)**

(b) You are the assistant management accountant of Zap plc. Preliminary discussions concerning the company budgets of the year ended 30 June 20X9 have already taken place, and the sales and production directors have produced the following forecasts.

Sales Director:

'I forecast that the total sales for the year will be 24,000 units of product A if we continue to sell them at $10.00 per unit for the first six months of the year and increase the price to $11.00 per unit thereafter. I estimate the quarterly sales to be as follows.

July – September	7,200 units
October – December	3,000 units
January – March	4,800 units
April – June	9,000 units

This represents a 20% increase over our present quarterly sales targets, and I expect that within each quarter the monthly demand will be equal. We can also sell up to 2,000 units of product B per month at a selling price of $8.00 per unit. This is a less profitable product, so we should concentrate on product A.'

Production Director:

'Our maximum capacity is at present limited by the available machine hours. Each unit of product A requires 2 machine hours, and on this basis we can usually produce 2,000 units per month. However, because of employee holidays in August, the number of machine operators is reduced, and in that month we can produce only 1,000 units. We have placed an order for new semi-automatic machines which are being installed in August 20X8. These should be capable of producing a further 2,000 units per month starting on 1 September 20X8.

Product B requires 4 machine hours per unit. The quantity that we can produce is limited because of the demands on the available machine time by making product A.'

You have predicted the costs per unit of the two products for the 20X9 budget year as follows.

	A	*B*
	$/unit	$/unit
Direct materials	1.50	1.60
Direct labour	2.50	3.00
Variable overhead	1.50	3.00
	5.50	7.60

Required

(i) Use the above information to calculate the extent of the limiting factor during the budget period. **(4 marks)**

(ii) Prepare monthly sales and production budgets, expressed in units, for the period *July to December 20X8*, based upon the limiting factor you determined in (i) above. Assume that inventories of products A and B cannot be held, and that Zap plc wishes to concentrate on production of product A. **(6 marks)**

(Total = 20 marks)

10 Zero based budgeting — 36 mins

You work for a large multinational company which manufactures weedkillers. It has been decided to introduce zero based budgeting in place of the more traditional incremental budgeting. The manager of the research and development department has never heard of zero based budgeting (ZBB).

Required

Write a report to the manager of the research and development department which explains the following.

(a) How zero based budgeting techniques differ from traditional budgeting
(b) How ZBB may assist in planning and controlling discretionary costs
(c) How ZBB will help to control budgetary slack

(20 marks)

11 Fixed or flexible budget — 36 mins

A company manufactures a single product and has the following flexible production cost budgets for a period.

Production quantity	12,000 units	15,000 units	18,000 units
Direct materials:			
Material AB	$3,600	$4,500	$5,400
Material CD	$17,760	$22,200	$26,196
Labour (direct and indirect)	$25,700	$29,900	$35,150
Overhead (excluding indirect labour)	$12,400	$13,180	$13,960

The budget is based upon the following assumptions.

(i) Each unit requires:
Material AB 0.2 kg
Material CD 0.4 kg
Direct labour 0.2 hours

(ii) The supplier of Material CD gives a 10% discount on the excess of purchases over 6,000 kg per period.

(iii) A premium of 25% on the direct labour basic hourly rate is paid on the excess of production over 15,000 units per period.

During the period, the company manufactured 17,000 units of the product and incurred the following production costs:

Direct materials	
Material AB	$5,025
Material CD	$25,118
Labour (direct and indirect)	$32,889
Overhead (excluding indirect labour)	$13,315

Required

(a) Outline the difference between a flexible budget and a fixed budget.

(b) Calculate the budgeted cost per kg of Material CD on the excess of purchases over 6,000 kg per period.

(c) Prepare a statement for the period showing for each of the four items of cost (ie Material AB, Material CD, labour and overhead):

(i) the flexible budget allowance;
(ii) the actual amount incurred;
(iii) the variance between the flexible budget and actual costs.

(d) The purchase price of Material AB in the period was as per budget.

Required

Calculate the material usage variance (in kg) for Material AB.

(Total = 20 marks)

12 Setting standards — 36 mins

(a) Describe the possible problems which could arise when setting standards.
(b) List possible advantages of standard costing.

(20 marks)

13 Milbri — 18 mins

Milbri, a manufacturing firm, operates a standard marginal costing system. It makes a single product, LI, using a single raw material AN.

Standard costs relating to LI have been calculated as follows.

Standard cost schedule – LI	*Per unit*
	$
Direct material, AN, 100 kg at $5 per kg	500
Direct labour, 10 hours at $8 per hour	80
Variable production overhead, 10 hours at $2 per hour	20
	600

The standard selling price of a LI is $900 and Milbri produce 1,020 units a month.

During December, 1,000 units of LI were produced. Relevant details of this production are as follows.

Direct material AN

90,000 kgs costing $720,000 were bought and used.

Direct labour

8,200 hours were worked during the month and total wages were $63,000.

Variable production overhead

The actual cost for the month was $25,000.

Inventories of the direct material AN are valued at the standard price of $5 per kg.

Each LI was sold for $975.

Required

Calculate the following for the month of December.

(a) Variable production cost variance
(b) Direct labour cost variance, analysed into rate and efficiency variances
(c) Direct material cost variance, analysed into price and usage variances
(d) Variable production overhead variance, analysed into expenditure and efficiency variances
(e) Selling price variance
(f) Sales volume contribution variance

(10 marks)

14 ES — 36 mins

ES installs complex satellite navigation systems in cars, at a very large national depot. The standard cost of an installation is shown below. The budgeted volume is 1,000 units installed each month. The operations manager is responsible for three departments, namely: purchasing, fitting and quality control. ES Limited purchases navigation systems and other equipment from different suppliers, and most items are imported. The fitting of different systems takes differing amounts of time, but the differences are not more than 25% from the average, so a standard labour time is applied.

Standard cost of installation of one navigation system

	$	Quantity	Price ($)
Materials	400	1 unit	400
Labour	320	20 hours	16
Variable overheads	140	20 hours	7
Fixed overheads	300	20 hours	15
Total standard cost	1,160		

The Operations Department has gathered the following information over the last few months. There are significant difficulties in retaining skilled staff. Many have left for similar but better paid jobs and as a result there is a high labour turnover. Exchange rates have moved and commentators have argued this will make exports cheaper, but ES Limited has no exports and has not benefited. Some of the fitters have complained that one large batch of systems did not have the correct adapters and would not fit certain cars, but this was not apparent until fitting was attempted. Rent, rates, insurance and computing facilities have risen in price noticeably.

The financial results for September to December are shown below.

Operating Statement for ES for September to December

	September	October	November	December	4 months
	$	$	$	$	$
Standard cost of actual output	1,276,000	1,276,000	1,102,000	1,044,000	4,698,000
Variances					
Materials Price	5,505F	3,354F	9,520A	10,340A	11,001 A
Usage	400A	7,200A	800A	16,000A	24,400 A
Labour					
Rate	4,200A	5,500A	23,100A	24,000A	56,800 A
Efficiency	16,000F	0	32,000A	32,000A	48,000 A
Variable overheads					
Expenditure	7,000A	2,000A	2,000F	0	7,000 A
Efficiency	7,000F	0	14,000A	14,000A	21,000 A
Fixed overheads					
Expenditure	5,000A	10,000A	20,000A	20,000A	55,000 A
Volume	30,000F	30,000F	15,000A	30,000A	15,000 F
Actual costs	1,234,095	1,267,346	1,214,420	1,190,340	4,906,201

A = adverse variance
F = favourable variance

Required

(a) Prepare a report to the operations manager of ES commenting on the performance of the company for the four months to 31 December. State probable causes for the key issues you have included in your report and state the further information that would be helpful in assessing the performance of the company. **(15 marks)**

(b) Prepare a short report to the operations manager of ES suggesting ways that the budgeting system could be used to increase motivation and improve performance. **(5 marks)**

(Total = 20 marks)

15 WH — 36 mins

WH is a member of a trade association which operates an inter-company comparison scheme. The scheme is designed to help its member companies to monitor their own performance against that of other companies in the same industry.

At the end of each year, the member companies submit detailed annual accounts to the scheme organisers. The results are processed and a number of accounting ratios are published and circulated to members. The ratios indicate the average results for all member companies.

Your manager has given you the following extract, which shows the average profitability and asset turnover ratios for the latest year (Year 4). For comparison purposes, WH's accounts analyst has added the ratios for your company.

	Trade association average	*WH Limited*
Return on capital employed	20.5%	18.4%
Net (operating) profit margin	5.4%	6.8%
Asset turnover	3.8 times	2.7 times
Gross margin	14.2%	12.9%

Required

As assistant accountant for WH, your manager has asked you to prepare a report for the Senior Management Committee. The report should cover the following points.

(a) An explanation of what each ratio is designed to show

(b) An interpretation of WH's profitability and asset turnover compared with the trade association average

(20 marks)

16 Supervans **72 mins**

Supervans is a freight delivery company. Its mission statement is 'to provide the quickest and most reliable delivery service to our customers and satisfactory returns to our shareholders'. The company currently has a total of 230 vans operating from eight depots making urgent deliveries of packages to small shops (mainly pharmacies) and businesses across the UK. Recently the company has started making deliveries of parcels to private households in the UK. The company is highly geared and cash flow as well as profitability is vital to its survival. Competition in its marketplace is fierce and customers expect a high standard of service. The depot managers are responsible for all the operations within their depot, a key role being route planning, as efficient routing of vehicles and drivers' schedules is a major cost driver. A typical depot includes the following operations: a depot manager; an administration and accounting department; vehicle maintenance; deliveries; and a sales and marketing team responsible for increasing business.

To date the company has judged the success of its depot managers on the basis of return on investment.

Required

(a) Explain the role of mission statements in performance measurement.

(b) Explain the balanced scorecard approach to performance measurement and discuss its advantages over traditional accounting performance measures such as return on investment.

(c) For each of the following categories suggest two critical success factors and accompanying key performance indicators that could be useful in measuring the performance of a depot:

- (i) financial success;
- (ii) customer satisfaction;
- (iii) process efficiency;
- (iv) growth.

(d) Explain how benchmarking could assist Supervans in assessing the performance of its depots and suggest three potential sources of benchmarking information.

(40 marks)

17 Three components **36 mins**

Your company manufactures and sells three components, but the purchasing manager has been asked to investigate the prices of an overseas producer. She provides the following cost and price information.

Component	X	Y	Z
Production (units)	20,000	40,000	80,000
	$	$	$
Direct material cost, per unit	0.80	1.00	0.40
Direct labour cost, per unit	1.60	1.80	0.80
Direct expense cost, per unit	0.40	0.60	0.20
Fixed cost per unit	0.80	1.00	0.40
Selling price each	4.00	5.00	2.00
Imported price	2.75	4.20	2.00

Required

Write a report to management which covers the following.

(a) A recommendation to management as to whether any component should be purchased on the basis of cost only.

(b) The profit figure the company will make by producing all the components itself.

(c) How your recommendation in (a) above is likely to affect the profit and by how much.

(d) Assuming management proposes to go ahead and import some of the components, the matters that you would bring to their attention.

(20 marks)

18 Ship **36 mins**

Ship has recently shut down its London factory which used to make cushions, although all the inventories of raw materials and machinery are still there awaiting disposal. A former customer has just asked whether he could be supplied with one last delivery of 500 cushions. You ascertain the following facts.

(a) There is sufficient covering material in inventory. This originally cost $400 but has a disposal value of $190.

(b) There is sufficient stuffing in inventory. This originally cost $350. It was to have been shipped to the Bristol factory at a cost of $80. The Bristol factory would currently expect to pay $500 for this quantity.

(c) Labour costs would be $450.

(d) A supervisor could be spared from the Bristol factory for the week needed to produce the cushions. His normal wage is $160 and his rail fare and hotel bill in London would amount to $135.

(e) Before the factory was closed, fixed overheads were absorbed at 200% of direct labour cost.

Required

(a) Calculate the minimum price that could be quoted.

(b) List the advantages and disadvantages of a marginal cost plus approach.

(20 marks)

19 Quality **36 mins**

RUS plc operates a chain of hotels. Its strategy has been to provide medium-priced accommodation for business people during the week and for families at weekends. The market has become increasingly competitive and RUS plc has decided to change its strategy. In future, it will provide 'a high-quality service for the discerning guest'.

(a) Explain the relevance of a programme of 'total quality management' for RUS plc in the implementation of its new strategy.

(b) Summarise the financial and organisational implications of RUS plc's new strategy.

(c) Discuss the contribution that RUS plc's management accountant could make to the new strategy.

(20 marks)

20 Cost reduction **36 mins**

It has been suggested that much of the training of management accountants is concerned with cost control whereas the major emphasis should be on cost reduction.

Required

(a) Distinguish between cost control and cost reduction. **(8 marks)**

(b) Give *three* examples *each* of the techniques and principles used for (i) cost control and (ii) cost reduction. **(12 marks)**

(Total = 20 marks)

Answers to Examiner's Sample Multiple Choice Questions

1 C The calculation in C applies the relative increase in the price index to the specific material X.

2 A B and C are features of a flexible budget. D is a description of an imposed budget.

3 B Residual Income (RI) = traceable profit – imputed interest charge on traceable investment

You are given the return on investment and know that:

ROI = traceable profit/traceable investment

Therefore to arrive at the traceable investment you can re-arrange the formula above to:

Traceable investment = traceable profit/ROI = \$80,000/25% = \$80,000/0.25 = \$320,000.

Substituting \$320,000 back into the first formula together with other information in the question gives an RI of \$22,400.

RI = \$80,000 – (\$320,000 × 0.18) = (\$80,000 – \$57,600) = \$22,400

4 B The actual production volume was 5000 units and 2 kg was budgeted to be used for each unit. 5,000 units × 2 kg = 10,000 kg and represents budgeted material at that activity level.

However the material actually used is the 13,000 kg purchased less the increase in raw material inventory (in kgs).

The increase in raw material stock in kgs is calculated as:

Raw material valuation/standard cost per kg = \$8,000/\$4 = 2,000 kg

Therefore 11,000 kg (13,000 kg – 2,000kg) was actually used compared to 10,000 kg budgeted at a production level of 5,000 units. This equates to an over-use of 1,000 kg of material and a \$4,000 adverse variance from budget at a standard cost of \$4 per unit.

The key to answering this question correctly is to remember you are calculating a usage (not a price) variance, therefore standard costs are used throughout. Do not get distracted by actual costs.

5 C Efficiency is the best way to describe the particular performance measure given.

6 A The calculation in A uses the high-low method but adjusts for the additional variable element over 7,000 units (by subtracting the affected 3,000 units of \$1 each).

If you selected B then you did not take into account the increase in the variable element for above 7,000 units.

If you selected C then you added instead of subtracted 3,000 units to adjust for the increase in the variable element.

If you selected D you performed an unadjusted high-low calculation initially and added the increase in variable element per unit at the end.

7 B (i) is true because linear regression analysis uses a series of observations to provide estimates. The high low method uses only two.

(ii) is not true. It can also be used to predict the variable element of a semi-variable cost.

(iii) is true as linear regression uses a line of best fit to estimate how costs vary with output.

(iv) is not true of linear regression. It is the high low method that uses only two observations.

8 A The correct calculation is as follows:

	Units	*Comment*
Sales	2,000	Current month sales
Less opening inventory	(400)	20% of sales (2,000) in the current month
Add closing inventory	480	20% of budgeted sales (2,400 × 20% = 480)
	2,080	

9 A If the margin on sales is 20%, then costs are 80% of sales (since sales less costs is margin).

$10 × 80% = ($10 × 80)/100 = $8

The new sales price will be 130% of costs.

$8 × 130% = ($8 × 130)/100 = $10.40

This is a $0.40 increase which is 4% of the original $10 price.

10 D They are all components of a time series analysis.

Section A: Answers to Multiple Choice Questions

1 B **Tactical planning** is used by middle management to decide how the resources of the business should be employed to achieve specific objectives in the most efficient and effective way.

Strategic planning (option A) is planning for the achievement of long-term objectives, and corporate planning (option D) is another name for this.

Operational planning (option C)is concerned with the very short term, day to day planning that is carried out by 'front line' managers such as supervisors and head clerks.

2 (a) (i) $ **12,480**

(ii) $ **10,850**

(iii) $ **6,700**

(iv) $ **14,040**

(b) (i) $ **104**

(ii) $ **108.50**

(iii) $ **83.75**

(iv) $ **117**

Workings

	P1	*P2*	*P3*	*P4*
	$	$	$	$
Direct material	4,800	5,000	2,400	7,200
Direct labour	3,360	2,100	1,120	2,520
Production overhead *				
Set up costs	1,500	1,250	1,000	1,500
Stores receiving	900	900	900	900
Inspection/quality control	600	500	400	600
Material handling and despatch	1,320	1,100	880	1,320
(a) Total cost	12,480	10,850	6,700	14,040
(b) Unit costs	(÷120) $104	(÷ 100) $108.50	(÷ 80) $83.75	(÷ 120) $117

* Overhead costs will be divided in the following ratios, depending upon the number of production runs, requisitions or orders per product.

	P1	*P2*	*P3*	*P4*
Production runs	6	5	4	6
Requisitions raised	20	20	20	20
Orders executed	12	10	8	12

3 A All of the overhead absorption methods are suitable, depending on the circumstances.

Method (i), direct labour hours, is suitable in a labour-intensive environment. **Method (ii)**, machine hours, is suitable in a machine-intensive environment. **Method (iii)**, a percentage of prime cost, can be used if it is difficult to obtain the necessary information to use a time-based method. **Method (iv)**, a rate per unit, is suitable if all cost units are identical.

4 C The insurance cost is likely to be linked to the cost of replacing the machines, therefore the most appropriate basis for apportionment is the value of machinery.

Options A, B and D would all be possible apportionment bases in the absence of better information, but option C is preferable.

5

		A or M
(a)	Closing inventory valued at marginal production cost	M
(b)	Closing inventory valued at full production cost	A
(c)	Cost of sales include some fixed overhead incurred in previous period in opening inventory values	A
(d)	Fixed costs are charged in full against profit for the period	M

6 D 2,000 more units of product have been produced than sold, resulting in the same increase in inventory levels.

Closing inventories will not include any fixed overheads where marginal costing is used as they are written off in the period incurred.

However where absorption costing is used, \$5 of additional fixed cost will be included per unit of increase in inventory over the period, accounting for the profit being \$10,000 higher under this method for the period.

7

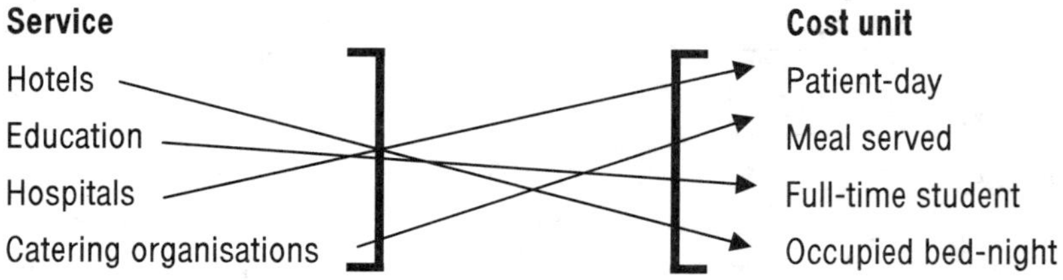

8 B **Systematic sampling** is a sampling method which works by selecting every n^{th} item (or m^{th} in this case) after a random start.

9 A = 6.5

B = 12

C = 16

D = 4.5

10 A (i) and (ii) are both true of a Paasche price index.

(iii) is true of a Paasche quantity index rather than a price index.

Laspeyre indices use weights from the base period so go out of date quicker than Paasche indices (where the weights are updated each period). Therefore (iv) is not true.

11 B As this is a multiplicative model, the seasonal variations should sum (in this case) to 4 (an average of 1) as there are four quarters.

Let x = seasonal variation for quarter 4.

$$0.45 + 1.22 + 1.31 + x = 4$$
$$2.98 + x = 4$$
$$x = 4 - 2.98$$
$$= 1.02$$

If you selected option A you subtracted the sum of the seasonal variations from 3 instead of 4.

If you selected option D, you forgot to subtract the sum of the seasonal variations for quarters 1-3 from 4.

12 D Long-term planning

13 C This is a detail budget.

14 (a) At the planning stage, a **flexible** budget can show what the effects would be if the actual outcome differs from the prediction.

(b) At the end of each period, actual results may be compared with the relevant activity level in the **flexible** budget as a control procedure.

(c) Master budgets are **fixed** budgets.

15

(a)	Targets and measures of performance	✓
(b)	Information for budgeting	✓
(c)	Simplification of inventory control systems	✓
(d)	Actual future costs	

Standard costing provides targets for achievement, and yardsticks against which actual performance can be monitored (**item (a)**). It also provides the unit cost information for evaluating the volume figures contained in a budget (**item (b)**). Inventory control systems are simplified with standard costing. Once the variances have been eliminated, all inventory units are evaluated at standard price (**item (c)**).

Item (d) is incorrect because standard costs are an estimate of what will happen in the future, and a unit cost target that the organisation is aiming to achieve.

16 A

	$	
5,800 hours should have cost (× $9.20)	53,360	
but did cost	55,100	
Labour rate variance	1,740	(A)
1,600 units should take (× 3.5 hours)	5,600	hrs
but did take	5,800	hrs
Variance in hours	200	hrs (A)
× standard rate per hour	× $9.20	
Labour efficiency variance	$1,840	(A)

If you selected option B you valued the efficiency variance in hours at the actual rate per hour instead of the standard rate per hour.

If you selected option C or option D you calculated the money values of the variances correctly but misinterpreted their direction.

17 A **Variable overhead total variance**

	$	
Budgeted 5,000 units should cost (× $4)	20,000	
But did cost	17,500	
Variable overhead total variance	2,500	(F)

The variance is favourable because the actual expenditure was less than the amount budgeted.

If you selected an incorrect option you misinterpreted the direction of the variance or calculated one element of it only.

18 C **Situation (i)** would result in an adverse sales volume variance because volumes were reduced.

Situation (ii) would result in a favourable sales volume variance, evaluated at the standard contribution achievable on the extra sales volume above standard.

A higher contribution per unit (**situation (iii)**) would not affect the sales volume variance because the variance is evaluated at standard contribution per unit.

Situation (iv) would lead to an increased sales volume and hence a favourable sales volume variance.

19 ROCE = profit margin × asset turnover

20 B ($1,300 + $1,250) ÷ $2,100 = 1.21

If you selected A you calculated the current ratio and included inventory in your calculation.

C is receivables divided by payables.

D is inventory divided by payables.

21 B A, C and D are all financial performance measures.

22 (a) (3)
(b) (2)
(c) (1)

23 D Residual income is an **absolute** measure (compared to Return on Investment which is a relative measure) which allows you to select a proposal that will maximise your wealth in absolute terms.

It measures divisional performance divisional performance based on a **single value** and as assets get older it generally **increases**. This is because the number subtracted from traceable profits decreases as the book value decreases.

24 C The fourth perspective not listed is process efficiency.

25 (a) $100,000 + (25% × $100,000) = $100,000 + $25,000 = $125,000

(b) Profit is 25 per cent of the selling price, therefore selling price should be written as 100%:

	%
Selling price	100
Profit	25
Cost	75

∴ Price = $100,000 × 100/75 = $133,333.

26 (a) (i)
(b) (iv)
(c) (ii)
(d) (iii)

27 Cost value (d)
Exchange value (b)
Use value (c)
Esteem value (a)

Section B: Answers to Questions

1 Wilton, Macdonald, Pearce & Co

(a) Management accounting involves providing and interpreting internal accounting information for managers to use for the following purposes.

(i) **Planning the organisation's activities in the short, medium and long term.**

For example, the management accounting system should provide information which will allow management to plan the future activities of the new, larger business.

(ii) **Controlling the activities of the organisation**

Management will have to learn to control a larger business. They will therefore need control reports so that they can compare actual results against plans or budgets. Action can then be taken to correct any differences between actual and plan and to help the organisation to continue in the direction set out by the plans.

(iii) **Making decisions**

For example, information will be needed for pricing architectural contracts for tendering purposes.

(iv) **Performance appraisal, both financial and non-financial**

For example, information on the percentage of jobs completed on time, percentage of successful tenders and so on should be provided.

(b) (i) Be training for or already possess a professional qualification in management accountancy both because he/she will have to deal with professionals and for technical reasons.

(ii) Be highly numerate.

(iii) Have excellent knowledge of the management accounting information requirements of a large architects' business.

(iv) Be able to critically appraise the existing systems and information to ensure their relevance to the future.

(v) Have excellent communication skills. This is particularly important because of the uncertainty caused by the major changes taking place. He or she must be able to explain and interpret management accounting information for those architects and other employees who have little or no financial background.

(vi) Be flexible and self-motivating. For example he/she must be willing to leave their office desk and visit sites when necessary.

(vii) Possess management perspective as well as being technically competent.

Of course you may have thought of completely different points to those noted above. The purpose of this question was to get you thinking about management accounting.

2 Products L and M

(a) **Traditional costing approach**

	Direct labour hours
Product L = 5,000 units × 1 hour	5,000
Product M = 7,000 units × 2 hours	14,000
	19,000

$\therefore$ Overhead absorption rate $\dfrac{\$285,000}{19,000}$ = \$15 per hour

Overhead absorbed would be as follows.

Product L	1 hour × $15	=	$15 per unit
Product M	2 hours × $15	=	$30 per unit

(b) **ABC approach**

	Machine hours
Product L = 5,000 units × 3 hours	15,000
Product M = 7,000 units × 1 hour	7,000
	22,000

Using ABC the overhead costs are absorbed according to the **cost drivers**.

	$			
Machine-hour driven costs	220,000	÷	22,000 m/c hours	= $10 per m/c hour
Set-up driven costs	20,000	÷	50 set-ups	= $400 per set-up
Order driven costs	45,000	÷	75 orders	= $600 per order

Overhead costs are therefore as follows.

		Product L		*Product M*
		$		$
Machine-driven costs	(15,000 hrs × $10)	150,000	(7,000 hrs × $10)	70,000
Set-up costs	(10 × $400)	4,000	(40 × $400)	16,000
Order handling costs	(15 × $600)	9,000	(60 × $600)	36,000
		163,000		122,000
Units produced		5,000		7,000
Overhead cost per unit		$32.60		$17.43

These figures suggest that product M absorbs an unrealistic amount of overhead using a direct labour hour basis. Overhead absorption should be based on the activities which **drive the costs**, in this case machine hours, the number of production run set-ups and the number of orders handled for each product.

3 ABC

(a) **Marginal costing**

	January – March		*April – June*	
	$'000	$'000	$'000	$'000
Sales (W1)		2,700		4,050
Opening inventory (W4)	–		165	
Variable production costs (W2)	1,155		1,650	
Closing inventory (W4)	(165)		(330)	
		(990)		(1,485)
Cost of sales		1,710		2,565
Variable selling costs (W5)		(90)		(135)
Contribution		1,620		2,430
Fixed production overhead (per quarter)		(100)		(100)
Fixed selling costs (per quarter)		(20)		(20)
Administration costs (per quarter)		(30)		(30)
Budgeted profit		1,470		2,280

(b) **Absorption costing**

	January – March		April – June	
	$'000	$'000	$'000	$'000
Sales		2,700.0		4,050.0
Opening inventory (W4)	–		177.5	
Production costs (W2)	1,242.5		1,775.0	
Closing inventory (W4)	(177.5)		(355.0)	
		1,065.0		1,597.5
		1,635.0		2,452.5
(Under-)/over-absorbed overheads (W6)		(12.5)		25.0
		1,622.5		2,477.5
Variable selling costs (W5)		(90.0)		(135.0)
Fixed selling costs (per quarter)		(20.0)		(20.0)
Administration costs (per quarter)		(30.0)		(30.0)
Budgeted profit		1,482.5		2,292.5

Workings

1 **Sales** are 60,000 or 90,000 × $45

2 **Production costs** are calculated as follows.

	Per unit	70,000 units	100,000 units
	$	$'000	$'000
Direct materials	10.00		
Direct wages	4.00		
Variable overhead	2.50		
Variable production cost	16.50	1,155.00	1,650
Variable production cost	16.50	1,155.00	1,650
Fixed production overhead (W3)	1.25	87.50	125
Total production cost	17.75	1,242.50	1,775

3 **Fixed production overhead per unit**

$$\frac{\text{Total cost}}{\text{Total absorption basis}} \quad \frac{\$400{,}000}{320{,}000 \text{ units}} = \$1.25$$

Fixed production overheads are absorbed on a per unit basis in the absence of alternative instructions.

4 **Closing inventory**

January – March	Units	Marginal costing $'000	Absorption costing $'000
Opening inventory	-		
Production (Jan-March)	70,000		
Sales	60,000		
Closing inventory – March (W2)	10,000	165	177.5
Production (April-June)	100,000		
	110,000		
Sales	90,000		
Closing inventory – June (W2)	20,000	330	355

5 **Variable selling costs**

	January – March	April – June
	$'000	$'000
60,000 × $1.50	90	
90,000 × $1.50		135

6 **(Under-)/over-absorbed fixed production overheads**

Budgeted production per quarter = 320,000 ÷ 4 = 80,000 units

		$
January – March	(70,000 – 80,000) × $1.25 (W3)	(12,500)
April – June	(100,000 – 80,000) × $1.25 (W3)	25,000

Note. If overheads are under absorbed, too little overhead is charged to profit and vice versa. The profit statement must be adjusted accordingly. The effect of the adjustment is to make *total* production costs equal whether marginal costing or absorption costing is used.

	Marginal costing			*Absorption costing*	
	$'000	$'000		$'000	$'000
Variable cost	(1,155)	(1,650)	Production cost	(1,242.5)	(1,775.0)
Fixed cost	(100)	(100)	Under-/over-absorbed	(12.5)	25.0
	(1,255)	(1,750)		(1,255.0)	(1,750.0)

4 Twist and Tern Co

(a) (i) **The direct materials cost is $ 6,440**

Workings

	$
Direct material Y (400 kilos × $5)	2,000
Direct material Z (800 – 60 kilos × $6)	4,440
Total direct material cost	6,440

(ii) **The direct labour cost is $ 4,560**

Workings

	$
Department P (320 hours × $8)	2,560
Department Q (200 hours × $10)	2,000
Total direct labour cost	4,560

In Department P, overtime premium will be charged to overhead. In Department Q, overtime premium will be charged to the job of the customer who asked for overtime to be worked.

(iii) **The full production cost is $ 12,500**

Workings

	$
Direct material cost	6,440
Direct labour cost	4,560
Production overhead (520 hours × $3)	1,560
	12,560

(b) (i) (1) **The selling price is $ 53.20**

(2) **The selling price is $ 42.20**

Workings

Expected orders per annum = 2 orders × 50 weeks = 100 orders

$$\therefore \text{ Fixed overhead per order} = \frac{\$1,000}{100} = \$10$$

Calculation of price per 1,000 leaflets

Batch size: (leaflets)	5,000	10,000
	$	$
Setting up machine	60.00	60.00
Artwork	20.00	20.00
Paper	90.00	180.00
Other printing materials	7.50	15.00
Direct labour cost	12.00	24.00
Fixed overhead	10.00	10.00
Total cost	199.50	309.00
Profit	66.50	103.00
Selling price	266.00	412.00
Price per 1,000 leaflets	53.20	41.20

The profit is 25% on selling price ie cost (75) + profit (25) = selling price (100), and thus profit = 1/3 cost

(ii) **The profit for the week was $ 282.50**

Workings

		$	$
Batch profit	$66.50 × 1		66.50
	$103.00 × 2		206.00
			272.50
Plus over-absorbed overhead:			
Overhead absorbed 3 batches × $10		30.00	
Overhead incurred $1,000/50 weeks		20.00	
			10.00
Profit for the week			282.50

5 Test the market

(a) The brewery could try to supply the beer to a **random sample** of beer drinkers, and then ask for their views. Such samples are taken in such a way that every member of the population (in this case, all beer drinkers and perhaps all potential beer drinkers) has an equal chance of being selected for the sample. The main advantage of random sampling is that it allows mathematical analysis of the data to be carried out. The main disadvantage is that a random sample can be difficult and expensive to collect. The brewery may well find that it is impossible to compile a list of all beer drinkers from which to select a sample.

(b) **Stratified sampling** may well be appropriate. The population would first be divided into groups, perhaps by age or by weekly beer consumption, and then samples would be selected from each group (reflecting the proportion of the population in the group). The main advantage of stratified sampling is that it ensures that each group is represented in the sample. The main disadvantage is that preliminary work is needed to determine which groupings are likely to be useful and the proportion of the population in each group.

(c) **Cluster sampling** may well be a practical alternative, giving some of the benefits of both random sampling and stratified sampling. The population could be divided geographically into beer drinkers at public houses in different regions of the country and beer purchasers at off licences within these regions. A sample of regions could be selected, and a sample of public houses and off licences in each selected region could be chosen. All consumers at the chosen public houses and off licences would then form the sample. The main advantage of cluster sampling is its relative cheapness. The main disadvantage is that the sample obtained will not be truly random, so some forms of statistical analysis will not be possible.

(d) **Quota sampling** has the advantage of being even cheaper than cluster sampling, but the disadvantage of producing a sample which is even further from being random. Researchers would simply visit a selection of public houses and off licences and interview the first beer drinkers they met until they had fulfilled some quota (say ten men and ten women).

6 Lemmi Bank

(a)

20X0	*20X1*	*20X2*
$'000	$'000	$'000
3,579	2,961	2,192
857	893	917
62	59	70
4,498	3,913	3,179

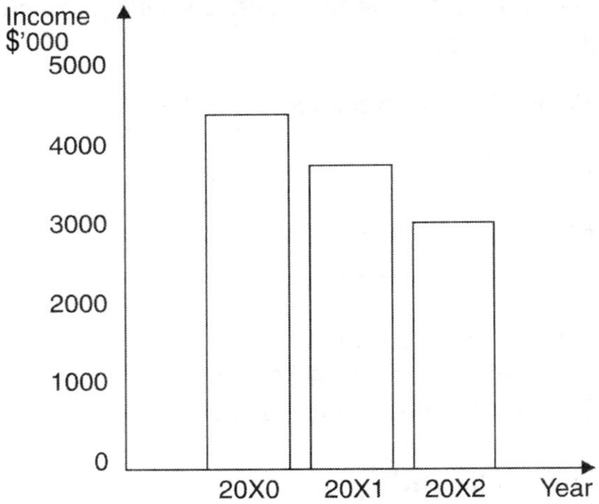

(b)

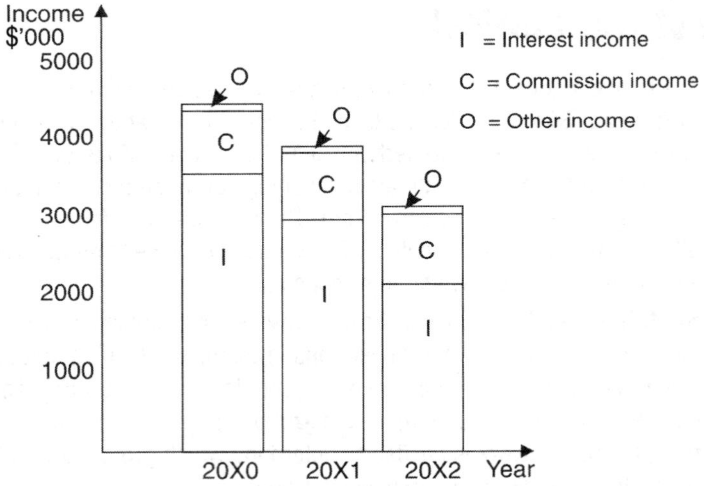

(c)

20X0		*20X1*		*20X2*	
$'000	%	$'000	%	$'000	%
3,579	80	2,961	76	2,192	69
857	19	893	23	917	29
62	1	59	1	70	2
4,498	100	3,913	100	3,179	100

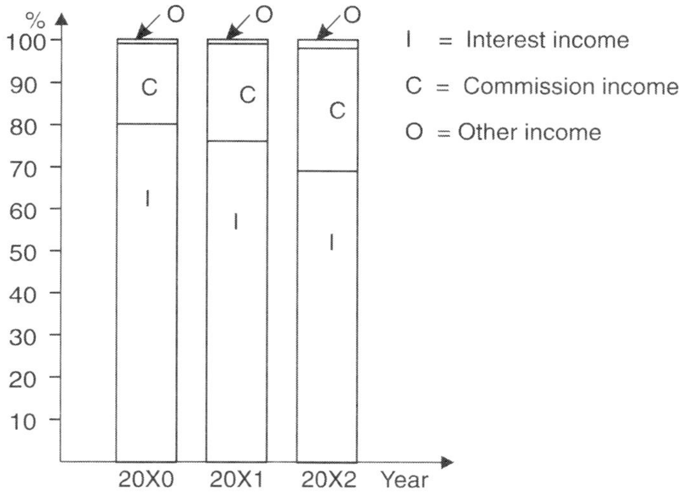

(d)

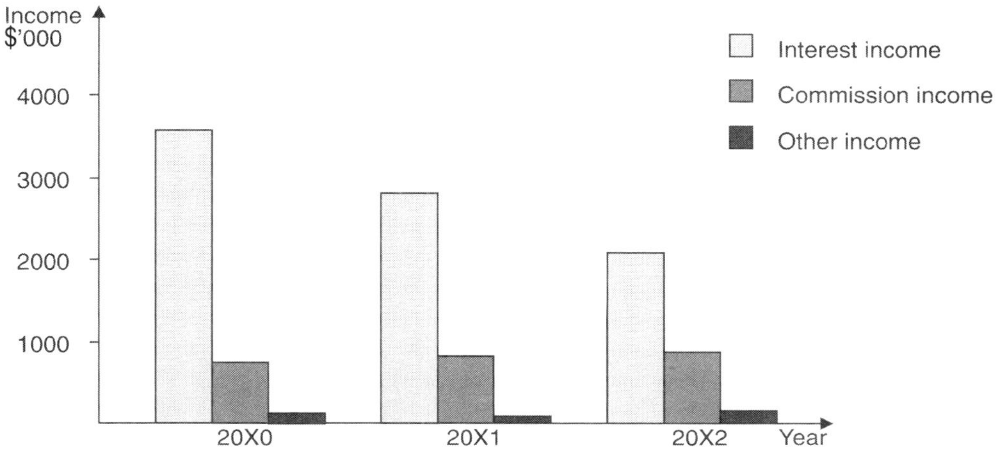

7 Product costing system

(a) **Adjustment factors**

Period 1	1.05 × 1.04 × 1.03	= 1.12476
Period 2	1.04 × 1.03	= 1.0712
Period 3		= 1.03

Adjusted costs

	Actual cost ($)	*Gross up by*	*Adjusted cost ($)*
Period 1	190,760	1.12476	214,559
Period 2	224,020	1.0712	239,970
Period 3	236,100	1.03	243,183
Period 4	255,600	1.00	255,600

(b)

	$		Units	
High	255,600		85,620	
Low	(214,559)		(64,200)	
Variable cost =	41,041	÷	21,420	= $1.916/unit

Fixed cost = $255,600 – (85,620 × $1.916) = $91,552

y = $91,552 + 1.916 x

(c)

Scattergraph and linear cost function

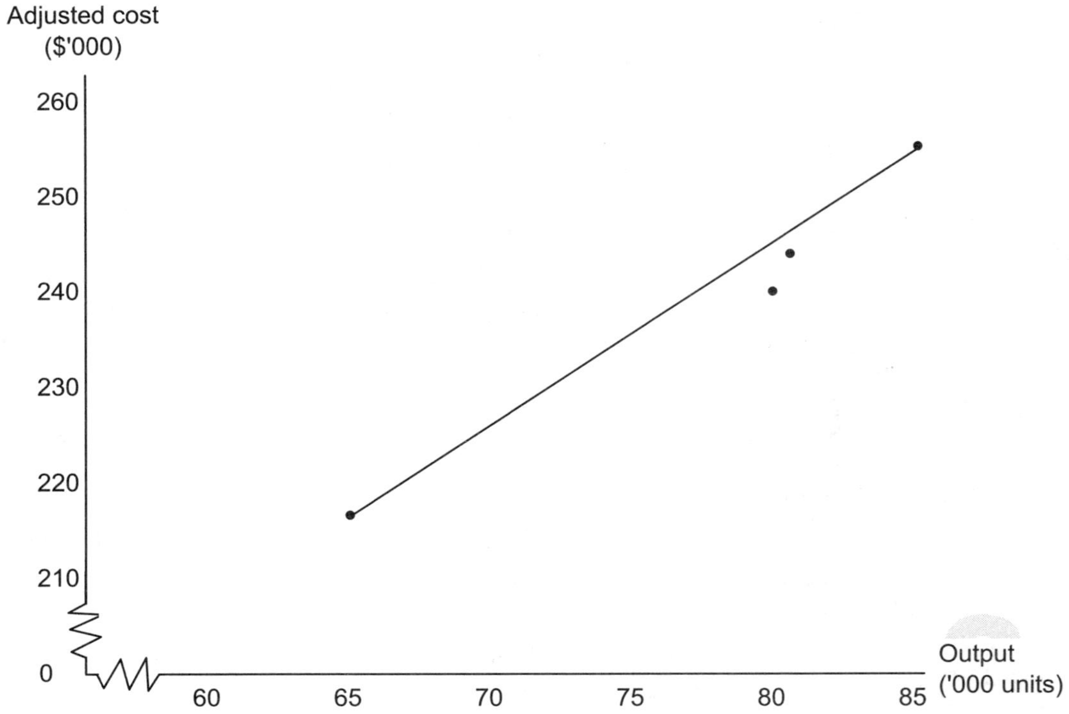

(d) **Period 5 costs**

	$
Fixed costs	91,552
Variable costs 87,500 units @ $1.916	167,650
	259,202
Gross up for inflation (2%)	× 1.02
Period 5 costs in total	264,386

(e) Limitations of the analysis

Part (a) The company's costs may not have suffered the same rate of inflation as average prices.

Part (b) The high/low method uses only two pairs of data and by definition these are at the extremes of the ranges concerned. The resulting function is not therefore very likely to be accurate.

Part (c) The scattergraph intermediate points illustrate the inaccuracy noted above.

Part (d) The computation is an extrapolation from the known data. That is, the output is greater than the maximum used in establishing the known function. There is no evidence that a linear cost function is appropriate outside the limits of the known data.

The further one goes from the known data, the greater is the likelihood that influences on cost will behave in new and different ways.

8 Planning and control systems

The provision of information for planning, control and decision making are all important aspects of management accounting, along with providing information for formulating strategy, safeguarding assets, optimising the use of resources and so on.

Planning

Planning involves establishing objectives and selecting appropriate strategies to achieve those objectives. If forces management to think ahead systematically in both the short term (via the setting of budgets) and the long term (via strategic planning).

Decision making

Decision making is carried out at all levels of an organisation. At the **strategic level**, a decision might be taken to close down a division, at the **tactical level** to terminate a member of staff's employment and at the **operational level** to reduce a customer's credit limit.

Control

Control involves two stages. The performance of an organisation as set out in detailed operational plans is compared with actual performance on a regular and continuous basis. Any deviations from the plans are identified (variance analysis) and corrective action is taken by the manager responsible for the area in question as part of a system of **responsibility accounting**. The plans are then reviewed in the light of the first stage of control and modified to take account of any changes to the parameters upon which the plans were based.

Planning, control and decision making all require different types of **information**. **Planning information** must be essentially forward looking and must include non- financial information relating to personnel, markets and so on. The most important requirements of decision-making information are that it is relevant, timely, accurate and appropriate. **Control information**, on the other hand, is mostly historic.

As mentioned earlier, **management accounting** is concerned with the provision of information for planning, control and decision making. In the past the most comprehensive information system was the **financial accounting system**. As the control function relies on historic information, the financial accounting system provides a ready source of suitable information. Moreover, its suitability has only been reinforced in the past by the concentration on the financial results of an organisation.

Such information is entirely unsuitable for planning and decision making, however. The use of absorption costing to comply with the requirements of SSAP 9, for example, produces information which is totally misleading for product and output decisions.

It is because accounting information is so readily available from the financial accounting system that organisations have tended to concentrate their efforts on control, either disregarding the planning and decision making functions because of a lack of suitable information *or* using totally inappropriate information for planning and decision-making purposes.

Financial results are no longer seen as the only way of assessing and organisation's performance, however, and it has recently become evident that effective control is possible using both financial and non-financial information. For example, there has been an increase in the use of non-financial indicators which are based on information more suited to planning and decision making. Moreover, the increase in the use of activity based costing and other activity based techniques means that information more relevant to planning and decision making is now available.

The nature of an organisation may of course have an impact on the relative importance of the control activity. For example, public sector organisations may place more emphasis on control. This may be due to the need for greater accountability and is not necessarily to the detriment of the other functions of management accounting.

Other factors which may influence the relative importance of planning and decision-making activities compared with control activities include the following.

(a) The **nature of the environment** in which the organisation operates. Dynamic environments may require more emphasis on planning.

(b) The **management accounting resources** and the **sophistication of the information system** available. Some organisations may wish to spend more effort on planning but they may not have the resources available.

(c) The **complexity of the organisation**. More complex organisations may need to expend more effort on the control activity.

It is therefore not necessarily detrimental for an organisation to emphasise the control function in its management accounting activity.

However, it may be that organisations have concentrated too much on the control aspect of management accounting simply because of a lack of suitable information for planning and decision-making purposes. It is possible that as the importance of non-financial results increases and more sophisticated management accounting techniques are employed, the provision of information for planning, control and decision making will all become equally important for the management accountant.

9 Zap plc

Top tips. You could have wasted quite a lot of time if you did not think very carefully about what you were doing in advance. You were given demand information in terms of Product A and Product B but capacity information in terms of product A only so you had to convert all the information into machine hours.

To determine how many of each product you could produce, you had to look at how many sets of one unit of each product (which uses six machine hours) could be produced in the available time.

(a) **What is the principal budget factor?**

Known as the key budget factor or limiting budget factor, this is the factor which, at any given time, effectively limits the activities of an organisation. The principal budget factor is usually sales demand: a company is usually restricted from making and selling more of its products because there would be no sales demand for the increased output at a price which would be acceptable/profitable for the company. The principal budget factor may also be machine capacity, distribution and selling resources, the availability of key raw materials or the availability of cash.

Its importance

Once this factor is identified then the rest of the budget can be prepared. For example, if sales are the principal budget factor then the production manager can only prepare his budget after the sales budget is complete.

Sales forecasting

There are two basic approaches to sales forecasting.

(i) **Use of internal estimates**

In-house sales staff can forecast future sales using their experience and knowledge and by considering the following factors.

(1) Past sales patterns
(2) Economic environment
(3) Results of market research
(4) Anticipated advertising
(5) Competition
(6) Changing consumer taste
(7) New legislation
(8) Distribution and quality of sales outlets and personnel

(ii) **Statistical techniques**

Such an approach is most appropriate if past sales patterns given some indication of future sales patterns (that is, extrapolation is valid). The techniques include regression analysis by the least squares method in combination with moving averages analysis.

Obviously both approaches can be used in conjunction with each other. Statistical forecasts can be considered and adjusted by sales personnel based on their knowledge and consideration of factors (1) to (8) listed above.

Use of computers

Computers are particularly useful for forecasting. They facilitate complex calculations within the statistical techniques, produce acceptably accurate estimates of future sales and are capable of performing 'what if' analysis, which shows management the effect of different sales levels on profit, cash flows and so on.

(b) (i)

	Demand		*Demand*	*Capacity*
	Units of A	Units of B	Hrs*	Hrs
July	2,400	2,000	12,800	4,000
August	2,400	2,000	12,800	2,000
September	2,400	2,000	12,800	8,000
October – December	3,000	6,000	30,000	24,000
January – March	4,800	6,000	33,600	24,000
April – June	9,000	6,000	42,000	24,000
	24,000	24,000	144,000	86,000

There is a shortfall of 144,000 – 86,000 = 58,000 machine hours.

* (2 × demand for A in units) + (4 × demand for B in units)

(ii) To prepare the budgets we produce the **maximum number of Product A** with the hours available and then use the **remaining hours to produce Product B**. In July, for example, we have 4,000 hours so we can produce only 4,000 ÷ 2 = 2,000 units of Product A whereas in September we can produce 2,400 units of Product A, using 4,800 of the 8,000 hours. The remaining 3,200 can be used to make 3,200 ÷ 4 hrs = 800 units of Product B. Likewise, in October, November and December, the demand for Product A can be met, leaving 8,000 – 2,000 = 6,000 hours to produce 6,000 ÷ 4 = 1,500 units of product B.

Production and sales budgets

July – December 20X8	*Product A*	*Product B*
	Units	Units
July	2,000	–
August	1,000	–
September	2,400	800
October	1,000	1,500
November	1,000	1,500
December	1,000	1,500
	8,400	5,300

10 Zero based budgeting

REPORT

To: R&D manager
From: Management accountant
Date: 01.01.X3
Subject: Zero based budgeting

(a) **Zero based budgeting and traditional budgeting**

The traditional approach to budgeting works from the premise that last year's activities will continue at the same level or volume, and that next year's budget can be based on last year's costs plus an extra amount to allow for expansion and inflation. The term 'incremental' budgeting is often used to describe this approach.

Zero based budgeting (ZBB) quite literally works from a zero base. The approach recognises that every activity has a cost and insists that there must be quantifiable benefits to justify the spending. ZBB expects managers to choose the best method of achieving each task by comparing costs and benefits. Activities must be ranked in order of priority.

(b) A **discretionary cost** is not vital to the continued existence of an organisation in the way that, say, raw materials are to a manufacturing business. ZBB was developed originally to help management with the difficult task of allocating resources in precisely such areas. **Research and development** is a frequently cited example; others are **advertising** and **training**.

Within a research and development department ZBB will establish priorities by ranking the projects that are planned and in progress. Project managers will be forced to consider the benefit obtainable from their work in relation to the costs involved. The result may be an overall increase in R&D expenditure, but only if it is justified.

(c) **Budgetary slack** may be defined as the difference between the minimum necessary costs and the costs built into the budget or actually incurred. One of the reasons why, under traditional budgeting, an extra amount is added to last year's budget may be because managers are overestimating costs to avoid being blamed in the future for overspending and to make targets easier to achieve. Slack is a protective device and it is self-fulfilling because managers will subsequently ensure that their actual spending rises to meet the (overestimated) budget, in case they are blamed for careless budgeting.

In an R&D department a further incentive to include slack is the nature of the work. Managers may well have 'pet' projects in which their personal interest is so strong that they tend to ignore the benefit or lack of benefit to the organisation which is funding them.

The **ZBB approach**, as described in (a) above, clearly will not accept this approach: all expenditure has (in theory) to be justified in cost-benefit terms in its entirety in order to be included in next year's budget. In practice it is more likely that managers will start from their current level of expenditure as usual, but ZBB requires them to work **downwards**, asking what would happen if any particular element of current expenditure and current operations were removed from the budget.

11 Fixed or flexible budget

(a) A fixed budget is based upon a single forecast level of activity and no allowance is made for possible changes to that level of activity.
A flexible budget takes account of possible variations in cost arising from different levels of activity.

(b) At 0.4 kg per unit, 6,000 kg would produce $\frac{6{,}000}{0.4}$ units = 15,000 units

Therefore, if 18,000 units incur a total cost of \$26,195 for Material CD, (18,000 – 15,000) units have incurred an incremental cost of \$26,195 – 22,200.

This gives an incremental cost for material CD of:

$$\frac{(\$26,195 - 22,200)}{18,000 - 15,000} \text{ per unit} = \frac{\$3,995}{3,000}$$

This must be divided by 0.4 to find the cost per kg

$$\frac{\$3,995}{3,000} \div 0.4 = \$3.33 \text{ per kg}$$

(c) **Production costs for the period**

	Budget $	*Actual* $	*Variance* $	*Working*
Direct material				
Material AB	5,100	5,025	75 (F)	1
Material CD	24,864	25,118	254 (A)	2
Labour	33,400	32,889	511 (F)	3
Overhead (excluding indirect)	13,700	13,315	385 (F)	4
Totals	77,064	76,347	717 (F)	

Workings

1 **Cost of material AB is constant**

$$\frac{\$3,600}{12,000} = \$0.3 \text{ per unit}$$

17,000 × $0.3 = $5,100

2 **Cost of material CD**

Units	*Kg*	*Cost/kg*	*Total cost* $
15,000	6,000	-	22,200
2,000	800	$3.33	2,664
17,000			24,864

3 Labour includes both direct and indirect; only the indirect attracts the 25% premium for outputs over $15,000. Cost must therefore be split into fixed and variable elements.

Variable cost per unit at 15,000 units output

Cost ($)	Units
29,900	15,000
(25,700)	(12,000)
4,200	3,000

$$\text{Variable cost per unit} = \frac{\$4,200}{3,000} = \$1.40$$

17,000 units incur costs:	$
15,000 (fixed and variable)	29,900
2,000 ×1.4 × 1.25 (variable)	3,500
17,000	33,400

4 **Overheads: fixed and variable costs**

Cost ($)		Units
13,960		18,000
(12,400)		(12,000)
1,560	÷	6,000

$$\text{Variable cost per unit} = \frac{\$1,560}{6,000} = \$0.26$$

13,960 – (18,000 × 26c) = $9,280 fixed cost

At output 17,000 units:

	$
Fixed	9,280
Variable (17,000 × 26c)	4,420
	13,700

(d) Total cost variance for material AB = $75 (F)

Material price variance is zero

0.2 kg of material per unit cost $0.3

Therefore 1 kg cost $1.50

$75 ÷ 1.50/kg = 50 kg

Therefore material usage variance is 50 kg (F)

12 Setting standards

(a) (i) Deciding how to incorporate inflation into planned unit costs.

(ii) Agreeing a short-term labour efficiency standard (current, attainable or ideal).

(iii) Deciding on the quality of materials to be used (a better quality of material will cost more, but perhaps reduce material wastage).

(iv) Deciding on the appropriate mix of component materials, where some change in the mix is possible (for example in the manufacture of foods and drink).

(v) Estimating materials prices where seasonal price variations or bulk purchase discounts may be significant.

(vi) Finding sufficient time to construct accurate standards. Standard setting can be a time-consuming process.

(vii) Incurring the cost of setting up and maintaining a system for establishing standards.

(viii) Dealing with possible behavioural problems. Managers responsible for the achievement of standards might resist the use of a standard costing control system for fear of being blamed for any adverse variances.

(b) (i) Carefully planned standards are an aid to more accurate budgeting.

(ii) Standard costs provide a yardstick against which actual costs can be measured.

(iii) The setting of standards involves determining the best materials and methods which may lead to economies.

(iv) A target of efficiency is set for employees to reach and cost consciousness is stimulated.

(v) Variances can be calculated which enable the principle of 'management by exception' to be operated. Only the variances which exceed acceptable tolerance limits need to be investigated by management with a view to control action.

(vi) Standard costs and variance analysis can provide a way of motivating managers to achieve better performance. However, care must be taken to distinguish between controllable and non-controllable costs in variance reporting.

13 Milbri

(a) This is simply a '**total**' **variance**.

	$
1,000 units should have cost (× $600)	600,000
but did cost (see working)	808,000
Variable production cost variance	208,000 (A)

(b) **Direct labour cost variances**

	$
8,200 hours should cost (× $8)	65,600
but did cost	63,000
Direct labour rate variance	2,600 (F)
1,000 units should take (× 10 hours)	10,000 hrs
but did take	8,200 hrs
Direct labour efficiency variance in hrs	1,800 hrs (F)
× standard rate per hour	× $8
Direct labour efficiency variance in $	$14,400 (F)

Summary	$
Rate	2,600 (F)
Efficiency	14,400 (F)
Total	17,000 (F)

(c) **Direct material cost variances**

	$
90,000 kg should cost (× $5)	450,000
but did cost	720,000
Direct material price variance	270,000 (A)
1,000 units should use (× 100 kg)	100,000 kg
but did use	90,000 kg
Direct material usage variance in kgs	10,000 kg (F)
× standard cost per kg	× $5
Direct material usage variance in $	$50,000 (F)

Summary	$
Price	270,000 (A)
Usage	50,000 (F)
Total	220,000 (A)

(d) **Variable production overhead variances**

	$
8,200 hours incurring o/hd should cost (× $2)	16,400
but did cost	25,000
Variable production overhead expenditure variance	8,600 (A)
Efficiency variance in hrs (from (b))	1,800 hrs (F)
× standard rate per hour	× $2
Variable production overhead efficiency variance	$3,600 (F)

Summary

	$
Expenditure	8,600 (A)
Efficiency	3,600 (F)
Total	5,000 (A)

(e) **Selling price variance**

	$	
Revenue from 1,000 units should have been (× $900)	900,000	
but was (× $975)	975,000	
Selling price variance	75,000	(F)

(f) **Sales volume contribution variance**

Budgeted sales	1,020 units
Actual sales	1,000 units
Sales volume variance in units	20 units (A)
× standard contribution margin ($(900 – 600))	× $300
Sales volume contribution variance in $	$6,000 (A)

Workings

	$
Direct material	720,000
Total wages	63,000
Variable production overhead	25,000
	808,000

14 ES

Top tips. It is important to start with well presented report headings, ie subject of the report, date, to whom it is addressed and the person writing it. The discussion must be balanced, including both what appear to be positive as well as negative factors.

It is important to relate the variances to probable causes based on the information given in the question. For each of these likely causes, identify additional information or investigation needed. Show originality and ensure you bring in your own ideas in the discussion.

Showing an understanding of the interrelationship of variances and the controllability principles is very important.

Easy marks. Easy marks will be gained by commenting on volume charges (including the November/December change) and on each of the eight rows of variances relating these to the information in the question.

For extra marks you need to comment on the interrelationship between variances, pose appropriate questions and identify further information needed.

(a) REPORT

To: Operations Manager of ES
Subject: Performance for period September to December
From: Management Accountant
Date: December 20X4

Output is lower in November and December as compared to September and October. This decline needs to be further investigated. Is this the beginning of a trend that should give cause for concern? Are there seasonal factors involved? Were there larger contracts in September and October?

Materials variances

Materials usage variance has been adverse throughout the four months.

This variance is related to the efficiency with which materials are used and is unaffected by volume. A possible explanation could be the large batch of systems that were found to include incorrect adaptors that would not fit certain cars. As this was not apparent until fitting was attempted (and it is probable that replacement parts may have been required), it could well be the main reason for the adverse usage variances over the period. Another area to explore is whether materials efficiency relates specifically to the incorrect adapters or any particular stage of the installation process or to any inexperienced fitters.

Materials price variance

This is favourable in the first two months and unfavourable in November and December. It is likely that the cause is the exchange rate movement which, if we are told would make exports cheaper, would imply sterling depreciation. As we are told that most items are imported, a sterling depreciation would cause prices of parts to rise. It would be helpful to quantify the effect of the exchange rate movement as well as the timing of it. This will help determine whether there are other factors involved.

The purchasing department will need to investigate this further and perhaps explore other sources of materials. As the company is dependent on stable import prices, a hedging contract could have been considered.

Labour rate

The labour rate variance is adverse throughout the period but seriously deteriorates in November and December increasing nearly six-fold in relation to September. This needs further investigation. We are told that the company had significant difficulties in retaining skilled staff and that many left for better paid jobs. This may mean that the company had to pay higher than budgeted rates to recruit staff at short notice to complete the jobs. Further investigation needs to be carried out to establish whether the budgeted labour rate was set too low.

Labour efficiency

The labour efficiency variance is favourable in September, zero in October and adverse in November. The timing of the problems of retaining skilled labour must be investigated.

Part of the adverse efficiency variance may be explained by the company having to recruit new workers who will have to be trained. Another possibility that should be investigated is whether the problematic batch led to wasted labour time.

It must also considered that labour may not actually be a totally variable cost as assumed by variable costing. As volumes are decreasing, more labour hours are attributed to each job. The labour efficiency variance should also be investigated in the context of the 25% variation that is expected to occur.

Overheads

There is a steady worsening from October onwards. This may indicate that variable overheads are not truly variable and as volumes decrease, these decrease proportionately less.

The total fixed overhead variance for November and December has also been deteriorating and is adverse for both the last two months in the period. We know that rent, rates, insurance and computing expenses have risen sharply. The increase of these may not have been budgeted.

(b)

Top tips. Start by clearly setting out report headings.

Discuss motivation and performance improvement **within a budgetary control** system. The question does not require you to look outside traditional budgeting.

Ensure it is all related to S and use all relevant information given in the question. The examiner is looking for answers tailored to the particular circumstances of the question, not answers regurgitating the theory.

Briefly explain the complexity of factors and interrelationships within the company that need to be considered.

Key ideas would include good planning, anticipating external factors (such as an adverse exchange rate movement) participation, setting of appropriate standards, feedback and feedforward control, clear communication, re-evaluation of budget where necessary, controllable and uncontrollable elements in the budgetary process and the recognition of the need for improved company co-operation and company-wide incentives.

Easy marks. There are five marks available for part (b) which would suggest that five ways to increase performance and improve motivation, well explained will earn these marks.

REPORT

To: Operations manager
Subject: Increasing motivation and improving performance
From: Management accountant
Date: December 20X5

The following ways could be used to enhance the budgeting system in order to increase motivation and improve performance.

Planning

Good planning, ahead of preparing the budget will ensure that external factors are taken into account as far as possible. For example, the risk of exchange rate movements where the company is reliant on import markets could be taken into account at this stage.

Participation

Participation in general is said to improve motivation and performance. Setting budgets with the participation of the managers in the three departments (purchasing, fitting and quality control) is likely to have the following advantages:

(a) The budgets will be based on relevant information from employees familiar with the three departments and are likely to be more realistic.

(b) Morale and motivation will be improved if the managers of the three departments are committed to the organisational objectives that they participated in setting.

(c) Co-ordination between the three departments will be improved and company wide targets set that do not conflict with departmental targets.

Feedback and revaluation of budget

A clear and timely two-way communication with managers and team leaders will increase motivation. The teams will be able to communicate the problems being faced and where appropriate the budget may be amended to reflect a planning variance. For example, the purchasing department cannot be held responsible for an adverse exchange rate movement if this was not forecast. Good communication should ensure that alternative sources of materials should be investigated in future.

Controllable/uncontrollable elements

Managers should not be held responsible for elements in the budget they do not control. The unsuitable batches were not the fault of the fitting department. Further investigation by the purchasing department to identify how this happened, should be taking place.

15 WH

WH

REPORT

To: Senior Management Committee — Date: 12 December Year 4
From: Assistant accountant
Subject: Profitability and asset turnover ratios

We have received the Trade Association results for year 4 and this report looks in detail at the profitability and asset turnover ratios.

(a) *What each ratio is designed to show*

(i) **Return on capital employed (ROCE)/Return on investment (ROI).** This ratio shows the percentage rate of profit which has been earned on the capital invested in the business, that is the return on the resources controlled by management. The expected return varies depending on the type of business and it is usually calculated as follows.

Return on capital employed = (Profit before interest and tax/capital employed) $\times$ 100%.

Other profit figures can be used, as well as various definitions of capital employed.

(ii) **Net (operating) profit margin.** This ratio shows the operating profit as a percentage of sales. The operating profit is calculated before interest and tax and it is the profit over which operational mangers can exercise day to day control. It is the amount left after all direct costs and overheads have been deducted from sales revenue.

Net operating profit margin = (Operating profit/sales revenue) $\times$ 100%

(iii) **Asset turnover**. This ratio shows how effectively the assets of a business are being used to generate sales.

Asset turnover = (Sales revenue/capital employed)

If the same figure for capital employed is used as in ROCE, than ratios (i) to (iii) can be related together: (i) ROCE = (ii) net operating profit margin $\times$ (iii) asset turnover.

(iv) **Gross margin**. This ratio measures the profitability of sales.

Gross margin = (Gross profit/sales revenue) $\times$ 100%

The gross profit is calculated as sales revenue less the cost of goods sold, and this ratio therefore focuses on the company's manufacturing and trading activities.

(b) **WH's profitability and asset turnover**

WH's ROCE is lower than the trade association average, possibly indicating that the company's assets are not being used as profitably as in the industry as a whole.

WH's operating profit margin is higher than the trade association average, despite a lower than average gross profit margin. This suggests that non-production costs are lower in relation to sales value in WH Limited than in the industry as a whole.

WH's asset turnover ratio is lower than the trade association average. This may mean that assets are not being used as effectively in our company as in the industry as a whole, which could be the cause of the lower than average ROCE.

WH's gross profit margin is lower than the trade association average. This suggests either that WH Limited's production costs are higher than average, or that selling prices are lower than average.

If you would like further information please do not hesitate to contact me.

16 Supervans

(a) Many organisations have clearly stated definitions of what they exist for and are trying to achieve, but equally, many do not and rely on an implied or cultural awareness of their objectives. Several groups of stakeholders may have a valid interest in the definition of mission. Where an explicit statement of the organisation's purpose exists, it may be used as a slogan for marketing purposes, as an important input into the management and motivation of staff at all levels and, specifically, here, as the apex of a system of performance management.

Performance implies purpose and directed rather than random action. Individual performance should contribute to group performance, group to department and so on all the way up to overall organisational performance. In the same way as **performance** at each level supports that at each higher level, so the **targets** at each level flow **downwards** from higher levels, deriving ultimately from the organisational mission.

(b) Kaplan and Norton likened the practice of judging overall performance by reference to a single measure such as ROI as like trying to fly an aircraft in cloud by reference to only one instrument: the picture is complex and must be observed through a number of perspectives. Kaplan and Norton suggested these four perspectives:

(i) Financial success
(ii) Customer satisfaction
(iii) Efficiency of internal processes
(iv) Learning and innovation (growth)

Such an approach has a range of advantages.

(i) The wider range of performance measures provides a clearer picture of both strengths and weaknesses.

(ii) Dysfunctional decision-making, short-termism and manipulation of single-measure outputs are discouraged and detected, since progress and performance are required on a broad front.

(iii) Managers understand more clearly that broader performance is important and are motivated to achieve it.

(iv) Only financial success can be easily measured using traditional monetary measures. The other three perspectives require careful attention to the overall **quality** of what the organisation does.

(c)

(i) **Perspective**

Financial success

Critical success factor	**Key performance indicator**
Profitability	ROI, gross margin, net margin, average margin per order
Cashflow	Daily bankings, accounts receivable collection days, accounts payable payment days, bank balance, cashflow forecast

(ii) **Customer satisfaction**

Critical success factor	**Key performance indicator**
Delivery on time	Ratio of late deliveries to those on time, number of complaints as a percentage of orders
Reliability	Number of deliveries lost as percentage of deliveries Number of parcels damaged as percentage of deliveries Percentage of late collections

(iii) **Process efficiency**

Critical success factor	**Key performance indicator**
Route efficiency	Fuel cost per delivery compared to budget and earlier periods * Vehicle and driver idle time
Transport costs	Van downtime, servicing cost per route mile, vehicle availability each day

* Route distances will vary from depot to depot

(iv) **Growth**

Critical success factor	**Key performance indicator**
Introduction of new services	Percentage of turnover from services introduced within previous year
Technical innovation	Growth in use of IT for planning and control/reduction in head count

(d) **Benchmarking, like a control system, is a process of comparison**. The difference is that under a normal control system comparison is made between target and actual performance; under benchmarking, two standards of actual performance are compared. Conclusions may then be drawn about the relative success of the activities compared. This process may be carried out across the whole range of an organisation's operations.

Three common approaches to benchmarking are **internal, external** and **best practice.**

Internal benchmarking at Supervans Ltd would involve comparisons between depots. This is an obvious thing to do anyway and could reveal areas for useful improvement.

External benchmarking requires comparison of performance with other companies in the same industry, that is to say, with competitors. This can be difficult to arrange but benchmarking schemes exist in many industries: steps are taken to achieve anonymity of data.

Best practice benchmarking makes comparisons between aspects of operations rather than operations as a whole. This allows comparisons with organisations in completely different industries, since only one aspect is compared at a time. Supervans for example, might compare its vehicle maintenance performance with that of a vehicle hire business.

17 Three components

REPORT

To: Management Group
From: Assistant Management Accountant
Date: 17 June 20X3
Subject: Components X, Y and Z: make or buy?

Following our meeting earlier in the week, I have analysed the cost and price information provided by the purchasing manager. This report sets out the results of my analysis and provides recommendations for management action.

(a) **Should any component be purchased from the overseas producer on the basis of cost only?**

On the basis of cost only, we should continue to produce components Y and Z but component X should be purchased from the overseas producer.

Workings to support this recommendation are shown in Appendix A.

(b) and (c) **The effect on profit of the above recommendation**

If we produce our three components in-house our total profits are $48,000 (see Appendix B for workings). If we buy component X from the overseas producer, however, total profit will increase by $1,000 to $49,000 (see Appendix C for workings).

(d) **Matters to be considered before importing components.**

(i) Will the quality be maintained by the overseas producer?

(ii) Will continuity of supply be guaranteed?

(iii) How long is the quoted price fixed for? Will exchange rate changes cause fluctuations in prices?

(iv) Can any profits be earned from the available capacity not used to produce component X?

(v) What will be the effect on labour morale of importing requirements of component X?

I hope the above information is useful. If you require any further assistance with this decision please do not hesitate to contact me.

Appendix A

	X	*Y*	*Z*
	$	$	$
Unit variable costs:			
direct material	0.80	1.00	0.40
direct labour	1.60	1.80	0.80
direct expense	0.40	0.60	0.20
Total variable cost	2.80	3.40	1.40
Imported price	2.75	4.20	2.00
Saving/(increased cost) of purchasing	0.05	(0.80)	(0.60)

Appendix B

	X	*Y*	*Z*	*Total*
	$'000	$'000	$'000	$'000
Sales value	80	200	160	440
Variable costs	56	136	112	304
Contribution	24	64	48	136
Fixed costs	16	40	32	88
Profit	8	24	16	48

Appendix C

The recommendation in (a) will increase profit because of the saving of $0.05 per unit of component X.

∴ Increased profit = $0.05 × 20,000 = $1,000

∴ Total profit will be $49,000

18 Ship

(a) **The minimum price is estimated from the relevant costs of producing the cushions**

	$
Covering material (the opportunity cost of this material is its scrap value of $190. The original cost is irrelevant because it is a historical cost, not a future cash flow)	190
Stuffing (the opportunity cost of the stuffing is the savings foregone by not sending it to Bristol, net of the transport costs of getting it to Bristol: $(500 – 80))	420
Labour: incremental cost	450
Supervisor's expenses: incremental expense item	135
Minimum price	1,195

The supervisor's basic wage and the overheads are irrelevant to the decision because these are costs that would be incurred anyway, even if the cushions were not produced.

(b) **Advantages of a marginal cost plus approach**

(i) It is a **simple and easy** method to use.

(ii) The **mark-up can be varied**, and so provided that a rigid mark-up is not used, mark-up pricing can be adjusted to reflect demand conditions.

BPP LEARNING MEDIA

(iii) It draws management attention to contribution and the effects of higher or lower sales volumes on profit. This helps to **create a better awareness of** the concepts and implications of **marginal costing and breakeven analysis**. For example, if a product costs $10 a unit and a mark-up of 150% is added to reach a price of $25 a unit, management should be clearly aware that every additional $1 of sales revenue would add 60c to contribution and profit.

(iv) Mark-up pricing is **convenient where there is a readily identifiable basic variable cost. Retail industries** are the most obvious example, and it is quite common for the prices of goods in shops to be fixed by adding a mark-up (20% or 33^1/3%, say) to the purchase cost. For example, a department store might buy in items of pottery at $3 each, add a mark-up of one third and resell the items at $4.

Drawbacks to marginal cost plus pricing

(i) Although the size of the mark-up can be varied in accordance with demand conditions, it **does not ensure that sufficient attention is paid to demand conditions, competitors' prices and profit maximisation**.

(ii) It ignores fixed overheads in the pricing decision, but the price must be high enough to ensure that a profit is made after covering fixed costs. Pricing decisions **cannot ignore fixed costs altogether.**

19 Quality

(a) **Relevance of TQM**

TQM is relevant to both the previous and the new strategy. It is a way of managing a business to achieve continually improving performance.

TQM is more than just a set of techniques. Developed in manufacturing industry, it is an approach to dealing with production, which involves getting things right first time and achieving zero defects. It tries to involve the customer's needs in the very process of production. This is obviously relevant to service industries, with the proviso that bad service cannot be inspected and scrapped after it is delivered: services are generally consumed as they are produced. As much of the success in a service industry depends on repeat business, getting things right first time (as that is, indeed, the only time) must be a priority.

TQM also involves a detailed analysis of the process of production. An aspect of TQM is **reduction in variation**. Restaurant service should be predictable; food quality must be consistently good, not outstanding one day and mediocre the next, otherwise the hotel will get a reputation for being unreliable.

The culture of TQM also must be considered. Employees must be encouraged to come forward with suggestions, and they must be engaged in the process of improving service. An almost obsessional interest in service quality should be encouraged.

There is no reason why these considerations should not apply to the family and medium-priced business accommodation as well as to the hotel's new strategy. However, as the new guests will be paying more, their expectations will be so much more exacting than before. The design quality of the service (what these new customers actually want) is paramount, and conformance quality (what is actually given) must be faultless.

(b) **Financial and organisational implications**

RUS is chasing a different market, targeting high spending customers whose requirements will be different. Investment in buildings and fixtures includes the following.

(i) Decoration
(ii) Changes to room sizes (eg conversion of pairs of single rooms into suites)
(iii) More luxurious furnishings
(iv) Perhaps expanded restaurant and kitchen facilities

(v) Swimming pool, gymnasium etc
(vi) More opulent spaces
(vii) Enhancing the hotel's grounds and gardens
(viii) Carparking facilities

Other expenditure will arise from the following.

(i) More staff, to provide the service required
(ii) More training
(iii) The greater variety of food offered to guests (hence kitchen costs will rise)
(iv) Advertising to reach the target segment

There will be few customers but they will be paying more.

Organisationally, the increased numbers in staff must be given more training, and existing staff will have to learn to cater differently for the new customers. Furthermore, there is unlikely to be the same deployment of staff as before, catering for family and business customers at different times. More effort will need to be spent on management and marketing. Quality circles could be introduced.

(c) **The management accountant's contribution to the new strategy is as follows.**

(i) To provide cost and revenue information in the initial research and planning phase, and to forecast future income and expenditure.
(ii) To cost any improvements to buildings and furnishings.
(iii) To suggest an appropriate pricing policy.
(iv) To raise external finance (eg from the bank) if substantial capital investment is needed and borrowing is necessary.
(v) To draw up tactical plans and budgets for the changeover.
(vi) To set up and operate new management accounting systems to monitor and control the hotel's performance.
(vii) To suggest appropriate non-financial performance measures, in particular with relation to quality of service.
(viii) To consider if the hotel's new clients will need services such as travellers cheques encashment etc, if they are from overseas.
(ix) To provide regular and suitable management information.

20 Cost reduction

(a) **Cost control** is the regulation of the costs of operating a business and is concerned with keeping costs within acceptable limits.

In contrast, **cost reduction** is a planned and positive approach to reducing expenditure. It starts with an assumption that current or planned cost levels are too high and looks for ways of reducing them without reducing effectiveness.

Cost control action ought to lead to a reduction in excessive spending (for example when material wastage is higher than budget levels or productivity levels are below agreed standards). However, a cost reduction programme is directed towards reducing expected cost levels below current budgeted or standard levels.

Cost control tends to be carried out on a routine basis whereas cost reduction programmes are often ad hoc exercises.

(b) **Three examples of cost control techniques**

(i) **Budgetary control**. Cost control is achieved by setting predetermined absolute levels for expenditure. If flexible budgeting is used then the budget cost allowance can be flexed in line with changes in activity. Control action is taken if actual expenditure differs from planned expenditure by an excessive amount.

(ii) **Standard costing**. Designed to control unit costs rather than absolute levels of expenditure, the use of standard costing depends on the existence of a measurable output which is produced in standard operations. Control action is taken if the actual unit costs differ from standard unit costs by an excessive amount.

(iii) **Limits on authority to incur expenditure**. Many organisations restrict the authority for their managers to incur expenditure. For example a budget manager may have an overall budget for overheads in a period, but even within this budget the manager may be required to seek separate authorisation for individual items of expenditure which are above a certain amount.

Three examples of cost reduction techniques

(i) **Value analysis**. CIMA defines value analysis as 'a systematic inter-disciplinary examination of factors affecting the cost of a product or service, in order to devise means of achieving the specified purpose most economically at the required standard of quality and reliability.' The aim in a value analysis exercise is to eliminate unnecessary costs without reducing the use value, the esteem value or the exchange value of the item under consideration.

(ii) **Work study**. This is a means of raising the production efficiency of an operating unit by the reorganisation of work. The two main parts to work study are method study and work measurement. Method study is the most significant in the context of cost reduction. It looks at the way in which work is done and attempts to develop easier and more effective methods in order to reduce costs.

(iii) **Variety reduction**. This involves standardisation of parts and components which can offer enormous cost reduction potential for some manufacturing industries. Variety reduction can also be used to describe the standardisation or simplification of an organisation's product range.

List of key terms and index

REVIEW FORM & FREE PRIZE DRAW

All original review forms from the entire BPP range, completed with genuine comments, will be entered into one of two draws on 31 January 2010 and 31 July 2010. The names on the first four forms picked out on each occasion will be sent a cheque for £50.

Name: ______________________ **Address:** ______________________

____

____

How have you used this Interactive Text?
(Tick one box only)

☐ Home study (book only)

☐ On a course: college ____________

☐ With 'correspondence' package

☐ Other ____________

Why did you decide to purchase this Interactive Text? *(Tick one box only)*

☐ Have used BPP Texts in the past

☐ Recommendation by friend/colleague

☐ Recommendation by a lecturer at college

☐ Saw advertising

☐ Other ____________

Which BPP products have you used?

☑ Text ☐ Kit ☐ i-Pass ☐ i-Learn

During the past six months do you recall seeing/receiving any of the following?
(Tick as many boxes as are relevant)

☐ Our advertisement in *ACCA Student Accountant*

☐ Other advertisement ____________

☐ Our brochure with a letter through the post

☐ Our website www.bpp.com

Which (if any) aspects of our advertising do you find useful?
(Tick as many boxes as are relevant)

☐ Prices and publication dates of new editions

☐ Information on Interactive Text content

☐ Facility to order books off-the-page

☐ None of the above

Your ratings, comments and suggestions would be appreciated on the following areas

	Very useful	*Useful*	*Not useful*
Introductory section (How to use this Interactive Text)	☐	☐	☐
Key terms	☐	☐	☐
Examples	☐	☐	☐
Activities and answers	☐	☐	☐
Key learning points	☐	☐	☐
Quick quizzes	☐	☐	☐
Exam alerts	☐	☐	☐
Question Bank	☐	☐	☐
Answer Bank	☐	☐	☐
List of key terms and index	☐	☐	☐
Structure and presentation	☐	☐	☐
Icons	☐	☐	☐

	Excellent	*Good*	*Adequate*	*Poor*
Overall opinion of this Interactive Text	☐	☐	☐	☐

Do you intend to continue using BPP products? ☐ Yes ☐ No

Please note any further comments and suggestions/errors on the reverse of this page. The BPP author of this edition can be emailed at paulsutcliffe@bpp.com

Please return this form to: Mary Maclean, CAT Range Manager, BPP Learning Media Ltd, FREEPOST, London, W12 8BR

REVIEW FORM & FREE PRIZE DRAW (continued)

Please note any further comments and suggestions/errors below

FREE PRIZE DRAW RULES

1. Closing date for 31 January 2010 draw is 31 December 2009. Closing date for 31 July 2010 draw is 30 June 2010.
2. No purchase necessary. Entry forms are available upon request from BPP Learning Media Ltd. No more than one entry per title, per person. Draw restricted to persons aged 16 and over.
3. Winners will be notified by post and receive their cheques not later than 6 weeks after the relevant draw date.
4. The decision of the promoter in all matters is final and binding. No correspondence will be entered into.